14th International Conference Information Systems 2021

Online
3 - 5 March 2021

ISBN: 978-1-7138-3582-0

Printed from e-media with permission by:

Curran Associates, Inc.
57 Morehouse Lane
Red Hook, NY 12571

Some format issues inherent in the e-media version may also appear in this print version.

Printed with permission by Curran Associates, Inc. (2021)

For permission requests, please contact International Association for Development of the Information Society (IADIS) at the address below.

International Association for Development of the Information Society (IADIS)
Rua Sao Sebastiao Da Pedreira
No. 100, 30, 1050-209
Lisbon, Portugal

Phone: 351 21 3151373
Fax: 351 21 3151244

secretariat@iadis.org

Additional copies of this publication are available from:

Curran Associates, Inc.
57 Morehouse Lane
Red Hook, NY 12571 USA
Phone: 845-758-0400
Fax: 845-758-2633
Email: curran@proceedings.com
Web: www.proceedings.com

14th IADIS International Conference Information Systems 2021

CONFERENCE PROGRAM

Wednesday 3rd, March 2021

09:15-09:30 Session O – Opening Session

OPENING SESSION
Profs.Philip Powell, Miguel Baptista Nunes and Pedro Isaías

09:30-10:30 Session KL – Keynote Presentation

"REFLECTIONS OF A SENIOR SCHOLAR"
Professor Robert M Davison, Dept of Information Systems,City University of Hong Kong, Hong Kong

10:30-10:45 Break

10:45-12:35 Session FSP 3.1
IS Design, Development and Management Issues and Methodologies
Chair: Philip Powell

12:35-14:00 Lunch Break

14:00-16:20 Session FSP 3.2
Design and Development Methodologies and Frameworks // IS in Practice, Technology Infrastructures and Organisational Processes
Chair: Xenia Mamakou

Thursday 4th, March 2021

08:00-10:30 Session FP 4.1
IS Management // Information Management // Knowledge Management
Chair: Hardy Pundt

10:30-10:45 Break

10:45-12:15 Session FP 4.2
Ethical, social, privacy, security and moral issues in an e-society // The role of information in the information society
Chair: Karsten Böhm

12:15-14:00 Lunch Break

14:00-16:05 Session FSP 4.3
IS Learning and Teaching / IS in Practice, Technology Infrastructures and Organisational Processes
Chair: Xenia Mamakou

Friday 5th, March 2021

08:40-10:30 Session FSP 5.1
Power, Cultural, Behavioural and Political issues // The centrality of IS and IT in Organisational Processes
Chair: Samiaji Sarosa

10:30-10:45 Break

10:45-12:10 Session FSP 5.2
Design and Development Methodologies and Frameworks // IS Project Management
Chair: Roger Maull

12:10-14:00 Lunch Break

14:00-15:50 Session FSRP 5.3
IS Research // Design Research and the Sciences of the Artificial in IS
Chair: Luis Claudio Barradas

15:50 Best Paper Awards Ceremony and Closing Session
Profs. Philip Powell and Miguel Baptista Nunes

Additional Papers:

E-SHOPS EVALUATION DURING COVID-19 LOCKDOWN USING E-S-QUAL AND AHP-TOPSIS

Xenia J. Mamakou and Konstantina – Porfyria Roumeliotou
Athens University of Economics and Business
76 Patission Str. Athens, Greece

ABSTRACT

This paper uses the E-S-QUAL model, analytic hierarchy process (AHP), and technique for order performance by similarity to ideal solution (TOPSIS) to evaluate e-commerce B2C websites among coffee-chain leaders in the Greek market. The research took place during the lockdown in Greece, due to COVID-19, which increased online sales. Our findings suggest that system availability and fulfillment are the two most important dimensions of the model, while credit card information protection and webpages that do not freeze during the ordering process are considered as the most crucial sub-dimensions. Our proposed 12-step approach can help web developers focus on the most important factors when designing e-shops, while companies can lead their efforts in improving service quality when offering their products and services to online customers. Moreover, the results of the evaluation process highlight the coffee-chain e-shop that could serve as a benchmark for best practices in online service quality.

KEYWORDS

E-commerce, Website Evaluation, E-S-QUAL, AHP, TOPSIS

1. INTRODUCTION

COVID-19 has changed the way people communicate, work, learn, travel, and behave during everyday life. Apart from the obvious health side-effects, business in many fields has decreased dangerously, causing company bankruptcies and loss of many jobs. In many cases, business and education can stay operational using available online technology. E-learning platforms help students in all educational levels continue the learning process, whereas online capabilities of corporate information systems and communication platforms assist professionals to continue their work from home. Recent studies (Contactpigeon, 2020, Eltrun, 2020) reveal that due to COVID-19 and the enforcement of lockdown in many countries, online shopping has increased, especially in the fields of consumer electronics and food & drink.

Businesses are required to respond immediately to such market changes, to satisfy customers, and to diversify from the competition. To achieve these goals, companies need to deeply understand the online customer experience. This way, they can improve the placement of their products and services as well as their communication. Past experiences could affect current and future experiences. Such experiences include e-shop navigation, searching capabilities, pricing policy, and after-sales service. According to (Grewal and Roggeveen, 2020) even the way a product is delivered and packaged could have a significant impact on current and future consumer experience.

In this vein, our research focuses on e-shops evaluation during COVID-19 lockdown in Greece. Our goal is to weight and rank the elements that affect online service quality and then evaluate the e-commerce websites of the top coffee-chains in the Greek market. The rest of the paper is organized as follows. Section 2 presents a literature review of service quality and its implementation in related studies. Section 3 outlines the research methodology implemented in the paper. Section 4 presents the results of this study and Section 5 discusses the conclusions.

2. LITERATURE REVIEW

Service quality has been a subject for research in many studies (Arcand et al., 2017, Suhartanto et al., 2019, Santos, 2003). Quality of services is one of the elements that build customer loyalty (Wirtz and Lovelock, 2016). Several instruments have been developed by researchers to measure service quality, with SERVQUAL (Parasuraman et al., 1988) to be one of the most known and widely used. The advent of the Internet and the spread of electronic services has created the need for different or modified instruments, to be able to measure electronic service quality. Such instruments include e-SQ (Zeithaml et al., 2000), which captures customers' interactions with a website, WebQual (Loiacono et al., 2002), based on 12 dimensions to measure website quality, SITEQUAL (Yoo and Donthu, 2001) and eTailQ (Wolfinbarger and Gilly, 2003) based on 4 dimensions. Criticism has been made to all these instruments, for either been used only to students, not capturing all aspects of the purchasing process, lacking internal consistency (Parasuraman et al., 2005), or focusing mainly on giving feedback to website designers (Zeithaml et al., 2002).

To overcome these limitations, Parasuraman et al. (Parasuraman et al., 2005) developed a four-dimension, 22 items instrument, called E-S-QUAL, that captures all phases of customers' interactions with a website. These dimensions include efficiency (eight items), system availability (four items), fulfillment (seven items), and privacy (three items). Efficiency refers to the ease and speed of accessing and using a website. System availability measures the technical functionality of the website. Fulfillment inspects the extent to which the website's promises about order delivery and item availability are fulfilled. Finally, privacy measures the degree to which a website is safe and protects customer information. Table 1 presents the dimensions and sub-dimensions of the E-S-QUAL model.

Table 1. Dimensions and sub-dimensions of E-S-QUAL model

Dimensions	Sub-dimensions
Efficiency	This site makes it easy to find what I need (SD_{11})
	It makes it easy to get anywhere on the site (SD_{12})
	It enables me to complete a transaction quickly (SD_{13})
	Information at this site is well organized (SD_{14})
	It loads its pages fast (SD_{15})
	This site is simple to use (SD_{16})
	This site enables me to get on to it quickly (SD_{17})
	This site is well organized (SD_{18})
System Availability	This site is always available for business (SD_{21})
	This site launches and runs right away (SD_{22})
	This site does not crash (SD_{23})
	Pages at this site do not freeze after I enter my order information (SD_{24})
Fulfillment	It delivers orders when promised (SD_{31})
	This site makes items available for delivery within a suitable time frame (SD_{32})
	It quickly delivers what I order (SD_{33})
	It sends out the items ordered (SD_{34})
	It has in stock the items the company claims to have (SD_{35})
	It is truthful about its offerings (SD_{36})
	It makes accurate promises about the delivery of products (SD_{37})
Privacy	It protects information about my Web-shopping behavior (SD_{41})
	It does not share my personal information with other sites (SD_{42})
	This site protects information about my credit card (SD_{43})

E-S-QUAL has been tested in many studies. Santouridis et al. (Santouridis et al., 2012) examined the applicability of E-S-QUAL and its factor structure in the context of e-commerce in Greece. Their findings confirmed the E-S-QUAL model and produced similar results to those of the initial research. Kandulapati and Bellamkonda (Kandulapati and Bellamkonda, 2014) measured the service quality of online shops using E-S-QUAL and validated the tool in an Indian context. Their study revealed that E-S-QUAL was valid for measuring service quality in the context of Indian online shopping. Ahmed et al. (Ahmed et al., 2020) employed E-S-QUAL to examine electronic banking service quality and customer satisfaction. Their finding confirmed an affirmative and potent impact of E-S-QUAL dimensions on customer's satisfaction. Dalbehera (Dalbehera, 2020) adopted the E-S-QUAL model to identify the criteria to assess the service quality of a University library website from the research scholars' viewpoints. The purpose of this study was to investigate the effects of E-S-QUAL dimensions that influence the digital library services on user's perceived value, e-service quality and e-loyalty. The findings revealed that the E-S-QUAL scale was a valid instrument for measuring e-service quality in the context of digital library services.

Website evaluation has been studied in the past. Masudin and Saputoro (Masudin and Saputro, 2016) evaluated B2C websites based on usability heuristics using fuzzy AHP & hierarchical fuzzy TOPSIS. Their results revealed that security and privacy is the most important factor followed by trust, loading time, easy transaction, and e-payment support. Soleymaninejad et al. (Soleymaninejad et al., 2016) evaluated two main online travel agencies in the US market with TOPSIS using a six-factor scale. They found that visibility and findability and functionality and accessibility were the most important criteria in their study. Ostovare and Shahraki (Ostovare and Shahraki, 2019) evaluated the status of websites and e-services provided by five-star hotels. They determined the main criteria and subcriteria using fuzzy Delphi method and weighted them using the Shannon entropy method. PROMETHEE and GAIA methods were then implemented to rank and develop the visual aid of websites. Their results revealed that customer orientation was the most important criterion, followed by marketing, security, and technology. Kang (Kang et al., 2016) presented a new method for evaluating B2C e-commerce websites, with the integration of E-S-QUAL and fuzzy hierarchical TOPSIS. To illustrate the efficacy of the proposed approach, they selected to evaluate six widely used Korean B2C e-commerce websites that provide similar services.

3. METHODOLOGY

This paper is based on a multiple criteria decision making (MCDM) approach that combines more than one research methodology, to overcome the limitations of the use of a single technique. In this vein, our research is based on AHP and TOPSIS, a combined methodology used in many studies (Zaidan et al., 2015, Hanine et al., 2016, Sharma and Joshi, 2019).

An online questionnaire was developed and used to capture experts' opinions regarding the importance of the dimensions related to website evaluation. The questionnaire consisted of three parts. The first part was asking experts to make pairwise comparison judgments between the 4 main dimensions and the 22 sub-dimensions of the E-S-QUAL model. The results of this analysis with AHP are used to evaluate the relative importance of the factors that influence users' decisions on choosing a website to make online purchases. The second part of the questionnaire was urging the experts to visit the websites under evaluation and to provide an answer for each of the model's sub-dimensions on a 9-level Likert scale. Their answers are analyzed using TOPSIS to provide a ranking of the evaluated websites. The final part of the questionnaire consisted of demographic questions.

Three B2C websites of Greek coffee-chains that rank among Europe's top 15 brands, according to FoodService Europe & Middle East magazine (Foodservice, 2019) were chosen to be evaluated. The research took place in the period of lockdown due to COVID-19, during April and May 2020. 25 experts agreed to take part in the research. They were all advanced web users, familiar with online purchases, professionals in website development, and/or UX design. Similar researches use sample sizes ranging from just 3 (Kang et al., 2016), to 27 (Ocampo et al., 2019). Thus, our sample size is considered acceptable for the proposed methodology.

Our methodology was based on the following steps, which are in accordance with the research of Ocampo et al. (Ocampo et al., 2019):

Step 1: Define the evaluation criteria and choose websites for evaluation. The evaluation criteria are based on the E-S-QUAL model and the chosen websites include three Greek coffee-chain B2C e-commerce websites.

Step 2: Construct a suitable instrument and collect experts' opinions. An online questionnaire is created, and experts accept to take part in the investigation, completing pairwise comparisons matrices among all dimensions and sub-dimensions, using the ratings: 1 = Equally preferred, 2 = Equally to moderately preferred, 3 = Moderately preferred, 4 =Moderately to strongly preferred, 5 = Strongly preferred, 6 = Strongly to very strongly preferred, 7 = Very strongly preferred, 8 = Very strongly to extremely preferred, 9 = Extremely preferred. Their ratings represent their judgment regarding the relative importance of one dimension over another based on the goal under investigation, as well as on the relative importance of one sub-dimension over another based on the parent dimension.

Step 3: Aggregate experts' opinions. To aggregate ratings made by experts, the geometric mean is used. Let $M^k = (m_{ij}^k)_{nxn}$ be a pairwise comparison matrix of the kth expert, where m_{ij} represents the importance of dimension (or sub-dimension) i over dimension (or sub-dimension) j. Then

$$M = (m_{ij})_{nxm} = (\sqrt[n]{\prod_{k=1}^{n} m_{ij}^k})_{nxm} \quad (1)$$

Step 4: Calculate local weights. To calculate the local priority weights of dimensions and sub-dimensions we use Eq. 2.

$$Mw = \lambda_{max} w \quad (2)$$

where λ_{max} is the maximum eigenvalue of M and w is the corresponding principal eigenvector, considered as the best estimate of the priority weights of the dimensions or sub-dimensions compared in the pairwise comparison matrix.

Step 5: Check for consistency. We compute the consistency index (CI) and consistency ratio (CR) for both dimensions and sub-dimensions, using Eq. 3 and 4.

$$CI = \frac{\lambda_{max} - n}{n-1} \quad (3)$$

$$CR = \frac{CI}{RI} \quad (4)$$

The random consistency index (RI) represents the consistency of a random pairwise comparison matrix. To have consistent ratings, CR value needs to be less than or equal to 0.10.

Step 6: Calculate global weights for sub-dimensions. To calculate the global weight of the sub-dimension w_j we multiply its local weight by the parent dimension's weight.

Step 7: Calculate a decision matrix. A decision matrix D is calculated, where d_{ij} represents the quality of the e-commerce website i = 1,2,3,…,m in the sub-dimension j = 1,2,3,…,n.

$$D = \begin{bmatrix} d_{11}\, d_{12} \dots d_{1n} \\ d_{21}\, d_{22} \dots d_{2n} \\ \dots \\ d_{m1}\, d_{m2} \dots d_{mn} \end{bmatrix} \quad (5)$$

Step 8: Compute the normalized decision matrix. The normalized decision matrix $R = (r_{ij})_{nxn}$ is computed using:

$$r_{ij} = \frac{d_{ij}}{\sqrt{\sum_{i=1}^{m} d_{ij}^2}} \quad (6)$$

Step 9: Obtain the weighted decision matrix. The weighted decision matrix V is obtained by:

$$V = (v_{ij})_{mxn} = (w_j r_{ij})_{mxn} \quad (7)$$

Step 10: Determine the ideal alternative. Both the ideal (A^+) and non-ideal (A^-) alternatives are determined according to

$$A^+ = \{(max_i(v_{ij})\ if\ j \in J); (min_i(v_{ij})\ if\ j \in J')\} \quad (8)$$

$$A^- = \{(min_i(v_{ij})\ if\ j \in J); (max_i(v_{ij})\ if\ j \in J')\} \quad (9)$$

where J and J' are beneficial and non-beneficial attributes, respectively.

Step 11: Calculate the distance of each alternative from the best and the worst alternative. We calculate the distance of each evaluated e-commerce website from the best and the worst website, using:

$$S_i^+ = \sqrt{\sum_{j=1}^{n}(v_{ij} - v_j^+)^2}\ ,\ i = 1,2,\dots,m \quad (10)$$

$$S_i^- = \sqrt{\sum_{j=1}^{n}(v_{ij} - v_j^-)^2}\ ,\ i = 1,2,\dots,m \quad (11)$$

Step 12: Rank the alternatives. We calculate the closeness coefficient C_i using Eq. 12 to rank the evaluated e-commerce websites. The website with the higher C_i is the more preferred one.

$$C_i = \frac{S_i^-}{(S_i^+ + S_i^-)} \quad (12)$$

4. RESULTS

To evaluate the quality of Greek coffee-chain e-commerce websites, according to the dimensions and sub-dimensions of E-S-QUAL model, we use the 12 steps of the proposed AHP – TOPSIS methodology, discussed in the previous section. Table 2 presents the local and global weights of the sub-dimensions, along with their rankings. Each sub-dimension's local weight represents its performance in the parent dimension, whereas its global weight represents its overall performance in the E-S-QUAL model, regardless of its parent dimension. Overall CR for our data was found to be less than 0.1, indicating the consistency of the resulting AHP model.

Table 2. Local and global weights and ranking of sub-dimensions

Dimensions	Sub-dimensions	Local weight	Global weight	Rank
Efficiency (0.185)	SD_{11}	0.157	0.0290	13
	SD_{12}	0.154	0.0285	14
	SD_{13}	0.145	0.0268	16
	SD_{14}	0.098	0.0181	19
	SD_{15}	0.083	0.0154	20
	SD_{16}	0.171	0.0316	12
	SD_{17}	0.079	0.0146	21
	SD_{18}	0.113	0.0209	17
System availability (0.284)	SD_{21}	0.160	0.0454	8
	SD_{22}	0.227	0.0645	5
	SD_{23}	0.196	0.0557	6
	SD_{24}	0.418	0.1187	2
Fulfillment (0.278)	SD_{31}	0.129	0.0359	10
	SD_{32}	0.050	0.0139	22
	SD_{33}	0.071	0.0197	18
	SD_{34}	0.293	0.0815	3
	SD_{35}	0.118	0.0328	11
	SD_{36}	0.240	0.0667	4
	SD_{37}	0.099	0.0275	15
Privacy (0.253)	SD_{41}	0.171	0.0433	9
	SD_{42}	0.186	0.0471	7
	SD_{43}	0.643	0.1627	1

4.1 Local Weights of Sub-Dimensions

Local weights of sub-dimensions under system availability - the dimension that ranks higher among all four - reveal that webpages functioning as expected, without freezing during the ordering process is the most important element. Therefore, companies that develop e-commerce websites with online ordering functionalities need to pay the necessary attention when implementing their ordering forms. Customers expect that after completing their order information on an online order form, pages will keep working, without freezing, presenting a message of either order completion or a prompt for making order changes. What customers do not expect is to come across a situation where nothing happens after they complete their order, leaving them wondering whether their order has been submitted or not. The second most important element under system availability is a website that lunches and runs immediately. Load speed is essential for the quality of a website. Many online tests offer insights and advice concerning online performance optimization. Following the page speed, the absence of crashes and the availability of the e-commerce website are prioritized. Customers would probably stop trying to make an online purchase from a website that stops working or is never available to visit.

The sub-dimension under fulfillment which obtains the higher weight is that the B2C e-commerce website sends out the ordered items. That is, it is not delivering wrong or incomplete products. The second-ranked element in this category is truthfulness about products and services offered to customers. Delivery of products when promised comes next, followed by posting truthful supplies. Last in this dimension is that the website makes items available for delivery within a suitable time frame.

The first ranked element in the privacy dimension is credit card protection. Online customers highly care about the safeguard of their sensitive personal information, giving this sub-dimension the higher score between all items in all four categories. The second-ranked item in this dimension is that the website does not share customer information with others and last comes the protection of personal information online.

The final ranked dimension is efficiency. In this dimension, simple of use comes first, having the highest local weight. Simplicity of search process and navigation follow, leaving page loading and quick access to customers at the final places.

4.2 Global Weights of Sub-Dimensions

Apart from the local weights, the global weights of sub-dimensions are very important, since they can provide a more complete understanding of the position of each item in relation to the overall service quality of a B2C e-commerce website. First in rankings, we find credit card information protection, followed by webpages working as expected (i.e. do not freeze) during the ordering process. Items sent as ordered come third and truthfulness about products and services follows.

4.3 Evaluation of B2C e-Commerce Websites

Using the results from our E-S-QUAL model with AHP methodology, we proceed in implementing TOPSIS for the evaluation of the three Greek coffee-chains B2C e-commerce websites. We first calculate the decision matrix, using expert opinions on how well each particular website (W1, W2, and W3) performs with respect to a sub-dimension, as discussed in Step 7. The results of this step are presented in Table 3.

Table 3. Decision matrix showing the evaluation made for each website with respect to each sub-dimension

	SD_{11}	SD_{12}	SD_{13}	SD_{14}	SD_{15}	SD_{16}	SD_{17}	…	SD_{32}	SD_{33}	SD_{34}	SD_{35}	SD_{36}	SD_{37}	SD_{41}	SD_{42}	SD_{43}
W1	8.08	7.77	7.55	7.51	7.54	7.43	8.24	…	7.84	7.53	8.36	8.25	7.80	7.83	8.56	8.77	8.91
W2	7.60	7.45	7.51	7.40	7.09	6.54	7.60	…	8.58	8.49	8.90	8.37	8.16	8.36	8.72	8.70	9.00
W3	7.25	6.95	6.81	6.67	7.14	6.63	7.74	…	8.62	8.17	8.25	8.50	8.51	8.62	8.34	8.62	8.72

We then normalize the decision matrix, using Eq. 6. Table 4 presents the normalized decision matrix, including the experts' evaluations for each website.

Table 4. Normalized decision matrix

	SD_{11}	SD_{12}	SD_{13}	SD_{14}	SD_{15}	SD_{16}	SD_{17}	…	SD_{32}	SD_{33}	SD_{34}	SD_{35}	SD_{36}	SD_{37}	SD_{41}	SD_{42}	SD_{43}
W1	0.61	0.61	0.60	0.60	0.60	0.62	0.61	…	0.54	0.54	0.57	0.57	0.55	0.55	0.58	0.58	0.58
W2	0.57	0.58	0.59	0.59	0.56	0.55	0.56	…	0.59	0.61	0.60	0.58	0.58	0.58	0.59	0.58	0.59
W3	0.55	0.54	0.54	0.53	0.57	0.56	0.57	…	0.60	0.58	0.56	0.59	0.60	0.60	0.56	0.57	0.57

Using Eq. 7, we then calculate the weighted normalized decision matrix, shown in Table 5.

Table 5. Weighted normalized decision matrix

	SD_{11}	SD_{12}	SD_{13}	SD_{14}	SD_{15}	…	SD_{32}	SD_{33}	SD_{34}	SD_{35}	SD_{36}	SD_{37}	SD_{41}	SD_{42}	SD_{43}
W1	0.018	0.018	0.016	0.011	0.0090	…	0.0076	0.011	0.046	0.0188	0.037	0.020	0.025	0.027	0.094
W2	0.017	0.017	0.016	0.011	0.0085	…	0.0083	0.012	0.049	0.0190	0.039	0.021	0.025	0.027	0.095
W3	0.016	0.016	0.015	0.010	0.0085	…	0.0083	0.012	0.045	0.0193	0.040	0.022	0.024	0.027	0.092

The next step is to determine the positive and the negative ideal alternatives, using Eq. 8 and 9 (Table 6), and finally to calculate the general distance from the best and the worst alternative (Eq. 10, 11) and the closeness coefficient (Eq. 12), to be able to rank the websites under evaluation. The results are presented in Table 7.

Table 6. Positive ideal solution and negative ideal solution

	SD_{11}	SD_{12}	SD_{13}	SD_{14}	SD_{15}	SD_{16}	…	SD_{32}	SD_{33}	SD_{34}	SD_{35}	SD_{36}	SD_{37}	SD_{41}	SD_{42}	SD_{43}
A^-	0.016	0.016	0.015	0.010	0.008	0.018	…	0.008	0.011	0.045	0.019	0.037	0.020	0.024	0.027	0.092
A^+	0.018	0.018	0.016	0.011	0.009	0.020	…	0.008	0.012	0.049	0.019	0.040	0.022	0.025	0.027	0.095

As Table 7 suggests, the best-ranked website is W2, followed closely by W1. Website W3 comes last in rankings.

Table 7. General distance, closeness coefficient, and ranking of websites

	S^+	S^-	C_i	Ranking
W1	0.0061	0.0070	0.5377	2
W2	0.0056	0.0068	0.5489	1
W3	0.0077	0.0050	0.3930	3

Consequently, B2C e-commerce website 2, scoring the highest rank in electronic service quality, can be considered as the benchmarking coffee-chain e-shop for the improvement of the service quality of the other websites in the same field.

5. CONCLUSIONS

In this study, we use the E-S-QUAL model and AHP methodology to weight the elements that affect electronic service quality and then we rank three coffee-chains' B2C e-commerce websites using the results of the AHP and TOPSIS. Our methodology consists of 12 steps. We first defined the evaluation criteria and chose the websites under evaluation. In our study, the evaluation criteria consisted of the dimensions and sub-dimensions of the E-S-QUEL model. We then constructed an online questionnaire and collected experts' opinions who made pair-wise comparisons on the model's evaluated criteria. Using their answers, we aggregated their opinions and calculated local weights for each dimension and sub-dimension. We checked for consistency using consistency index (CI) and consistency ratio (CR) and we moved on to calculating the global weights for the sub-dimensions. The next step was to apply TOPSIS to construct a decision matrix, which was normalized and weighted using the results from AHP. Finally, we calculated the distance of each alternative from the best and the worst alternative, to rank the coffee-chains e-shops.

Our results indicate that the most important dimension in evaluating B2C e-commerce websites is system availability, which measures the functionality of the website from a technical point of view. Fulfillment comes next, which controls the extent to which promises about item availability and order delivery is fulfilled. Privacy, which inspects the degree to which a website safeguards customer information comes third, leaving efficiency that refers to the easiness of accessing and using a website at the final place.

Website designers can benefit from our study since they can focus on the most important elements when developing an e-commerce website. Security of credit card information, webpages that do not freeze during the ordering process, a website that launches immediately and does not crush are four of the most important evaluation sub-dimensions a developer should consider.

Our study also has managerial implications, since companies offering their products and services online can control the performance of their e-commerce websites, considering the ranking of the E-S-QUAL model's dimensions and sub-dimensions. Apart from making checks for their existing website to see if it meets the requirements and to demand alterations, companies should also control whether other important factors, like items sent to customers as ordered and truthfulness about their products and services, are fulfilled. In nowadays changing and demanding environment, business survival is more crucial than ever before. The exploitation of our study's results could offer companies the opportunity to make improvements that matter to their online customers and witness an increase in sales during the pandemic.

Our proposed methodology is not limited to the scope of our research. It can also be applied for the evaluation of websites from different sectors and even for the evaluation of other areas, apart from B2C e-commerce websites, where pairwise comparisons are important in providing improvements to service operations.

REFERENCES

Ahmed, R. R., Romeika, G., Kauliene, R., Streimikis, J. & Dapkus, R. 2020. ES-QUAL model and customer satisfaction in online banking: evidence from multivariate analysis techniques. *Oeconomia Copernicana,* 11, 59-93.

Arcand, M., Promtep, S., Brun, I. & Rajaobelina, L. 2017. Mobile banking service quality and customer relationships. *International Journal of Bank Marketing*.

Contactpigeon. 2020. *How has COVID-19 Impacted Ecommerce Trends?* [Online]. Available: https://blog.contactpigeon.com/covid-19-ecommerce-impact/ [Accessed 23/10/2020].

Dalbehera, S. 2020. Measuring Service Quality in Digital Library Services by the Research Scholars of SOA University of Odisha Using ES-QUAL Model. *International Perspectives on Improving Student Engagement: Advances in Library Practices in Higher Education.* Emerald Publishing Limited.

Eltrun, R. I. O. R. C. G. A. 2020. *Greek Consumers Significantly Increase Use of E-commerce* [Online]. Available: https://greece.greekreporter.com/2020/04/07/greek-consumers-significantly-increase-use-of-e-commerce-survey-shows/ [Accessed 23/10/2020].

Foodservice. 2019. *Top 80 coffee bar brands in Europe* [Online]. Available: https://www.food-service.de/international/int-news/ranking-top-80-coffee-bar-brands-in-europe-45918 [Accessed 26/10/2020].

Grewal, D. & Roggeveen, A. L. 2020. Understanding retail experiences and customer journey management. *Journal of Retailing,* 96, 3-8.

Hanine, M., Boutkhoum, O., Tikniouine, A. & Agouti, T. 2016. Application of an integrated multi-criteria decision making AHP-TOPSIS methodology for ETL software selection. *SpringerPlus,* 5, 263.

Kandulapati, S. & Bellamkonda, R. S. 2014. E-service quality: a study of online shoppers in India. *American Journal of Business*.

Kang, D., Jang, W. & Park, Y. 2016. Evaluation of e-commerce websites using fuzzy hierarchical TOPSIS based on ES-QUAL. *Applied Soft Computing,* 42, 53-65.

Loiacono, E. T., Watson, R. T. & Goodhue, D. L. 2002. WebQual: A measure of website quality. *Marketing theory and applications,* 13, 432-438.

Masudin, I. & Saputro, T. E. Evaluation of B2C website based on the usability factors by using fuzzy AHP & hierarchical fuzzy TOPSIS. IOP Conference Series: Materials Science and Engineering, 2016. IOP Publishing Ltd, 012091.

Ocampo, L., Alinsub, J., Casul, R. A., Enquig, G., Luar, M., Panuncillon, N., Bongo, M. & Ocampo, C. O. 2019. Public service quality evaluation with SERVQUAL and AHP-TOPSIS: A case of Philippine government agencies. *Socio-Economic Planning Sciences,* 68, 100604.

Ostovare, M. & Shahraki, M. R. 2019. Evaluation of hotel websites using the multicriteria analysis of PROMETHEE and GAIA: Evidence from the five-star hotels of Mashhad. *Tourism Management Perspectives,* 30, 107-116.

Parasuraman, A., Zeithaml, V. A. & Berry, L. L. 1988. Servqual: A multiple-item scale for measuring consumer perc. *Journal of retailing,* 64, 12.

Parasuraman, A., Zeithaml, V. A. & Malhotra, A. 2005. ES-QUAL: A multiple-item scale for assessing electronic service quality. *Journal of service research,* 7, 213-233.

Santos, J. 2003. E-service quality: a model of virtual service quality dimensions. *Managing Service Quality: An International Journal*.

Santouridis, I., Trivellas, P. & Tsimonis, G. 2012. Using ES-QUAL to measure internet service quality of e-commerce web sites in Greece. *International Journal of Quality and Service Sciences,* 4, 86.

Sharma, M. & Joshi, S. 2019. Brand sustainability among young consumers: an AHP-TOPSIS approach. *Young Consumers*.

Soleymaninejad, M., Shadifar, M. & Karimi, A. 2016. Evaluation of two major online travel agencies of us using TOPSIS method. *Digital Technologies,* 2, 1-8.

Suhartanto, D., Helmi Ali, M., Tan, K. H., Sjahroeddin, F. & Kusdibyo, L. 2019. Loyalty toward online food delivery service: the role of e-service quality and food quality. *Journal of foodservice business research,* 22, 81-97.

Wirtz, J. & Lovelock, C. 2016. *Services marketing: People, technology*, World Scientific Publishing Company.

Wolfinbarger, M. & Gilly, M. C. 2003. eTailQ: dimensionalizing, measuring and predicting etail quality. *Journal of retailing,* 79, 183-198.

Yoo, B. & Donthu, N. 2001. Developing a scale to measure the perceived quality of an Internet shopping site (SITEQUAL). *Quarterly journal of electronic commerce,* 2, 31-45.

Zaidan, A. A., Zaidan, B. B., Al-Haiqi, A., Kiah, M. L. M., Hussain, M. & Abdulnabi, M. 2015. Evaluation and selection of open-source EMR software packages based on integrated AHP and TOPSIS. *Journal of biomedical informatics,* 53, 390-404.

Zeithaml, V. A., Parasuraman, A. & Malhotra, A. 2000. *A conceptual framework for understanding e-service quality: implications for future research and managerial practice*, Marketing Science Institute Cambridge, MA.

Zeithaml, V. A., Parasuraman, A. & Malhotra, A. 2002. Service quality delivery through web sites: a critical review of extant knowledge. *Journal of the academy of marketing science,* 30, 362-375.

USER-ADAPTIVE NOTIFICATION SOUND ASSIGNMENT FOR NOTIFICATION MESSAGES

Marina Sakai[1], Junko Shirogane[2], Hajime Iwata[3] and Yoshiaki Fukazawa[1]
[1]Waseda University, Fukazawa Lab., Building 63, Waseda University, 3-4-1 Ohkubo, Shinjuku-ku, Tokyo 169-8555, Japan
[2]Tokyo Woman's Christian University, 2-6-1 Zempukuji, Suginami-ku, Tokyo 167-8585, Japan
[3]Kanagawa Institute of Technology, 1030 Shimo-Ogino Atsugi Kanagawa 243-0292, Japan

ABSTRACT

When using software, various notification messages are displayed in response to users' operations. Although each notification message has its own importance level, users often do not perceive the importance level. For example, they just proceed with an operation without reading the content or they do not notice the notification itself. Meanwhile, sound is a common resource used to convey the importance of a situation and is often employed to make users aware of notification messages. Thus, it is effective to represent the importance of the notification message by sound. However, sound importance depends on the user. This paper proposes a determination method of notification sounds by evaluating the importance level of sounds by users. Then sounds are assigned to notification messages according to users' input.

KEYWORDS

Notification Messages, Notification Sound, User-Adaptive, Assignment

1. INTRODUCTION

Notification messages are displayed as users interact with software to indicate what the user has done, to represent a problem, or to convey information. There are various kinds of notification messages, and each one has a different level of importance. However, there are many cases in which users do not properly understand the importance of a notification message. For example, users often proceed with an operation without reading the content of the message or they completely miss a notification message. If users execute an operation without recognizing the intent of the notification message, important operations, which cannot be undone such as deleting files or paying money may be unconsciously performed.

Meanwhile, sound is a common resource used to convey the importance of a situation. Examples include sounds of an ambulance siren and an earthquake early warning. Sound can be recognized even when users do not pay attention to the situation. In addition, a notification sound can alert users to a notification message. Thus, it is effective to represent the importance of the notification message by sound. However, the feeling of a sound depends on the user. For example, when some people hear a scratching sound on a blackboard, they want to run away immediately, while others feel it is unpleasant but bearable. Thus, what sounds sound important depends on the user's perception.

In this study, we propose a method to assign notification sounds to notification messages according to individual user's senses so that users notice and respond appropriately to important notification messages. In a previous study (Sakai et al., 2019), we assumed that users paid attention to unpleasant sounds. Thus, we proposed a method to assign more unpleasant sounds to more important notification messages. The results of user experiments based on the proposed method showed that the assumption was appropriate. If appropriate sounds can be assigned, they can be useful for notification messages according to individual user's feelings. However, the feedback contained many comments about the assigned sound such as "I noticed the sound, but the sound is too strong for the intent of the notification message" or "The sound startled me", and "the evaluation of the sound assigned to the notification message was exaggerated compared to the message". Thus, we concluded that unpleasant sounds are inappropriate for users to notice important notification messages. In this study, we survey characteristics of sounds to inform of important messages in an effort to improve our method to evaluate and assign sounds to notification messages. This study should help users recognize the importance of notification messages according to their feelings, even if the notice is not read.

2. BACKGROUND

2.1 Earthquake Early Warning

According to the Japan Meteorological Agency (2007), the Earthquake Early Warning (EEW) System is designed to predict the arrival time and intensity of strong earthquakes in various areas and then inform the public as quickly as possible before strong earthquakes arrive. It is intended to protect people, slow down trains, and control machinery in factories. In other words, an earthquake early warning can be considered a high-importance notification that alerts people to danger and allows them to respond immediately and appropriately. The earthquake early warning is accompanied by a sound. Ifukube (2013), the creator of the earthquake early warning sound, mentioned the following points when creating the sound: (1) the sound conveys urgency, (2) it does not give a sense of uncomfortability or anxiety, (3) it is audible even in noisy environments, (4) it is audible to people with mild hearing impairment, and (5) it is not similar to a sound heard somewhere else.

Since this study aims to enable users to recognize important notification messages and take appropriate actions, we believe that the emergency earthquake early warning is an appropriate reference for high-importance notifications.

2.2 Notification Sound

The macOS Human Interface Guidelines (2021) mention that sound is a great way to get users' attention when they are not viewing the screen. Thus, the guidelines instruct developers to provide sound to supplement notification messages. As an example, the To-Do list app plays a notification sound to inform of the time to perform an important task. The guidelines mention that apps can use custom or built-in sounds, but if developers use custom sounds, they should ensure that the sounds are short, distinctive, and professional.

Microsoft Windows Dev Center (2020) mentions that sound is the audio element of the user experience, and when used properly, can be an effective form of communication that establishes a non-verbal and even emotional relationship with users. Windows also states that sound can be used as a supplement to the visual UI (User Interface). For example, adding sound effects to notifications makes them more easily noticed, especially if the user is not viewing the screen when an event occurs.

3. RELATED WORK

3.1 Feeling of Notification Message Color

Sillic (2016) conducted a study on how the color of a warning banner message affects a user's decision-making process. They employed different colored warning banner messages: black, blue, yellow, red, green, and white. They conducted their experiment in two different countries: the United States and India. Yellow, red, and green were more effective warning colors. However, in the United States, red was the most effective warning color, while yellow was the most effective one in India. Thus, users' feelings depend on the cultural environment. Their study investigated how users feel about the notification message color, but did not consider the notification message sound.

3.2 Information Display by Signaling Sounds

Wake noted that humans originally used the five senses to collect information, but most information was received visually. It was thought that representing information with sound is an effective alternative to representing information with sight, and that the use of a sine (non-verbal) sounds plays an important role. Hence, Wake (2005) proposed using non-verbal sounds in a SUI (Sound User Interface). Similar to a GUI (Graphical User Interface), which has both functionality and aesthetics, Wake believed that a SUI must also satisfy both functionality and aesthetics. However, both characteristics of the current sign sounds have yet to be fully considered. Hence, these characteristics should be studied to improve the design methodology and guidelines from a functional point of view as well as to improve developers' awareness of sign sounds from a design point of view. Wake's study investigated the use of sound to display information, but did not consider the use of sounds according to users' feelings.

4. SOUND-ASSIGNMENT METHOD

This chapter describes a method to assign sounds to notification messages based on the importance of the messages and users' feelings.

4.1 Assignment Flow

Figure 1 overviews the process of assigning sounds to notification messages. Software developers classify notification messages into levels according to the notification message importance guidelines, which are described in Section 4.2. In addition, software developers should prepare candidate sounds. Then a user listens to the candidate sounds and evaluates them according to a sound evaluation questionnaire. Based on the answers in the questionnaire, sounds are assigned to notification messages by the sound-assignment algorithm of our method.

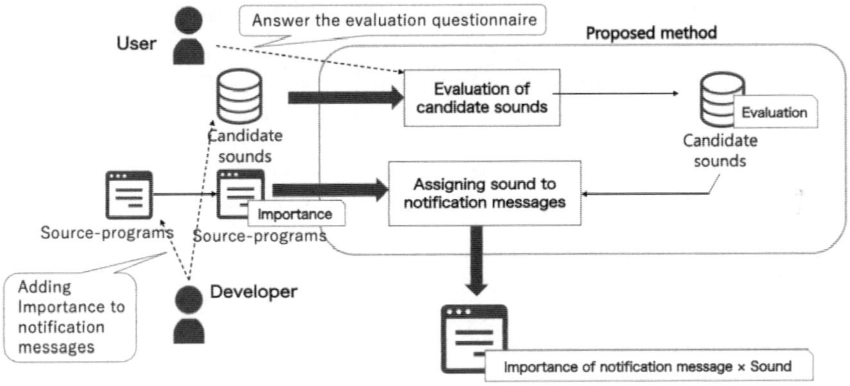

Figure 1. Sound-assignment process for notification messages

4.2 Guidelines to Determine Importance Levels of Notification Messages

There are various types of notification messages. Although user interface guidelines often define several types of notification messages, it is defined in terms of software behavior and not necessarily defined according to the importance level recognized by users. In this study, we define guidelines for software developers to determine the importance levels of software notification messages (Table 1). There are four importance levels, where level 1 is least important and level 4 is most important.

Table 1. Guidelines to determine the importance levels of notification messages and their examples

Importance level	Content	Example
level 4	The user needs to respond immediately or something may be lost	Purchase confirmation Permanent deletion of files
level 3	Users do not necessarily have to respond immediately, but something may be lost	Low battery notification Password authentication failure
level 2	Some users need to respond	Email notifications OS update notifications
level 1	Users do not have to respond	News and other information

4.3 Evaluation of the Importance Felt for Sound

To assign sounds, the appropriateness of sounds for notification messages according to users must be measured. Thus, a scale is required to measure the sound characteristics. Iwamiya et al. (2009) conducted a rating experiment using adjective pairs to investigate the possibility of assigning chords as sounds to convey messages. Table 2 shows the 10 adjective pairs for the sound impressions. These adjectives were used to evaluate chords and not necessarily the appropriateness of sounds for notification messages. To measure the appropriateness of sounds for notification messages, appropriate adjectives for the scales must be selected and weighted.

Here, we investigate the applicable levels of the adjectives to actual notification sounds. Nine sounds were prepared: Earthquake Early Warning Sound, XP Alert, Windows Error Sound, Windows User Account Control, Windows Low Battery, Windows Notify Calendar, LINE Message Ringtone, Windows Information Bar, and Windows Notify System Generic. We assumed that the earthquake early warning sound, XP warning sound, and Windows error sound are importance level 4, Windows user account control and Windows low battery are level 3, Windows Notify Calendar and LINE message ringtones are level 2, and Windows Notify System Generic and Windows information bar are level 1. Nineteen subjects listened to these sounds and were asked to rate their impressions on a six-point Likert scale, where a higher value indicated a higher importance. For example, for the adjective pair "relaxed/tense", there were 6 levels of evaluation, where 0 means no tension and 5 means a lot of tension.

Table 3 shows the average results of the questionnaire for each sound. Although Table 3 does not include characteristics of each importance level, the earthquake early warning sound has a relatively high value compared to the other sounds. A t-test was conducted to calculate the distance between the sound of earthquake early warning and the other sounds for each of the 10 adjective pairs of sound impressions. A significant difference was set to the commonly used p-value of 0.05. Table 4 lists the t-values for each adjective. There were 166 degrees of freedom. According to the t-distribution table, the t-value for the 166 degrees of freedom is 1.9744. Because the values of all 10 adjective pairs significantly differ from those of the earthquake early warning, the sound value of the earthquake early warning is greater than the mean value of the other sounds for all 10 adjective pairs.

As mentioned in Section 2.1, we believe that the earthquake early warning sound is an appropriate reference for high-importance notifications. Because all adjective pairs have high values for the earthquake early warning sound, all 10 adjective pairs of sound impressions can be used as a scale to measure the appropriateness of sounds for notification messages. A higher value indicates a higher appropriateness. In addition, the sound of earthquake early warning must (1) give a feeling of urgency but (2) not give a feeling of uncomfortability or anxiety. Accordingly, it is necessary to exclude uncomfortable sounds. Thus, the "comfortable/uncomfortable" adjective pair was used as a cut-off point to exclude extreme values. The other adjectives were scored and used. In the scoring, we divided the evaluation into three groups: 0–1.67 out of a maximum value of 5 is the low-scoring group, 1.6–3.33 is the medium scoring group, and 3.33–5 is the high-scoring group.

According to the evaluation of each adjective pair for the earthquake early warning sound in Table 3, no adjective pair belongs to the low-scoring group, two adjective pairs, "bright/dark" and "light/heavy", belong to the medium-scoring group, and the other seven adjective pairs belong to the high-scoring group. Hence, the higher the score, the more appropriate the sound.

In our method, the sounds are compared. First, the scores of the high-scoring group are compared. If two sounds have the same score using the high-scoring group, the scores of the medium-scoring group are also used.

Table 2. Ten adjective pairs of sound impressions

Adjectives
relaxed / tense
familiar / unfamiliar
comfortable / uncomfortable
quiet / noisy
bright / dark
safe / dangerous
slow / busy
stable / unstable
light / heavy
common / unique

Table 3. Experimental results of the evaluation for sound adjectives

	relaxed tense	familiar unfamiliar	comfortable uncomfortable	quiet noisy	bright dark	safe dangerous	slow busy	stable unstable	light heavy	common unique
Earthquake Early Warning	4.45	4.15	4.2	3.9	3.3	4.6	4.25	4.45	2.5	4.05
XP Alert	2.25	2.95	2.65	1.8	3.5	2.7	2.3	2.15	3.8	2.47
Windows Error	2.11	2.16	2.32	1.79	1.11	2.16	1.95	2.39	0.84	1.84
Windows User Account Control	1.47	1.74	1.63	0.95	1.89	1.79	1.21	1.95	1.26	2.37
Windows Low Battery	1.68	2.16	2.32	1.58	2.21	2.0	1.63	2.16	1.47	1.84
Windows Notify Calendar	0.82	1.24	1.35	1.12	1.35	1.12	1.0	1.88	1.29	2.29
LINE Message Ringtone	1.56	1.11	2.06	2.17	1.17	1.22	2.78	1.5	0.72	2.56
Windows Information Bar	2.67	3.28	3.17	2.78	1.83	2.78	2.67	2.78	1.67	2.89
Windows Notify System Generic	0.94	1.56	1.78	1.17	1.78	1.39	1.06	1.5	1.5	2.83

Table 4. T-values for each of the other sound adjectives compared with the sound of earthquake early warning

	relaxed tense	familiar unfamiliar	comfortable uncomfortable	quiet noisy	bright dark	safe dangerous	slow busy	stable unstable	light heavy	common unique
t-value	13.96	6.76	8.96	9.64	4.08	18.85	8.72	12.92	2.72	6.66

4.4 Appropriateness Evaluation of Sounds

In our method, sounds are assigned to notification messages according to the following algorithm:

(1) Users listen to candidate sounds prepared by the software developer and rate each sound on a 6-point Likert scale from 0 to 5 for the 10 adjective pairs of sound impressions shown in Table 2. As explained in Section 4.3, a higher score indicates a higher appropriateness. Table 5 shows an example of an evaluation.

(2) For each sound, the scores are calculated according to Formula (i), using the ratings of each adjective pair for the high-scoring group ("relaxed/tense", "familiar/unfamiliar", "quiet/noisy", "safe/dangerous", "slow/busy", "stable/unstable", and "common/unique") and medium-scoring group ("bright/dark" and "light/heavy") defined in Section 4.3. In this formula, *n* is the number of adjectives in a group, *v* is the user rating for each adjective, and *t* is the t-value for each adjective shown in Table 4. Table 6 shows an example of the results.

$$score = \sum_{i=1}^{n} v_i t_i \qquad \text{(i)}$$

(3) Sounds that are very uncomfortable are excluded (i.e., those that have a "comfortable/uncomfortable" adjective value of 5 among the candidate sounds). As an example, Sound 4 in Table 5 is excluded due to this criterion.

(4) Based on the scores of the high-scoring group, the remaining sounds in step (3) are ranked in descending order by score. If sounds have the same score, then the scores of the medium-scoring group are evaluated. If the scores in the medium-scoring group are the same, then the sounds are assigned the same rank. Table 6 shows an example ranking.

(5) The remaining *k* sounds from step (3) are divided into four groups of *k*/4 sounds in order of rank in step (4). Table 7 shows an example. The highest-ranked sound in the highest-ranked group is assigned to a notification message of importance level 4, as shown in Table 1. For the second group, the sound of the middle rank within the group is assigned to importance level 3. For the third group, the sound of the middle rank within the group is assigned to importance level 2. Finally, the lowest-ranked sound within the lowest-ranked group is assigned to importance level 1. Table 7 shows an example of the assignment results, where a circle indicates an assigned sound.

Table 5. Example of each sound evaluation by the number of users

	relaxed tense	familiar unfamiliar	comfortable uncomfortable	quiet noisy	bright dark	safe dangerous	slow busy	stable unstable	light heavy	common unique
Sound 1	2	3	3	3	3	4	2	4	2	2
Sound 2	2	4	4	4	3	3	3	3	3	2
Sound 3	2	2	1	3	1	2	1	1	1	2
Sound 4	4	5	5	5	2	3	3	4	2	2
Sound 5	0	4	3	3	2	2	2	2	2	3
Sound 6	3	2	2	2	3	2	2	2	3	3
Sound 7	1	1	1	3	0	2	1	1	0	0
Sound 8	3	2	2	4	1	3	3	2	1	1
Sound 9	2	3	3	3	1	3	3	3	2	4
Sound 10	2	3	3	3	1	3	3	3	2	4

Table 6. Example of the high- and medium-scoring groups' scores, their rankings, and assigned importance levels

	High-scoring group scores	Medium-scoring group scores	Rank	Assigned importance level
Sound 1	235.31	17.71	2	-
Sound 2	241.94	20.44	1	4
Sound 3	143.16	6.81	7	-
Sound 4	292.60	13.62	-	-
Sound 5	163.80	13.62	6	2
Sound 6	175.86	20.44	5	-
Sound 7	109.09	0	8	-
Sound 8	209.39	6.81	4	3
Sound 9	106.12	6.81	9	1
Sound 10	225.53	9.54	3	-

Table 7. Example groupings of candidate sounds by importance level

Importance level	Grouped candidate sounds
4	○Sound 2, Sound 1, Sound 10
3	○Sound 8, Sound 6
2	○Sound 5, Sound 3
1	Sound 7, ○Sound 9

5. EXPERIMENT

To investigate the effectiveness of the proposed sound-assignment method, we conducted an experiment involving 20 subjects.

5.1 Experimental Design

The 20 subjects listened to the 10 candidate sounds and rated each one (Table 2). The candidate sounds were free materials (Kurage-kosho, 2014). These sounds were selected based on the intention according to the authors. The intentions were written as tags and comments such as "sounds that can be used as error sounds" and "bright images". We assumed that these sounds were appropriate for importance levels 1 to 4 of notification messages. For each sound, the subjects selected which level of importance they thought was appropriate for the notification message (Table 1). However, if a subject felt that a sound was inappropriate for any level, they selected none and provided their reason.

5.2 Experimental Results

To determine the sounds assigned to the four importance levels of notification messages for each subject, the sound-assignment algorithm in Section 4.4 was applied to the subject's answers. Table 8 shows subjects' answers of the appropriate levels for the assigned sounds by importance level of the notification message. For example, when Sound 1 was assigned to importance level 1 of notification message, but a subject thought the sound was appropriate for importance level 2, Table 8 shows a "2" in the cell of importance level 1 by subject. Then the gap between the importance level of the assigned sound and the importance level of the notification message that the subject thought was appropriate for the sound was calculated. For example, Subject 1 felt that the sound assigned to importance level 3 should be assigned to level 4, the gap is |4−3| = 1. Table 9 shows the total number of gaps and the average of the gaps for all subjects for each importance level. However, here "other" indicates the case when a subject responded that the sound was inappropriate for all importance levels. One reason for the lack of appropriate importance level was that a long sound was perceived as an OS boot sound rather than a notification sound. Additionally, all subjects selected either importance level 1 or importance level 2 as appropriate for any of the 10 candidate sounds, but some subjects did not identify any sound as appropriate for importance level 3 or 4.

Table 8. Importance assignment sound levels selected by subject

Subject	Importance level 4	Importance level 3	Importance level 2	Importance level 1
1	3	3	1	1
2	3	2	N/A	1
3	2	3	1	1
4	2	2	2	1
5	2	1	1	1
6	3	2	1	2
7	3	3	3	1
8	2	4	1	1
9	3	2	1	1
10	3	1	1	1
11	4	2	1	1
12	3	1	2	1
13	3	3	1	1
14	2	1	N/A	1
15	3	1	1	1
16	3	2	1	1
17	3	1	1	1
18	4	1	1	1
19	3	2	3	1
20	2	2	1	1

Table 9. Gap of importance levels for notification messages between the assignment by our method and users' feelings to the sounds

Gap	Total number
0	30
1	35
2	13
3	0
4	0
other	2
average	0.7625

5.3 Discussion

The average gap of the importance levels for notification messages between the assignment by our method and users' feelings to the sounds was 0.7625, which was less than 1 (Table 9). In the cases with a gap of 2, in 7 of the 13 cases, the subjects did not select level 3 or level 4 as an importance level appropriate for the candidate sounds. In all but one of the remaining six cases, although the subject selected level 3 or higher for candidate sounds, these sounds were omitted in step (3) of our sound-assignment algorithm in Section 4.4. Hence, the average gap was small and in the case where the gap was large, the candidate sound did not match the subjects' feelings. Overall, the sound-assignment method described in Section 4 is considered to be effective.

6. CONCLUSION

Herein we propose a method to assign notification sounds to notification messages according to the user's individual feelings. Our method allows users to notice and take appropriate actions for important notification messages.

Future works include to:

1) build a support system to develop software with an assignment function of the notification sound based on our method, and
2) confirm the appropriateness of users' actions based on the assigned notification sounds by our method.

REFERENCES

Ifukube, A, 2013, The Birth Story of the Earthquake Early Warning Chime. *JAS Journal,* Vol. 53, No. 2, pp.4-10.

Iwamiya, S. et al, 2009. On the Effectiveness of Using Musical Chords for Auditory Signals. *The Japanese Journal of Ergonomics,* Vol. 45, No. 6, pp. 329-335.

Japan Meteorological Agency, 2007. What is an Earthquake Early Waring?. Available at: https://www.jma.go.jp/jma/en/Activities/eew1.html [Accessed 3 Jan. 2021].

Kurage-kosho, 2014. System Sound and Electronic Sound. Available at: http://www.kurage-kosho.info/system.html [Accessed 3 Jan. 2021].

MacOS Human Interface Guidelines, 2021. Notifications. Available at: https://developer.apple.com/design/human-interface-guidelines/macos/system-capabilities/notifications/ [Accessed 3 Jan. 2021].

Microsoft, 2020. Sound. Available at: https://docs.microsoft.com/en-us/windows/win32/uxguide/vis-sound [Accessed 3 Jan. 2021].

Sakai, M. et al, 2019. Assigning sounds according to the importance of notification messages and users' feelings. *The 81st National Convention Lecture and Paper Collection*, Vol. 2019, No. 1, pp. 257-258 (in Japanese).

Sillic, M. et al, 2016. Understanding Colour Impact on Warning Messages: Evidence from US and India. *Proceedings of the 2016 CHI Conference Extended Abstracts on Human Factors in Computing Systems. San Jose, USA,* pp. 2954-2960.

Wake, S, SUI(Sound User Interface) : Auditory Information Display used Sign Sound and Its Design. *Proceedings of the Human Interface Symposium.* Fujisawa, Japan, pp. 105-110.

MEDIATING SOCIAL TOURISM EXPERIENCES THROUGH A MOBILE APPLICATION

Luís C. S. Barradas[a, b], João Nascimento[a], Sandra Oliveira[a, c], Susana Leal[a, d], Carla Vivas[a] and André Alves[a]

[a] *Instituto Politécnico de Santarém, Complexo Andaluz, Apartado 295, 2001-904 Santarém, Portugal*

[b] *Digital Services, Applications and Content Research & Development Unit, Av. do Empresário, 6000-767 Castelo Branco, Portugal*

[c] *Centre for Health Studies and Research, University of Coimbra, Avenida Dias da Silva 165, 3004-512 Coimbra, Portugal*

[d] *Life Quality Research Centre, Complexo Andaluz, Apartado 279, 2001-904 Santarém, Portugal*

ABSTRACT

Nowadays, mobile devices are an essential mean for accessing information. Over time, industries and businesses have been exploring this phenomenon extensively to gain market share and competitive advantage. This is especially true in the tourism industry where mobile applications are crucial in the modern e-Tourism model. This paper presents a mobile application that aims to support the management of social tourism initiatives and the mediation of tourist experiences, within the context of a senior exchange programme in social economy organisations. The mobile application design was guided by the Dynamic Systems Development Method framework and takes a set of requirements and specific needs of each stakeholder into account. The developed software artefact is a mobile hybrid application that provides an almost native user experience, fulfilling its design objectives and purpose.

KEYWORDS

Social Tourism, Mobile Applications, Tourism Experience Mediation, Elderly

1. INTRODUCTION

The desire to travel to meet and establish relationships with other people and civilisations has been a constant throughout the history of mankind. Since time immemorial, travel has been important not simply to ensure subsistence (Cunha, 2013) but for a host of other reasons, be they religious, commercial, political, territorial expansion, or even mere curiosity. Although tourism is typically seen as "travelling for fun", this definition has recently been expanded to include any displacement outside the normal area of work or residence. Nowadays, tourism is a gigantic international industry in constant change that embraces various other industries such as transportation, hotels, restaurants, handicrafts, etc. Information and communication technologies quickly assumed a significant role in this process, supporting not only core activities in the tourism industry value chain (Cunha, 2013, Kazandzhieva and Santana, 2019, Osei *et al.*, 2020) but also innovative business models (Presenza *et al.*, 2020) and the mediation of tourism experiences (Hyun *et al.*, 2009) where mobile applications emerge as a key element (Figueiredo, 2014, Raposo *et al.*, 2012).

Opportunities to travel and experience touristic offers are not transversal to all sectors of modern society for several reasons, even in the so-called "developed countries". European Union (EU) countries are facing an ageing process due to the increase in overall life expectancy and Portugal is no exception to this trend. It is estimated that the old-age dependency ratio of the EU population in 2070 will be 51.2% with 266.24 million people over the age of 65 (European Union, 2018). As in the health industry, a process of adaptation is underway in the tourism industry to meet this new demand. The rise in active ageing practices alongside the growing importance of quality of life for the elderly has led to a greater willingness to participate in this sort of touristic offer. Moreover, many seniors lack financial or economic resources and face increased social difficulties as the population grows (Oliveira *et al.*, 2019); indeed, a large proportion of Portuguese seniors cannot afford the touristic packages targeting this group. This is particularly true for the elderly population in institutions who often face economic and social difficulties and, many of those from inland regions have never even seen the sea or travelled outside their municipality. Touristic packages targeting this group need to be specially adapted to their profile. To address this problem, the VOLTO JÁ Project (Oliveira *et al.*, 2019) proposes a social tourism business model supported by information and communication technologies.

This paper presents the VOLTO JÁ Mobile Application (VJAPP) which aims to support and mediate the three critical stages of the tourist experience (Figueiredo, 2014) within the scope of social tourism addressed by the VOLTO JÁ Project.

The paper is organised as follows: Section 2 presents a survey on mobile tourism applications and the challenges related to their use by the elderly. Section 3 presents the mobile application development methodology, main functionalities, architecture building blocks, supporting technology, and how the application mediates the users' tourism experience. This is followed by the discussion in Section 4. Finally, Section 5 presents the conclusions and limitations, and proposes future research avenues.

2. MOBILE TOURISM APPLICATIONS AND ELDERLY USERS

Modern mobile e-Tourism has allowed tourists to deal with almost every aspect of travel a using a mobile application: (1) choosing the destination; (2) finding attractions and points of interest; (3) booking transportation, accommodation, and activities; (4) receiving on-site support; and (5) sharing their experience. Some aspects of travel planning were formerly reserved to travel agencies. Today, mobile technologies can assist tourists in every stage of their travel and many mobile applications are available for this purpose. Kennedy-Eden and Gretzel (2012), Wang and Xiang (2012), Gavalas *et al.* (2014), Borràs *et al.* (2014), and Wörndl and Herzog (2020) conducted surveys aiming to classify these mobile tourism applications. According to Wörndl and Herzog (2020) taxonomy, they can be classified into four major groups, as shown in Table 1.

Table 1. Classification of mobile applications for tourism. Adapted from Wörndl and Herzog (2020)

Application category	Purpose	Examples
Information and Sharing	Destinations Points of Interest Activities	TripAdvisor FourSquare TripAdvisor
Booking	Accommodation Transportation Activities	Booking.com; Trivago; Airbnb TAP Air Portugal; eDreams; Booking.com TripAdvisor
On-trip Services	Help & Support Navigation & Transport Safety	National Park Passport Book; Louvre Travel Guide Lisboa Viagem; Uber Can I Go?
Sharing & Interaction	Social Virtual Tourism Others	Instagram; FourSquare Swarm VR Travel; Iran Tour; Google Arts & Culture Google Translator

Despite this segmentation, many of the applications often combine functionalities from several application categories. For example, TripAdvisor combines features from Information and Sharing and Booking categories. Although some other applications, such as Pokemon Go!, cannot be included in any of the above categories, they are used by both travellers and the general population.

Mobile applications can provide a pleasant user experience to travellers by assisting them with personalised services and helping tourism service providers to understand their customers and adapt their offers accordingly. However, the intrinsic characteristics of mobile devices (e.g., screen size) present some interaction challenges to users, notably the impaired and elderly (Ribeiro *et al.*, 2018a). The acceptance and use of mobile devices and applications by the elderly remains an active field of study. There are several mobile applications on the market for the elderly but they seldom meet the specific needs of this target group due to their physical and cognitive impairments (Klimova, 2018).

The literature reveals some remarkable projects addressing the use of mobile applications for the elderly in tourism. For example, E^2 (Khadraoui *et al.*, 2014) comprises a web system and a mobile application that aims to allow the elderly to plan their trips in line with their constraints and preferences; Trip 4 All (Signoretti *et al.*, 2015) is a mobile application that works as a gamified virtual assistant to the elderly during a walking tourist visits; Sweet Mobility (Borrelli *et al.*, 2015) is a smartphone-based system to promote walking for the elderly and empower tourism; and finally, iTourism Travel Buddy (Ismail *et al.*, 2016) is a mobile tourism application that supports tourism information with assistive travel features to help tourists by using technology that is closest to them.

The elderly population is of growing importance in e-Tourism and the supporting technologies must be adapted to their specific needs.

3. VOLTO JÁ MOBILE APPLICATION

The VOLTO JÁ Mobile Application is a component of the VOLTO JÁ Information System (VJIS). The design of the VJIS was guided by the Dynamic Systems Development Method framework (Anwer *et al.*, 2017, DSDMC, 2014). This paper encompasses only the Business study (partially), the Functional Model Iteration, and the Implementation Iteration.

3.1 The VOLTO JÁ Business Model

The VOLTO JÁ Project focuses on Social Tourism for low-income groups, particularly institutionalised seniors in homes for senior citizens or nursing homes who would not otherwise go on holiday. Special emphasis is given to what motivates the elderly populations to have new cultural experiences and the impact this may have on their active ageing and quality of life. The project is essentially a social senior exchange programme in Social Economy Entities (SEE) that promote cultural, touristic, and artistic experiences. It encompasses a set of activities that directly impact the mobility and active ageing of seniors.

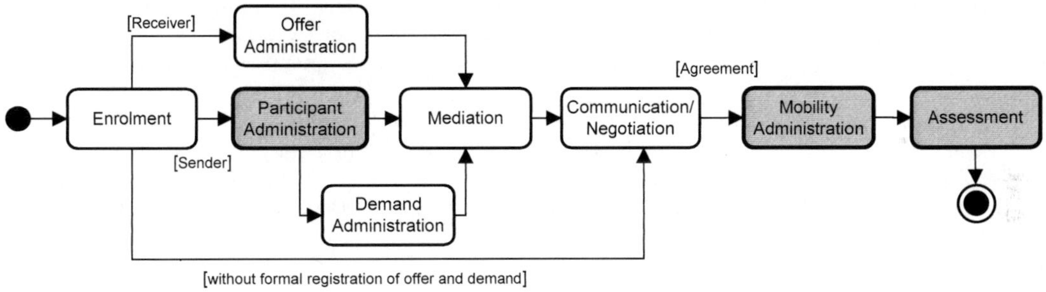

Figure 1. VJBM business processes co-supported by VJAPP. Adapted from (Author Citation)

The VOLTO JÁ Business Model (VJBM) lies on eight core business processes (see Figure 1) and considers four key players: (1) Social Economy Entities that provide housing and care services to the elderly; (2) the Social Economy Entities Directors (SEED), who are the main representatives of SEEs; (3) SEE users (also referred to as participants), who are the institutionalised elderly in SEE; and (4) the SEE companions (also referred to as teammates) who are the SEE people who accompany the participants in the mobilities (senior interchanges). The VJBM is operationalised by VJIS comprising a web platform (Barradas *et al.*, 2019) and a mobile application. While the web platform, far more complex, aims to support the whole set of business processes of the VJBM, the mobile application seeks to co-support only three core business processes. Figure 1 highlights the subset of VJBM core business processes (in grey) co-supported by the mobile application from the SEE perspective.

3.2 Requirements and Functionalities

As noted above, the mobile application is a component of VJIS. The list of VJIS requirements was produced based on the VJBM business processes presented in Figure 1. The consolidated list of requirements comprised sixty-one items, which was shortened to forty-five (27 mandatories; 9 important; 8 suggested; 1 excluded) after refinement through the MoSCoW technique (DSDMC, 2014). All the non-excluded requirements became part of the list of VJIS functionalities, fifteen of which were relative to the mobile application. Figure 2 presents the top-level UML use case diagram of the mobile application. In addition to showing technical requirements (Login and Abandon session) and a generic requirement (View public contents), it also represents the supported VJBM core business processes as packages.

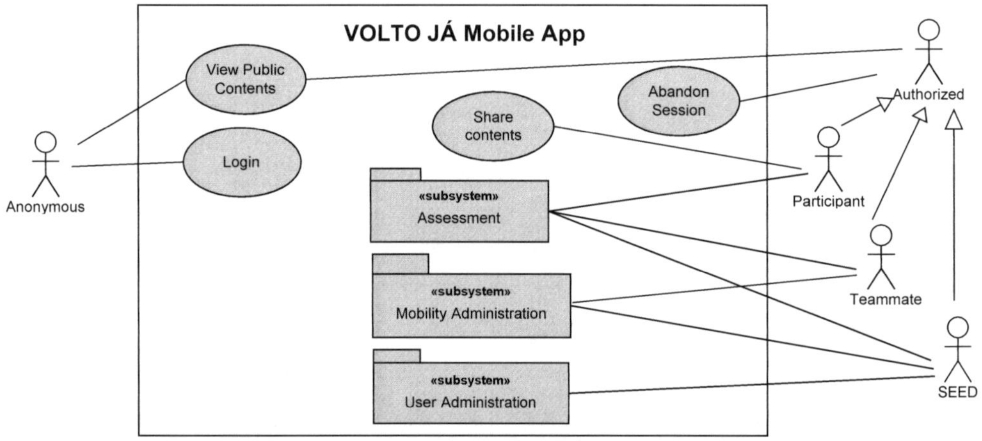

Figure 2. VJAPP top-level UML use case

Public content refers to any that can be viewed in an unrestricted environment; this includes information about the project, the offers or demands as a result of a search process, the elderly mobilities that have already taken place, and the content shared (posts tagged as public, containing comments and photos) by the participants in the scope of those mobilities, reflecting their lived tourism experience. The Teammates and the SEEDs assess participants' posts. Finished mobilities are also assessed quantitatively by the Participants and SEEDs.

SEEDs can administrate both the users of the system (only participants and Teammates) and mobilities; they are able to: (1) open mobilities; (2) view details about the mobilities (e.g., listing details of participants involved and teammates, tourism programme of mobilities, transportation and feeding aspects of mobilities); and (3) close the running mobilities. Teammates can also view details about the participants and the mobilities in which they are involved.

3.3 Application Architecture and Development Technology

The mobile application builds on a modular three-tier layered architecture (see Figure 3). The presentation layer, responsible for the user interface (UI), comprises four functional modules. The "anonymous" module provides access to general functionalities for which no authentication is required for access, such as searching for offers and demands, accessing contents of mobilities carried out (with public access), generic information about the mobility programme, partner entities, and their geographic location. The SEED module is aimed at SEEDs and provides access to features related to the administration of participants and Teammates, administration of mobilities (consulting data, opening mobilities and closing mobilities), validation of published content, and mobility evaluation by participants. The Companion module is aimed at Teammates and provides functionalities for consulting data on mobilities in which they participate or have participated and validating content published by participants. The Participants module is for participants and provides functionalities for consulting data on mobilities in which they participated, sharing content about these mobilities, and assessing mobilities based on their experience.

The Application layer comprises models and components and is responsible for the application logic and task orchestration in line with business rules.

Finally, the Service layer offers an abstraction layer for accessing persistent data, integrating the mobile application with the web platform through the consumption of REST services. It provides a set of services that deal with functional, security/authentication, or utility concerns.

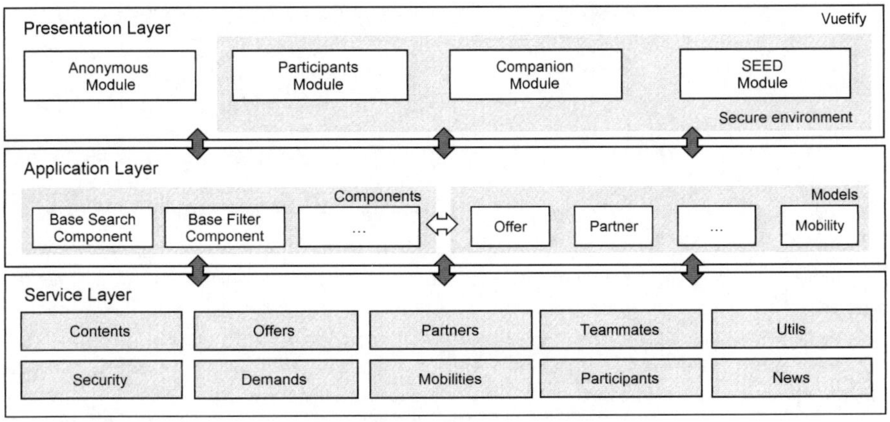

Figure 3. VJAPP architecture

In the current scenario of mobile application development, three types of applications can be considered: (1) native applications; (2) cross-platform applications; and (3) hybrid applications (Majchrzak *et al.*, 2018). In this research work, the development technology was selected using three main criteria: (1) independence of the platform/execution environment; (2) time to market; and (3) familiarity with the development technologies. To meet these criteria, it was decided to construct a hybrid application, allowing the development of a mobile application based on web technologies (familiarity) running on the WebView component present in the Android and iOS platforms. Although this approach provides lower performance when compared to other alternatives, this criterion was considered as not relevant for the technology selection decision-making process.

The Vue.js JavaScript framework was the selected technology for implementation. This framework allowed the application to be developed in a single-page model using the Vue Router component (Rojas, 2020). The UI was developed using Vuetify, a complete UI framework built on top of Vue.js. This framework provides semantic UI components based on the Material Design specification, which permits a UI design that offers engaging, native-like mobile user experiences. The development of Vue.js applications follows the Model-View-ViewModel pattern; this allows reactive behaviours, i.e., any changes made in the models, are immediately reflected in the UI and vice versa.

Concerning security aspects, the communication between the web platform and the mobile application involves a 32-byte token exchange (bearer authentication). Even the consumption of unrestricted content requires the use of tokens to avoid denial of service attacks.

Ionic Capacitor (Huber *et al.*, 2020) was selected as cross-platform native runtime, which allows transparent access to the device resources (such as camera, location services, network status, file system, etc.) through plugins; and to export/deploy them to Android or iOS platforms.

3.4 Mediating Participants' Tourism Experience

According to Milano *et al.* (2011), on a technology-mediated tourism experience, three phases are influential in the travel experience formation process: (1) pre-experience, built on other people's travel stories before travelling; (2) experience during travel or stay, now shared increasingly in real-time through mobile applications; and (3) post-experience, which disseminates comments, evaluations, and emotions. Figure 4 depicts the participants' mobility experience mediation through the VOLTO JÁ Mobile Application. The pre-experience phase begins when the participants list mobilities carried out and see the contents (comments, photos) shared by people about their experience in that mobility (see Figure 5a, b); or search for available offers/demands in a destination of their preference.

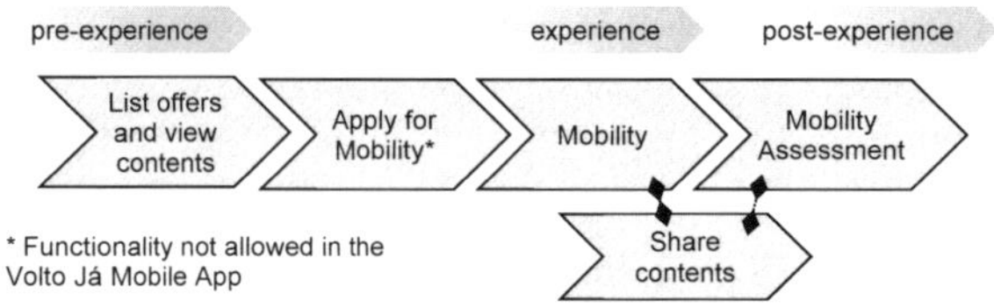

Figure 4. Participants' mobility experience activities supported by VJAPP

After applying for mobility, and once negotiations between the partner institutions are concluded, the experience phase starts with the arrival of the participants at the host institution. During the mobility, participants can feed the system with comments and photos about their own mobility tourism experience (see Figure 5c). Participants can define the visibility level of their published content. Only the content defined as "public" can be accessed in unrestricted environments. Participants can set a shared content as "private", "visible to the group", "visible to the Institution", "visible to the mobility", "visible to authorised users", or "public". A Teammate or a SEED is responsible for reviewing any shared content, and only approved content can be made available.

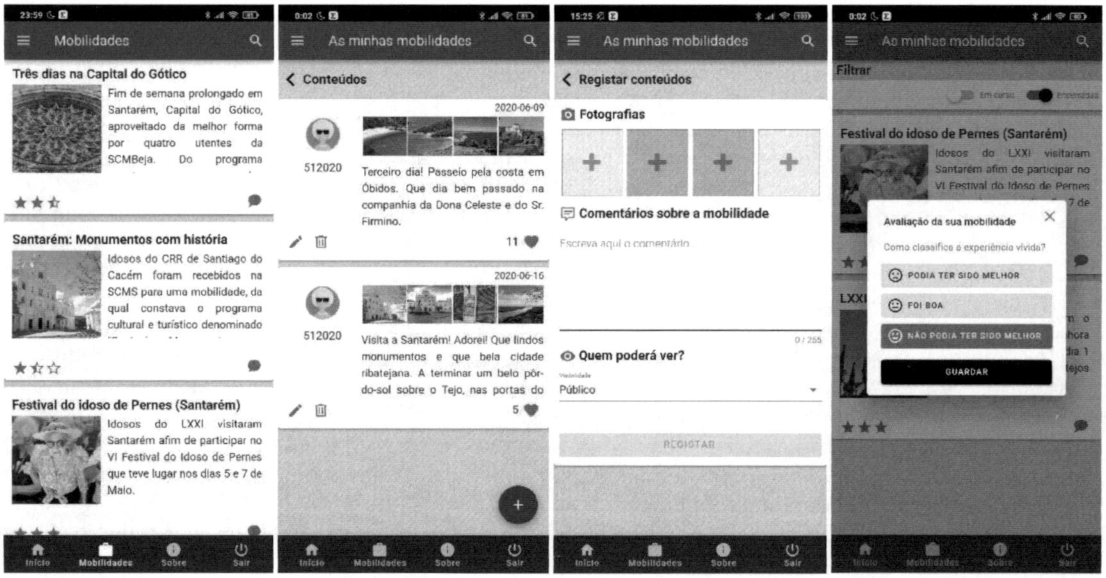

a) b) c) d)

Figure 5. Participants' mobile views related to mobility experience mediation

The post-experience phase begins when the mobility ends (participants arrive at their home institution). At this stage, participants can review and rate their experience (see Figure 5d). Participants can continue to share and publish content while the mobility status remains "open".

4. DISCUSSION

The mobile application developed has two fundamental objectives: to facilitate the administration of mobility to SEED and companions through their ubiquity; and to mediate the participants' tourist experience. Despite its simplicity, we believe the application fulfils the purpose for which it was designed. This simplicity is due to the target user population, notably participants, whose physical and cognitive conditions require special requirements in the application design (Klimova, 2018). Within the scope of e-Tourism, Ribeiro *et al.* (2018a) and Ribeiro *et al.* (2018b) have already proposed a Framework for accessible tourism mobile application development, although focused on people with disabilities.

The list of requirements and features initially planned for the application included a wider range of features. However, following recommendations made by the social economy entity partners during focus groups with stakeholders, some functionalities were removed as a result of the very specific characteristics of the elderly in institutions.

5. CONCLUSION

From a macro perspective, this work aims to establish a link between senior tourism and a business model for the social economy to promote active ageing and social value creation. To that end, an information system was designed and developed to operationalise the business model and support the underlying processes. While the web platform strives to provide support for the heavy work of operationalising the entire business model, the mobile application presented here aims to mediate the tourism experiences of participants during their mobilities and provides SEED and Teammates with a pocket tool to manage the mobilities in which they are involved.

Mobile applications are now part of our way of life and dozens of mobile applications with varied objectives are used throughout the tourism industry value chain, some of which have similar objectives to the Volta Já mobile app. However, the originality of this work lies in the nature and particularities of the target group.

Due to the world COVID-19 pandemic, the application has only been tested in a controlled environment because it could not be used in a real scenario. However, this situation will be rectified as soon as the necessary security health conditions are restored to assess its utility. Unit, integration, and functional tests were performed to assess the quality and efficiency of the application.

Given the national scope of this research project, the business specificities and the implemented business rules are only applicable to the Portuguese context. In the future, we aim to internationalize the project by extending the concept to other countries and realities and expand the application by adding new utility services (e.g., weather forecast) and context-aware functionalities.

ACKNOWLEDGEMENT

The authors wish to thank the Fundação para a Ciência e a Tecnologia (FCT), which is the financing support entity of the project “VOLTO JÁ: PROGRAMA DE INTERCÂMBIO SENIOR” Ref: ALT20-03-0145-FEDER-024111. The authors are also grateful to all the Social Economy Entities that have been active collaborators in the project.

REFERENCES

Anwer, F., Aftab, S., Waheed, U. & Muhammad, S. S. (2017). Agile Software Development Models Tdd, Fdd, Dsdm, and Crystal Methods: A Survey. *International journal of multidisciplinary sciences and engineering,* Vol: 8, pp:1-10.

Barradas, L. C., Nascimento, J., Martins, L., *et al.* (2019). Developing an Information System for Social Value Creation. *Procedia Computer Science,* Vol: 164, pp:547-552.

Borràs, J., Moreno, A. & Valls, A. (2014). Intelligent Tourism Recommender Systems: A Survey. *Expert Systems with Applications,* Vol: 41, pp:7370-7389.

Borrelli, G., Pistoia, M., Fruttarol, B. & Paolo, C. (2015). A System to Promote Walking for the Elderly and Empower Tourism: The Sweet Mobility Project. *In:* Andò, B., Siciliano, P., Marletta, V. & Monteriù, A. (eds.) *Ambient Assisted Living: Italian Forum 2014.* Cham: Springer International Publishing.

Cunha, L. (2013). *Economia E Política Do Turismo,* Lisboa, Lidel.

DSDMC (2014). *The Dsdm Agile Project Framework Handbook,* Ashford, Kent, UK, DSDM Consortium.

European Union (2018). The 2018 Ageing Report - Economic & Budgetary Projections for the 28 Eu Member States (2016-2070). *In:* Union, E. (ed.) *European Economy.* online: http://data.europa.eu/doi/10.2765/615631.

Figueiredo, C. (2014). A Complexidade Da Experiência Turística Mediatizada E Tecnologicamente Mediada: Uma Reflexão. *In:* Martins, M. d. L. & Oliveira, M. (eds.) *Comunicação Ibero-Americana: Os Desafios Da Internacionalização.*

Gavalas, D., Konstantopoulos, C., Mastakas, K. & Pantziou, G. (2014). Mobile Recommender Systems in Tourism. *Journal of network and computer applications,* Vol: 39, pp:319-333.

Huber, S., Demetz, L. & Felderer, M. (2020). Analysing the Performance of Mobile Cross-Platform Development Approaches Using Ui Interaction Scenarios. *In International Conference on Software Technologies.* Cham: Springer International Publishing.

Hyun, M. Y., Lee, S. & Hu, C. (2009). Mobile-Mediated Virtual Experience in Tourism: Concept, Typology and Applications. *Journal of Vacation Marketing,* Vol: 15, pp:149-164.

Ismail, A., Kadir, S. A. S. A., Aziz, A., *et al.* (2016). Itourism Travel Buddy Mobile Application. *In:* 2016 10th International Conference on Next Generation Mobile Applications, Security and Technologies (NGMAST), 2016. IEEE, 82-87.

Kazandzhieva, V. & Santana, H. (2019). E-Tourism: Definition, Development and Conceptual Framework. *Turizam: međunarodni znanstveno-stručni časopis,* Vol: 67, pp:332-350.

Kennedy-Eden, H. & Gretzel, U. (2012). A Taxonomy of Mobile Applications in Tourism. *e-Rev Tour Res (eRTR),* Vol: 10, pp:47-50.

Khadraoui, D., Ayed, H. & Nicolas, D. (2014). Sustainable E2 Mobility Services for Elderly People - Platform System Architecture. *2014 Science and Information Conference.* London: IEEE.

Klimova, B. (2018). Acceptance and Use of Mobile Devices and Apps by Elderly People. *In:* Al-Sharhan, S. A., Simintiras, A. C., Dwivedi, Y. K., Janssen, M., Mäntymäki, M., Tahat, L., Moughrabi, I., Ali, T. M. & Rana, N. P., eds. Challenges and Opportunities in the Digital Era, 2018 Kuwait City. Springer International Publishing, 30-36.

Majchrzak, T. A., Biørn-Hansen, A. & Grønli, T.-M. (2018). Progressive Web Apps: The Definite Approach to Cross-Platform Development? *Hawaii International Conference on System Sciences.* Hawaii.

Milano, R., Baggio, R. & Piattelli, R. (2011). The Effects of Online Social Media on Tourism Websites. *ENTER - International Conference on Information Technology and Travel & Tourism.* Innsbruck.

Oliveira, S., Leal, S., Vivas, C., *et al.* (2019). A Social Business Model for Active Ageing: The Case of Volto Já Project. *I Luso-Brazilian Meeting of Social Education (AGEINGCONGRESS2019).* Coimbra, Portugal: Thomson Reuters.

Osei, B. A., Ragavan, N. A., Kandappan, B. & Mensah, H. K. (2020). "Hospitality Revolution 4.0": A Literature Review on a Unified Typology of Ir 4.0 Technologies for the Tourism and Hospitality Industry in the Era of Covid-19. *Asia-Pacific Journal of Innovation in Hospitality and Tourism (APJIHT),* Vol: 9, pp:25.

Presenza, A., Panniello, U. & Messeni Petruzzelli, A. (2020). Tourism Multi-Sided Platforms and the Social Innovation Trajectory: The Case of Airbnb. *Creativity and Innovation Management,* Vol: n/a, pp:1-16.

Raposo, R., Pereira, P. M. B., Figueiredo, C. & Santos, H. (2012). A Abordagem Do E-Tourism Como Um Ecossistema De Inter-Influências Composto Por Rizomas De Redes Pessoais. *Revista Turismo & Desenvolvimento,* Vol: 1, pp:351-361.

Ribeiro, F. R., Silva, A., Barbosa, F., *et al.* (2018a). Mobile Applications for Accessible Tourism: Overview, Challenges and a Proposed Platform. *Information Technology & Tourism,* Vol: 19, pp:29-59.

Ribeiro, F. R., Silva, A., Metrôlho, J. C., *et al.* (2018b). A New Framework for Accessible Tourism Mobile Application Development. *International Journal of Mobile Computing and Multimedia Communications (IJMCMC),* Vol: 9, pp:31-46.

Rojas, C. (2020). Making Your First Progressive Web App. *Building Progressive Web Applications with Vue.Js: Reliable, Fast, and Engaging Apps with Vue.Js.* Berkeley, CA: Apress.

Signoretti, A., Martins, A. I., Almeida, N., *et al.* (2015). Trip 4 All: A Gamified App to Provide a New Way to Elderly People to Travel. *Procedia Computer Science,* Vol: 67, pp:301-311.

Wang, D. & Xiang, Z. (2012). The New Landscape of Travel: A Comprehensive Analysis of Smartphone Apps. Vienna: Springer Vienna.

Wörndl, W. & Herzog, D. (2020). Mobile Applications for E-Tourism. *In:* Xiang, Z., Fuchs, M., Gretzel, U. & Höpken, W. (eds.) *Handbook of E-Tourism.* Springer, Cham.

ANALYSIS, DESIGN AND IMPLEMENTATION OF A VACCINATION INFORMATION SYSTEM

Blirona Keraj[1] and Igli Hakrama[2]
[1]*Data Science & AI, Saarland University, Saarbrücken, Germany*
[2]*Computer Engineering, Epoka University, Tirana, Albania*

ABSTRACT

Nowadays, we cohabit with technology in an inseparable way. Acknowledging the importance of Immunization in population's health we emphasize the necessity of an intervention in the process of record-keeping and information flow that occurs during the vaccination and immunization procedures. This paper elaborates the process of analyzing, designing and implementing a Vaccination Information System e-Vacc using Unified Modelling Language

KEYWORDS

Vaccination Information System, UML, Data Processing, Vaccination Providers/Receivers, Design

1. INTRODUCTION

The way data is managed and handled is one of the main indicators of the efficiency and accuracy of the activity related to that data. Vaccination efficiency is a crucial metric that measures the quality of the national health care system. We are currently witnessing the collapse that can cause a contagious disease proving the importance and seriousness of this delicate topic. Undoubtedly, a qualitative and accurate information and historical data derived from vaccination is the best coach for future steps toward vaccination improvement.

Vaccination in Albania needs and deserves more than being handled manually and on paper registers and archives. The digitalization of this process will bring closer every party involved in vaccination, intensifying the cooperation for a better immunization procedure. To serve this need, a good solution would be a vaccination information system. This is an outcome of an iterative process from the analysis and design to the implementation of the system. Some of the steps are briefly presented in this paper using UML diagrams.

2. BACKGROUND

The interrelation between informatics and immunization is described by the transition from paper based to electronic health record. The systems already implemented in other countries and important indicators are put forward to support the idea of implementing a vaccination management system.

2.1 Transition from Paper Based to Electronic Health Record

An electronic health record is a repository of electronically maintained information about an individual's health status and health care, stored such that it can serve the multiple legitimate uses and users of the record. (Clement J. McDonald, 2014) Paper based record is a repository of individual's health information but stored in a media that constraints its functionality, paper.

EHR is flexible and takes the form user requires it, in contrary paper-based record which remains in the form it was stored, requires manual, time consuming manipulation with a high probability of errors. Health care and particularly vaccination is an information-intensive field. Vaccination providers are constantly collecting, gathering, reviewing, analyzing, communication information from many sources to make decisions. Information software related to health care is intended to facilitate the use of this information in different stages of delivery process. (A.B. Wilcox 2013) Main functions of health care related information systems are; acquiring, storing, summarizing and displaying data, generating reminders or other forms of decision support, facilitating communication and information exchange, supporting educational research and public health initiatives

2.2 Successful Implementations

One of the first countries that invested on immunization's improvement by implementing an IIS is the US (Novick, Lloyd F. MD, MPH 2014). These IIS are created based on the CDC criteria and are subject to some predefined Functional Standards whose main goal is to implement the best practices of immunization, address changes in technology and prioritize the IIS goals (Centers for Disease Control, 2019). The absence of a unified system causes lack of synchronization and ones that are privately funded are vulnerable toward privacy leaks. The four main strategic priorities for IIS are: enhancing performance, promote adherence to IIS standards, sustain the IIS community and influence and monitor the health IT environment.

Another country with a consolidated immunization system is England. The vaccination procurement and data management procedures are handled by 2 separated systems; ImmFrom, which is a Public Health England website used to both collect data on vaccine uptake for the national immunization program and provide ordering facilities for vaccines. CHIS is build in 3 sections (NHS England, August 2015); child health information service system, a child health record department (CHRD), a parent held child health record (PCHR). In Europe, also, many countries use an IIS but there are a few cases that implement the vaccination reminders, which are crucial for preventing latencies and other related consequences.

3. ANALYSIS AND DESIGN OF VACCINATION INFORMATION SYSTEM (E-VACC)

The process of developing an application includes a series of steps such as analyzing, designing, implementing and testing the application. The most useful tool used throughout these steps is Unified Modeling Language. UML is a standard language for writing the software blueprints. The UML diagrams are used to visualize, specify, construct the components of a software (Pressman, 1987).

The development of the application includes a series of interleaved iterative processes such as requirement elicitation, analysis, validation which are part of the requirement engineering activity. Each step is visualized using UML, starting with behavioral diagrams to continue with interaction diagrams, followed by the design process of the system with the structural diagrams and so on. The rest of the paper describes briefly some of the processes and steps toward the final design and implementation of the system.

3.1 Requirement Analysis

Requirement analysis is the process of collecting services, operations, features of a system, which are generally defined after consultation with all system stakeholders. (Terolli,2013). A detailed analysis on the vaccination process was conducted in collaboration with immunization service providers to have a clear idea what is expected from the application. The system will provide for each user their accounts and their functionalities, and this way ensure the data flow and user data interaction. The account creation cannot be done directly by the user himself, but according to the privileges and dependencies that users have with each other, to ensure a data protection at some extent.

Four priority points of e-Vacc are:

- Generating geographical and provider-level childhood vaccination coverage estimates
- Vaccination documentation including information of person vaccinated and the details related to the vaccines injected; vaccine type, lot number, manufacturer; injection site; dosage; and name, of person who injects the vaccine.
- Client reminder and feedback for provider/patient
- The inventory data registration, record of every order and automatic update calculations of available doses
- The patient side of the system including every detailed information for immunization processes and historical data

Use case diagrams are used to illustrate the interactions user has with the system and the user's perspective of the application. These diagrams include main functionalities system has for each actor.

The system can be used by 8 users:

Admin: the main system manager. The admin's account credentials are provided by the systems' creators. The account creation of the vaccination providers will be done by registration requests. Admin will receive and decide upon the registration requests from Main Depot Managers and Local Admins.

Local Admin: shall manage every user employee categorized by position on the Health Center he has been assigned. Local admin zones to patronage nurses, who gain access to all the children's personal cards and vaccination schedules living inside that zone of the geographical area covered by the Health Center.

Maternity nurse: registers the child into the system through the New Born section, pass the security step, fill the form with personal and the maternity information. Proceeds with child's account creation specifying the credentials which will be given to child's parents. The last step is the personal card creation based on baby's personal number, Health Center and the zone.

Vaccinator Nurse: records every vaccination and this vaccination entry will be automatically entered in the Main Register of Vaccination and in the individual's personal card. Besides the vaccination entry, in case of any incident or unusual situation the vaccinator shall document it on the Special Cases section for later reference and historical data maintenance. The nurse must record the used and wasted items to update the local depot inventory. Vaccinator shall generate the quarterly coverage report.

Patronage Nurse shall access every patients' personal immunization schedule and health card, can view the Main Register of the zone assigned to. The patronage Nurse shall view the upcoming vaccination in weekly and monthly plan and must trigger the function that automatically calculates and sends the email reminders for upcoming vaccination 3 days in advance to every vaccination receiver.

Local Depot Manager: shall send vaccine orders each trimester to the Main Depot. Maintain orders from Health Centers of the district he covers and subtract the distributed doses. Specify the received order date so the system does the addition of the new doses and subtracts these amounts of doses from the inventory of the supplier Main Depot. Generate the Vaccine Demand Trimester Plans.

Main Depot Manager: shall view the list of all Local Depots and their managers, also, manage the orders requested by the local depots and also request doses from the main suppliers. Generate the Vaccine Demand Trimester Plans. Maintain inventory by checking the low doses warnings sent by the system.

Child(parent): is the child account used by the parent to follow his child's immunization. Each of them can view their vaccination history and track it based on the official vaccination schedule. Changes can be made at the profile section and a feedback form is provided. Three days before the vaccination appointment every individual is notified through email reminder.

3.2 System Design

System design is related to constructing the system architecture and also defines the system abstractions and their relationships. Realization of software design based on a set of programs represents the implementation of the system (Sommerville 2011). After an intensive requirement analysis the main modules of the e-Vacc Vaccination System are identified; Depots and vaccine inventory, Child's account and Vaccination data, Health Centers and vaccination providers organization.

Activity diagram provides a graphical representation of the flow of actions and their interaction. In the activity diagram is represented the process of child's registration in the system, the personal card initialization and the child account access. This process is done by the maternity nurse in every maternity in Albania.

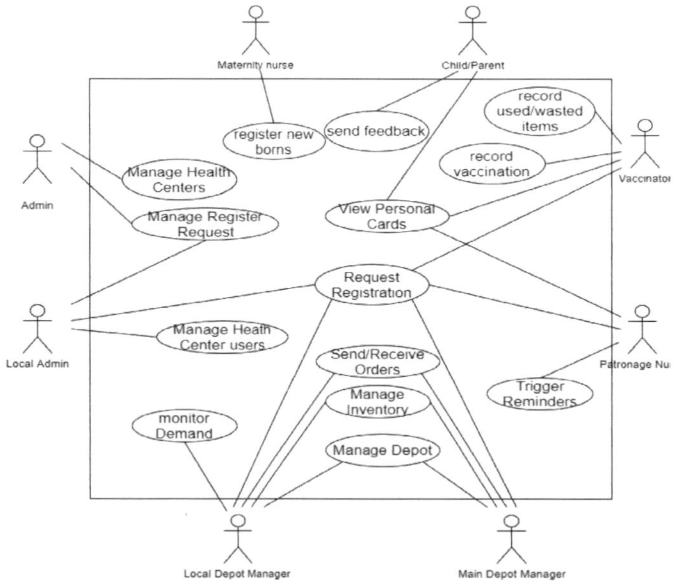

Figure 1. e-Vacc Use Case

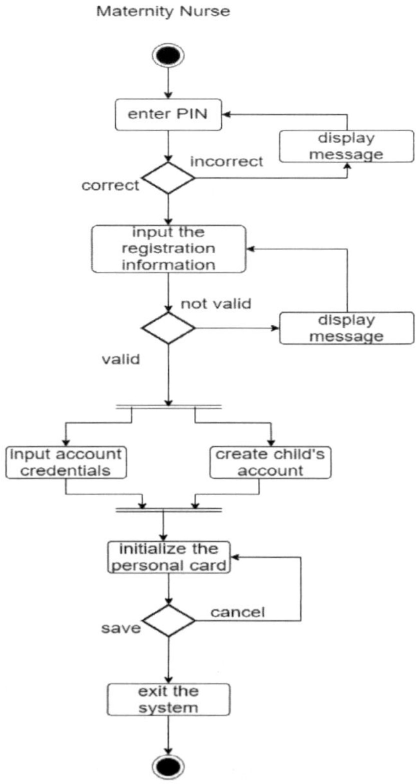

Figure 2. Child Registration Activity Diagram

Sequence diagrams are part of behavioral diagrams with the aim to represent the transition from one object to another as a function of time caused by different event. This sequence diagram is shown the vaccination entry record process done by the vaccinator for each child registered in a specific health centerThe personal Card of each child is generated by these vaccination entries. The main register, which holds the entries for every vaccination done, after each entry, fetches the data and gets updated.

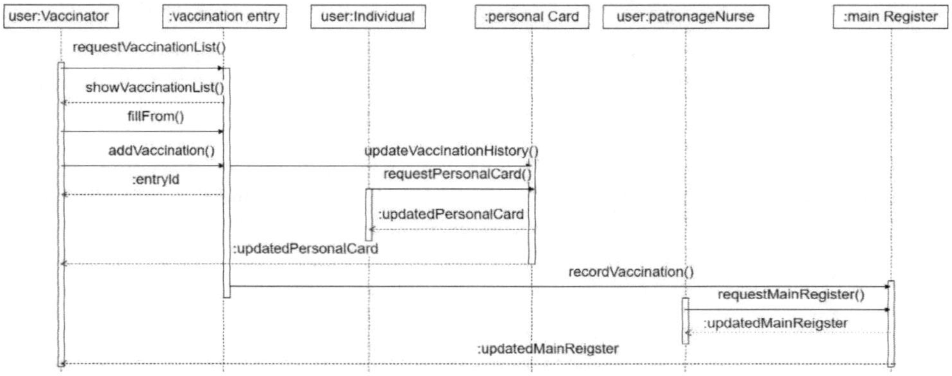

Figure 3. Vaccination entry Sequence Diagram

The most important features of the system are the reminders. Everyday the system calculates the upcoming vaccination for the following 3 days, based on birthdays in the database. The patronage nurse triggers the reminder everyday just by pressing a button, and the child's parents receive the email reminders.

4. IMPLEMENTATION

The e-Vacc is developed as a web-application in order to be easily accessed requiring only a device with internet connection. This way not only vaccination providers but also individuals can access their vaccination data anytime they want. The technologies used for building this web-application are PHP, MySql, CSS, Bootstrap, HTML, Java Script, JQuery the interconnection of which manipulates data and offers a responsive and user-friendly web application. The process is ongoing and the system is tested only on experimental made-up data, because it is not yet implemented on Albanian Vaccination since it is a private initiative.

The system follows the actual Albanian Vaccination processes, despite some procedures that are not necessary when using e-Vacc. Such a case is the child registration which traditionally is done by the patronage nurse who has to deliver and receive the documents in person to and from the maternity. This task of registering the child in the system, opening a personal card and specifying the Health Center is done by the maternity nurse when the infant is born.

The implemented version of Vaccination Information System can be found on: http://stud-proj.epoka.edu.al/~evaccine/Vaccination%20System/index.php

5. CONCLUSION

The success of immunization systems already implemented in different countries and the favorable infrastructure conditions in Albania push further the necessity of having a dedicated system for vaccination. The expected outcomes consist in reducing the vaccination providers workload, overcoming the lack of labor force, provide data efficiency, prevent vaccination latency, raise health institutions flexibility toward unexpected situations, data accuracy and availability to every individual.

Undoubtedly, aforementioned features require to be expanded adding more functionalities and modules to achieve a fully developed Immunization System. One of them is the module of health records from routine check-ups, by the Family's Doctor, of children from 0 to 6 years old. This will be the right complementary part for this application to settle a fully functioning and incorporative Immunization System.

REFERENCES

Centers for Disease Control and Prevention. (2019, October 7). Basics of Immunization Informatoin Systems. Retrieved from https://www.cdc.gov/vaccines/programs/iis/about.html

Clement J. McDonald, P. C. (2014). *Biomedical Informatics* (Vol. Electronic Health Record Systems). London: Springer . doi:https://doi.org/10.1007/978-1-4471-4474-8_12

NHS England. (2015, August 10). Child Health Information Services (CHIS)Provider Service Specifications. Retrieved from https://www.england.nhs.uk/commissioning/wpcontent/uploads/sites/12/2013/05/chis-provider-service-spec.pdf

Novick, L. F. (2014, June 6). Immunization Information Systems. *Journal of Public Health Management and Practice* . doi:10.1097/PHH.0000000000000111

Pressman, R. S. (1987). *Software Engineering: A practitioner's approach.* New York: McGraw-Hill. Retrieved from https://dinus.ac.id/repository/docs/ajar/Pressman-Software_Engineering-9ed.pdf

Somerville, I. (2011). *Software Engineering* (9th ed.). Addison-Wesley.

Terolli, E. & Hakrama, I., 2013, Modeling a Career Office Information System with UML, 2nd International Symposium on Computing in Informatics and Mathematics, Tirana, Albania, pp. 98-108.

BEHAVIORAL PROGRAMMING WITH A SUBSET OF NATURAL LANGUAGE: AN EVALUATION STUDY

Michal Gordon-Kiwkowitz[1] and David Harel[2]
[1]*Holon Institute of Technology, Holon, Israel*
[2]*Weizmann Institute of Science, Rehovot, Israel*

ABSTRACT

We consider the idea of behavioral programming by writing controlled natural language requirements, which are then compiled directly into executable code. Our motivation is to bridge the gap between system requirements and a final system. We claim that formal structured natural language requirements can serve as the means and the end to programming the behavior of reactive systems, if one utilizes a fully executable language that supports story-like sentences, such as *live sequence charts* (LSC). We use natural language processing methods combined with user interaction in order to understand English requirements, and translate them into LSCs, disambiguating and clarifying intentions with the user when necessary. We test a multi-modal user interface we term *show & tell*, where natural language is interspersed with *play-in*, and model-based co-reference resolution. Our approach is domain general and builds the underlying model of the system leading to direct execution. The paper presents novel evaluation studies that show its potential as an effective tool for natural language programming of reactive system behavior.

KEYWORDS

Live Sequence Charts, Controlled Natural Language, Modeling, Behavioral Programming, Scenario-Based Programming, Human Computer Interfaces

1. INTRODUCTION

The language of *live sequence charts (LSCs)* (Damm & Harel, 2001) and the subsequent challenge of "liberating programming", by which system behavior will be easily definable by making programming more similar to how people think (Harel, 2008), are the motivation for this paper. Many languages and interfaces have been invented in recent years for end-user programming (Cypher et al., 2010; Schlegel et al., 2019). Here we evaluate an interface for reactive systems' programming by engineers. LSCs are an executable visual formalism that describes natural "pieces" of behavior in a manner similar to telling someone what they may and may not do, and under what conditions, using short scenarios. The question we address here is: can we capture the desired behavior of a system in a far more natural style than is common? We want a style that is intuitive and less formal, and which can serve both as the system's behavioral specification and as its final executable artifact, bridging the gap between requirements and implementation.

Most system requirements are short and fragmented, and require further analysis in order to tie them together; in this sense they can be considered appropriate for automatic execution using LSC. The method we propose, termed *controlled natural language play-in (CNLPI)* assists requirement engineers, using a parser and a dialog system that guide them in writing structured controlled natural language (CNL) requirements, with a system model, that can be directly executed.

Natural language processing (NLP) has been used in computer-aided software engineering tools to assist human analysis of the requirements (Zhao et al., 2020). One such use is in extracting the classes, objects, methods or connections from the natural language description (Bryant & Lee, 2002; Mich, 1996). Another is applying NLP to use cases, in order to create simple sequence diagrams with messages between objects (Segundo et al., 2007), or to assist in initial design (Drazan & Mencl, 2007). A tool has been developed for capturing requirements in controlled natural language, backed by a formal requirements analysis engine and to automatically generate a complete set of requirements-based test cases (Moitra et al., 2019). Another tool has introduced the generation of core requirements from product requirements written in a natural language (Reinhartz-Berger & Kemelman, 2020).

Neural networks have been used to assist modeling elements of use case documents (Madala et al., 2020), and statistical methods have been used to transform natural language specifications into program input parsers (Lei et al., 2013) and into LSCs, using the CNL we describe (Tsarfaty et al., 2014). NLP has also been used to parse requirements and to extract executable code by generating object-oriented models using a two-level grammar (Bryant & Lee, 2002), and for reasoning in the Attempto language (Fuchs & Schwitter, 1995). NLP is widespread in end-user programming, for example, in web programming (Cypher et al., 2010). However, we note that in these efforts the resulting code is not scenario-based ; in most cases it describes the behavior of each object separately under the various conditions, and is usually limited to sequential behavior. The resulting code is rarely aligned with the system's requirements, and neither do these systems allow user interaction for complete system requirements translation.

An end-user interface for programming in Python was also developed and evaluated for programmers and non-programmers (Schlegel et al., 2019). Recently, deep learning algorithms for natural language programming have also been introduced (Desai et al., 2016). However, they require a large corpus of data for training.

In (Harel, 2001; Harel & Marelly, 2003), the mechanisms of *play-in* and *play-out* were described as means for making programming more practical. In play-in, the system engineer specifies scenarios by playing-them-in directly from a graphical user interface (GUI) of the system being developed. The developer interacts with the GUI that represents the objects in the as-of-yet behavior-less system, in order to show, or teach, the scenario-based behavior of the system by example (e.g., by clicking buttons, changing properties or sending messages). Play-in was developed independently, but is similar to other methods like programming by demonstration (PBD) (Cypher et al., 1993, 2010) in that it is a way of demonstrating behavior, and the behavior is generalized into recurring behavior. In play-in, demonstration is used to specify explicit requirements, usually GUI-based, in a scenario-based fashion. Play-in includes negative and possible scenarios, and always results in a full executable. The notion of demonstrating an example and having the system generalize it is but one facet of play-in. This paper focuses on the controlled natural language as an interface for programming, rather than on the idea of generalizing from examples.

In *play-out*, the execution phase, multiple scenarios are integrated into a fully executable artifact (Harel & Marelly, 2003). Since overall system behavior is defined by an incremental set of separate behaviors, it is usually underspecified, and may contain contradictions. Over the past few years, advanced algorithms for executing a set of LSC scenarios have been developed, employing synthesis (Harel & Segall, 2012), planning algorithms (Harel, 2006) and model-checking (Harel et al., 2002) to help alleviate this problem. In the present paper we focus on methods for creating LSCs, rather than executing them.

Thus, the main contribution of the current paper is an evaluation conducted to better understand the advantages and shortcoming of controlled natural language programming with LSCs as compared to other LSC interfaces and the ability to teach them.

The paper is organized as follows: Section 2 describes the LSC language and the CNL method for creating LSCs. Section 3 describes the evaluation studies and Sections. The paper concludes with Sec. 4.

2. THE LANGUAGE OF LSC

An LSC specifies behavior, stating what can be done, what must be done and what is forbidden. The behavior is a sequence of messages between object instances, with additional constructs that can add conditions. Thus, an LSC can assert mandatory behavior - what must happen, possible behavior - what can, or may happen, as well as forbidden behaviors and other possibilities and combinations. The LSC language (Damm & Harel, 2001; Harel & Marelly, 2003a) extends message sequence charts (MSC) (ITU: International Telecommunication Union, 1996), which in the UML are termed sequence diagrams (UML, 2007). In both formalisms, objects are represented by vertical lines, or lifelines, and messages between objects are represented by horizontal arrows between objects. Time advances along the vertical axis and the messages entail an obvious partial ordering.

A sample LSC is seen in Figure 1. The cold monitored events (dashed blue arrows) mean that the events are monitored and if they occur, the next event in the partial order should be monitored or executed. A hot execute event (solid red arrows) means that the system should perform the event eventually. The LSC language also includes conditions, assertions, loops and switch cases. Additionally, in (Harel & Marelly, 2003) the language was enriched to include also time, scoped forbidden elements and symbolic instances that allow reference to a class in general, not only to an instance, with the instantiation being carried out at runtime.

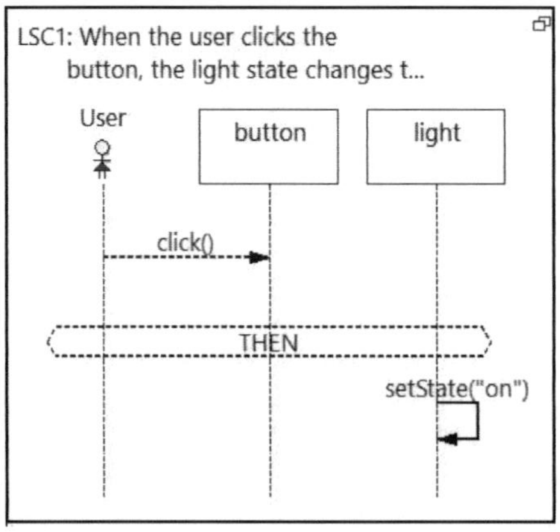

Figure 1. A sample LSC. The monitored message click is shown as a dashed blue arrow. A THEN synchronization invariant synchronizes executed events to occur only after the monitored events. The executed event here setState(''on'') is depicted as a solid red arrow. One possible sentence that creates this LSC is: "When the user clicks the button, the light state changes to on"

A set of LSCs is executed using the *play-out* mechanism (Harel & Marelly, 2003) . *Play-out* monitors at all times what must be done, what may be done and what is den and proceeds accordingly, yielding a complete execution of the LSC specification. The execution can be naïve, considering only the current state and progressing by choosing arbitrarily from all possible next events to be triggered, or use methods from model-checking or planning (Harel et al., 2002), to look-ahead and choose an execution order in a smarter fashion.

In this contribution, we focus on the interactive interface for programming LSCs, the basic one being *Play-in*. While programming by demonstration is meant for programming software applications using preferences, macro recordings, scripts, etc.; play-in uses demonstration to specify formal rules explicitly in order to describe a system's behavior. We believe play-in is more relevant to the requirement's engineering community, than to those making changes to customized software.

The play-in method works well for some operations, mostly those that involve the GUI. More complex operations, such as the "if-then" or "when some X then some Y" are less convenient to demonstrate, and are done, e.g., using menus. The CNL interface attempts to alleviate these difficulties, taking a further step towards liberating programming.

2.1 Controlled Natural Language Interface

The natural language interface for LSCs consists of a context free grammar (CFG) bottom-up parser (Jurafsky & Martin, 2008), a dialog system, and a knowledge base that also serves as the system model. The parser uses a CFG adapted for LSCs and is an extension of the active chart parser of Kay (Kay, 1986). The grammar is domain general and is composed from a set of rules and terminal symbols. The terminal symbols include static terminals / reserved words, that are used as language directives such as *if, then, must, may,* etc. and dynamic terminals are processed by a dictionary or taken from the working system model.

The grammar used in the current study is described in (Gordon & Harel, 2009), it includes the ability to specify in CNL the following elements: messages, condition, forbidden messages, symbolic entities and some additional constructs not tested in this research.

To resolve imprecise and ambiguous requirements with the help of the engineer, we have implemented a dialog system using an interface similar to the *quick fix* interface of programming environments like Eclipse

IDE (Carlson, 2005). The engineer may then select one of the options from the dialog (a quick option that fixes the problem) or make a different change on his/her own once the problem is known. Figure 2 shows a sample problem and available solutions.

The problems encountered may be a result of different types of analysis: a grammatical analysis, an LSC disambiguation or a model connected analysis. In the first type, a word may have two different meanings, e.g., *value* can be used as a verb or a property. In the second type, a sentence can be interpreted differently when creating the LSC. For example, in the partial sentence "the controller toggles the light", when no information about model elements exists, one interpretation is a message toggles from object controller to light and another is a self message toggles from object controller to itself with the message parameter of the light.

In the third type, the analysis checks that the terms the engineer refers to appear in the *system model*. The system model is a tree structure containing all the objects in the specification, each object with its properties and methods. Figure 2 displays the system model of the wristwatch example. Some objects may be represented in the GUI, while others may not.

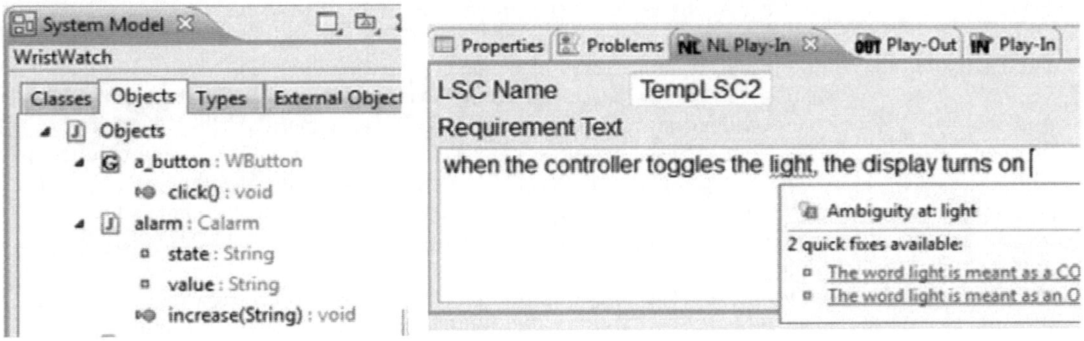

Figure 2. The tool. On the left is the system model view with a model of a wristwatch. On the right is a sample of quick fix options for resolving an ambiguity. The problem location is indicated by the squiggly line and the quick box dialog that appears when hovering with the mouse over the problem displays the problem's description and possible solutions, if available. Tool available at http://wiki.weizmann.ac.il/playgo/index.php/PlayGo_Feature_List#Natural_language_play-in

3. EVALUATION STUDIES

We next describe three preliminary evaluation studies which aim to better understand the CNL behavioral approach to development. In study 1 we conducted a user study with a novice programmer, interviewing her while she created 2 full projects using the language. Our main question was: how long would it take a novice programmer to learn the language. Study 2 was more elaborate and included a class of graduate students attempting to comprehend the language in a shorter time frame. The next tree sections report on our preliminary findings.

3.1 Study 1: Novice Programmer Example

We asked the novice programmer to learn the CNL for LSCs on her own, using the PlayGo website [http://wiki.weizmann.ac.il/playgo/index.php/Main_Page] and the tutorial used in (Gordon & Harel, 2012).

As for the novice programmer, after a week, she was able to complete the task from the first experiment and was then able to program systems of her own choice. She created modest examples of a cell phone [http://wiki.weizmann.ac.il/playgo/index.php/Phone_Specification] and a chess game [http://wiki.weizmann.ac.il/playgo/index.php/Chess_Game_Example]. This participant was in her twenties, fresh out of undergraduate school, and a non-native English speaker. Her ability to write in CNL increased and eventually she created systems with 20 requirements. Some syntax choices in the grammar, like the necessity to add a determinant before an object, were not naturally occurring in her English. Her learning of the CNL included learning the CNL syntax, which is similar to learning the syntax of other programming languages and specifically she had to learn to add a determinant before object names. Part of writing the CNL requirements was dedicated to figuring out what type of behaviors were low-level and require further implementation in Java. For example, in the chess game, calculating the possible location of all pieces was done in Java code. The examples are available [http://wiki.weizmann.ac.il/playgo/index.php/Chess_Game_Example].

Since we concluded that knowledge of LSC is required, we continued to test comprehension and creation of LSC in a shorter time frame.

3.2 Study 2: Quick Comprehension and Creation

In this study, we focused the evaluation on using PlayGo to model a coffee machine system. We concentrated on the following research questions: (i) Is the controlled natural language play-in method sufficient for writing and reading requirements? (ii) Can it be learned and used effectively in two sessions?

Participants. The experiment took place at Tel Aviv University (TAU) and the Academic College of Tel Aviv-Yafo (MTA). Participants were recruited from computer science graduate students, who had taken advanced classes on software modeling. Students were offered a small monetary reward for their time, independent of performance in the experiment. No grades were involved. A single three hour class meeting, conducted a week before the experiment, was dedicated to introducing the ideas of scenario-based programming and to presenting the LSC language and the PlayGo tool. The meeting included a short live demo.

In total, 19 graduate students participated, sixteen male and three female. All had over three years of programming experience, in languages such as Java and C#. Each received a booklet with instructions and questions, as well as a copy of a pre-prepared PlayGo workspace, running on Eclipse in one of the two universities student labs. Each of the participants spent between 2 and 2.5 hours to complete the experiment. sixteen participants completed all parts of the experiment, while three had to leave before completion due to other unrelated scheduled obligations (we left them out of the analysis for the questions they did not answer). Participants signed a consent form and the study was approved by the institutional IRB.

Protocol. We designed an evaluation study with small tasks and questions that attempt to get user preference and abilities in qualitative and quantitative measurements. Participants received a set of tasks divided into five parts, roughly going from basic and easy tasks to more complex and difficult ones. We had the participants add requirements to increase the system's complexity, while also gaining experience using the play-in approach. Part I dealt with LSC comprehension, and parts II and IV dealt with play-in, examining the process of creating an LSC, both in CNL text and graphically. Parts III and V were related to play-out and will be reported upon in a future publication. We gave participants a high-level description of a new requirement and asked them to write it down more formally, first by writing it in general English, then by drawing it, and finally by using the CNLPI interface in PlayGo to define the new LSC.

Each of the three parts included a mix of multiple-choice questions for quantitative analysis and open-ended questions for a more qualitative analysis. We planned to perform the experiment in a 2-3 hour session, allowing participants to advance at their own pace. We estimated times after a test run with two developers from our group.

The LSCs used in the experiment were adapted from several variants of the vending machine specifications described in (Maoz & Sa'ar, 2012, 2013). They consist of 5-7 LSCs, and involve a user, a water heater, a panel, a cashier, and a dispenser. When designing an example application for the experiment, we chose to adapt this previously studied example, in order to eliminate the risk of our own bias (e.g., to create an application that is unfairly simple) .

The questionnaire was designed to test the hypothesis using qualitative and quantitative questions. Table 1 summarizes the type of questions and their goal. The complete questionnaire is available in supporting materials (https://drive.google.com/file/d/1hn2bGmPZBw5fVyiy2454leNyZIOyO3zg/view?usp=sharing).

Part I. The tasks in part I intended to examine the participants understanding of basic LSC concepts and their ability to read and understand a given single LSC and a given specification that consisted of several LSCs, presented both graphically and in controlled natural language text. Given a specification with four LSCs, we asked participants to distinguish system events from environment-controlled events, to describe in their own words what the system does, to select a correct, short high-level description of what the system does (e.g, "serves coffee", "counts coins and returns change"), etc. We then asked the participants to reflect on which of the presentation forms they used more often in order to understand the system's behavior and answer the questions: the diagrams or the textual description in controlled natural language.

Part II. The task in part II was to define a requirement in which the panel shows the word error whenever the user asks for coffee but coffee cannot be served. Participants had to figure out that this situation occurs when the user requests coffee but three coins have not yet been inserted.

Part IV. In part IV, the task was a bit more complicated, in the context of a more complex specification (two new LSCs were introduced). The participants had to add a cancellation functionality that would allow the user of the vending machine to retrieve her coins.

Table 1. Goal and type of questions in the questionnaire. Q_i is the question number, and P_i is the part number, as some parts had an unnumbered open question

Description	Goal	Multiple Choice	Open Ended
Programming background	Establish knowledge level	Q1	Q2
LSC background	SubjectiveLSC understanding	Q3, Q5, Q44	Q4, Q45
LSC Comprehension	Understanding existing specification	Q6, Q7, Q9	P1, Q8
Comprehension preference	Subjectivepreference	Q10	
LSC generation	Creating LSCs in NL, CNL, drawing		Q11-13, Q15, Q16, Q27-29, Q32
Generation preference	Preferred creation method	Q14, Q30	Q15, Q31

Due to the limited time, we did not ask participants to create the LSCs in diagram form using PlayGo, nor did we allow for time to try and run the new specification with the LSC that was added using CNLPI. However, participants were asked to reflect on which of the activities they preferred, drawing or writing natural language text.

3.2.1 Results

Comprehension. All participants were able to complete the comprehension task, which made their results relevant for further analysis. All but four rated their understanding of LSCs after the single lesson as 'not so good', two rated their understanding as 'good', and two as 'not good at all'. In the second class we added a question of LSC understanding also at the end of the last task, and for the seven participants who answered the understanding question before and after the experiment there was a significant difference between the two answers (Wilcoxon 1-tail signed-rank test $W(5) = 0,\ p \leq 0.05$). For the comprehension task in part I, we found a significant preference to use the diagram over the text, which is in line with the fact that the text can be ambiguous while the diagram contains complete and formal information ($W(13) = 3.5, p \leq 0.05$).

Play-in. For part II, all participants were able to provide a single LSC that captured the requirement; some of these LSCs were correct while others were almost correct. Most participants entered a requirement that caused an error if there were less than 3 coins, while others showed an error, when the number of coins was different than 3. We did not find a tendency to prefer the CNLPI over the drawing, or the other way around ($W(14) = 49, p > 0.05$).

As one participant mentioned: *"You cannot work only on the text, you must have the diagram in order to verify that the text was correctly understood"* [translated]. We therefore feel that the question might have caused confusion between using CNLPI with or without the diagram as feedback, versus creating the diagram directly. We also believe that since participants drew freely on paper, without getting any feedback on whether the syntax was correct, it was not appropriate to compare to the CNLPI, where they did use the tool and had to adhere to the exact syntax.

No preference was found also in part IV ($W(17) = 52, p > 0.05$). However in task two, we got a larger variety of LSCs; participants used between one and three LSCs. Most participants attempted to handle not only the requirement we asked for, i.e., the cancel functionality, but also the problems that may be caused by cancelling in mid-operation.

Overall, it seems that participants were able to express their requirements in LSCs, both in diagram format, and in CNL. In some cases, the CNL was similar to the general requirement description. For example, participant #3 wrote the requirement as: *"When the user requests coffee from the panel, if the cashier coins are less than 3, the panel shows 'error'."*, and the CNL was exactly the same. There were additional participants who chose to use the CNL examples for their description, when they were asked to use the controlled English as example for their own requirements. Thus, we also had participants who wrote text fragments that were replaced later by text that was acceptable by the CNL parser. For example, participant #5 started with: *"When the user requests coffee from the panel, if the dispenser cannot serve coffee, the panel shows 'error'."*. This requirement, which includes a condition on an event (not supported in LSCs), was changed to: *"When the user requests coffee from the panel, if the dispenser status is 'cannot serve coffee', the panel shows an error."*

Participants were able to work with PlayGo, after a very short tutorial session. Participants were able to specify useful requirements in CNLPI mainly by using the examples provided. Some did complain about understanding the syntax errors and commented as an example: *"The parser error are not very informative. You need to hit the correct syntax. If you could draw the LSC while the user is typing it could help a lot"*. However they were ultimately able to solve the problems with little help.

Most participants were able to complete the task, comprehend the system, and extend it with some LSCs, in expected time, with very little tutoring and practice. We believe this hints to the learnability of the language and the PlayGo tool. Those participants that did not complete the second task were all in the second group, which participated in the experiment in the afternoon, and we believe, since it was voluntary, that they preferred to leave due to the late hour. However, this might have been due to the task difficulty.

4. CONCLUSION

In answer to some of the questions raised in the introduction about the knowledge necessary to program LSCs with CNL, it was important in all cases for the participants to have knowledge of the LSC visual language, and to verify that their text was translated as they expected. Natural language even in the controlled form we discussed, is not formal enough for execution. With the help of a system model, the CNL requirements are less ambiguous, but it is only with the LSC chart that the formalism is completely clear. Therefore, the writer verifies her requirements with the visual representation of the LSCs and is expected to understand them. Another question, is how long it takes an engineer to learn the method. Our evaluation has shortcomings, and a better tool and longer evaluation are required, yet we show a possibility of using CNL for LSC after two short sessions allowing comprehension and creation of a demo system.

Creating complex reactive systems is not a simple task and neither is understanding natural language requirements. We have presented a method that translates controlled NL requirements into LSCs, which are fully executable. Moreover, we have expanded the power of this NL interface by combining it with play-in, yielding the hybrid show & tell method. The implementation of the system is thus a set of fragmented, yet structured requirements/ namely the LSCs, which are fully executable.

The ability to translate a controlled natural language into the formal language of LSCs is a step in the direction of making programming more readily available in our developing digital world. The translation we suggest is tailored for the LSC language, but can be extended to support other languages too. It can also be integrated with other non-programmer approaches.

Some of the key features this work offers include formal rules, fragmented and scenario-based descriptions in the spirit of behavioral programming, and an executable and verifiable system with an intelligent natural interface. These ideas take a step towards having the computational tools adapt to human nature than to have humans adapt and learn computational concepts.

The current situation regarding the execution of LSCs is not without its limitations. LSCs do not always result in a deterministic execution and the execution is not always optimal. Nor are LSCs yet scalable to very large systems. However, progress is being made on the execution methods; see for example, (Harel et al., 2002; Harel & Segall, 2012). The work presented here shows how NLP and the LSC formalism, together with the behavioral programming approach, take programming closer to how humans specify requirements.

ACKNOWLEDGEMENT

We would like to thank Shahar Maoz and Smadar Szekely for their help with the evaluation experiment, Shmuel Tishberowitz for assisting in recruiting participants for it, and Jayasree Nair for helping with the checkers example. This work was supported in part by grant number 857/12 to D.H. from the Israel Science Foundation.

REFERENCES

Bryant, B. R., & Lee, B.-S. (2002). Two-Level Grammar as an Object-Oriented Requirements Specification Language. *Proc. 35th Annual Hawaii Int. Conf. on System Sciences (HICSS'02)*, 280–289.

Carlson, D. (2005). *Eclipse Distilled*. Addison-Wesley.

Cypher, A., Dontcheva, M., Lau, T., & Nichols, J. (2010). *No Code Required: Giving Users Tools to Transform the Web*. Morgan Kaufmann Publishers Inc.

Cypher, A., Halbert, D. C., Kurlander, D., Lieberman, H., Maulsby, D., Myers, B. A., & Turransky, A. (Eds.). (1993). *Watch What I Do: Programming by Demonstration*. MIT Press.

Damm, W., & Harel, D. (2001). LSCs: Breathing Life into Message Sequence Charts. *Formal Methods in System Design*, *19*(1), 45–80.

Desai, A., Gulwani, S., Hingorani, V., Jain, N., Karkare, A., Marron, M., R, S., & Roy, S. (2016). Program Synthesis Using Natural Language. *Proceedings of the 38th International Conference on Software Engineering*, 345–356.

Drazan, J., & Mencl, V. (2007). Improved Processing of Textual Use Cases: Deriving Behavior Specifications. *Proc. 33rd Int. Conf. on Trends in Theory and Practice of Computer Science*, 856–868.

Fuchs, N. E., & Schwitter, R. (1995). Attempto: Controlled natural language for requirements specifications. *Proc. 7th ILPS Workshop on Logic Programming Environments*.

Gordon, M., & Harel, D. (2012). Evaluating a Natural Language Interface for Behavioral Programming. *Proc. of IEEE Symp. on Visual Languages and Human-Centric Computing*, 17–20.

Gordon, M., & Harel, D. (2009). Generating Executable Scenarios from Natural Language. *Proc. 10th Int. Conf. on Computational Linguistics and Intelligent Text Processing*, 456–467.

Harel, D. (2001). From Play-In Scenarios To Code: An Achievable Dream. *Computer*, *34*(1), 53–60.

Harel, D. (2008). Can Programming be Liberated, Period? *Computer*, *41*(1), 28–37.

Harel, D. (2006). Playing with Verification, Planning and Aspects: Unusual Methods for Running Scenario-Based Programs. *Proc. 18th Int. Conf. on Computer Aided Verification*, 3–4.

Harel, D., Kugler, H., Marelly, R., & Pnueli, A. (2002). Smart Play-Out of Behavioral Requirements. *Proc. 4th Int. Conf. on Formal Methods in Computer-Aided Design*, 378–398.

Harel, D., & Marelly, R. (2003). *Come, Let's Play: Scenario-Based Programming Using LSC's and the Play-Engine*. Springer-Verlag.

Harel, D., & Segall, I. (2012). Synthesis from scenario-based specifications. *J. of Comp. and Sys. Sci.*, *78*(3), 970–980.

ITU: International Telecommunication Union. (1996). *Recommendation Z.120: Message Sequence Chart (MSC)*.

Jurafsky, D., & Martin, J. H. (2008). *Speech and Language Processing: An Introduction to Natural Language Processing, Computational Linguistics, and Speech Recognition*. Prentice-Hall.

Kay, M. (1986). *Readings in Natural Lang. Processing* (B. J. Grosz, K. Sparck-Jones, & B. L. Webber, Eds.; pp. 35–70).

Lei, T., Long, F., Barzilay, R., & Rinard, M. (2013). From Natural Language Specifications to Program Input Parsers. *Proc. Annual Meeting Assoc. for Computational Linguistics*.

Madala, K., Piparia, S., Blanco, E., Do, H., & Bryce, R. (2020). Model elements identification using neural networks: A comprehensive study. *Requirements Engineering*. https://doi.org/10.1007/s00766-020-00332-2

Maoz, S., & Sa'ar, Y. (2012). Assume-Guarantee Scenarios: Semantics and Synthesis. *MoDELS*, 335–351.

Maoz, S., & Sa'ar, Y. (2013). Counter Play-out: Executing Unrealizable Scenario-based Specifications. *Proc. 2013 Int. Conf. on Software Engineering*, 242–251.

Mich, L. (1996). NL-OOPS: From Natural Language to Object Oriented Requirements Using the Natural Language Processing System LOLITA. *Natural Language Engineering*, *2*(2), 161–187.

Moitra, A., Siu, K., Crapo, A. W., Durling, M., Li, M., Manolios, P., Meiners, M., & McMillan, C. (2019). Automating requirements analysis and test case generation. *Requirements Engineering*, *24*(3), 341–364.

Reinhartz-Berger, I., & Kemelman, M. (2020). Extracting core requirements for software product lines. *Requirements Engineering*, *25*(1), 47–65. https://doi.org/10.1007/s00766-018-0307-0

Schlegel, V., Lang, B., Handschuh, S., & Freitas, A. (2019). Vajra: Step-by-Step Programming with Natural Language. *Proceedings of the 24th International Conference on Intelligent User Interfaces*, 30–39. https://doi.org/10.1145/3301275.3302267

Segundo, L. M., Herrera, R. R., & Herrera, K. Y. P. (2007). UML Sequence Diagram Generator System from Use Case Description Using Natural Language. *Electronics, Robotics and Automotive Mechanics Conf.*, *0*, 360–363.

Tsarfaty, R., Pogrebezky, I., Weiss, G., Natan, Y., Szekely, S., & Harel, D. (2014). Semantic Parsing Using Content and Context: A Case Study from Requirements Elicitation. *Proc. Int. Conf. on Empirical Methods in Natural Language Processing (EMNLP)*, 1296–1307.

UML. (2007). *Unified Modeling Language Superstructure, v2.1.1* (formal/2007-02-03; Issue formal/2007-02-03). Object Management Group.

Zhao, L., Alhoshan, W., Ferrari, A., Letsholo, K. J., Ajagbe, M. A., Chioasca, E.-V., & Batista-Navarro, R. T. (2020). Natural Language Processing (NLP) for Requirements Engineering: A Systematic Mapping Study. *ArXiv Preprint ArXiv:2004.01099*.

A HOLISTIC FRAMEWORK FOR INFORMATION SYSTEM FOR THE MANAGEMENT OF INDOOR ENVIRONMENTAL QUALITIES (IEQ) IN BUILT FACILITIES

Ahmed M. Ibrahim[1], Mohammad A. Hassanain[2] and Ibrahim A. Hameed[1]
[1]*Department of ICT, Norwegian University of Science and Technology, Ålesund, Norway*
[2]*Architectural Engineering Department, King Fahd University of Petroleum and Minerals, Dhahran, Saudi Arabia*

ABSTRACT

Because every building is considered as a long-run investment, regardless of its scale, at least to its owner, broadly by collectively impacting the national development of built assets. It is a vital aspect to ensure the qualities which define its inhabitance experience. Buildings' indoor environments have been undermined being observed as an uncontrolled expensive application of systems, targeted for research, while indoor environmental quality (IEQ) is one of the assembly of aspects that aim to appraise almost any built facility performance. There have been research efforts in literature, with global and contextual limitations, covering dispersed relations and topics in the IEQ domain, such as the control, and analysis of occupants' satisfaction and facilities systems performance in respect to standards. These research efforts were more focused on investigating results rather than allowing for an automated solution for the creation of universal standards. Therefore, emerged a need for modelling IEQ management in an inclusive manner, to allow for the sustainable management and understanding of facilities components' impacts, on both occupants' experiences and wellbeing, whereas the power of information systems with the capabilities of todays' hardware and technologies, set a new era, for the architectural science in digital means. This research paper proposes a conceptual information system framework modelled in Integrated Computer Aided Manufacturing Definition for Function Modeling (IDEF$_0$) diagram, to enable the architects and the facility managers to sustainably manage and monitor IEQs in built facilities. The proposed framework is based on a standardized big data analytics that can provide architects and facility managers with meaningful insights for achieving an evidence based, and informed design thinking, as well as sustainable monitoring of built facilities in real time.

KEYWORDS

Framework, IEQ, Information System, Open Database, Big Data Analytics, Universal, Facilities Management, Life Cycle Assessment (LCA), Sustainable Development Goals (SDGs)

1. INTRODUCTION

Facilities management is the science which encompasses people, process and technology endeavoring highest quality of occupation, services, and operation of the built environment. Built facilities are considered as a long run investment by their owners, (either as organizations or individuals), that need to maintain satisfactory conditions for its indoor environments. The challenge is in alignment of users' satisfaction, while maintaining control over the variety of systems in facilities, through the continuous appraisal of operational performance, on the macro-urban and micro-indoor environments (Alexander, 1992; Bröchner et al., 2019; Lindkvist et al., 2020).

The advancement of facilities is evaluated by benchmarking of facilities with similar functionalities, in different indoor environmental quality (IEQ) elements that are not limited to the air cooling, heating, ventilation, conditioning, thermal comfort, indoor air quality (IAQ), spaces acoustics, illumination, aesthetics and recently to the exposure of electromagnetic frequencies (Dan Norbäck, 2020; Ribino et al., 2020; Wei et al., 2020). Unsatisfactory conditions impact occupants by several means, such as sick building syndrome, noise, contamination, thermal discomfort, and loss of productivity (Hameen et al., 2020). Thus, many researchers worked on different research objectives, by focusing on relational impacts of building systems design, selection and operation on occupants. In a sense where IEQ is put into question, from a holistic point of view.

International organizations, *e.g.* American Society of Heating, Refrigerating and Air-Conditioning Engineers (ASHRAE) provides an international standard based on collected global data, to develop a thermal comfort database. Unfortunately, the limitation was always geographical, varying based on the providing countries systematic research and collection methods, undertaking IEQ data. The resulting database was in excel format and limited to specific regions (such as: Australia, Belgium, Brazil, Canada, China, Denmark, France, Germany, Greece, India, Indonesia, Italy, Japan, Malaysia, Mexico, Nigeria, Pakistan, Philippines, Portugal, Singapore, Slovakia, South Korea, Sweden, Thailand, Tunisia, UK and USA). Furtherly the database included a limited number of indicators and facilities, Yet, considered to be one of the most comprehensive data for designers and facility managers (Földváry et al., 2018). Other organizations such as Chartered Institution of Building Services Engineers (CIBSE), U.S. Green Building Council (USGBC), and online benchmarking tools also developed an emerged sources of data but with geographical and contextual limitations, serving only specific focus on subjective or objective measures, that lack holisticness in the making (Heinzerling et al., 2013).

What if there is an enabling platform, along with the advancement of technology, that can be implemented at a wider prospect, openly over the planet, without commercial interests, that can release precise and interoperable standards for all. Allowing designers to an access for a globalized standard, where engineers from a specific region can open access standards for another, by then, newer business opportunities would emerge in an accelerating world of demands.

There are different standards that developed indices and requirements to maintain satisfactory indoor environment, based on research conducted at different facilities, such as: *Center for the Built Environment at Berkley*, *Center for Sustainable Built Environment at New York University*, and *Centre for a Sustainable Built Environment at KTH royal institute of technology*. Despite the innovative tools developed by such organizations, usually, the process of developing such standards and recommendations holds time, comprise extensive costs for funding, to measure, review and analyze built environment IEQ data, as well as they do not deliver an open and universal database, that allows for an accustomed analyses, of a longtime historical and accurate ranges, that can effectively enhance the understanding, design and operation of the indoor environments of facilities. Different tools and formulae can be used for measuring IEQ indices, these organizations have made a distinguished advancement being able to collect specific features about the space. The collected measurements and calculation of IEQ indices allow architects and facility managers to analyze evidence for future design projects and operation of existing facilities. Different regions have developed own standards, to promote guidelines for designers and facility managers to improve its indoor environment targeting sustainable design and operation of facilities. With time the standards developed serve to enrich a knowledge base that contains analyzed data in various formats.

Since, people spend 90% of their time in built facilities (Danza et al., 2020) being critical to their wellbeing. Thus, the dispersed research efforts in literature establish research questions, that needs to be investigated.

2. RESEARCH AIMS AND QUESTIONS

- How can IEQ indicators be updated systematically in an agile and collective manner?
- How can the IEQ be assessed in a holistic manner? combining physical measurements and subjective feedbacks from the users about their built environment?
- How can IEQ be assessed to serve a universal geographical context allowing for watch over different types of facilities?
- How can IEQ serve the sustainability and operation of facilities?
- How can IEQ data be processed to provide a consistent, and an on-demand reporting?
- What are the potentials of a holistic IEQ database? for researchers, designers as well as regulators?

3. RESEARCH METHODOLOGY

The research is designed to comprise of three main stages:

1) Review of select of recent journal publications in the literature, within the domain of facilities management and IEQ research, on the holisticness of approaches for the assessment and management of built facilities, questioning for the evaluation tools, techniques, and methods producing the IEQ indicators. Also, to review the literature upon geographical contexts and buildings typologies coverage for IEQ research.

2) Development and proposal of a systematic framework allowing for a universal IEQ data collection, assessment, reporting, benchmarking. This is for allowing the sustainable operation and maintenance of built facilities and keeping of design recommendations of new facilities.

3) Conclusion and recommendations for the proposed framework and further considerations that can lead to effective validation.

4. LITERATURE REVIEW

Scopus search engine was utilized to synthesize journal publications in 2020, on the topic of IEQ. Keywords searched for were: "Indoor environmental quality framework", "IEQ", "Assessment of IEQ" and "IEQ benchmarks". A plethora of research results emerged in the database, yet, most of the references focused on investigating relational performance elements between demographics of the occupants and the IEQ, while some references focused on the development of compass tools for visually representing the IEQ indicators, other references focused on utilizing different measurement devices for physical and subjective measurements of IEQ performance, Yet the references did not serve the need for a holistic framework for the management of IEQ, on a high level of processes. Fast readings of the papers' contexts were conducted to synthesize recent references that are critical to provide an overall impression of the research magnitudes, contexts as in the literature on IEQ, the review findings were as follows:

Ioannou *et al.* (2019) researched the possibility of using a free software to calculate a prediction for heat strain of individuals at a built facility (based on equations and formulae elaborated in ISO 7933:2018). This is for optimization of calculating the heat strain, the developed software model is namely: FAME Lab PHS Calculator software (PHS_{FL}). The researchers reviewed further related standards of different regionality. The validation of the software has shown high predictability in accordance with standards by 95% significance. This finding promotes the potential behind the historical IEQ data and its collection accuracy to predict a facility IEQ indicator, and report it in accordance to different standards. The authors discussed that "*it is not always possible to perform the necessary physiological assessments in workers due to, for instance, lack of equipment, expertise, resources, time, and/or inability to recruit volunteers*". Despite this statement, A project by the European Union was funded to develop a model for predicting heat strain (PHS) over a group with known environmental and physiological conditions. Based on dynamically variant inputs and parameters, the researchers discovered high significance, by comparing predicted results to field experiments. Such predictability, enables physiologists, industrial hygienists, and occupational physicians to enhance workers' health and improve productivity by improving the built environment.

Hassanain (2007) evaluated IEQ by conducting an indicative Post Occupancy Evaluation (POE) on students housing facilities, at a public university in Saudi Arabia. The research involved investigations of historical maintenance data, frequent complains and areas of discomfort raised by the occupants, as well as the conduct of surveys to obtain their feedback qualitatively. The analyses lead to recommendations directed for designers, planners and operation and maintenance teams upon satisfactory requirements for similar type of facilities projects (future students' housings). The elements investigated were an IEQ requirements of thermal, acoustical, visual comfort, and IAQ. Several standards were referenced to benchmark the facilities existent conditions. The research involved processes of data analyses, were plans of the facility were referenced to provide a schematic understanding of design impacts in relevance to occupation. An overall satisfaction mean was calculated, to represent the sampled opinions. The research was produced in a manner, that it can be applied to a similar type of educational housing facilities, especially in Saudi Arabia.

Cao *et al.* (2020) researched the impacts of Heating Ventilation and Air Conditioning (HVAC) system and controls, on wellbeing of occupants. The research highlighted the role of IEQ investigations, in relevance to Chinese standards of performance criteria. This was initiated by a promoting requirement in china to induce passive elements in facilities, that can allow for the realization of near-zero energy buildings. The authors highlighted that HVAC systems can be responsible for more than 50% of a total energy consumption in built facilities. Moreover, because that HVAC can directly affect the IAQ, where pollutants transferability is a subject of concern. The IEQ Elements under investigations were Particulate matters with different sizes such as (PM_{10}, and $PM_{2.5}$), Volatile Organic Compounds (VOC_s) and Nitrogen oxides (NO_x), Airborne fungi, Ozone (O_3), radon and Carbon dioxide CO_2 concentrations. Since pollutants have undesirable impacts on human health by impacting the overall wellbeing of occupants, thus, its needed to understand the correlations, allowing better regulation of air to enhance quality and reduce such risks. Thus, the study researched correlation between different IEQ and HVAC systems performance under the check of compliance to Chinese specifications, for the better understanding of the systems performance. The research recommended the need for establishing a systematic feedback mechanism by regulation, to assess the correlation between the environmental control and human behaviors.

Yoseph (2020) investigated a set of parameters in residential built facilities, located at Borg el Arab region in Egypt. This is to relate the IEQ design elements and performance with urban formation of units, for future developments of residential urban communities and evaluation of the regulatory standards comprehensiveness. The author discussed several buildings characteristics that affected the IEQ, along with the design of openings in each unit (*e.g.* orientation, size, and positioning). The spatial and environmental standard of Egypt was assessed, to validate performance of the facilities. A parametric simulation performed identified links between microclimate parameters (exterior of the building) and IEQ (interior of the building). The study highlighted that, despite satisfactory design of the units to the legislations, there is still a need to update the impacts of the urban morphology on the IEQ.

Geng *et al.* (2020) investigated intensity of energy use (EUI) in link to the performance of IEQ, for elements such as: *thermal comfort, air quality and visual environment*. The research encompassed a synthesis of three million sets of environmental data, and a relevant sample of 1,756 users' satisfaction surveys. The findings indicated that users were less satisfied about the *thermal comfort and indoor air quality* in facilities with high EUI due to the limitations of environmental control, in compare to users within low EUI facilities. Furtherly, facilities with high EUI scored higher conformity to local standards more than facilities with low EUI, while both groups of facilities seemed to confirm similarly to local standards in aspects of *visual performance*. The findings of this study indicated that, the investigated, green facilities suffered from overcooling and overheating, due to the minimal conformity to thermal comfort requirements. Furtherly, the study introduced an environmental energy efficiency indicator, for a linked evaluation of IEQ performance and energy consumption comprehensively, claiming that IEQ of a facility should not contradict with the energy efficiency. Thus, the authors reviewed IEQ and Energy use in literature and reported negative energy performance of green buildings and concluded that LEED buildings did not save energy compared to non-LEED buildings. Furtherly, they highlighted that there was a gap in literature focusing on this correlation in different regional localities.

Danza *et al.* (2020) discussed the challenge of zero energy buildings (ZEN), to deliver a quality of IEQ. The authors referred that there is not a unified standard for the comprehensive evaluation of IEQ. The reviewed literature indicated that research cases are dispersed in their findings and there is a need to rank importance of several factors affecting IEQ, in the built environment. Thus, the authors carried investigative surveys on 100 occupants of different ZEN buildings, to solicit their levels of comfort and satisfaction. Furtherly, physical measurements were taken in specific ZEN facilities conditions. The analyses of the surveys led to ranking of several indoor environmental factors. The authors highlighted the need to investigate the same indicators over different ZEN facilities with varying conditions. As research was conducted over a short exposure time, it was considered a limitation for the findings. A longer exposure time of sensors collecting measurements information and users' satisfaction data, would alter the research results and findings, to be more stable against wider fluctuation in environmental conditions.

Kishi and Araki (2020) discussed the need for improvement of IEQ as they are directly linked to sustainability. As built facilities design, where characteristics of a building such as increased air tightness can lead to symptoms of a sick home syndrome (SHS); according to a case from japan. The symptoms of SHS are not limited to *sensory irritation, headache, dry cough, nausea, dermal itches, and dizziness*.

Since, health of occupants in a built facility is linked to the controls over its IEQ performance, a healthy indoor environment can achieve the realization of many of United nations (UN) sustainability development goals (SDG), such as:

- SDG 3 of maintaining good health and wellbeing.
- SDG 5 of gender equality.
- SDG6 of clean water and sanitation.
- SDG7 Affordable and clean energy.
- SDG 8 decent work and economic growth.
- SDG 9 industry, innovation, and infrastructure.
- SDG 10 sustainable cities and communities.
- SDG 12 of responsible production and consumption.
- SDG 13 climate action.

IEQ is related to wellbeing of occupants, *e.g.* understanding the functional use of spaces and variation of men and women, such as exposure to cooking and combustible gases. As well as the treatment of drinking water and sanitation and ability to prevent infections, reduction of emissions that result and pollute from non-clean energy sources utilization, the adoption of environmental materials and assets, while making clean indoor environments and reducing exposure to hazardous remains. Moreover, according to world health organization (WHO) in 2018, air polluted household environments are responsible for 3.8 million deaths annually. Usually, SHS happens for occupants under the age of 20 as they stay more at homes, where in office buildings its referred to as a sick building syndrome (SBS), with similar symptoms, that takes place but for older age groups ranging from 20-60 years old. In office buildings the occupancy levels are larger than in households, thus, it is easier to identify the causes of SBS than SHS. The study also investigated different research efforts from 1984 to 2010, indicating that yet all studies were dispersed in approach and limited over different geographical regions, such as: Europe, US, China, Brazil, and Egypt (Kishi and Araki, 2020).

Vilčeková *et al.* (2020) investigated the lifecycle assessment (LCA) of wooden housing units against short time measurement of IEQ indicators. Physical parameters were investigated such as *temperature, relative humidity, air circulation and acoustical performance*; the monitoring included measuring *CO_2 concentration (expressed in kilograms per space)* and other *volatile and non-volatile compounds*. The findings highlighted that wooden houses with zero energy characteristics are considerably green buildings that have potential of improved IEQ conditions. The study linked the production of raw materials used in construction of wooden houses, to the environmental aspects, as a potential for achieving a high quality IEQ. The measurements taken, utilized different instruments, and sensing devices, that can provide quantified data for further analyses of the units' performance. The limitation of this study is that it focused on collection of measurements during short period of time (cold period of the heating season). The study indicated that wooden houses possess satisfactory IEQ performance conditions for its occupants.

Asojo, *et al.* (2020) conducted a POE on 2,275 occupants at 30 different workplaces, located at Minnesota, USA. The study indicated that male occupants were more satisfied of the thermal conditions of the workplaces, than their female counterparts. The study was performed on ranging group of occupants within the facilities who experienced a span ranging up to 9 years of time. The findings indicated that those occupants who stayed for 2 years or less periods were more satisfied about the environmental conditions, than those who occupied the work facilities for periods longer than 2 years. The elements investigated were related to different IEQ aspects, such as *acoustic quality, ability to hear desired sounds, ability to limit noise, aesthetical appearances, quality of cleaning and maintenance, accessibility to and amount of daylight, illuminance performance, adjustability of ambient and task lighting, ergonomics of furniture, privacy, indoor air quality (IAQ), technological readiness, humidity, vibrations and view conditions*. Consequently, the study recommendations aimed to inform designers of workplace facilities about considerations for IEQ, that may lead to satisfactory future occupation. The study was limited to subjective means of satisfaction and lacked the measurements of IEQ due to the physical buildings' characteristics.

Hameen *et al.* (2020) aimed to investigate IEQ performance in educational facilities, using the national environmental assessment toolkit, of USA. The research included measurements and satisfaction surveys collected from eight schools, over a period of eight years' time. The research highlighted the need to distinguish the post occupancy evaluation and measurements of school facilities, from workplace facilities. The research indicated that there is a lack of implementation of POE studies and measurements of IEQ in educational facilities, on a national and international level. Different types of data were collected ranging from excel sheets, photos, videos, interviews narrative, MySQL, and hand sketches. The IEQ elements under study were: *glare on computer screens, audio visual discomfort, illuminance, optimal air quality, adequacy of monitoring devices, assessment of air temperature and movement, relative humidity, radiant temperature, acoustic attenuation, background sound levels and spatial qualities*. A report was provided by the end of the study, listing every categorized element of IEQ against its performance with evaluation recommendations. The findings of this research allowed stakeholders of the educational facilities, to make informed decisions, about allocation of resources and investments toward the improvement of their facilities.

Romero Herrera *et al.* (2020) investigated the impact assessment reporting of IEQ comfort elements in two different office buildings, that have varying organizational cultures. The facilities were equipped with indoor environmental devices, and sensors that were used to collect, and analyze indoor climatic conditions. The study was conducted over 2 weeks. The study findings led to recommendations about the effective reporting reliability, of thermal comfort aspects. The recommendations highlighted the need for continuous monitoring of comfort elements, and the facility performance, over longer periods, to avoid simplification of findings and to foster contextual understanding of complex occupational behaviors, in facilities. The authors indicated that "*A major shortcoming of most commonly used comfort parameters and scales is that they are based on lab research while often applied in real-world setups*". Thus, the research indicated that there is a need to focus efforts on the role of ICT in supporting effective measurements and data capturing techniques in a systematic manner, serving the comprehensive need of understanding built indoor environmental performance; in link with energy use. The research also concluded, the need for avoiding averaging IEQ comfort related aspects, as applied by many of the short-term studies, trying to understand IEQ performance in buildings. The study utilized a specific mobile application, to collect users' subjective indicators, along with an accustomed sensor box to take field measurements, around the under-study facilities. The reports produced (from the analyses of collected data) were then used to assess comfort elements within the facilities under investigation.

Martin *et al.* (2020) utilized a benchmarking online platform, used to analyze POE data from 11 different higher education classrooms, as a survey collected from 3140 students, over 9 years, at Minnesota, USA. The study indicated the importance of specific IEQ elements, in relation to the gender of students. Yet, the research concluded the need for a benchmarking tool, that extends physical measurements along with the objective survey responses, from the students. Stating that benchmarking automation needs to be unified universally to allow for the better understanding and comparison of specific facilities performance under equivalent categories.

Valderrama-Ulloa *et al.* (2020) conducted a systematic literature review, on more than 100 IEQ studies, over different regional contexts. This is to synthesize the domain coverage and typologies of facilities which are lacked in IEQ research. The findings indicated that Argentina and Brazil fronted other countries in number of IEQ research studies, by contexts on residential and educational facilities. The study identified gaps in IEQ research, based on facilities types, such as nursery schools, senior homes, and health facilities. The study recommended the need for more IEQ research, to improve the regulatory standards and design of future facilities. As well as to improve operation, maintenance, and management of existing facilities. The alarming finding of this review is that different studies, comprising a total of 88 facilities in Latin America indicated that 67.5% of occupants are uncomfortable with their IEQ.

Larsen *et al.* (2020) developed an innovative tool, for the holistic evaluation of IEQ, to facilitate a graphical understanding and reporting of a facility IEQ performance. The tool comprised of elements such as: *potential indoor air quality (IAQ), thermal, visual, and acoustical qualities*. The holisticness of the tool can be set under question as it did not consider users subjective influences, as well as only 16 parameters that can be measured physically, but practically easy to measure. The parameters are then weighted to provide an overall rating indicator for IEQ of the built facility, in letters ranging from A to G, next to a scale of percentage scores. The tool assists facility managers and designers to identify IEQ problems and warrant about aspects for future design. The research did not introduce the potential for adding further parameters, yet the tool is considered as an innovative representation that can be replicated for reporting facilities IEQ performance.

5. A FRAMEWORK FOR THE MANAGEMENT OF IEQ IN BUILT FACILITIES

A framework has been developed utilizing Integrated Computer Aided Manufacturing Definition for Function Modeling ($IDEF_0$) graphical modelling technique to represent the processes involved in the holistic management of IEQ, in built facilities, while supporting the needs for sustainable monitoring and update of IEQ indices. The framework assigns responsibilities, while inform on constraints that must be considered for the implementation of the processes. The framework comprises of 5 main processes: measure IEQ indicators, store data for IEQ indicators, Evaluate IEQ indicators, Update IEQ indicators, and implement the corrective measures. Each of the processes have multiple inputs to perform each of its underlying activities, and outputs as outcomes. The processes can be expressed, as follows (as shown in *Figure 1*):

5.1 (P1) - Measure IEQ Indicators

This process aims to uphold all the functions related to identifying the built facility characteristics, ensures identification, running communication to the physical measuring devices, sensors, and wearables of occupants. To initiate the collection functions of measured raw data in quantitative means, in forms of a big multi-dimensional table, for identified set of IEQ elements, as attributes. Inputs of collectors as data should be time stamped and logged in real-time. The output will be a big table of keyed raw data on a shell of dimensions. This process will be constrained by costs of the hardware, and communication infrastructure that will be invested in the facility and human gadgets in context. Table 1 enlists the proposed inputs for the system.

5.2 (P2) - Store Data for IEQ Indicators

This process aims to ensure the security and storage of data and serves to send the facility data, from its local storage, from an edge to a cloud end. This serves as a terminal for categorization of raw data into specific tables, for classification of data types based on units of measure, and facilities space attributes. This process must ensure the quality for validity, consistency, accuracy, timeliness, and completeness of data. The output will be a structured batch of data. This process is constrained by time stamp, where it is necessary to uplink to cloud continuously without latency.

5.3 (P3) - Evaluate IEQ Indicators

This process aims to analyze IEQ structured data to report the IEQ indicators and create meaningful insights about the facility's indoor environmental performance. The process inputs of structured data allow a bigger pool for indoor environmental quality categorization. Relations will be formulated between different attributes to calculate specific IEQ indicators. The users, on demand, may define the relationships between different attributes of data, to generate insightful graphs that can provide informed decisions about the operation and maintenance of the facility. These relationships can be accustomed and saved as coded queries, this can be referred to as the built facility intelligence reporting, where prediction analysis of IEQ can then take place based on the frequent queries of reports. The evaluation will be constrained by the national sustainability regulations, and time stamp for submission of reports. The output of this process is a batch of IEQ indices, that are analyzed with a status statement based on occupants' feedback. A weighted 5-points Likert scale can be utilized ranging from Satisfactory to unsatisfactory, to solicit the users' feedback. This process will be constrained by the time stamp, where cloud analytics should be run continuously without latency, to ensure that the reporting dashboards are updated with minimal processing latency.

5.4 (P4) - Update IEQ Indicators

This process allows the facility team to update their newly discovered IEQ indicators to a server of standardized IEQ indices, while at the same time ensures that the facility indices are updated to a national standard of IEQ. The output will be a request to update indices through detailed documentation of needed data and physical devices of measure, this is combined with a description of its underlying analyses. This process should be coordinated between the facility team and a sustainability team that represents a national authority at the other end, its responsibility to maintain quality sets of unified IEQ indices.

5.5 (P5) - Implement Corrective Measures

This process serves to inform the facility management teams about the needed corrective measures prior for producing a comprehensive IEQ benchmark report. The functions involves a system ability to store and revoke recommended actions, based on the IEQ indices that were evaluated, the ability to control operation and maintenance tasks and report the action taken by the team within the facility. The process is controlled by operation and maintenance (O&M) schemes, being cyclic or noncyclic O&M to implement the corrective measures. The corrective measures are also constrained by the sustainability measures governing the facility. The output of this process is going to be a standardized report of categorized data schema that can be classified based on the built facility characteristics and profile.

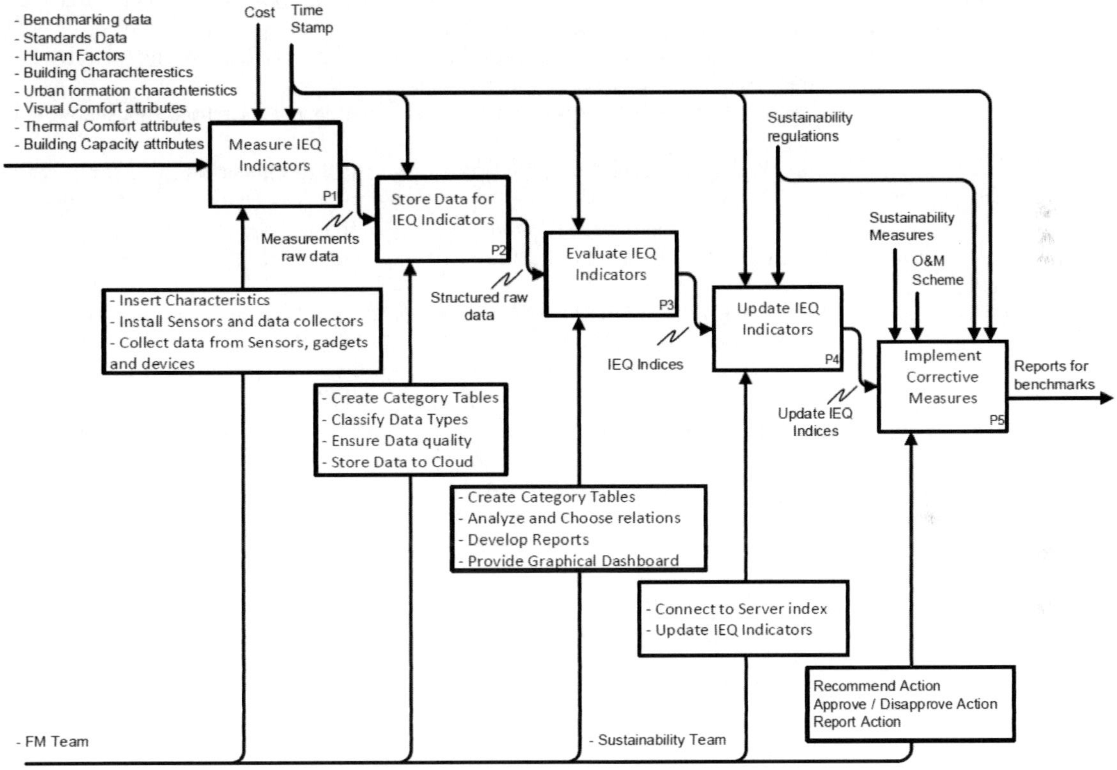

Figure 1. An IDEF$_0$ framework for the management of IEQ in built facilities

6. DISCUSSIONS AND CONCLUSION

The proposed framework introduces a systematic process for the holistic management of IEQ in built facilities. The framework utilizes IDEF$_0$ modelling technique to ensure the inclusion of several activities, inputs, outputs and identified constraints that can be managed by different stakeholders. The emergence of internet of things (IoT), machine learning and artificial intelligence applications, serve the desired need for analysis of a universal IEQ database. There are variety of opportunities and potentials from collecting big data of built facilities performance and occupants perspectives, such as: 1) enabling researchers to generate and analyze accustomed relations between different attributes, at almost any locality, with ultimate enablement of classification and categorization of occupants' demographics and functional typologies of facilities, this can be expanded to micro climatic aspects as well as urban formulation impacts on indoor environmental qualities, 2) its universal implementation will allow for the interoperability of IEQ sensors and measuring devices by accommodating different inputs and output formats of data, 3) the framework uncovers the potential for starting a global open benchmarking tool, by proposing the use of accustomed dashboards, 4) the framework calls for focusing efforts on reducing costs of measuring devices and improving connectivity for ease of data collection, by introducing a management process, 5) the proposed framework implementation will serve urgent needs toward the realization of sustainability development goals (*e.g.* SDG 3 of maintaining good health and wellbeing, SDG 5 of gender equality, SDG6 of clean water and sanitation, SDG7 Affordable and clean energy, SDG 8 decent work and economic growth, SDG 9 industry, innovation and infrastructure, SDG 10 sustainable cities and communities, SDG 12 of responsible production and consumption and SDG 13 climate action) by allowing for a universal update of IEQ indicators and methods of calculation, 6) the implementation of the framework serves the need to maintain a historical record of IEQ performance of facilities, as many IEQ studies focused on the time dimension being a limitation of its findings, 7) the proposed framework allows for future integration of further processes; being dynamic in the making, 8) the framework widens IEQ management from being a research area to a job creation by integrating new mechanisms that can be applied on almost any type of facilities, 9) the framework supports the informed decision making upon operation and maintenance of facilities. Considerations for implementation of the framework include:

A. The development of platforms which serve its functions, must ensure user friendliness and unity of design.

B. The platforms must allow users to accustom the features and attributes that are needed for the analyses (Ioannou et al., 2019)

C. The implementation of socio-technical reporting techniques must serve the need for accuracy and representativeness of subjective voting and data collection for the active reporting of the occupants (Romero Herrera et al., 2020).

D. The machine learning capabilities based on the historical data and its characteristics, must allow for exploration of a large number of future scenarios, being predictive in approach.

More research is needed simultaneously with the implementation of the framework to experiment the impact of newly deployed collection devices, and sensors on real time performance. Furtherly a cost effective, precise, and secure modes of data communication need to be established for allowing transfer of a varying range of data types. The implementation of the proposed framework can allow for the graphical evaluation of complex scenarios using third-party computer simulations. Sustainability aspects are identified by the impacts of IEQ measures on global environment and earth simultaneously by green design of the built environment. The sustainability buildings standards such as Leadership in Energy and Environmental Design (LEED), Building Research Establishment Environmental Assessment Method (BREEAM), International Energy Conservation code (ICEC) and the American society for heating refrigeration and air condition engineers (ASHRAE) are all developed standards that can be synthesized by the sustainability experts world wide under the supervision of UN to globalize and ensure an international and wider aspect for implementation of the reporting processes. Leading technology providers can collaborate to develop a universal standardized code in collaboration with the UN and international standardization organization (ISO) to ensure a wider consensus of the framework and create an international definition book to ensure sustainability for the Triple Bottom Line (TBL) aspects from cultural, social and environmental perspectives; an emerging initiative such as Architecture 2030 could be an enabler for the implementation of the framework. Furtherly, the framework provides a process that engages sustainability experts in formulating codes by updating lessons learned, and concerns dealt with in professional practice; such link will adequately initiate a more effective development of standards and enhance realization of a sustainable built environment and future designs by evidence.

REFERENCES

Alexander, K. (1992). An Agenda for Facilities Management Research. Facilities, 10(7), 6–12.

Bae, S., Asojo, A. O., and Martin, C. S. (2020). Impact of occupants' demographics on indoor environmental quality satisfaction in the workplace. Building Research and Information, 48(3), 301–315.

Bae, S., Martin, C. S., and Asojo, A. O. (2020). Higher education students' indoor environmental quality satisfaction benchmark. Building Research and Information, 0(0), 1–16.

Bröchner, J., Haugen, T., and Lindkvist, C. (2019). Shaping tomorrow's facilities management. Facilities, 37(7–8), 366–380.

Cao, S., Yu, C. W., and Luo, X. (2020). Indoor and Built Heating, ventilating and air conditioning system and environmental control for wellbeing. 0(0), 1–4.

Dan Norbäck, A. A. R. K. (2020). Indoor environmental quality and health risk toward healthier environment for all.

Danza, L., Barozzi, B., Bellazzi, A., Belussi, L., Devitofrancesco, A., Ghellere, M., Salamone, F., Scamoni, F., and Scrosati, C. (2020). A weighting procedure to analyze the Indoor Environmental Quality of a Zero-Energy Building. Building and Environment, 183(July).

Földváry Ličina, Veronika et al. (2018), ASHRAE Global Thermal Comfort Database II, Dryad, Dataset,

Geng, Y., Lin, B., and Zhu, Y. (2020). Comparative study on indoor environmental quality of green office buildings with different levels of energy use intensity. Building and Environment, 168(August 2019), 106482.

Hameen, E. C., Ken-Opurum, B., and Son, Y. J. (2020). Protocol for post occupancy evaluation in schools to improve indoor environmental quality and energy efficiency. Sustainability (Switzerland), 12(9).

Hassanain, M. A. (2007). Post-Occupancy indoor environmental quality evaluation of student housing facilities. Architectural Engineering and Design Management, 3(4), 249–256.

Heinzerling, D., Schiavon, S., Webster, T., and Arens, E. (2013). Indoor environmental quality assessment models: A literature review and a proposed weighting and classification scheme. Building and Environment, 70, 210–222.

Ioannou, L. G., Tsoutsoubi, L., Mantzios, K., and Flouris, A. D. (2019). A free software to predict heat strain according to the ISO 7933:2018. Industrial Health, 57(6), 711–720.

Kishi, R., and Araki, A. (2020). Importance of Indoor Environmental Quality on Human Health toward Achievement of the SDGs (pp. 3–18).

Larsen, T. S., Rohde, L., Jønsson, K. T., Rasmussen, B., Jensen, R. L., Knudsen, H. N., Witterseh, T., and Bekö, G. (2020). IEQ-Compass – A tool for holistic evaluation of potential indoor environmental quality. Building and Environment, 172.

Lindkvist, C., Temeljotov Salaj, A., Collins, D., Bjørberg, S., and Haugen, T. B. (2020). Exploring urban facilities management approaches to increase connectivity in smart cities. Facilities, ahead-of-print (ahead-of-print).

Ribino, P., Bonomolo, M., Lodato, C., and Vitale, G. (2020). A Humanoid Social Robot Based Approach for Indoor Environment Quality Monitoring and Well-Being Improvement. International Journal of Social Robotics.

Romero Herrera, N., Doolaard, J., Guerra-Santin, O., Jaskiewicz, T., and Keyson, D. (2020). Office occupants as active actors in assessing and informing comfort: a context-embedded comfort assessment in indoor environmental quality investigations. Advances in Building Energy Research, 14(1), 41–65.

Valderrama-Ulloa, C., Silva-Castillo, L., Sandoval-Grandi, C., Robles-Calderon, C., and Rouault, F. (2020). Indoor environmental quality in Latin American buildings: A systematic literature review. Sustainability (Switzerland), 12(2), 1–19.

Vilčeková, S., Harčárová, K., Moňoková, A., and Krídlová Burdová, E. (2020). Life Cycle Assessment and Short-Term Measurements of Indoor Environmental Quality of a Wooden Family House. The 11th International Conference Environmental Engineering 11th ICEE Selected Papers, May, 21–22.

World Health Organization (2018). Household air pollution and health. Fact Sheets. Retrieved from URL: https://www.who.int/news-room/fact-sheets/detail/household-air-pollution-and-health#:~:text=3.8%20million%20people%20a%20year,fuels%20and%20kerosene%20for%20cooking

Wei, W., Wargocki, P., Zirngibl, J., Bendžalová, J., and Mandin, C. (2020). Review of parameters used to assess the quality of the indoor environment in Green Building certification schemes for offices and hotels. Energy and Buildings, 209.

Yoseph, W. E.-S. (2020). Parametric Assessment for Achieving Indoor Environmental Quality (IEQ) in Egypt's New Urban Communities: Considering New Borg El-Arab City Urban Morphology and Openings' Specifications BT - Urban and Transit Planning: A Culmination of Selected Research P (H. Bougdah, A. Versaci, A. Sotoca, F. Trapani, M. Migliore, and N. Clark (eds.); pp. 87–100). Springer International Publishing.

ENTERPRISE ARCHITECTURE ARTIFACTS FACILITATING DIGITAL TRANSFORMATIONS' STRATEGIC PLANNING PROCESS

Frank Grave, Rogier van de Wetering and Rob Kusters
Department of Information Science, Open University, The Netherlands
Valkenburgerweg 177, Heerlen, The Netherlands

ABSTRACT

The exploitation of new value propositions enabled by disruptive digital technologies—also known as digital transformations—influences firms' configurations of people, processes, and technology and must be considered in the enterprise's strategy. Strategic planning, i.e., the process that determines strategy, is facilitated by enterprise architecture (EA). Hence, strategic plans are reflected in EA documents called artifacts. Our objective is to construct an overview of essential EA artifacts that are used to facilitate the strategic planning process for digital transformations. Therefore, we analyzed popular EA sources, performed a systematic literature review, and organized an expert session using the Metaplan method. Building on EA's current knowledge, we propose 15 EA artifacts that facilitate digital transformations' strategic planning process.

KEYWORDS

Enterprise Architecture, Digital Transformation, Strategic Planning, Artifacts, Frameworks

1. INTRODUCTION

Integrating and exploiting new digital technologies into an organization's value propositions as a response to digital disruption requires organizations to leverage digital capabilities (Ross, Beath, & Mocker, 2019; Vial, 2019). These digital capabilities are delivered using digital technologies. Furthermore, new digital technologies, such as analytics, cloud, Internet of Things, cyber-physical, and related technologies, present both game-changing opportunities and existential threats (Sebastian et al., 2017). Digital transformation (DT) is a process that aims to create new value propositions by triggering significant changes to the properties of an organization through combinations of information, computing, communication, and connectivity technologies (Vial, 2019). In other words, DT defines value propositions made possible by the capabilities of digital technologies (Ross et al., 2019). The enterprise architecture (EA) is affected by strategic initiatives that utilize these technologies for DTs (Ahlemann et al., 2012). Therefore, EA's practice attempts to bridge the gap between strategic planning and implementation efforts (Bernard, 2012; Gong & Janssen, 2019; Kotusev, 2018; Radeke, 2011; Simon, Fischbach, & Schoder, 2014). EA artifacts are used to facilitate transformations by describing the enterprise from an integrated business and IT perspective. EA artifacts are documents that describe the fundamental organization of an enterprise as a socio-technical system, along with the principles governing its design and development (Ahlemann et al., 2012).

However, until today, EA has had a strong framework orientation. Very little is known about the practices that are used and followed, how well they fit with their purposes, what the challenges are, and how different stakeholders act in successful EA practices (Gong & Janssen, 2019; Kotusev, 2018). Moreover, our theoretical and practical understanding of how EA can be leveraged to create business value for firms remains limited (Van de Wetering, 2020). Popular frameworks, such as The Open Group Architecture Framework (TOGAF) (The Open Group, 2018) and the Department of Defense Architecture Framework (DoDAF) (United States Department of Defense [DoD], 2010) introduce EA artifacts but give no insight into which EA artifacts are fundamental for facilitating DTs.

A major problem seems to be the absence of empirically validated best practices for EA artifacts (Gong & Janssen, 2019; Kotusev, 2018; Roth et al., 2013). Kotusev (2018) essentially invalidates the conceptualization of EA as a set of business, information, application, and technology architectures and the conceptualization of EA as a current state, future state, and transition roadmap. Hence, framework conceptualizations, such as TOGAF and DoDAF, contradict empirical evidence from numerous established EA practices (Kotusev, 2018). Overall, there is a scarcity of studies that provide a clear, up-to-date description of EA artifacts—such as repositories, maps, objects, or models—and which elucidate the use of these artifacts.

Additionally, there is a call for a reconceptualization of EA that should focus on new realistic models that align with genuine industry best practices (Kotusev, 2018) and fill the research gap on leveraging EA for DTs (Hafsi & Assar, 2016). Our research aims to understand the set of EA artifacts that are used by organizations to support the strategic planning process for DTs. Moreover, we want to establish the purposes for creating EA artifacts, and how they are used. Therefore, our research aims to explore and synthesize current knowledge on EA artifacts that facilitate DT's strategic planning process. Thus, our research question is as follows:

RQ: What is currently known about EA artifacts that facilitate the strategic planning process for digital transformations?

We analyzed popular EA sources, conducted a systematic literature review, and organized an expert session as an initial empirical validation of the results of our synthesis of popular EA sources and the literature review.

This paper is structured as follows. First, in Section 2 we give more background information about our research subject. Next, Section 3 describes the methodology for our study. We present and discuss the results in Section 4. Then, Section 5 provides a discussion on the implications for practice and theory. Finally, Section 6 presents our conclusions, limitations, and suggestions for future research.

2. BACKGROUND

EA is a collection of documents describing an organization from an integrated business and IT perspective (Bernard, 2012; Kotusev, 2018). EA documents, also known as EA artifacts, describe the EA in its current, future, or transition states. Additionally, these artifacts can contain principles, and they always serve a purpose (Bernard, 2012; Kotusev, 2018; The Open Group, 2018). Examples of EA artifacts are landscape diagrams, catalogs with principles, solution designs, and application/data matrixes. EA artifacts are the products of an EA practice (Kotusev, 2018). An EA practice delivers EA artifacts to facilitate strategic planning, technology optimization, project delivery, and operations to achieve business-IT alignment (BITA) (Kotusev, 2018). With this, we define BITA as a state where IT is applied in an appropriate and timely way (Luftman & Kempaiah, 2007). Thus, EA artifacts are used to align strategic business objectives with state-of-the-art technologies (Ross, Weill, & Robertson, 2006; Van de Wetering, 2020).

A business strategy promotes creating future competitive advantage faster than one's competitors (Johnson, Scholes, & Whittington, 2008). Generally, the business strategy's strategic function can be divided into strategy planning, strategy implementation, and strategy evaluation (Ahlemann et al., 2012; Simon et al., 2014). The goal of the strategy planning process, in particular, is to formulate the long-term future course of action (Ahlemann et al., 2012; Kotusev, 2018; Simon et al., 2014).

EA-based capabilities are the capabilities that organize and use organization-specific resources to align strategic objectives with the use of technology (Kotusev, 2018; Van de Wetering, 2020). In other words, EA-based capabilities promote BITA and do so by producing EA artifacts that facilitate decision-making about standardizing processes, integrating data, standardizing applications, and standardizing the IT infrastructure (Ross et al., 2006; Van de Wetering, Kurnia, & Kotusev, 2020). However, DTs concern changes that are so fast that traditional EA-based capabilities cannot cope with them (Drews, Schirmer, Horlach, & Tekaat, 2017). The current digital technologies and DTs era has created a marketplace that demands speed and flexibility (Ross et al., 2019). Hence, there is an apparent tension between standardization and flexibility. For this reason, two types of EA-based capabilities have emerged: specifically, a traditional type and a fast type (Drews et al., 2017; Ross et al., 2019). However, it is unclear how digital transformation changes EA artifacts' role (Korhonen & Halén, 2017). Moreover, studies, such as (Kotusev, 2020), state that it is implausible that EA is based on strategy.

3. METHOD

In line with our research question's breadth, we used a broad range of sources to establish a list of EA artifacts that facilitate DTs' strategic planning process. First, we analyzed popular EA sources. Next, we performed a systematic literature review (SLR), and finally, we organized a Metaplan session with experts to deepen our understanding of the literature review results. Our method's goal was to synthesize existing knowledge, identify gaps in current research, and provide a background to appropriately position new research activities (Kitchenham, 2007) on EA artifacts that facilitate DTs' strategic planning process.

As a starting point, we used the following popular EA sources: Zachman (1987), Spewak and Hill (1992) Van den Berg and Van Steenbergen (2004), Ross et al., (2006), DoD (2010), Bernard (2012), United States Office of Budget and Management [OMB] (2013), and The Open Group (2018). We analyzed these popular EA sources and synthesized twelve EA artifacts we believe are relevant for the strategic planning process for DT's.

Following the analysis of popular EA sources, we performed an SLR. Therefore, we used online database searches in scientific databases and assumed that the major research results in books and reports are also usually described or referenced in scientific papers. We used the ACM Digital Library, AIS, EBSCO Host, IEEE Xplore, Science Direct, Springer Link, and Web of Science databases to perform our search. These seven databases provide access to many journals and publications with a high rating in ranking lists and include the essential articles from journals and proceedings. The AISeL database, for instance, focuses mainly on scholarly publications, and the contents of IEEE Xplore tend to be more focused on practice. We generated search terms based on the research question. Next, we paired the search terms to create appropriate search strings. This led to the search strings "enterprise architecture" AND ("artifact" OR "document"), "enterprise architecture" AND "strategic planning," "enterprise architecture" AND "digital transformation", and "digital transformation" AND "strategic planning." Finally, we performed a title search on the four strings in Google Scholar to determine if we had covered all the relevant articles. The search was conducted between December 7, 2019, and December 13, 2019. The selection of studies was performed through the following processes. First, we performed a search in the databases to identify relevant studies. We performed the database search in the title, keywords, and abstract fields, except Google Scholar, where we only searched the titles. This search resulted in 1,080 articles for the next step in the process. Second, we removed duplicate studies. Third, we excluded irrelevant studies based on an analysis of their titles and if titles were not in English. We scanned all article titles for the likelihood of containing relevant information as described in the inclusion criteria. Fourth, we excluded irrelevant studies based on the analysis of their abstracts, introductions, and conclusions. We scanned all abstracts, introductions, and conclusions of the articles that were still included after the previous step for their likelihood to contain relevant information described in the inclusion criteria. Fifth, we evaluated the selected studies based on a full-text read. Finally, we obtained the primary studies that resulted after the fifth step. Moreover, we evaluated each paper, using questions to assess quality in qualitative research suggested by Mays and Pope (Mays & Pope, 2000). Our explorative research aims to establish a set of EA artifacts that can be used to facilitate the strategic planning process for DT. Each paper was evaluated by reviewing the clarity of the research aims and objectives, design of the research, research process, data display concerning the interpretations and conclusions, and appropriateness of the method. Finally, 39 articles remained after the quality assessment. From these 39 articles, we extracted the source and full references, EA artifacts listed in the article, strategic planning process characteristics, and DT characteristics. We extracted the data by identifying text segments that were related to the research questions. Next, we adapted the steps for thematic synthesis, as recommended by Cruzes and Diba (Cruzes & Dyba, 2011), to analyze the extracted data. First, we read each article; then, we identified specific text segments that could be relevant for answering our research question; next, we labeled the text segments; and after that, we reduced overlap and translated codes into themes. Finally, we analyzed the themes and linked them with our relevant theoretical theme families, i.e., strategic planning, digital transformation, EA, and EA artifacts. The SLR did not result in any additional EA artifacts, but it did add to our understanding of the relation between the different EA artifacts and the strategic planning process for DTs.

As an initial empirical validation and to further deepen our knowledge of EA artifacts, we conducted an expert session using the Metaplan method (Metaplan, 2009). The Metaplan method is a card sorting technique based on a group discussion that facilitates a structured classification process. The team that performed the Metaplan session consisted of a full professor, an associate professor, two Ph.D. candidates, and three Master's students who are all highly knowledgeable in the area of EA. Before the session, we prepared a document to inform the participants of the session's goal and give background information on the subject and the literature review findings. The session itself was divided into the following phases: (1) Describe the goal. (2) Present the findings of the literature review. (3) Brainstorm EA artifacts that facilitate DT's strategic planning process (4) Determine a final list of EA artifacts. (5) Recap and conclude. The Metaplan session resulted in three additional EA artifacts and, additionally, we agreed to rename an artifact in line with the participants' practical experience.

4. RESULTS

4.1 EA Artifacts from Popular EA Sources

The list of EA artifacts that follows is the result of our analysis and synthesis of popular EA sources. We synthesized a total of 12 different EA artifacts that facilitate the strategic planning process for DTs and briefly describe their goal and use here.

Future development will be affected by the anticipation of emerging technologies, software/hardware products, and skills expected to be available in a given time frame. The purpose of the **technology and skills forecast** artifact is to facilitate the reduction of dependence on legacy systems and technologies, to improve the technical efficiency and reliability of the IT landscape, to make use of newly available possibilities, and to serve as input for SWOT analyses (DoD, 2010; Bernard, 2012; OMB, 2013; Kotusev, 2018).

A **SWOT analysis** is a view of the organization's position in terms of strengths, weaknesses, opportunities, and threats to provide a foundation for the strategic plan (Bernard, 2012; OMB, 2013). This analysis analyzes internal and external factors to determine areas the enterprise should focus on to exploit strengths and take advantage of opportunities and areas where the enterprise should reduce threats and remove weaknesses (Bernard, 2012).

A **strategic plan** is a document containing the mission, vision, and strategic goals of an organization (Zachman, 1987; Spewak & Hill, 1992; DoD, 2010; Bernard, 2012; OMB, 2013; Kotusev, 2018; The Open Group, 2018). The overall vision for transformational endeavors provides a strategic context for digital transformation with a high-level scope. Furthermore, the strategic plan facilitates conceptual consistency between general business and IT directions. It also presents the composition of and relationships among organizational performers (organization model), business drivers, and competitor analysis. Thus, the strategic plan serves as input for a high-level operational context and a business function development plan.

A **high-level operational concept** is a high-level graphical and/or textual description of the future state of the operational concept, including the organizational context, role, or other relationships among organizations (Zachman, 1987; Spewak & Hill, 1992; Van den Berg & Van Steenbergen, 2004; Ross et al., 2006; DoD, 2010; Bernard, 2012; OMB, 2013; Kotusev, 2018; The Open Group, 2018). This is a one-page picture with a high-level view of processes, data, and technologies. It is used mostly to plan the implementation of new solutions and their integration into the current environment, and it is periodically updated to reflect the evolution of the organizational landscape—for example, after new IT systems are deployed. It provides a common context for discussions between business and IT leaders and facilitates strategic dialog and alignment. Furthermore, a high-level operational concept helps architects understand, analyze, and modify the enterprise landscape structure.

A **capability development plan** provides structured views of all organizational business capabilities on a single page, sometimes together with other supporting information such as business strategy, objectives, main customers, and partners (Spewak & Hill, 1992; DoD, 2010; Kotusev, 2018; The Open Group, 2018). The purpose of this artifact is to facilitate the alignment of strategic business goals with priorities for IT investments and thereby improve strategic business and IT alignment.

The purpose of an **operating model** is to determine the necessary level of business process integration and standardization for delivering goods and services to customers (Ross et al., 2006). An operating model describes how a company aspires to thrive and grow by providing a more stable and actionable view of the company than strategy. The operating model drives the design of the foundation for execution.

Common or infrastructural components are tackled by joint developments that deliver results to specific capabilities. To be able to do this, a form of overall enterprise architecture is needed in the form of an **enterprise portfolio** (Zachman, 1987; Spewak & Hill, 1992; Van den Berg & Van Steenbergen, 2004; Bernard, 2012; OMB, 2013; Kotusev, 2018; The Open Group, 2018). An enterprise portfolio provides information about the architecture as a whole, including interrelations among the involved components. This artifact aims to align developments based on the content of the developments, control the duplication and reuse of IT assets, and facilitate the analysis of the IT landscape and its overall organizational fitness.

A **conceptual data model** contains abstract definitions of the main data entities that are critical for an organization's business and their relationships (Zachman, 1987; Spewak & Hill, 1992; DoD, 2010; Kotusev, 2018; The Open Group, 2018). The purpose of this artifact is to achieve better global data consistency and uniform handling of information in all IT systems.

Principles and guidelines are high-level global guidelines that influence all decision-making and planning in an organization and IT-specific implementation-level prescriptions applicable in narrow technology-specific areas or domains (Kotusev, 2018; The Open Group, 2018). This artifact facilitates the reuse of proven best practices and reduces the general technical complexity of the IT landscape. Additionally, principles and guidelines promote consistent approaches to IT and facilitate better conceptual homogeneity of IT-related decision-making.

A **security and privacy plan** provides both high-level and detailed descriptions of the security program that is in effect throughout the enterprise (Bernard, 2012; OMB, 2013). This includes physical data, personnel, and operational security elements and procedures. It constitutes a description of the agency's enterprise security and privacy programs, policies, and procedures. The purpose of this artifact is to improve security, compliance, and overall conceptual consistency.

A **stakeholder communication plan** is a plan which elaborates the "what, when, how, and by whom" relating to communicating about architecture in order to facilitate correct, complete, and timely communication with all relevant stakeholders (Van den Berg & Van Steenbergen, 2004; The Open Group, 2018). The purpose of this artifact is to foster effective communication of targeted information to the right stakeholders at the right time.

A **technology standards list** is a list of all technologies used in an organization. It includes generic reusable solutions to commonly occurring problems in the design of IT systems (Spewak & Hill, 1992; DoD, 2010; Bernard, 2012; OMB, 2013; Kotusev, 2018; The Open Group, 2018). This artifact aims to reduce technical risks and heterogeneity of the IT landscape, achieve better technological consistency, and reduce the complexity of the IT landscape.

4.2 SLR Results

Although the SLR did not lead to any additional EA artifacts, it did produce insights into the strategic planning process for DT's and its relation to EA practice processes. We synthesized the strategic planning process for DTs based on Johnson et al. (2008), Ahlemann et al. (2012), Simon et al. (2014), Chanias, Myers and Hess (2019), Ross et al. (2019) and Vial (2019). This process starts sensing disruptions, followed by creating or adjusting the digital transformation strategy and ends with conceptualizing digital transformations. Furthermore, to enable development teams to do their work, they need a governance framework describing decision rights and accountabilities, insights into stakeholders, technological standards, a conceptual data model, and security and privacy guidelines. The EA practice processes are based on Drews et al. (2017), Korhonen and Halén (2017), Sebastian et al. (2017), and Chanias et al. (2019). Three EA practice processes facilitate the strategic planning process for digital transformation. The first EA practice process is surveillance, technology watch, and business watch. This process leverages technology to sense and make sense of information to support and facilitate a strategic response. This first EA practice process is achieved through technology and business foresight, continuous supervision of signals, identification of events, data synthesis, and evaluation (Drews et al., 2017; Korhonen & Halén, 2017). The surveillance, technology watch, and business watch process facilitates sensing disruptions and delivers input for creating or adjusting a DT strategy. The second EA practice process is impacting analysis and simulations. This EA practice runs impact analyses and simulations on hypothetical change scenarios (Chanias et al., 2019; Korhonen & Halén, 2017). This process facilitates the design aspect of creating or adjusting a DT strategy and conceptualizing DTs. Finally, the third EA practice process is distributed decision-making facilitation. Rules, guidelines, and principles support decision-making to make flexible use of promising and unexpected opportunities as they present themselves (Drews et al., 2017; Korhonen & Halén, 2017; Sebastian et al., 2017). This process facilitates the decision-making aspect of creating or adjusting a DT strategy and conceptualizing DTs.

4.3 Metaplan Session Results

The Metaplan session resulted in an adjustment of the name of an EA artifact and three additional EA artifacts.

The participants of the Metaplan session agreed that in practice, the term 'function' is more common than the term 'capability'. Therefore, we changed the name **capability development plan** to the **business function development plan**.

Furthermore, we added the **impact and risk assessment** EA artifact. New facts may come to light that invalidate existing aspects of the architecture. This EA artifact assesses the current EA to identify changes that should be made and its implications to identify an architectural adjustment's impacts and risks. Risks can be regarded to be additional constraints on the architecture engagement—for example, upcoming organizational changes, other programs and initiatives running in parallel, or the use of unproven technology.

Moreover, a **governance structure document** specifies decision rights and accountability to encourage desirable behavior (Ross et al., 2006). We did not recognize this EA artifact to be relevant for the strategic planning process for DTs due to our literature review. However, the Metaplan session participants proposed to include this EA artifact because of the importance of transparency in decision rights and accountability.

Finally, the **services and products overview** maps the lifecycle of each revenue-producing service or product that the enterprise produces for business lines that support one or more phases of the service/product life cycle. We did not recognize this EA artifact to be relevant for the strategic planning process for DTs as a result of our literature review. Nonetheless, the Metaplan session participants proposed this EA artifact because this overview allows the enterprise to see where the vertical and horizontal (crosscutting) business service/product activities are located and help define ownership of those processes.

5. DISCUSSION: IMPLICATIONS FOR PRACTICE AND THEORY

Driven by the call for a reconceptualization of EA, this study shows how EA practice and EA artifacts can facilitate DTs' strategic planning process. In doing so, we make various substantial contributions to the information systems practice and literature.

A SWOT analysis and technology and skills forecast can help with sensing disruptions. Moreover, these two artifacts deliver input for creating or adjusting a DT strategy.

Furthermore, the DT strategy, which is created in the DT strategy creation or adjustment sub-process as part of the strategic planning process, is assumed to consist of a strategic plan, a high-level operational concept, and a business function development plan. Also, an impact and risk assessment help to make explicit the impact and risk of DTs. The EA artifacts that are outputs of the DT strategy creation or adjustment sub-process guide developers by providing them with boundaries. Moreover, these four artifacts are products of the impact analysis and simulation EA practice process and provide input for the DT conceptualization sub-process from the strategic planning process.

Finally, the majority of EA artifacts facilitate distributed decision-making to enable development teams to conceptualize DTs. The enterprise portfolio facilitates alignment among different development teams. Moreover, principles and guidelines provide best practices and help to manage the complexity of the IT landscape. Additionally, the governance structure provides clarity on who can make any particular decisions. Furthermore, the conceptual data model assures the enterprise-wide use of the right data definitions. Besides, the security and privacy plan delivers the security and privacy rules to which the development team needs to adhere. The services and product overview informs teams about who owns which services and or products.

Moreover, the technology standards are a toolbox for developers, which they can use. Subsequently, the stakeholder's communications plan helps to involve the right stakeholder at the right time. Hence, all the EA artifacts from the distributed decision-making facilitation process contribute to conditions that enable emergent, bottom-up strategic planning. Table 1 summarizes the EA practice processes and the EA artifacts they produce.

Table 1. EA practice processes related to the EA artifacts they produce

EA practice process	EA artifacts
Surveillance, technology watch, and business wat	1. SWOT analysis
	2. Technology and skills forecast
Impact analysis and simulations	1. Business function development plan
	2. Operating model
	3. High-level operational concept
	4. Impact and risk assessment
	5. Strategic plan
Distributed decision-making facilitation	1. Conceptual data model
	2. Enterprise portfolio
	3. Governance structure
	4. Principles and guidelines
	5. Security and privacy plan
	6. Services and products overview
	7. Stakeholder communication plan
	8. Technology standards

6. CONCLUSIONS AND LIMITATIONS

Our research on EA artifacts that facilitate DTs' strategic planning process highlights a fragmented body of literature. Our findings underline the changing role of EA to support fast IT provisioning with a fast EA-based capability that co-exists with the traditional EA-based capability. Based on a discussion of DTs' strategic planning process, we proposed a strategic planning process for DTs. The strategic planning process senses disruptions creates or adjusts the DT strategy, and conceptualizes DTs. Additionally, founded on a broad range of EA artifacts sources, we presented a list of EA artifacts that facilitate DT's strategic planning process. The list of 15 EA artifacts can be used as a guideline to facilitate the strategic planning process for DTs. Moreover, we derived three EA practice processes that facilitate strategic planning for DTs. These three processes have been related to the strategic planning process, providing insight into EA practice processes' facilitating role for DTs' strategic planning process. Finally, we related the EA artifacts with the EA practice processes that produce them.

We believe the initial set of EA artifacts and the proposed EA practice processes may serve as a basis for future empirical studies. Consequently, this study has a limitation in that only the Metadata session participants empirically validated the EA artifacts and EA practice processes. Thus, despite using a large body of literature and validation of results by an expert team, future research needs to examine the real, practical value of our results.

REFERENCES

Ahlemann, F., Stettiner, E., Messerschmidt, M., & Legner, C. (2012). *Strategic enterprise architecture management: challenges, best practices, and future developments*. Springer Science & Business Media.

Bernard, S. A. (2012). *An introduction to enterprise architecture* (3rd ed.). Bloomington, IN: AuthorHouse.

Chanias, S., Myers, M. D., & Hess, T. (2019). Digital transformation strategy making in pre-digital organizations: The case of a financial services provider. *The Journal of Strategic Information Systems*, *28*(1), 17–33.

Cruzes, D. S., & Dyba, T. (2011). Recommended steps for thematic synthesis in software engineering. *2011 International Symposium on Empirical Software Engineering and Measurement*, 275–284.

Drews, P., Schirmer, I., Horlach, B., & Tekaat, C. (2017). Bimodal enterprise architecture management: The emergence of a New EAM function for a BizDevOps-based fast IT. *2017 IEEE 21st International Enterprise Distributed Object Computing Workshop (EDOCW)*, 57–64.

Gong, Y., & Janssen, M. (2019). The value of and myths about enterprise architecture. *International Journal of Information Management*, *46*, 1–9.

Hafsi, M., & Assar, S. (2016). What enterprise architecture can bring for digital transformation: An exploratory study. *2016 IEEE 18th Conference on Business Informatics (CBI)*, *2*, 83–89.

Johnson, G., Scholes, K., & Whittington, R. (2008). *Exploring corporate strategy: text & cases*. Pearson Education.

Kitchenham, B. (2007). *Guidelines for performing Systematic Literature Reviews in Software Engineering* (S. Charters (ed.); 2.3).

Korhonen, J. J., & Halén, M. (2017). Enterprise architecture for digital transformation. In I. Xplore (Ed.), *2017 IEEE 19th Conference on Business Informatics* (Vol. 1, pp. 349–358).

Kotusev, S. (2018). *The Practice of Enterprise Architecture: A Modern Approach to Business and IT Alignment*. SK Publishing.

Kotusev, S., Kurnia, S., Taylor, P., & Dilnutt, R. (2020). Can Enterprise Architecture Be Based on the Business Strategy?. In Proceedings of the 53rd Hawaii International Conference on System Sciences.

Luftman, J., & Kempaiah, R. (2007). An update on business-IT alignment: "a line" has been drawn. *MIS Quarterly Executive*, *6*(3), 165–177.

Mays, N., & Pope, C. (2000). Assessing quality in qualitative research. *Bmj*, *320*(7226), 50–52.

Metaplan. (2009). *Metaplan Basic Techniques Moderating group discussions using the Metaplan approach*.

Radeke, F. (2011). Toward Understanding Enterprise Architecture Management's Role in Strategic Change: Antecedents, Processes, Outcomes. *Wirtschaftsinformatik*, *16*(18), 1–11.

Ross, J. W., Beath, C. M., & Mocker, M. (2019). Designed for Digital: How to Architect Your Business for Sustained Success. In *Management on the cutting edge*. The MIT Press.

Ross, J. W., Weill, P., & Robertson, D. (2006). *Enterprise architecture as strategy: Creating a foundation for business execution*. Harvard Business Press.

Roth, S., Hauder, M., Farwick, M., Breu, R., & Matthes, F. (2013). Enterprise Architecture Documentation: Current Practices and Future Directions. *Wirtschaftsinformatik*, *58*.

Sebastian, I. M., Ross, J. W., Beath, C., Mocker, M., Moloney, K. G., & Fonstad, N. O. (2017). How Big Old Companies Navigate Digital Transformation. *MIS Quarterly Executive*, *16*(3), 197–213.

Simon, D., Fischbach, K., & Schoder, D. (2014). Enterprise architecture management and its role in corporate strategic management. *Information Systems and E-Business Management*, *12*(1), 5–42.

Spewak, S. H., & Hill, S. C. (1992). *Enterprise Architecture Planning: Developing a Blueprint for Data, Applications, and Technology*. Jhon Wiley & Sons. Inc., New York.

The Open Group. (2018). *Togaf® Version 9.2*. Van Haren Publishing.

United States Department of Defense. (2010). *Department of Defense Architecture Framework*.

United States Office of Management and Budget. (2013). *Federal enterprise architecture framework (FEAF)*.

Van de Wetering, R. (2020). Dynamic enterprise architecture capabilities and organizational benefits: an empirical mediation study. *Twenty-Eigth European Conference on Information Systems*.

Van de Wetering, R, Kurnia, S., & Kotusev, S. (2020). The Effect of Enterprise Architecture Deployment Practices on Organizational Benefits: A Dynamic Capability Perspective. *Sustainability*, *12*(21), 8902.

Van den Berg, M., & van Steenbergen, M. (2004). *DYA: Stap voor stap naar professionele enterprise-architectuur*. TenHagenStam Uitgevers.

Vial, G. (2019). Understanding digital transformation: A review and a research agenda. *The Journal of Strategic Information Systems*.

Zachman, J. A. (1987). A framework for information systems architecture. *IBM Systems Journal*, *26*(3), 276–292.

PRODUCT MANAGEMENT FOR INDUSTRIAL PRODUCT SERVICE SYSTEMS: A MODEL TOWARDS THE UNDERSTANDING OF THE ROLE OF PRODUCT MANAGEMENT

Marina Brunner and Christian Schieder
Technical University of Applied Sciences Amberg-Weiden
Hetzenrichter Weg 15, 92637 Weiden, Germany

ABSTRACT

Due to increasing competition and new consumer trends, the importance of innovation for industrial product service system is continuously increasing. Industrial companies must constantly come up with new ways to differentiate themselves from cheaper competitors, which also increases the complexity of product management tasks. In this paper, we aim to improve the understanding of the individual tasks of product management in an industrial environment, to identify their interrelationships and to measure and optimize the quality of the executed processes. In total, we defined 22 different industrial product management tasks along the product lifecycle, determined by five maturity levels within 14 maturity dimensions for each object. Subsequently, the model was tested in several industrial companies. Initial validations of the model's structure and content show that the model is transparent, easy to use, and has proven its applicability in real business environments.

KEYWORDS

Product Management, Maturity Model, Industrial Product Service Systems, Design Science Research

1. INTRODUCTION

Globalization and increasing international competition mean that companies need to innovate products and processes in order to continue to withstand rising cost and time pressures (Großmann et al. (2015)). As a result of the increasingly global division of labor, the complexity of work organization has increased. In addition, complex customer requirements and the trend toward product customization pose major challenges for companies (Großmann et al. (2015); Helo et al. (2017)). New product variants have to be developed, tested, documented and supported once. This situation leads to more resources, increased workload, and difficulties in implementing product roadmaps. Only companies that follow a market-oriented production approach are successful in the long run. The implementation of such processes requires a lot of discipline and commitment and, above all, competent employees (Steinhardt (2017)). Therefore, a company must coordinate these processes in order to develop customer-oriented products, bring them successfully to market, and optimize the product life cycle.

The product manager plays an increasingly important role in the sustainable development of products. Product managers must plan, implement, and control all product-related activities in a goal-oriented manner as part of a systematic management process (Stark (2018); Dawid et al. (2017)). However, compared to other areas, there is a lack of understanding of the tasks of product management. As a result, the scope of product management is defined and lived differently from company to company, making it difficult to compare and optimize processes. A correct definition and structuring of the roles and tasks of product management would lead to a more efficient and productive use of company resources, resulting in better yields and higher quality products (Steinhardt (2017)).

Therefore, the goal of this work is to develop a maturity model that evaluates whether product management and its functionality are suitable to support the complexity of the management processes of product service systems. A maturity model comprises a sequence of maturity levels for a class of objects and thus describes the desired development path of these objects. Progress along this development path usually means a steady increase in the performance or quality of the object (Pöppelbuß et al. (2011); Mettler (2010)).

2. THEORETICAL BACKGROUND

2.1 Product Management

Product management (PM) is a management concept that ensures product-related task structuring while maintaining functional structures. PM coordinates all product-related topics for products or product groups across all functional areas. It is thus an information, coordination, and control platform for all product-related topics inside and outside the company (Behrens et al. (2014); Pranam (2018)).

Over time, the role of product management in the corporate context has been redefined again and again (Behrens et al. (2014)). Similar to professional fields such as program and project management or product development, product management emerged from the defense industry in the United States after World War II. The field of product management is still misinterpreted today, which is why it needs a more precise definition. A specifically defined scope would ensure better execution, optimization and comparability of processes, roles and tasks in the future (Steinhardt (2017)).

2.2 Industrial Product Service Systems

For a long time, industrial manufacturers were able to hold their own in the market by offering technically and qualitatively superior products. In recent years, however, the framework conditions that can generate competitive advantages have changed. Products are becoming increasingly similar as a result of globalization, and price is becoming the decisive purchasing criterion for physical products. More and more industrial companies are responding to this change by supplementing physical products with accompanying service components. Companies that embrace this development can expect higher customer loyalty, increased revenue streams, stable sales, and new customer segments (Helo et al. (2017); Behrens et al. (2014); Schweitzer et al. (2010); Song (2019)). The so-called product service system manufacturers offer lifecycle-oriented service products that effectively support customers in the use of physical products. Customer support is thus ensured throughout the entire life cycle of the products. With an appropriate IT infrastructure, companies can also continuously gain information about the use of the physical products, the customers and the current market situation (Schweitzer et al. (2010)).

Industrial product service systems (IPSS) consist of product and service components that together meet customer needs in an industrial business-to-business context. The product components can be mechanical, electronic, or software (Großmann et al. (2015); Helo et al. (2017)). The service components may change depending on the life cycle phase. The design and implementation of IPSS takes place within the extended value network of the IPSS provider, while the production network includes, for example, suppliers of parts for manufacturing. The service network is responsible for providing service products and consists of the subsidiaries, contract and service partners. Above all, the network and infrastructure are specific characteristics for IPSS (Schweitzer et al. (2010); Ceschin (2014)).

3. RESEARCH APPROACH

According to Becker et al. (2009), a maturity model can be considered an artifact and is therefore subject to the principles of design-oriented research. The Design Science Research (DSR) approach was chosen because it has the potential to bridge the gap between theory and practice by both solving practical problems and generating knowledge that can be used as a basis or to improve scientific theories.

Becker et al. (2009) provide the following requirements for developing a maturity model: (1) comparison with existing maturity models, (2) iterative approach, (3) evaluation, (4) multi-method approach, (5) evidence of problem relevance, (6) problem definition, (7) provision of results appropriate to the target audience, (8) scientific documentation. Figure 1 shows how the requirements are adapted in the development of this maturity model.

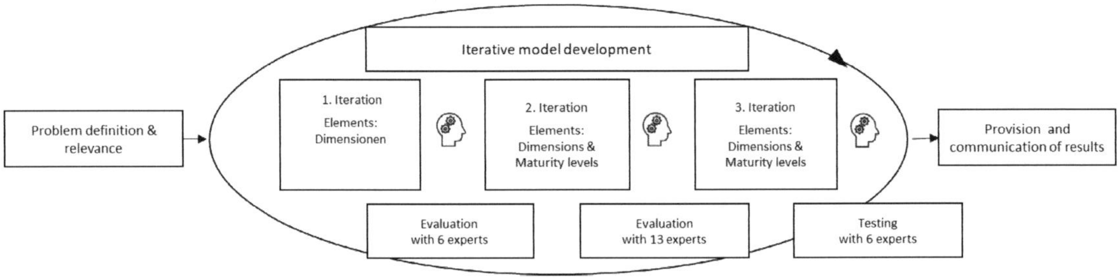

Figure 1. Iterative development of the maturity model

4. METHODOLOGY

4.1 Literature Research

The basis for the development of this maturity model for IPSS product management is a systematic literature review based on the specifications of Vom Brocke et al. (Vom Brocke et al. (2015)). The literature review serves as a basis for the definition of the product management task areas and the subsequent determination of the maturity levels. Table 1 shows the flow of the applied method.

For this thesis, it was decided to use an iterative search process. In this process, the literature search is continued and repeated several times. Since this thesis uses a design science research approach, an iterative approach is preferred over a sequential one. In this work, free services such as Google Scholar, publication databases, such as ScienceDirect, AISeL, Emerald Insight, and university libraries have been used. Covering the topic of product management of product service systems is laborious, as there is little accessible literature on this particular topic. Therefore, it was not possible to build on similar work or on seminal work in this area. Nevertheless, a representative literature review, based on the individual components of the topic, was conducted. To ensure representativeness, the defined tasks of PM had to be described by different sources (Vom Brocke et al. (2015)). This procedure resulted in 41 publications and books that were evaluated by the researchers.

4.2 Expert Interviews

In addition to the information derived from the literature review, the iterative nature of the DSR approach allows us to include further insights from expert interviews. In this work, expert interviews are used to review the state of research on product management for product service systems and to extract relevant information that has not yet been addressed in the literature (Wilberg et al. (2017)). As part of the research project, we collected and analyzed the opinions of 25 experts through semi-structured interviews and expert surveys.

The first six interviews provided overarching insights into the scope of product management for IPSS. The insights from the following 13 expert interviews were collected through a survey to verify the quality of the maturity model based on the criteria explained in Chapter 6. The remaining 6 experts tested the optimized maturity model in their company's product management.

Table 1 provides an overview of the interview partners (IP) and their background. Listed are the number of experts in chronological order, their current position, their area of experience, a distinction between physical products (PP), services (S) and software products (SW), their experience with product management or product service systems in years and the industry in which they work.

Table 1. Overview of expert's background

IP	Position	Area of Experience	Experience in years	Industry
		1. Iteration		
1	**Head of Product Management**	PP	2	Machine construction
2	**Head of Product Management Lifecycle**	S	10	Machine construction
3	**Product manager**	PP / S	3 ½	Components construction
4	**Product management consultant**	PP	20	Consulting
5	**Professor**	S	10	Education
6	**General Manager**	PP	5	Components construction
		2. Iteration		
7	**Junior Product Manager**	PP / SW	3	Automation
8	**Product Manager**	SW	4	Wellness SaaS
9	**Product Manager B2C**	S	5	Utilities
10	**Industry Strategy Manager**	PP / SW / S	12	Industrial automation
11	**Industry Portfolio Manager**	PP	10	Industrial automation
12	**Industry Strategy Manager**	PP	9	Industrial automation
13	**Strategic Incubation Manager**	SW / S	1	Industrial automation
14	**Product Manager**	PP	3	Furniture industry
15	**Head of Product Management**	PP	3	Industrial automation
16	**Industry Management**	PP	20	Electrical industry
17	**Product Manager**	PP / S	30	Automobile
18	**Product Manager**	PP / SW / S	10	Industrial automation
19	**Product Manager**	S	22	Automobile
		3. Iteration		
20	**Product Manager**	PP	5	Food
21	**Product Manager**	PP	5	Electrical
22	**Product Owner**	S	2	Service industry
23	**Product Manager**	S	6	Insurance
24	**Head of Product Management**	PP / SW / S	7	Machine construction
25	**Industry Strategy Manager**	PP / SW / S	3	Media

5. ARTEFACT DESCRIPTION

5.1 Definition of Tasks of Product Management

The development and management process of product service systems encompasses all lifecycle phases. Product management represents a cross-functional organizational unit that accompanies the development and management from the creation to the execution of the product. To get a better overview of the scope of all critical product management tasks, the tasks are assigned chronologically to the different lifecycle phases (see Figure 2). The final model contains 22 tasks that are relevant for the product management of industrial product service systems.

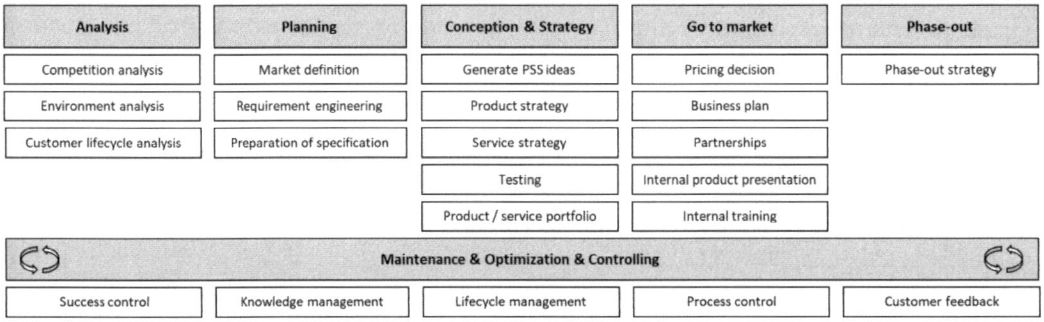

Figure 2. Objects of the maturity model

5.2 Definition of Maturity Levels for Product Management

The essential elements of a maturity model are the various maturity levels at which the quality of the object of investigation is assessed. Depending on the model, four to six different maturity levels are usually defined. As already mentioned, this work examines the quality of the tasks performed by product management. For this reason, a maturity model that measures the quality of the processes is suitable. A successful process flow depends on various criteria (Hammer et al. (2007)). Most maturity models work with cumulative maturity levels that contain several criteria. Since product management is a very practical business domain, this work focuses on the problem adequacy of the model. Cumulative maturity levels can lead to confusion in practical applications, as rarely all criteria of a maturity level are met. Therefore, assignment to a particular maturity level can be difficult. In addition, a cumulative assessment can lead to the risk that the cause of the process problem cannot be clearly identified when analyzing the problems later.

Therefore, the maturity levels for this model are divided into different criteria. The criteria, referred to below as maturity dimensions, were derived from existing business process maturity models. It was possible to identify 14 process maturity dimensions. And it was found that not every dimension has five maturity levels. Some dimensions require a certain basic structure to be applied by companies, such as optimization. Most companies optimize their processes only after they have already established a structured process. Other dimensions play a significant role only in the first stages of maturity, such as the need for action, which is an important process driver at the beginning but usually cannot be improved further once it is established. The distribution and definition of dimensions and maturity levels is shown in Figure 3. The following dimensions are used to assess the maturity level of the individual product management tasks: Need for Action (NfA), Frequency of Execution (FoE), Standardization (Stand), Documentation (Doc), Measure and Control (M&C), Process Context (ProCon), Optimization (Opt), Skills, Training (Train), Networking and Communication (N&C), Tool Usage (TU), Key Performance Indicator (KPI), Adaptation and Agility (Adapt), and IT Infrastructure (IT).

NfA describes the extent to which an organization sees the need to accomplish the task. The FoE dimension measures the frequency with which the task is performed. State and Doc describe the extent to which the task is standardized and documented. The M&C dimension gives an impression of the extent to which the execution of the task is measured and controlled. ProCon measures the employees' understanding of the process context in which the task is embedded and which other areas are affected by its execution. Opt shows the optimization opportunities applied. The Skills and Train dimensions refer to the skills of the employees and the extent to which they are trained for the task. N&C refers to interdisciplinary networking to solve the task within the company and the communication of important information across companies. TU and IT describe whether and to what extent tools are used and how well the IT infrastructure is developed. The KPI dimension measures the use and quality of the metrics used. Adapt gives an indication of how quickly the company reacts to changes in the market or the competition.

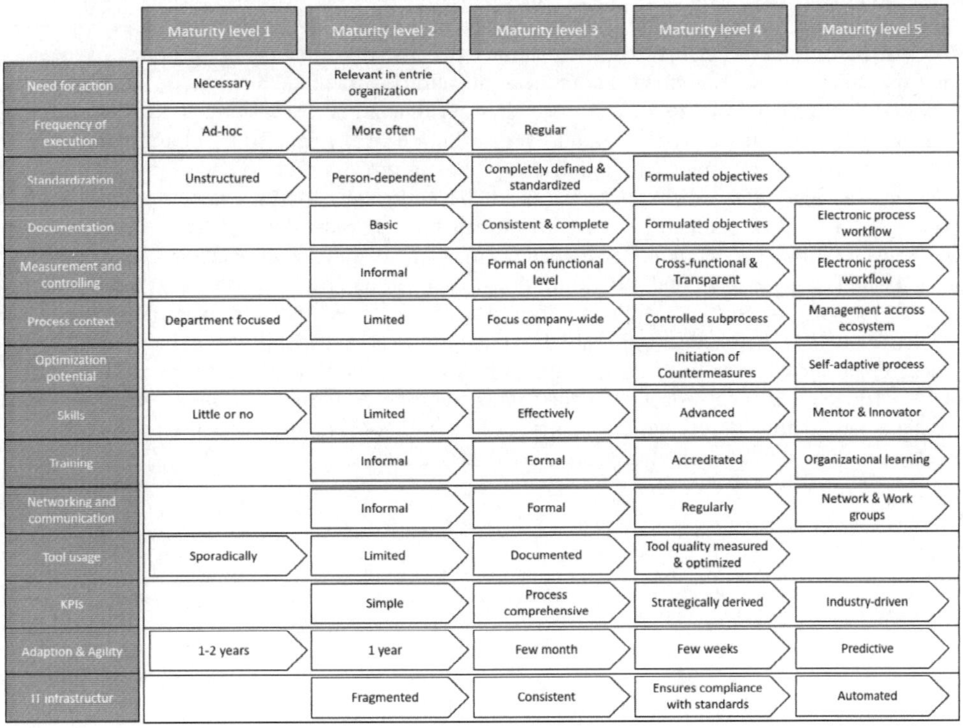

Figure 3. Overview of maturity levels

6. EVALUATION

Becker et al. plan for this step to check and evaluate the developed results for completeness, consistency, and problem adequacy (Pöppelbuß et al. (2011)). The participants of the second evaluation assessed the existing model within the assessment dimensions quality of the objects, quality of the maturity levels, quality of the maturity model, and quality of problem solving (Pöppelbuß et al. (2011)) (Dresch et al. (2015)). The criteria to be evaluated can be seen in figure 4.

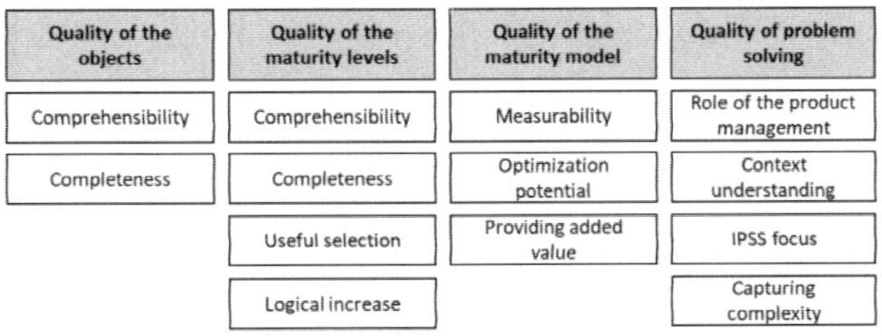

Figure 4. Overview of evaluation criteria

The experts assessed the maturity model as a consistent tool for evaluating product management for industrial product-service-systems. Many of the requirements are already satisfactorily fulfilled in the status quo.

Furthermore, the model was used by six other experts as proof of feasibility. The company received a questionnaire per e-mail to allow for reflected assessment of their internal situation on their own time. Nevertheless, it should be borne in mind that mere implementation cannot provide proof of an increase in the quality of product management for IPSS as a result of implementing the model. Such proof would require, on the one hand, a larger and longer-term test phase and, on the other hand, the definition of key figures to measure success. The purpose of this test is to determine the current status in the area of product management maturity in order to be able to make statements about the applicability of the model.

Network diagrams are used to present the overall result at a glance. Visualization in the form of a network diagram provides an overview of the maturity distribution of the individual object within the 14 different maturity dimensions. Companies can thus identify gaps in process performance for each individual task. To provide an overview of the differences between the companies in the evaluation, the results of the six companies for the object "competition analysis" are analyzed in more detail below.

The gray line shows the maximum achievable maturity level for each dimension. None of the six companies achieves the highest level in all maturity dimensions. Within the individual company results, strong differences can be seen in the assessment of the various maturity dimensions. For example, company 6 rates the competitive analysis process at levels 3 and 4 in the optimization, capabilities and tool use dimensions, while the measurement and controlling and adaptation to market conditions dimensions are rated as non-existent (level 0). This trend is also reflected in the maturity rating of the other objects. This approach enables a differentiated and detailed presentation. In further investigations, more concrete recommendations for action can be derived than with the cumulative maturity measurement.

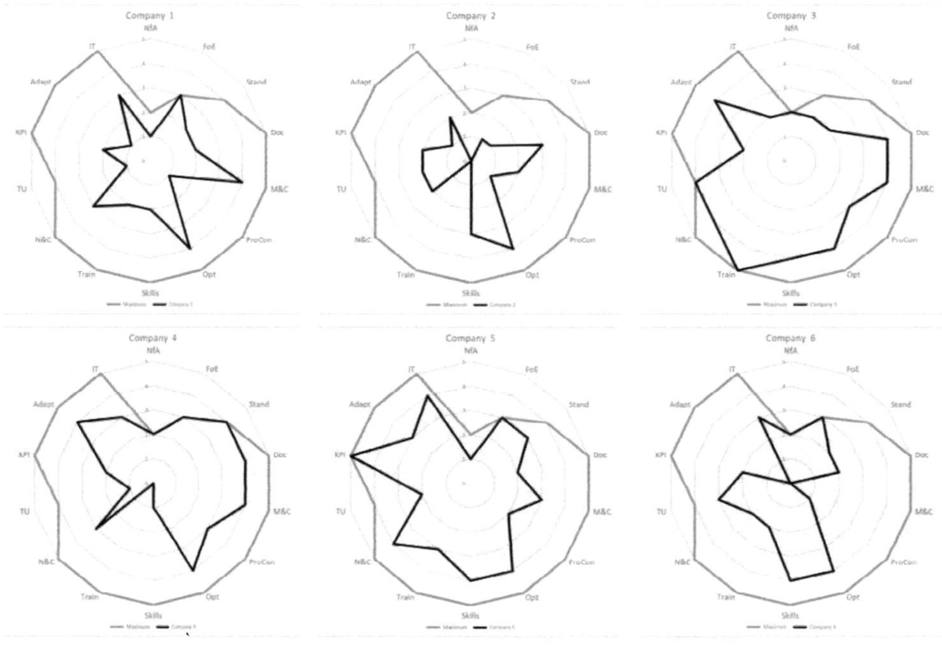

Figure 5. Overview of the evaluation results for the task "competition analysis"

7. CONCLUSION

As part of the study, a complete maturity model was created through several iterations. This study was conducted to develop a model to facilitate the assessment and improvement of product management maturity of industrial product service systems. Many models exist in the literature to facilitate the assessment or improvement of business process management maturity. Such models prove to be most effective when specialized for a particular business domain. While many general maturity models are available in the literature, no product management-specific model has been found. To support the improvement of product management maturity for industrial product service systems and thereby contribute to the understanding of the role of product management and the quality of IPSS, a new maturity model was developed.

The model was developed using various scientific methods. Through literature review, expert interviews, and surveys, data was collected on the possible structure and content of a product management maturity model. The final model contains 22 tasks that are relevant for product management of industrial product service systems. These objects can be measured along different maturity levels. The maturity levels have 14 dimensions and between two and five maturity levels depending on the dimension. Assessing product management along the maturity model provides an overview of the domain's maturity level, which identifies areas for improvement. This assessment helps to create awareness of current problems in product management and provides the starting point for future improvements. Thus, the model can help to achieve better quality of industrial product service systems. In view of this, the development of the model fulfills both organizational and scientific requirements and answers the previously posed research questions.

REFERENCES

Behrens, B.; Nyhuis, P.; Overmeyer, L.; Bentlage, A.; Rüther, T.; Ullmann, G.: Towards a definition of large scale products. In: Prod. Eng. Res. Devel. 8 (1-2), S. 153–164. (2014)

Ceschin, F.: Sustainable product-service systems. Between strategic design and transition studies. Cham: Springer International Publishing (2014)

Dawid, H.; Decker, R.; Hermann, T.; Jahnke, H.; Klat, W.; König, R.; Stummer, C.: Management science in the era of smart consumer products. Challenges and research perspectives. In: Central European Journal of Operations Research 25 (1), S. 203–230 (2017)

Dresch, A.; Lacerda, D.; Antunes Júnior, J.: Design science research. A method for science and technology advancement. Cham: Springer International Publishing. (2015)

Großmann, D. J.; Kasperek, D.; Stahl, B.; Lohmann, B.; Maurer, M.: Supporting IPSS Innovation Processes by an Integrating Model Grid. In: Procedia CIRP 30, S. 227–232. (2015)

Hammer, M.: The Process Audit. A new framework, as comprehensive as it is easy to apply, is helpingcompanies plan and execute process-based transformations. Harvard Business Review, Vol. 85 No. 4, pp. 111-23. (2007)

Helo, P.; Gunasekaran, A.; Rymaszewska, A.: Designing and Managing Industrial Product-Service Systems. Cham.: Springer International Publishing (2017)

Mettler, T.: Thinking in Terms of Design Decisions When Developing Maturity Models. In: International Journal of Strategic Decision Sciences 1 (4), S. 76–87. (2010)

Pöppelbuß, J.; Röglinger, M.: What makes a useful maturity model? a framework of general design principles for maturity models and its demonstration in business process management. paper presented at 19th European Conference on Information Systems. (2011)

Pranam, A.: Product management essentials. Tools and techniques for becoming an effective technical product manager. Berkeley, California, New York, Springer Science (2018)

Schuh, G.; Rozenfeld, H.; Assmus, D.; Zancul, E.: Process oriented framework to support PLM implementation. In: Computers in Industry 59 (2-3), S. 210–218. (2008)

Schweitzer, E.; Aurich, J. C.: Continuous improvement of industrial product-service systems. In: CIRP Journal of Manufacturing Science and Technology 3 (2), S. 158–164 (2010)

Song, W.: Customization-Oriented Design of Product-Service System. Singapore: Springer Singapore. (2019)

Stark, J.: Product Lifecycle Management (Volume 3): The Executive Summary. Cham: Springer International Publishing (2018)

Steinhardt, G.: The product manager's toolkit. Methodologies, processes and tasks in high-tech product management. Second edition. Cham, Switzerland: Springer (2017)

Vom Brocke, J.; Simons, A.; Riemer, K.; Niehaves, B.; Plattfaut, R.; Cleven, A.: Standing on the Shoulders of Giants: Challenges and Recommendations of Literature Search in Information Systems Research. In: Communications of the Association for Information Systems 8-2015 // 37. (2015)

Wilberg, J.; Schafer, F.; Kandlbinder, P.; Hollauer, C.; Omer, M.; Lindemann, U.: Data analytics in product development: Implications from expert interviews (IEEE International Conference on Industrial Engineering and Engineering Management (IEEM)), S. 818–822 (2017)

AN ONTOLOGY-BASED APPROACH TO STRUCTURE BUSINESS MODEL INNOVATION CASES

Marco Peter
FHNW University of Applied Sciences and Arts Northwestern Switzerland
Riggenbachstrasse 16, 4600 Olten, Switzerland

ABSTRACT

For companies to be able to adapt to market circumstances, they need to reconfigure or even reinvent their current business model. For this, companies need support to know their possibilities for business model innovations. Using a design science approach, this research developed an ontology to systematically represent business model innovation cases. Through this ontology, reasoning on business model innovation cases can be conducted to recommend promising business models. This ontology has been successfully applied to eight cases of business model innovation.

KEYWORDS

Business Model, Business Model Innovation, Case Structure, Ontology

1. INTRODUCTION

Today, more and more competition takes place not only between products, services, or processes but between business models (Gassmann, Frankenberger and Csik, 2014). Therefore, companies must be able to adapt their business model since companies that have decided to undertake an innovative transformation of their business model have found themselves to be more competitive in today's market (Chesbrough, 2010; Witschel *et al.*, 2019).

Several strategies on how to perform business model innovation (BMI) exist (Breuer, 2013; Smit *et al.*, 2016; Geissdoerfer *et al.*, 2017), such as the four phases method introduced by Gassmann et al. (2014) with initiation, including analysis of the ecosystem, ideation, including adaption of patterns, integration, including defining the business model in detail, and the fourth phase implementation, including the realization of the plan. But to develop software supporting the BMI process, it is crucial to have an efficient and systematic approach to collecting and representing detailed business model innovation cases. This facilitates the functionality of providing previously collected BMI cases as suggestions of new business models and thus, learn from other companies' successes or failures through the BMI cases. Nevertheless, the level of detail needs to be higher than given by the state of the art tools such as the Business Model Canvas (BMC) from Osterwalder and Pigneur (2010) or the magic triangle from Gassmann et al. (2014). The reason for this is that to compare business models only on the nine dimensions from the BMC or the four dimensions from the magic triangle would be too superficial as several BMI cases would have the same dimensions and thus, more in-depth distinctions are required. Therefore, a new structure for BMI cases is needed.

This research has the objective to answer the following research question: how does an ontology for cases of business model innovation look like? The outcome of this research will be used for a web-based tool, which should support businesses on their BMI process by facilitating the BMI process by providing previously collected real BMI cases or developed fictional BMI cases and match them to the company's business model and thus, show the impact the proposed new business model would have on the current one and provide information to estimate the transformation costs.

This paper is organized as follows: the section research method introduces the applied research method, while the section key insights describes the proposed solution for an ontology for structuring BMI-cases. The section discussion and conclusion closes this research paper with a discussion of the developed ontology based on a real-life example from the insurance sector, also, areas of further research are presented in a concluding manner.

2. RESEARCH METHOD

The objective of creating an appropriate ontology for cases of business model innovation has led to the decision to apply a design-oriented research approach. I follow the Design Science Research process model proposed by Vaishnavi and Kuechler (2004), with its five research phases. In the first phase, the awareness phase, besides the literature research on BMI and ontologies, I collected two cases of BMI through semi-structured interviews with BMI experts and six cases of BMI through desk research. The cases are from companies of different sizes and different sectors to have a diversified dataset for the analysis as well as for the evaluation of the ontology. The results of this analysis in combination with the knowledge from the literature analysis were used to build the BMI case ontology. This ontology was developed using the approach from Noy and McGuinness (2001) and thus, as they suggest iterations for its development, the development and evaluation of the ontology were done iteratively to create a sophisticated outcome. The evaluation of the artefact was done by using the qualitative methods expert interviews and application of test scenarios based on the collected BMI cases to evaluate the outcome provided by the ontology. For the test scenarios, I first formulated assumptions and expectations regarding the results, which then were compared to the results within the ontology. The research results were documented and represent the groundwork for developing a recommender system of BMI cases based on individual company criteria.

3. KEY INSIGHTS

The concept of ontologies is promising to bring positive results regarding the capability to structure business model innovation cases systematically and to be able to perform reasoning algorithms on this structure. An ontology is a fundamental concept in knowledge representation (van Harmelen, Lifschitz and Porter, 2008) and can be defined as a "[...] formal, explicit specification of a shared conceptualization" (Studer, Benjamins and Fensel, 1998). Thus, ontologies can be used to describe a concept within a model or a program (Studer, Benjamins and Fensel, 1998). This representation enables reasoning over models of a specific concept (Bonifati *et al.*, 2010), such as the concept of BMI.

The developed ontology for BMI cases consists of two ontologies: the business innovation case ontology and the business model ontology. The reason to develop two separate ontologies and to later merge them was because of the goal to have the ontology as reusable as possible. Thus, researchers and practitioners can reuse the combined ontology or only one ontology, depending on their needs. This results in a reduction of complexity regarding the application of the ontology.

The business innovation case ontology represents the aspects (classes) a business innovation case has according to the analyzed data from the collected BMI cases. This includes aspects such as barriers that need to be overcome to introduce the innovation, drivers and required resources for the innovation, involved parties as well as the benefits of the business innovation. In total there are 27 classes within the ontology, which are required to define a business innovation case.

The business model ontology was developed starting from the widely used tool to describe a business model in a structured way: the Business Model Canvas. This tool was developed by Osterwalder and Pigneur (2010). The tool consists of nine building blocks: customer segments, value proposition, channels, customer relationships, revenue streams, key resources, key activities, key partnerships, and cost structure (Osterwalder and Pigneur, 2010). This tool originates from four main components any business model has: offering, customer interface, infrastructure, and financial aspects. The component offering focuses on the products and services a company offers to its customers and can be seen as a value proposition delivered to the customer (Osterwalder, 2004; Zarei *et al.*, 2011). Customer interface represents the value delivery and includes the channels used to interact with a customer and thus, the go-to-market strategy, as well as the customer segments and the relationships towards the company's customers (Osterwalder, 2004; Zarei *et al.*, 2011). The infrastructure component is essential to determine the needs to deliver the offering according to the customer interface and represents the value creation of a business (Osterwalder, 2004; Zarei *et al.*, 2011). Financial aspects involve the cost structure as well as the revenue model of a company and thus, reflect the value capturing attempts of a business. This knowledge of business models was altogether included in the business model ontology and expanded by different methods from the literature. One of these methods was the innovation ecosystem approach for creating new innovations and new business models. Innovation ecosystems can be represented in quadruple helixes including individuals, the government, academic institutes, and businesses (Rabelo and Bernus, 2015; Schütz *et al.*, 2018). In total there are 97 classes within the ontology, which are required to define a business model in detail.

Figure 1 illustrates an excerpt of the developed ontology to structure BMI cases systematically. The excerpt only shows the modeled part for the infrastructure of the BMI case ontology since the entire ontology would be too big to be illustrated on a single page.

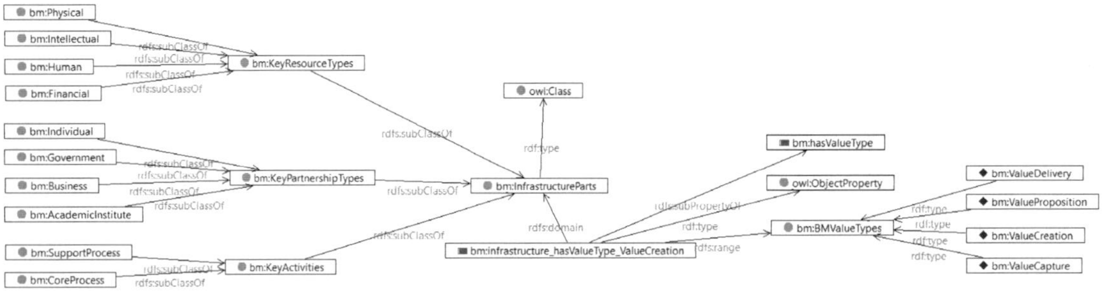

Figure 1. Excerpt of the business model infrastructure parts from the BMI case ontology

4. DISCUSSION AND CONCLUSION

As part of the evaluation of the BMI case ontology, the eight previously collected BMI cases were applied to the ontology to assess its applicability for cases of different sectors and company sizes. An excerpt from one of these cases, an insurance company related case, is shown in Figure 2, where the infrastructure aspect of the case is shown within the ontology.

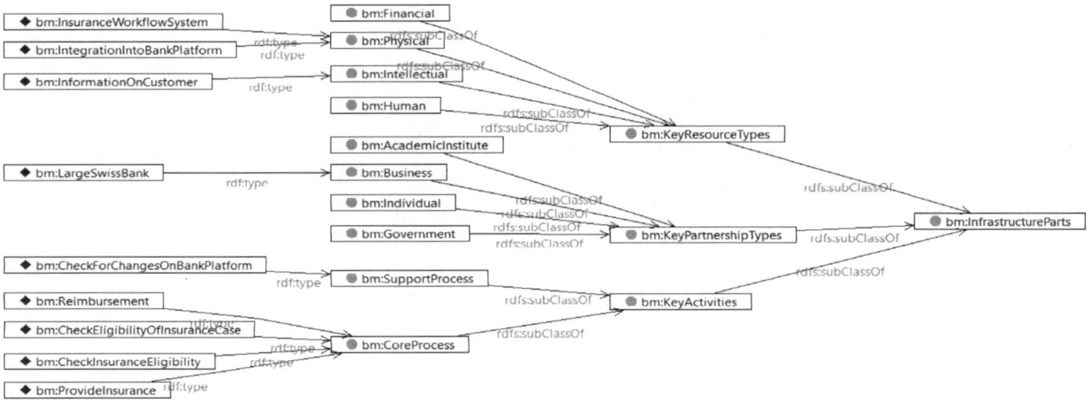

Figure 2. Excerpt of the business model infrastructure parts from the BMI case ontology for the insurance case example

The evaluation showed that the ontology is capable to handle BMI cases of different sectors and company sizes. Nevertheless, to provide more details of a BMI case, it would be useful to provide industry-specific information within the ontology as well. For example, within the construction sector, the aspect of the partnership is essential, while for the hotel industry the customer relationship is key. Thus, it would be helpful to have an even higher level of detail for specific aspects of the BMI case ontology depending on the related sector of the BMI case.

There are other business model innovation tools such as the 55 business model cards from Gassmann (2014) or the business model pattern tool by Remane et al. (2017). These tools are helpful for a business, especially the 55 business model cards as they provide suggestions for business models during the ideation phase of the BMI process. Yet, it would be helpful to have a recommendation for a new business model based on a current business model to estimate the consequences of implementing the proposed business model. Thus, this BMI case ontology is the first step towards the development of a business model recommender system to facilitate the innovation process of businesses. Nevertheless, the two tools by Gassmann (2014) and Remane et al. (2017) can be integrated into the ontology and act as partial business model innovation cases and therefore, enrich the case database of the BMI case ontology.

This paper aims to contribute an ontology for systematically structuring BMI cases. Therefore, this paper has discussed an ontology for potential cases of BMI and showed that it is not only technically possible, but it also advances the current state of the art. Thus, the research question of how an ontology for cases of business model innovation could look like has been answered. Further research is now required regarding the integration of the ontology into a recommender system (Bonifati *et al.*, 2010; Witschel *et al.*, 2015) and adapting the ontology to different sectors. Thus, further research on this topic is necessary and promising and might lead to relevant academic and practical insights.

REFERENCES

Bonifati, A. *et al.* (2010) 'Ontological Matchmaking in Recommender Systems', pp. 1–28. Available at: http://arxiv.org/abs/1010.2148.

Breuer, H. (2013) 'Lean Venturing: Learning to Create new Business Through Exploration, Elaboration, Evaluation, Experimentation, and Evolution', *International Journal of Innovation Management*, 17(3), pp. 1–22. doi: 10.1142/S1363919613400136.

Chesbrough, H. (2010) 'Business model innovation: Opportunities and barriers', *Long Range Planning*, 43(2–3), pp. 354–363. doi: 10.1016/j.lrp.2009.07.010.

Gassmann, O., Frankenberger, K. and Csik, M. (2014) *The business model navigator : 55 models that will revolutionise your business*. Harlow, England: Pearson Education Limited.

Geissdoerfer, M., Savaget, P. and Evans, S. (2017) 'The Cambridge Business Model Innovation Process', *Procedia Manufacturing*, 8(October 2016), pp. 262–269. doi: 10.1016/j.promfg.2017.02.033.

Noy, N. F. and McGuinness, D. L. (2001) 'Ontology Development 101: A Guide to Creating Your First Ontology', *Stanford Knowledge Systems Laboratory*, p. 25. doi: 10.1016/j.artmed.2004.01.014.

Osterwalder, A. (2004) *The business model ontology - a proposition in a design science approach, Ph.D. dissertation*. University of Lausanne.

Osterwalder, A. and Pigneur, Y. (2010) *Business Model Generation*. Hoboken, New Jersey: John Wiley & Sons Inc.

Rabelo, R. J. and Bernus, P. (2015) 'A holistic model of building innovation ecosystems', *IFAC-PapersOnLine*, 28(3), pp. 2250–2257. doi: 10.1016/j.ifacol.2015.06.423.

Remane, G. *et al.* (2017) 'The Business Model Pattern Database-A Tool For Systematic Business Model Innovation', *International Journal of Innovation Management*, 21(1). doi: 10.1142/S1363919617500049.

Schütz, F. *et al.* (2018) 'Defining functional roles for research institutions in helix innovation networks', *Journal of Technology Management & Innovation*, 13(4), pp. 47–54.

Smit, S. *et al.* (2016) 'Business Model Boutique: A Prêt-à-Porter Solution for Business Model Innovation in SMEs', in *IFIP International Federation for Information Processing*, pp. 579–587. doi: 10.1007/978-3-319-45390-3_49.

Studer, R., Benjamins, V. R. and Fensel, D. (1998) 'Knowledge Engineering: Principles and methods', *Data & Knowledge Engineering*, 25, pp. 161–197. doi: https://doi.org/10.1016/S0169-023X(97)00056-6.

Vaishnavi, V. and Kuechler, B. (2004) 'Design Science Research in Information Systems Overview of Design Science Research', *Ais*, p. 45. doi: 10.1007/978-1-4419-5653-8.

van Harmelen, F., Lifschitz, V. and Porter, B. (2008) *Handbook of Knowledge Representation*. 3rd edn. Elsevier Science.

Witschel, H. F. *et al.* (2015) 'A new Retrieval Function for Ontology-Based Complex Case Descriptions', *International Workshop Case-Based Reasoning CBR-MD 2015*.

Witschel, H. F. *et al.* (2019) 'Case Model for the RoboInnoCase Recommender System for Cases of Digital Business Transformation: Structuring Information for a Case of Digital Change', in *IC3K 2019 - Proceedings of the 11th International Joint Conference on Knowledge Discovery, Knowledge Engineering and Knowledge Management*, pp. 62–73. doi: 10.5220/0008064900620073.

Zarei, B., Nasseri, H. and Tajeddin, M. (2011) 'Best practice network business model for internationalization of small and medium enterprises', *Journal of International Entrepreneurship*, 9(4), pp. 299–315. doi: 10.1007/s10843-011-0080-3.

A DEEP LEARNING BASED TRAFFIC CLASSIFICATION IN SOFTWARE DEFINED NETWORKING

Rahma Hammedi
Prince Lab, ISITCOM, University of Sousse, Sousse, Tunisia

ABSTRACT

Moving from legacy internet applications, such as web, and e-mail, to dynamic complex applications, such as video streaming, and file sharing, improves the underlying network architectures to provide new services with high QoS requirements. Thus, a new network paradigm is developed and deployed; Software Defined Networking (SDN). As a result of the significant impact of using the internet, network traffic is growing up, and the network itself is becoming more overloaded. Therefore, new tools that can cover new requirements for high-quality services are becoming mandatory. Inherently, traffic classification (TC) has gained continuous interest as an important decision- centric approach to deliver the quality of service. The current main challenge is how to classify flows efficiently. In this work, a new method of classification for incoming flows is proposed. It is based on Deep learning and consists of using the MultiLayer Perceptron Model (MLP) to classify flows according to its constraints throughput and delay. Experimental results prove that the proposed approach outperforms parallel solutions in terms of precision. It can classify traffic with more than 97.7% precision compared to the Linear Regression classification and the Fuzzy Decision- tree model.

KEYWORDS

SDN, Traffic Classification, Deep Learning, Artificial Neural Network

1. INTRODUCTION

Current technological advancements in the field of networking do not cease evolving. Emerging applications require high demands on Quality of Service (QoS) such as delay and bandwidth to satisfy users. Thus, it is necessary to introduce new QoS- delivery approaches to meet the current application requirements. The current internet architectures provide only best-effort services, which cause traffic management problems. To solve this problem, it was thought to optimize the traffic classification as it is essential for the network functionality (Nguyen & Armitage, 2008). A promising solution to address the complexity of traffic classification is SDN. SDN is a novel architecture that offers centralized management of the network (routing, classification, monitoring.) through programmable interfaces. This may ensure flexibility and fine-grained flow control. Unfortunately, current classification techniques are not evaluative. This current work aims to overcome the lack of sufficient support for performing tasks related to TC (Da Silva et al., 2015). Thus, we create a new classification method to solve these problems and to guarantee QoS. The traffic classification model is formulated to optimize traffic scheduling according to the appropriate class. The rest of this paper is structured as follows. Section 2 presents an overview of the current public architecture and techniques. In Section 3, we detail the characteristics of our proposed architecture. Finally, discussion on results and performance evaluation are presented in Section 4.

2. RELATED WORK

Traffic classification (TC) is defined as linking and identifying flows to traffic classes (Ng et al., 2015). For two decades, it is becoming a fundamental network function to a wide range of applications (Rezaei & Liu, 2019) and has attracted increasing research efforts. To address this network function, some work, such as the differentiated service model (DiffServ) (Chan et al, 2006) , core on early-stage traffic identification, i.e., techniques that use the information contained in the Differentiated Service Code Point (DSCP) byte in each packet which is associated to a Per-Hop Behavior (PHB). According to network management problems, three types of PHB have been defined:

-BEST EFFORT (BE): The network provides no quality of service. It does neither guarantee the transmission delay nor the required resource allocation.

-ASSURED FORWARDING (AF): This PHB is intended for bandwidth-sensitive flows, allowing transmitting real-time data which have the constraint of resource allocation.

-EXPEDITED FORWARDING (EF): Designed for traffic that requires strict delay. EF can also be used to build a service that requires very low latency, jitter, and packet loss.

As shown in (Burgstahle et al, 2003), defining the code (DSCP) in each incoming packet is helpful, but it suffers from scalability problems. Authors in (Karagiannis et al, 2004) proposed an approach that is based on logical port numbers. It depends on investigating the standard ports used by well- known applications. However, novel applications either use well-known port numbers to disguise their traffic or do not use standard registered port numbers. (Li & Li J., 2014) Present traffic classifiers which dependent on Deep Packet Inspection (DPI). They focus on finding patterns or keywords in packets. These methods are only relevant to unencrypted traffic and have a lofty computational overhead. As a result, a new method is based on flow statistics. Usually, these methods employ classical machine learning (ML) algorithms (Sen et al., 2004). The effectiveness and accuracy of port-based classification, DPI, and classical machine learning methods have been declined due to the increasing variety and complexity of recent Internet applications. Recent research on network TC focuses on deep learning (Da Silva et al., 2015). Deep learning obviates the need to select features by a domain expert since it automatically selects features through training. Thus, deep learning has a considerably higher capacity of learning and efficient approach (Karagiannis et al, 2004), (Nandy, 2013) for TC. Authors in (Sandhya et al., 2017) show that SDN is a promising architecture to build efficient TC model due to its network-wide visibility (Hayes & Ng, 2018). The current SDN controller can enhance TC in large-scale networks (Morzhov & Nikitinskiy, 2018).

SDN can face the legacy IP architecture's limitations by decoupling the control plane from the forwarding plane and moving it to a centralized node, called the SDN controller. Network devices become simply Forwarding Elements (FE) (Pérez et al., 2019).The application of deep learning in SDN networks to classify flows is divided into supervised learning and unsupervised learning. In Unsupervised Learning or clustering, no information is required on the class label of the data or the number of classes; the goal is to discover similar instances in the data. The purpose of supervised classification is to learn using training set a classification procedure, allowing classifying new instances into predefined classes. Supervised learning has two main stages:

- Training: the learning phase analyses the data provided (training dataset) and forms a classification model.

-Validation/testing: the model created during the training stage is used to classify the new illustrations. The performance of the classification system is assessed during this step.

The literature (Nandy, 2013), (Sandhya et al., 2017) determines that supervised classification outperformed unsupervised clustering. A comparison between the hierarchical classification and a battery of different supervised classification algorithms (Nandy, 2013) reveals that the hierarchical classification approach is unable to obtain a precision as precise as the supervised classification. Consequently, supervised classification is more efficient than hierarchical classification.

3. PROPOSED ARCHITECTURE

In this section, the proposed classification approach is described, and phases of this approach are detailed. Finally, an illustrative example of the routing application of this model is presented.

3.1 Overall Structure

Our approach consists on classifying the incoming flows according to two features, Delay and Throughput, into three classes defined by the DiffServ approach (ref. section 2). The selection of these features is imposed because the delay and the throughput are considered the most relevant to define the constraints required by a flow to guarantee the application routing's optimal quality. Thus, flows are classified: AF for applications with bandwidth constraints and implicitly bit rate, EF for applications with delay constraints, and BE for applications without constraints. The proposed approach is based on two phases, a phase of preparation of the dataset (feature extraction) and a flows classification phase. This process is depicted in the figure 1.

3.1.1 Phase1: Feature Extraction

The extraction model receives a set of data as a pcap file obtained by capturing packets with the Wireshark tool (Kogan et al., 2013), invisibly in "promiscuous" mode, without jeopardizing data routing.

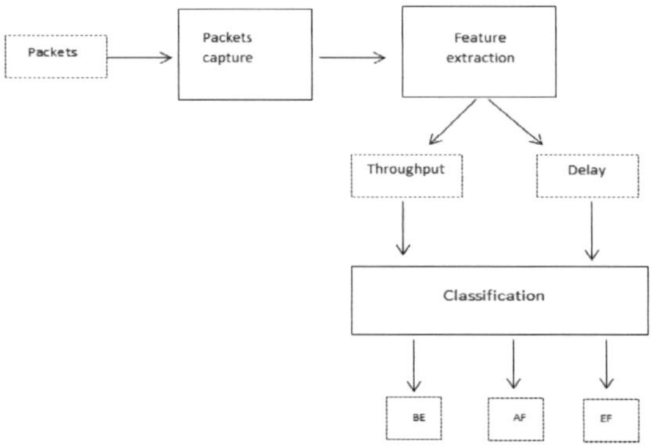

Figure 1. Process of the proposed classification model

Then, captured packets are decoded to find the required information, delay, and throughput of each flow.

Algorithm1: Feature extraction

Require: packets from PCAP file *ListPackets, number of* packets per window *WindowSize*
ListFeatures← []
while *listPackets.size≥WindowSize* ***do***
NextPackets← List Packets.take (WindowSize)
LengthPackets← 0
For *Packet ∈ListPackets* **do**
LengthPackets← LengthPackets + Packet.size
end for
Delay← Normalize (NextPackts.last.time – NextPackets.first.time
Throughput← Normalize (LengthPackets/Delay)
Features ← (Delay, Throughput)
ListFeatures.append (Features)
End while
return list of features vectors *ListFeatures*

3.1.2 Classification

Increasing learning algorithm parameters is related to several factors, including the number of hidden layers, the activation function, choice of necessary tests, and algorithms learning. The proposed model is based on the Multilayer Perceptron (MLP) algorithm.

It is recognized as the most used model due to its highest overall accuracy (Yan et al., 2015). A neuron acquires a weighted sum of its inputs and passes it over an activation function to create an output. In this algorithm, the input vector represented the throughput and the delay values, referred to as. At the output, the three PHBs defined in the DiffServ architecture are adopted so that each flow must be classified at BE, EF, or AF class.

B: Bias

Inputs: $X = (x1, x2)$

Outputs: $Y = (y1, y2, y3)$

w_i^j : The weight of link coupling the node i from the previous layer to the node j from the next layer

F: The Sigmoid Activation function is used as follows:

$$f_{Sig}(x) = \frac{1}{1+e^{-x}} \tag{1}$$

The sum of the weights pre-activation is defined by the function Z(X) as follows:

$$Z(x1, x2) = w_1^1 x_1 + w_2^1 x_2 + B \qquad (2)$$

In the second stage, we use an aggregation function whose association weights calculated in the previous phase are combined. N refers to the number of nodes in the neural network.

$$Z(X) = \sum_1^N w_i^j x_i \qquad i = 1 \ldots N \qquad (3)$$

In the last step the function Z can be computed using the activation function Sigmoid (equation 1) to determine the final sum of weights.

$$Y(X) = Sig[Z(X)] \qquad (4)$$

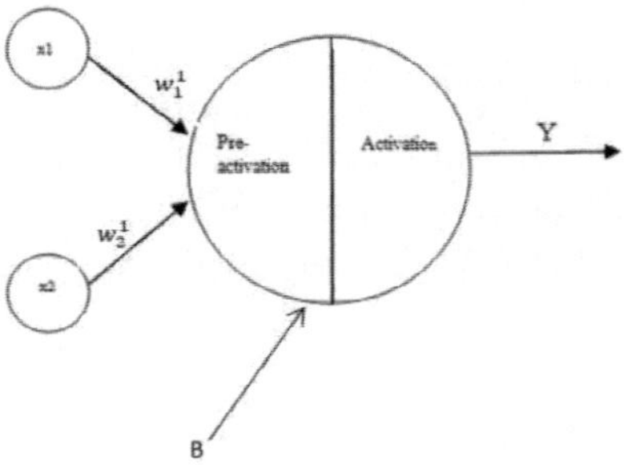

Figure 2. Pre-activation and activation phase within anode

Thus, a classification algorithm is used to classify an entry using the pre-trained learning model as follows.

Algorithm2: Flows classification

Require: pre-trained weights matrices $W^{"} \in R^{5*2}$ and $W^{"} \in R^{3*5}$, pre-trained biases vectors $B' \in R^5$ and $B^{"} \in R^3$, features vector (delay, throughput) x $\in R^2$
$\gamma \leftarrow$ ()
For I ← 1 → 5 **do**
$\gamma_i^1 \leftarrow$ x $*W_i^1 + B_i^1$
End for
$\partial^{"} \leftarrow$ ()
For I ← 1 → 3 **do**
$\partial_i^n \leftarrow \partial' *W_i^n + B_i^n$
End for
$\partial \leftarrow$ Softmax ($\partial^{"}$)
Return vector of classes probabilities $\partial \in R^3$

3.2 Information Routing

In SDN (Morzhov & Nikitinskiy, 2018), coupling the control plane and the data plane has invented another method of routing packets. Routing becomes a communication between switches and SDN controllers instead of consulting a routing table in the routers. The classification method's mechanism is illustrated as follows: When the incoming traffic arrives at the switch, a "packet_In" is sent from the switch to the SDN controller indicating the characteristics of this stream. Since he has a general view of the network, the controller should calculate and make decisions (based on the proposed classification model). It then answers the switch with a 'paket_Out,' providing the decision for what host and how it will be directed. Assuming that this message is received, the switch can successfully orient the packet as the SDN controller indicates.

4. EVALUATION AND EXPERIMENTAL RESULTS

In this section, we will describe the datasets selected for the experimental analyze and evaluate the proposed classification model's performance.

4.1 Feature Extraction

One of the most important steps in network traffic classification is the feature extraction as it is a crucial pre- processing task.

4.1.1 Collect Data

In reason of the lack of public and recent datasets available for research purposes, to achieve this step, forming an adequate dataset is mandatory. Traffic is captured during different periods with Wireshark. Obtained packets are saved into PCAP files. Initially, the program extracts the following features: duration for fixed packets, number of bytes, min packet length, max packet length, min interval packet time, max interval packet time and average interval packet time, the standard deviation of interval packet time, and the duration for fixed packets. Obtained features allow calculating the necessary inputs to our classification model: throughput and delay.

4.1.2 Normalization

Some inputs assume a finite number of values (discrete type) or continuous type. The data is normalized because it can have large order range values and different magnitudes, which can create problems in the classification. Thus, the values of the characteristics are normalized by applying a standard transformation to each characteristic. The normalization function is represented as follows.

$$X = (x - x_{min}) - (x_{max} - x_{min}) \qquad (5)$$

x: The original value.
x_{min}: The minimum value of all attributes.
x_{max}: The maximum value of all attributes.
X: The normalized value ∊ [0.1].

4.1.3 Training and Test Data

A large and representative set of data is one of the most important requirements for a deep learning model. The nodes of theL_i; i> 1 automatically choose and merge the information in the layer based on a weighted summation and an activation function. At the output layer, a measure of the average error is determined then used to adjust the weights throughout the network. This phase is named « Feed-forwarding» The final model is then used to predict the observations' responses in the second set of data called the validation dataset. We experiment with the proposed model on different sets of data. Each set will be automatically divided into 75% for the training and 25% for the validation.

4.2 Performance

In this section, we present the experimental results to evaluate our proposed classification model's performance in terms of precision.

4.2.1 Settings of the Experiments

To evaluate our model, the performance is measured in terms of precision. This metric is often defined as the proportion of the instances that correctly belong to class X amidst all those classified as X. In this part, we evaluate our model with different epochs on the dataset generated during the phase of extraction of the characteristics: delay and throughput. The variation in precision is presented in figure 3.

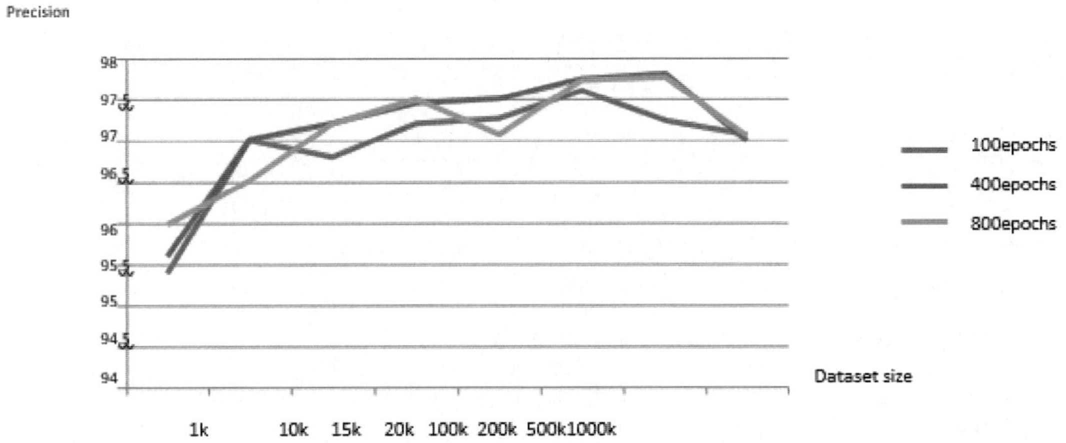

Figure 3. Precision of our model

Results shown in figure 3 present two phases: learning and over-learning. Testing data with a maximum number of flows 200k allows the model to learn continually, reaching a high accuracy of 97.74%.The second phase starts with a dataset bigger than 200k. The precision curve decreases slightly but always has a significant value of precision equal to 96.99%.As a result, the model achieved better than 97.5% Precision. This result allows the classifier to ensure an accurate classification over time.

Testing data in the flow interval] 200k, 500k [with 400 pockets allows the model to learn, achieving high accuracy of 97.8% gradually. The second phase begins when the number of incoming flows exceeds 500k. The precision curve decreases slightly. It is a saturation phase i, e. A phenomenon appears when the weighted sum of the signals that most neurons receive as input is too large. A saturated network is often in a situation of over-learning. Therefore, we fixed the size of the learning bench at 200k in the rest of our experiment. This decision is made to finalize a compromise between execution time and accuracy. The results are illustrated in table 1.

Table 1. Comparative study of execution time and precision between 200k and 500k models

	200k	500k
Precision %	97.74	97.8
Execution time in sec	24926.977	50188.597

4.2.2 Comparison

To have a correct comparison, all the experiments are applied to the same dataset, including a standard performance measure. This section reviewed two supervised classification approaches, Logistic regression and Fuzzy decision tree, to accomplish this experience. The choice was based on the classification time, and accuracy. The indicators obtained in (Yan et al., 2015) reflect that the decision tree technique predicts students dropping out with more accuracy and a lower percentage of errors. In (Enajjari et al., 2010), it is shown that logistic regression takes a "Train Time" more than "Test Time," however, these two values are significantly minimized compared to other algorithms, namely the KNN. Therefore, these two algorithms have low complexity and show better results in various fields, namely prediction (Enajjari et al., 2010), and diagnostics (Sujatha et al., 2018).

- **The proposed model vs. Logistic regression (LR)**

Logistic regression (LR) is a mathematical model (Enajjari et al., 2010) with real observations. The principle of LR is to make optimization loops. To ameliorate LR's learning parameters and to find its higher precision value, we simulate it with a varied number of iterations.

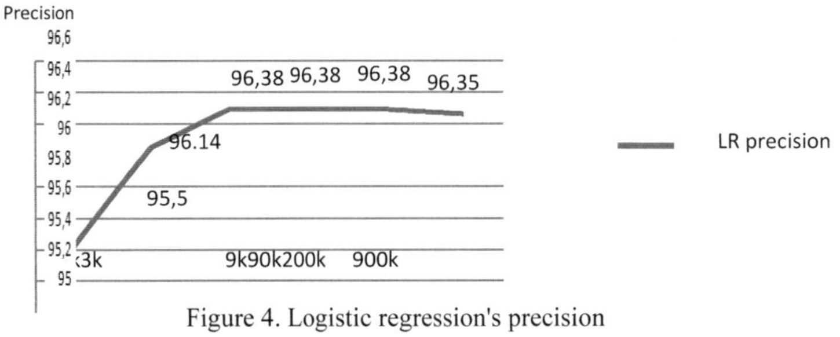

Figure 4. Logistic regression's precision

The highest precision obtained with LR is 96.38%, which is lower than the proposed model's precision.

- **The proposed model vs. Fuzzy decision tree (FDT)**

The fuzzy decision tree is a sequential connected graph representing the succession of decisions (Sujatha et al., 2018). In (Olaru & Wehenkel., 2003) is claimed that the performance of an FDT was based on the determination of its size. Thus, we try to build a tree, ensuring the best possible performance. Figure 5 shows the different results obtained. The decision tree presents a high accuracy, with 76.53%.

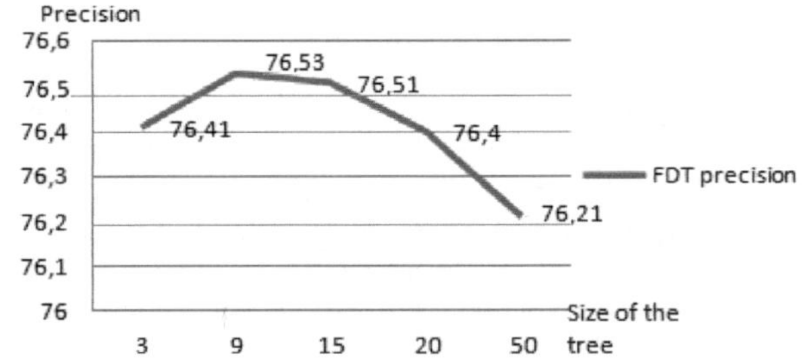

Figure 5. Precision of FDT

FDT is executed with its optimal depth (9 altitudes of nodes). We notice that the proposed model results are significantly better than FDT results in terms of precision.

5. RESULTS

We have shown that the proposed classification model based on Multilayer Perceptron is highly efficacious in precision, reaching approximately 97.74% with a high flows number reaching 500k flow, which presents a higher value compared to other solutions such as Fuzzy Decision Tree and Logistic regression.

6. DISCUSSION AND FUTURE WORK

In this paper, we have demonstrated an artificial neural network application to classify traffic by features. We investigate and propose an efficient model that can be deployed within SDN networks. It aims to classify flows into three classes: AF, EF, and BE, based on delay and throughput. We illustrated the performance in terms of precision. The results indicate that our approach can achieve about 97.74% precision. Although the proposed method presents high precision performance, we must optimize it equally to its parameter execution time to start the system with a rapid time-based execution if applied to a real-time application.

ACKNOWLEDGEMENT

We want to thank everyone who helps to achieve this work. We made the used algorithms and the dataset openly accessible for the community working on this area.

REFERENCES

Bar M., Ambaw i A. & Doroslovacki M. (2018), "Comparison of Machine Learning Algorithms for Raw Handwritten Digits Recognition".

Burgstahler L., Dolzer K., Hauser C., Jahnert J., Junghans S., Macian C., & Payer W. (2003), "Beyond technology: the missing pieces for QoS success", Association for Computing Machinery, New York, NY, USA, 121–130. DOI:https://doi.org/10.1145/944592.944597

Chan K., Babiarz J. & Baker F. (2006), "Configuration guidelines for DiffServ service classes".

Da Silva A. S., Schaeffer-Filho A. E. & Granville L. Z. (2015), "Identification and Selection of Flow Features for Accurate Traffic Classification in SDN".

En-Najjary, T. (2010). "Traffic classification: Application-based feature selection using logistic regression".

Hayes M., Ng B., Pekar A. & Seah W. K. G. (2018), "Scalable Architecture for SDN Traffic Classification".

Karagiannis T., Broido A., Brownlee N., Claffy K., & Faloutsos M. (2004), "Is P2P dying or just hiding?" in IEEE Globecom.

Kogan K., Nikolenko S., Culhane W., Eugster P. & Ruan E. (2013), "Towards efficient implementation of packet classifiers in SDN/OpenFlow," in Proc. 2nd ACM SIGCOMM Workshop Hot Topics Softw. Defined Netw.

Li Y. & Li J. (2014), "MultiClassifier: A combination of DPI and ML for application-layer classification in SDN", The 2014 2nd International Conference on Systems and Informatics (ICSAI 2014), pp. 682-686.

Lin J. (2013), "Mapreduce is good enough? If all you have is a hammer, throw away everything that's not a nail!," Big Data, vol. 1, pp. 28–37.

Moore, A., & Papagiannaki, K. (2005). "Toward the Accurate Identification of Network Applications". *PAM.*

Morzhov S. V. & Nikitinskiy M. A. (2018), ``Development&research of the prerewall network application for oodlight SDN controller," in Proc. Moscow Workshop Electron. Netw. Technol. (MWENT), pp. 14.

Nandy M. (2013), "An Analytical Study of Supervised and Unsupervised Classification Methods for Breast Cancer Diagnosis", 2nd International conference on Computing Communication and Sensor Network (CCSN-2013).

Ng B., Winston M. H. & Seah K.G. (2015), "Developing a Traffic Classification Platform for Enterprise Networks with SDN: Experiences and Lessons Learned", New Zealand.

Nguyen T. & Armitage G. (2018) "A survey of techniques for internet traffic classification using machine learning," IEEE Communications Surveys Tutorials,Fourth.

Olaru C. & Wehenkel L. (2003), "A complete fuzzy decision tree technique", Fuzzy Sets&Systems, Issue 2.

Pérez A., Grandón E., Caniupán M. & Vargas G. (2019), "Comparative Analysis of Prediction Techniques to Determine Student Dropout: Logistic Regression vs Decision Trees".

Quoc D. L.,Alessandro V.D, Park B., Romano L. & Fetzer C. (2015), "Scalable network traffic classification using distributed support vector machines," in Proc. IEEE 8th Int. Conf. Cloud Comput., New York, NY, USA.

Rezaei, S. & Liu X. (2019), "Deep Learning for Encrypted Traffic Classification: An Overview", Data Science and Artificial Intelligence for Communications.

Sandhya, S., Purkayastha, S., Joshua, E., & Deep, A. (2017). Assessment of website security by penetration testing using Wireshark. 2017 4th International Conference on Advanced Computing and Communication Systems (ICACCS), 1-4.

Sen, S., Spatscheck, O., & Wang, D. (2004). "Accurate, scalable in-network identification of p2p traffic using application signatures". WWW '04.

Sujatha R., AnithaNithya R., Subhapradha S., Srinithibharathi S. (2018), "Decision Tree Classification for Traffic Congestion",", International Journal of Engineering&Techniques, India.

Yan J., Zhang H., Shuai Q., Liu B. & Guo X. (2015), "HiQoS: An SDN-based multipath QoS solution", China Communications, 12(5): 123-133.

A NETWORK ANALYSIS OF IT-CMF

Fábio Longo De Moura and Filipe De Sá-Soares
Centro ALGORITMI – University of Minho – Guimarães, Braga, Portugal

ABSTRACT

Information Systems and Technology (IST) have been a great support in meeting business challenges, providing organizational agents with information to better perform their tasks. However, IST also requires attention to ensure that they continue to be valuable to all areas of the enterprise. In order to help organizations get value from IST several management models have emerged. IT-CMF is a comprehensive reference to guide the evolution in 36 different areas of the organization, in terms of its relationship with IST. The adoption of IT-CMF requires managers to decide on the areas to be enhanced, in order to make better use of organizational resources to add value to the organization's business, and to find the best path for improvement of IST. To assist managers in this process, this study presents a network analysis of IT-CMF, by the use of graphs as a means to clarify development paths, which include areas to prioritize for the use of resources, and that are aligned with the objectives of the organization.

KEYWORDS

IT-CMF, Capability, Competency, Graph, Information Systems, Information Systems and Technology

1. INTRODUCTION

Improving business performance, or even maintaining the competitive potential, is a daily and constant challenge for an enterprise. To strength its position in the market, an organization needs to change certain characteristics to a different state while preserving those characteristics that meet desirable parameters (Business Dictionary, 2012). This requires managers to make decisions from which a path to be followed by the organization towards defined goals should be derived. To best support their decisions, managers need information about the current situation and alternative options. Thus, Information Systems and Technology (IST) play a central role in organizations as fundamental resources to synthetize information.

Peppard and Ward (2004) identified three different eras of evolution for organizations, concerning their exploitation of IST, namely Data Processing, Management Information Systems, and Strategic Information Systems. These ages presented different challenges for the evolution of organizations, which influenced the development of different evolution models and maturity models. Such models depicted scenarios that might be faced by organizations and suggested paths for their evolution concerning technology, intending to achieve success in different aspects of the organization's operating environment. The increase in complexity inside and outside organizations, and in the amount of available information, led to an increased dependence of organizations on IST, requiring organizations to better manage their information-related resources.

To help organizations respond to this information management challenge, new evolution models and maturity models that formulate relationships between IST and organizations emerged. One of the latest models is the Information Technology Capability Maturity Framework (IT-CMF). The design of the IT-CMF reflects the demand for differentiated analyzes about the possibilities of improving organizations by the exploitation of IST. The framework indicates knowledge and skills that an organization should hold in order to manage efficiently and effectively the organization's IST function (Duarte and Da Silva, 2013). According to the provisions of the IT-CMF (IVI, 2016), it is possible to carry out diagnostic and in-depth analysis for each of the 36 management areas that make up the framework. The framework also points out relationships between management areas and how improvements in one area may contribute to improvements in other areas.

The organization that wishes to evolve, based on new demands or on any factor that influences the alteration of any of its characteristics, should consider evolution paths that may enhance certain management areas that make up the IT-CMF, with the prospect of rising its business performance. However, there may be alternative paths to choose from, taking into account not only the objectives established for the areas of IT-CMF, but also considering the relationship between the areas. Given the interdependences between the 36 management areas, organizations may face a complex task identifying and making sense of different evolution paths. From this observation stemmed the motivation to carry out this study. To facilitate the selection of evolution paths by organizations through better use of IST, we conducted a network analysis of IT-CMF. For this aim, we resort to graph theory to make explicit the interrelationships, scope, and possibilities when prioritizing improvements in one or more areas of IST in an organization. Such a proposal also allows managers more clarity in decision making, in addition to greater assertiveness and efficiency in the deployment of resources for the evolution of organizations through IST.

The following section covers the literature review, setting the stage for a new way to apply IT-CMF according to the specificities of each organization. After the literature review, this work is composed of two other sections, related to graph theory and the proposition of using IT-CMF and graph theory to improve the application of organizational resources, highlighting different views about the relevance of each area covered by IT-CMF. At the end of this paper, conclusions are drawn and future work involving the application of this proposal is advanced.

2. LITERATURE REVIEW

In this section, organizational success and measurement are discussed, taking into account the role that IST play both for that end and in that task. Then, evolution and maturity models for the exploitation and management of the organization's IST are briefly reviewed. Afterwards, the structure of IT-CMF and the relationship between the areas composing this framework are put into perspective.

2.1 Organizational Success

The availability of information on a large scale does not guarantees, by itself, the success of organizations. The business practices of organizations must keep up with constant changes, as practices that are known to be successful in the past may not indicate success in the future (Fong, 2010), as illustrated by what happened to companies with predominant market share a few years ago, such as Kodak, Blockbuster, and BlackBerry, that today no longer dominate the market, transmuted into a different business or just disappeared.

The measurement of the organization's success should not be static and should not be based on simplistic and isolated measures. A tool widely used to measure the success of organizations is the Balanced Scorecard (BSC) (Kaplan and Norton, 1992). BSC aims to overcome weaknesses of indicators such as Return Over Investment (ROI) and Earning Per Share (EPS), noting that these are not sufficient indicators for continuous improvement and innovation, factors which are necessary for the survival of the organization in the environment in which it operates. The BSC authors advocate the integration of complementary indicators to assist in the evaluation of the success of the organization, taking into account the customer perspective, internal business processes perspective, learning and growth perspective, and the financial perspective.

The success of an organization depends on its sustainability and growth, requiring the orchestration of very different tasks, such as segment identification and market niche, development of products and services, acquisition of resources, development of operating systems, development of management systems, and development of the corporate culture (Flamholtz and Aksehirli, 2000). In order to obtain a competitive advantage, an enterprise needs to align resources with the business strategy (Khani, Md Nor and Samani, 2011).

Whether for the purpose of measuring the level of success, which in itself has become more demanding since it has to consider a multitude of parameters (Curley, 2008), as instruments to know what is happening or as products or services by themselves, IST are a fundamental part of and for the success of organizations. It is therefore easy to understand the emergence of models to guide the exploitation and management of organizations' IST.

2.2 Evolution and Maturity Models

Through changes in the characteristics of organizations, which occurred over several decades, the concepts of evolution and maturity were adopted in order to envision the progress of the organization and its maturity regarding the use of IST. Common to most models of evolution and maturity, designed to guide organizations to obtain greater support in business processes from IST, several factors were used to measure the current state of organizations and to indicate aspects to improve, based on concepts, such as, information systems planning, strategic planning of information systems, organizational learning, information systems management, alignment of IST with the business, and user involvement (McFarlan *et al.*, 1983; Hirschheim *et al.*, 1988; Galliers and Sutherland, 1991).

The factors that help to assess the evolutionary stage of organizations, regarding their IST, are usually called variables, and should guide organizations to answer the following questions: Where are we? Where are we going? What will we do to get there? (Santos and Valdesuso, 1985).

Although different concepts are employed in different models, the fundamental difference between evolution models and maturity models concerns the support given to the actions to be developed, in the search for a better relationship between organizations and IST (Rocha and Vasconcelos, 2004). Hence, maturity models may offer greater support to managers regarding the desired improvements, in comparison to the simplified architecture of the evolution models, which limit themselves to present characteristics of situations experienced by organizations and failing to suggest actions to be taken for improvement of the current situation.

Given the increase in complexity, regarding the possibilities of evolution and maturity of organizations, proposing directions that unveil evolutionary paths for the organization becomes challenging. The scope of most of the models designed so far has become limited due to the numerous possibilities provided by the use of IST. Ergo, there is a need for a holistic approach to extract value from IST, that pays attention to different sectors of the organization, their specific demands and relationships, making explicit the influences and dependencies existing between them.

2.3 IT-CMF

Based on the various scientific contributions conceived over decades of studies on the relationship between organizations and IST, the IT-CMF appears as a composite of maturity models, not limited to analyzing a specific context. The framework architecture includes 36 contexts for analysis, each with a maturity model that indicates a possible path to be taken by the organization that seeks to improve its relationship with IST in a management area, in an attempt to do more for less, concerning financial investments made in IST (Carcary, Doherty and Thornley, 2015). Each IT-CMF maturity model is composed of five evolutionary stages, and the areas covered by the framework have guiding questions to assess the level of maturity, guidelines for the evolution of the area, typical challenges for the intended evolution, as well as actions necessary to be performed by those responsible for the evolution of the organization. The areas, called Critical Capabilities (CC), are organized into four large groups, called Macro Capabilities (MC). These groups bring together areas that have equivalent objectives, which according to the provisions of IVI (2016), are:

- Managing IT like a business (MC1): Composed of 14 CCs, it proposes to change the vision of how IT is considered, migrating from a cost center to a value center view, offering solutions to customers and existing problems in the business;
- Managing the IT budget (MC2): Formed by 4 CCs, it includes challenges related to the cost of IT, such as unplanned costs, maintenance of legacy systems, and the difficulty of strategically investing in new technologies;
- Managing the IT capability (MC3): It covers 15 CCs and refers to the maintenance of the services provided by the IT function and the development of new services, stimulating innovation in the organizational environment through services and solutions provided by IT; and
- Managing IT for business value (MC4): It involves 3 CCs, which aim to ensure that IT investments will enable business benefits, fostering the view that IT projects are not technology projects, but projects that generate business value.

Theories and practices proposed by several of the maturity and evolution models known until the conception of the IT-CMF in 2016 were incorporated in this framework. The process of diagnosing the necessary improvements for the organization, which is also included in the framework architecture, will indicate a set of CCs that should be improved, according to the current situation of the organization and its business objectives.

Through the diagnosis of the organizational scenario, in line with what the framework suggests, the benefits from the improvement actions applied to a single CC or a group of CCs may contribute to several areas of the organization. Analyzing the relationships between the CCs, contributions to the improvement of several CCs are observed, which may be the result of isolated actions, but with comprehensive results. The relationships between the 36 CCs that make up the IT-CMF involve 230 contributions, either between CCs from the same MC or between CCs from other MCs, as shown in Table 1.

Considering the significant number of relationships existing between the CCs, the prioritization of CCs on the path to be followed for the improvement of the areas of the organization becomes complex. Therefore, it is necessary to understand better such relationships, specifically regarding the contributions provided and received by each CC, in order to assist managers on the selection of the best evolutionary path to be followed. This argument is related to the purpose of IT-CMF, to do more with less, making it possible to add value to the business through assertive investment in IST.

Table 1. Contributions between IT-CMF MCs

Contributions →	MC1	MC2	MC3	MC4
MC1	52	8	47	7
MC2	6	6	2	3
MC3	34	2	45	1
MC4	4	7	4	2

According to the data provided in Table 1, the relevance of MC1 is patent, both in the contributions provided by the CCs that compose it and in the contributions received by their CCs. On the other hand, there is a lower weight of the CCs of MC2, regarding the contribution to the other CCs, as well as the contributions received by the CCs that make up MC4. To enable a better representation of the CCs, visually indicating the existing relationships between them, making clear their contribution to improvement actions, we resort to graph theory, using representations as well as applying algorithms on the data compiled from IT-CMF. The application of algorithms enables the identification of communities of CCs that show greater proximity, identification of CCs with greater relevance in the framework, either in general or in the contributions received or provided, as well as showing the affected CCs through the improvements made in a single CC. The representations were made using software Gephi (version 0.9.2).

3. GRAPH THEORY

Graph theory is a branch of mathematics concerned with the study of structures – graphs – that model relationships between objects. A graph is a representation formed by a set of points (vertices) and connections between points (edges), which can be used to represent different situations in the real world (Bondy and Murty, 1976). The history of graph theory began in 1736, in the famous dilemma of the Königsberg bridges. In this dilemma, the seven bridges (edges) and four regions (nodes) of the city of Königsberg were involved, which were cut by the river Pregel (Goldbarg and Goldbarg, 2012). Figure 1, developed by Rouse Ball (Gross and Yellen, 2003), exemplifies the dilemma mentioned when he called the concept of graph. This example came from the challenge of the Königsberg population, which was to walk through all regions of the city without crossing the same bridge more than once.

One of the most used examples for graphs is about representing people, with lines representing the relationship between people, being able to demonstrate large concentrations and displacements on a map. Such a scenario is of great relevance for macro analysis and makes it possible to obtain results regarding the spread of diseases in the world. A current case for analysis is the evolution of the pandemic caused by the SARS-CoV-2 virus (COVID-19). When traveling, people end up transporting the virus to their cities but passing by large points of concentration of people, such as large airports (hubs).

Regarding displacement, the theory of graphs can also be applied to chess games, with each piece having a specific graph that indicates its displacement, citing the Queen, for example. The Queen is the piece that has the greatest number of opportunities in its displacement on the board and may have up to 8 possible edges and several vertices for its final position on the board, as shown in Figure 2. The queen is at the center of the graph, indicated by the non-empty point, having 25 vertices as the final position, depending on whether there is an impediment to displacement, caused by any other piece of the board.

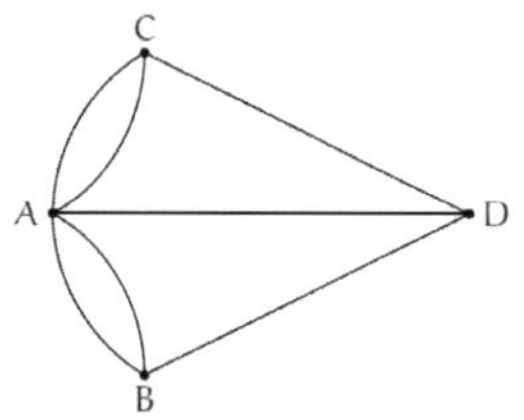

Figure 1. Graph diagram of the Königsberg bridges

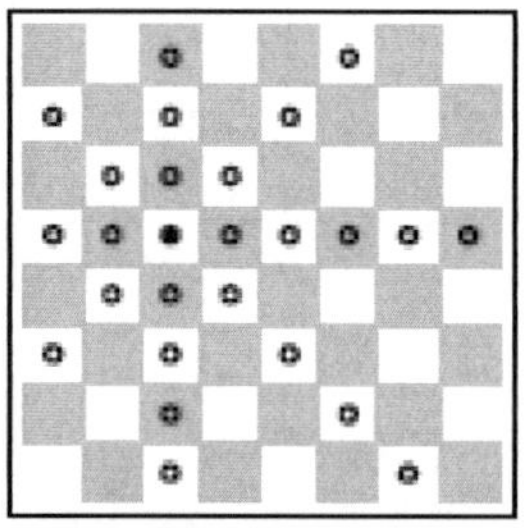
Figure 2. Chessboard

These are just a few examples of the use of graphs, from a myriad of applications in chemistry, operations research, social sciences, and computer science, to name a few. In this work, graphs will be used to represent the CCs and MCs of IT-CMF, to clarify how CCs are related and how they can indicate paths for the evolution of organizations, regarding their relationship with IST. The path to follow is based on the diagnosis of the improvements to be made, according to the objectives defined for the organization. In other words, the graph makes a clear sequence of actions related to the various CCs that make up the IT-CMF, through the improvements identified as necessary to the organization. In addition, it may indicate necessary paths to follow, that is, in the evolutionary path proposed for the organization, it might prove essential to mobilize certain resources in order to make feasible improvements in a specific area of the organization.

4. ANALYZING THE IT-CMF WITH GRAPH THEORY

The use of the concept of graphs for this work was thought of as a means to facilitate the understanding of the existing relationships between the areas addressed by IT-CMF, as set out in Table 1. Hence, it became possible to analyze all the CCs that make up the framework, as depicted in Figure 3, as well as a subset of CCs, such as those that make up each MC, as shown in Figure 4. In the figures, CCs are identified by a numeral and an abbreviation in square brackets (the meaning of each abbreviation is provided in Appendix A).

In both Figures 3 and 4, CCs are arranged following the distribution proposed by the Force Atlas 2 algorithm, being dimensioned according to their degree (corresponding to the inputs and outputs of each node – CC). The color of each node corresponds to the application of the Heat Map, with an emphasis on the CC with the highest degree in the analysis performed, except for MC2. This exception is because the CCs BOP(16) and FF(17) have the same degree, so the CCs are dimensioned by their centrality, and the colors with the application of the Heat Map are based in the CC with greater centrality.

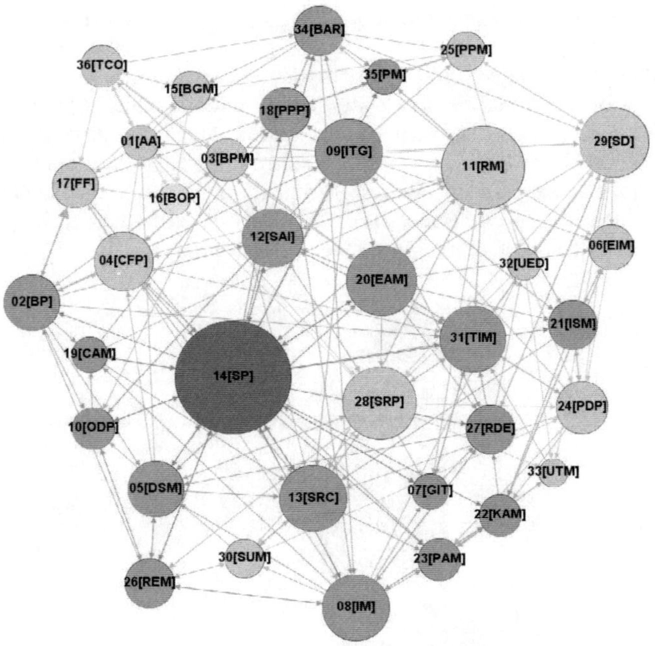

Figure 3. IT-CMF Critical Capabilities

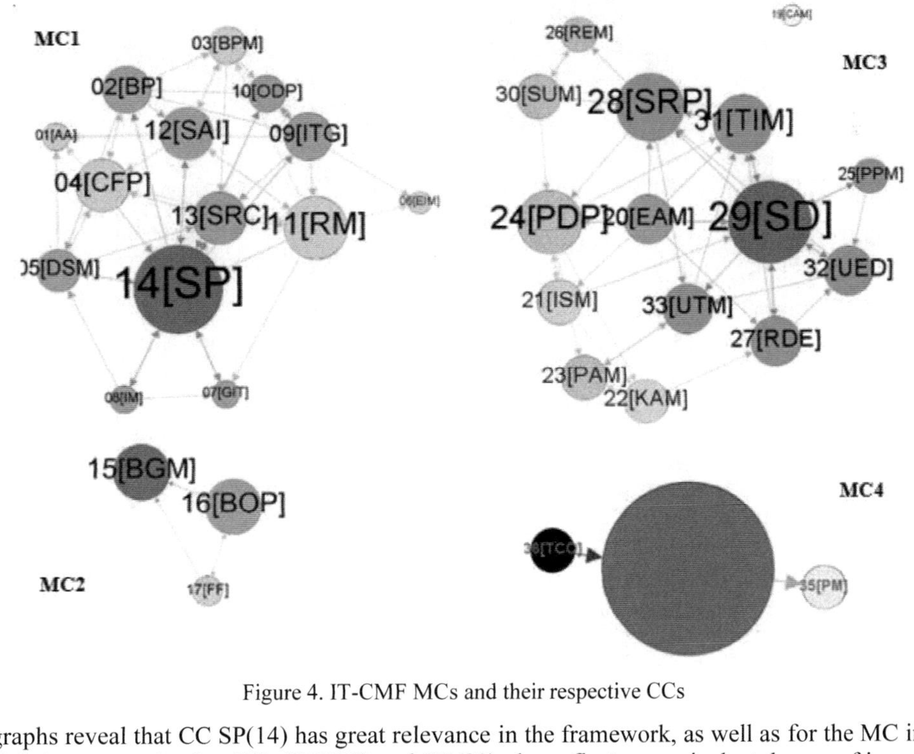

Figure 4. IT-CMF MCs and their respective CCs

The graphs reveal that CC SP(14) has great relevance in the framework, as well as for the MC in which it is located. It is noteworthy that CCs SRP(28) and SD(29) also reflect an equivalent degree of importance for MC, but in the global framework, they are less important. Concerning the contributions between CCs, it is noted that CC CAM(19) does not co-participate in the MC in which it is located, exercising relations in large part with the CCs of MC1 (7 CCs) and MC3 (1 CC). This fact strengthens and clarifies the essence of the framework, namely that the relationships between different sectors enable the organization to evolve. Thus, although CC CAM(19) works to raise the quality of MC3, its improvement will also facilitate improvements intended for MC1 and MC3.

Figure 5 strengthens this statement, presenting another point of view on the IT-CMF CCs. In this figure, the CCs are presented in colors that represent their communities, rendering the CCs that have the strongest relationship. This result was obtained through the distribution using Force Atlas 2 algorithm and the calculation of Modularity (0.238). It is noted, therefore, the existence of different communities from the corresponding organization with the MCs (presented in Figure 6), emphasizing again the argument of IT-CMF that although each CC has a main objective, leading to classify it in an MC according to its purpose, its evolution may contribute to the improvement of another area of the organization.

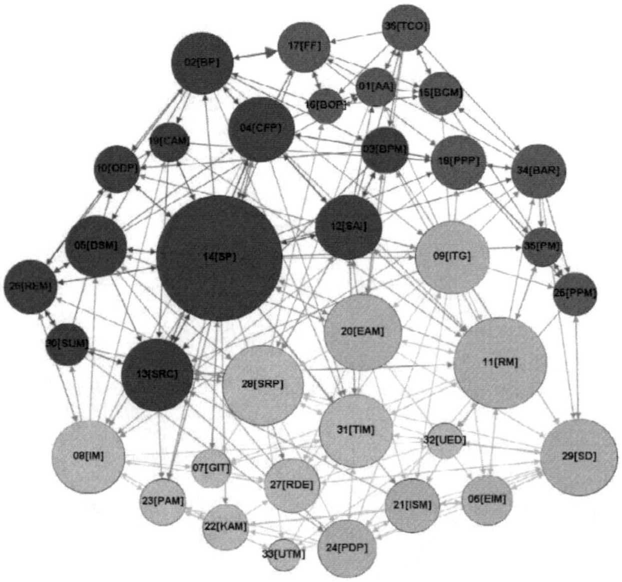

Figure 5. IT-CMF emphasizing the representation of CC communities

Another representation derived from Figure 5 and shown in Figure 7 is to scale the nodes according to the degree value of each node, dividing it into two figures, one to represent the degree of the input and the other to represent the degree of the output. This representation is expected to contribute to the definition of paths to be followed to carry out activities related to the CCs, considering what should be prioritized in an evolutionary path of the organization. Such an argument considers the following scenario: let us imagine that managers identify as necessary to make improvements in CC BPM(03), belonging to MC1. Knowing that BPM is part of a community (resulting from the modularity of the graph) whose main facilitators are CCs BP(02), CFP(04), and SP(14), it makes sense to consider the contributions by these CCs, which will help to improve the organization's BPM(03). It is noteworthy that CC BP(02) contributes directly to CC BPM and can assist in its evolution. On the other hand, the contribution provided by BPM to the other CCs should also be considered, regarding the relevance of these CCs to the organization. In this case, contributions resulting from improvements made in the context of BPM are directed to CCs ODP(10), SAI(12), SRC(13), EAM(20), and SD(29). If these CCs are also considered relevant to the business, the importance of using resources to improve BPM(03) is even greater. Another important insight is that CC EAM(20) has a high degree of output, contributing to several other CCs, as shown in Figure 7(B).

It is also relevant to consider that there are four MCs, as documented in IT-CMF, coinciding with the number of CC communities identified by calculating the graph's modularity. The similarities observed through the representation, shown in Figure 6, cover the fact that MC2 and MC4 are practically united in one community, with only one CC of MC3 grouped in that community. In the other communities, all CCs correspond to MC1 and MC3, being well balanced in their division between communities.

Referring to the relevance of MCs to the framework, it is evident that MC1 and MC3, by efficiently and effectively employing organizational resources in the evolution of their CCs, tend to enable a radical change in the organization, resulting from improvements in line with the objectives of CCs. However, although MC2 and MC4 have substantially fewer CCs, when employing organizational resources to improve these CCs, the contributions to the other CCs in the framework are above the average of the number of contributions provided by the CCs of MC1 and MC3. Table 2, as a complement to Table 1, shows the average of contributions per CC, taking into account the number of CCs in each MC.

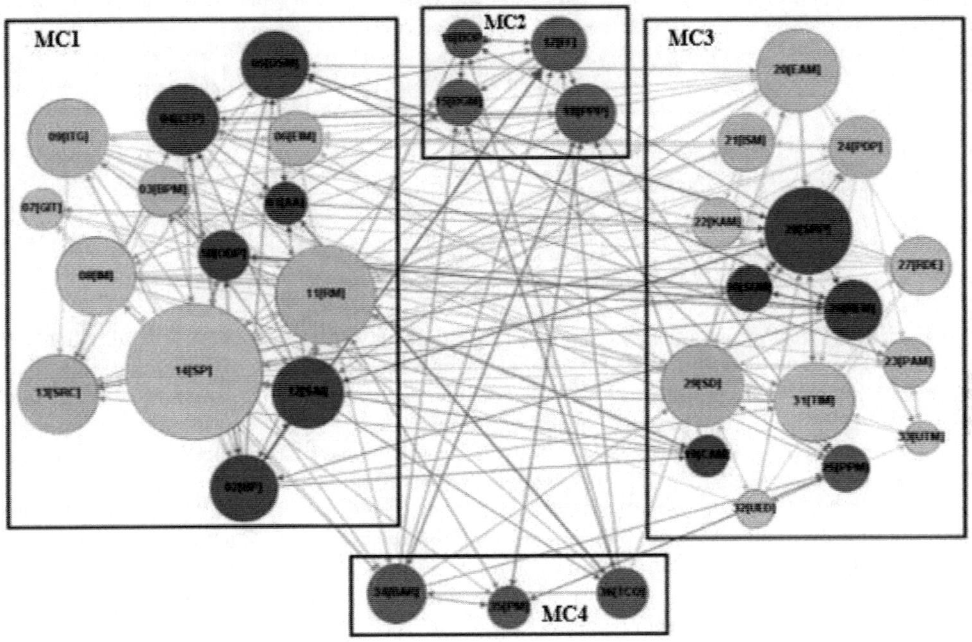

Figure 6. Organization of CCs according to MCs

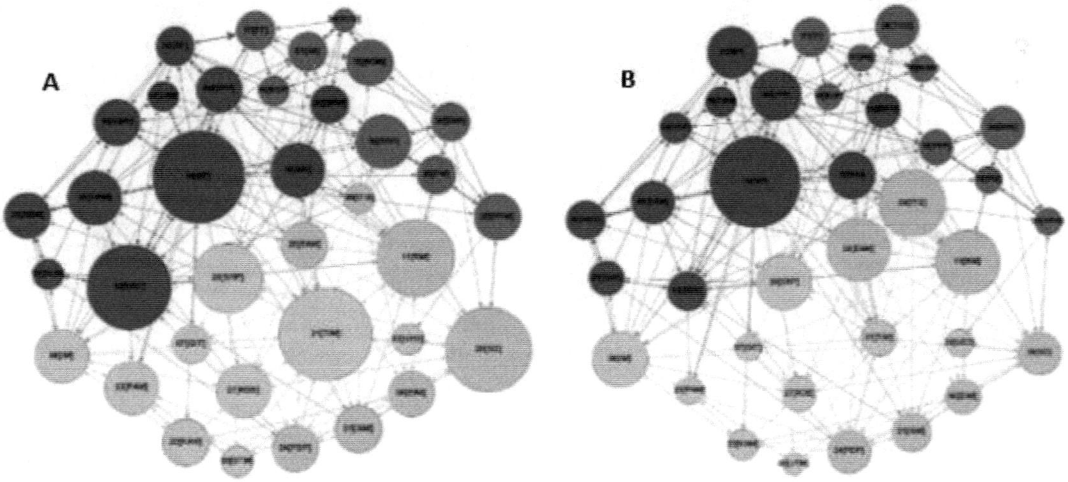

Figure 7. Input and output degree comparison of CCs

Considering the contributions featured in Table 2, one notes that the relationship between the CCs of MC1 and MC3 are very strong, as well as the relationships that exist internally, that is, between the CCs of MC1 and MC3 themselves. However, when directing the relationship between these MCs and the other smaller MCs, the contribution is much lower than the contributions provided by the MCs composed of a lower number of CCs. The weakness, nevertheless, is part of the internal relations between the CCs, since, comparatively, the smaller MCs have, on average, less internal relations than the most numerous MCs. Therefore, when defining an IST improvement plan in an organization, it is necessary to visit the contributions provided by the smaller

MCs, because at first, these MCs indicate that they have a more comprehensive impact in the potential results from the correct use of organizational resources. Being more specific about this example, when considering the CCs with the highest degree in the graph, in MC2 and MC4, respectively PPP(18) and BAR(34) (see Figure 4), and also because they are in the same community (see Figure 5), it is advisable that, even if such CCs are not prioritized, the contribution provided by them is validated, based on what the organization wants to achieve and if, indirectly, the path to the objective cannot be facilitated.

Table 2. Average contributions from CCs (Grouped by MCs)

Average contributions →	MC1	MC2	MC3	MC4
MC1	3.71	0.57	3.36	0.50
MC2	1.50	1.50	0.50	0.75
MC3	2.27	0.13	3.00	0.07
MC4	1.33	2.33	1.33	0.67

To clarify the relationships and contributions existing between the CCs of the MCs that make up the IT-CMF, Figure 8 makes a comparison of the direct relationship between the MCs. In Figure 8(A), the thickness of the edges (the size of the edge arrow) conveys, through the direction of the arrow, the contribution provided from one MC to another. It can be noted, therefore, the strength of the relationship between MC1 and MC3, as previously mentioned, in addition to also demonstrating the connectivity of the CCs that make up MC1 and MC3 (as revealed by the self-loops). Figure 8(B) depicts the total contributions divided by the number of CCs that make up the MC. In this representation, it is evident that, in all relationships, MC2 and MC4 provide more contributions to MC1 and MC3 than receive contributions from these MCs, making clear the need to provide attention to MC2 – Managing the IT Budget and MC4 – Managing IT for Business Value, even though, quantitatively, they are less expressive than the other MCs. The CCs that makeup MC2 and MC4 can act as great facilitators for improvements to be performed in different areas of management of the organization.

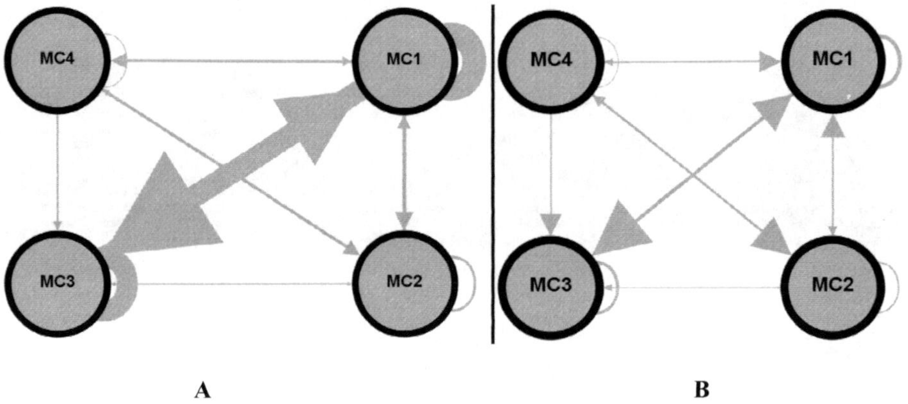

Figure 8. Relations and contributions between MCs and CCs

5. CONCLUSION

In the face of a challenge, it is necessary to act. To act, the action must be well-founded, that is, be based on elements that support that the action performed was identified as the best option for the given moment. The decision for a path to be followed to make improvements in the organization needs to be as assertive as possible, as many organizations have no margin for errors, or, even if errors are part of the evolutionary path that the organization takes, they are never desirable. The proposal to use graphs as an aid to find the evolutionary paths for the organization, which are adapted to its needs, seeks to maximize the use of organizational resources in the adoption and use of IT-CMF.

Considering that IT-CMF is one of the most robust and mature references in the evaluation of the relationship between organizations and IST, it is of great relevance to explore it, to present different points of view for its application, seeking to facilitate the immersion of managers in the content provided. By conducting a network analysis of IT-CMF based on graph theory, it is possible to demonstrate, with greater clarity, how the management areas that make up IT-CMF are related, as well as revealing the paths that can be covered by the organization, in order to improve its use of IST. The possibilities for combining the graph concept with the framework are numerous, and it is believed that sufficient guidelines have been provided in this paper to suggest how managers can build the best roadmap to be followed, deploying organizational resources as efficiently and effectively as possible, focusing on the creation of aggregate value to the business by using IST.

For future work, we consider the application of this proposal in different organizations to be extremely relevant. This would assist in the validation of the proposal of using graph theory for planning improvement actions to be carried out based on the IT-CMF.

ACKNOWLEDGEMENT

This work has been supported by FCT – Fundação para a Ciência e Tecnologia within R&D Units Project Scope: UIDB/00319/2020.

REFERENCES

Bondy, J. A. and Murty, U. S. R. (1976) *Graph Theory with Applications*. Ontario: Macmillan.

Business Dictionary (2012) *Evolution*. Available at: http://www.businessdictionary.com/definition/evolution.html (Accessed: 15 August 2019).

Carcary, M., Doherty, E. and Thornley, C. (2015) 'Business innovation and differentiation: Maturing the IT capability', *IT Professional*. IEEE Computer Society, 17(2), pp.46–53.

Duarte, A. and Da Silva, M. M. (2013) 'Cloud Maturity Model', in *2013 IEEE Sixth International Conference on Cloud Computing*. Santa Clara (Califórnia), pp.606–613.

Flamholtz, E. G. and Aksehirli, Z. (2000) 'Organizational success and failure: An Empirical Test of a Holistic Model', *European Management Journal*, 18(5), pp.488–498.

Fong, K. (2010) *The Five Elements of Organizational Success*. Available at: http://elementalpartners.net/downloads/5_Elements.pdf (Accessed: 20 October 2019).

Galliers, R. D. and Sutherland, A. R. (1991) 'Information systems management and strategy formulation: the "stages of growth" model revisited', *Information Systems Journal*. Wiley/Blackwell (10.1111), 1(2), pp.89–114.

Goldbarg, M. and Goldbarg, G. (2012) *Grafos: Conceitos, Algoritmos e Aplicações*. Rio de Janeiro: Elsevier.

Gross, J. and Yellen, J. (2003) *Handbook of Graph Theory*. New York: CRC.

Hirschheim, R. *et al.* (1988) 'An exploration into the management of the information systems function: key issues and an evolutionary model', in *Proceedings of the Joint International Symposium on Information Systems*. Sidney, pp. 4.15-4.38.

IVI (2016) *IT Capability Maturity Framework (IT-CMF) – The Body of Knowledge Guide*. Maynooth: Innovation Value Institute.

Kaplan, R. S. and Norton, D. P. (1992) *The Balanced Scorecard—Measures that Drive Performance*, *Harvard Business Review*. Available at: https://hbr.org/1992/01/the-balanced-scorecard-measures-that-drive-performance-2 (Accessed: 13 August 2019).

Khani, N., Md Nor, K. and Samani, M. B. (2011) 'A Proposed Research Model for the Relationship between Organizational IS capabilities , Organizational Performance and Strategic Planning', in *Innovation and Knowledge Management: A Global Competitive Advantage*. Isfahan, Najafabad, pp.770–782.

McFarlan, F. W., McKenney, J. L. and Pyburn, P. (1983) 'The information archipelago--plotting a course.', *Harvard Business Review*, 61(1), pp.145–156.

Peppard, J. and Ward, J. (2004) 'Beyond strategic information systems: towards an IS capability', *The Journal of Strategic Information Systems*, 13(2), pp.167–194.

Rocha, A. and Vasconcelos, J. (2004) 'Os Modelos de Maturidade na Gestão de Sistemas de Informação', *Revista da Faculdade de Ciências e Tecnologia da Universidade Fernando Pessoa*, pp.93–107.

Santos, J. R. and Valdesuso, C. (1985) *Planejamento Estratégico e Tático da Informática*. 2nd edn. Rio de Janeiro: SCI-Editora.

APPENDIX A – LIST OF CRITICAL CAPABILITIES

Abbreviation	Description
AA	Accounting and Allocation
BAR	Benefits Assessment and Realization
BGM	Budget Management
BOP	Budget Oversight and Performance Analysis
BP	Business Planning
BPM	Business Process Management
CAM	Capability Assessment Management
CFP	Capacity Forecasting and Planning
DSM	Demand and Supply Management
EAM	Enterprise Architecture Management
EIM	Enterprise Information Management
FF	Funding and Financing
GIT	Green Information Technology
IM	Innovation Management
ISM	Information Security Management
ITG	IT Leadership and Governance
KAM	Knowledge Asset Management
ODP	Organization Design and Planning
PAM	People Asset Management
PDP	Personal Data Protection
PM	Portfolio Management
PPM	Programme and Project Management
PPP	Portfolio Planning and Prioritization
RDE	Research, Development and Engineering
REM	Relationship Management
RM	Risk Management
SAI	Service Analytics and Intelligence
SD	Solutions Delivery
SP	Strategic Planning
SRC	Sourcing
SRP	Service Provisioning
SUM	Supplier Management
TCO	Total Cost of Ownership
TIM	Technical Infrastructure Management
UED	User Experience Design
UTM	User Training Management

TRUST EVALUATION IN ONLINE SOCIAL NETWORKS

Christina Sanchita Shah and Mankoottathil Paulose Sebastian
Indian Institute of Management
Kozhikode, India

ABSTRACT

Online social networks (OSNs) are among the most commonly accessed sites on the internet. People use OSNs to share activities, memories, events and concerns with their family, friends and acquaintances. OSNs are important means for information exchange and collaboration also. Though OSNs make correspondence and data sharing much easier, it has adverse impacts such as being able to receive meaningless, unnecessary, and inaccurate information through connections proposed by the recommending system. This might also escalate to the exploitation of user's data by recommending false information. This generates a pressing need to assess the trustworthiness of links between users in order to guarantee the safety of their everyday social networking interactions. The aim of this paper is to understand trust evaluation in OSNs which is accomplished by addressing three research questions. The contribution of this study is threefold. First, we present a comprehensive understanding of trust in OSNs. Second, we present the research trends and profile of studies examining trust evaluation is OSNs. Third, we outline the key challenges present in trust evaluation in OSNs.

KEYWORDS

Trust Evaluation, Online Social Networks, OSN, Trust

1. INTRODUCTION

Online social networks (OSNs) are very commonly accessed by people to share activities, memories, events and concerns with their family, friends and acquaintances (Xiao et al., 2018). Furthermore, with increased accessibility to the internet through personal computers, tablets and smartphones, social networking platforms have become omnipresent (Sherchan, Nepal, and Paris, 2013). However, with the rise of OSNs, concerns about the privacy of information have been raised. While the pattern of link-based data sharing makes communication and collaboration much easier, it also has adverse impacts (Li et al., 2016). Recent times have witnessed massive breaches of user privacy. In 2018, big firms such as Facebook, Under Armor, Quora and Panera Bread were victims of large-scale data breaches. Personal identifiable information (PII) of users were stolen, which included personal email addresses, physical addresses, passwords, card numbers, phone numbers, passport data, and more (Strain, 2018). Thus, trust is becoming a significant element in social networks and communities (Sherchan et al., 2013), giving rise to an imperative need to evaluate the trustworthiness of links between users in order to safeguard their daily interactions.

Trust plays a big role in people's lives without which our everyday social lives would have been different. Trust is a key component of decision making and its value intensifies in OSNs as there are no real-life physical interactions (Jiang et al., 2016). However, the concept of trust is complex and therefore, quantifying trust is not easy. OSNs leverage trust to increase accessibility and ease of use, but trust remains a key challenge as individuals are typically anonymous and do not talk face to face. In this sense, trust becomes a precondition for online social behaviour (Liu et al., 2019).

While trust in OSNs is a relatively new concept, it is a growing field of research. In their review of trust in social networks, Sherchan et al. (2013) explained the concept of social trust and its aspects such as trust dissemination, trust information collection and trust evaluation. Their review, however, did not include OSNs. To bridge this gap, Jiang et al. (2016) reviewed graph-based trust evaluation techniques in OSNs. Their review, however, was limited only to trust evaluation in graph-based methodologies. In a broader review, Ureña et al. (2019) studied a different aspect of trust, namely trust propagation and opinion dynamics in OSNs. While these reviews are informative, there remains a gap in understanding trust in OSNs. Our paper attempts to bridge this gap by synthesizing the literature and analyzing trust evaluation in OSNs, leading to the following research questions: *RQ1:* What is meant by trust in OSNs? *RQ2:* What is the research profile of studies on trust evaluation in OSNs? *RQ3:* What are the key challenges present in trust evaluation in OSNs? The contribution of this research is threefold. First, we present a comprehensive understanding of trust in OSNs (Section 2 and 3). Second, we present the research trends and profile of studies examining trust evaluation is OSNs (Section 4 and 5). Third, we outline the key challenges present in trust evaluation in OSNs (Section 6).

2. REVIEW METHODOLOGY

This study used a systematic review method to evaluate research into the notion of trust in OSNs. The articles used for this study were extracted from Academic Search Premier (EBSCO) database, ScienceDirect and ProQuest database. Academic Search Premier (EBSCO) was primarily used to search for papers as (i) it is a leading database for peer-reviewed academic articles (ii) it has a large volume of published papers, books, magazines and reports indexed and (iii) it has a considerable amount of interdisciplinary literature indexed as well. Other databases like ProQuest and ScienceDirect have also been used to search for literature that was absent in EBSCO. A check for duplication was done to find a unique and distinct list of academic papers. 266 articles were obtained as a result of using keywords such as online social network, OSN and trust. From 266 articles, 44 were shortlisted based on specific inclusion and exclusion criteria. The inclusion criteria were: (i) Studies on the concept of trust and its evaluation in OSN (ii) Studies published in academic peer-reviewed journals only and (iii) studies published in English. The exclusion criteria were: (i) Studies on OSN but not about trust evaluation (ii) Studies on trust evaluation in domains other than OSNs and (iii) conference papers. It must also be mentioned here that during our literature search, we came across previous reviews on trust and OSN that we have considered separately to delineate the concept of trust and OSN.

3. TRUST

Since trust is a complex concept, multiple interpretations of trust exist. Table 1 describes varying definitions of trust according to different authors. While these definitions differ, they all suggest a shared nature of trust. In all the descriptions of trust, two common elements emerge: risk and interdependence. Risk is the ambiguity regarding the purpose of the other member and interdependence refers to the common and related goals of linked members which cannot be accomplished without depending on each other. These two conditions form the crux of any trust relationship (Sherchan et al., 2013). Table 2 describes the various terms associated with trust concepts taken from Jiang, Wang, & Wu (2014), Josang et al. (2007) and Sherchan et al. (2013).

Table 1. Various definitions of trust

Reference	Definition of Trust
(Sherchan et al., 2013)	"Trust is a measure of confidence that an entity or entities will behave in an expected manner despite the lack of ability to monitor or control the environment in which it operates."
(Golbeck, 2005)	Trust is "a commitment to an action, based on a belief that the future actions of that person will lead to a good outcome."
(Josang et al., 2007)	Trust is "the subjective probability by which one user expects that another user performs a given action."
(Ruohomaa and Kutvonen, 2005)	Trust is "the extent to which one party is willing to participate in a given action with a given partner, considering the risks and incentives involved."
(Grandison and Sloman, 2016)	Trust is "the firm belief in the competence of an entity to act dependably, securely and reliably within a specified context."

Table 2. Common terms associated with trust

Terms	Definitions
Trustor	A person who is attempting to understand another user's degree of integrity/trust is the trustee.
Trustee	A person whose degree of trust is being assessed is the trustee.
Recommender	The recommender is an intermediate person who assists the trustee judge the degree of trustworthiness / trust of the trustee.
Trusted Path	It is the path that connects the source (the trustor) with the destination (the trustee).
Trusted Graph	This graph is comprised of all trusted paths between two nodes i.e., trustor and trustee. It is a subsidiary of a trust network.
Referral Trust	This is the trust in the ability (of a recommender) to suggest a successful provider of service (i.e., trustee).
Functional Trust	Trust in genuinely being a trustee is functional confidence.
Topic	It is the reason why a trustor wishes to understand the trustee.
Domain	This refers to a basic unit whose members share a common interest.
Active domain	All the domains a user has been part of.

3.1 Properties of Trust

Based on the research, trust has the following properties:

Context-specific: Trust always has a specific context. "Trust context" is the environment in which trust relationships occur (Liu et al., 2018).

Dynamic: Trust is dynamic in nature and changes with time, interactions and observations. While sometimes trust may increase with more interactions, sometimes it may also decrease with time (Ghavipour and Meybodi, 2018; Josang et al., 2007; Li, Xu, and Tang, 2018; Shehada et al., 2018).

Propagative: This is one of the most studied properties of trust in OSNs. For instance, if Alice trusts Bob and Bob trusts John then based on the amount of trust Alice has on Bob, Alice can gain a certain level of trust in John (Ghavipour and Meybodi, 2018; Josang et al., 2007; Sherchan et al., 2013; Wu et al., 2019).

Non-transitive: While trust is propagative, it is not transitive. Transitivity presupposes propagation, however, propagation does not imply transitivity (Sherchan et al., 2013).

Composable: Increasing trust and distrust across social networks enables a user to trust another member who is not directly associated with the user. If, however, several links in the network suggest a varying level of trust for the member, then the trustor is left to his own devices to compose trust information about that member (Golbeck, 2005).

Subjective: Trust is not objective but somewhat subjective. This results in customization of trust calculation where the trustor's preconditions directly influence the calculated trust value (Chen, Wang, and Jia, 2015; Farivar, Turel, and Yuan, 2017; Pavleska and Jerman Blažič, 2017).

Asymmetric: Trust is asymmetric. The amount of trust shared between a trustor and trustee may or may not be equal. For instance, Alex trusts Bob more than Bob trusts her (Sherchan et al., 2013).

Self-reinforcing: A trustor interacts positively with a trustee when he/she trusts that person. Conversely, positive interaction is less between members who do not trust each other, leading to further distrust (Kim and Ahmad 2013; Wang, Qiao, and Zhang, 2018).

Event sensitive: While trust takes time to build, it takes as little as one event to destroy it (Sherchan et al., 2013).

4. ONLINE SOCIAL NETWORKS (OSN)

An OSN can be described as a social graph in which a user is represented by a node and the edge between nodes signifies the connection between the users (Barnes, 1954). Social networks have entered a fresh era in OSNs with technological growth and the fast growth of accessibility. The numerous social networking sites lead to the development of complex and large social networks (Grandison and Sloman, 2016). There are three kinds of entities within an OSN: users (nodes), links (edges) and the information that flows between nodes via edges. The users generate links between each other which depend on the topic and are time-sensitive. The information exchanged between the users through the connections may be large and independent of time and space. Thus, it can be said that information diffusion in a primary function of OSN ((Arnaboldi et al., 2016; Jiang et al., 2016).

4.1 Trust in OSNs

The aim of OSN is to connect as many people as possible, and this makes trust a core element in OSNs. People use social networks to connect with others, and trust is one of the key determinants in the way they interact and relate with other members.

4.2 Factors Affecting the Formation of Online Social Trust

Since trust is a complex idea, it is not possible to exhaustively explain all the aspects that affect the formation of trust in a user. Moreover, when trust formation and propagation is online in social networks, it becomes even more difficult to understand trust as it is not based on real-life physical interactions. Below are a few aspects that affect online social trust (Zolfaghar and Aghaie, 2012).

Knowledge-based: This refers not to knowledge obtained indirectly but to the direct knowledge about the trustee. Here, users directly get acquainted by interactions and then predict the conduct of people based upon the data obtained from prior interactions. However, in an OSN, direct interactions between users are limited and therefore not much data is available to help in the formation of trust by the trustor in the trustee (Farivar et al., 2017; Lu, Zhao, and Wang, 2010; Lu et al., 2010; Xiao et al., 2018; Zolfaghar and Aghaie, 2012).

Reputation-based: Reputation-based trust implies the mechanism for forming trust in which a trustor combines previous interactions or results of the trustee to evaluate their future behaviour. Rating systems are a typical example wherein users rate their experience to express the trustworthiness of the trustee. However, rating systems are also subject to manipulation by friends of the trustee to artificially increase their value of trustworthiness (Kim, Kandampully, and Bilgihan, 2018; Zolfaghar and Aghaie, 2012).

Relationship-based: This is based on a subjective evaluation of social links. While trust is not transitive, it is helpful to view the expanded relationships of the trustee. The distribution of user-specified trust relations can often be interpreted as being analogous to the power-law with a small proportion of customers specifying many trust relationships (Arnaboldi et al., 2016; Asim et al., 2019).

Similarity-based: Common aspects between users in terms of interests, values, demography can potentially *lead* to trust relationships. It has also been proven experimentally that the trust formed between users and the degree of similarity between them as recommended by the system, is significantly correlated (Kim and Ahmad, 2013).

Personality based: The personality-based trust argues that the trust between two users is based on the trustor's personality. If a trustor has a generally high tendency to trust people, it is more likely to build more positive high valued trust relations. Conversely, if a trustor is suspicious generally by nature, then he is more likely to have negative low valued trust relationships with others. However, quantifying trust propensity is a complex task as no scale exists for it (Kim and Ahmad, 2013; Lu et al., 2019; Zhang et al., 2018; Zolfaghar and Aghaie, 2012).

5. RESEARCH PROFILE

5.1 Publishing Trends

Figure 1 shows the publishing pattern of papers on trust evaluation in OSNs. We note a rising interest in the last ten years as the proliferation of OSNs in society increases. Table 3 shows the leading journals that have published the most significant number of papers on trust evaluation in OSNs. It appears that Knowledge based systems have published the maximum articles followed by IEEE, Social Network Analysis and Mining, ACM Transactions on Internet Technology, Future Generation Computer Systems, Information Sciences, Journal of Network and Computer Applications and Neurocomputing. Other journals that have published only one article include ACM Transactions on Knowledge Discovery from Data, Applied Intelligence, Computational Intelligence, Computer Communications, Computer Networks, Computers & Security, Cybernetics & Systems, IEEE Transactions on Computers, IEEE Transactions on Dependable and Secure Computing, IEEE Transactions on Emerging Topics in Computational Intelligence, IEEE Transactions on Services Computing, IEEE Transactions on Systems, Man, and Cybernetics: Systems, IEICE Transactions on Communications, IEICE Transactions on Information and Systems, Information Security Journal, Information Systems Frontiers, International Journal of Digital Content Technology and its Applications, International Journal of Distributed Sensor Networks, International Journal of High Performance Computing and Networking, Journal of Computational Science, Journal of Cyber Security and Mobility, Journal of Supercomputing, KSII Transactions on Internet and Information Systems, Kybernetes, Physica A: Statistical Mechanics and its Applications, Telematics & Informatics.

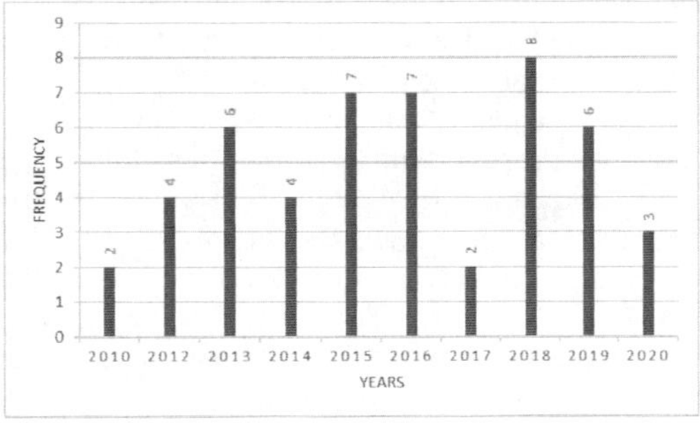

Figure 1. The yearly trend of papers published

Table 3. Journal wise publishing trend

Journal	Count
Knowledge-Based Systems	4
IEEE Access	3
IEEE Transactions on Knowledge & Data Engineering	3
Social Network Analysis & Mining	3
ACM Transactions on Internet Technology	2
Future Generation Computer Systems	2
Information Sciences	2
Journal of Network and Computer Applications	2
Neurocomputing	2

5.2 Paper Analysis

We have followed the categorization as suggested by Sherchan et al., (2013). According to them, social trust evaluation models can be divided into three groups, namely graph-based models, interaction-based modes and hybrid models. Graph-based models focus on the network topology of social trust. These models leverage the structure of the OSN. Typically for each participant, a trust network is established. The other members of the social network of the participant are represented as nodes. The edges denote the magnitude of the trust the participant has for that member. Interaction based models, on the other hand, focus on social interactions between a participant and another member, to evaluate trust. Such models ignore the structure of the OSN. Combining these two approaches results in hybrid models that use both network structure and social interactions in OSNs. Table 4 shows that most of the papers on trust evaluation are either graph-based or hybrid papers with only a handful of studies being purely interaction-based.

Table 4. Categorization of trust evaluation studies

Category	Count
Graph-based	20
Hybrid	19
Interaction-based	5
Grand Total	44

Further, from the review of the selected papers, we found certain parameters used to evaluate trust to be common across multiple studies. These are feedback, relationship, reputation, knowledge, similarity, history, history, share session, quality of trust, user behaviour and features, transitivity, trust bias, the density of interactions, degree of separation, the decay of friendship effect, experience, context information, social distance, ratings, expertise, uncertainty, reciprocity, and distrust. However, there were only a handful of studies that used theories to evaluate trust in OSNs. The theories used are small world theory, Dempster–Shafer theory for trust, the theory of weak ties, signalling theory and social theory of Dunbar. Of these Dempster-Shafer theory for trust and small world theory were most commonly used.

For testing their models, the most commonly used datasets were Epinions, Advogato, Facebook, Ciao, Slashdot and DBLP. Other less commonly used datasets include MySpace, FilmTrust, Douban, Flixster, Toabao, Kaitiaki, CyVOD, Trustlet, Cit-HepTh, Twitter, LiveJournal, Stanford Large Network Dataset Collection, Pretty Good Privacy (PGP), and Alibaba. Many studies also proposed novel trust evaluation methods. These include SocialTrust, SUNNY, PolarityTrust, Multimedia Social Networks Trust Model (MSNTM), Multiple Foreseen Path-Based Heuristic (MFPB-HOSTP), Joint Social Network Mining (JSNM), SWTrust, MATRI, Recommendation-Aware Trust Evaluation (RATE), k-FuzzyTrust, Trust-Oriented Social Influence (TOSI), GFTrust, HT-TRUST, Time-variant Stochastic Trust Evaluation (TSTE), DyTrust, RHT, User-Will, DLATrust, SNTrust, AssessTrust, TrustCTR and Trust Relevancy, Strong Social Graph (SSG), and eTrust.

6. RESEARCH CHALLENGES

The methods for trust evaluation, while being efficient and profusely used, are not devoid of limitations and challenges.

Path limitation: Path limitation needs to be specified in graph simplification methods. Too small a limit may result in fewer paths while too large a limit might lead to an inaccurate conclusion. Till date, the best-trusted path length and the correct number of paths are not clear, even in a context.

Normalization: For graph analogy-based methods, proper normalization requires as results are often out of range.

Scale: Due to time and space complexity constraints, the network should not be large.

Path dependence: Path dependence is often an issue in trusted graphs as some paths may overlap with others. This becomes a challenge as some paths may share edges.

Trust decay: Because trust depends on time, time can alter or decline the level of trust. Thus, the decay of trust becomes an issue as the trust value is not constant over time. There are two kinds of decay, namely decay with time and decay with space. When trust is decayed due to iterative recommendations, it is called decay with space. Therefore, patterns of decay impact the final trust value.

Trust and distrust: Lack of trust does not imply distrust. Only a few papers deal with the concept of distrust as it may not be propagative. In OSN, researchers have to be wary of distrust to avoid negative feedback. Thus, it is more difficult to manage distrust than to manage with trust. While they might be closely related, the rules of evaluation may be different for trust and distrust.

Privacy issues: Privacy concerns limit feedback from users in OSN, which restricts the performance of the trust evaluation system. Therefore, ways to collect feedback can be quite a challenge for researchers.

Information sharing: Trust evaluation models assume that information is shared by users explicitly. However, in actuality, because of privacy concerns, it is difficult to get trust details from users. It is, therefore, quite a challenge to collect evidence while persevering user privacy.

Human language: In hybrid or interaction-based studies, which use comments, reviews or any statement made by users as their input for trust evaluation, understanding the human language becomes challenging. Features of human language such as sarcasm, irony, ambiguity and metaphors, make it difficult for any software agent to analyze human language.

Temporary trust information: Information that is used to evaluate trust is often subjective and changeable. Sometimes it is complicated to obtain and can be resource consuming.

Lack of social context: Trust is a social phenomenon, dependent on the social context. However, very few studies incorporate social context when evaluating trust in OSNs. For instance, the reliability of information available in an e-commerce context is low as a result of its openness.

7. CONCLUSION

The tremendous growth of technology has made it easier to transmit data quickly through complicated interpersonal networks or OSNs. In spite of many benefits, OSNs have limitations such as being able to receive meaningless, unnecessary, and inaccurate information through connections proposed by the recommending system. This can also lead to the exploitation of user's data by recommending false information. So, there is a need to assess the trustworthiness of links between users for better guaranteeing the safety of the interactions. It is expected that by improving the precision of the trust assessment, both client experience and quality of service will improve.

In this paper, we have comprehensively explained the concept of trust in OSNs (RQ1) and articulated the research profile of the studies included in this review (RQ2). This included publishing trends and various aspects of paper analysis such as the grouping of papers, theories and datasets used, common parameters used for trust evaluation and novel trust evaluation methods. Finally, we have highlighted the key challenges faced during the evaluation of trust in OSNs (RQ3). There are certain limitations to this review. First, this review is subject to inclusion and exclusion criteria which limits its scope. Future research can broaden this scope to include more articles. Second, while this review is about trust in OSNs, it focuses on trust evaluation only. Future research can, therefore, include other aspects of trust.

REFERENCES

Arnaboldi, Valerio, Massimiliano La Gala, Andrea Passarella, and Marco Conti. 2016. "Information Diffusion in Distributed OSN: The Impact of Trusted Relationships." *Peer-to-Peer Networking and Applications* 9(6):1195–1208. doi: 10.1007/s12083-015-0395-2.

Asim, Yousra, Ahmad Kamran Malik, Basit Raza, and Ahmad Raza Shahid. 2019. "A Trust Model for Analysis of Trust, Influence and Their Relationship in Social Network Communities." *Telematics and Informatics* 36:94–116. doi: 10.1016/j.tele.2018.11.008.

Barnes, John. 1954. "Class and Committees in a Norwegian Island Parish." *Human Relations* (7):39–58.

Chen, Shuhong, Guojun Wang, and Weijia Jia. 2015. "κ-FuzzyTrust: Efficient Trust Computation for Large-Scale Mobile Social Networks Using a Fuzzy Implicit Social Graph." *Information Sciences* 318:123–43. doi: 10.1016/j.ins.2014.09.058.

Farivar, Samira, Ofir Turel, and Yufei Yuan. 2017. "A Trust-Risk Perspective on Social Commerce Use: An Examination of the Biasing Role of Habit." *Internet Research* 27(3):586–607. doi: 10.1108/IntR-06-2016-0175.

Ghavipour, Mina, and Mohammad Reza Meybodi. 2018. "A Dynamic Algorithm for Stochastic Trust Propagation in Online Social Networks: Learning Automata Approach." *Computer Communications* 123:11–23. doi: 10.1016/j.comcom.2018.04.004.

Golbeck, J. 2005. "Computing and Applying Trust in Web-Based Social Networks." University of Maryland.

Grandison, T., and M. Sloman. 2016. "A Survey of Trust in Internet Applications." *IEEE Communications Surveys and Tutorials* 3(4):2016. doi: http://dx.doi.org/10.1109/COMST.2000.5340804.

Jiang, Wenjun, Guojun Wang, Md Zakirul Alam Bhuiyan, and Jie Wu. 2016. "Understanding Graph-Based Trust Evaluation in Online Social Networks: Methodologies and Challenges." *ACM Computing Surveys* 49(1):1–35. doi: 10.1145/2906151.

Jiang, Wenjun, Guojun Wang, and Jie Wu. 2014. "Generating Trusted Graphs for Trust Evaluation in Online Social Networks." *Future Generation Computer Systems* 31:48–58. doi: 10.1016/j.future.2012.06.010.

Josang, A., R. Ismail, and C. Boyd. 2007. "A Survey of Trust and Reputation Systems for Online Service Provision." *Decision Support Systems* 43(2):618–44.

Kim, Soyeon, Jay Kandampully, and Anil Bilgihan. 2018. "The Influence of EWOM Communications: An Application of Online Social Network Framework." *Computers in Human Behavior* 80:243–54. doi: 10.1016/j.chb.2017.11.015.

Kim, Young Ae, and Muhammad A. Ahmad. 2013. "Trust, Distrust and Lack of Confidence of Users in Online Social Media-Sharing Communities." *Knowledge-Based Systems* 37:438–50. doi: 10.1016/j.knosys.2012.09.002.

Li, Meizi, Yang Xiang, Bo Zhang, Zhenhua Huang, and Jiawen Zhang. 2016. "A Trust Evaluation Scheme for Complex Links in a Social Network: A Link Strength Perspective." *Applied Intelligence* 44(4):969–87. doi: 10.1007/s10489-015-0734-2.

Li, XiaoMing, Guangquan Xu, and Minghu Tang. 2018. "Community Detection for Multi-Layer Social Network Based on Local Random Walk." *Journal of Visual Communication and Image Representation* 57:91–98. doi: 10.1016/j.jvcir.2018.10.003.

Liu, Guanfeng, Yi Liu, An Liu, Zhixu Li, Kai Zheng, Yan Wang, and Xiaofang Zhou. 2018. "Context-Aware Trust Network Extraction in Large-Scale Trust-Oriented Social Networks." *World Wide Web* 21(3):713–38. doi: 10.1007/s11280-017-0485-6.

Liu, Guangchi, Qing Yang, Honggang Wang, and Alex X. Liu. 2019. "Three-Valued Subjective Logic: A Model for Trust Assessment in Online Social Networks." *IEEE Transactions on Dependable and Secure Computing* 1–1. doi: 10.1109/TDSC.2019.2916366.

Lu, Junwen, Guanfeng Liu, Bolong Zheng, Yan Zhao, and Kai Zheng. 2019. "Social Context-Aware Trust Paths Finding for Trustworthy Service Provider Selection in Social Media." *Multimedia Tools and Applications*. doi: 10.1007/s11042-019-7158-7.

Lu, Yaobin, Ling Zhao, and Bin Wang. 2010. "From Virtual Community Members to C2C E-Commerce Buyers: Trust in Virtual Communities and Its Effect on Consumers' Purchase Intention." *Electronic Commerce Research and Applications* 9(4):346–60. doi: 10.1016/j.elerap.2009.07.003.

Pavleska, Tanja, and Borka Jerman Blažič. 2017. "User Bias in Online Trust Systems: Aligning the System Designers' Intentions with the Users' Expectations." *Behaviour & Information Technology* 36(4):404–21. doi: 10.1080/0144929X.2016.1239761.

Ruohomaa, S., and L. Kutvonen. 2005. "Trust Management Survey." *Proceedings of the 3rd International Conference on Trust Management (2005)* 77–92.

Shehada, Dina, Chan Yeob Yeun, M. Jamal Zemerly, Mahmoud Al-Qutayri, Yousof Al-Hammadi, and Jiankun Hu. 2018. "A New Adaptive Trust and Reputation Model for Mobile Agent Systems." *Journal of Network and Computer Applications* 124:33–43. doi: 10.1016/j.jnca.2018.09.011.

Sherchan, Wanita, Surya Nepal, and Cecile Paris. 2013. "A Survey of Trust in Social Networks." *ACM Computing* Surveys 45(4):1–33. doi: 10.1145/2501654.2501661.

Strain, Logan. 2018. "2018: The Year of the Data Breach Tsunami." *Malwarebytes Labs*. Retrieved August 9, 2019 (https://blog.malwarebytes.com/101/2018/12/2018-the-year-of-the-data-breach-tsunami/).

Ureña, Raquel, Gang Kou, Yucheng Dong, Francisco Chiclana, and Enrique Herrera-Viedma. 2019. "A Review on Trust Propagation and Opinion Dynamics in Social Networks and Group Decision Making Frameworks." *Information Sciences* 478:461–75. DOI: 10.1016/j.ins.2018.11.037.

Wang, Jian, Kuoyuan Qiao, and Zhiyong Zhang. 2018. "Trust Evaluation Based on Evidence Theory in Online Social Networks." *International Journal of Distributed Sensor Networks* 14(10):155014771879462. doi: 10.1177/1550147718794629.

Wu, Jian, Jiali Chang, Qingwei Cao, and Changyong Liang. 2019. "A Trust Propagation and Collaborative Filtering Based Method for Incomplete Information in Social Network Group Decision Making with Type-2 Linguistic Trust." *Computers & Industrial Engineering* 127:853–64. doi: 10.1016/j.cie.2018.11.020.

Xiao, Yang, Qingqi Pei, Xuefeng Liu, and Shui Yu. 2018. "A Novel Trust Evaluation Mechanism for Collaborative Filtering Recommender Systems." *IEEE Access* 6:70298–312. doi: 10.1109/ACCESS.2018.2871681.

Zhang, Zhiyong, Jing Wen, Xiaoxue Wang, and Changwei Zhao. 2018. "A Novel Crowd Evaluation Method for Security and Trustworthiness of Online Social Networks Platforms Based on Signaling Theory." *Journal of Computational Science* 26:468–77. doi: 10.1016/j.jocs.2017.05.018.

Zolfaghar, Kiyana, and Abdollah Aghaie. 2012. "A Syntactical Approach for Interpersonal Trust Prediction in Social Web Applications: Combining Contextual and Structural Data." *Knowledge-Based Systems* 26:93–102. doi: 10.1016/j.knosys.2010.10.007.

A CASE STUDY FOR SUMMARY WRITING WITH A GRAPHIC ORGANIZER IN WEB-BASED INVESTIGATIVE LEARNING

Oriko Harada and Akihiro Kashihara
Graduate School of Informatics and Engineering, The University of Electro-Communications
1-5-1, Chofugaoka, Chofu, 182-8585, Tokyo, Japan

ABSTRACT

In Web-based investigative learning (WBIL), learners construct knowledge on a question by navigating and collecting information from Web resources. Previous works have designed a learning model as well as a cognitive tool to support learners to conduct deep and wide investigation instead of building superficial knowledge. On the cognitive tool, learners can create a learning scenario representing the navigation path between Web resources, save keywords extracted from Web resources, create a table of contents (TOC) to linearize their knowledge, and build text structure for the summary of a paper to report their respective investigations. In Harada and Kashihara (2020), we proposed a method for summary writing in WBIL, where learners use graphic organizers (GOs) to structure the summary. The current paper will report on the between-subjects case study conducted to evaluate this method. Results showed that while there was little difference between the experimental and contrast group, learners in the experimental group considered the method effective for organizing and visualizing their knowledge.

KEYWORDS

Web-Based Investigative Learning, Summary Writing, Graphic Organizer, Learner-Created Learning Scenario

1. INTRODUCTION

With the prevalence of personal computers and mobile devices, gathering information online has become an everyday activity. The Web has become the main information resource especially for students, who have been reported to use information online to complete most of their assignments (Julien and Barker, 2009). Information seeking on the Web consists of multiple processes, such as selecting suitable resources and navigating between pages, and various research has been conducted to provide support. For example, Nishihara et al (2006) aimed to support learners in selecting resources according to their knowledge of the topic. To this end, they developed an application which extracts keywords from Web resources and provides learners with a difficulty of each resource and the order of reading resources to understand a certain topic. Aramaki et al (2016) aimed at supporting elementary school students to internalize what they read from resources by providing a tablet application where students can save images from resources and a note attached to each image. Our aim, on the other hand, is to deepen and widen the learners' investigation on the Web. To do so, we have defined a learning model where learners seek information with not only a single query but multiple search queries.

"Web-based investigative learning (WBIL for short)" is defined as a form of learning where learners use search engines to investigate any question with Web resources to construct knowledge. In WBIL, learners are provided with a learning model and a cognitive tool where they can create a learning scenario visualized as a tree with each search query as its node and the progress of one search query to another as links between the nodes. WBIL targets beginners in searching information online, but basic knowledge of using computers and reading skills to comprehend online articles are presupposed. In practice, university students would be the main targets of WBIL, and our past experiments have been conducted on undergraduate and graduate students (Kashihara and Akiyama, 2016; Morishita et al, 2020; Harada and Kashihara, 2020). The learning model and iLSB has then progressed to encompass not only investigation online but also reflecting, organizing and presenting knowledge constructed from resources. The current work focuses on the last learning process, where learners are expected to write a paper reporting the investigation.

While information on iLSB, such as keywords extracted from resources and learning scenarios, are useful for the learners themselves in investigating or reflecting upon information, they cannot be used by other learners to understand another learners' investigation. For the learners to communicate their learning outcomes to peers or instructors, they must convert the information stored in iLSB into a paper. On the other hand, the paper includes everything a learner investigated and contains a substantial amount of information for the readers of the paper. Therefore, a summary for the paper is necessary as an advance organizer for learners to effectively communicate what they investigated. As there have been no established method for learners of WBIL to write a summary, which itself is not a simple task, our previous work (Harada and Kashihara, 2020) proposed a method to support summary writing in WBIL. This method uses graphic organizers which represent the text structure of a summary for learners to organize information. The current paper focuses on the evaluation of our method and will report on a case study conducted with 16 participants.

2. SUPPORTING SUMMARY WRITING FOR WBIL

In this chapter, we will briefly discuss how summary writing for Web-based investigative learning (WBIL) is supported with the learning support system iLSB (interactive Learning Scenario Builder) (Akiyama and Kashihara, 2016) and graphic oranizers (Harada and Kashihara, 2020).

2.1 Web-based Investigative Learning (WBIL)

WBIL aims to support learners using Web resources to collect information (Akiyama and Kashihara, 2016). A learning model and a learning support system iLSB (interactive Learning Scenario Builder) was designed. In the model, In the model, learners begin their investigation with a question, which is called the "initial question." Learners construct knowledge for the initial question in the "Knowledge construction process" by expanding the initial question into sub-questions and creating a learning scenario on the iLSB. Next, in the "Knowledge linearization process", learners order and hierarchize their knowledge by creating a table of contents (TOC) from the learning scenario. The goal of creating the TOC is for the learners to write a paper for the learner to report on their findings. The paper consists of a summary and body. Our work focuses on supporting learners in writing the summary. We will explain the framework in the next section.

2.2 Framework

Our method uses graphic organizers (GOs) to support learners in organizing various pieces of information stored in the iLSB (Harada and Kashihara, 2020). Graphic organizers represent the text structure of the summary, which is categorized into the following five types (Roehling et al, 2017): *description*, *sequence and order*, *cause and effect*, *compare and contrast*, and *problem and solution*. Figure 1 shows GOs for each text structure. Given the table of contents (TOC), iLSB generates a list of GOs based on the relationships between nodes in the TOC. Learners then supplement the information in GOs by adding "node annotations" and "link annotations" on the iLSB. Node annotations are information added to the nodes of a GO and selected by learners from the keywords collected in the knowledge construction process. Link annotations are information for links between nodes in a GO, where learners describe relationships between nodes in their own words.

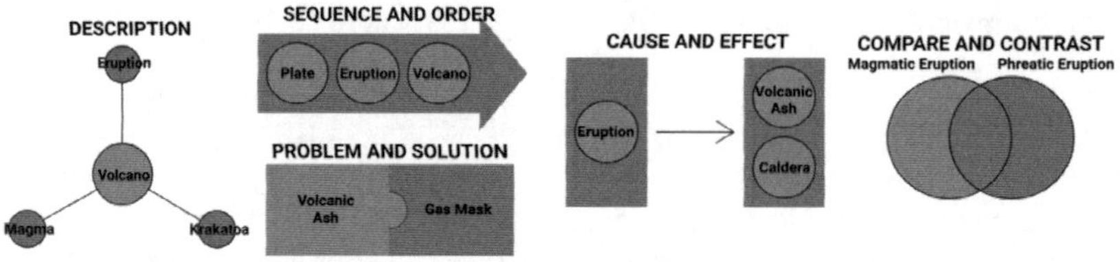

Figure 1. GOs and corresponding text structure

2.3 Interactive Learning Scenario Builder (iLSB)

Interactive Learning Scenario Builder (iLSB) is a Firefox add-on we developed as a cognitive scaffolding (tool) for iLSB (Akiyama and Kashihara, 2016). In the knowledge construction process, learners first enter keyword representing the initial question into a search engine. This keyword is called the "q-keyword". For example, the keyword for the initial question "What is 'tax'?" would be "tax". Next, they select resources to gather information from the list of Web pages given by the search engine. For each resource, the learners read the contents and save relevant keywords in the "keyword repository" of iLSB. Once learners feel they have gathered enough information for the initial question, they select the next question to investigate, or the "sub-question". To do so, learners select a new keyword for further investigation among the repository keywords and add them as child nodes in the "question tree", which is a tree structure representing the learning scenario. For each sub-question, learners repeat the above process to enter the q-keyword in the search engine, navigate Web resources, extract keywords, and discover sub-questions. Once learners feel there is no need for expanding questions into sub-questions, the knowledge construction process is completed.

In the knowledge linearization process, learners aim to write a written report on their findings from the knowledge construction process. For this, learners first create a TOC for their paper using iLSB (Morishita et al, 2020). Then, learners structure the summary with the screens shown below. First, learners view the TOC they constructed (Figure 2), from which iLSB generates a list of GOs (Figure 3). Learners then add node and link annotations as shown in Figure 4 and Figure 5. Finally, iLSB displays a list of GOs with annotations.

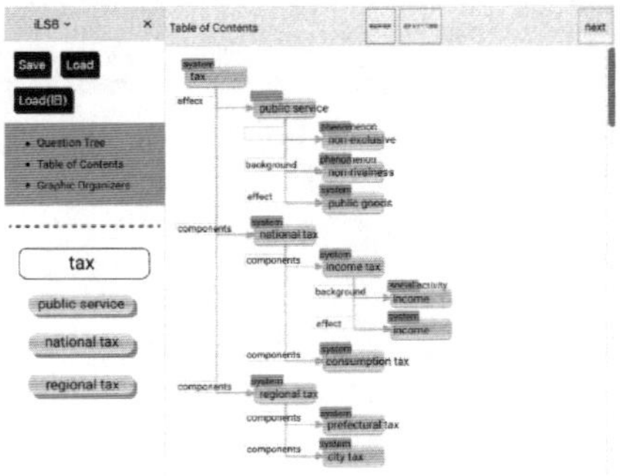

Figure 2. An example of TOC

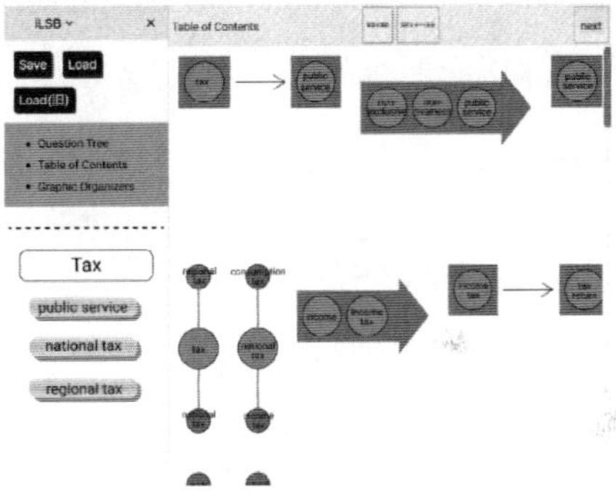

Figure 3. List of GOs

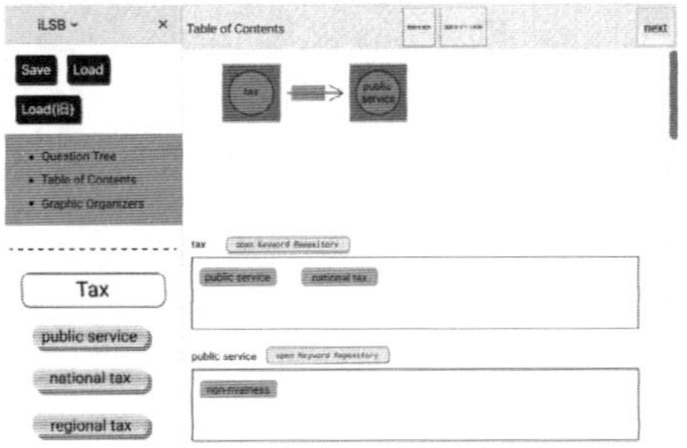

Figure 4. Adding node annotations

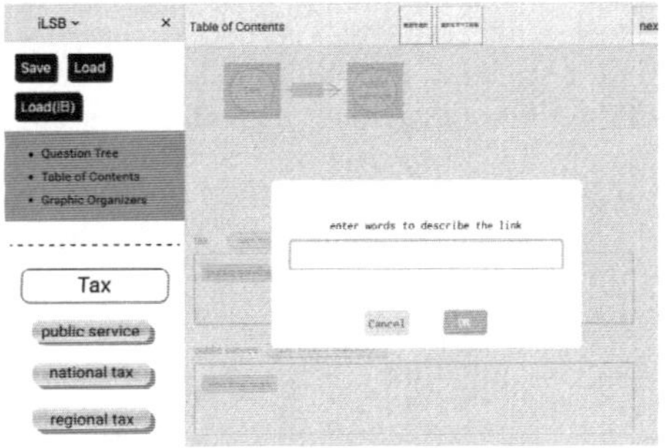

Figure 5. Adding link annotations

3. CASE STUDY

To assess the effectiveness of our method in helping learners come up with a better written report more easily, we conducted a case study. We evaluated the proposed method on 1) exhaustiveness of the summary with respect to TOC, and 2) cognitive load of writing the summary with two learner groups.

3.1 Methods

Sixteen undergraduate and graduate students at the University of Electro-Communications, Japan, participated as subjects of this experiment. As the university focuses on informatics and engineering education, all subjects are assumed to have sufficient computer literacy and therefore meet the criteria for WBIL targets. The case study was conducted under a between-subjects design. As the case study was planned to take 210 minutes at the maximum, within-subjects design was considered too time-consuming and exhausting for the subjects. Moreover, potential learning effects would confound any differences found in the study. As such, subjects were equally divided into either the experimental group (8 subjects) and the contrast group (8 subjects).

The subjects first used iLSB for investigating the initial q-keyword "Tax", then created TOC for the paper to report on their investigation also using iLSB, and finally wrote their summaries. In the summary writing, the experimental group could use graphic organizers to build text structure from their TOC and to view the text structure while writing the summary. On the other hand, the contrast group was required to write their summaries using only the TOC and did not create graphic organizers.

Data were collected according to the two evaluation perspectives mentioned above: exhaustiveness of the summary and cognitive load of summary writing. For the former, we analyzed the summaries for its exhaustiveness and letters per q-keyword. We also asked for a subjective assessment of how exhaustive subjects were able to write their summaries in questionnaire #1, answered both by the experimental and contrast group. For the latter, the summaries were analyzed for writing duration per letter and the number of letters. Questionnaire #1 asked the subjective difficulty of writing a summary, and questionnaire #2, answered only by the experimental group, asked the ease of use for iLSB in creating GOs as well as their general impressions on our method.

3.2 Results

3.2.1 Analysis of Summary

To analyze the summary text, we collected data for 1) exhaustiveness of summary, 2) length of summary, and 3) seconds spent for writing the summary. The results for the contrast and experimental group are shown in Table 1.

First, 1) the exhaustiveness of summary was calculated as the ratio of q-keywords in summary to q-keywords in TOC. The contrast group on average covered 91% (SD: 0.12) of the TOC q-keywords in their summary, and the experimental group average was 96% (SD: 0.06). For 2) the length of summary, we collected the total number of letters of the summary as well as the number of letters per q-keyword. For the former, the contrast group average was 332 letters (SD: 99.71) and the experimental group average was 558 letters (SD: 343.74). For the latter, the contrast group average was 29.43 letters/q-keyword (SD: 13.96) and the experimental group average was 42.97 letters/keyword (SD: 12.08). Finally, for 3) seconds spent for writing the summary, the contrast group on average took 4.05 seconds/letter (SD: 1.77) and the experimental group average was 2.97 seconds/letter (SD: 0.99).

While there were trends between the contrast group and experimental group where the experimental group tended to cover more of the q-keywords in TOC, take less time to write their summaries, and write more for each q-keyword, there was no statistically significant difference between the two groups.

Table 1. Results of summary analysis

Data	Contrast		Experimental group	
	Average	SD	Average	SD
Q-keywords in summary/ q-keywords in TOC	91%	0.12	96%	0.06
# of letters	332 letters	99.71	558 letters	343.74
# of letters/q-keyword	29.43 letters/keyword	13.96	42.97 letters/keyword	12.08
seconds/letter	4.05 s/letter	1.77	2.97 s/letter	0.99

3.2.2 Reviewer Assessment

In the reviewer assessment, we asked two reviewers to first read each summary and then to draw TOC which can be assumed that the summary was written from. TOC for each subject by the two reviewers were then compared to the original TOC created by the subject, and the Tree Edit Distance (TED) (Zhang and Shasha, 1989) between TOCs were calculated. This assessment aimed to measure how well the summaries reflected the structure and contents of TOC.

The correlation between the two reviewers were calculated to be 0.71. As such, we have used the average of the two reviewer's TED to be the distance between reviewer's TOC and subject's TOC. The average TED for the contrast group was 8.88 (SD: 2.98) and 6.38 (SD: 3.31) for the experimental group. While a trend was seen for the experimental group to have shorter TED than the contrast group, there was no statistical significance.

As it was perceived that some subjects in the contrast group possessed high writing skills having shorter TEDs than the experimental group average, we attempted to evaluate the difference between the contrast and experimental groups by separating the former into sub-groups with low skill level and high skill level and comparing the experimental group with the contrast group's low skill level subgroup. This subgroup consisted of three subjects who had longer TEDs than the contrast group average. The results showed the contrast subgroup's average to be 11.67 (SD: 2.83). A t-test between the experimental group and the contrast subgroup showed the two group's difference to be statistically significant at the 0.05 level ($p = 0.049$).

3.2.3 Questionnaire #1

Questionnaire #1 was asked to both the experimental and contrast groups. Subjects answered three questions on a five-point Likert scale. Questions and the average scores for each group are shown in Table 2.

Question 1-1 asked the subjective difficulty of summary writing, where 1 on the Likert scale indicated "very easy" and 5 "very difficult". The contrast group average was 2.50 (SD: 0.93) and the experimental group average was 2.38 (SD:0.74). Question 1-2 asked the exhaustiveness of the written summary from the subjects' own points of view, 1 indicating "not exhaustive at all" and 5 indicating "very exhaustive". The contrast group average was 4.13 (SD: 0.83) and the experimental group average was 4.25 (SD: 0.46). Question 1-3 asked the subjective effect of summary writing in gaining an overview of the topics learned in their investigation, 1 indicating "not effective at all" and 5 indicative "very effective". The contrast group average was 4.38 (SD: 0.52) and the experimental group average was 4.50 (SD: 0.53).

Table 2. Results of questionnaire #1

Question number	Question	Contrast group average	Experimental group average
Q1-1	How difficult was the summary writing?	2.50 (SD: 0.93)	2.38 (SD:0.74)
Q1-2	How much were you able to cover what you investigated in the summary?	4.13 (SD:0.83)	4.25 (SD: 0.46)
Q1-3	Did writing the summary help you achieve an overview of what you investigated?	4.38 (SD:0.52)	4.50 (SD: 0.53)

3.2.4 Questionnaire #2

Questionnaire #2 was asked only to the experimental group and consisted of the following three sections: A) ease of using iLSB to create text structures with graphic organizers, B) effect of creating text structures with graphic organizers, and C) process of summary writing with graphic organizers. Questions were either answered by a five-point Likert scale or open-ended questions. The following tables will show average scores for the former. Open-ended questions are marked with "-" in the table.

Table 3 shows the results for questions concerning the use of iLSB (section A). For this section, 1 on the Likert scale indicated "very difficult", and 5 "very easy". First, the overall ease of using iLSB scored an average of 4.1 (SD: 0.83). From the open-ended descriptions answers to Q2A-2, it was observed that subjects perceived some difficulty when entering link annotations, viewing node annotations or the list of graphic organizers, and moving between graphic organizers to enter annotations. One subject commented that the GOs generated by iLSB was different from what the subject predicted, and that this led to some difficulty especially when adding annotations. The ease of entering node annotations averaged 4.1 (SD: 0.99) and 3.8 (SD: 1.58) respectively. For the visual ease of using the list of graphic organizers, the average was 4.1 (SD: 0.99).

Table 3. Questionnaire results regarding the use of iLSB

Question number	Question	Average	SD
Q2A-1	Was the iLSB easy to use for creating text structure with graphic organizers?	4.1	0.83
Q2A-2	(continued from previous question) What were the difficulties?	-	-
Q2A-3	Was it easy to enter node annotations?	4.1	0.99
Q2A-4	Was it easy to enter link annotations?	3.8	1.58
Q2A-5	Was the list of graphic organizers easy to grasp visually when writing the summary?	4.1	0.99

Table 4 shows the results to questions regarding the learning effect of GOs. Questions 2B-1 and 2B-2 asked whether GOs contributed to organizing information to determine relevant information for the summary. Results from Q2B-1 show that GOs on average scored 3.8 (SD: 1.04) on the effectiveness of organizing information from TOC on a Likert scale where 1 indicated "not helpful at all" and 5 "very helpful". Similarly, results from Q2B-2 showed the effectiveness of GOs in organizing the entire information on iLSB such as the learning scenario and TOC to be 4.1 (SD: 1.04). Q2B-3 aimed to measure how well the subjects understood the text structure represented by the GOs on a Likert scale with 1 indicating "could not understand at all" and 5 "understood very well". The average for this question was 4.0 (SD: 0.93). Finally, Q2B-4 was an open-ended question which aimed to identify factors of GOs to be improved in future research. Subjects raised the following points as difficulties in using GOs:

- inability to change GOs from those generated
- necessity of the GOs to be one of the five types
- not being used to GOs in general and therefore needing to check the type of text structure represented by each GO

Table 4. Questionnaire results regarding the learning effect of GOs

Question number	Question	Average	SD
Q2B-1	Did GOs help you organize information in TOC?	3.8	1.04
Q2B-2	Did GOs help you organize information from your investigation?	4.1	1.04
Q2B-3	How well did you understand text structures and other information represented by GOs?	4.0	0.93
Q2B-4	What were the factors of GOs that made it difficult to use?	-	-

Table 5 shows the results for questionnaires regarding the process of summary writing with GOs. Questions 2C-1 and 2C-2 asked how much subjects used the information in node and link annotations, respectively. The average scores on a Likert scale with 1 indicated "not useful at all" and 5 "very useful" were 4.6 (SD: 0.52) for the node annotations and 4.1 (SD: 0.99) for link annotations.

Q2C-3 asked the perceived effectiveness of the GOs in writing an exhaustive summary. Subjects answered on a Likert scale with 1 indicating "not effective at all" and 5 "very effective". The average score for this question was 3.9 (SD: 0.83). Q2C-4 asked the specific factors contributing the effectiveness, to which subjects listed the following:

- no need to take notes for writing
- visualization of the thought process
- visualization of the relationships and relevance between topics
- ease of ordering the topics in the summary
- ability to gain an overview of the topics

Q2C-5 asked the difficulty of writing text from the GOs to which subjects answered on a Likert scale with 1 indicating "very easy" and 5 "very difficult". The average score was 1.9 (SD: 0.64). Q2C-6 asked factors which made the above process difficult. Some subjects commented that as nodes in the GOs are represented with keywords, there was some difficulty in creating sentences from keywords and recalling what they learned from the investigation. Q2C-7 asked for comments regarding summary writing with GOs in general. It was observed that the ability to visualize, record, and organize information from the investigation as well as their own ideas was perceived to be an advantage of GOs, and that subjects overall felt GOs made summary writing easier.

Table 5. Questionnaire results regarding the process of summary writing with GOs

Question number	Question	Average	SD
Q2C-1	How useful were the node annotations for writing the summary?	4.6	0.52
Q2C-2	How useful were the link annotations for writing the summary?	4.1	0.99
Q2C-3	How effective were the GOs in writing an exhaustive summary?	3.9	0.83
Q2C-4	What were the factors of GOs that made it easy to write text?	-	-
Q2C-5	Was writing text from GOs difficult?	1.9	0.64
Q2C-6	What were the factors of GOs that made it difficult to write text?	-	-
Q2C-7	Please write any other comments on GOs and summary writing.	-	-

3.3 Discussion

We will discuss the case study results with respect to the two aims of our method, which are 1) to support writing an exhaustive summary and 2) to decrease the cognitive load of the writing process. For the first aim, the experimental group was expected to create longer and more exhaustive summaries in less time compared to the contrast group using the GOs. However, results from the case study revealed no statistically significant differences. By observing individual data, this can be partly attributed to subjects in the contrast group already having high skills of organizing information and summarizing the information in text. For example, while the experimental group performed well on the summary's exhaustiveness, covering on average 96% of the q-keywords in TOC in their summary, the contrast group average also reached 91%. By looking at the number of q-keywords in TOC which were not included in the summary, the experimental group subjects omitted 0 or only 1 keyword(s) except from one subject who omitted 2 keywords. For the contrast group 7 out of 8 subjects in the contrast group also omitted 0 or only 1 keyword(s), resulting in the two groups having similar results.

Results from questionnaire #1 also support the hypothesis that the contrast group already had high writing and summarizing skills. From Q1-1, it can be observed that the perceived difficulty of summary writing was the same for both contrast and experimental group even though the contrast group had no support for the learning process. It can be said that some subjects in the contrast group did not require learning support for summary writing in WBIL and therefore were not targets of our research. As such, we conclude that the experimental group could write a summary in which the learners explained all or most of the q-keywords in TOC.

From the above evaluation, it can be concluded that using GOs to support summary writing was partially successful in achieving the two goals of the support set in our research. However, further research is required to evaluate the difference between the process where GOs are not used, especially those with a larger number of subjects and subjects targeted in our support.

Finally, reviewer assessments revealed that compared to the low-skill level subgroup of the contrast group, the experimental group's summary better reflected TOC. The utility of the application used for the learning support is evaluated from section A of questionnaire #2, whose results indicate to iLSB was relatively easy to use and that the presentation of the information was clear.

4. CONCLUSION

Web-based investigative learning (WBIL) has been proposed as a method to support learners in effectively gathering information from the Web and building knowledge from the information. With the cognitive tool interactive Learning Scenario Builder (iLSB), learners can structure their processes according to the model designed in previous studies and use such functions as visualizing navigation paths and saving keywords from Web resources. This paper targets the process of summary writing in WBIL, which is an essential process for learners to share their learning outcomes to their peers or instructors.

In our previous work, we have designed a method for helping learners build text structure with graphic organizers that allows learners to write a summary for their investigation in WBIL. Five types of graphic organizers which correspond to the five basic structures (*description*, *sequence and order, cause and effect*, *compare and contrast*, and *problem and solution*) were used to reorganize nodes included in TOC created during the knowledge construction process in WBIL. Our current work focused on the evaluation of this method. From the case study, it was suggested that text structure with graphic organizers were effective as a scaffold for writing a comprehensive summary with less effort. While differences between the contrast and experimental group were not found to be statistically significant, questionnaire results from the experimental group showed an overall positive attitude toward the method. Subjects observed that graphic organizers helped them by visualizing the order and relationships among information to be written in the summary. They also noted that writing the summary led to gaining an overview perspective of what they learned in their investigation. Along with the data obtained from analyzing the summaries, we have concluded that graphic organizers were able to decrease learners' cognitive load in writing a summary and making its contents exhaustive.

As the statistical insignificance for the results arose partly from the experimental design, where there was not enough control over the individual subjects' writing/organizing skills, further evaluation is necessary. In our future work, we plan to conduct a refined case study with more control over subjects' skills as well as a larger sample size.

ACKNOWLEDGEMENT

The work presented here is partially supported by JSPS KAKENHI Grant Number 17H01992 and 18H01053.

REFERENCES

Aramaki, M. et al, 2016. A Web-based Investigative Learning Support System (in Japanese), *Proceedings of the 78th National Convention of IPSJ*, Vol. 1, pp. 673-674.

Harada O. and Kashihara, A. 2020. A Graphic Organizer for Supporting Summary Writing in Web-based Investigative Learning, *The 17th International Conference on Cognition and Exploratory Learning in Digital Age (CELDA 2020)*, Lisbon, Portugal (in press).

Julien H. and Barker, S. 2009. How high-school students find and evaluate scientific information: A basis for information literacy skills development. *Library & Information Science Research*, Vol. 31, No. 1, pp. 12-17.

Kashihara, A. and Akiyama, N., 2016. Learning scenario creation for promoting investigative learning on the Web, *The Journal of Information and Systems in Education*, Vol. 15, No. 1, pp. 62-72.

Roehling, J. et al, 2017. Text structure strategies for improving expository reading comprehension. *The Reading Teacher*, Vol. 71, No. 1, pp.71-82.

Morishita, N. et al, 2020. Reconstructing Question tree in Web-based Investigative Learning. *44th Annual Conference of Japanese Society for Information and Systems in Education. in Japanese*. Hamamatsu, Japan, pp. 169-176

Nishihara, Y. et al, 2006. Information Understanding Support by Using Informational complexity and Continuity (in Japanese). *IEICE TRANSACTIONS on Information and Systems*, Vol. 89, No. 9, pp. 1963-1975.

Zhang, K., & Shasha, D. 1989. Simple fast algorithms for the editing distance between trees and related problems. *SIAM journal on computing*, Vol. 18, No. 6, pp.1245-1262.

KNOWLEDGE MANAGEMENT: THE TRUTH BEHIND THE CONCEPT

Sidney Viana[1], Luis Vellacich[2], Marcos Miranda[1] and Carolina Pereira[1]
[1]*Itaipu Technological Park, Hernandarias, Paraguay*
[2]*Itaipu Binacional, Hernandarias, Paraguay*

ABSTRACT

Knowledge has become the most precious asset of any organization, being the main ingredient for the success and innovation of the products and services offered. Currently there are different proposals of Knowledge Management models, with the implications of implementing them. Most of them are unrealistic in the context of the organizations and their implementation can be summarized in the document management. Consequently, in a short period of time, they fail in their attempt to adequately manage this precious asset, information. In context, this work proposes an efficient implementation of Knowledge Management, based on a model of four interrelated axes, successfully implemented in a real and complex environment: The Dam Safety project. This project is divided into three phases, where the above-mentioned axes are detailed. It also describes the difficulties encountered throughout the implementation, the actions taken to overcome these difficulties, the results and experiences obtained in the first phase of the project, ending with proposals for improvements for its second phase. The results are very encouraging and have the approval of the final users, who, for many years, were part of the search for a solution that could satisfactorily provide Knowledge Management in their work context.

KEYWORDS

Knowledge Management, Knowledge Management Models, Innovation, Dams

1. INTRODUCTION

Knowledge has characteristics of a commodity, which adds value to products or services and becomes one of the basic components necessary for market evolution. The knowledge resulting from the experience acquired over time, also known as tacit knowledge, has an added value that tends to increasing, according to the different experiences lived by people.

However, explicit knowledge is the materialization of knowledge. Generally, its value is despised over time, as experiences are embodied in documents, reports, articles, thesis, books, and other artifacts. It is also known as a static source of information. So, it can generate knowledge projected into the future, becoming current knowledge or obsolete knowledge.

Explicit knowledge is a very important mechanism for transmitting knowledge to others and when it is associated with technology, it becomes efficient. For example, the Internet is a way of capturing information at high speed, capable of providing large volumes of information, which must be classified to obtain those that are reliable and useful to knowledge. Figure 1 shows the data that are the raw material for information. The information, contextualized and with quality, associated with a domain, points to knowledge. The last one generates information that subsequently results in stored data.

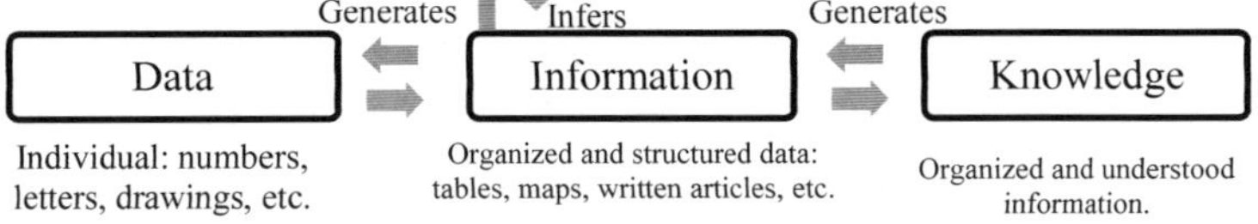

Figure 1. Evolutionary cycle of knowledge

2. STATE OF THE ART

A variety of Knowledge Management models exist in literature. Below are some of the Knowledge Management (KM) models and a brief description of them (Pérez, et. al, 2004; Espinoza, 2006):

The knowledge – creator organization (Nonaka and Takeuchi, 1995): It is based on the mobilization and conversion of tacit knowledge (epistemological dimension) and the creation of organizational knowledge versus individual knowledge (ontological dimension). It is a cyclical and infinite model that contemplates five phases: sharing tacit knowledge, creating concepts, justifying concepts, building an archetype, and expanding knowledge. Basically, they propose the creation of knowledge maps, self-organizing teams, and group dialogue sessions, where individuals reveal and share their tacit knowledge with the rest of the group, through schemes, models, metaphors, and analogies. The people involved in the process of creation and management of knowledge, will be part of the so-called knowledge-creating team, which will consist of knowledge practitioners, knowledge engineers and knowledge officers.

Knowledge Management as a "humanist" vision (Marulanda Echeverry, et. al, 2012): In the words of its author: "[...] it focuses its operation on the commitment of the organization's workforce, in such a way that, where others have emphasized technology as the basis of a system for managing knowledge, here the person, his or her stability within the organization and his or her involvement and alignment with the general objectives and the organizational project, are given prime importance". The model is made up of four phases: management consulting, organizational consulting, implementation of knowledge management plans and verification and monitoring measures. It proposes the development of knowledge maps, establishment of practice communities, creation of a knowledge warehouses, discussion forums, meetings and seminars. The people involved are members of the organization, internal experts, and external experts.

Knowledge Management from the organizational culture (Marsal and Molina, 2002): It is based on the type of organizational culture existing in the institution. It is also composed of five phases based on studying, interpreting, and changing, if necessary, the organizational culture: Self-diagnosis, strategic management, definition and application of the KM model, change management and indicators to measure the impact of KM. They propose the elaboration of yellow pages, learning communities, good practices, assistance and help meetings. Participants: KM managers (people with communication, technological and management skills); members of the organization.

Knowledge Management in education (Sallis and Jones, 2013): They start from the fact that each educational organization should possess and build its own structure, its own KM system, based on its characteristics, its strengths, and weaknesses. KM in education, is a model of KM centered on education centers, fundamentally higher-level education. The phases that make up the model are classification of knowledge, reference framework for KM, knowledge audit, knowledge measurement, technology and knowledge management and knowledge exploitation. They propose knowledge maps, creation and development of virtual communities and collaborative work. The different educational agents participate in the conception, planning and development of the KM system of their own institution.

Gamification in Knowledge Management Systems (Murawski, 2020): In the last decade, gamification has experienced a major popularity boom. Murawski summarized existing human resource management (HRM) related literature of gamification and systemized the findings in this regard into four potential application areas of gamification, being (1) supporting employee motivation, engagement, and performance, (2) improving training outcomes, (3) supporting talent management measures, and (4) foresting knowledge management activities. He found that within these categories, the use of game design elements to enhance motivation, engagement, and performance within the workplace is the most used area of focus.

As Murawski explains, current proponents of gamification emphasize the importance of holistic approaches to gamification design, considering the employee's needs and characteristics, as they have major impact on the effectiveness of the use of game design elements. It must be mention that the use of gamification in the knowledge management system for The Dam Security must take a long time, because it would be necessary develop different kinds of materials to represent the knowledge presented in books, documents, and in the expert's tacit knowledge, considering the existence of fluid communication among the stakeholders. Gamification has proven to work in the specific area of application. As the mentioned author explains, research on gamification in HRM lacks rigor in a few major aspects. He explains that HR scientists are at the beginning of a journey to explore the phenomenon of gamification. Therefore, larges companies, with well-defined policies, a cost-benefit evaluation should be carried out to determine if it is appropriate to implement a knowledge management system applying gamification techniques.

2.1 Difficulties and Limitations

The main constraints and difficulties that can be encountered during the implementation of a KM project are (Pérez et. al, 2004; Jennex, 2005; Rodríguez, 2006; Jennex et. al, 2014):

- **Lack of objectives:** The absence of objectives for KM or the lack of clarity is an impediment to the success of a project. In fact KM, is merely a way to achieve organizational goals, make decisions, or resolve problems and conflicts identified in the organization.
- **Lack of planning:** this is not an exclusive problem with KM projects, but it is obviously something that must be taken into consideration. The novelty and complexity of KM processes causes organizations to focus and invest a lot of resources in pilot planning and forget the subsequent extension of that project to the rest of the organization.
- **Diffuse responsibility:** KM initiatives can be headed to failure if a set of responsibilities are not clarified or established among people who are responsible for the entire process. A dedicated KM team is recommended for the design, development, and evaluation of the KM process.
- **Contextualization:** KM projects cannot be generalized; they must be designed according to the characteristics of the organization (values and objectives, structure, relational system, and organizational functions).
- **Conceptual confusion:** many organizations tend to confuse information management with knowledge management and use technology (e.g., intranets) potentially valid for KM processes, such as simple organizational document stores.
- **Lack of an adequate culture:** the absence of an adequate culture for KM leads irremediably to the failure of every effort.
- **Absence of the Specialist:** Knowledge Management should consider the role of the specialist as an essential element in the orientation of the knowledge base in the domain of the problem or the requirements to be outlined in the organization.

Information management can be defined as the set of activities carried out in order to control, store and, subsequently, adequately recover the information produced, received, or retained by any organization in its operative state. At the heart of information management is the be management of documentation (the information that is reflected in documents) (Bustelo and Amarilla, 2001).

The data source must be reliable; the data must be of quality and verifiable. Choosing good references requires experience and insight. The efficiency of Knowledge Management requires a technological component, a group of technicians dedicated to the task of management, one or more specialists in the domain of knowledge and very well-defined processes that guarantee the maintenance of management over time.

The following section describes the corporate environment considered to carry out Knowledge Management practices. In this environment, initiatives such as Knowledge Management did not have the credibility of high authorities since it had gone through its fourth attempt, made by commercial companies that did not achieve results that justified the financial investments made (Saz, 2001; Ruesta and Iglesias, 2001). Having a solution that meets the challenges and expectations of the requesting company is essential to follow up on the many projects that can be carried out in this area of science.

3. DESCRIPTION OF THE ENVIRONMENT

In a long-established organization, thousands of documents are usually produced each year, containing explicit knowledge accumulated over the course of the organization's history.

In the context of dams, small or large hydroelectric plants, this knowledge comes from two important stages: the first one refers to the construction, and the next one refers to the maintenance of the structure. In such stages, tacit knowledge of great importance is generated, mainly in the initial stage, due to the experiences accumulated in the construction phase. Not all constructions steps have been documented, those documentations generated was very simple, lack of techniques support. So, having the support of a technician that participate at the early stage of operations it would be very luck.

Currently, it's very hard to find an enterprise that has the courage to invest an amount of financial resource in a task force to deal with Corporate Knowledge Management. To attempt these demand, most of them take advantage of Document Management System, which allows access to the digital version of the documents created in the above-mentioned stages. However, these systems turn out to be document repositories (i.e. database engine), generating the need for specific knowledge (search engine by keywords). These systems are not optimal for dealing with the current problems faced by power generation companies, since the origin of the problems may be at the beginning of the work. For examples, if someone needs information about "crack in the wall", in detail, with explanation's video, photos, similar problems occurred on others Dam, the theory necessary to understand the problem and all technical report on the affected area and others information, could be informed by the System's modules, at the Figure 3.a.

The challenge is to minimize the time needed to transfer the tacit knowledge of senior officials of an organization, to the younger ones. This is because it has taken decades for such officials to accumulate the technical knowledge they now use. In addition, this problem is aggravated once they begin their retirement process, discovering the fact that there are no professionals prepared with the minimum necessary knowledge and do not have the time required to prepare a training program and delivering it, due to their daily activities.

On the other hand, staff members who participate in work scales activities need to constantly remember the hundred similar tasks they performed in the past. However, there is concern about probably mistakes face the work overload occurrence, caused by lack of technical reports information elaborated by the newest technicians, personnel actualization, and contextual technical changes among other reasons. Look for the personal adequate to receive the right information (tacit and explicit knowledge in an efficient and agile way), at the right time is a challenge (Papoutsoglou, et. al, 2017). As a result of lack of cumulative daily knowledge management, in its broad spectrum, this work presents an approach for Knowledge Management modeling and your correspondence implementation. Furthermore, it is generic and therefore applicable to other cases related to other areas of knowledge.

4. SOLUTION PROPOSAL

The proposed solution (Figure 3.a) consists of a continuous process, which begins with the capture of knowledge; this is based on technical reports available in information management systems, specialist personal notes and tacit knowledge from experts and technical users who can contribute with recent information.

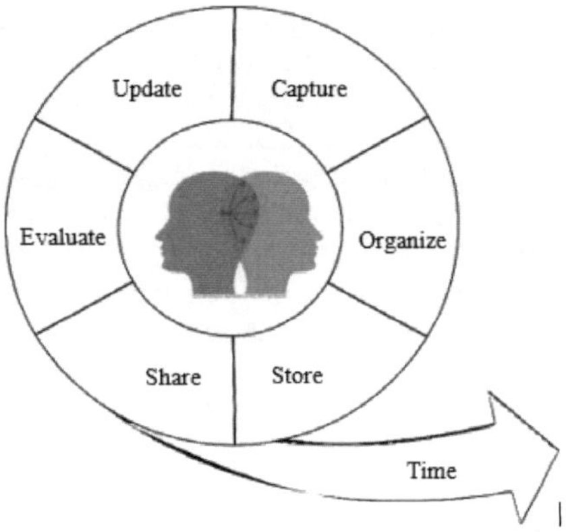

Figure 2. Knowledge management processes adopted

Subsequently, such knowledge is organized into correlative ideas, and classified according to the degree of importance and complexity, by a three-level taxonomy (basic, intermediate, and advanced). Once the information is organized, it is stored through the usage of Information and Communication Technologies (ICTs), and shared, so that it is easily accessible through personal computers and mobile devices. This information is shared with all those involved, so that they can make evaluations, suggestions and test the efficiency of the system in terms of its performance.

The information visualized by the end user is a multimedia document, composed of information in three (3) dimensions, with movement, added audio and a system that facilitates the search for information by subject and complexity. This process allows reductions in time for the explanation process of any content.

Once a presented topic was understood, it is possible to say that the knowledge was transferred to the end user. Finally, the next step is to update the information, or add new information. This process is carried out continuously so that knowledge lasts through time.

The proposed solution requires support tasks to validate the process. One of them is measurement the knowledge acquired by the end user. In other words, it is necessary to guarantee that the user evolves his knowledge on the subject, through time, and for this, the role of his superior in the organization is fundamental. In the same way, the mentioned user must have the information available in any place of the organization and at any time (through internet connection). In the end, learning related to state of mind.

4.1 Knowledge Management Model (4 Axes)

The proposal of a Knowledge Management Model for real problems, is based on four (4) interrelated axes. These axes are (i) the specialist's knowledge, (ii) information and communication technologies, (iii) organizational culture, and (iv) time.

Specialist's Knowledge: The first axis of the model covers the main asset of the organization, which is knowledge. Explicit knowledge is easier to deal with, once it is within everyone's reach. In this sense, the internal order of all this documentation is fundamental. Regarding tacit knowledge, it is provided by the specialist, who is usually the senior employee of the company, and sometimes, retired role. However, those who have not yet done so, are not willing to undertake the task of reviewing documentation and translating it into a language understandable to all. In addition, they do not have the necessary time to take on this new task. The senior available, must have a set of basic characteristics to play the role, such as the ability to share experiences with younger people, good communication skills and good writing skills.

Information and Communication Technologies: Technology is a way and not an end to the knowledge management process. Choosing the right technology is critical, because it must support the changes that will occur over time. One alternative is to use free technologies, which are not necessarily the most appropriate. This is because it can be discontinued, and it will probably be necessary to migrate to another platform. It is important considering the cost/benefit ratio of this. An important factor to be considered is the amount of accesses that must be supported by the system, especially when supporting multimedia data. Therefore, optimal performance is required from the hardware used to maintain the information.

Organizational Culture: The organizational culture is affected by users and their processes. For the end user to have an active participation throughout this transfer of knowledge, it is necessary that he commits himself to it, through his experience, his reviews, and comments in general. When the management process is imposed on the end user, rejection usually occurs when feeling pressure from the imposition. The user must participate through his creative process, at the moment he identifies with the system, understanding that his participation is a way of continuous improvement, tending to participate more often. Some of the processes that can be applied are: (i) Classification of information and knowledge by the specialist. (ii) Validation of the documents generated by the end users. (iii) Inclusion of end users, both in the validation and improvement of the solution.

Time: This must last as long as the knowledge management process is used. Mechanisms must be sought to guarantee actions over time. In the proposed system, time is very well framed through the participation of the superior or boss, where he verifies that knowledge tests were performed, information was updated, periodic meetings with technicians to know what should be added or improved on the proposed environment, among other actions.

The connection between the model and the Systems developed to support de Knowledge Management is about take into account the methodology used to catch the data, organize it and analyze whom will take advantage from it. To offer the information in a strategic and intuitive way, the Systems contain a lot of perspective that complement the user knowledge in any scalable perspective, practical cases, simulations, quiz (supervised by the manager) and searching tool. The manager knows who accessed de Systems, the grade obtained at the quiz (Papoutsoglou, 2017).

4.2 Computer System Modules

The basis of the proposed solution is a centralized computer system, where knowledge is available on a web environment and is accessed from both mobile devices and desktop computers. Figure 3.a shows the architecture of the solution. The Systems is supported by .NET framework, C# Language, ASP.NET y MVC architecture. The KM teams include a Dam specialist (retired employee), Solidworks technician, PMI Manager, among others. The specialist deeply knows the needs and the value of the business since worked last decade before him retired. He has accessed the information, translated many sheets into audiovisual and pleasant explanation, changing the reading on paper documents by visual navigation (Figure 3.a and Figure 4). The results obtained is delivered in business values. The feedback helped us to improve for the next delivered. All the time, technicians feed the system with more previously selected information that in turn notifies the end users involved in the topic, in a cyclic way.

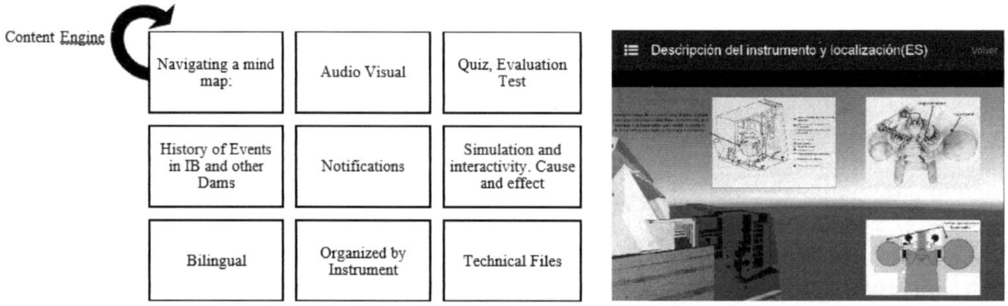

(a) Modules of the solution presented. (b) Audio visual material generated.

Figure 3. Presented solution

The computer system is composed of a set of ten (10) modules (Figure 3.a). Each of these modules is briefly described below.

- **Web navigation:** Structured content according to levels, basic, intermediate, and advanced. Navigation occurs in an intuitive way, facilitating access to different types of content. Each content can be repeated as many times as necessary, until the user feels capable enough to continue advancing with the content.
- **Audio visual:** The content is presented in an audio-visual way, facilitating the transfer of knowledge (see Figure 3.b). It is understood that the user does not have time to read technical information or understand certain drawings in representation of three (3) dimensions. For this reason, representations with animation and audio strongly help the user's understanding.
- **Quiz, evaluation test:** Contains an evaluation of the knowledge acquired. In this way it is possible to know if there was knowledge retention. These results are sent to the person in charge who has the objective of guaranteeing the active participation of the majority of the employees.
- **Simulation and interactivity:** Cause and effect: The simulation and interactivity cause-effect is an environment where the user can play with variables on models of the problem to understand the participation and the importance of each one of them. For example, what is the effect of increasing temperature, or pressure, among other variables.
- **Technical files:** Access to technical files produced by the organization. These files are technical references in the organization. From the system you can access this information for the purpose of complementing the knowledge in question.
- **Organized by instrument:** The instruments are rated according to the data they capture from the dam. Some are more important than others. Users can organize their studies according to these priorities.
- **Bilingual:** Possibility of learning in two languages: Spanish and Portuguese.
- **History of events in Itaipu Binational and other Dams:** To complement the knowledge of the organization's officials. Examples external and correlated to the area of operation, such as disasters occurred, are very important, so as to prevent this from happening in their future work environment.
- **Notifications:** System of notifications of the latest content updates and news in general.
- **Content engine:** Enabling the use of filters to search for specific content as it shown in Figure 4.b.

5. DISCUSSION

The solution presents a knowledge transfer methodology based on the use of multimedia data, in a highly interactive and easy to navigate environment, since it is based on web navigation. It is possible to identify the evolution of knowledge by the user. The base of this solution was the previous information about the working environment of the final users and the knowledge of their daily routine. It was understood that proposing a solution that introduces a degree of difficulty on their activities could lead the user to stop using it. This is because everything is known to have a degree of priority, and the system cannot compete with the priority of their tasks. Another important point was to consider that the end user should use the system in the organization, otherwise there would be no commitment on his part. Figure 4.a shows one of the results of this content creation process, where it can be seen that extensive (top left margin), and sometimes complex (top right margin) documentation is transformed into much more attractive content for the user (animated three-dimensional image with audio).

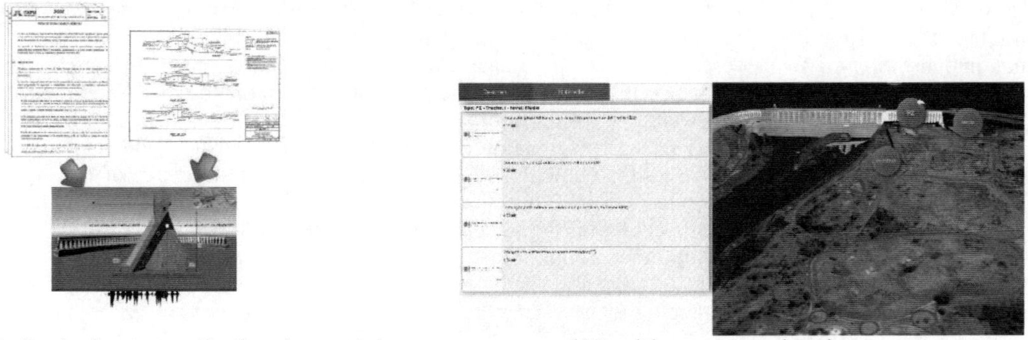

(a) Audio-visual content creation from documentation. (b) Result by context search engine.

Figure 4. Audio-visual content creation from technical documentation

6. RESULTS

The proposed Knowledge Management system was evaluated, considering a Dam staff member as a population. A non-probabilistic or targeted sample was taken based on the representativeness of the population, made up of 14 system users (ranging from 23 to 50 years of age), officials from the Technical Area of the mentioned Dam staff with experience ranging from 1 to 10 years. Grouping was made according to: (P1) focus given to the tool's content, (P2) Distribution of the tool's content, (P3) interaction with the KM Systems tool, and (P4) usefulness of the KM tool in terms of user experience.

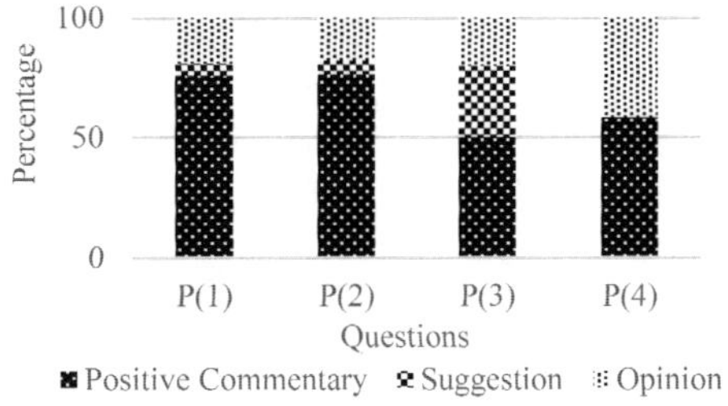

Figure 5. Test results applied to the computer systems users

Tests to the proposed Knowledge Management System were conducted through open questions posed to professionals in the area with extensive experience.

Considering the groupings described above, four levels of responses were obtained which were classified in the following level: basic, intermediate, advanced, and general. Finally, each one of them has been labeled according to its content as: positive comment, suggestion, and opinion.

The results obtained are summarized in the figure 5. As can be seen, a large percentage of positive comments from the users has been obtained.

7. CONCLUSION AND FUTURE WORK

The proposed solution is adaptable to different areas of human knowledge and can be expanded to other branches of knowledge such as medicine, physics, and administration, among others. The proposed solution is based on the presence of the specialist, who knows the domain of the problem and has the skills to carry out the challenge and the technicians who are committed to participate actively throughout this process.

Technology is important but not fundamental, as there are many options available, all depending on the resources required for this priority. The threats lie in the fact that the representatives of the organizations do not take the decision in time to solve a very serious problem that is the loss of senior staff members who do not intend to return to the organization to participate in Knowledge Management programs. This is an intangible but real problem that generates millions of dollars, resulting from the loss of information.

The results achieved so far were very satisfactory and motivating at the same time. One of the most important results was the recovery of tacit information from retired employees that provided vital information for the understanding of technical issues related to the maintenance of civil structures of the organization. Therefore, it is strongly recommended to apply concepts related to **"PEOPLE ANALYTICS"** to face a varied public, always framed in a strategic context that guarantees the continuity of the project.

It is intended to be followed by other frontline instruments, that is, the most important ones. In the same way, to implement these solutions in other areas of action. It is also expected to evolve the solution currently proposed so that it can make the digital inclusion, for new technologies, of the users of the organization.

REFERENCES

Bustelo Ruesta, C., and Amarilla Iglesias, R., 2001. Gestión del conocimiento y gestión de la info. Revista PH, 226.

Espinoza, H E., 2006. *Gestión de la información engranaje estratégico para la gestión del conocimiento..* "intempres". vol. 15, n. 2006. http://www.bnv.bib.ve/pdf/GestionHeisbellEspinoza.pdf

Jennex, M. E. et al, 2014. Knowledge Management Success in Practice. *47th Hawaii International Conference on System Science,* pp. 3615-3624.

Jennex, M.E., 2005. *Case Studies in Knowledge Management San Diego State University., USA.*, Idea Group Publishing.

Marsal, M.; Molina, J. L., 2002. *La gestión del conocimiento en las organizaciones"*, Coleccion de Negocios, Empresa y Economıa. Books on the net.

Marulanda Echeverry, C. E. et al, 2012. Modelos de gestión del conocimiento [Knowledge Management Models]. Ventana Informatica, 26.

Murawski, L., 2020. Gamification in human resource management. Status quo and quo vadis. *German Journal of Human Resource Management.* Zeitschrift für Personalforschung. I-19.

Nonaka, I.; Takeuchi, H., 1995. *The knowledge-creating company: how Japanese companies create the dynamics of innovation.* New York, Oxford University Press.

Papoutsoglou M., et. al, 2017. Mining People Analytics from StackOverflow Job Advertisements. *43rd Euromicro Conference on Software Engineering and Advanced Applications (SEAA)*, Vienna, pp. 108-115.

Pérez, S. et al, 2004. Managing knowledge: the link between culture and organizational learning. *Journal of Knowledge Management.* Vol. 8, núm 6, pp. 93-104.

Rodríguez-Gómez, D., 2006. Modelos para la creación y gestión del conocimiento: una aproximación teórica. *Educar*, ISSN 0211-819X, Nº 37, 2006 (Ejemplar dedicado a: La gestión del conocimiento a través de la red), pp. 25-39.

Ruesta, B. C. R. Iglesias, A., 2001. Gestión del Conocimiento y Gestión de la Información, INFORAREA S.L., *Boletín del Instituto Andaluz de Patrimonio Histórico*, ISSN 1136-1867, Año nº 9, Nº 34 (Ejemplar dedicado a: Especial Monográfico: Museos), pp. 226-230.

Sallis, E.; Jones, G., 2013. *Knowledge Management in Education: enhancing leaning and education*. Londres: Kogan.

Saz, M., 2001. Gestión del conocimiento: Pros y contras. *El profesional de la información,* ISSN 1386-6710, Vol. 10, Nº 4, 2001, pp. 14-28. 10. 10.1076/epri.10.4.14.6527.

A THREE-YEAR STUDY OF THE GDPR AND THE CONSUMER

Wanda Presthus and Hanne Sørum
Kristiania University College, Prinsens gate 7-9, 0107 Oslo, Norway

ABSTRACT

This paper presents an empirical study of the General Data Protection Regulation (GDPR) from the consumer perspective. Based on data collected through an online survey questionnaire over a period of three years (2018–2020), we identify trends and patterns among Norwegian consumers. The findings show that the GDPR has not significantly affected consumer awareness, nor level of control over their own personal data. Concerning the enhanced rights of deletion, data portability and access to personal data, the patterns are similar, revealing that most of our respondents 'might execute' their rights. Pertaining to website cookies, most of the respondents are unsure, and the general trend from 2019 to 2020 reveals a greater uncertainty. This paper contributes with new insights for the industry and to the information privacy research field.

KEYWORDS

Information Privacy, the General Data Protection Regulation (GDPR), Consumer Rights, Empirical Study

1. INTRODUCTION

The General Data Protection Regulation (GDPR) was introduced in 2018. There were many thoughts and opinions about the regulation regarding consequences for private persons and companies (Jarbekk & Sommerfeldt, 2019; Presthus, Sørum, & Andersen, 2018). The GDPR replaces about 40 privacy laws from European countries with one unified regulation (The European Parliament and the Council, 2016). The GDPR affects any company that handles personal data and has customers belonging to the EU or EEA. Existing research has revealed that consumers do not care too much about their privacy, especially when the benefits surpass the challenges, for example when shopping online (Krasnova & Veltri, 2010). However, privacy has interested researchers since the invention of the hand-held camera in the 1900-century (Solove, 2020), but people reacts differently regarding their privacy (Westin, 2003). In the wake of the GDPR, this paper is guided by the following research questions: (1) *to what extent has the GDPR affected consumer awareness of privacy rights* and (2) *to what extent do consumers make use of their enhanced rights?* Herein, the focus is on before and after the introduction of the regulation.

2. RELATED RESEARCH OF PRIVACY AND SECURITY

Research on information privacy enjoys substantial attention from researchers. Privacy as a concept is blurred (Solove, 2005) and has sparked interest for more than 100 years among almost all types of researchers (Westin, 2003, Dinev, Xu, Smith, & Hart, 2013; Lowry, Dinev, & Willison, 2017). In 1890, Warren and Brandeis defined privacy as the 'right to be left alone' (Bélanger & Crossler, 2011). This was before the information age, but information privacy became subsumed under the umbrella of privacy sometime after (Smith, Dinev, & Xu, 2011). Due to its long and inter-disciplinary existence, several studies have aimed to define information privacy. Definitions tend to take either an individual or an organisational perspective. An example of an individual perspective includes *'one's ability to manage information about oneself'* (Bélanger, Hiller, & Smith, 2002). From the organisational perspective, we find *'a set of problems arising from the ways organizations process personal information'* (Solove, 2005). Despite the many definitions, a reoccurring theme is control over personal information (Popovič, Smith, Thong, & Wattal, 2018). Control, however, has been debated.

It has been argued that an individual's perception of control does not lead to information privacy: *'Conversely, the individual may not perceive (s)he has control, yet the environmental and interpersonal elements may create perceptions of general privacy'* (Laufner and Wolfe, 1977, cited in Smith et al., 2011, p. 995). Thus, control is only a mediating variable in the general privacy system. According to Smith et al. (2011), there is also a debate on the distinction between security and privacy. Along with anonymity and secrecy, this has added to the confusion about information privacy (Dinev et al., 2013). Culnan and Williams claim that security is one aspect of privacy: *'Security is about protecting personal information, while privacy is broader and encompasses permission and use of personal information. Privacy is difficult to achieve without security'* (Culnan & Williams, 2009 p. 674). However, in this study, information privacy and security are viewed as interdependent. When it comes to the evolution of research, papers have been typically conceptual, falling into three categories: literature reviews, forward-looking research agendas and measurement instruments for other empirical researchers. Another theme is antecedents of information privacy, such as the perception of individuals with *trust* as a major issue. A third theme has focused on consequences, such as the reduced effectiveness of direct marketing and resistance to new technologies. The fourth theme is protecting the individual (Popovič et al., 2018). Finally, research has evolved from motivation for studying information privacy, via guidelines for companies and consequences, to privacy-protecting algorithms and privacy in healthcare and social networks.

2.1 Violations, Consequences, Concerns, and Attitudes

A breach or violation of information privacy can entail many consequences, both for the individual and for the organisation. It is not only the organisation who is the 'bad wolf'; hackers are examples of individuals that can harm organisations. According to (Chatterjee, Sarker, & Valacich, 2015), hacking, phishing and spoofing have become a major security concerns for society, individuals and organisations. Other risks from a pure networking site perspective, such as cyber-attack risks and privacy abuse risks, have been identified (Dinev et al., 2006). The same applied to e-business consumers who were concerned with the misuse of personal information, monitoring, spam, hackers and viruses and risk with payment (Kaapu & Tiainen, 2009). Security in usage of computer systems is a vital component for many stakeholders (Novakovic, McGill, & Dixon, 2009). From an individual perspective, examples include harmful consequences like surveillance, identification, blackmail, and decisional interference (Solove, 2005).

The advances in technology do not only entail harmful activities. Martin presents beneficial and questionable uses of big data (Martin, 2015), such as treating cancer (beneficial) versus discrimination in insurance (questionable). However, there is yet another actor at play: algorithms. If an algorithm makes questionable decisions, who is to blame? An attempt to solve this issue, known as algorithmic transparency, has emerged from artificial intelligence and machine learning (Watson & Nations, 2019). Watson and Nations also study the balance of beneficial and questionable uses by introducing a 'creepiness scale' that goes from *'this is helpful'* on the one end to *'this is so wrong'* on the other. Examples of *'this is helpful'* include movie suggestions on Netflix. *'This is so wrong'* include targeted ads from personal injury lawyers after visiting an emergency room at a hospital and health insurance decisions based on your friends on Facebook. However, Watson and Nations express the need for more research on creepiness as a construct.

2.2 Conceptual Frameworks

Several conceptual frameworks have been developed and tested over the years. Numerous studies have drawn on the *privacy calculus* and the *privacy paradox*. The *privacy calculus model* deals with how the individual makes an informed decision of trading personal data for benefits, such as discounted merchandise or maintaining friends on social media (Presthus & Vatne, 2019). In other words, the benefits will surpass the risk of losing one's privacy (Krasnova & Veltri, 2010). However, the *privacy paradox model* suggests that individuals tend to make decisions that contradict their dispositional privacy concerns (Alashoor, 2019). Thus, the *privacy calculus model* aims to predict an individual's decision, while the privacy paradox phenomenon reflects a weak relationship (or a mismatch) between dispositional privacy concerns and disclosure behaviours. The debate surrounding these frameworks is ongoing; for example, some argue that the *privacy calculus* is obsolete (Knijnenburg et al., 2017).

Mason's privacy, accuracy, property and accessibility (PAPA) framework is seminal in Information Systems (Mason, 1986). Even though the PAPA framework was created in 1986, it is still highly relevant according to (Peslak, 2006; Parrish, 2010; Presthus & Andersen, 2017). Law professor Solove's taxonomy of privacy has four categories: information collection, information processing, information dissemination and invasion. Building on Solove (2005), Culnan and Williams (2009) identify two main potential problems in data breach: information reuse and unauthorised access. Bélanger and Crossler's framework conjoins individual, group, organisation and societal information, and illustrates various privacy concern constructs (Bélanger & Crossler, 2011); however, it does not include illegal parties. The *extended privacy model* (Conger, Pratt, & Loch, 2013) includes illegal parties in addition to individuals/consumers, vendors/providers, data sharing partners and illegal entities. The model illustrates how advanced technologies can evade individuals/consumers and make it possible for illegal entities to collect data. Thus, the *privacy calculus* or *privacy paradox* become obsolete. Some of the aforementioned frameworks also comprise government involvement and legal regulations.

2.3 The General Data Protection Regulation (GDPR)

The GDPR was implemented in 2018, replacing about 40 privacy laws from European countries with one unified regulation (The European Parliament and the Council, 2016). The GDPR consists of 99 Articles, and it can be found here: https://gdpr-info.eu/. As observed in the information privacy literature, there are several stakeholders related to the GDPR. Colesky, Hoepman, & Hillen (2016) present an overview with three actors and eight strategies for organisations to comply with the GDPR. As reported by Lomas (2016), the opportunities were fewer than the challenges for companies, but one benefit typically dealt with cleaning up data. Other potential benefits are that GDPR compliance can lead to satisfied customers and competitive advantages (Lomas, 2016). An empirical study conducted by Kleindienst et al. (2017) revealed that customers will value companies that offer insights before the customers have asked for them. Somewhat contradictory to other studies, the empirical paper by Crossler and Posey warns companies against using individual privacy concerns as promotion, though it might be tempting. Developers and marketers should rather focus on the company's ability, benevolence and integrity. These three factors constitute a company's trustworthiness (Crossler & Posey, 2017). The GDPR Article 17: The right to erasure, also known as 'The right to be forgotten', has gained interest. For example, Mantelero points out that it is not anything new and can be traced back to Warren and Brandeis in 1890 (Mantelero, 2013), while others discuss practical difficulties in removing data posted on the Internet (Koops, 2011; Korenhof et al., 2015). In addition, the GDPR does not give individuals the right to be completely forgotten. They can only claim this right if consent has not been given or if data are being used for other purposes than first stipulated (Lee & Pickering, 2016). An empirical study amongst 62 companies found that Article 17 was considered the most challenging (Presthus et al., 2018). Despite being a European regulation, researchers outside the EU have started to incorporate the GDPR in their research, with Watson and Nations (2019) as one example.

Summing up the related work, one conclusion is that information privacy and the GDPR are about protecting the individual from potential harmful activities. Another conclusion is that if one should attempt to conjoin all the models and concepts into one illustration, it would likely be enormous and difficult to grasp, however there are some common denominators amongst the models.

3. METHOD

Collecting primary data is encouraged within privacy and security research (Lowry et al., 2017). This article is based on an empirical, online survey questionnaire that has been distributed three times. In addition to related research, the survey is grounded in the legal document regulation (EU) 2016/679 of the European Parliament and of the council of 27 April 2016, which can be downloaded as a PDF from here: https://gdpr-info.eu/. The document lists 173 recitals and 99 Articles. A person, individual, consumer, citizen or alike is referred to as a 'data subject' in the regulation. The survey started with three questions concerning the data subject's perceived awareness about privacy, control over personal data and knowledge about the GDPR. These are some of the reasons why the GDPR was implemented and are based on the recitals. Second, four selected rights were investigated: right to erasure (Article 17), data portability (Article 20), right of access (Article 15) and cookies/consent (Recitals 30/32 and Articles 6 and 7).

The empirical study was carried out over a period of three years (2018–2020). We visited the classrooms during lectures and the students completed the survey while we were present. This way, we could address any practical issues that arose (but there were none). The questionnaire included Likert–scale, multiple choice and open–ended questions (requesting qualitative answers). The software tool SurveyMonkey® was used for conducting the survey, and the data were collected through a web-link created by the software. The same survey was replicated for all three years, except from a few changes that were needed concerning the questions, as the first survey was distributed before implementation of the GDPR, while the two last surveys was distributed after. It should also be noted that the survey in 2018 had fewer open comment fields compared to 2019 and 2020. After completing the first survey in 2018, the respondents commented that they wanted more opportunities to write text in addition to the predefined answer alternatives. As a result of this, additional open comments fields were included in the questionnaire in 2019 and 2020. Moreover, not everyone who started the survey completed it. The average time to complete the survey was five minutes (reported by the survey tool). After the surveys were completed, the data were visualised by using Microsoft Excel®. The aim was to generate overall trends and patterns.

The survey was replicated three times, with some minor adjustments due to the time the surveys were conducted (pre- and post-implementation of the GDPR). Pilot testing of the questionnaires was carried out before launching the survey and adjusted according to the feedback from the respondents. The aim was to ensure that the respondents understood the meaning of the questions and the use of answer alternatives.

4. FINDINGS AND DISCUSSION

The number of respondents in 2018 was 220, in 2019 it was 327 and in 2020 it reached 444. In 2018 and 2019, the typical respondent was male between 18–25 years old. Meanwhile, in 2020, the typical respondent was female but still in the same age group. Consequently, younger students in higher education in Norway dominated. While it must be acknowledged that it was not the same respondents that participated in all three surveys, they are still from the same target group (namely younger people).

As described above, the first investigation was the data subjects' own perceptions of the general awareness of privacy, whether they think they have control over their personal data and knowledge about the GDPR. The results are virtually identical for all three years. There is a clear peak of respondents who state that they have medium awareness, followed by a high degree. Regarding to what extent the respondents experience control over personal data: the majority state that they have partial control, followed by having no control at all.

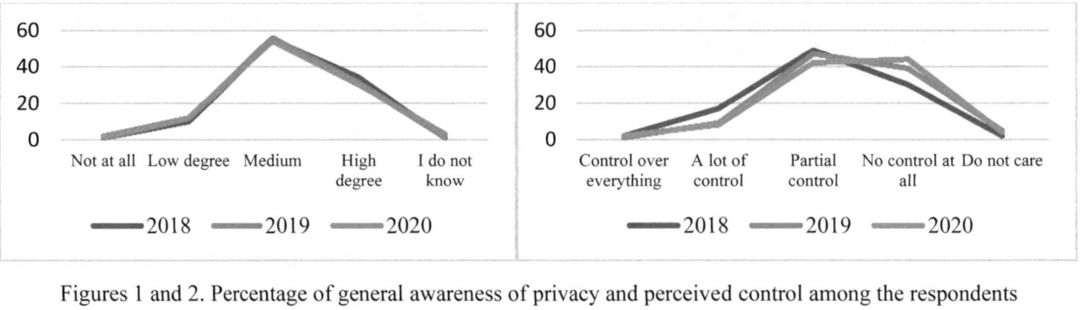

Figures 1 and 2. Percentage of general awareness of privacy and perceived control among the respondents

The graphs in Figures 1 and 2 has a similar pattern for all three years. Does this mean that the effect of the GDPR has not been as desired, at least not in the short term? The respondents experienced less control in 2020 compared to 2018. One possible explanation could be that today, people have more knowledge about all the data that is out there versus what they were aware of in 2018. Regarding knowledge of the GDPR, the findings show that the variations are greater among the three years. Consequently, the respondents demonstrate a greater disparity than is the case of the two other background questions. Moreover, the respondents had the greatest knowledge of the GDPR in 2019 and the lowest in 2020. This can have many explanations. In 2020, this hype of the GDPR may have decreased, and less attention is given by newspapers, TV and web news.

4.1 Enhanced Rights

As illustrated in Figure 3, more respondents stated in 2018 that they would 'definitely' make use of these rights (green columns), while fewer had actually executed them in 2019 and in 2020 (amber columns). Furthermore, there has been a small decline in the number who have used the new rights when comparing the numbers between 2019 and 2020. One reason can be that our respondents are different during the three years.

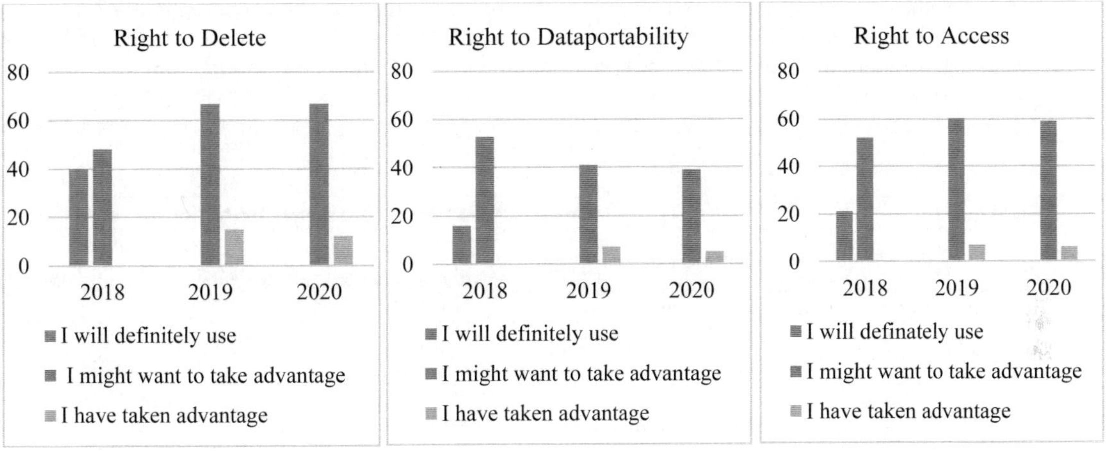

Figure 3. Percentage of the respondents' perception of the deletion of data; data portability and access

Regarding Article 17 about deletion, some comments from the respondents in 2019 read: *'Unless this is serious, I will not take advantage of this. May be good if suspected of illegal activity'*, while another wrote: *'Feeling poorly informed about how to get personal data deleted'*. One example of a comment from the survey conducted in 2020 is: *'Doesn't seem like it works particularly well anyway since they are just retrieving the same information again'*. This is a testament to the fact that not all consumers trust that information is indeed deleted. Article 20: Right to Data Portability, allows the data subject to get selected data that the company has acquired about him or her in a machine-readable format (Jarbekk & Sommerfeldt, 2019). For example, Facebook and Google have created an automated service (Sørum & Presthus, 2020). The trend and interest have declined somewhat over the years. Compared to 2018, where over 15 % said that this is something they would 'definitely' use, the data reveal that in 2019 and 2020, relatively few have used the right to data portability. Some comments pertaining to this topic from the respondents in 2019 were: *'Downloaded all the data Facebook has about me over time. Quite interesting'*; *'Very good that you do not have to lock yourself in to a bad service'*; and *'If needed, I will probably use it'*. However, not all respondents clearly see the same value in this, as explained in the following: *'Not sure in what context it might be useful'*.

The right of access by the data subject, Article 15, is highly comprehensive. It states that the data subjects can request both access to data about him/her, but also information about the purpose, how long it is stored, if it is shared, how to correct or delete and more (Jarbekk & Sommerfeldt, 2019). Our results are similar. The majority respond that this is something of which they *might* want to take advantage. Some of the open comments concerning this from 2019 are as follows: *'Scary to read everything Facebook has stored about you. Even things I've deleted.'* and *'It is a very good thing that companies must send it in a readable format, because then there is a greater chance that people will bother to read what they answer. If they send you 10 pages of lawyer response, there are many including myself who do not bother to engage me further because it requires too much energy'*.

A cookie is a text file that is downloaded on the data subject's computer or mobile device (Presthus & Andersen, 2017). The GDPR only mentions cookies once (in recital 30); however, it can be argued that the cookie-issue is truly about consent. Recital 32 states: *'Consent should be given by a clear affirmative act establishing a freely given, specific, informed and unambiguous indication of the data subject's agreement to the processing of personal data (...) This could include checking a box when visiting an internet website, (...) Silence, pre-checked boxes or inactivity should not therefore constitute consent'*. Article 7: Conditions for consent informs that the data subject has the possibility to consent to the processing of personal data. In addition, withdrawal must be easy. However, research has found that 90 % of websites are not allowing users the proper opt-out services regarding cookies and consent (Dabrowski et al., 2019; Sanchez-Rola et al., 2019).

Regarding the questions about website cookies, the respondents are unsure, and the general perception from 2019 to 2020 is a greater uncertainty. A summary of the findings from 2018 is as following: Almost 40 % do not believe that every company will follow the new rules and almost 30 % are unsure how the rule will work in practice. Moreover, 6 % answered that they do not care and 1 % did not know what cookies are. Comparing these findings to the results from 2019 and 2020, we do not see large differences in the respondents' perceptions of cookies. Some of the respondents provided open-ended comments: *'Seems to be nice, but it's hard to pay attention to everything in a day-to-day life that consists of a lot of information. That's why I press ok most of the time'*, and another one reads: *'Better, but many do not offer the option of refusing, without that box taking over the entire screen'*.

Based on three years of studying the GDPR, this paper offers accumulated insights (presented in Table 1).

Table 1. Accumulated insights about the consumer's perspectives on privacy

Insight topic	Consumer's perspective	Typical comments from the survey
General awareness of privacy	Medium degree	The consumers value their personal data, but acknowledge that they lack knowledge and control
Control over personal data	Partial control	
Knowledge of the GDPR	Have heard of, but do not know what it means	The consumers have heard about the regulation, but express uncertainty of the content
Right to be forgotten	Might execute	The consumers are in favor of the regulation, but express concerns about the enforcement
Right to data portability		
Right to access		

Based on the findings, the general pattern is dominated by "medium", "partial" and "might". Why the lack of concern and action from individuals? Based on related research, there are three possible answers. First: The concept is blurred (Solove, 2005), and we do not understand the technology at work behind the scenes of our computers (Presthus & Andersen, 2017), nor do we understand the 99 paragraphs of the GDPR (Jarbekk & Sommerfeldt, 2019). Many websites that consumers visit collect large amounts of data about individuals, our usage patterns and how we behave in a digital world. In many ways, it can be positive, but on the other hand, it is useful to know the questionable uses as well. Existing research has revealed that some companies fail at announcing this, for example on their websites. At the same time, it can be challenging to familiarize yourself with the regulations, considering legal rights and what they mean for the individual. Second: We make (more or less) calculated decisions about trading our information for benefits (Dinev et al., 2006), however, we are probably selling ourselves short, or there is a lack of business models that offer monetary payment rather than paying with personal data (Presthus & Vatne, 2019; Solove, 2020). Consequently, as consumers, we should become more aware of what our personal data is used for in a business purpose context and the high price consumers may end up paying by not being more conscious. Third: Some individuals have resigned (Few, 2018; Solove, 2020), as have companies in a supply chain, thinking 'everyone does it, why should not we' (Martin, 2015). Martin further describes negative externality, meaning that the big data industry is causing indirect harm to individuals. However, only the companies will profit from the passive attitudes of consumers.

5. LIMITATIONS AND FURTHER RESEARCH

No research is without limitations. Regarding method, Lowry et al. advise *against* using student sampling or sampling from one organization when it comes to privacy research (Lowry et al., 2017). This paper is guilty of both; however, the chosen organization is large, and the student body consists of a wide range of disciplines. Other limitations related to method are the focus on younger people, and their opinions do not necessarily reflect those of the rest of the population. Future research can compare younger people and seniors. Moreover, this study is relatively descriptive, but the aim was to paint an overall picture, as there is a lack of empirical research. Another limitation is the use of survey questions. Further research could therefore include qualitative interviews. International studies are also encouraged. For example, the California Consumer Privacy Act

(CCPA) went into effect on January 1st, 2020 in the US (Watson & Nations, 2019). It should be interesting to observe the influence of the CCPA in the future and how it relates to the GDPR. As demonstrated in the Related Research section, the conceptual models for information privacy are numerous, and we are therefore somewhat reluctant to add yet another at this point.

6. CONCLUSION

This study has investigated to what extent the GDPR affects consumer awareness of privacy rights and whether consumers make use of their enhanced rights. The data from a survey replicated three times indicate that the GDPR has not affected the consumer. The respondents state virtually the same level of awareness and control over personal data over the three years. Regarding knowledge about the GDPR, the pattern shows that it declined in 2020 compared to the level of knowledge in the two previous years. Concerning deletion, data portability and access to personal data, the patterns are similar and reveal that most of the respondents 'might execute' their enhanced rights. Pertaining to website cookies, most respondents are unsure, and the general perception from 2019 to 2020 reveals a greater uncertainty. This study contributes with practical insights based on empirical data to industry and to the information privacy research field.

REFERENCES

Alashoor, T. (2019). Explaining the Privacy Paradox through Identifying Boundary Conditions of the Relationship between Privacy Concerns and Disclosure Behaviors. *Doctor of Philosophy Dissertation, Georgia State University*.

Bélanger, F., & Crossler, R. E. (2011). Privacy in the Digital Age: A Review of Information Privacy Research in Information Systems. *MIS Quarterly, 35*(4), pp. 1017-1041.

Bélanger, F., Hiller, J. S., & Smith, W. J. (2002). Trustworthiness in electronic commerce: the role of privacy, security, and site attributes. *The journal of strategic Information Systems, 11*(3-4), 245-270.

Chatterjee, S., Sarker, S., & Valacich, J. S. (2015). The behavioral roots of information systems security: Exploring key factors related to unethical IT use. *Journal of Management Information Systems, 31*(4), 49-87.

Colesky, M., Hoepman, J.-H., & Hillen, C. (2016). *A critical analysis of privacy design strategies.* Paper presented at the Security and Privacy Workshops (SPW), 2016 IEEE.

Conger, S., Pratt, J. H., & Loch, K. D. (2013). Personal information privacy and emerging technologies. *Information Systems Journal, 23*, pp.401-417.

Crossler, R. E., & Posey, C. (2017). Robbing Peter to pay Paul: Surrendering privacy for security's sake in an identity ecosystem. *Journal of the Association for Information Systems, 18*(7), pp. 487-515.

Culnan, M. J., & Williams, C. C. (2009). How ethics can enhance organizational privacy: lessons from the choicepoint and TJX data breaches. *MIS Quarterly*, pp. 673-687.

Dabrowski, A., Merzdovnik, G., Ullrich, J., Sendera, G., & Weippl, E. (2019). *Measuring cookies and web privacy in a post-gdpr world.* Paper presented at the International Conference on Passive and Active Network Measurement.

Dinev, T., Belletto, M., Hart, P., Russo, V., Serra, I., & Colautti, C. (2006). Privacy calculus model in e-commerce – a study of Italy and the Unites States. *European Journal of Information Systems, 4*(15), pp. 389-402.

Dinev, T., Xu, H., Smith, J. H., & Hart, P. (2013). Information privacy and correlates: an empirical attempt to bridge and distinguish privacy-related concepts. *European Journal of Information Systems, 22*(3), pp. 295-316.

Few, S. (2018). *Big Data, Big Dupe. A little book about a big bunch of nonsense*: Analytic Press.

Jarbekk, E., & Sommerfeldt, S. (2019). *Personvern og GDPR i praksis*: Cappelen Damm, ISBN 9788202604066.

Kaapu, T., & Tiainen, T. (2009). Consumers' Views on Privacy in E-Commerce. *Scandinavian Journal of Information Systems, 21*(1), pp. 3-22.

Knijnenburg, B., Raybourn, E., Cherry, D., Wilkinson, D., Sivakumar, S., & Sloan, H. (2017). Death to the Privacy Calculus? *Available at SSRN 2923806.*

Koops, B.-J. (2011). Forgetting footprints, shunning shadows: A critical analysis of the right to be forgotten in big data practice. *SCRIPTed, 8*, 229.

Korenhof, P., Ausloos, J., Szekely, I., Ambrose, M., Sartor, G., & Leenes, R. (2015). Timing the right to be forgotten: A study into "time" as a factor in deciding about retention or erasure of data *Reforming European data protection law* (pp. 171-201): Springer.

Krasnova, H., & Veltri, N. (2010). *Privacy Calculus on Social Networking Sites: Explorative Evidence from Germany and USA".* Paper presented at the 43rd Hawaii International Conference on System Sciences, Honolulu, HI, USA. January 5-8.

Lee, P., & Pickering, K. (2016). The general data protection regulation: A myth-buster. *Journal of Data Protection & Privacy, 1*(1), pp. 1-5.

Lomas, E. (2016). Data Protection and GDPR Opportunites and Challenges. *IRMS London Particpatory workshop hosted by UCL, 7 July 2016.*, pp. 1-6.

Lowry, P. B., Dinev, T., & Willison, R. (2017). Why security and privacy research lies at the centre of the information systems (IS) artefact: proposing a bold research agenda. *European Journal of Information Systems, 26*, pp. 546-563.

Mantelero, A. (2013). The EU Proposal for a General Data Protection Regulation and the roots of the 'right to be forgotten'. *Computer Law & Security Review, 29*(3), pp. 229-235.

Martin, K. E. (2015). Ethical issues in the big data industry. *MIS Quarterly Executive, 14*(2), pp. 67-85.

Mason, R. O. (1986). Four ethical issues of the information age. *MIS Quarterly, 10*(1), pp. 5-12.

Novakovic, L., McGill, T., & Dixon, M. (2009). Understanding User Behavior towards Passwords through Acceptance and Use Modelling. *International Journal of Information Security and Privacy, 3*(1), pp. 11-29.

Parrish, J. L. (2010). PAPA knows best: Principles for the ethical sharing of information on social networking sites. *Ethics and Information Technology, 12*(2), pp. 187-193.

Peslak, A. R. (2006). PAPA revisited: A current empirical study of the Mason framework. *Journal of Computer Information Systems, 46*(3), pp. 117-123.

Popovič, A., Smith, H. J., Thong, J. Y. L., & Wattal, S. (2018). Information Privacy. *MIS Quarterly Research Curations, Ashley Bush and Arun Rai, Eds., http://misq.org/research-curations,.*

Presthus, W., & Andersen, L. R. (2017). *Information Privacy from a Retail Management Perspective.* Paper presented at the In Proceedings of the 25th European Conference on Information Systems (ECIS), Guimarães, Portugal, June 5-10, 2017.

Presthus, W., Sørum, H., & Andersen, L. R. (2018). GDPR compliance in Norwegian Companies. *Norsk konferanse for organisasjoners bruk av IT (NOKOBIT). Svalbard 18-20 September 2018.*

Presthus, W., & Vatne, D. M. (2019). A Survey on Facebook Users and Information Privacy. *Procedia Computer Science, 164*, pp. 39-47.

Sanchez-Rola, I., Dell'Amico, M., Kotzias, P., Balzarotti, D., Bilge, L., Vervier, P.-A., & Santos, I. (2019). *Can I Opt Out Yet? GDPR and the Global Illusion of Cookie Control.* Paper presented at the Proceedings of the 2019 ACM Asia Conference on Computer and Communications Security.

Smith, H. J., Dinev, T., & Xu, H. (2011). Information Privacy Research: An Interdisciplinary Review. *MIS Quarterly, 35*(4), pp. 989-1015.

Solove, D. J. (2005). A taxonomy of privacy. *U. Pa. L. Rev., 154*, pp. 477-560.

Solove, D.J. (2020) Privacy + Security Blog. News, Developments, and Insights. https://teachprivacy.com/cartoon-the-history-of-privacy/ Visited November 11, 2020.

Sørum, H., & Presthus, W. (2020). Dude, Where's My Data? The GDPR in Practice, from a Consumer's Point of View. *Information Technology & People,* pp.1-18.

The European Parliament and the Council. (2016). REGULATION (EU) 2016/679 OF THE EUROPEAN PARLIAMENT AND OF THE COUNCIL of 27 April 2016. *Official Journal of the European Union, available through https://gdpr-info.eu/*, pp. 1-88.

Watson, H. J., & Nations, C. (2019). Addressing the Growing Need for Algorithmic Transparency. *Communications of The Association for Information Systems, 45*(1), 26, pp. 488-510.

Westin, A.F. (2003) Social and Political Dimensions of Privacy. *Journal of Social Issues, 59*(2), pp. 431-453.

DETERMINATION OF RESEARCH TRENDS IN COVID-19 LITERATURE USING TOPIC MODEL APPROACH

Eda Sonmez and Keziban Seckin Codal
Ankara Yildirim Beyazit University, Department of Management Information Systems
Ankara Yıldırım Beyazıt University Business School, Building B, Esenboga Campus, 06760 Ankara, Turkey

ABSTRACT

The world is currently facing a significant global health crisis that threatens millions of lives. Researchers and scholars have united to create a network and knowledge maps for the novel crisis of coronavirus (COVID-19) pandemic. During a pandemic, identifying the fields of scientific study that have attracted greater research attention with the pandemic is of paramount importance in managing the pandemic. This paper aims to identify a number of popular subjects of research related to COVID-19 through topic modeling, as well as to demonstrate the role of information systems (IS) to raise awareness of new research. In this context, a corpus of 7,395 English articles related to COVID-19 published in the Web of Science database was analyzed by using the Latent Dirichlet Allocation (LDA) and the topics were identified, which are classified into five main themes: epidemiological studies, clinical studies, global impacts of COVID-19, guidelines regarding the challenges of COVID-19, and the role of information systems to manage the COVID-19 outbreak. The findings suggest that epidemiological and clinical studies are the core research topics in this respect, in line with the findings of a number of previous studies, while global impacts of COVID-19, guidelines regarding the challenges of COVID-19, and use of information systems in COVID-19 pandemic are new trend topics of COVID-19 research.

KEYWORDS

COVID-19, Topic Modeling, LDA, Research Trends, Information Systems

1. INTRODUCTION

The World Health Organization (WHO) announced the COVID-19 as a global pandemic on March 11, 2020 (WHO, 2020a). Earlier in this year, on January 11, the first deadly case due to coronavirus was reported in China (WHO, 2020a). Although the city of Wuhan was quarantined soon afterwards, the virus had already begun spreading to other countries exponentially by January 23 (Taylor, 2020). The distribution of the total COVID-19 cases, deaths and new cases in the past 24 hours by region as of August 10,2020 are presented in Table 1. There were 19,718,030 cases and 728,013 deaths globally(WHO, 2020b). COVID-19 has received huge attention in recent months because it has been affecting millions of people all around the world (Tran et al., 2020).It has significant impacts on security, politics, economy, society or technology(Etyang, 2020).

Table 1. Total cases, deaths, and new cases and deaths in the past 24 hours as of August 10, 2020 (WHO, 2020b)

	Total cases	New cases in the past 24 hrs.	Total deaths	New deaths in the past 24 hrs.
Globally	19,718,030	253,409	728,013	5,719
Africa	895,696	10,706	16,713	310
Americas	10,590,929	143,668	388,673	3,597
Eastern Mediterranean	1,644,359	9,419	43,433	353
Europe	3,582,911	17,627	216,693	258
South-East Asia	2,632,773	66,973	53,677	1,108
Western Pacific	370,621	5,016	8,811	93

Due to its recent emergence as an infectious disease, COVID-19 is a currently popular research subject (Xiang et al., 2020). In the absence of vaccines and antiviral care, a good number of laboratories, researchers and corporations have been working to find a medication or vaccine for the treatment of COVID-19 (Haleem et al., 2020). There are other researchers who have been investigating the impacts of COVID-19 in social, economic, health-related and many other domains. Naturally, the number of academic studies in many fields have significantly increased over time (Tran et al., 2020). According to Dimensions (2020), while the number of clinical trials focusing of COVID-19 was 60 in the first week of January 2020, this number was 5,516 by the end of August, 2020 and there were 96,449 articles and 25,012 preprints. 7,395 articles in English became available in the Web of Science database until August 2020. On February 11-12, 2020, large number of scientists were brought together by the WHO in Geneva, and an R&D Blueprint was created to provide ideas on COVID-19-related issues (WHO, 2020c). The R&D Blueprint facilitates communication between scientists and has two main purposes: to find solutions that would slow the progression of the epidemic and a cure, and to support global research platforms against a new pandemic that may occur afterwards (WHO, 2020c). The WHO has also created a database where it collects international findings and information related to COVID-19. This regularly updated database has become a comprehensive resource for those who want to work on COVID-19 (WHO, 2020c). Scientific studies are of paramount importance in reducing the impacts of COVID-19 and preparing for a possible new pandemic (Tran et al., 2020). Identifying and studying the academic research about COVID-19 is, therefore, an urgent need (Haleem et al., 2020).

This paper aims to classify the current research topics related to COVID-19 and to illustrate the role of information systems based on a corpus of articles published in English through a systematic literature review in the Web of Science database. The paper reveals the research foci related to COVID-19 to increase the visibility of new research by using the Latent Dirichlet Allocation (LDA). In the next section, we briefly discuss some areas adversely affected by COVID-19 and section 3 describes the methodology used and provides some information about the topic modeling and LDA. Section 4 presents our findings and interpretations of the results. The final section is the conclusion section.

2. LITERATURE REVIEW

COVID-19 has a remarkable influence on individuals' daily life and routine of corporations. COVID-19 is considered a disease that has primarily affected the healthcare sector, but it has also harmed many other sectors. The COVID-19 outbreak has caused long-standing damage to the economy, education, and tourism and aviation. The potential impacts have prompted researchers to work on longer-term effects of the spread and to determine the dynamics of COVID-19.

The health sector has been heavily disrupted due to COVID-19. A rapid rise in the number of patients has caused a shortage of equipment, beds and personnel leading to healthcare systems' collapsing (Etyang, 2020). Some researchers concentrate on the treatment and diagnosis of COVID-19 (Gautret et al., 2020; X. Li et al., 2020; Tang et al., 2020). There are also studies focusing on the healthcare infrastructures of different countries (Etyang, 2020; Paintsil, 2020). These studies examine how prepared countries are against such a patient overload. Healthcare professionals are at the forefront and they directly communicate with COVID-19 patients; hence, psychological disorders and mental problems might occur. Moreover, a large number of cases, excessive workload, shortage of certain medications and lack of protective equipment might negatively affect healthcare workers (Lai et al., 2020; Chew et al., 2020). Several research studies have been conducted to integrate new technologies into the healthcare sector and use them in COVID-19 treatments in order to reduce the risks threatening healthcare workers and to provide an uninterrupted supply of medications (Bamber & Fernandez-Stark, 2020; Javaid et al., 2020).

There are many studies on how the manufacturing of products has slowed down and the supply has been disrupted(Govindan et al., 2020; Reardon et al., 2020; Rizou et al., 2020). Economic harm both at the micro and macro levels is emphasized in the literature. United Nations Industrial Development Organization (UNIDO) points out that countries were severely affected by COVID-19 between December 2019 and April 2020, regardless of income level (UNIDO, 2020).

Additionally, some researchers focus on the volatility in the revenue growth (Atkeson, 2020; Fernandes, 2020; McKibbin & Fernando, 2020; Usman et al., 2020) and there are studies analyzing the stock market reactions in the literature (Baker et al., 2020; Huo & Qiu, 2020; Khanthavit, 2020; Zhang et al., 2020). According to the OECD data, while the unemployment rate was 5.2% in February 2020 , this rate was 8.4% in May 2020 that is the highest unemployment rate in a decade. Moreover, in the fourth quarter of 2020, this rate is estimated to reach 9.4% (OECD, 2020).

Most of the governments have temporarily closed their educational institutions to prevent the spread of COVID-19. UNESCO stated that as of March 4, 2020, schools were closed in 22 countries (UNESCO, 2020a). Sixty percent of the student population in the world has been affected by these closures (UNESCO, 2020b). Many countries' education systems have sustained their operations by shifting from traditional learning to digital learning. This unexpected transition to digital education is also studied in the literature (Barnes, 2020; Özer, 2020; Teräs et al., 2020). Furthermore, there are many studies focusing on the mental health of students during an epidemic (Cao et al., 2020; Li & Leung, 2020; Zhai & Du, 2020).

Many countries suffer from the disruption of tourism activities, vacation travel and passenger transportation. According to the data of UNWTO, international tourism shrank by 22% in the first quarter of the year, and this number is anticipated to reach 60-80% over the year (UNWTO, 2020). In this context, passenger mobility at airports worldwide declined by 12% in the first quarter of 2020 (ACI, 2020). The International Air Transport Association (2020) announced that the sector's revenue loss might reach 314 billion dollars (IATA, 2020). Most of the studies in this area analyze the impacts of the pandemic on cruises, air travel and accommodations (Farzanegan et al., 2020; Türker, 2020). Researchers also examine how much damage COVID-19 has caused to domestic and international aviation industry (Akipinar & Seckin Codal, 2020; Çora, 2020; Macit, 2020).

Information systems have a crucial role in countering the COVID-19 pandemic by radically changing the dynamics of sectors, such as healthcare, education, businesses and etc., in addition to providing effective communication. Various information system strategies have been adopted by different countries in dealing with COVID-19 (C. Liu, 2020). With many people in lockdown, thousands of people dying, businesses going bankrupt, and many sectors and organizations suffering, several countries have imposed restrictions to prevent the spread of the disease. Researchers in different disciplines have cooperated against the challenges of COVID-19, and information systems scholars have also been making a great effort to fight COVID-19 (Ågerfalk et al., 2020). IS scholars have contributed new knowledge to the existing literature and proposed new areas for IS research that can be alternative solutions for such challenges (Pan & Zhang, 2020). Research on IS is grouped under three main headings: diffusion and adoption of new technology, technology adaptation and tackling with the problems of technology use, impact of technology on well-being during the COVID-19 pandemic (Dey et al., 2020).

3. METHODOLOGY

We specifically address the following question in our study: What topics has research focused on in the scientific literature on COVID-19? For an answer to this question, firstly we collected the articles related to COVID-19 in the Web of Science database. The search was made with the keyword "COVID-19" and the document type was specified as articles are preferred. No category restrictions were applied while searching. Our data covers the period from December 2019 to August 2020. The article abstracts were exported to an Excel sheet. Non-English articles were not included in the analysis. Finally, the number of data entries for analysis was 7,395.

The second step was the data cleaning and preparation step to make the analysis easier and ensure we get more accurate results. The Excel sheet was converted to a csv file to make it more suitable for Pandas, a library in Python. All letters were converted to lowercase. All stop words were removed thanks to NLTK, the text-processing library of Python. Biagrams and trigrams were created. Python's Gensim library was imported and the functions corpora, simple_preprocess and CoherenceModel were run. While the tokenization was done through Gensim's function simple preprocess, lemmatization was analyzed by spacy's NLP library. A dictionary was created by Gensim's function corpora.Dictionary. The articles were finally converted into a document corpus via the function doc2bow to analyze distribution of semantic word clusters, i.e. the topic modeling. The flow diagram of LDA's preprocessing steps is presented in Figure 1.

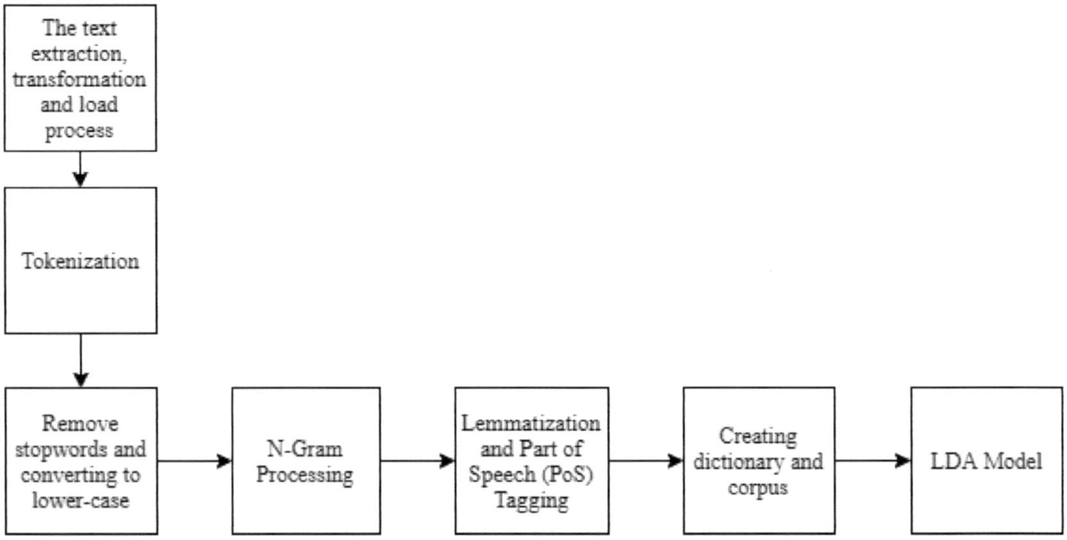

Figure 1. The preprocessing step for LDA

In this study, the topic modeling method was used to determine what topics have been focused on in the scientific literature on COVID-19. LDA was preferred because it is the most well-known topic modeling method (Habibabadi & Haghighi, 2019).Unsupervised machine learning algorithms and probabilistic topic models are utilized by researchers to extract hidden information from various text automatically. LDA, one of the probabilistic topic models, shows great performance in the fields of information retrieval, text classifications and text annotations (Bellegarda, 2008; Blei, 2012; Z. Liu, 2013). The main logic of LDA is that documents are symbolized as random mixtures over latent topics, and every topic is qualified by a distribution over words (Jordan et al., 2003). Compared to other probabilistic models, LDA is advantageous as it trains models directly with mature probability algorithms, it is more stable than non-hierarchical models and it provides better semantic conditions and a stronger descriptive power (Girolami & Kabán, 2003; Z. Liu, 2013). Additionally, since LDA's logic is based on the probability distribution of topics, it eases the generative process and efficiently works on large-scale datasets (Z. Liu, 2013; Masada et al., 2008). Chen and colleagues (2020) have studied an effective model for forecasting preoperative critical disease with the help of LDA. LDA is a commonly applied method to determine customer profiles and retrieve information from customer comments in marketing areas (H. Li, 2020; Sutherland et al., 2020). Moreover, it is beneficial to identify hot topics on specific issues on social media (Abd-Alrazaq et al., 2020; Xue et al., 2020). Mori and colleagues (2020) propose an automated evaluation system for improving working skills by using LDA. Y. Liu and Cheng (2020) reveal the transit patterns using the LDA technique on personalized smart card data. They understand passenger behaviors by interpreting these inferences with geodemographics data.

LDA Mallet is used in this study. "*MALLET is a Java-based package for statistical natural language processing, document classification, clustering, topic modeling, information extraction, and other machine learning applications to text*" (Mallet, 2020). The MALLET package contains an highly scalable and fast implementation of Gibbs sampling. For the second part of the analysis, we tried a few numbers of topics to determine the best number by using the CoherenceModel package. We compared the coherence scores for four different numbers of topics: 5, 10, 15, and 20. The best score was yielded by 10, which was then adopted as the number of topics. Then, the topics were labeled with the help of opinions of three researchers. A consistency analysis was performed across the opinions of the researchers.

4. RESULTS AND DISCUSSION

This paper contributes to the literature by specifying the current research foci related to COVID-19, illuminating some crucial gaps that previous studies have not addressed. Previous studies about COVID-19 literature have generally concentrated on bibliometric analysis (Verma & Gustafsson, 2020). In our study, using the topic modeling method, we examine the current literature not only on the basis of text, but also with its semantic structure. The current study reveals a shift in the topics of COVID-19 publications and contributes to determining the current topic subjects. We used the 7,395 articles we found in the Web of Science database, and applied LDA only for the abstracts of these articles in Python. Based on the fact that the highest coherence score was obtained with 10 topics, the most appropriate labels were defined for the 10 topics by help of three independent researchers. A list of the ten research topics related to COVID-19 and their respective top ten most frequent words are presented in Table 3.

Table 3. Ten research topics related to COVID-19 and their respective top ten most frequent words

Topic	Top Ten Most Frequent Words
1.Epidemiological situation of COVID-19	case, number, measure, control, epidemic, rate, model, transmission, country, spread
2. COVID-19 impacts on mental health and psychological well-being	covid, health, study, risk, level, high, factor, result, survey, mental
3. COVID-19 research for the progress of diagnostic values	result, test, method, study, covid, base, positive, datum, model, perform
4. Laboratory and clinical examination on patients admitted to the hospital	patient, covid, infection, symptom, disease, case, report, present, clinical, severe
5. Prevention of the COVID-19	virus, viral, potential, drug, human, cell, target, treatment, infection, study
6. The global impact of COVID-19 on the socio-economic status	pandemic, crisis, impact, social, policy, world, paper, economic, global, change
7. Developing an emergency risk management plan for health-care organizations	care, patient, risk, management, medical, hospital, covid, emergency, pandemic, procedure
8. Supportive advice for coping with the pandemic-related challenges	pandemic, challenge, experience, support, work, provide, face, practice, service, research
9. The role of IS to manage the COVID-19 outbreak	health, public, covid, response, information, system, strategy, global, provide, spread
10. Risk stratification of COVID-19 cases	patient, group, clinical, severe, age, high, day, study, year, compare

The topics listed in Table 3 can be divided into five categories: epidemiological studies (Topic 1), clinical studies (Topic 3, 4, 5, 10), global impacts of COVID-19 (Topic 2, 6), guidelines regarding the challenges of COVID-19 (Topic 7, 8), and the role of information systems to manage the COVID-19 pandemic (Topic 9). Our findings are in line with previous LDA studies, which demonstrate that epidemiological and clinical studies are core research foci (Tran et al., 2020).

Some researchers work on faster and more accurate methods for the diagnosis, treatment and control of the spread of the virus (Jiao et al., 2020; Sheikhzadeh et al., 2020). COVID-19 causes medical problems of different clinical severities, manifesting with both extra-respiratory and respiratory symptoms. There are studies examining how manifestations vary between severe and non-severe COVID-19 cases in terms of nature and frequency, to help researchers specify a treatment method and determine high-risk patient groups (Bao et al., 2020; Dalal et al., 2020). Besides the clinical aspects of COVID-19, some researchers actively work on the whole range of short-term and long-term impacts of COVID-19. They intensely study how people have been affected in economic, social and psychological terms and make suggestions to reduce the negative impacts of the crisis (Choudhari, 2020; Song, 2020; Vindegaard & Eriksen Benros, 2020). A group of researchers investigate the relationship between possible impacts of the pandemic on mental health and socio-demographic factors. Healthcare workers who are at the forefront of combating the pandemic, students who have undergone academic disruptions, and workers who lost their jobs are frequently chosen as subjects in research (Cao et al., 2020; Greenberg et al., 2020; Lai et al., 2020). Since there is still little known about COVID-19, the WHO and many countries have been publishing many informative articles for the public and healthcare professionals. The WHO has determined the major themes of informative articles: public guidance, national healthcare systems and technical consulting, situation updates, research and development, and scam alerts. The WHO has also published its COVID-19 Emergency Use Listing Procedure and generated a COVID-database that gathers the academic research related to COVID-19 (WHO | World Health Organization, 2020).

A topic determined in this study which is different from those of previous studies is the role of IS to manage the COVID-19 outbreak. Information systems have a crucial role in responding to COVID-19; hence, IS scholars concentrate on the existing literature to create a new approach to tackle the challenges of COVID-19 (Pan & Zhang, 2020). The struggle with pandemic has been gradually more dependent on technology and information systems.

Some researchers focus on the adoption and adaptation of new technological applications, such as new social media-based applications, video and voice call software, etc. (Dey et al., 2020). Some video meeting applications have rapidly become widespread and moved beyond social and national borders. Many industries now operate their businesses remotely by means of such platforms (Barnes, 2020). A number of governments have ordered to continue education by shifting from traditional learning to digital learning due to the school closures (Özer, 2020). Web conferencing systems and digital monitoring are also used to provide patients with remote healthcare (Whitelaw et al., 2020). Moreover, AI methods enable more rapid diagnosis. Images can be processed in seconds and results differentiated from the manifestations of other lung diseases; hence, diagnosis times substantially decline with AI methods (McCall, 2020). Many governments have integrated digital technologies into their pandemic policies to perform planning, testing, surveillance, quarantine, contact tracing and clinical management in order to reduce COVID-19 cases and deaths. The people are tracked by using facial recognition technology, security cameras, global positioning systems (GPS) and bank card records (Fisher & Sang-Hun, 2020). In Singapore, the distance between any two individuals is determined by Singapore Ministry of Health via a mobile phone application called UpCode using Bluetooth signals. Moreover, UpCode is also used to estimate the tendency for COVID-19 cases to infect others by sex, age, location and recovery time (Dick, 2020). In Germany, a smartwatch application provides useful data for individual temperatures, sleep patterns and pulses (Busvine, 2020). The Turkish Ministry of Health has launched the application "Hayat Eve Sığar" to identify recent physical contacts of infected persons with a HesCode (Sağlık Bakanlığı, 2020). In China, people are tracked through migration maps. Migration maps collect real time data from mobile phones, social media and mobile payment applications (Hu et al., 2020). The Taiwan government requires health checks for airline travelers by using the national health insurance database and individual migration records (Wang et al., 2020). Sweden authorities have announced a platform to track the number of COVID-19 patients, protective healthcare equipment, hospital bed capacity, and other resources (Drees, 2020).

5. CONCLUSION

This study analyzed, through the LDA method, English manuscripts submitted during and related to the Covid-19 pandemic as available crisis in the Web of Science database. In this paper, the high-priority research landscape of the COVID-19 publications is outlined and the importance of information systems in this respect is highlighted. The topics determined through LDA are as follows: epidemiological situation of COVID-19, COVID-19 impacts on mental health and psychological well-being, COVID-19 research for the progress of diagnostic values, laboratory and clinical examination on patients admitted to the hospital, prevention of the COVID-19, the global impact of COVID-19 on the socio-economic status, developing an emergency risk management plan for health-care organizations, supportive advice for coping with the pandemic-related challenges, the role of IS to manage the COVID-19 outbreak and risk stratification of COVID-19 cases. The role of information systems to manage the COVID-19 outbreak is a revolutionary new trend to tackling the pandemic. This study contributes to the determination of current topics and it could inspire researchers in the process of identifying the topics of new research and potential directions for future work.

The analysis was conducted by searching the Web of Science with the keyword "COVID-19", and the LDA method was applied to the abstracts of the articles retrieved because the abstract of an article provides a powerful statement, including the scope, purpose, results, and contents of the work while the rest of the article provides comprehensive information. The only language preferred for searching the articles was English, which introduces a challenge for examining other studies written in different languages. For further studies, the methodology used in this study to analyze COVID-19 research can be progressively improved, using different databases, greater number of keywords, and more advanced text mining techniques.

REFERENCES

Abd-Alrazaq, A., Alhuwail, D., Househ, M., Hamdi, M., & Shah, Z. (2020). Top Concerns of Tweeters During the COVID-19 Pandemic: Infoveillance Study. *Journal of Medical Internet Research*, *22*(4), e19016. https://doi.org/10.2196/19016

ACI. (2020). *The impact of COVID-19 on the airport business: preliminary assessment.*

Ågerfalk, P. J., Conboy, K., & Myers, M. D. (2020). Information systems in the age of pandemics: COVID-19 and beyond. *European Journal of Information Systems*, *29*(3), 203–207. https://doi.org/10.1080/0960085X.2020.1771968

Akipinar, M. T., & Seckin Codal, K. (2020). *The Impact of the Coronavirus (COVID-19) Outbreak on Asia-Pacific Airways Stocks Prices : An Event-Study Approach. 2.*

Atkeson, A. (2020). What Will Be the Economic Impact of COVID-19 in the US? Rough Estimates of Disease Scenarios. In *NBER Working Paper Series* (Issue 595, p. 25). https://doi.org/10.3386/w26867

Baker, S., Bloom, N., Davis, S., Kost, K., Sammon, M., & Viratyosin, T. (2020). The Unprecedented Stock Market Impact of COVID-19. *National Bureau of Economic Research*. https://doi.org/10.3386/w26945

Bamber, P., & Fernandez-Stark, K. (2020). *Why global value chains remain essential for COVID-19 supplies*. https://www.researchgate.net/publication/343190696

Barnes, S. J. (2020). Information management research and practice in the post-COVID-19 world. *International Journal of Information Management*, 102175. https://doi.org/10.1016/j.ijinfomgt.2020.102175

Bellegarda, J. R. (2008). Latent Semantic Mapping: Principles & Applications. *San Rafael: Morgan and Claypool Publishers*.

Blei, D. M. (2012). Probabilistic topic models. *Communications of the Acm*, *55*(4).

Busvine, D. (2020). *Germany launches smartwatch app to monitor coronavirus spread | Reuters*. https://www.reuters.com/article/us-health-coronavirus-germany-tech-idUSKBN21P1SS

Cao, W., Fang, Z., Hou, G., Han, M., Xu, X., Dong, J., & Zheng, J. (2020). The psychological impact of the COVID-19 epidemic on college students in China. *Psychiatry Research*, *287*. https://doi.org/10.1016/j.psychres.2020.112934

Chen, Y., Zhang, L., Zhang, J., Yi, B., & Qin, X. (2020). PREOPERATIVE RISK PREDICTION OF HEART FAILUREWITH NUMERICAL AND TEXTUAL ATTRIBUTES. *International Journal of InnovativeComputing, Information and Control*, *16*(6).

Chew, N. W. S., Lee, G. K. H., Tan, B. Y. Q., Jing, M., Goh, Y., Ngiam, N. J. H., Yeo, L. L. L., Ahmad, A., Ahmed Khan, F., Napolean Shanmugam, G., Sharma, A. K., Komalkumar, R. N., Meenakshi, P. V., Shah, K., Patel, B., Chan, B. P. L., Sunny, S., Chandra, B., Ong, J. J. Y., … Sharma, V. K. (2020). A multinational, multicentre study on the psychological outcomes and associated physical symptoms amongst healthcare workers during COVID-19 outbreak. *Brain, Behavior, and Immunity*, *88*, 559–565. https://doi.org/10.1016/j.bbi.2020.04.049

Çora, H. (2020). IMPACT OF COVID-19 ON GLOBAL AND TURKISH AVIATION SECTOR – PROACTIVE AND PREEMPTIVE MEASURES DURING AND AFTER PANDEMIC. *International Journal of Advanced Science and Technology*, *29*(8), 2825–2851.

Dey, B. L., Al-Karaghouli, W., & Muhammad, S. S. (2020). Adoption, Adaptation, Use and Impact of Information Systems during Pandemic Time and Beyond: Research and Managerial Implications. *Information Systems Management*. https://doi.org/10.1080/10580530.2020.1820632

Dick, S. (2020). *Singapore's COVID-19 temperature scans and tracking leading the way*. https://thenewdaily.com.au/news/national/2020/03/19/singapore-coronavirus-temperature-scans/

Dimensions. (2020). *COVID19 | Dimensions*. https://www.dimensions.ai/covid19/

Drees, J. (2020). *Swedish Health Services taps Microsoft to build app that tracks COVID-19 patients, hospital capacity*. https://www.beckershospitalreview.com/healthcare-information-technology/swedish-health-services-taps-microsoft-to-build-app-that-tracks-covid-19-patients-hospital-capacity.html

Elmer, T., Mepham, K., & Stadtfeld, C. (2020). Students under lockdown: Comparisons of students' social networks and mental health before and during the COVID-19 crisis in Switzerland. *PLOS ONE*, *15*(7), e0236337. https://doi.org/10.1371/journal.pone.0236337

Etyang, O. (2020). *COVID-19 Pandemic and its Potential Impact on The Health Sector in the COMESA Region*. https://au.int/sites/default/files/documents/38326-doc-cov-

Farzanegan, M. R., Gholipour, H. F., Feizi, M., Nunkoo, R., & Andargoli, A. E. (2020). International Tourism and Outbreak of Coronavirus (COVID-19): A Cross-Country Analysis. In *Journal of Travel Research*. SAGE Publications Ltd. https://doi.org/10.1177/0047287520931593

Fernandes, N. (2020). Economic Effects of Coronavirus Outbreak (COVID-19) on the World Economy. *SSRN Electronic Journal*. https://doi.org/10.2139/ssrn.3557504

Fisher, M., & Sang-Hun, C. (2020). *How South Korea Flattened the Coronavirus Curve*. The New York Times. https://www.nytimes.com/2020/03/23/world/asia/coronavirus-south-korea-flatten-curve.html

Gautret, P., Lagier, J. C., Parola, P., Hoang, V. T., Meddeb, L., Mailhe, M., Doudier, B., Courjon, J., Giordanengo, V., Vieira, V. E., Tissot Dupont, H., Honoré, S., Colson, P., Chabrière, E., La Scola, B., Rolain, J. M., Brouqui, P., & Raoult, D. (2020). Hydroxychloroquine and azithromycin as a treatment of COVID-19: results of an open-label non-randomized clinical trial. *International Journal of Antimicrobial Agents*, *56*(1). https://doi.org/10.1016/j.ijantimicag.2020.105949

Girolami, M., & Kabán, A. (2003). On an equivalence between PLSI and LDA. *26th Annual International ACM SIGIR Conference on Research and Development in Informaion Retrieval*, 433–434.

Gössling, S., Scott, D., & Hall, C. M. (2020). Pandemics, tourism and global change: a rapid assessment of COVID-19. *Journal of Sustainable Tourism*, 1–20. https://doi.org/10.1080/09669582.2020.1758708

Govindan, K., Mina, H., & Alavi, B. (2020). A decision support system for demand management in healthcare supply chains considering the epidemic outbreaks: A case study of coronavirus disease 2019 (COVID-19). *Transportation Research Part E: Logistics and Transportation Review*, *138*, 101967. https://doi.org/10.1016/j.tre.2020.101967

Greenberg, N., Docherty, M., Gnanapragasam, S., & Wessely, S. (2020). *Managing mental health challenges faced by healthcare workers during covid-19 pandemic*. https://doi.org/10.1136/bmj.m1211

Habibabadi, S. K., & Haghighi, P. D. (2019). Topic Modelling for Identification of Vaccine Reactions in Twitter. *ACM International Conference Proceeding Series*, 1–10. https://doi.org/10.1145/3290688.3290735

Haleem, A., Javaid, M., Vaishya, R., & Deshmukh, S. G. (2020). Areas of academic research with the impact of COVID-19. In *American Journal of Emergency Medicine* (Vol. 38, Issue 7, pp. 1524–1526). W.B. Saunders. https://doi.org/10.1016/j.ajem.2020.04.022

Hu, Z., Ge, Q., Li, S., Jin, L., & Xiong, M. (2020). *Artificial Intelligence Forecasting of Covid-19 in China*. http://arxiv.org/abs/2002.07112

Huo, X., & Qiu, Z. (2020). How does China's stock market react to the announcement of the COVID-19 pandemic lockdown? *Economic and Political Studies*, 1–26. https://doi.org/10.1080/20954816.2020.1780695

IATA. (2020). *IATA - Home*. https://www.iata.org/

Javaid, M., Haleem, A., Vaishya, R., Bahl, S., Suman, R., & Vaish, A. (2020). Industry 4.0 technologies and their applications in fighting COVID-19 pandemic. *Diabetes and Metabolic Syndrome: Clinical Research and Reviews*, *14*(4), 419–422. https://doi.org/10.1016/j.dsx.2020.04.032

Jiao, J., Duan, C., Xue, L., Liu, Y., Sun, W., & Xiang, Y. (2020). DNA nanoscaffold-based SARS-CoV-2 detection for COVID-19 diagnosis. *Biosensors and Bioelectronics*, *167*. https://doi.org/10.1016/j.bios.2020.112479

Jordan, M., Blei, D. M., Ng, A. Y., & Edu, J. B. (2003). Latent Dirichlet Allocation Sampling and Bayesian inference View project EM and optimization algorithms in statistical models View project Latent Dirichlet Allocation Michael I. Jordan. In *Journal of Machine Learning Research* (Vol. 3). https://www.researchgate.net/publication/221620547

Khanthavit, A. (2020). *World and National Stock Market Reactions to COVID-19*. https://doi.org/10.13140/RG.2.2.22792.57606

Lai, J., Ma, S., Wang, Y., Cai, Z., Hu, J., Wei, N., Wu, J., Du, H., Chen, T., Li, R., Tan, H., Kang, L., Yao, L., Huang, M., Wang, H., Wang, G., Liu, Z., & Hu, S. (2020). Factors Associated With Mental Health Outcomes Among Health Care Workers Exposed to Coronavirus Disease 2019. *JAMA Network Open*, *3*(3), e203976. https://doi.org/10.1001/jamanetworkopen.2020.3976

Li, H. (2020). Charting the Path to Purchase UsingTopic Models. *Journal of Marketing Research*, *57*(6), 1019–1036.

Li, T. M. H., & Leung, C. S. Y. (2020). Exploring student mental health and intention to use online counseling in Hong Kong during the COVID-19 pandemic. In *Psychiatry and Clinical Neurosciences*. Blackwell Publishing. https://doi.org/10.1111/pcn.13117

Li, X., Geng, M., Peng, Y., Meng, L., & Lu, S. (2020). Molecular immune pathogenesis and diagnosis of COVID-19. In *Journal of Pharmaceutical Analysis* (Vol. 10, Issue 2, pp. 102–108). Xi'an Jiaotong University. https://doi.org/10.1016/j.jpha.2020.03.001

Liu, C. (2020). Health information systems amid COVID-19 outbreak: Lessons from China. *Health Information Management Journal*. https://doi.org/10.1177/1833358320947557

Liu, Y., & Cheng, T. (2020). Understanding public transit patterns with open geodemographics to facilitate public transport planning. *Transportmetrica A: Transport Science*, *16*(1), 76–103. https://doi.org/10.1080/23249935.2018.1493549

Liu, Z. (2013). *High Performance Latent Dirichlet Allocation for Text Mining. September*.

Macit, A. M. D. (2020). *Türk Sivil Havacılık Sektöründe Covid-19 Pandemisinin Yönetimi*. https://www.researchgate.net/publication/341327367_Turk_Sivil_Havacilik_Sektorunde_Covid-19_Pandemisinin_Yonetimi

Mallet. (2020). *MALLET homepage*. http://mallet.cs.umass.edu/

Masada, T., Kiyasu, S., & Miyahara, S. (2008). Comparing LDA with pLSI as a dimensionality reduction method in document clustering. *LKR'08 Proceedings of the 3rd International Conference on Large-Scale Knowledge Resources: Construction and Application*, 13–26.

McCall, B. (2020). COVID-19 and artificial intelligence: protecting health-care workers and curbing the spread. *The Lancet Digital Health*, *2*(4), e166–e167. https://doi.org/10.1016/s2589-7500(20)30054-6

McKibbin, W. J., & Fernando, R. (2020). The Global Macroeconomic Impacts of COVID-19: Seven Scenarios. *SSRN Electronic Journal*. https://doi.org/10.2139/ssrn.3547729

Mori, K., Nakajima, H., & Hata, Y. (2020). Automated worker skill evaluation for improving productivity based on labeled LDA. *International Journal of Machine Learning and Cybernetics*.

OECD. (2020). *Tackling coronavirus (COVID-19) Contributing to a global effort*. https://www.oecd.org/coronavirus/en/#highlights

Özer, M. (2020). *COVİD-19 SALGINI SONRASI DÜNYADA EĞİTİM*. MEB. http://www.meb.gov.tr/covid-19-salgini-sonrasi-dunyada-egitim/haber/20936/tr

Paintsil, E. (2020). COVID-19 threatens health systems in sub-Saharan Africa: The eye of the crocodile. In *Journal of Clinical Investigation* (Vol. 130, Issue 6, pp. 2741–2744). American Society for Clinical Investigation. https://doi.org/10.1172/JCI138493

Pan, S. L., & Zhang, S. (2020). From fighting COVID-19 pandemic to tackling sustainable development goals: An opportunity for responsible information systems research. *International Journal of Information Management*, *55*(June), 102196. https://doi.org/10.1016/j.ijinfomgt.2020.102196

Reardon, T., Bellemare, M. F., & Zilberman, D. (2020). How COVID-19 may disrupt food supply chains in developing countries. *IFPRI Book Chapters*, 78–80. https://ideas.repec.org/h/fpr/ifpric/133821.html

Rizou, M., Galanakis, I. M., Aldawoud, T. M. S., & Galanakis, C. M. (2020). Safety of foods, food supply chain and environment within the COVID-19 pandemic. In *Trends in Food Science and Technology* (Vol. 102, pp. 293–299). Elsevier Ltd. https://doi.org/10.1016/j.tifs.2020.06.008

Sağlık Bakanlığı. (2020). *hayatevesığar*. https://hayatevesigar.saglik.gov.tr/hes.html

Sheikhzadeh, E., Eissa, S., Ismail, A., & Zourob, M. (2020). Diagnostic techniques for COVID-19 and new developments. In *Talanta* (Vol. 220). Elsevier B.V. https://doi.org/10.1016/j.talanta.2020.121392

Sutherland, I., Sim, Y., Lee, S. K., Byun, J., & Kiatkawsin, K. (2020). *Topic Modeling of Online Accommodation Reviews via Latent Dirichlet Allocation*.

Tang, Y. W., Schmitz, J. E., Persing, D. H., & Stratton, C. W. (2020). Laboratory diagnosis of COVID-19: Current issues and challenges. In *Journal of Clinical Microbiology* (Vol. 58, Issue 6). American Society for Microbiology. https://doi.org/10.1128/JCM.00512-20

Taylor, D. B. (2020). *A Timeline of the Coronavirus Pandemic*. The New York Times. https://www.nytimes.com/article/coronavirus-timeline.html

Teräs, M., Suoranta, J., Teräs, H., & Curcher, M. (2020). Post-Covid-19 Education and Education Technology 'Solutionism': a Seller's Market. *Postdigital Science and Education*, 1–16. https://doi.org/10.1007/s42438-020-00164-x

Tran, B. X., Ha, G. H., Nguyen, L. H., Vu, G. T., Hoang, M. T., Le, H. T., Latkin, C. A., Ho, C. S. H., & Ho, R. C. M. (2020). Studies of novel coronavirus disease 19 (Covid-19) pandemic: A global analysis of literature. *International Journal of Environmental Research and Public Health*, *17*(11), 1–20. https://doi.org/10.3390/ijerph17114095

Türker, G. Ö. (2020). How Covid-19 pandemic affects tourism sector? An evaluation from tourism academics perspective. *International Journal of Social Sciences and Education Research*, 207–224. https://doi.org/10.24289/ijsser.760790

UNESCO. (2020a). *290 million students out of school due to COVID-19: UNESCO releases first global numbers and mobilizes response*. https://en.unesco.org/news/290-million-students-out-school-due-covid-19-unesco-releases-first-global-numbers-and-mobilizes

UNESCO. (2020b). *School closures caused by Coronavirus (Covid-19)*. https://en.unesco.org/covid19/educationresponse

UNIDO. (2020). *Coronavirus: the economic impact – 10 July 2020 | UNIDO*. https://www.unido.org/stories/coronavirus-economic-impact-10-july-2020

UNWTO. (2020). *International Tourist Numbers Could Fall 60-80% in 2020, UNWTO Reports | UNWTO*. https://www.unwto.org/news/covid-19-international-tourist-numbers-could-fall-60-80-in-2020

Usman, M., Ali, Y., Riaz, A., Riaz, A., & Zubair, A. (2020). Economic perspective of coronavirus (COVID-19). In *Journal of Public Affairs*. John Wiley and Sons Ltd. https://doi.org/10.1002/pa.2252

Verma, S., & Gustafsson, A. (2020). Investigating the emerging COVID-19 research trends in the field of business and management: A bibliometric analysis approach. *Journal of Business Research 118*, *January*, 253–261.

Wang, C., NG, C., & Brook, R. (2020). *Response to COVID-19 in Taiwan*. https://doi.org/10.1001/jama.2020.3151

Whitelaw, S., Mamas, M. A., Topol, E., & Van Spall, H. G. C. (2020). Applications of digital technology in COVID-19 pandemic planning and response. *The Lancet Digital Health*, *2*(8), e435–e440. https://doi.org/10.1016/S2589-7500(20)30142-4

WHO. (2020a). *Archived: WHO Timeline - COVID-19*. https://www.who.int/news-room/detail/27-04-2020-who-timeline--covid-19

WHO. (2020b). *Coronavirus disease (COVID-19) Situation Report-203*.

WHO. (2020c). *R&D Blueprint and COVID-19*. https://www.who.int/teams/blueprint/covid-19

WHO | World Health Organization. (2020). https://www.who.int/

Xiang, Y. T., Li, W., Zhang, Q., Jin, Y., Rao, W. W., Zeng, L. N., Lok, G. K. I., Chow, I. H. I., Cheung, T., & Hall, B. J. (2020). Timely research papers about COVID-19 in China. In *The Lancet* (Vol. 395, Issue 10225, pp. 684–685). Lancet Publishing Group. https://doi.org/10.1016/S0140-6736(20)30375-5

Xue, J., Chen, J., Chen, C., Zheng, C., Li, S., & Zhu, T. (2020). Public discourse and sentiment during the COVID19 pandemic:Using Latent Dirichlet Allocation for topic modeling on Twitter. *PLOS ONE*, *15*(9).

Zhai, Y., & Du, X. (2020). Mental health care for international Chinese students affected by the COVID-19 outbreak. In *The Lancet Psychiatry* (Vol. 7, Issue 4, p. e22). Elsevier Ltd. https://doi.org/10.1016/S2215-0366(20)30089-4

Zhang, D., Hu, M., & Ji, Q. (2020). Financial markets under the global pandemic of COVID-19. *Finance Research Letters*, *36*, 101528. https://doi.org/10.1016/j.frl.2020.101528

AGILE LEARNING LOOPS – COMBINING AGILE APPROACHES IN HIGHER EDUCATION PROGRAMS

Karsten Böhm and Yvonne Unnold
FH Kufstein Tirol – University of Applied Sciences
Andreas-Hofer-Str.7, A-6330 Kufstein, Austria

ABSTRACT

Learning processes within higher education programs increasingly focus on applying concepts rather than just facilitating the comprehension of concepts studied. Some of the curricular elements commonly used can be classified as project-based exploratory learning activities that usually pose unique challenges for students. Examples of such activities include theses or individual projects. To be successful in these tasks, students require more agility and flexibility in designing, managing and implementing their project. This contribution addresses those requirements by introducing introduces a concept that adopts the SCRUM methodology to facilitate project-based learning processes in higher education. It discusses application scenarios and benefits of a more iterative and agile approach called *Agile Learning Loops (ALL)*, describes the new methodology in detail and addresses its application potential.

KEYWORDS

SCRUM, Learning Framework, Project-Based Learning, Agile Learning, Learning Loops

1. INTRODUCTION

Higher education should enable students to build advanced scientific and abstract thinking skills for problem-solving that they can apply in their professional career after their studies in their respective subjects. Thus, courses should not only provide an opportunity for the acquisition of knowledge. It is imperative that they train students to apply this knowledge in chalenging and real-worldscontexts. Project-Based Learning (PBL) (Chen and Yang, 2019) provides valuable learning opportunities to apply their knowledge, including previously acquired knowledge or new insights that students discover as part of the project. Generally, PBL activities are student-driven and involve limited supervision or guidance by lecturers. The open character of PBL poses a particular challenge for students and facilitators because much flexibility is required to reach curricula learning outcomes.

Learning Loops (Kolb, 2014) has been distinguished in didactic literature as an effective way to deepen understanding and enhance skills via iterations that allow opportunities to learn from mistakes and incorporate insights gained through feedback loops (e.g., iteration). However, due to the time and resource constraints in many curricula, the provision of opportunities for circular learning is not always feasible.

In the realm of computer sciences, SCRUM (Schwaber, 2007; Srivastava, Bhardwaj and Saraswat, 2017) has been established as a methodology to develop software systems in an agile way, using iteration in individual development cycles to improve the process and to react to changed environmental conditions or project goals. However, SCRUM methodology can also enable the implementation of learning loops for specific projects. The present study's core goal is to demonstrate the applicability of the SCRUM methodology for teaching purposes in higher education subjects that corporate PBL.

Surprisingly, research published on this topic is limited. There are a few papers on the use of SCRUM for educational purposes in schools (i.e., Royle and Nikolic, 2016). In the realm of e-learning, SCRUM has been used to manage the process of designing course content (Supangat *et al.*, 2019; Vogelzang, Admiraal and Driel, 2019). However, to the authors best knowledge, SCRUM has not yet been used for an educational design in the area of higher education.

The paper is organised as follows: Section 2 describes the concept of Agile Learning Loops (ALL) as a learning design framework with references to loop-style learning models and presents the ALL process, including associate roles and activities. Section 3 elaborates on the current application of ALL in the context of a higher education program, and section 4 outlines the present-day IT-tools supporting the implementation of ALL. Finally, section 5 concludes the paper with a summary and an outlook on planned next steps.

2. THE CONCEPT OF AGILE LEARNING LOOPS

The concept of *Agile Learning Loops* (ALL) focuses on a methodological transfer of the SCRUM methodology (Schwaber, 2007) and of the organisational concepts of loop-oriented learning models, such as Single-, Double- and Triple-Loop-Learning (Argyris and Schön, 1978), as an organisational design framework into the context of a learning situation in higher education, and, thus, into a *learning design framework for PBL*. The intention of this transfer is to provide an agile supporting framework for student-oriented tasks that (a) helps the learner structure the learning process while maintaining maximal flexibility for the project and (b) affords coaching opportunities for the lecturer to assist the student throughout the project with minimal interference in the learning process.

The aspects that are taken into account for this transfer include a) the roles, b) the activities, and c) the process defined in SCRUM that need to be transferred in a meaningful way to the ALL methodology.

2.1 Loop Style Learning Models

The research on Loop Style Learning Models refers back to (Argyris and Schön, 1978), who primarily studied organisational learning processes and developed several loop learning models, shown in figure 1, namely Single-Loop-Learning (SLL), Double-Loop-Learning (DLL), and Triple Loop Learning (TLL). Applications of these learning models are also relevant for higher education processes and can be applied to our framework.

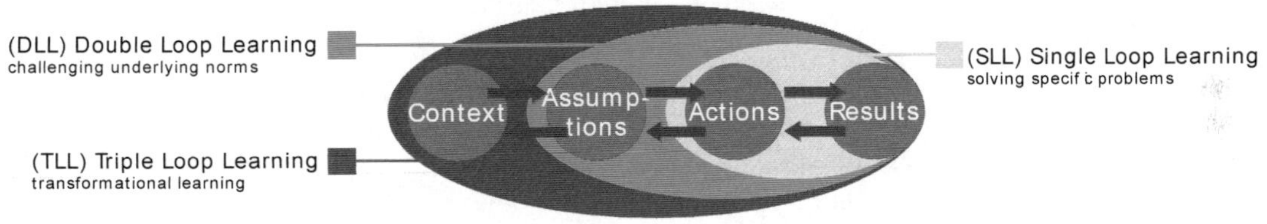

Figure 1. Association of the different Loop Learning Methods with increasing reflection and learning impact process per (Argyris and Schön, 1978)

SLL refers to solving a specific problem and is usually the primary tool for building necessary problem-solving skills in the first phases of higher education programs (e.g., by solving exercises). It represents a simple control loop that provides a stimulus and a response which generates a positive effect when the right solution is found. Learning also occurs when mistakes are identified on a repetitive execution of this loop ("trial and error"). Formerly, students were asked to find solutions on problems that are posed by the professors and thus finding the right solution is the standard mode for most students. This type of learning remains on the level of solving a specific problem and does not challenge the underlying assumptions or norms. However, developing critical thinking skills ("asking why" attitude) is one of the core features of a higher education program and reflected in DLL, which requires students to solve problems, question underlying norms, and identify root causes. Students often struggle when transitioning from SLL to DLL because the latter requires solving more complex scientific tasks. Support methodologies, like ALL, can assist students with this transition.

The optimal learning methodology in higher education is Triple Loop Learning (TLL), which can be described as transformational learning. TLL trains students to take the underlying context into account and enables them to derive universal patterns that are valid independently of the specific application context – leading to a transformational change in the learner.

2.2 The Agile Learning Loop (ALL) Process

The general SCRUM process is illustrated in figure 2 below. It already includes some slight adaptations to the ALL methodology. The iterative nature of the process is organised into so-called sprints, each of which addresses a part of the possible product features. Sprints have a typical duration of about 2-3 weeks and reflect the stakeholders' project plan and development team's timeline of task sequence and completion. When planing the project, tasks are divided into subtasks, organised via the Product Backlog, and assigned a sprint phase based on relevance and complexity. The Sprint Backlog contains all planned activities for each consecutive sprint. During a sprint, the development team holds brief daily meetings to plan the day's work (Daily Scrum) and identify problems (impediments) that may affect the timely completion of tasks. The latter is usually depicted in Kanban-style planning boards and progress charts. This process helps coordinate the team and provides transparency among all stakeholders. Upon completion of a sprint, the team evaluates the results and reflects on the lessons learned (a process called 'retrospective'). Then the cycle starts again. Retrospectives provide an opportunity to evaluate the development process, the (current) product features, and the productivity of the involved team members. Moreover, they enable the team to improve the mentioned aspects by identifying and removing impediments from the process.

The ALL framework adopts most SCRUM concepts and integrates them into the context of a learning framework. The product backlog can be adopted in a very similar way: the artefact of a product backlog helps the learner organise and document the project tasks and determine the tasks' level of usefulness (relevance) and difficulty in the planning phase. For the lecturer, this opens up another opportunity for coaching and to give guidance on product backlog items. In contrast to other learning frameworks, the tasks' detailed documentation makes the process much more transparent and specific for all stakeholders (student, supervisors, and eventually peers).

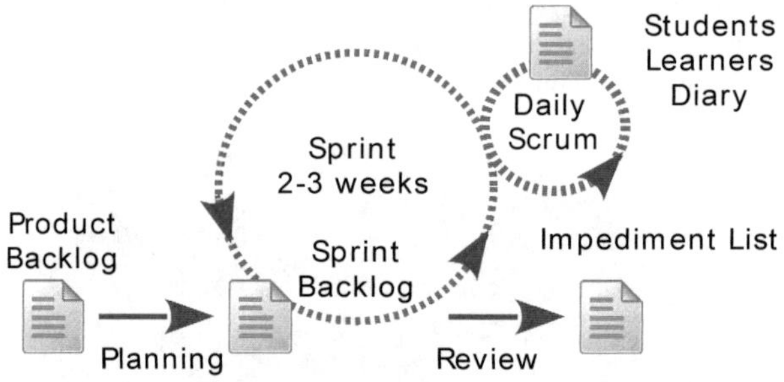

Figure 2. Illustration of a Sprint within a SCRUM process with some adaptions to the ALL methodology

The user stories (the term used for functional requirement in SCRUM) in the backlog describe the specific learning outcomes from the learners' perspective. The task of articulating their learning outcomes represents the students' first step towards grasping the complexity of the problem; simultaneously, this provides a coaching possibility for the lecturer.

Students complete the planned tasks during a sprint and reflect daily on their progress in their learners' diary. This effort, which is usually executed by the development team, might initially appear redundant; however, it serves two purposes in ALL methodology. (1) It encourages students to reflect on achievements and upcoming tasks. When articulated in this way, project problems and overall progress become explicit (e.g., adding problems to the impediment log) and can more easily be discussed with the lecturer. Furthermore, (2) it helps students plan a clear daily timeline for their tasks. This is important, as daily timelines help students stay on task when completing complex projects (such as a thesis).

After a sprint, students and lecturers hold a sprint review. They reflect on the performance of the last sprint, evaluate their progress in the sprint backlog and the impediment list. This retrospective phase is a prime opportunity for coaching, as it highlights deficits and unresolved questions. Moreover, it helps improve student performance on the next iteration (sprint). Without the backlog and impediment list, effective coaching poses a challenge because lecturers are not involved in the sprint execution. Without ALL, the situation lacks the transparency required for thorough analysis. In contrast, with ALL methodology, progress is much more visible due to the framework structure. With every iteration, it becomes easier to have an open reflection because the benefit becomes more obvious for the students. This also helps improve the relationship between the students and their lecturer, as students recognise that the lecturer is supporting rather than judging their work's quality and progress. Well-executed retrospectives improve team performance and create trust among the group (Paasivaara *et al.*, 2013), (McHugh, Conboy and Lang, 2012).

An important aspect for the retrospective is a proper "Definition of Done" (DoD) within the ALL methodology. It is a good way of discussing an outcome in terms of its relation to scientific work (rigour and relevance). Moreover, it is much more useful from a didactic point of view because discussing important aspects of scientific work is not abstract for students when it is closely related to their specific project or task. This makes for a good learning opportunity. Table 1 summarises and compares the most relevant process artefacts in SCRUM and ALL.

Table 1. Comparison of the most important process artefacts in SCRUM and ALL

Artefact	SCRUM Methodology	ALL Methodology
Product Backlog	Planned product features	Planned project activities
Sprint Backlog	Features developed in the current sprint	Activities tackled in the current sprint
Impediment List	List of project impediments for the team	List of project impediments for the student
Daily Scrum	Daily team meeting for coordination	Individual reflection of the student on progress
Learners' Diary	(n/a)	Brief documentation of Daily Scrum outcomes

2.3 Roles in the ALL Methodology

Multiple roles must be assigned to implement SCRUM effectively, execute the overall process, and meet specific sub-tasks and associated goals. While one role focuses on the capability to react to unprecedented changes and unexpected challenges, another focuses on the proper application of SCRUM methodology. SCRUM methodology is designed to be implemented without any changes or adaptations. However, in the context of ALL methodology, some adaptations or interpretations are necessary.

The primary roles in SCRUM include the Scrum Master (SM), the Product Owner (PO), and the Development Team (DEV). Table 2 provides a brief definition of these roles in SCRUM and ALL methodologies.

Table 2. Comparison of the most important process aspects in SCRUM and ALL

Role	SCRUM Methodology	ALL Methodology
SCRUM Master (SM)	A facilitator for the process that supports the SCRUM process and removes impediments for the team	A supervisor (lecturer) who guides students in the agile process and sprints to help them achieve their planned outcomes
Product Owner (PO)	The stakeholder that is responsible for the quality and functional requirements of the final product and an expert in the domain that the product is designed for	A 'shared role' between student and supervisor (lecturer) with both being accountable for different aspects of the final result
Development Team (DEV)	A group of developers that carries out the product development tasks in an iterative and agile development process	The role of the lead student. Potentially, peers may be involved at given moments; however, this role is not designed to be carried out by a team.

In a higher education context, students assume two roles: the role of the product owner and the role of the developer[1]. This is because the student is responsible for implementing the project as well as for the final result. For this reason, the DEV role is usually not designed as a team role in ALL methodology. Instead, it is a role to be carried out by a single student who may be supported in this role through collaboration by peers involved in the project or the project review.

1 We are using the role definition 'developer' here as it is defined that way in SCRUM. However, ALL is not restricted to software developing projects, thus the developer-role can be understood as the role the builder or creator of the various project artefacts.

In contrast, the lecturer (supervisor) primarily assumes the role of Scrum Master (SM), who is responsible for supporting the overall process and serves as a liaison for other main stakeholders involved (e.g., an external project sponsor). When applying ALL methodology, the SM's role is not limited to ensuring the application of the methodology. Here, the role of SM also includes counselling and coaching students in the field of scientific work. Moreover, the lecturer defines some of the formal requirements (e.g., scientific rigour). Therefore, the PO's role is shared to some extent. In SCRUM, this could pose a potential source of conflict as roles are usually not split in this methodology. However, when applying ALL, the shared role allocation can serve as a specific coaching opportunity to improve the project result.

2.4 Activities and Artifacts in the ALL Process

Some activities and artefacts are central to SCRUM methodology and are used to support teams in executing their development processes in an agile and efficient way. In order to integrate SCRUM activities and artefacts with the ALL methodology for application in higher education, some important aspects need to be adapted to suit the new context. Table 3 articulates the changes necessary.

Table 3. Adaptation of typical SCRUM activities & artefacts to the ALL Methodology

Artefact	Description in SCRUM	Adaptation for use in ALL
Product Increment	The development progress between different sprints	Used to measure the progress in the project (reflection on learnings)
Velocity	The amount of functional requirements implemented in comparison to previous sprints, measured with Story Points; represents the development speed of the team over time	Only useful if stories are equipped with story points, and the estimations are correct; as the DEV is a person and the project objective often of exploratory nature, velocity will vary significantly, and estimations may be more or less correct
Story Point Estimation	A measurement to express the usefulness and the complexity of a functional requirement described in a user story	Used to quantify the complexity of the tasks in the planning and the retrospective phases; the supervisor could provide a usefulness estimation
Definition of Done	An agreement among the team on the properties that an implementation of a functional requirement must meet to be considered complete	In an academic context, a project-specific definition of rigour and relevance may be a variable used to define the outcomes that must be achieved in order for a task to be considered done
Code Review	Quality assessment of the resulting code via peer review of individual segments	As the DEV is not a team effort, this aspect is of little importance for ALL; might be used for specific feedbacks
Burndown Chart	A chart listing the number of open tasks in the backlogs over time, presenting a graphic depiction of the development speed	Could be used in later stages of ALL with projects involving a large number of stories and when story points are used
Kanban-Board	A table listing the different activities in a given sprint, reflecting their current status; a primary method used to coordinate DEV	Used to facilitate reflection and coaching; serves to make the student-centric process (more) transparent and to provide coaching opportunities for the supervisor.
Backlog Grooming	The process of reviewing the backlogs for functional requirements that are no longer relevant and can be removed; carried out by the PO	Used as a part of the retrospective; enables the supervisor to evaluate and help to adjust the project focus
Story Writing Workshop	An activity to formalise the definition of work done in the project; usually a team effort at the commencement of the project or sprint	Used to help students set up their project and get started (assist in overcoming potential writers' block)

User Story	A description in layman's terms of the functional requirements so that these can be understood by the domain expert (PO) as well as the team (DEV)	Used to define project tasks and outcomes; can also be used to coach and help improve individual stories
Epic	An aggregation of different user stories that have a close relation to each other or represent a more abstract description that is not (yet) specific enough to be implemented	Used for pre-structured individual projects, such as a final thesis, to provide an initial and abstract structure for the components that should be part of the final product

3. APPLICATION OF ALL METHODOLOGY

The ALL methodology has shown to be applicable across the curriculum at the author's university as many lecturers and courses now regularly integrate PBL-oriented teaching and learning. This trend is likely to grow even further, given the increased focus on applied learning in our education programs across all subjects and domains.

This study proposes that the new methodology be used for two primary purposes: (1) to facilitate the supervision of final thesis projects (both in the Bachelor's and Master's programs), in which all students are assigned a mentor for their specific topic, and (2) to guide Individual Projects (IP) associated with a Bachelor's program.

An IP is a course that allows students to work individually on a wide range of topics while coached by degree program faculty. In contrast to final thesis projects, IPs are introduced at the commencement of the program and are designed to help students (a) build a scientific skillset and (b) provide an opportunity to in the program to "fail without failing"[2]. Both settings require a learning process tailored to students learning needs and progress. Thus, the support of the lecturer needs to respond to students' individual needs and requires an agile teaching approach.

The ALL method provides a specific framework for the required coaching processes and retains flexibility for addressing individual needs. Figure 3 illustrates the application of ALL over the course of one semester (roughly three months). The four cycles planned for the individual projects are designed for a duration of approx. three weeks each.

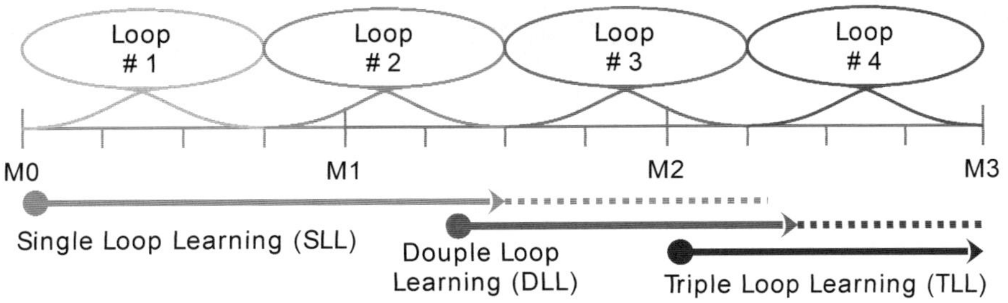

Figure 3. Relationship between the loops within a semester cycle and the distinct types of loop learning occuring over time

In each cycle (or loop), students resolve individual tasks within the project under faculty supervision. Initially, loops will be primarily problem-focused and constitute SLLs. Using ALL methodology, a transition to DLL and finally TLL will occur over the course of the project.

2 Usually, courses and assessments are designed with the requirement to reach a successful result in a first attempt. Such an expectation tends to discourage students risk-taking. However, when students are allowed to make and reflect on errors and mistaken initial approaches these can constitute optimal situations for successful and sustainable learning. Thus it is important that IPs provide a space for trial and error, reflection and assessment.

4. IT-TOOLS TO SUPPORT ALL METHODOLOGY

For the implementation of ALL methodology, tools designed to support the SCRUM process can be used to help organise and facilitate the ALL process. Commercial tools, such as JIRA[3] from Atlassian, may be used for this purpose (Li, 2018); however, the author decided to use Redmine[4] (Lesyuk, 2016) with the Agile Plugin and the Boostmine Theme[5]. The reason for this tool choice is two-fold. For one, Redmine is an extensible and stable open-source software system; it is hence user-friendly and free of charge in terms of license fees. Secondly, students in computer sciences are generally familiar with the software from other contexts of their studies, which reduces their learning curve.

Redmine applies the concept of ticket-based activities assigned to members of the project team. The Agile Plugin implements a Kanban-style depiction of the different tickets based on status. The tool can be easily adapted to different needs, e.g. the activity status, the implicit workflows that result from activites status transitions, or the definition of custom attributes. Therefore, it can be effortlessly configured to meet the needs of ALL methodology. To configure the tool for use with ALL, two roles must be defined (Student and Supervisor). Moreover, the status of activities should include "New-SprintBacklog", "New-ProjectBacklog", "InProgress", "Feedback" and "Done". Figure 4 provides an interactive Kanban chart that displays the current activities together with their current status and the corresponding assignee.

Another important aspect of ALL methodology is a way to take notes on the individual project without adhering to a formal structure. The note-taking function is needed for two purposes: collecting random ideas and maintaining the research diary. 'Random ideas' are notes on thoughts that might not fit into a specific project activity or do not serve a specific purpose. Usually, they are written down in an ordinary notebook; however, the Redmine system provides the possibility to use the included Wiki-system for a quick and low-tech way of taking these notes.

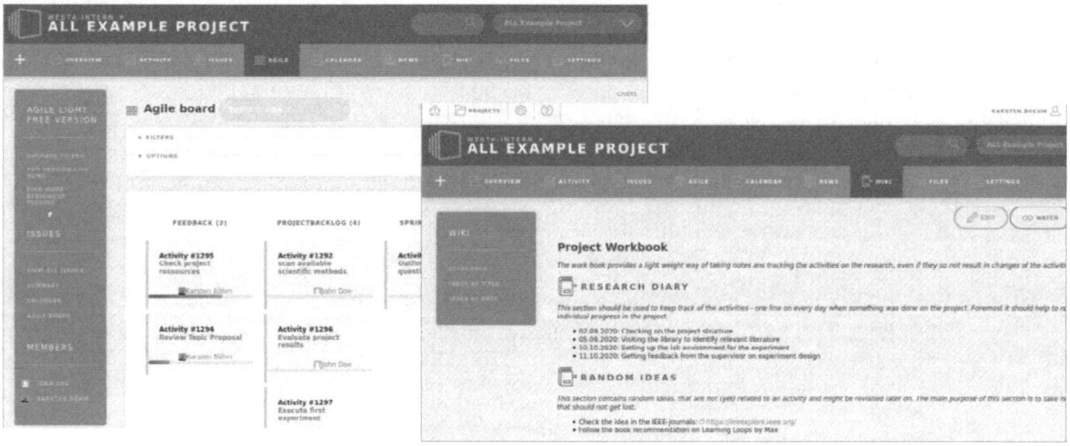

Figure 4. Kaban Board (left) to display and manage active tasks together with their status and Workbook for ALL (right) based on the existing Wiki-functionality in Redmine

The system's note-taking function allows students to link random ideas to other parts of the project (e.g. activities or documents). Figure 4 shows an example of such a wiki entry. The other crucial note-taking purpose of the project workbook is the Research Diary, which student keep to report their daily progress via a single-line entry. This daily routine provides an opportunity for students to reflect on the time spent on the project and the specific progress achieved. Moreover, these entries capture the project process and can be helpful when coaching or addressing (unexpected) challenges during the project.

3 The JIRA product is described here: https://www.atlassian.com/de/software/jira/scrum-boards

4 More information on RedMine can be found here: https://www.redmine.org/

5 More on the Agile Plugin can be found here: https://www.redmineup.com/pages/plugins/agile and the used theme is documented here: https//bestredminetheme.com/boostmine/

5. SUMMARY

This study outlines the methodology of Agile Learning Loops (ALL), a learning design framework inspired by the SCRUM methodology, and shows how it can be applied to PBL-oriented learning situations in higher education settings. Through minor modification and adaptation, SCRUM features can be integrated into ALL to help students transition between the three Loop Learning Methods, from SLL to DLL and then to TLL. Moreover, this approach strengthens students' problem solving and critical thinking skillsets and fosters appropriate time and task management skills. Finally, this unique integration of methodologies enables lecturers to enhance their mentorship in PBL, gives students relevant experience in project management, and utilises tools established and proven effective in their career field.

The respective process, activities and roles of the methodology in a Higher Education setting have been described and the application scenario and the tooling support have been outlined. The formal evaluation of this learning design framework will be subject to further research, but first experiences from the ongoing application of ALL will be reported at the conference.

REFERENCES

Argyris, C. and Schön, D. A. (1978) *Organizational Learning: A Theory of Action Perspective*. Addison-Wesley Publishing Company.

Chen, C.-H. and Yang, Y.-C. (2019) 'Revisiting the effects of project-based learning on students' academic achievement: A meta-analysis investigating moderators', *Educational Research Review*, 26, pp. 71–81. doi: 10.1016/j.edurev.2018.11.001.

Kolb, D. A. (2014) *Experiential Learning: Experience as the Source of Learning and Development*. FT Press.

Lesyuk, A. (2016) *Mastering Redmine*. Packt Publishing Ltd.

Li, P. (2018) *Jira Software Essentials: Plan, track, and release great applications with Jira Software, 2nd Edition*. Packt Publishing Ltd.

McHugh, O., Conboy, K. and Lang, M. (2012) 'Agile Practices: The Impact on Trust in Software Project Teams', *IEEE Software*, 29(3), pp. 71–76. doi: 10.1109/MS.2011.118.

Royle, K. and Nikolic, J. (2016) 'A modern mixture, agency, capability, technology and "scrum": agile work practices for learning and teaching in schools', *3*. doi: 10.30845/jesp.

Paasivaara, M. *et al.* (2013) 'Teaching students global software engineering skills using distributed Scrum', in *2013 35th International Conference on Software Engineering (ICSE). 2013 35th International Conference on Software Engineering (ICSE)*, pp. 1128–1137. doi: 10.1109/ICSE.2013.6606664.Schwaber, K. (2007) *The Enterprise and Scrum*. Microsoft Press.

Srivastava, A., Bhardwaj, S. and Saraswat, S. (2017) 'SCRUM model for agile methodology', in *2017 International Conference on Computing, Communication and Automation (ICCCA). 2017 International Conference on Computing, Communication and Automation (ICCCA)*, pp. 864–869. doi: 10.1109/CCAA.2017.8229928.

Supangat, S. *et al.* (2019) 'E-Learning Development as Interactive System with Scrum Methodology', in. *2nd International Conference on Vocational Innovation and Applied Sciences 2019*, Wyndham Hotel, Surabaya. Available at: http://icvias.com/ (Accessed: 24 October 2020).

Vogelzang, J., Admiraal, W. F. and Driel, J. H. van (2019) 'Scrum Methodology as an Effective Scaffold to Promote Students' Learning and Motivation in Context-based Secondary Chemistry Education', *Eurasia Journal of Mathematics, Science and Technology Education*, 15(12), p. em1783. doi: 10.29333/ejmste/109941.

STRUCTURING A COMPETENCY REPOSITORY - APPLICATION TO THE DOMAIN OF INFORMATION SYSTEMS

Ahmed Bounekkar[1], Corine Cauvet[2], Cyrille Desmoulins[3], Daniel Marquie[4], Michel Schneider[5], Carine Souveyet[6] and Cédric Teyssie[4]

[1]*Université de Lyon, France*
[2]*Université d'Aix-Marseille, France*
[3]*Université Grenoble Alpes, CNRS, Grenoble INP, France*
[4]*Université de Toulouse, France*
[5]*Université de Clermont Auvergne, France*
[6]*Université de Paris 1 Panthéon Sorbonne, France*

ABSTRACT

In this paper, we propose a method for structuring a competency repository based on 5 principles. Two of them consist in using a composition relation to define competencies at several levels of abstraction and a prerequisite relation to establish prerequisites between competencies. To illustrate the contributions of these principles, an application in the domain of information systems design and implementation is fully developed. This application is based on the discussions that were carried out within the "Competency Working Group" of the French network of MIAGE (Méthodes Informatiques Appliquées à la Gestion des Entreprises) Masters and within the framework of the IDEFI-N OPENMIAGE project funded by the French ANR (Agence Nationale de la Recherche). The proposed repository, in addition to a new structure, incorporates new competencies compared to existing repositories, in particular with regard to strategic management of the IS, development techniques, interpersonal competencies, prerequisites coming from basic disciplines. This repository aims primarily to help the organization of academic and professional training and to allow the assessment of personal skills.

KEYWORDS

Competency, Repository, Composition Relationship, Prerequisite Relationship, Information System, Learning Outcome

1. INTRODUCTION

The usefulness of a competency-based approach is now well recognized both in the professional world to characterize activities and help recruiting, and in the academic world to characterize educational objectives and help organizing training. The term competency refers to a complex concept covering different points of view and whose precise definition remains controversial. Recall that the most common acceptance distinguishes three inseparable components in a competency: knowledge, know-how, interpersonal competency. Furthermore, a competency can only be understood in relation to the context in which it is considered. In the professional world, it is know-how and interpersonal competencies that are highlighted while academics focus primarily on knowledge and reasoning.

Competency repositories have been developed in various fields. A repository can be structured in various ways. A structure can be characterized by three main criteria: i) the way in which competencies are divided into groups and possibly sub-groups; ii) the way in which the links between competencies are expressed within a group or between groups; iii) the level of detail with which competencies are expressed. It is clear that the more detailed the competencies are, the greater the volume of specifications is and the greater the need for adequate structuring is.

The structuring directly impacts the ease of use of the repository. Several types of users are concerned (repository designer, human resources manager, recruiter, teacher and trainer, student and listener) and their needs are different. But the ease of locating a competency in the repository and positioning it in relation to close competencies or prerequisites interests all users.

Our objective in this paper is to show how the use of several principles can help improve the structuring of a competency repository and consequently facilitate its use. More specifically, we want to facilitate the following activities: searching for a competency in the repository, inserting a new competency, developing initial and vocational training, developing competencies assessments, searching for training to meet a learning objective.

We first establish a state of the art to identify different forms for structuring a competency repository. We then explain our five principles and discuss their impact on structuring. We then apply these principles to structure a competency repository in the domain of information systems design and implementation. The starting point of this application is the MIAGE repository, developed by the "competency working group" of the MIAGE Masters network. We suggest another structuring of this repository and we show how useful extensions can be inserted.

2. STATE OF THE ART

We first study the structuring of three competency repositories in the field of information systems. However, competencies are generally derived from typical activities of the domain and it is useful to also focus on the structuring of trade repositories. Finally, we mention some works that have addressed the study of relationships between competencies.

Competency repositories in the IS domain

We analyse hereafter three competency repositories: the e-CF (European e-Competence Framework) (e-CF, 2019), the MSIS (Master of Science Information Systems) (Topi, 2016), and the SFIA (Sfia, 2018).

The e-CF repository has been developed by the CEN (European Committee for Standardization). It consists of 40 competencies grouped into 5 main types of activities (Plan, Develop, Use, Facilitate, Manage). Each competency is defined globally by general activities denominated through action verbs. Five competency levels are considered. Each competency is associated with examples of know-how and knowledge. The e-CF does not include any explicit interpersonal competencies. It has a fairly general aim. It can be used both to characterize business activities and training objectives.

The MSIS repository, which is more precisely titled "Global Competency Model for Graduate Degree Programs in Information Systems", was developed under the aegis of the Association for Information Systems (AIS) and the Association for Computing Machinery (ACM). It was specifically designed for a Master degree in information systems. It covers the topics of information technology and information systems management. It is divided into five main sectors: Pre-Master Competencies; Information Systems Competencies; Domain Competencies such as management, law, health; Specialized Competencies and Individual Foundational Competencies. The Information Systems Competencies sector is itself divided into nine areas, one relating to ethics and sustainability issues and another relating to innovation and entrepreneurship. In each of these areas, competencies are specified at two levels of abstraction: the first level for categories and the second level for examples. Each of these levels is described with sentences using action verbs (in the infinitive for categories, in the present imperative for examples) and represent an activity.

The SFIA repository, in version 7, focuses on information and communication technologies, digital transformations and software engineering. It describes 95 professional competencies, which are organized into 6 categories and 17 sub-categories. Each competency is defined in the form of responsibility levels (up to seven levels are possible). These levels are characterized by five attributes (Autonomy, Influence, Complexity, Knowledge and Business Competencies).

We can see that the organization of these three repositories is presented in an ad-hoc hierarchical form. We can consider that this hierarchy implicitly underlies a composition.

The "Competency Working Group" of the French MIAGE network has also elaborated a version V0 for a competency repository in the domain of information systems. Its objective is to offer a competencies booklet to streamline the development of training. This booklet has also an ad-hoc hierarchical organization. It is in the form of teaching topics (TT) which are organized into 6 areas. Each topic is divided into LU (Learning Unit) and each LU is characterized by a set of ELO (Expected Learning Outcomes). An ELO specifies the objectives to be achieved through action verbs using the BLOOM classification (Bloom, 1956; Churches, 2008). ELO are then distributed according to a three-level classification. Each MIAGE Master training can be positioned in relation to this booklet to identify any adaptation to be made in order to meet the trade needs.

Trade repositories in the IS domain

Many organizations have developed repositories to describe the objectives of trades related to information systems and the corresponding activities. At the European level, CEN has proposed a repository for trades and more recently a repository for roles (Cen, 2018). A role is a coherent set of activities. A role can be part of a trade. In France, the CIGREF repository (Cigref, 2018) is the best known and most often referenced. Other French organizations have also published professional repositories in the information systems domain, notably the OPIIEC (Opiiec, 2018) and the ANAP (Anap, 2020). The ANAP repository is targeted at health information systems. All these repositories have roughly the same sections for each profession: mission, typical activities, expected competencies, required training, deliverables and potential developments.

These repositories organize trades into families. Thus, the CEN repository is organized into 7 families and that of CIGREF into 9 families. In both cases, these families correspond roughly to a breakdown of activities into major processes. This type of organization can be a way to organize a competency repository.

The O*NET database (O*NET On Line, 2020) is an important initiative that brings together more than 1,000 trades covering the entire US economy. For each trade, it provides information on the following attributes: Tasks, Technology competencies, Knowledge, Competencies, Abilities, Work activities, Detailed work activities, Work context, Job zone, Education. ICT and information systems professions are well represented.

Competency repositories in other domains

Competency repositories have been proposed in many domains. Here are references to some of them: (Embo & all, 2015; Lundqvist & all, 2008; Sastre-Fullana & all, 2014; Vandeweerd & all, 2014; Whitehead & Kuper, 2015). In a same domain, particularly in the medical domain, propositions can be multiple, overlapping, and heterogeneous. The idea of reconciling points of view is now often expressed.

Conceptual models of competencies relationships

Several works have been interested in the conceptual modeling of competencies with various objectives. For example, in (Schmidt & Kunzmann, 2006) and (Paquette, 2006), ontologies are proposed, one for human resource management and the other to support e-learning systems. Relationships between competencies have been highlighted, particularly prerequisite, composition and subsumption relationships.

Either composition or subsumption relationships can be useful for organizing a competency repository by showing competencies at multiple levels of abstraction in hierarchical form.

We propose to use the composition relation to remain consistent with the implicit structuring of existing repositories in the IS domain. The novelty we introduce is that all hierarchical levels are expressed in a uniform way. We associate it with the prerequisite relationship. These two relationships constitute two of the principles of our proposal which also includes three other principles. We explain these five principles in the next section.

3. STRUCTURING PRINCIPLES

In this section, we present the five principles we propose for structuring a competency repository.

Principle 1: Identification of competencies from trade activities

An activity in a trade implies a competency for its good realization. This competency must then be characterized. It is generally a know-how. It can also be knowledge or interpersonal competencies. The context can be specified if necessary. It is important to note that, from the same activity, one or more know-how, knowledge and interpersonal competencies can be extracted simultaneously. It depends on the context in which this activity is expressed. Consider, for example, the "Analysing Needs" activity that can be found in the description of the business analyst job. This sentence induces a know-how which is associated with knowledge (knows the procedures to analyze needs, knows the different types of needs) and interpersonal competencies (has the qualities to dialogue with users, to lead a meeting, to write a report). The attitude of analyzing business activities to elicit competencies is natural and therefore general. The main problem is to select and organize them. Principles 2 to 5 defined below contribute to this essential task.

Principle 2: Hierarchical organization by a composition relationship

We suggest using the composition relationship to organize competencies at different levels of abstraction. The semantic interpretation of a composite competency is then obtained from its component competencies.

This relationship induces a hierarchy insofar as a component competency can itself be the subject of a composition. However, we impose a weak unshared composition to mean that the deletion of a composite does not entail that of its components and that a component is linked to only one composite. We can then consider that this relation introduces a kind of semantic map.

We propose a hierarchical organization on four levels: general, main, specific, elementary.

The general level corresponds to very broad competencies for the domain (this level, for example, correspond to the main types of activity for the e-CF repository). The main level corresponds to the major competencies of the repository (this level could for example correspond to the 40 competencies of the e-CF repository). The specific level corresponds to an interpretation of the main level. The elementary level corresponds to the lowest level. The word elementary is used here to mean that it is no longer useful to decompose again. We will see that a specification at the elementary level contains all the ingredients to characterize the underlying learnings and their assessments.

The general, main and elementary levels are mandatory. The specific level is optional. Indeed, in some cases, the number of elementary competencies for a main competency may not be very large and the introduction of specific competencies is not necessary for the interpretation of the main competency.

This composition relationship and the resulting hierarchical organization are important for assessing the achievement of objectives. At the elementary level, the specification must make it possible to deduce unequivocally the test or tests to be performed (with the learner or with a job candidate) to assess the satisfaction of the competency.

Principle 3: Expression of the ability level by the use of action verbs respecting the BLOOM classification

The notion of LO (Learning Outcome) or ELO (Expected Learning Outcome) has been widely explored to describe training objectives, competencies and results. Universities, especially North American universities, have become accustomed to characterizing their training by LO which can be placed at the level of a course or at the level of a module. The ACM also defines its curricula using LO (Acm, 2016).

An effective solution for specifying LO is to use the classification of BLOOM and its associated action verbs (Bloom, 1956; Churches, 2008). Recall that the original BLOOM classification distinguishes six cognitive levels ranging from memorization to synthesis. This initial classification was the subject of several variants. Various studies have worked on how to express LO from action verbs corresponding to the BLOOM classification (Kennedy, 2006; Oster & Tiu, 2008). A LO normally includes the following elements: an action verb, the object and conditions of this action, an element to allow the assessment of the ability to perform this action.

With action verbs respecting the BLOOM classification, we can express levels of ability to be achieved for know-how, knowledge and interpersonal competencies. Here are some examples:

- "Collecting the needs": know-how at ability level 3, assessed through observations in real or simulated conditions;
- "Describing the different types of needs": knowledge at ability level 1, assessed by oral or written tests;
- "Communicating in a professional environment": interpersonal competency at ability level 3, assessed through observations in real or simulated conditions.

In the three cases, the context is implicitly the company information system and the parties concerned are the users of the system.

We propose to extend the use of action verbs respecting the BLOOM classification to characterize the competencies of the four levels (general, main, specific, elementary).

It is clear that the verbs used in the different levels of a hierarchy must be specified consistently: the competency level of a compound competency must be in coherence with the levels of its component competencies.

It is important to note that action verbs respecting the BLOOM classification correspond to action verbs of the cognitive type. Affective or psychomotor action verbs have also been proposed and can be used as far as an assessment is possible.

Principle 4: Choice of general competencies

General competencies constitute the roots of the hierarchical organization and will directly condition the structure of the repository. They should therefore be chosen with care according to the objectives sought. This choice obviously depends on the domain covered, which must be defined beforehand. Many approaches can be considered to guide this choice: respecting the major processes that govern the domain, adapting trade classes in the domain, using cognitive classes (case of the e-CF repository), reusing the division of the domain into sectors of training.

This notion of general competency must be compared with the notion of block of competencies. In the French context, training and certification bodies are strongly encouraged to define blocks of competencies. In the labor code, a block of competencies is defined as a "homogeneous and coherent set of competencies contributing to the independent exercise of a professional activity and which can be assessed and validated". It is the respect of principles 2 and 3 which makes it possible to guarantee that a general competency can be considered as a block of competencies.

One wonders if more restrictive properties should be assigned to these blocks (and therefore to general competencies). For example, a form of semantic independence between blocks could make it easier to read, delete and add competencies to the repository. The use of a weak non-shared composition to organize hierarchy goes in the direction of this semantic independence.

We may need two different types of general competencies: superior competencies which are in direct correspondence with the activities of the trades in the domain; primary competencies which serve as support for the previous ones. These are necessary to acquire superior competencies, but they are not necessarily specified through an activity of a trade.

Principle 5: Explicit representation of prerequisites

In a competency repository covering a wide area, there are generally prerequisites between competencies. It is important to explain the most significant prerequisites. They will be very useful, for example, to an employee who would like to master a given competency; its prerequisites indicate the most efficient way to that aim, given the competencies already acquired. They will also be useful for a training manager who would like to design training that must include some competencies; the prerequisites help him to elaborate a complete and coherent set of training actions.

We wish to give flexibility to this relation. First, some prerequisites are obvious and there is no need to explain them. In addition, the number of competencies being able to be high, in particular at the elementary level, it would be tedious to make a complete explanation of it. We therefore propose to define explicit prerequisites only between the competencies of the first three levels (general, main, specific).

To allow instantiation of the prerequisites, it will be necessary to identify the competencies with labels.

4. APPLICATION TO THE DOMAIN OF INFORMATION SYSTEMS

In this section, we propose to apply the principles defined above to structure a competency repository in the domain of information systems design and implementation. The trades can be found in the CIGREF and CEN repositories. This competency repository is a priori oriented towards Master training: the competencies are those that a Bachelor or Master graduate should assess from his/her training. But this repository must also be able to allow a professional to position his competencies and determine ways of progression. We want to cover all the competencies in the domain and thus objectify all the variants of Master training in the domain.

The proposed repository, in addition to a novel structuration, incorporates topics which are not specified in existing repositories: concrete approaches for strategic alignment of IS, methods and techniques for designing and implementing software, prerequisites in basic disciplines (computer science, management science, discrete mathematics), interpersonal competencies.

In accordance with principle 4, we propose to separate the general competencies into two parts: the superior competencies which report directly on the activities of the trades in the domain and the primary competencies which serve as a basis for the previous ones. This gives five superior general competencies that correspond to a breakdown of the domain into major processes (see Table 1).

There are also five general primary competencies (see Table 1). The breakdown globally respects the training disciplines. Competencies I, G, M, which refer respectively to computer science, management science and mathematics, bring together the knowledge and competencies of these disciplines which are useful or necessary for the acquisition of superior competencies. They are located at levels 2, 3, 4 of the BLOOM classification. CP competency brings together the interpersonal competencies required for the activities of trades. These competencies are broad and the prerequisite relationship makes it possible to specify those which relate more specifically to each case. IE competency corresponds to innovation, R&D and entrepreneurship activities.

Table 1. Ten general competencies for the domain of information systems

Domain	**Information systems design and implementation**
General superior competencies	PS-Managing the information system at the strategic level
	PO-Managing the information system at the operational level
	CD-Designing and implementing computer applications and systems
	FO-Maintaining in operation IT infrastructures and implementing their evolutions
	SS-Implementing an information system in a specific sector
General primary competencies	I-Choosing and using computer science models, methods and techniques
	G-Analyzing company operation and its interactions with its environment
	M-Implementing mathematical models to evaluate or optimize a product, a process, a service
	CP-Assessing and improving interpersonal competencies
	IE-Developing innovation, research and entrepreneurship projects

These primary competencies can be considered as global prerequisites. They could be the subject of a pre-master training. But it is not necessary to master all primary competencies before superior ones. Some may correspond to advanced topics whose mastery may be deferred. The prerequisite can be used to organize the training chronology. In addition, a training is not intended to integrate all the competencies of the repository. There is therefore a certain flexibility to compose an academic or a professional course from the repository.

In order to save space, we explicit only the levels "main" and "specific" for the 5 general superior competencies. Each one is described through a table. In a table, prerequisites are installed by using labels associated to the first three levels. We give textual descriptions for the 5 general primary competencies. For these 10 general competencies, we indicate the main correspondences, when they exist, with the e-CF and MSIS repositories. We also present an example to illustrate elementary competencies. The complete repository can be viewed from the URL: http://miage.univ-lyon1.fr/referentiel-anglais/.

The PS competency corresponds to the strategic steering activities of the IS which are carried out in close association by actors of general management, business lines and IT department. It mainly concerns the elaboration of a map of the existing IS at all levels (business processes, functions, applications, infrastructures), the detection and the characterization of problems or any wish for change and evolution, the choice of a solution, the initialization of the implementation of this solution through a strategic project. This block covers and extends competencies A1, A3, A4, D10, E1, E2, E3, E5, E7 of e-CF. There are correspondences with the "Enterprise Architecture", "IS Strategy and Governance" and "Business Continuity and Information Assurance" areas of the MSIS repository.

Table 2

PS-Managing the information system at the strategic level		
Main competencies	**Specific competencies**	**Prerequisite**
Car-Elaborating a global IS map		
Fes-Formalizing a solution for a strategic evolution	a-Characterizing a strategic need in its context	G-Str, G-Dof, CD-Sbe
	b-Studying potential solutions to meet a strategic need and choose a solution	G, PO-Msi-d, CP-Car-f
	c-Developing a macroscopic formalization of a solution to meet a strategic need	CD-Mod, PS-Car
Oes-Studying opportunity of typical solutions of strategic evolution	a-Using an ERP software	G
	b-Unifying separate information systems	G
	c-Outsourcing activities and services	G
	d-Using a decisional system	G
Gps-Managing portfolio of strategic projects		M-Rop-a, M-Gra, G-Str, CP-Car
Gcc-Managing strategic change and ensure the continuity of business processes		G
Gco-Managing knowledge	a-Identifying forms of knowledge and issues of knowledge management in organizations	G
	b-Formalizing knowledge	I-Bdd, M-Log
	c-Implementing a knowledge management system	I-Bdd
Gdd-Organizing data governance		I-Bdd

The PO competency corresponds to operational steering activities which are mainly carried out by actors of the Information Systems Department: determining solutions for the evolution of applications and infrastructures, managing project, managing quality and security, managing resource. This block corresponds to competencies D1, D2, D8, E2, E6, E7, E8, E9 of e-CF. There are connections with the MSIS repository for project management, quality, security, IS management.

Table 3

PO-Managing the information system at the operational level		
Main competencies	**Specific competencies**	**Prerequisite**
Eai-Managing requests for evolution of applications and infrastructures	a-Designing a solution for a request for changes in applications and infrastructures	PO-Msi-d
	b-Managing the portfolio of application projects and infrastructure projects	M-Rop-a, M-Gra, CP-Car
Sai-Studying typical solutions for evolution of applications and infrastructures	a-Explaining the iso-functional reengineering of an application	
	b-Explaining migration of infrastructures	
Ppr-Managing a project	a-Analyzing the objectives and constraints of a project	PO-Msi-d
	b-Breaking down a project into tasks	
	c-Choosing a project management methodology	
	d-Elaborating and watching a schedule for a project	M-Gra
	e-Managing the risks of a project	
	f-Coordinating the project team	CP-Car
	g-Communicating with the client of a project	CP-Car
Qua-Organizing IS quality	a-Identifying potential approaches for IS quality	
	b-Defining an IS quality policy	
	c-Controlling IS quality	G-Aud
Ssi-Organizing IS security	a-Defining an IS security policy and the terms of its application	I-Sec, FO-Gin-d, G-Aud
	b-Analyzing incident history and updating IS security policy	M-Sta-a, G-Aud
Msi-Managing the IS	a-Managing human resources	G-Dof
	b-Managing financial resources	G-Dof, G-Out
	c-Defining contract policy	G-Jur
	d-Organizing and supervising IS activities	G-Out, G-Aud

The CD competency refers to all activities related to the design and production of IT solutions. It also relates to know-how for the implementation of specific systems and applications relating to decision-making, multimedia and mobility. The prerequisites come from competencies inside this block or inside blocks I, M, G. Correspondences exist with competencies B1 to B6, A6 and D11 of the e-CF. This block also corresponds to the "System Development and Deployment" area of the MSIS repository.

Table 4

CD-Designing and implementing solutions		
Main competencies	**Specific competencies**	**Prerequisite**
Mod-Using modeling languages	a-Modeling with the Entities Associations (EA) model	
	b-Modeling with UML	
	c-Modeling with BPM	
	d-Identifying other modeling languages	
	e-Using meta modeling	
Sbe-Identifying and specifying requirements	a-Acquiring and formalizing requirements	CP-Car-a/d
	b-Using formal specification of requirements	
Mco-Using design and development methods	a-Choosing a development process	
	b-Choosing a design and development method	
	c-Applying a design and development method	
Sdc-Developing conceptual diagrams for data and behavior	a-Developing a conceptual diagram for data	CD-Mod, CD-Sbe
	b-Developing a conceptual diagram for behavior	CD-Mod, M-Pet, CD-Sbe
Alo-Implementing software architecture with design patterns, architectural patterns and frameworks		I-Pro-b CD-Mod-b

Ihm-Designing and developing human-machine interfaces (HMI)	a-Describing the elements which compose an interface	
	b-Designing an interface	CP-Car-a/d
	c-Implementing an interface	CD-Alo
Pas-Organizing the programming of an application or a system	a-Using the principles of software quality assurance	
	b-Using automatic code generation	
	c-Using good practices for manual coding	
	d-Documenting the code	
	e-Using test-driven development	CD-Tas
Tas-Organizing dynamic tests of an application or system	a-Explaining the different types of dynamic tests	
	b-Elaborating dynamic test plans	
	c-Automating dynamic testing	
Moa-Managing the installation of an application	a-Managing the configurations of an application	
	b-Managing the deployment of an application or a software package	
	c-Managing the maintenance of an application	
Dsd-Developing decisional applications and systems	a-Collecting decision-making needs	CD-Sbe
	b-Implementing decisional data structures	I-Bdd
	c-Using an ETL to integrate data	
	d-Using OLAP and reporting tools	
	e-Using data mining and AI to solve decision problems	M-Dat, M-Ina, M-Sta
Dmm-Developing multimedia applications and systems		CD-Ihm CD-Alo
Dmo-Developing mobile applications and systems		I-Sys-e, CD-Ihm, CD-Alo
Erp-Installing an ERP software		G-Dof, I-Sys, CD-Mod, CD-Moa

The FO competency brings together the activities which ensure the proper functioning of the hardware and software infrastructures and which implement the changes decided at the PS and / or PO level. The prerequisites are mainly in computer science. In the e-CF, we can note a correspondence with D10. There are correspondences with the MSIS repository for all the competencies in this block.

Table 5

FO- Maintaining the proper functioning of IT infrastructures and implementing their evolutions		
Main competencies	**Specific competencies**	**Prerequisite**
Gin-Managing hardware and software infrastructures	a-Managing systems, networks, services	I-Sys, G-Aud
	b-Managing maintenance of infrastructure	I-Sys
	c-Optimizing performances of infrastructure	I-Sys, M-Sta
	d-Implementing infrastructure security	I-Sec, CP-Car-a, IE-Vei, G-Aud
	e-Organizing infrastructure service continuity	I-Sys
	f-Integrating a new hardware or software component	I-Sys
Gap-Managing applications		G-Dof, I-Sys
Gdo-Managing data	a-Administrating DBMS and data bases	I-Sys, I-Bdd, CP-Car-j
	b-Administrating data	I-Sys, I-Bdd

The SS competency corresponds to the implementation of an IS in a specific sector. Certain sectors, such as health for example, indeed require adapted approaches. A main competency is introduced for each sector. We propose, here, specific competencies for the health sector. It is essentially about knowing the structure and functioning of the health system and identifying the potentials that a digital information system can provide.

Table 6

SS-Implementing an Information System in a specific sector		
Main competencies	**Specific competencies**	**Prerequisite**
San-Implementing an Information System in the health sector	a-Explaining organization and operation of the health system	
	b-Explaining challenges of the personal health record	
	c-Explaining operation of care networks	
	d-Explaining organization and operation of the hospital	G-Dof
	e-Explaining data processing in epidemiology	
	f-Explaining assessment of medical practices	M-Sta
	g-Explaining standards and classifications used for medical knowledge	PS-Gco
	h-Explaining the major uses of ICT in health	I-Bdd, I-Iot, M-Sta, M-Dat, M-Ina

Other sectors can be considered: finance, transport and distribution, tourism and leisure, telecommunications, public sector and e-government. The MSIS repository expresses competencies for several specific sectors.

These 5 general superior competencies are mainly found at competency levels 3, 4, 5 of the BLOOM classification. Remember that we are aiming for a level of ability corresponding to an early career in the various trades of the domain.

The I competency aims at a deep knowledge of the foundations of IT and its foreseeable evolution, the aptitude to develop software in any type of language, the aptitude to install and operate the different computer systems which a company can use to support its information system. A good mastery of these competencies is necessary for the five superior general competencies and more particularly for the CD and FO competencies. The e-CF does not structure this type of competencies. It includes references to data management and programming. The MSIS repository structures competencies relating to data management, the management of IT systems and networks, the management of IT security and risks.

The G competency is about understanding the models, reasoning and tools used by business managers. This block mainly brings together knowledge relating to the economic and legal environment of companies, the business strategy, the operation of different units, the business processes, the control via accounting mechanisms. It also includes know-how relating to internal audit. This knowledge and know-how are essential for the proper implementation of activities in the PS, PO, CD blocks. The e-CF and MSIS repositories do not directly structure competencies about these topics. The e-CF repository, on the other hand, defines competencies relating to the functions of buying and selling products and services in the IS domain (D4, D5, D6, D7).

The M competency aims, on the one hand, at understanding the main theories of discrete mathematics and artificial intelligence, their constraints and limits, and, on the other hand, the ability to reuse and improve algorithms for analysis and optimization through languages and software packages. These competencies are useful and necessary for data processing, development of assessment models and decision support at the level of PS, PO, CD blocks. This type of competencies is partially expressed in the MSIS standard.

The CP competency brings together interpersonal competencies. Many interpersonal competencies have been characterized and classified (Scouarnec, 2019; Bonnstetter & Brooks, 2003; Oecd, 2014). The objective here is to specify those which relate more specifically to the trades in the domain. For each of them, it is a question of understanding its effects, having its level of ability assessed or self-assessed, identifying ways of improvement and implementing them. The prerequisites, established in the other blocks, make it possible to specify the interpersonal competencies which are more especially expected to carry out a particular activity. This block also offers competencies to strengthen his professionalism and manage his professional career. Interpersonal competencies are not explicitly present in the e-CF. Some are developed in the MSIS repository. The FNEGE framework (Scouarnec, 2019), positioned on general management and business management, is organized around this type of competencies.

The IE competency brings together competencies relating to technology watch, innovation, R&D, entrepreneurship. The IS domain is very favorable for the development of new scientific and technological advances and the acquisition of this type of competencies should be recommended. The e-CF repository incorporates a technology watch competency (A7) and an innovation competency (A9). The MSIS repository includes competencies relating to innovation and entrepreneurship.

We now give some comments about elementary competencies. Remember that an elementary competency is not intended to be broken down. Through its specification, any industrial or academic tutor must be able to interpret without ambiguity the knowledge, know-how and interpersonal competencies that it covers. In particular, he/she may deduct the teaching activities to be implemented in order to acquire the competency and the assessments to be carried out to verify that the competency is well mastered. For illustrating, we give below the elementary competencies that we propose for the specific competency "Administrating DBMS and databases" of the main competency "Managing data" in the FO block. We have highlighted teaching activities enabling to master these elementary competencies. Assessment can be easily deduced: MCQ, exercises, analysis report of a case, analysis report about an experimentation, observation in simulated conditions, etc. These types of teaching activities and assessments are easily practicable in face-to-face configurations. In the field of ICT, there are now various solutions that allow them to be reproduced remotely.

Table 7. Example of elementary competencies and teaching activities

Specific competency: a-Administrating DBMS and databases	
Elementary competencies	**Teaching activities**
• Installing a DBMS	Explaining the principles of the operation and the variants of the implementation process according to the characteristics of the server and the DBMS. Illustrating the operation through an experiment. Asking the apprentice to do the operation.
• Performing version upgrades of a DBMS	Idem
• Administrating databases (security, access rights, storage optimization, request optimization, backup, restoration, ...)	Idem (for each operation)
• Identifying and correcting problems or incidents related to DB and DBMS	Idem (for each type of incident)
• Performing a technology watch on DBMS	Explaining important points to watch and potential sources to consult.
• Assisting data base users	Explaining the difficulties that users generally encounter. Explaining the behavior to adopt towards each type of user and each type of assistance process. Accompanying the apprentice in real situations.
• Contributing to the choice of a DBMS	Explaining the parameters to take into account. Explaining how to elaborate an argumentation according to the constraints of the choice. Explaining the behavior to adopt during a meeting organized for the choice.

5. EVALUATION

In this section, we give elements for evaluating our proposals.

Evaluation of the structuring approach

The proposed approach is based on five principles and makes it possible to organize competencies in the form of composition hierarchies with four levels of abstraction: general, main, specific, elementary. The general level corresponds to the notion of competency block. At all levels, competencies are specified in the same way using action verbs that may relate to the classification of BLOOM. These verbs make it possible to clearly set the objectives. At the elementary level, they allow to induce the type of assessments to be carried out to measure their achievement. The measures can then be propagated by aggregation in the upper levels. In addition, it is recommended to instantiate prerequisites between competencies. This kind of structuration is general and can be considered for building a competency repository in any domain.

Thus organized, a competency repository provides the facilities we aimed at:

- Easily searching for a competency. The repository is similar to a semantic map which can be browsed from general competency to more detailed ones (main, specific, elementary).

- Easily inserting a new competency. The semantic map makes it possible to identify the most appropriate positioning for inserting a new competency (main, specific, elementary).

- Easily developing initial and vocational training. The issue is to derive a specific competency repository for a certification or a training. It is possible to proceed from objectives or from trades or roles. Each hierarchical level defines a learning objective. One can select one or more objectives and assemble the corresponding competencies by attaching all the lower level competencies linked by composition and prerequisites. Filtering can be carried out. The resulting repository has as many blocks as separate hierarchies in the assembly. We can do the same by trades: the competencies-to-trades correspondence brings together all the competencies corresponding to the selected trades.

- Drawing up a competency assessment. Anyone can identify the competency included in its profile and can perform a self-assessment (using the elementary competencies specifications) to draw up a competency assessment in relation to the area covered by the repository.

- Easily finding training courses that meet a learning objective. Suppose that a set E of existing training courses have been previously indexed by competencies, searching for courses that satisfy a learning objective identified by X then consists in searching for the training of E indexed by X.

Evaluation of the competency repository in the domain of information systems

The repository we propose is elaborated from an initial repository designed by the French network of MIAGE Masters. We first structured the initial repository according to the principles of the proposed approach. The new repository includes 10 composition hierarchies (therefore 10 competency blocks) and a significant part of the existing specifications has been recovered. We then suggested extensions. In this new repository, we find, not surprisingly, most of the competencies offered by the repositories in the domain and in particular those of the e-CF and MSIS repositories. However, this repository has several particularities. First, it distinguishes superior competencies which correspond directly to the activities of the trades in the domain and primary competencies which serve as the basis for the previous ones. The latter bring together knowledge and competencies from the three basic disciplines of computer science, management science and discrete mathematics. Superior competencies are directly based on this type of knowledge and know-how. The prerequisites make it possible to express the most significant dependencies. The importance of these primary competencies will increase in the future as information systems evolve towards increased technicality, closer coupling with business processes, higher requirements in terms of data analysis and assistance to decision processes. Then, the "Designing and developing applications and systems" block was the subject of various enhancements to cover the ever widening range of development methods and technologies. A majority of students graduating in information system begin their professional career with activities corresponding to this block and it is necessary to take into account new approaches. In addition, we separated strategic management of the information system from operational management because they involve different actors. The two corresponding blocks have been enriched with competencies relating to design and implementation of typical solutions for the evolution and adaptation of an information system. Finally, we paid a particular attention to the block "Developing interpersonal competencies and professionalism". Interpersonal competencies (i.e. soft skills) have become essential in all trades in the domain. The recommendation that is made is that an individual be able, not only to identify the importance of an interpersonal competency relative to a trade, but also to assess his level of ability and to choose solutions to improve it.

Some competencies may depend on national contexts. This is particularly the case with corporate law. We have worded them in a neutral way. So, the proposed repository can be normally used in an international context.

6. CONCLUSION

In this paper we propose a general model to organize a competency repository and its instantiation in the domain of information systems. Numerous competency repositories have been suggested in different areas and surprisingly no proposal has been made to structure them. Our model is general and can be used to structure any type of repository. Such a proposal constitutes an effective way to facilitate understanding by users and maintenance by designers. In the domain of information systems, several competency repositories have been proposed. Our suggestion integrates the main points of these repositories and introduces many other points, in particular in terms of interpersonal competencies. It can be used both to guide the development of training and to assess individual competencies. We are implementing it in the context of the French network of MIAGE Masters. It is used in particular to help in the development of distance learning modules.

ACKNOWLEDGEMENT

The authors would like to thank M. Gilles DESSAGNE, Head of the Urban Planning Division of IS at SNCF, for fruitful discussions. They want also to thank the French ANR (Agence Nationale de la Recherche) who funded this work.

REFERENCES

Acm. (2016). Computer Engineering Curricula. https://www.acm.org/binaries/content/assets/education/ce2016-final-report.pdf

Anap. (2020). Référentiel de compétences en système d'information. Retrieved from http://ressources.anap.fr/ressourceshumaines/publication/196

Bloom, B. S. (1956). Taxonomy of educational objectives: the classification of educational goals, Handbook 1: Cognitive domain. White Plains, N.Y., Longman.

Bonnstetter, B.J. & Brooks, B. (2003). List of soft skill competencies with description, Nielson Group. Retrieved from http://www.nielsongroup.com/articles/list_of_competencies.pdf

Cen. (2018). European ICT Professional Role Profiles built on the e-CF. Retrieved from www.ecompetences.eu/ict-professional-profiles/

Churches, A. (2008). Bloom's taxonomy blooms digitally, Tech & Learning, 2008, vol. 1, p. 1-6.

Cigref. (2018). Nomenclature CIGREF des métiers du système d'information, Club Informatique des Grandes Entreprises Françaises. Retrieved from www.cigref.fr/wp/wp-content/uploads/2018/07/Cigref-Nomenclature-RH-Metiers-Competences-2018_v2.pdf

e-CF. (2019). European e-Competence Framework. Retrieved from www.ecompetences.eu

Embo, M., Driessen, E., Valcke, M., & Van der Vleuten, C. P. (2015). Integrating learning assessment and supervision in a competency framework for clinical workplace education. Nurse Education Today, 35(2), 341-346.

Kennedy, D. (2006). Writing and using learning outcomes: a practical guide, University College Cork.

Lundqvist, K. O., Baker, K., & Williams, S. (2008). An ontological approach to competency management.

Oecd. (2014). Competency framework. Retrieved from www.oecd.org/careers/competency_framework_en.pdf

Opiiec. (2018). Référentiels métiers de la branche du numérique. Retrieved from www.referentiels-metiers.opiiec.fr/

Osters, S., & Tiu, F. S. (2008). Writing measurable learning outcomes. In 3rd Annual Texas A&M Assessment Conference.

O*NET On Line. (2020). Organization of Data in the O*NET Database and O*NET Online. Retrieved from https://www.onetonline.org/.

Paquette, G. (2007). An Ontology and a Software Framework for Competency Modeling and Management, Educational Technology & Society, 10(3), 1-21.

Sastre-Fullana, P., De Pedro-Gómez, J. E., Bennasar-Veny, M., Serrano-Gallardo, P., & Morales-Asencio, J. M. (2014). Competency frameworks for advanced practice nursing: a literature review. International nursing review, 61(4), 534-542.

Schmidt, A., & Kunzmann, C. (2006). Towards a human resource development ontology for combining competence management and technology-enhanced workplace learning. In : OTM Confederated International Conferences "On the Move to Meaningful Internet Systems". Springer, Berlin, Heidelberg, p. 1078-1087.

Scouarnec, A., & all. (2019). Les compétences de demain - « Management et Gestion des Affaires », Fnege. Retrieved from www.fnege.org/publications/referentiel-prospectif-des-competences-management-gestion-des-affaires.

Sfia. (2018). The global skills and competency framework for a digital world, version 7. Retrieved from https://www.sfia-online.org/en.

Topi, H. & all. (2016). MSIS 2016 Global Competency Model for Graduate Degree Programs in Information Systems. Retrieved from www.acm.org/binaries/content/assets/education/msis2016.pdf.

Vandeweerd, J. M., Cambier, C., Romainville, M., Perrenoud, P., Desbrosse, F., Dugdale, A., & Gustin, P. (2014). Competency frameworks: which format for which target?. Journal of veterinary medical education, 41(1), 27-36.

Whitehead, C. R., & Kuper, A. (2015). Competency-based training for physicians: are we doing no harm? Cmaj, 187(4), E128-E129.

A SYSTEMATIC LITERATURE REVIEW ON THE SOCIAL AFFORDANCES OF SOCIAL MEDIA FOR INFORMAL LEARNING ENVIRONMENTS

Maryam Meshari Almukhaylid, Salah Kabanda and Nawal Nasser Al-Haidari
University of Cape Town, South Africa

ABSTRACT

Social media becomes a mediator in an informal learning environment where learners are responsible for their own learning activities. Many studies acknowledge that informal learners tend to use social media as a learning tool in modern times, but social media was not created with this purpose in mind. This study therefore aims to review and analyse the literature on social media and informal learning from an information system (IS) perspective to identify the social affordances. The study is based on e English publications in peer-reviewed journals and conferences from 2010 to 2020. 136 papers in the field of social media and informal learning have been analysed. Thematic analysis has been used to identify the social affordances. Social affordances of social media that have been identified can help learners to evaluate the success of their informal learning via social media, while learners who are currently not engaged in social media can gain a better understanding of how to utilize social media platforms to enhance their informal learning. This review contributes to the growing field of research on the role of affordance in social media and informal learning fields.

KEYWORDS

Social Media, Informal Learning, Social Affordances

1. INTRODUCTION

Social media platforms are vital to people living in the 21st Century. Social media provides an informal learning environment where people engage and learn socially with others to help them understand new ideas (Conner, 2012). Informal learning is not organized learning and it usually occurs outside of educational institutions (Garcia, Elbeltagi, Dungay, & Hardaker, 2015; Hsi, 2015; Lay Shi, Siew Ming, & Noorizah Mohd, 2018). Informal learning through social media has helped learners to overcome many of the challenges and barriers present in formal learning settings. This type of learning it provides an opportunity to support the development of learner competencies and skills (Blaschke, 2014).

Several studies such as Hamat and Abu Hassan (2019), Tallent (2014), Osborne (2014), and Baruh and Watson (2014) have highlighted social media's value for building and maintaining relationships with a variety of stakeholders in informal learning environments, thereby creating a space for continuous professional development and empowering people in their search for information.

Social media provides more advantages than traditional media, the major benefits being interactivity (Al-Sabaawi & Dahlan, 2018; Alsaadat, 2018; Ersoy & Güneyli, 2016; Fox & Ralston, 2016; Genden, 2018; McCarthy, 2015), familiarity (Al-Sabaawi & Dahlan, 2018; Blaschke, 2014; Genden, 2018), popularity (Garcia et al., 2015), and engagement (Al-Sabaawi & Dahlan, 2018; McPherson, Budge, & Lemon, 2015). The use of social media as learning tools could be crucial at these difficult times of the Covid-19 crisis.

Although social media was not initially created for learning purposes (McCarthy, 2015), the social aspect in learning activities is extremely crucial (Taibi, Gentile, Fulantelli, & Allegra, 2010). In informal learning contexts, learners use social media differently based on their needs and therefore each user applies different affordances (Balci, Rosenkranz, & Schuhen, 2014). The affordances provide a useful lens for studying learning technologies and their impact on human learning (Mao, 2014). (Wang, Wang, & Tang, 2018) , in their review of application of affordance theory in IS, found that IS scholars should consider social affordances and improve our understanding of IS-related social media use in social processes. Social affordances describe "the relationship between the properties of an object and the social characteristics of a group that enable particular kinds of interactions among members of that group" (Bradner, Kellogg, & Erickson, 1999).

Social media platforms offer many social affordances (Moreno & Uhls, 2019). It is important to understand how users apply these social affordances of social media within the setting of an informal learning scenario, is important because social affordances is often used in the context of social technology. A prominent perspective within information systems regarding how to understand this relationship, between the technology (social media) and the user in the informal learning context, is through the study of affordances (Anderson & Robey, 2017; Stendal, Thapa, & Lanamäki, 2016; Volkoff & Strong, 2017). Also, informal learning is generally a social process, and social affordances include a sense of belonging to a group which may be created through a shared interest or experience (Moreno & Uhls, 2019). Moreover, social affordances assist people to learn informally by helping them to engage, build social connections and to be aware of other users' thoughts, opinions and feedback (Ahuja, 2009; Kavanaugh et al., 2012). The experience social media usage by informal learners needs to be considered in academia (Song & Lee, 2014). Not all informal learners who use social media as tools for their learning have the same knowledge of the social media affordances, and informal learners need to know how to use social media tools effectively to accomplish their learning goals (Li, 2013).

In academia, there is also a lack of social affordance knowledge in general. Researchers have not paid much attention to the social affordances of technology especially in the field of informal learning and social media. More research is needed to consider the social affordances because they provide an explanation of how the social construction of technology impacts the practices afforded by that environment (Fayard & Weeks, 2014). Moreover, an understanding of the specific affordances in the selected field will further our understanding of users' activities and their relationships with this technology (Pozzi, Pigni, & Vitari, 2014; Van Osch & Mendelson, 2011). All these reasons support the importance of identifying the social affordances of social media platforms for informal learners to help them gain a better understanding of how social media platforms can be utilized to enhance informal learning.

Considering this background and the limited work done on informal learning (Aramo-Immonen, Karkkainen, Jussila, Joel-Edgar, & Huhtamaki, 2016; Kanwar, Balasubramanian, & Umar, 2013; Klomsri, Grebäck, & Tedre, 2013; Sangrà & Wheeler, 2013; Yakin & Gencel, 2013), this study seeks to identify the social affordances of social media as an informal learning tool for learners. This systematic review aims to answer the question: What are the social affordances of social media tools in an informal learning context?

The paper is structured as follows: the systematic review methodology and analyses is presented in section 2. Section 3 discusses the findings of literature synthesis. Finally, section 4 presents conclusions with potential directions for future research.

2. METHODOLOGY

2.1 Research Approach

The main purpose of this study is to identify the social affordances of social media in informal learning. Thus, a qualitative systematic literature review approach is used in this paper which was informed by the Okoli guidelines for IS researchers (Okoli, 2015). There are five major stages for conducting literature reviews on IS, and they are as follows: (1) Define the protocol, (2) Search the literature, (3) Select the papers, (4) Analyse, synthesise, and interpret the data, (5) Write the review aiming to identify the research gap (Oosterwyk, Brown, & Geeling, 2019).

2.2 Data Collection

In order to identify papers in the field of social media and informal learning, the initial step was to identify papers from IS journals and conferences. Bandara, Furtmueller, Gorbacheva, Miskon, and Beekhuyzen (2015) recommended the use of top-ranked journals and conference papers. These include the Association for Information Systems' (AIS) electronic library and the basket of eight IS journals (European Journal of Information Systems, Information Systems Journal, Information Systems Research, Journal of the Association of Information Systems, Journal of Management Information Systems, MIS Quarterly, Journal of Strategic Information Systems, and Journal of Information Technology) were searched.

Thus, journal articles and conference papers in the field of social media and informal learning were collected from the Web of Science database and Google Scholar, as these databases are frequently used for IS literature reviews (Bandara et al., 2015; Schryen, 2015). Studies and searches included only publications in Englishfrom the year 2010 – to date. This period was chosen because going back through ten years of research should be sufficient for IS literature reviews (Oosterwyk et al., 2019; Templier & Paré, 2015). In order to identify papers relating to social media and informal learning, the search key terms that were used were specific to the main goal of the study. Key terms used included "informal learning" and "social media." In addition, to track down more literature, we also added "social networking," "web 2.0," and "user-generated content," as keywords in the search (Zeng & Gerritsen, 2014). This process led to a data corpus of 136 papers which were used for analysis. All papers have been uploaded to EndNote. Okoli (2015) recommended the use of EndNote as a helpful tool to manage references when conducting literature reviews.

2.3 Analysis

Collected papers were exported from EndNote to Excel sheets for analysis. Microsoft Excel is a popular tool for literature reviews and a helpful instrument to analyse papers (Bandara et al., 2015). The data analysis commenced by reviewing each paper's title, topic, abstracts, and keywords. From this initial analysis, the following were identified and removed from the data corpus: book reviews, posters, duplicated papers, and those that did not deal with social media and informal learning. For example, papers such as the "Construction of Informal Learning Knowledge Network Based on Social Network Analysis" paper by (Ma, Wen, & Wang, 2019) were removed. After the initial analysis, 55 papers that focused specifically on social media and informal learning remained. The second phase of analysis entailed a careful examination of the remaining papers to identify the social affordances of social media in informal learning contexts. Each paper was examined based on its introductions, conclusions, and main objectives in relation to whether they offered social affordances of social media for informal learning. From the 55 papers, one was omitted on the basis that did not offer social affordances of social media in informal learning contexts. After this second phase, the data corpus stood at 54 papers (see table 1 and figure 1).

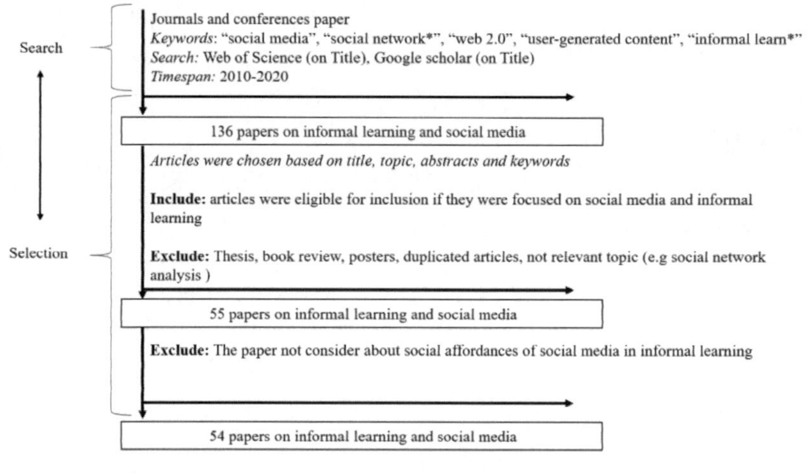

Figure 1. Search and selection process (after the fashion of Günther et al., 2017)

The third phase of analysis involved the use of thematic analysis using NVivo for literature review synthesis to identify social affordances of social media in informal learning environments. NVivo is a qualitative data analysis tool with powerful abilities to analyse, synthesize, and write up IS literature reviews (Bandara et al., 2015; Schryen, 2015). The major themes related to the social affordances of social media for informal learning that emerged from common patterns in the paper corpus, as well as examples of authors are shown in Table 1.

Table 1. Findings of Social affordances of social media for informal learning

Social affordances		Instance of social affordance	Example of authors
Interaction		Online forums and chat, afforded the interactivity for those who wanted to interact with others and discuss.	(Akpomuje & Akinsooto, 2016), (Babu, 2015) ,(Hamat & Abu Hassan, 2019).
Engagement		Engaging in social conversations with one another and build a stronger online community.	(Osborne, 2014), (Michel, Touré, & Marty, 2018), (Al-Sabaawi & Dahlan, 2018).
Sharing		Share common interests within online communities.	(Lisbôa & Coutinho, 2011), (Lundgren, Crippen, & Bex, 2020), (Sclater, 2016).
Posting		Posting questions, pictures, and videos.	(Klomsri et al., 2013), (Oliveira & Figueira, 2017), (Bagdy, Dennen, Rutledge, Rowlett, & Burnick, 2018).
Participation		The participation tool which makes the learners simultaneously become the producer.	(Yoo & Kim, 2013), (Zhang & Gao, 2014), (Oliveira & Figueira, 2017).
Discussion		The synchronous and asynchronous discussion in the walls of social networks sites.	(Sato, Kageto, & Kirkpatrick, 2013), (Thaler, 2011), (Kumar & Gruzd, 2019).
Connection		Connecting learners with alumni, outside communities, and experts around the world.	(Zhao & Kemp, 2012), (Heo & Lee, 2013), (Jones, 2014).
Networking		Allowing learners to build, expand and develop their relationships through social networks.	(Ferguson, Faulkner, Whitelock, & Sheehy, 2015), (Blümcke, 2011), (Yakin & Gencel, 2013).
Communication		Communication with teachers and peers (group discussion, asking questions, receiving feedback).	(Greenhow & Lewin, 2016), (Jones, 2014), (Klomsri et al., 2013).
Commenting		Posting comments and receiving comments from other users.	(Melrose, 2012), (Song & Lee, 2014), (Aghili, Palaniappan, Kamali, Aghabozorgi, & Sardareh, 2014).
Collaboration		Collaboration with peers through blog commentaries and wiki's collaborative editing and commenting features.	(Zhao & Kemp, 2012), (Michel et al., 2018), (Rehm, Littlejohn, & Rienties, 2018).
Communities		Hashtags allow the creation of an online community by use of a particular term or topic.	(Babu, 2015), (Jiménez-Cortés, 2015), (Che & Ibrahim, 2018).
Social emotional affordances	Online friendships	Suggestion friends for a user based on their friends' friends.	(Drlik & Beranek, 2016), (Akpomuje & Akinsooto, 2016), (Ab Rashid, Yahaya, Rahman, & Yunus, 2016).
	Identity development	The ability of creating and sharing online identities which might be different than the offline identities.	(Bagdy et al., 2018), (Popescu, 2012),(Dabbagh & Kitsantas, 2012)

Self-expression	Learners can express themselves in a more relaxed manner and provide a different and perspective on their learning experiences.	(Sato et al., 2013), (Parmigiani & Pennazio, 2012), (Heo & Lee, 2013).
Celebrities' inspiration	Learners take inspirations from hero's profile or page	(Fox & Ralston, 2016), (Islam & Rabbi, 2016), (Klomsri et al., 2013).

3. FINDINGS AND DISCUSSION

The purpose of this study was to identify the social affordances of social media in informal learning environments. Following a systematic review process of the articles on social media and informal learning from the peer reviewed papers; the findings identified the following themes as shown in Table 2. These themes are discussed in the following subsections.

3.1 Interaction

This study found that more than 80% of the literature mentioned *interaction* as a significant social affordance. Informal learners who are willing to use social media for informal learning purposes should interact socially using different social features to achieve their highest learning goals. Interaction is at the core of every virtual community, as it often facilitates a user's need to solve problems and/or learn (Zehrer & Grabmüller, 2012). Fox and Ralston (2016) in their study refer to interaction affordance as the first phase for learners to start online informal learning in social media environments. Hence, the more learners interact with others, the greater the benefits of using social media platforms for learning. However, not all learners' interactions on social media may lead to may lead to achieving learning goals

3.2 Engagement

Social media is about encouraging engagement with other people in a socially interactive environment. From the literature analysis, about 70% of the research on social media and informal learning point to engagement as one of the main social affordances that allow learners to learn informally. Learners engage with peers in collaborative problem-solving and discussions by liking, commenting, posting questions, and sharing tips on posted topics (Babu, 2015). Also, hashtags, for example, afford people the capability to engage in life-long and life-wide learning processes asynchronously across space and time (Kumar & Gruzd, 2019). "The type of engagement informal learners have with people on social media depends on their goals. Those who are actively engaged may create more successful communities (Zhang & Gao, 2014).

3.3 Sharing

The majority (85%) of the publications refer to *sharing* as an essential social affordance for informal learning. Learners learn when they receive knowledge from others, but they learn more when they share their thoughts, opinions, and information with others. Using social media platforms as informal ways to share their information and experience with others allows informal learners to become more confident as they can prepare themselves to share their ideas and thoughts without fear of criticism or disapproval (Akpomuje & Akinsooto, 2016; Fox & Ralston, 2016; Lisbôa & Coutinho, 2011; Meace: Sophie, Naamani: Catherine, & Fiona Carroll, 2018; Wan, Prain, & Collet, 2014). The affordance of sharing allows users to share ideas, resources, articles, photos, videos, ratings, tags, and links (Greenhow & Lewin, 2016; Islam & Rabbi, 2016; Yoo & Kim, 2013). Therefore, the opportunities for learners to share are greater in informal learning environments than in formal learning environments.

3.4 Posting

According to the literature, around 50% of social media and informal learning papers indicate that *posting* is a substantial social affordance. Social media afforded posting features as a tool of communication and contacting that allows informal learners to communicate with peers and their teachers anytime and anywhere (Aghili et al., 2014; Sato et al., 2013). Learners can post different types of content, such as questions that are answered by others through reply posts and they may also post their photographs and their own educational videos (Fox & Ralston, 2016; Sato et al., 2013). Heo and Lee (2013) indicates that many learners spend more time creating and managing their own postings and writing their own experiences and thoughts.

3.5 Participation

Participation is one of the essential social affordances that were found during the analysing process. Learners participate on social media when they take part in informal learning activities. Participation is also a learning process (Jiménez-Cortés, 2015). Participating is more than sharing with others. Learners can create, refine, and share knowledge, information, and interests through participating with others in social media platforms (Yoo & Kim, 2013; Zhao & Kemp, 2012).

3.6 Discussion

The analysis of the literature showed that 55% of papers mention *discussion* as a way of informal learning through social media platforms. Social media allows learners to have discussions in a relaxed atmosphere with others who have similar interests (Babu, 2015; Kumar & Gruzd, 2019). In addition, social media is used to facilitate working on projects, as learners discuss project activities online (Sato et al., 2013). However, social media might reveal students' identities to the public and some learners are not aware that their discussion on social media might be publicly available (Chen & Bryer, 2012). Learners should be able to participate in the informal discussion to have their voice heard by others and to gain the maximum learning benefits.

3.7 Connection

Around 70% of the reviewed literature highlighted the importance of having *connection*. Being connected through social media tools allow users to build communities and to socialize with others. Social media has the ability to maintain social connections and to overcome isolation (Aghili et al., 2014; Li, Gray, Verspoor, & Barnett, 2017; Osborne, 2014). Connecting with people via social media, for the purpose of giving and receiving information, is a way of informal learning (Babu, 2015; Zhao & Kemp, 2012). Informal learners exchange knowledge through connecting to others by using social media tools, such as Wikipedia, LinkedIn, and WordPress, to name a few; it also connects learners with peers, experts in the field, and communities across the world (Chen & Bryer, 2012; Fox & Ralston, 2016). Additionally, social media community members could use hashtag features strategically to connect their messages to a wider topic for more interaction (Lundgren et al., 2020). On other hand, increasing the number of connections doesn't mean that informal learners are learning efficiently and effectively. Taibi et al. (2010) emphasize that those who use social media informally, should not only to be connected to other people, but that they should be connected to the right people, depending on learner aims.

3.8 Networking

Research showed that creating *networks* or being in a network is a fundamental phase of informal learning on social media. Social media platform tools can be used to promote the development of social learning networks. People connect with others in well-known social media platforms mainly to build their networks with people they may already know, and with strangers based on shared interests (Heo & Lee, 2013). Social media builds a knowledge network by linking learning resources to a set of competences to be developed, and by connecting people who wish to share, create, and evaluate their knowledge with peers in the network (Zhao & Kemp, 2012). Learners acquire important network capital by using these technologies and generating collaborative informal learning spaces (Sánchez-Navarro & Aranda, 2013). However, building networks take time and needs constant learner engagement and social presence while using social media. Social presence is defined as the ability of learners to present themselves as real persons in the online community (Aghili et al., 2014).

3.9 Communication

From the research, 76% of papers provide evidence that social media has been used as a general communication tool. The affordances of *communication* on social technologies allow users to communicate synchronously or asynchronously, and to maintain social relationships informally and authentically in the virtual environment of the Internet (Dogan, 2014; Heo & Lee, 2013). For most learners, online communication has become simpler than communicating personally because of the geographical distance between people (Islam & Rabbi, 2016). Research on social media in learning suggests that integrating social media into learning environments may yield new forms of communication that facilitate knowledge exchange (Greenhow & Lewin, 2016; Klomsri et al., 2013). Learners can use different social tools to effectively communicate such as texting, microblogging, commenting, liking, skyping, recording, and video conferencing.

3.10 Commenting

The findings show that more than 50% of the reviewed publications identified *comments* as major social part of social media. Commenting is a typical social media feature that promotes individual users (Greenhow & Lewin, 2016), and it can be considered a tool for communication and expression (Michel et al., 2018). One of the advantages of using social media for informal learning purposes is the possibility of receiving comments from both friends and non-friends, thus enabling the informal learners to receive multiple perspectives from others (Ab Rashid et al., 2016; Sato et al., 2013). In addition, learners on social media engage by reading each other's posts and discussions, and answering questions by commenting on posted topics (Babu, 2015; Yoo & Kim, 2013). Fox and Ralston (2016) indicate that social media allows learners to comment, ask questions, and share things they would not necessarily feel comfortable sharing with learners who know the individuals they are referring to. However, the large number of comments, especially those that are irrelevant and negative, can be an issue for informal learners. Learners may miss key instructions and knowledge if it gets lost within too many comments (Sclater, 2016).

3.11 Collaboration

About 75% of reviewed papers mention the collaborative environment provided by social media for informal learners. Informal learners who use social media for learning purposes are not only the consumers but also the producers of the knowledge (Ab Rashid et al., 2016). Learners are using social media as tools to collaborate with their instructors and peers (Dabbagh & Kitsantas, 2012; Meace: Sophie et al., 2018). *Collaboration* is a social process and one of the pillars of any learning process. Learners who do not aspire to collaborate with others usually do not complete their informal learning. The affordance of collaboration allows learners to build a knowledge base by commenting for feedback and expressing their thoughts and ideas to each other (Babu, 2015; Zhang & Gao, 2014).

3.12 Communities

The findings indicate that building *communities* is one of the major social affordances of social media for learning purposes. The sense of belonging to a community is important to enable informal learning processes as informal learners use social media for building appropriate online learning communities (Sato et al., 2013; Zhang & Gao, 2014). Learning communities are described as groups that have shared interests who communicate informally using social media to achieve their goals (Hamat & Abu Hassan, 2019). This expands the concept of community of practice (CoP) where people share their knowledge and skills (Bagdy et al., 2018; Burnick, 2018). CoP has been used as the framework in many studies of social media-based learning. For example, Bagdy et al. (2018) used CoP to explore how teens engage in informal learning via social media.

3.13 Social-emotional Affordances

In the literature we found that there are several social-emotional affordances that have an impact on informal learning processes. Social media is used by learners to deepen their feelings and understanding of the subject and their learning (Meace Sophie, Naamani Catherine, & Fiona Carroll, 2018). We pointed out some of the social emotional affordances, such as online friendship, identity development, self-expression, and celebrities' inspiration.

3.13.1 Online Friendships

The need to coexist with others drives people to form relationships with friends. The literature illustrates the importance of learners' socialization with online friends during the informal learning process. Nowadays people of all races, ages, religions, occupations, and socio-economic backgrounds use social media to maintain existing relationships and to make new online friendships (Aghili et al., 2014; Lisbôa & Coutinho, 2011). Through interaction by chatting and sharing information with online friends, people find ways to learn informally (Akpomuje & Akinsooto, 2016). Informal learners would prefer to share their thoughts and opinions with their friends on social media as opposed to people they knew in real life. The affordances of creating friendship on the networking technology allows for quick and rich responses by allowing learners to ask questions online rather than meeting friends face-to-face (Ab Rashid et al., 2016). The more friends are included, the greater the chance for sociability, interaction, possibilities of support, and information acquisition (Sánchez-Navarro & Aranda, 2013).

3.13.2 Identity Development

One in every three papers from previous studies indicated the impact of social media for developing identity. Social media plays a role in identity creation (Melrose, 2012). The learner identity development in an online learning environment is a key feature that prompts the learner on what to share, what not to share, and who to share it with (Dabbagh & Kitsantas, 2012). Learners in informal learning environments could build their online identity to be whoever they want to be. However, the world of social media is not completely anonymous, as offline relationships can be anchored to online relationships (Barkhordari & Willemyns, 2016).

3.13.3 Self-expression

The findings indicate that informal learners had a tendency to express themselves. The informal nature of social media allows users a space to express themselves in a more relaxed manner (Heo & Lee, 2013; Sato et al., 2013). By participating in discussions, they engage in positive self-expression that develops their communication skills (Islam & Rabbi, 2016). Learners' social presence in social media influences their self-expression. Having a social presence on social media enables users to feel comfortable and safe when expressing their ideas, opinions, and points of view (Lisbôa & Coutinho, 2011).

3.13.4 Celebrities' Inspiration

Despite many celebrities who use social media, the study found few papers that addressed users following celebrities to learn informally. However, these papers indicate that celebrities inspire learners and have a social-emotional impact on them. Social media is a tool you can use to become a celebrity and it allows celebrities to communicate and inspire their followers. Social media users draw inspiration from their heroes' profiles or pages (Islam & Rabbi, 2016). Informal learners may learn and be uplifted by celebrities on social media (Fox & Ralston, 2016).

4. IMPLICATION

Social media in learning has become the focus of several studies over the last few years (Maria, 2019). However, the analysis of this systematic review found that there are limited papers on Social media and informal learning sectors from an IS perspective. IS researchers should focus more on the social media and informal learning phenomena from an individual point of view. Moreover, a few studies mentioned the term "social affordances". During the analysis of the literature, many factors have been highlighted which circumnavigate social affordances; by contrast, this study focuses on identifying the major social affordances in order to help learners reap the benefits of these affordances and learn effectively. Also, in future studies the key construct of social affordances could be clearly defined and conceptualized.

5. LIMITATIONS

In this paper, we could have used an additional database to get more papers on social media and informal learning. Also, a comparative measurement could have been used, to justify the conclusions.

6. CONCLUSION

Despite the interest shown by many researchers in social media and informal learning for the past decade, it can be concluded that the topic of social affordances of social media is still under research and. This systematic review contributes to the knowledge by identifying the social affordances and social-emotional affordances of social media to help the people who are willing to learn informally to be aware of the many benefits of using these social affordances for learning effectively. 12 social affordances and 4 social-emotional affordances have been identified during the literature analysis.

The research findings suggest a growing interest in using these social affordances of social media in the informal learning process, which marked an increasing trend in informal learning for everyone who would like to develop themselves based on their interests. Future studies should utilize the social affordances and existing social media related frameworks to provide a lens through which study results can be analyzed and interpreted in an informal learning context. Also, an experimental design of research methodology could provide empirical evidence on informal learning activities on social media.

REFERENCES

Ab Rashid, R., Yahaya, M. F., Rahman, M. F. A., & Yunus, K. (2016). Teachers' Informal Learning via Social Networking Technology. *International Journal of Emerging Technologies in Learning, 11*(10), 76-79. doi:10.3991/ijet.v11i10.5908

Aghili, M., Palaniappan, A. K., Kamali, K., Aghabozorgi, S., & Sardareh, S. A. (2014). Unifying informal and formal learning environments: Educational use of social network sites through implementing community of inquiry framework. *International Journal of e-Education, e-Business, e-Management and e-Learning, 4*(3), 191.

Ahuja, S. (2009). *A Tale of Two Sites: An explorative study of the design and evaluation of social network sites.* Virginia Tech,

Akpomuje, P., & Akinsooto, T. (2016). Adults' Informal Learning Experiences Using the Social Media in a Nigerian University.

Al-Sabaawi, M. M. Y., & Dahlan, H. M. (2018). *Acceptance Model of Social Media for Informal Learning.* Paper presented at the the 2nd International Conference of Reliable Information and Communication Technology (IRICT 2017), Cham.

Alsaadat, K. (2018). The impact of social media technologies on adult learning. *International Journal of Electrical and Computer Engineering, 8*(5), 3747-3755. doi:10.11591/ijece.v8i5.pp3747-3755

Anderson, C., & Robey, D. (2017). Affordance potency: Explaining the actualization of technology affordances. *Information and Organization, 27*(2), 100-115. doi:https://doi.org/10.1016/j.infoandorg.2017.03.002

Aramo-Immonen, H., Karkkainen, H., Jussila, J. J., Joel-Edgar, S., & Huhtamaki, J. (2016). Visualizing informal learning behavior from conference participants' Twitter data with the Ostinato Model. *Computers in Human Behavior, 55*, 584-595. doi:10.1016/j.chb.2015.09.043

Babu, R. (2015). Blind Students' Challenges in Social Media Communication: An Early Investigation of Facebook Usability for Informal Learning. *International Journal of Online Pedagogy and Course Design, 5*(1), 58-73. doi:10.4018/ijopcd.2015010105

Bagdy, L. M., Dennen, V. P., Rutledge, S. A., Rowlett, J. T., & Burnick, S. (2018). *Teens and Social Media: A Case Study of High School Students' Informal Learning Practices and Trajectories*. Paper presented at the Proceedings of the 9th International Conference on Social Media and Society, Copenhagen, Denmark. https://doi.org/10.1145/3217804.3217920

Balci, B., Rosenkranz, C., & Schuhen, S. (2014). Identification of different affordances of information technology systems: An empirical study.

Bandara, W., Furtmueller, E., Gorbacheva, E., Miskon, S., & Beekhuyzen, J. (2015). Achieving Rigor in Literature Reviews: Insights from Qualitative Data Analysis and Tool-Support. *Communications of the Association for Information Systems, 37*, 154-204. doi:10.17705/1CAIS.03708

Barkhordari, R., & Willemyns, M. (2016). *Young adults' construction of social identity on Facebook: a structural equation model.* Paper presented at the 3rd European Conference on Social M di R h Media Research EM Normandie, Caen, France.

Baruh, L., & Watson, H. (2014). *Using Twitter for what? A segmentation study of Twitter usage during Gezi protests.* Paper presented at the Proceedings of the European Conference on Social Media.

Blaschke, L. M. (2014). Using social media to engage and develop the online learner in self-determined learning. *Research in Learning Technology, 22*, 1-23. doi:10.3402/rlt.v22.21635

Blümcke, K. P., Friederike. (2011). Interactive Social Media for Informal Learning and Empowerment–the Project Isabel.

Bradner, E., Kellogg, W. A., & Erickson, T. (1999). The Adoption and Use of 'BABBLE': A Field Study of Chat in the Workplace. In S. Bødker, M. Kyng, & K. Schmidt (Eds.), *ECSCW '99: Proceedings of the Sixth European Conference on Computer Supported Cooperative Work 12–16 September 1999, Copenhagen, Denmark* (pp. 139-158). Dordrecht: Springer Netherlands.

Burnick, L. M. B. V. P. D. S. A. R. J. T. R. S. (2018). *Teens and Social Media: A Case Study of High School Students' Informal Learning Practices and Trajectories*. Paper presented at the Proceedings of the 9th International Conference on Social Media and Society, Copenhagen, Denmark. https://doi.org/10.1145/3217804.3217920

Che, C. W. I. R. B., & Ibrahim, W. (2018). Social Media Tools for Informal Language Learning: A Comprehensive Theoretical Framework. *Asian Social Science, 14*(4).

Chen, B., & Bryer, T. (2012). Investigating Instructional Strategies for Using Social Media in Formal and Informal Learning. *International Review of Research in Open and Distance Learning, 13*(1), 87-104. doi:10.19173/irrodl.v13i1.1027

Conner, M. (2012). Learning Through Social Media. In N. M. Seel (Ed.), *Encyclopedia of the Sciences of Learning* (pp. 1986-1989). Boston, MA: Springer US.

Dabbagh, N., & Kitsantas, A. (2012). Personal Learning Environments, Social Media, and Self-Regulated Learning: A Natural Formula for Connecting Formal and Informal Learning. *Internet and Higher Education, 15*(1), 3-8. doi:10.1016/j.iheduc.2011.06.002

Dogan, M. E. (2014). *Bringing informal communication to the fore in e-learning: Physicians and health educators opinions on using social media for health and healthcare education.* Paper presented at the EdMedia + Innovate Learning 2014, Tampere, Finland. https://www.learntechlib.org/p/147816

Drlik, M., & Beranek, L. (2016). *Social Networks and Their Role in Informal Learning.* Paper presented at the 3rd European Conference on Social M di R h Media Research EM Normandie, Caen, France.

Ersoy, M., & Güneyli, A. (2016). Social Networking as a Tool for Lifelong Learning with Orthopedically Impaired Learners. *Journal of Educational Technology & Society, 19*(1), 41-52.

Fayard, A.-L., & Weeks, J. (2014). Affordances for practice. *Information and Organization, 24*(4), 236-249. doi:https://doi.org/10.1016/j.infoandorg.2014.10.001

Ferguson, R., Faulkner, D., Whitelock, D., & Sheehy, K. (2015). Pre-teens' informal learning with ICT and Web 2.0. *Technology, Pedagogy and Education, 24*(2), 247-265.

Fox, J., & Ralston, R. (2016). Queer identity online: Informal learning and teaching experiences of LGBTQ individuals on social media. *Computers in Human Behavior, 65*, 635-642. doi:https://doi.org/10.1016/j.chb.2016.06.009

Garcia, E., Elbeltagi, I. M., Dungay, K., & Hardaker, G. (2015). Student use of Facebook for informal learning and peer support. *International Journal of Information & Learning Technology, 32*(5), 286-299. doi:10.1108/IJILT-09-2015-0024

Genden, S. N. (2018). Informal Learning Through Social Media: Opportunities for Learning Professionals. In M. J. Spector, B. B. Lockee, & M. D. Childress (Eds.), *Learning, Design, and Technology: An International Compendium of Theory, Research, Practice, and Policy* (pp. 1-23). Cham: Springer International Publishing.

Greenhow, C., & Lewin, C. (2016). Social media and education: reconceptualizing the boundaries of formal and informal learning. *Learning, Media and Technology, 41*(1), 6-30. doi:10.1080/17439884.2015.1064954

Hamat, A., & Abu Hassan, H. (2019). Use of Social Media for Informal Language Learning by Malaysian University Students. *3l-Language Linguistics Literature-the Southeast Asian Journal of English Language Studies, 25*(4), 68-83. doi:10.17576/3l-2019-2504-05

Heo, G. M., & Lee, R. (2013). Blogs and Social Network Sites as Activity Systems: Exploring Adult Informal Learning Process through Activity Theory Framework. *Educational Technology & Society, 16*(4), 133-145. Retrieved from <Go to ISI>://WOS:000327764400011

Hsi, S. (2015). Technology for Informal and Out-of-School Learning of Science. In R. Gunstone (Ed.), *Encyclopedia of Science Education* (pp. 1053-1055). Dordrecht: Springer Netherlands.

Islam, R., & Rabbi, F. (2016). *Researching Students' Experience of Social Media Use as an Informal Learning Platform.* Paper presented at the International Confernece on Teaching and Learning (ICTL).

Jiménez-Cortés, R. (2015). The influence of informal learning processes of social network sites on the subjective well-being of women in rural areas / La influencia de procesos de aprendizaje informal en las redes sociales digitales en el bienestar subjetivo de mujeres de zonas rurales. *Culture and Education, 27*(2), 407-439. doi:10.1080/11356405.2015.1034534

Jones, A. (2014). Social media for informal minority language learning: exploring Welsh learners' practices. *ECSM 2014 University of Brighton Brighton, UK 10-11 July 2014*, 226.

Kanwar, A. S., Balasubramanian, K., & Umar, A. (2013). Lifelong learning in South Africa. *International Journal of Continuing Education & Lifelong Learning, 5*(2), 17-39.

Kavanaugh, A., Gad, S., Neidig, S., Pérez-Quiñones, M. A., Tedesco, J., Ahuja, A., & Ramakrishnan, N. (2012). *(Hyper) local news aggregation: designing for social affordances*. Paper presented at the Proceedings of the 13th Annual International Conference on Digital Government Research, College Park, Maryland, USA. https://doi.org/10.1145/2307729.2307736

Klomsri, T., Grebäck, L., & Tedre, M. (2013). *Social media in everyday learning: How Facebook supports informal learning among young adults in South Africa.* Paper presented at the Proceedings of the 13th Koli Calling International Conference on Computing Education Research.

Kumar, P., & Gruzd, A. (2019). *Social Media for Informal Learning: a Case of# Twitterstorians.* Paper presented at the Proceedings of the 52nd Hawaii International Conference on System Sciences.

Lay Shi, N., Siew Ming, T., & Noorizah Mohd, N. (2018). The Usage of Social Networking Sites for Informal Learning: A Comparative Study Between Malaysia Students of Different Gender and Age Group. *International Journal of Computer-Assisted Language Learning and Teaching (IJCALLT), 8*(4), 76-88. doi:10.4018/IJCALLT.2018100106

Li, X., Gray, K., Verspoor, K., & Barnett, S. (2017). Understanding the context of learning in an online social network for health professionals' informal learning. *Studies In Health Technology And Informatics, 235*, 353-357.

Li, Y. (2013). Informal learning in the Web 2.0 environment: how Chinese students who are learning English use Web 2.0 tools for informal learning.

Lisbôa, E. S., & Coutinho, C. P. (2011). Informal learning in social networks: A study of the Orkut social network. *Issues in Educational Research, 21*(2), 162.

Lundgren, L., Crippen, K. J., & Bex, R. T. (2020). Social Media Interaction as Informal Science Learning: a Comparison of Message Design in Two Niches. *Research in Science Education.* doi:10.1007/s11165-019-09911-y

Ma, Y., Wen, B., & Wang, J. (2019). *Construction of Informal Learning Knowledge Network Based on Social Network Analysis.* Paper presented at the 2019 IEEE International Conference on Computer Science and Educational Informatization (CSEI).

Mao, J. (2014). Social media for learning: A mixed methods study on high school students' technology affordances and perspectives. *Computers in Human Behavior, 33*, 213-223. doi:https://doi.org/10.1016/j.chb.2014.01.002

Maria, R. (2019). Professional development in the digital age. Benefits and constraints of social media for lifelong learning. *Form@re - Open Journal per la formazione in rete, 19*(2). doi:10.13128/formare-25353

McCarthy, J. (2015). Learning in the "Café": Pilot Testing the Collaborative Application for Education in Facebook. *Australasian Journal of Educational Technology, 31*(1), 67-85. doi:10.14742/ajet.1500

McPherson, M., Budge, K., & Lemon, N. (2015). New Practices in Doing Academic Development: Twitter as an Informal Learning Space. *International Journal for Academic Development, 20*(2), 126-136.

Melrose, P. (2012). Irish Students and Facebook: Informal learning choices in a Web 2.0 world. *Irish Journal of Academic Practice, 1*(1), 5.

Michel, C., Touré, C., & Marty, J.-C. (2018). *Adapting Enterprise Social Media for Informal Learning in the Workplace: Using Incremental and Iterative Design Methods to Favor Sustainable Uses.* Paper presented at the International Conference on Computer Supported Education, Cham.

Moreno, M. A., & Uhls, Y. T. (2019). Applying an affordances approach and a developmental lens to approach adolescent social media use. *DIGITAL HEALTH, 5*, 2055207619826678. doi:10.1177/2055207619826678

Okoli, C. (2015). A Guide to Conducting a Standalone Systematic Literature Review. *Communications of the Association for Information Systems, 37*. doi:10.17705/1CAIS.03743

Oliveira, L., & Figueira, Á. (2017). *Social Network Analytics in Formal and Informal Learning Environments with EduBridge Social.* Paper presented at the International Conference on Computer Supported Education, Cham.

Oosterwyk, G., Brown, I., & Geeling, S. (2019). *A Synthesis of Literature Review Guidelines from Information Systems Journals.* Paper presented at the Proceedings of 4th International Conference on the.

Osborne, N. (2014). *Learning from others mistakes: how social media etiquette distorts informal learning online.* Paper presented at the Proceedings of the European Conference on Social Media.

Parmigiani, D., & Pennazio, V. (2012). Web and tool 2.0 affordances for formal and informal learning strategies: the role of the educational project. *REM-Research on Education and Media, 4*(1), 71-84.

Popescu, A. (2012). Social Media, Informal Language Learning, and Knowledge Management. A Case Study. *Synergies Roumanie.*

Pozzi, G., Pigni, F., & Vitari, C. (2014). Affordance Theory in the IS Discipline: a Review and Synthesis of the Literature.

Rehm, M., Littlejohn, A., & Rienties, B. (2018). Does a formal wiki event contribute to the formation of a network of practice? A social capital perspective on the potential for informal learning. *Interactive Learning Environments, 26*(3), 308-319.

Sánchez-Navarro, J., & Aranda, D. (2013). Messenger and social network sites as tools for sociability, leisure and informal learning for Spanish young people. *European Journal of Communication, 28*(1), 67-75.

Sangrà, A., & Wheeler, S. (2013). New Informal Ways of Learning: Or Are We Formalising the Informal? *RUSC, 10*(1), 286-293.

Sato, S., Kageto, M., & Kirkpatrick, G. (2013). Analysis of informal use of social media in formal project-based learning. *International Journal for Educational Media and Technology, 7*(1), 26-37.

Schryen, G. (2015). Writing qualitative IS literature reviews – Guidelines for synthesis, interpretation and guidance of research. *Communications of the AIS, 37*, 286-325. doi:10.17705/1CAIS.03712

Sclater, N. (2016). MOOCs, Open educational resources and social networking: bridging the gap between informal and formal learning. *Revista Mediterranea Comunicacion-Journal of Communication, 7*(2), 9-19. doi:10.14198/medcom2016.7.2.1

Song, D., & Lee, J. (2014). Has Web 2.0 revitalized informal learning? The relationship between Web 2.0 and informal learning. *Journal of Computer Assisted Learning, 30*(6), 511-533. doi:10.1111/jcal.12056

Sophie, M., Catherine, N., & Carroll, F. (2018). *Building the 'Connection'Between the Student, their Peers and the Lecturer: How Social Media can Enhance Student Engagement and Afford Informal Learning Opportunities*. Paper presented at the 10th International Conference on Education and New Learning Technologies.

Sophie, M., Catherine, N., & Carroll, F. (2018). Building the 'Connection'Between the Student, their Peers and the Lecturer: How Social Media can Enhance Student Engagement and Afford Informal Learning Opportunities.

Stendal, K., Thapa, D., & Lanamäki, A. (2016). *Analyzing the concept of affordances in information systems.* Paper presented at the 2016 49th Hawaii International Conference on System Sciences (HICSS).

Taibi, D., Gentile, M., Fulantelli, G., & Allegra, M. (2010). An Ontology to Model e-portfolio and Social Relationship in Web 2.0 Informal Learning Environments. *International Journal of Computers Communications & Control, 5*(4), 578-585. doi:10.15837/ijccc.2010.4.2516

Tallent, G. (2014). *The Social Media Canvas and Its Use in Strategy Formulation.* Paper presented at the European Conference on Social Media.

Templier, M., & Paré, G. J. C. o. t. A. f. I. S. (2015). A framework for guiding and evaluating literature reviews. *37*(1), 6.

Thaler, A. (2011). *Informal learning with social media and its potential for a democratisation of education.* Paper presented at the Proceedings of the 9th Annual IASSTS Conference on Critical Issues in Science and Technology Studies, 2th–3th May.

Van Osch, W., & Mendelson, O. (2011). A typology of affordances: Untangling sociomaterial interactions through video analysis.

Volkoff, O., & Strong, D. M. (2017). Affordance theory and how to use it in IS research. In *The Routledge companion to management information systems* (pp. 232-245): Routledge.

Wan, C. W. I. R. C., Prain, V., & Collet, P. (2014). Perceived learning strategies of Malaysian university students in Web 2.0-based English as a Second Language informal learning. *GEMA Online® Journal of Language Studies, 14*(1).

Wang, H., Wang, J., & Tang, Q. (2018). A Review of Application of Affordance Theory in Information Systems. *11*(1), 56-70.

Yakin, I., & Gencel, I. E. (2013). The Utilization of Social Media Tools for Informal Learning Activities: A Survey Study. *Mevlana International Journal of Education, 3*(4), 108.

Yoo, S., & Kim, S. (2013). How and why college students use Web 2.0 applications: The role of social media in formal and informal learning. *Int. J. of Web Based Communities, 9*, 174-187. doi:10.1504/IJWBC.2013.053242

Zehrer, A., & Grabmüller, A. (2012). Social media marketing in tourism education:Insights into the development and value of a social network site for a higher education institution in tourism. *18*(3), 221-228. doi:10.1177/1356766712449368

Zeng, B., & Gerritsen, R. (2014). What do we know about social media in tourism? A review. *Tourism Management Perspectives, 10*, 27-36. doi:https://doi.org/10.1016/j.tmp.2014.01.001

Zhang, K., & Gao, F. (2014). Social media for informal science learning in China: A case study. *Knowledge Management & E-Learning: An International Journal, 6*(3), 262-280.

Zhao, F., & Kemp, L. (2012). Integrating Web 2.0-based informal learning with workplace training. *Educational Media International, 49*(3), 231-245. doi:10.1080/09523987.2012.738015

DEVELOPING A MOBILE SOCIAL LEARNING APPLICATION FOR INTERDISCIPLINARY TECHNOLOGY COURSES

Brian Thoms[1] and Evren Eryilmaz[2]
[1]*CSU Channel Islands, Camarillo, California, USA*
[2]*CSU Sacramento, Sacramento, California, USA*

ABSTRACT

Smartphone adoption has grown steadily and now represents roughly 50% of all Internet traffic. Advances in mobile application development along with its widespread adoption offers unique opportunities within computing education to quickly offer knowledge and information directly into the hands of the learner. Adopting a mobile-first approach, this paper introduces the construction of a mobile social learning platform, built on top of existing social learning software and measures its adoption in interdisciplinary computing courses. The goal of the mobile app is to complement the browser-based system and provide access to course notifications, gradebook and discussion posts. Initial results found 50% of students adopting the smartphone app regularly, while most students preferred to use the browser-based system. Students adopting the mobile application indicated that they liked the ability to view course notifications, assignments, grades and instructor feedback from within the mobile app.

KEYWORDS

Computing Education, Social Networking, Mobile Application

1. INTRODUCTION

Across North America, colleges and universities are facing significant increases in enrollment in undergraduate computing courses and programs (Camp et al., 2017). This trend reflects projections produced by the U.S. Bureau of Labor Statistics (Bureau of Labor Statistics, Occupational Projections, 2020), which cites substantial increases in opportunities over the next ten years in various areas of computing, such as software developers and information security analysts (25% and 31% respectively). Interest in CS by non-majors has also substantially increased (Camp et al., 2017) as students attempt to build technical skills that are transferrable into the workplace (Camp et al., 2015). In some cases, this has led to CS majors taking courses along-side non-CS majors. This interdisciplinary approach to CS education works particularly well when natural synergies and overlap exist in the CS and non-CS curriculum.

During this same timeframe, the world has seen a steady rise in smartphone adoption and mobile computing, specifically with regards to accessing online content. Today, smartphones comprise over 50% of all Internet traffic (Clement, 2019). Consequently, in order to support the fact that students are using mobile technologies, they require tools on such devices to support individual learning, as identified in (Gikas and Grant, 2013). Yet delivery of effective education content over mobile devices remains challenging and face added workloads and costs on increasingly taxed educational systems.

In this paper, we introduce mobile social learning software, built atop an existing web-based social learning platform. More specifically, this paper describes the construction of a cross-platform mobile application for iOS and Android, and its implementation across interdisciplinary technology courses. The goal of this system is to offer students with a mobile-first system for instructional content and course features such as notifications, assignments, grades and peer-interactions. Initial results found that the mobile app, while useful as an informational resource was less utilized than the browser-based learning environment. This paper chronicles this experience.

2. BACKGROUND

2.1 Course Design

The Computer Science course COMP449 – Human Computer Interaction (HCI), studies the ways in which people interact with computing devices and design technologies to support interaction with these devices in novel ways. The course is cross-listed with Psychology and serves as an undergraduate upper-division general education course required for graduation. Cross-listed computing courses are becoming more popular and offer unique opportunities for computing programs and introduce more reluctant students to areas of computing through the integration of theories and concepts of other disciplines (Carter, 2014). In 2020, the software for COMP449 was enhanced with a mobile application, to provide students with a mobile-first alternative to accessing the gradebook, quizzes, discussion-board and blogs. In Version 1, the goal was to offer a complementary app to the web-based system and to measure students' satisfaction with the system.

2.2 SocialXYZ OSN Design

Constructivist learning places individuals at the center of the learning experience (Piaget, 1952). Instructional software embracing this approach often leverages social components common in online social networking (OSN) software (Thoms, Garrett and Ryan, 2009), (Boulos, Maramba and Wheeler, 2006) that have been shown to elevate learning, software satisfaction and course satisfaction, compared to traditional learning management systems (Thoms and Eryilmaz, 2014).

The primary system in this paper is SocialXYZ, which is software built atop Elgg, an open source social networking engine. Designed specifically for browser-based interaction, Elgg comes bundled with online discussion boards, blogs, file gallery, profile building and peer-to-peer connection-making. Illustrated in Figure 1, the course landing page highlights content from across the site including assignments and provides quick access to the course gradebook, syllabus, files and peer-connections. Illustrated in Figure 2 is the center of student-to-student interaction, the asynchronous online discussion board. Critical to SocialXYZ, the discussion board facilitates cognitive, on-topic, on-task, and sustained discussion among students (Pituch and Lee, 2006), and allows peers to communicate using similar language styles (Caldwell, 2007). In previous design iterations, SocialXYZ was enhanced to include a recommender system based on the sentiment and quality of discussion posts (Thoms et al., 2020), (Thoms et al., 2017). While effective in the browser, the system interface breaks down across mobile devices, where screen real estate is constrained. In this paper, we attempt to improve the user experience across mobile devices.

Figure 1. SocialXYZ Landing Page

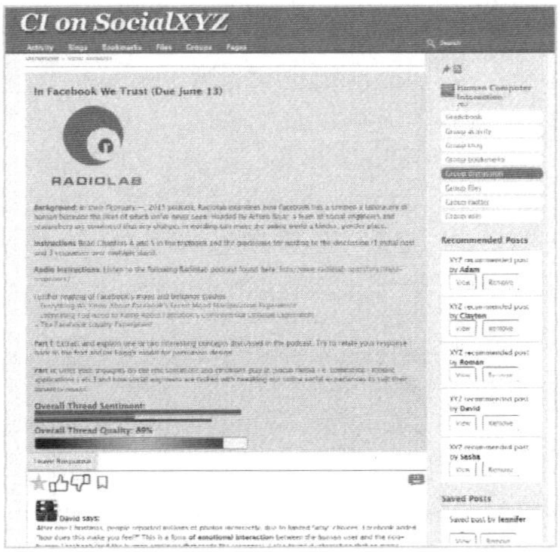

Figure 2. SocialXYZ AOD

2.3 SocialXYZ Mobile App Design

Built for Android and iOS, a mobile app was developed using the React Native JavaScript programming language and leverages a REST architecture for backend processing. Version 1 of the system includes critical features including course announcements, syllabus, discussion board and gradebook. The Home screen, which is illustrated in Figure 3, provides access to this primary application feature-set. Course assignments, depicted in Figure 4, also provides functionality for grades and instructor feedback. The threaded asynchronous online discussion board is illustrated in Figure 5 and Figure 6 illustrates the screen for a typical discussion response. Response metrics highlighted in Figure 6 were studied in previous design iterations of the web-based platform (see [Thoms et al., 2020], [Thoms et al., 2017]). Enhanced mobile app features leveraged native smartphone functionality such as automated delivery of system notifications and gesture-based screen swiping.

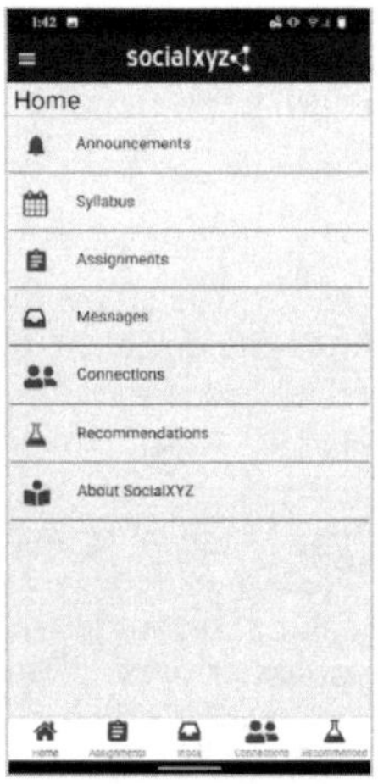

Figure 3. Home Screen

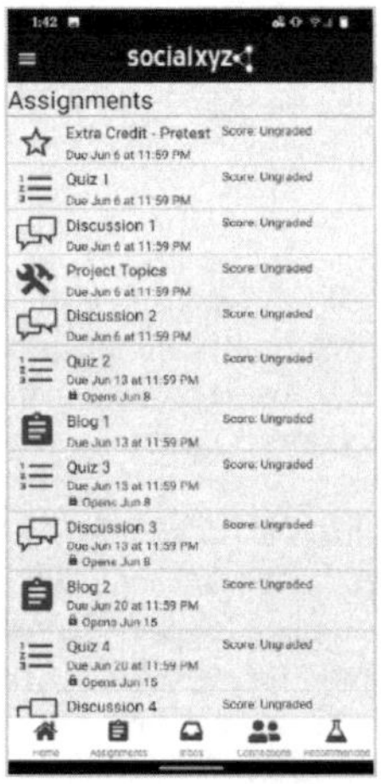

Figure 4. Assignments

Figure 5. Discussion Board

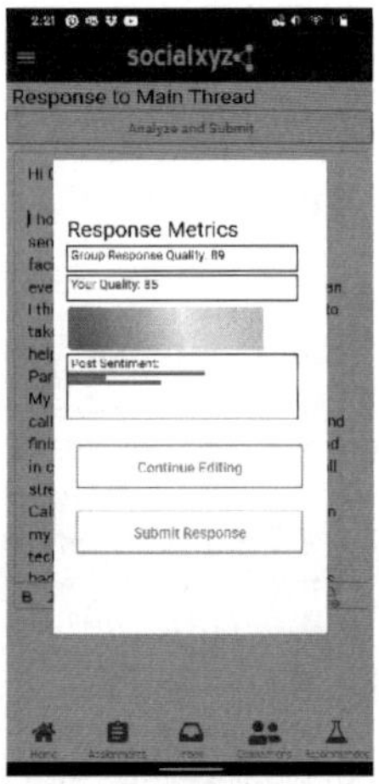

Figure 6. Response Screen

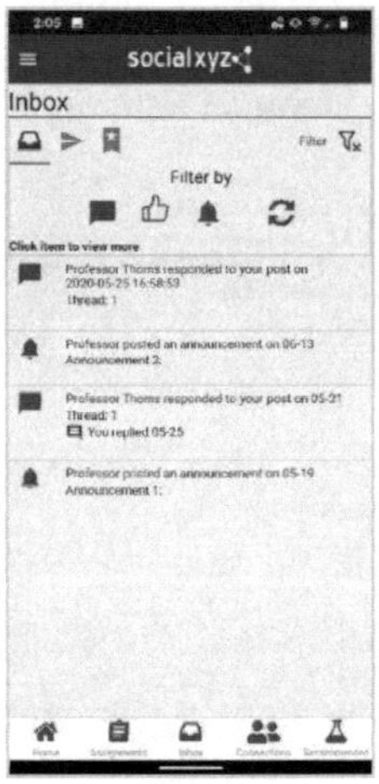

Figure 7. Inbox

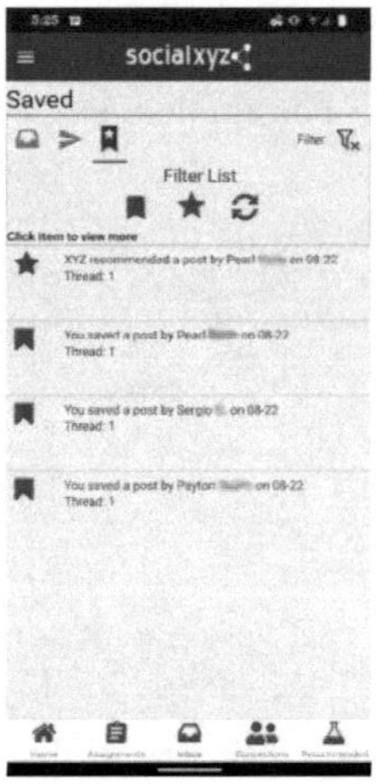

Figure 8. Bookmarks

Figure 9. Connections

Figure 10. User Posts

Figure 7 and Figure 8 illustrate app messages, announcements and bookmarks. All content created by or directed to a user can be found in the user's Inbox, Sent Box and Bookmarks screens. Figure 9 and Figure 10 illustrate screens for direct peer-to-peer interactions across the system. In short, users may quickly navigate to peer content via the Connections screen, where they can thumbs-up / thumbs-down content, which is saved directly to their Inbox. System Recommendations are available through the 'flask' icon and highlight top-rated content from across the system.

3. RESULTS

In summer of 2020, the system was tested across an online, asynchronous upper-division technology course, serving students looking to satisfy general education requirements for graduation. A total of 20 students participated in the course.

3.1 System Usage

Broken down in Figure 11, the composition of the course was 60% computer science and information technology majors and 40% non-computing majors including psychology, business and health sciences. Anonymous pretest data identified 100% of students having experience with learning management software such as Blackboard or Canvas and 91% having experience with social networking technologies such as Facebook and Twitter.

The total number of web views accessed through the browser-based system was 8,874, while the number of API calls from all mobile devices was 2,655. For results on web-based usage, we refer you to previous research in (Thoms et al., 2007). An analysis of device operating systems found that 65% of users used the app on iOS devices and 35% used the app on Android devices. All students attempted to use both the website and the mobile app initially, while the browser-based system was used considerably more and accounted for 75% of total interactions across the system. Posttest survey data identified 50% of respondents indicating that they used the mobile application frequently. Detailed in Figure 12, an analysis of API log files found that the primary use of the mobile app was largely informational. Viewing mobile messages and announcements accounted for 40% of all API calls. An additional 29% of API calls accessed the discussion board and system recommendations. Assignments and grades accounted for 13% of API calls as did API calls for peer-to-peer connections, which was also 13%. User generated content represented a much smaller percentage of overall interactions with the system. 3% of API calls made added discussion board posts and 3% of API calls made accessed the mobile quizzes. In total, the mobile discussion board was accessed 358 times, while the browser-based discussion board was accessed 791 times.

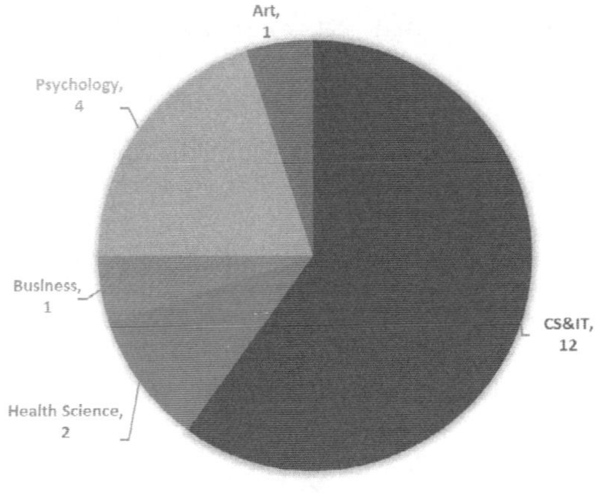

Figure 11. System Demographics

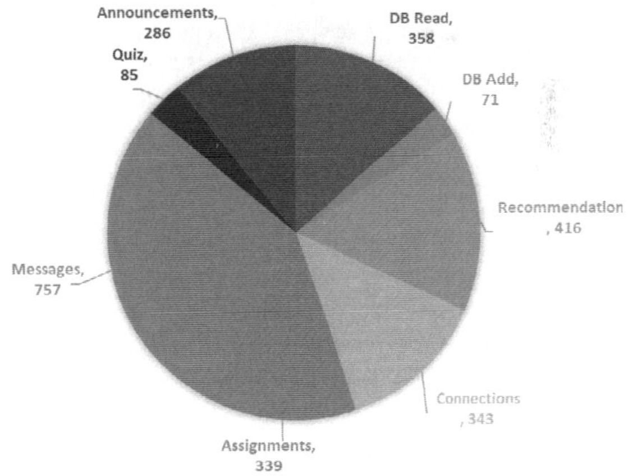

Figure 12. Mobile App Usage by REST Call

3.2 System Satisfaction

Detailed in Table 1, posttest survey data helped to gauge general satisfaction with the mobile app. Of the 18 students responding to the posttest, 78% indicated satisfaction with the mobile application compared to 100% indicating satisfaction with the browser-based system. More specifically related to the mobile app, 50% stated that it was easy to use and 50% stated it as an excellent way to receive updates from the instructor. Additionally, 50% of respondents indicated that the mobile app was an excellent way to view updates from their classmates. It was found that 28% of respondents strongly disagreed that the mobile app was an excellent way to post to the discussion with only 22% of respondents agreeing with this statement.

Table 1. Posttest Survey Results

Posttest Questions (n=18)	SA	A	N	D	SD
I used Mobile SocialXYZ frequently.	2	7	5	2	2
I preferred to use Mobile SocialXYZ over the Website.	3	1	6	6	2
Mobile SocialXYZ was easy to use.	2	7	6	3	0
Mobile SocialXYZ provided useful functionality.	3	5	8	2	0
Mobile SocialXYZ was an excellent way to view course content.	5	2	7	4	0
Mobile SocialXYZ was an excellent way to view updates by the instructor.	5	4	9	0	0
Mobile SocialXYZ was an excellent way to view updates by my classmates.	5	4	8	1	0
Mobile SocialXYZ was an excellent way to post to the discussion.	2	2	9	3	2

SA=Strongly Agree, A=Agree, N=Neutral, D= Disagree, SD= Strongly Disagree

4. CONCLUSION

This experiential paper introduces the design, development and implementation of Mobile SocialXYZ built atop existing open source social networking software. Overall, the mobile app complemented the browser-based system providing students with a mobile-first approach to accessing content such as announcements, gradebook and discussion posts and provides students with features for interacting with their peers through social networking and notifications. Additionally, this paper presents on Version 1 of the mobile app. New features for direct messaging, AWS cloud storage integration and an advanced content-based recommendation system are under construction.

REFERENCES

Boulos, M., Maramba, I., Wheeler, S. (2006). "Wikis, blogs and podcasts: a new generation of web-based tools for virtual collaborative clinical practice and education," *BMC Medical Education*, 6(41).

Bureau of Labor Statistics, Occupational Projections (2020). Retrieved online on June 21, 2020 from https://data.bls.gov/projections/occupationProj.

Caldwell, JE. (2007). "Clickers in the Large Classroom: Current Research and Best-practice Tips", *CBE-Life Sciences Education*, 6(1).

Camp, T., Adrion, W.R., Bizot, B., Davidson, S., Hall, M., Hambrusch, S., Walker, E. and Zweben, S. (2017). Generation CS: The Growth of Computer Science. *ACM Inroads* 8(2), pp. 44–50.

Camp, T., Zweben, S., Walker, E., and Barker, L. (2015). Booming enrollments: Good times? In *Proceedings of the 46th ACM Technical Symposium on Computer Science Education* (Kansas City, United States, (March 04-07, 2015). SIGSCE '15. ACM, New York, NY, 80–81.

Carter, L. (2014). "Interdisciplinary computing classes: worth the effort," In *Proceedings of the 45th ACM technical symposium on Computer science education* (SIGCSE '14). ACM, New York, NY, USA.

Clement, J. (2019). "Percentage of all global web pages served to mobile phones from 2009 to 2018," *Statistica.* Retrieved online from https://www.statista.com/statistics/277125/share-of-website-traffic-coming-from-mobile-devices/ on August 20, 2020.

Gikas, J., Grant, MM. (2013). "Mobile computing devices in higher education: Student perspectives on learning with cellphones, smartphones & social media," *The Internet and Higher Education*, v19, pp 18-26.

J. Piaget, *The Origins of Intelligence in Children.* New York, NY: International University Press, 1952.

Pituch, K., Lee, Y. (2006). "The influence of system characteristics on e-learning use," *Computers & Education*, 47(2).

Thoms, B., Eryilmaz, E. (2014). "How Media Choice Affects Learner Interactions in Distance Learning Classes," *Computers & Education*, v75.

Thoms, B., Eryilmaz, E. Dubin, N. Hernandez, R. Colon-Cerezo, S. (2020). "Real-Time Visualization to Improve Quality in Computer Mediated Communication," *Web Intelligence Journal*, v18(1), 2020.

Thoms, B., Eryilmaz, E. Mercado, G. Ramirez, B. Rodriguez, J. (2017). "Towards A Sentiment Analyzing Discussion Board," *Hawaiian International Conference on System Sciences* (*HICSS 50*).

Thoms, B., Garrett N. and Ryan, T. (2009). "Online Learning Communities in the New 'U'. *International Journal of Networking and Virtual Organisations*, 6(5), pp. 499-517.

Thoms, B., Garrett, N., Soffer, M. and Ryan, T. (2007). "Resurrecting Graduate Conversation through an Online Learning Community", *IADIS Multi Conference on Computer Science and Information Systems* (*IADIS-2007*).

TOWARDS SMART GOVERNMENT WITH A THEORETICAL STRATEGY MODEL

Meriem Bensaid and Salah Baina
ENSIAS, Mohammed V University in Rabat- Morocco

ABSTRACT

The concept of smartness gains more and more significant importance in public sector transformation and the governments are beginning to take the paradigm of electronic government to a new stage to engage with citizens, co-develop policies, adopt creative thinking, enable a citizen-centric public service, and adopt innovation as a core value to raise the quality of life of citizens and enhance economic growth. In this respect, this paper performed a comprehensive literature review analysis to the identified smart government approaches. The Most important outcome is a Smart Government Strategy Meta Model which shows that Smart government is a whole effort which can be thought of in terms of three paradigms: 1.Smart participation approach 2.Competentness approach 2.Entrepreneurial approach. These three pillars rely on three enablers: Data, Smart capabilities and innovation.

KEYWORDS

Smart Government, Innovation, Digital Transformation, Smart Services, Smart Citizen

1. INTRODUCTION

The Digital Transformation of the public sector is a continuous process of transformational change of the way government work internally and externally in which the ICT role is changing over the time ***(Lips/2012, Millard et al. /2007, Huijboom et al. /2009b, Traunmüller et al. /2003)***. In the literature, the ICT use in public administration is seen as a driver of efficiency and effectiveness by rationalizing existing process or as a tool to radically re-think the public sector and its external relationships re-engineer processes and organizations (***Cordella et al./2012***) and build new ways of interacting with citizens and businesses. Several concepts exist to assess the level of digital transformation development in the public sector. Indeed, as public administration grew in maturity in their use of ICT, they shift from Electronic Government where information and communication technologies (ICTs), and particularly the internet is seen as a tool to achieve better government (***OECD/2014***) to Digital Government where the use of digital technologies is an integrated part of governments' modernization strategies, to create public value.

However, on the one hand Public Administration faces the challenge of integrating emerging technologies more coherently and sustainably, on the other hand the technology and sup-ply-side focus of most benchmarks, indexes and rankings fail to explain the discrepancies between the availability and the use of online public services (***Meyerhoff Nielsen/2014; Meyerhoff Nielsen and Igari/2012***).

This fact also applies to the Moroccan Public Sector which is committed over the past two decades to embed ICT as a core function for public administrations to increase government effectiveness, efficiency, accountability and to establish better governance, responsive and open government (***Digital Government Review of Morocco, OECD/2018***).The COVID-19 pandemic has certainly confirmed the role of ICT as an important tool to improve the performance of the administration, while maintaining the physical distance with the citizen. But the challenge today for the Moroccan public sector is no longer to introduce emerging technologies into public sector but to align with advances in smart technologies, better informed and connected citizens, and global connected economies, this force Moroccan public administration to rethink their role and to take steps to become Smart (Smart government) and resilient; it's about a continuous effort and not a specific goal.

Many approaches exists that present different perspectives to Smart Government according which, the concept of smartness in the public sector are the outcome of a set of the element : open data , Sharing , Service Integration, Innovation, citizen participation, information transparency, co-develop policies all supported by emerging technologies (e.g., big data, open government data, IOT ….etc.).

The aims of this research is to use the descriptive analysis for the identified academic literature, governmental and non-governmental report that relates to both smart government and Digital Transformation evolution and driving forces of the enterprise. The objectives is to extract the knowledge and expertise obtained in the private sector and to discuss how such efforts and their results can be applied to existing research perspectives to smart government in order to identify the majors paradigms of smartness in the Public Sector and map them into a Smart Government Strategy Meta Model model for smart citizen (***DIY Citizenship", Ratto and Boler /2014***).

To do so, firstly this paper provides related literature on the subject of Smart Government. The next section enlightens about features of Smart Government throught the theoretical strategy model proposed, and finally conclusion and future work.

2. LITERATURE REVIEW

2.1 Understanding Smart Government

In the narrower sense, the term SMART is used as a synonym of modern and intelligent and it is increasingly used in different contexts with different meanings (smart phones, smart home, smart industry, smart cities, smart governance, smart government ... etc). In Smart Government context, the concept of SMART refers to (***Petrov/2014***):

- Social : Personalized and citizen-friendly service delivery ;
- Mobile : Using the latest mobile technologies to deliver information and services, and get contributions from citizens, wherever and whenever they want ;
- Radical-openness : "open by design" transforms accountability and transparency, engages citizens in co-creation and enable businesses to use data to innovative new services ;
- Trust: Effective cybersecurity so that services are resilient, available and protection privacy.

The smart government term initially appeared in 2010 and various smart government meanings have been provided by scholars since then, however there is a common consensus according to which, Smart Government has been coined to describe the next generation of government transformation (Table 1).

Table 1. The paradigm shift for smart Government (***Charalabidis/ 2015***)

	e-Government	***Open government***	***Smart Gov***
Concept	that work well	that opens to people	that think
Goal	how to do internal : Process innovation	how to do external : Governance innovation	what to do-Policy : innovation
Key ICT area	Infrastructures & Organisation	People & Data	Machine Intelligence & IoT

Some of these approaches are given by ***anowski/2015, Cornadie and Choenni/2014***, who relate the smartness of the public sector to the power (data-smart government). From a similar viewpoint, ***Harsh and Ichalkaranje/2015*** consider that governments utilize the power of "data" in their attempt to improve public services; to enable an integrated, seamless service experience; to engage with citizens; to co-develop policies; and to implement solutions for well-being of the community. While ***Mellouli et al./2014, Cellary/2013 and Puron-Cid /2014*** define it as the extensive use of technology by governments to perform governmental tasks. On the other hand, ***Gil Garcia et al./2014*** conclude that smart government is a creative mix of emerging technologies and innovation in the public sector. Other corresponding definitions to smart government consider it as the next step for e-government, with the use of innovation (***Savoldelli et al. /2014***) or as the next step of open government with the engagement of citizens, accountability and interoperability (***Veljković et al./2014, Jiménez et al/2014***).Smart government is also defined by ***Kliksberg's/2000*** as government that focuses on its strategic roles in society, with an institutional design and a development of managerial capacities that enable it to perform its roles in a highly effective; Moreover, ***Netten et al. /2016, Rubel/2014*** approaches Smart government as: "Interoperability, The implementation of a set of business processes and underlying ICT capabilities that enable seamless information flow across government agencies and programs, to become intuitive in providing high quality citizen services across all government programs and activity domains". Finally, ***L.G.Anthopoulos/2017*** define smart government as the evolution of both digital (e-government and open government and of smart city at a local level. The most important outcome of his study is "A unified smart government framework" that he compared with the Smart government conceptual framework given by ***Gil-Garcia et al. /2016***.

2.1.1 Smart Government Conceptual Framework (Gil-Garcia et al, 2016)

The dimensions are: Openness as a synonym of transparency, information access, and accountability; Citizen Centricity by providing personalized information and service; Citizen Engagement as synonym of e-Participation as an enabler for a stronger and more intelligent collaboration between citizens and governments; Evidence-based decision making as intensive use of data to make better decision; Entrepreneurialism as an enabler of an attractive ecosystem for businesses and a better quality of life for individuals; Effectiveness and Efficiency as a benefit of e-government; Technology savviness as o tool to have an expert knowledge on the use of information technology tools; Creativity as the process through which new ideas are produced in both public service, internal process or public governance; Innovation as the process through which those ideas are implemented; Integration as an enabler for better communication, response, coordination; Sustainability which refers to the ecological implications of growth; Equality in order to reduce social exclusion by ensuring that citizens have equitable access to education, training, and services...etc; Resiliency as the ability to respond to their citizens in cases of emergency and disaster.

2.1.2 Unified Smart Government Framework (Anthopoulos, 2017)

It is a scientific Model according which building a Smart government is a whole effort which can be thought of in terms of three pillars: Digital Government, Open Government, and Smart City at a local level. The principal aims of Digital Government are to transform the relation-ship between government and citizens via smart services, key-enablers deployment and Interoperability and result in an increased government effectiveness and efficiency. On the other hand, open Government can modernize public service delivery via openness and promote more citizen engagement in politics, it has the potential to change the way that people view government as more accountable. Moreover, Smart cities are more likely to address smart city government, while smart solutions enhance local economic growth and evidence-based policy making. Finally, Data and emerging technologies accompanied by innovation in the public sector depicts the key components that drive the development of the second ring.

2.1.3 Analysis - Literature Review

- The smart government conceptual framework (Gil-Garcia et al. /2016), which is a multidimensional concept with very diverse components and elements, identifies and defines the goals (WHY) that a smart administration should achieve in the future without describing the means (HOW) to achieve them. In addition, those dimensions are related, some of them are the values attained from smart government; while most of them may be seen as a means to this values. In the following table (Table 2), we propose a classification of these dimensions :

Table 2. Smart gov Outcomes/ Outputs/Means

Outcome/ Why	Means / How	Description
Citizen engagement	Openness	Openness provides information for citizens and lead to better communication which actively engages citizens
	Innovation	in terms of Policy innovation
	Technology savviness	Networked technologies also provide new opportunities for citizens to participate in and influence, develop, and test smart city policies (*Pereira, Cunha, Lampoltshammer, Parycek & Testa/2017*)
Efficiency & Effectiveness	Evidence-based decision making	Exploiting data in a more systematic rather than ad-hoc way to.
	Creativity	creative thinking as a way of removing rigid preconceptions and of opening ourselves to complex phenomena which cannot always be dealt with in a strictly logical manner (Landry /2012)
	Integration	Information integration in government can reduce duplication of data collection, coordinate efforts, and help local, state, and national level administrations become more efficient, transparent, and deliver better quality services (*Gil-Garcia/2012a, 2012b*).
	Technology savviness	ICT in government can reach goals beyond costs reduction and service quality improvement
	Innovation	innovation and intelligence for local or governments as the means to increase their efficiency and effectiveness (*Taylor/2015 and Gil-Garcia et al./2013, 2015a*)
Entrepreneurialism	Citizen Centricity	Meeting the Needs of the Customer
	Equality	equal accessibility to public services
	Resiliency	Proactiveness as a key dimension of (Covin & Slevin/1989; Miller/1983; Morris & Sexton/1996) Anticipatory Government: Prevention Rather than Cure
	Sustainability	By promoting the concept of entrepreneurship, Smart government initiatives can contribute in many ways to the achievement of the sustainable development goals
	Technology savviness	Creating public value through smart technologies
	Innovation	Innovative Public Services

Thus, it can be concluded that implementation of strategic approaches to transition towards smart government can focus on three core values supported by Technology, Innovation and Data: 1. Citizen Engagement, 2. Efficiency & Effectiveness as a result of creativity which is related to human capital, horizontal and vertical integration and Evidence-based decision making…etc., 3. Entrepreneurialism whish which is essentially based on smart services.

- Unified smart government framework (L.G. Anthopoulos/2017): by analyzing the three pillars on which this model is based, we can consider Digital Government, Open Government, and Smart City at a local level as complementary and interrelated concepts. Indeed, the potential of digital facilitate instant interaction with citizens and promote accountability. In addition Open government data and information based on technological trends foster innovation in the public and the private sector and promote social and economic development of a society as a whole (economic growth); these same trends are transforming citizens into coproducers of information (citizens engagement). In fact , the Unified smart government framework consider that the Smart Government is a multidimensional approach which encompasses both Digital/Open Government initiatives and Smart City at a local level ., but it doesn't propose a clear process to enable better decisions about the development of smart government strategies and projects (When does a smart government transformation start? And, where to begin?).

To conclude, Figure 1 synthesize all the smart government approaches given by the literatures above.

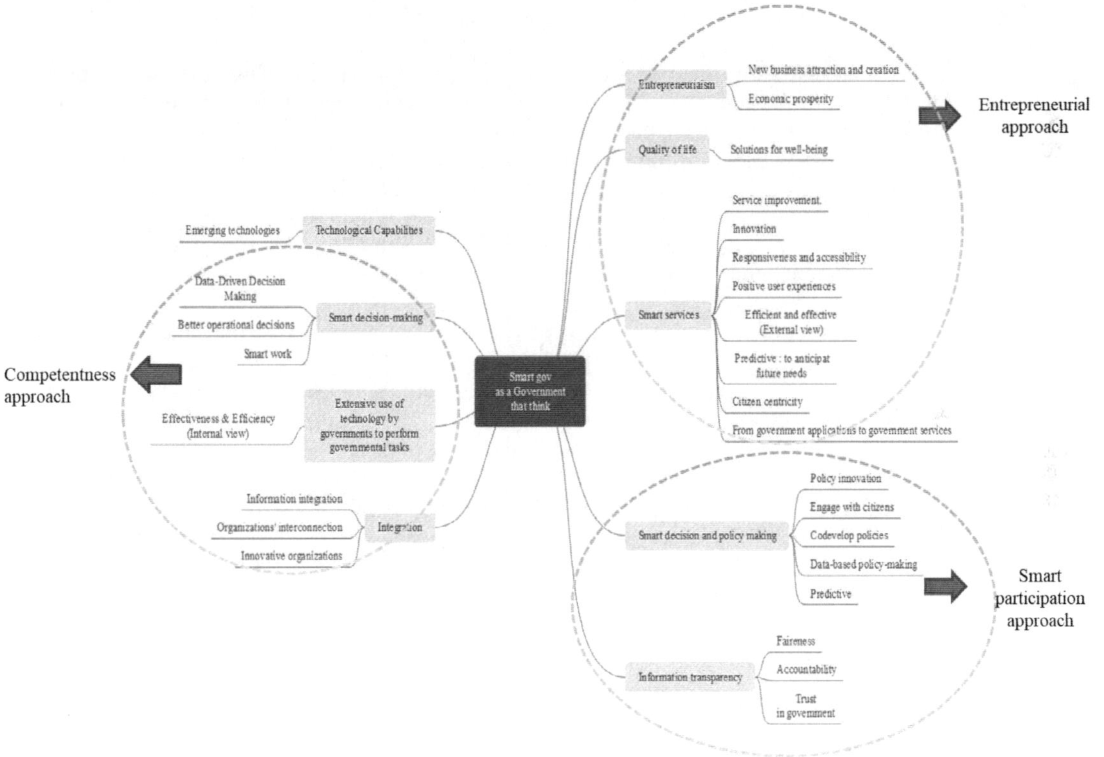

Figure 1. Smart government approaches synthesis

3. SMART GOVERNMENT STRATEGY META MODEL

Based on all those definitions to smart government (Figure 1), we can conclude that creating a Smart Government ecosystem does not only require just the appropriate digital tools but also well-functioning teams able to implement these smart technologies, along with necessary policies through co creation with citizens and policy innovation (smart engagement).

Thus, government transformation towards smart government may be seen as relies on three major paradigms (Figure 2):

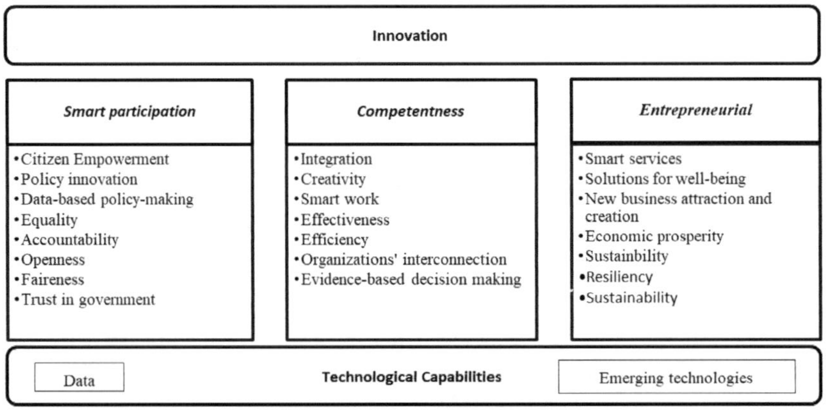

Figure 2. Smat govenrment Strategy Meta Model

- **Smart participation approach**: in term of policy making, this paradigm focuses on policy making processes to increase the society's trust and confidence in government and to promote e-democracy through more participatory and more responsibility; This approach represents the shift from open participation (reactive, responsive disclosure of public information) to smart participation which really gives power to citizens and aims to strength Citizen Empowerment. According to the categorization given by the OECD/2001 to the interaction between citizens and government, this smart participation covers the following three stages:
  - Smart Enabling : government produces and delivers information for use by citizens (information transparency, Open Any Data) ;
  - Smart Engagement : governments ask for and receive citizens' feedback on a policy issue (evidence-based policy making) ;
  - Smart Empowerment : in which citizens actively engage in the policy-making process (Codevelop policies and Policy innovation) ;

- **Competentness approach:** aims to enhance internal efficiency and effectiveness through a set of concepts: creativity, smart work, Data-Driven Decision Making cross-organizational information as well as knowledge integration. In addition while the need for interdisciplinary teams is important to any Electronic Government initiatives, it is particularly crucial for implementing Smart Government concept.

- **Entrepreneurial approach**: mainly aims at increasing the accessibility, responsiveness, smartness of public services and economic growth as well as citizens' well-being. This approach refers to the ability of governments to anticipate a need and to respond effectively in the face of external change.

This Smart government Strategy Meta Model aims to describe a standard in order to help governments developing and implementing their Smart government Strategy.

4. CONCLUSION

Governmental transformation to become smart is about a continuous effort and not a specific goal, this new phenomenon disrupt on the one hand the process of public policy making through data-based decisions and citizen engagement, on the other hand it provide predictive, adaptable, innovative, sustainable, effective and efficient public services which are accessible anytime, anywhere and from any device. Thus, Smart government that relies on smart technologies (IOT, Big Data, and IA…etc) complement both the e-government and open government concepts and introduce new ones such as innovation, creativity, entrepreneurialism, resilience and sustainability (***Gil-Garcia and al. /2016***). For future work, on the one hand, we will continue to develop the model shown in figure 4 by trying to cover the maximum amount of literature concerning smart gov. On the other hand, we will enhance this model with inter-national smart government and digitalization strategies well as the advances in the private sector in terms of digital transformation; the principal objective is to identify the underlying factors that control those elements and to examine the interrelationship between these components.

REFERENCES

Anthopoulos, L., 2017. Smart Government: A New Adjective to Government Transformation or a Trick? *Public Administration and Information Technology*, pp. 263-293.

Charalabidis, Y., Loukis, E., Alexopoulos, C. and Lachana, Z., 2019. The Three Generations of Electronic Government: From Service Provision to Open Data and to Policy Analytics. *Lecture Notes in Computer Science*, pp. 3-17.

Cordella, A. and Bonina, C., 2012. A public value perspective for ICT enabled public sector reforms: A theoretical reflection. *Government Information Quarterly*, 29(4), pp. 512-520.

Featherman, C., 2016. DIY citizenship: Critical making and social media. *New Media & Society*, 18(4), pp. 672-674.

Gil-Garcia, J., Helbig, N. and Ojo, A., 2014. Being smart: Emerging technologies and innovation in the public sector. *Government Information Quarterly*, 31, pp. I1-I8.

Gil-Garcia, J., Zhang, J. and Puron-Cid, G., 2016. Conceptualizing smartness in government: An integrative and multi-dimensional view. *Government Information Quarterly*, 33(3), pp. 524-534.

Kliksberg, B., 2000. Rebuilding the State for Social Development: Towards 'Smart Government'. *International Review of Administrative Sciences*, 66(2), pp. 241-257.

Lips, M., 2012. E-Government is dead: Long live Public Administration 2.0. *Information Polity*, 17(3, 4), pp. 239-250.

Mellouli, S., Luna-Reyes, L. and Zhang, J., 2014. Smart government, citizen participation and open data. *Information Polity*, 19(1,2), pp. 1-4.

Nam, T., 2013. Government 3.0 in Korea. *Proceedings of the 7th International Conference on Theory and Practice of Electronic Governance*.

Nceg.gov.in. 2021. [online] Available at: <https://www.nceg.gov.in/sites/default/files/nceg2014/presentation/day1_session3_World_Bank_Oleg_Petrov.pdf> [Accessed 20 February 2021].

Oecd.org. 2021. [online] Available at: <http://www.oecd.org/gov/digital-government/recommendation-digital-government-strategies.pdf> [Accessed 20 February 2021].

Public Administration and Information Technology, 2017. Government 3.0 – Next Generation Government Technology Infrastructure and Services.

Sun, P., Ku, C. and Shih, D., 2015. An implementation framework for E-Government 2.0. *Telematics and Informatics*, 32(3), pp. 504-520.

Viale Pereira, G., Cunha, M., Lampoltshammer, T., Parycek, P. and Testa, M., 2017. Increasing collaboration and participation in smart city governance: a cross-case analysis of smart city initiatives. *Information Technology for Development*, 23(3), pp. 526-553.

Winstanley, P., 2017. Public Administration for the Next Generation. *Public Administration and Information Technology*, pp. 27-36.

EXPLORING THE IMPACT OF PERSONALITY TRAITS AND TECHNICAL AFFINITY ON THE APPEARANCE OF TECHNOSTRESS

Maximilian Lang and Christian Schieder
Ostbayerische Technische Hochschule Amberg-Weiden, Germany

ABSTRACT

Information and communication technologies, such as instant messengers, have become an essential part of every person's work and private life. Undesirable side effects, such as technostress accompany this trend. The present study examines the relationship between the Big Five personality traits and the technical affinity to the appearance of technostress and its effect on the general task fulfillment. The experimental design's central component was an online memory game, combined with the NEO Five-Factor Inventory and a technical affinity questionnaire. The experiment with 13 participants was monitored with a gaze tracking device and corresponding software. This study showed that people with certain personality traits perceive technostress at a higher or lower level. Furthermore, technostress lowers task performance. However, this effect can be mitigated by a higher level of technical affinity. This paper is ongoing research. Therefore, future research should consider a higher number of participants and a variation of stressors.

KEYWORDS

Technostress, Personality Traits, Technical Affinity, Task Performance

1. INTRODUCTION

Digitization connects the entire world. Thanks to the increasing spread of information and communications technology (ICT), people are effortlessly connected anytime, anywhere. Of course, individuals, students, and employees alike benefit from this development through faster decision-making, smooth communication, and increased productivity. However, this trend is associated with adverse side effects, such as technology-induced stress, characterized as technostress. It is defined as "a modern adaptive disorder caused by the inability to use new computer technologies in a healthy way" (Brod, 1984).

Previous studies have focused primarily on the technostress creators' influence on a particular outcome (Sarabadani, Carter and Compeau, 2018; Benzari, Khedhaouria and Torrès, 2020). However, little is known about the relationship between the different personality traits and the emergence of technostress. The same applies to the influence of technical affinity on the occurrence of technostress. Therefore, this study aims to measure the influence of technostress on the overall task performance, based on the following research questions (RQ):

RQ1: "Which influence do personality traits have on the occurrence of technostress?
RQ2: "Which influence does technical affinity have on the occurrence of technostress?
RQ3: "Which influence does technostress have on the performance of tasks?

To answer these questions, a research model, including seven hypotheses, was developed. An experiment based on an online memory game was conducted to test the hypotheses. The personality traits of the participants were determined using the NEO Five-Factor Inventory. The attendees answered the questionnaire to determine their technical affinity. Also, eye-tracking software had monitored the entire experiment. The paper is structured as follows. First, the ethical explanation is mentioned, followed by the hypotheses and the research model. Then the analysis and the results are described. A discussion of the results follows this, and finally, a conclusion, the limitations, and future research are presented.

2. EXPERIMENT

2.1 Research Model and Hypotheses

In order to answer the defined research questions, the following research model and hypotheses were made:

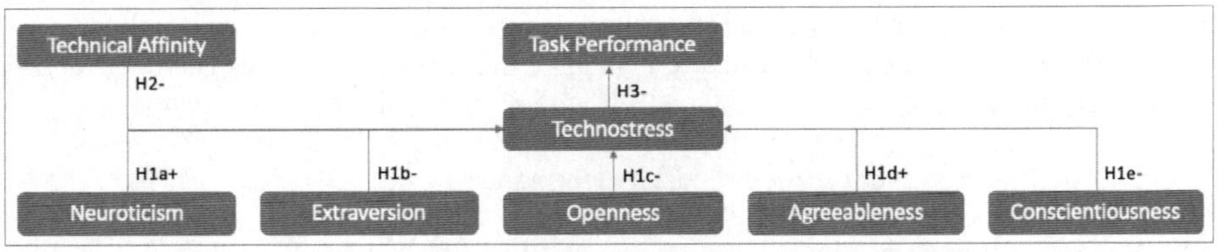

Figure 1. Research Model and Proposed Hypotheses

Neuroticism: According to Costa & McCrae, individuals with this personality trait can be defined as "anxious, generally apprehensive, and prone to worry" (Costa and McCrae, 1992). Furthermore, these people are described as "being poor at controlling [their] impulses and desires, and [they are] unable to handle stress well" (Costa and McCrae, 1992). Based on the definition of neuroticism, the following hypothesis can be made up:

H1a: Neuroticism is positively related to the appearance of technostress.

Extraversion: An individual with a high level of extraversion can be described as "having a high level of energy and likes to keep active and busy" (Costa and McCrae, 1992). Devaraj et al. suggested that those persons tend to use technologies to maintain their social image. Hence, it is likely for them to perceive technostress as an opportunity rather than a threat (Devaraj, Easley and Michael Crant, 2008). Based on the definition of extraversion, the following hypothesis can be made up:

H1b: Extraversion is negatively related to the appearance of technostress.

Openness: These Individuals are open to new ideas and strive for new opportunities. In this way, highly valued people in the dimension of openness will have positive insights about technostress. These circumstances are seen as an opportunity to perform better (Chandra, Srivastava and Shirish, 2015). Based on the definition of openness, the following hypothesis can be made up:

H1c: Openness is negatively related to the appearance of technostress.

Agreeableness: Persons with a high level of agreeableness are "kind, considerate, likable, helpful and cooperative" (Graziano and Eisenberg, 1997). Due to their personality, they experience technostress as a threat (Srivastava, Chandra and Shirish, 2015) Based on the definition of agreeableness, the following hypothesis can be made up:

H1d: Agreeableness is positively related to the appearance of technostress.

Conscientiousness: Following Costa & McCrae, these individuals are "reasonably efficient and generally sensible and rational in making decisions" (Costa and McCrae, 1992). Consequently, it is more likely for them to perceive technostress as a positive appearance. Based on the definition of conscientiousness, the following hypothesis can be made up:

H1e: Conscientiousness is negatively related to the appearance of technostress.

Technical affinity: Is defined as a personal behavior that expresses itself in a positive attitude, enthusiasm, and trust towards technology (Karrer et al. 2009). It consorts with interest and acceptance of the technology. Technical affinity also has a positive effect on knowledge and experience with technology (Karrer et al. 2009). Based on the definition of technical affinity, the following hypothesis can be made up:

H2: Technical affinity is negatively related to technostress.

Task Performance: According to Burton-Jones & Straub, task performance is defined as the "extent to which an individual's task output is effective in meeting task objectives" (Burton-Jones and Straub, 2006). Moreover, interruptions can lead to a reduction in task performance (Tams, Thatcher and Grover, 2018). Based on the definition of task performance, the following hypothesis can be made up:

H3: Technostress is negatively related to task performance.

2.2 Materials and Methods

The experimental setting is designed as a true experiment. The participants should play an online memory game, followed by a survey referring to the technical affinity and the NEO-Five-Factor Inventory (NEO-FFI). Due to restrictions caused by the corona pandemic, the participants were selected using the convenience sampling method. 13 persons with german citizenship (six male, seven female) in the age group of 22-28 with a mean age of M=25 were selected randomly into two groups: The first group was defined as test group with n=8 (four male, four female), the second group as the control group with n=5 (two male, three female). A person can only be assigned to one of the two groups and participated in an order. The characteristics of the final sample are shown in Table 1.

Table 1. Sample Selection

Measure	**Items**	**Quantity**	**%**
Age	22-25	9	69
	>25	4	31
Test group	Male	4	50
	Female	4	50
Control group	Male	2	40
	Female	3	60

The online memory consisted of 4x8 cards with cartoon-like images in different colors. The task was to find matching pairs of images by flipping two cards in each round. In the beginning, the cards were displayed face down. Whenever the participants identified matching pairs, the cards remained open. Otherwise, the cards were turned back to their original position (Tams, et al. 2018). The task was fulfilled when all 16 pairs were matched correctly. The number of moves and the time it took to complete the task was recorded to measure the task performance. The memory was selected due to easiness and understandability to cause as little stress as possible (Washburn et al. 2007).

The control group fulfilled the task without any interruptions. On the opposite, the test group was affected by upcoming instant messages on the screen's right bottom. These messages were sent in a pre-defined frequency (15 seconds) containing fun facts. Furthermore, the notifications were combined with a typical audio signal. All participants conducted the task in the same environment and setting to ensure a ceteris paribus condition.

An eye-tracking device has been used for both groups to receive a reliable set of physiological data. This instrument should detect whether and how often the test group was distracted by the upcoming notifications. First, the eye movement of the participants was calibrated by the system. They were asked to reduce their head movement during the experiment to a very minimum to ensure accurate measurement. A so-called area of interest (AOI) was defined to quantify the test group results. This area precisely reflects the area of the popup notifications. The measured time and count of views were the decisive variables to measure the appearance of technostress.

To determine the influence of technical affinity a survey was conducted. Karrer et al. developed the chosen questionnaire (Karrer et al. 2009), which included 19 questions about the personal assessment of technical and electronic devices. For the measurement, a five-point Likert-Scale with the following statements (5=strongly agree, 4=agree, 3=neutral, 2=disagree, 1=strongly disagree) has been used. Negative statements were inverted. Consequently, the higher the mean-value, the higher the degree of technical affinity. The reliability and validity of the survey were proven. For validation, it was tested on a large heterogeneous sample. The survey includes several factors of technical affinity and has satisfactory quality criteria (Karrer et al. 2009).

The NEO-FFI by Costa & McCrae was applied to identify the participants' personalities. The NEO-FFI (Costa and McCrae, 1992) was applied to investigate the five-factor model of personality. Consequently, a questionnaire containing 60 questions referring to the dimensions of the normal personality (neuroticism, extraversion, openness, agreeableness, and conscientiousness) was used (Schmitz et al. 2001). The survey is categorized into five dimensions, with 12 questions each. Again, a five-point Likert-Scale with the following statements (5=strongly agree, 4=agree, 3=neutral, 2=disagree, 1=strongly disagree) was deployed. It shows the quota sample representative of the population with T-values (50+10z). Table 2 shows the defined ranges of the participants' standard value.

Table 2. Categorization of NEO-FFI Results

Description	SD	Lower Limit	Upper Limit	SD
Far below average	–3SD	20	30	–2SD
Below average	–2SD	30	40	–SD
Average	–SD	40	60	+SD
Above average	+SD	60	70	+2SD
Far above average	+2SD	70	80	+3SD

The reliability and validity of the NEO-FFI were proven by a large sample and is one of the most applied tests to evaluate the five-factor model dimensions (Schmitz et al. 2001).The factors treatment and counterbalance were considered to increase the general validity of the experiment (Bhattacherjee, 2012). The experimental design aims to moderate different experience levels. Also, the duration was kept as short as possible to minimize boredom. There was no uncontrolled contact between the participants (Cassar, Friedman and Schneider, 2009).

All participants submitted a written declaration of consent following the General Data Protection Regulation (GDPR). After the experiment, the participants were informed about the study's purpose and the further data analysis process. All persons participated voluntarily and agreed to the use of their data for the research work.

2.3 Results

In the following chapter, the results of the experiment are analyzed based on the Research Question and the associated hypotheses. Figure 2 shows a summary of the results.

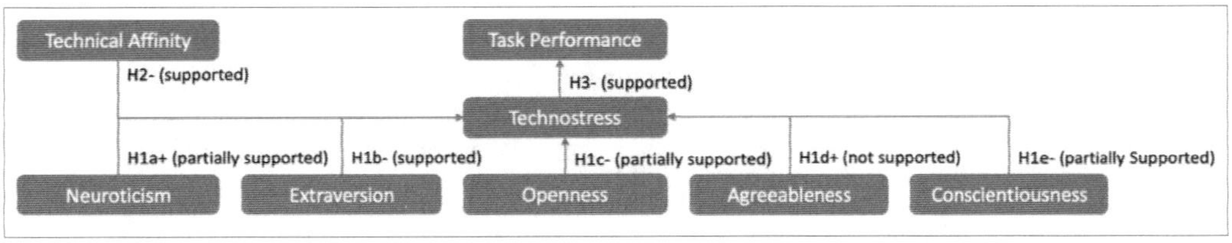

Figure 2. Summary of Results

2.3.1 Relationship between Personality Traits and the Appearance of Technostress

Neuroticism: The average time and the average number of views in the AOI were measured to test H1a. Three participants of the test group exposed a degree of neuroticism below average. The average time was

2.713 sec, and the average count of views in the AOI was 9.67. The four individuals with an average score of neuroticism had 1.413 sec, and 14 views in the AOI. 1 participant was above average and performed with a time of 5,48 sec and 15 views in the AOI. Figure 2 shows a positive relation between neuroticism and the number of views. At the same time, no relation between neuroticism and time occurs. A tendency arises since the participant with the highest value of neuroticism had the longest time in the AOI. Overall, H1a: Neuroticism is positively related to the appearance of technostress is partially supported.

Extraversion: The average time and the average number of views in the AOI were measured to test H1b. Within the test group, six participants showed an average degree of extraversion. They had an average time in the AOI of 3.084 sec and an average number of 16 views. Two participants had an above-average value of extraversion. The average time in the AOI was 0.381 sec, with an average number of two views. Based on this evidence, the higher the degree of extraversion, the lower the degree of distraction, as shown in Figure 3. Thus, H1b: Extraversion is negatively related to the appearance of technostress is supported.

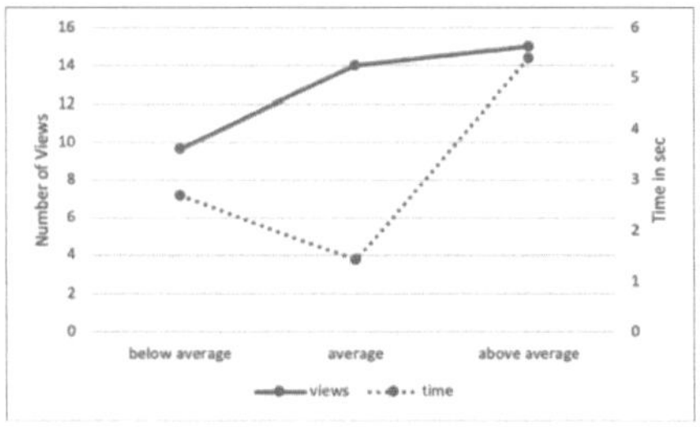

Figure 3. Results of Neuroticism

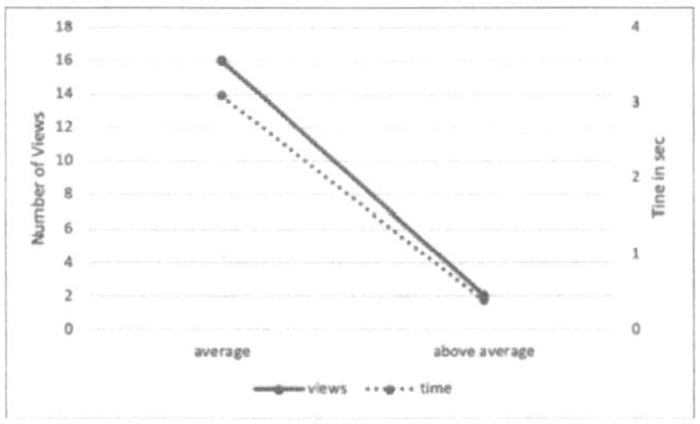

Figure 4. Results of Extraversion

Openness: The average time and the average number of views in the AOI were measured to test H1c. Two participants of the test group had a below-average degree of openness with a time of 2.611 sec and 25.5 views. Five persons had an average personality trait with a time of 2.690 sec, and 9.6 views in the AOI. 1 individual had an above-average score on openness, which leads to a time of 0.598 sec and one view. Figure 4 shows, in terms of views, the higher the degree of openness, the lower the number of views. A negative trend is recognizable except the average value, which is slightly higher, referring to the time. Thus, H1c: Openness is negatively related to the appearance of technostress is partially supported.

Agreeableness: The average time and the average number of views in the AOI were measured to test H1d. Two test group candidates showed below-average agreeableness with a time of 0.683 sec and a count of 2.5 views in the AOI. Four participants showed an average score on agreeableness. Therefore, the average time of 4.285 sec and 22.75 views were examined. Two individuals were above-average, with a time of 0.381 sec and 2.0 views. From the results in Figure 5, no trends and relations due to the hypothesis can be identified. Hence, H1d: Agreeableness is positively related to the appearance of technostress is not supported.

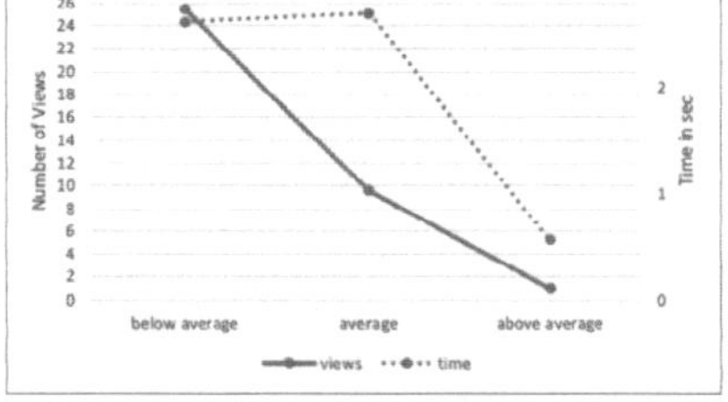

Figure 5. Results of Openness

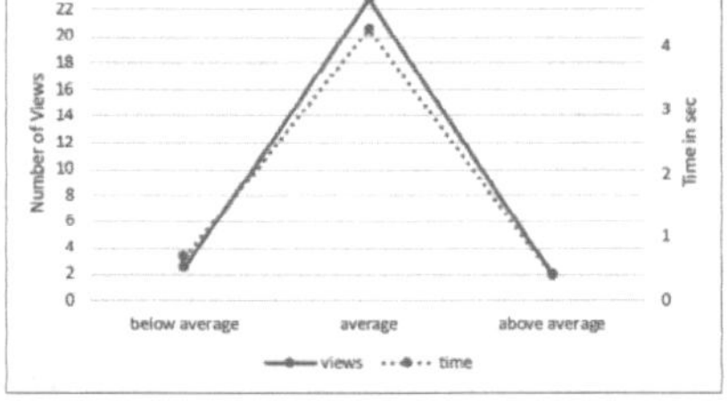

Figure 6. Results of Agreeableness

Conscientiousness: The average time and the average number of views in the AOI were measured to test H1e. Two participants showed a below-average score, with a time of 2.873 sec and 8.5 views in the AOI. In contrast, five candidates had an average conscientiousness. They pointed time of 2.585 sec and 16.4 views. 1 participant scores far above average in conscientiousness. Therefore, a time of 0.598 sec and 1.0 views in the AIO was measured. As presented in Figure 6, the higher the conscientiousness, the lower time in the AOI. In terms of the number of views, no trend is recognizable. Thus, H1e: Conscientiousness is negatively related to the appearance of technostress is partially supported. The Appendix provide an overview of all results of the participants' personality.

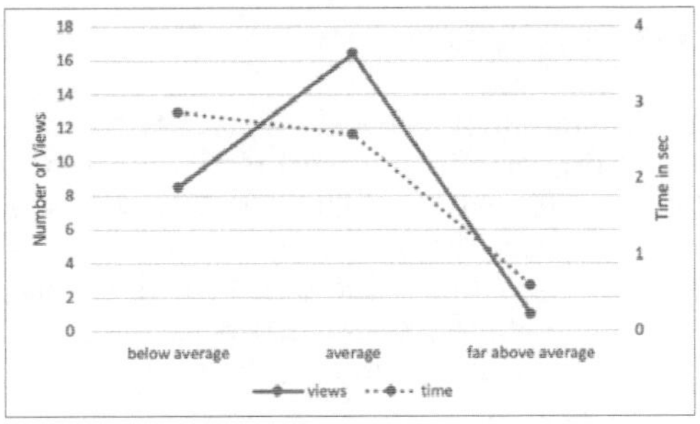

Figure 7. Results of Conscientiousness

2.3.2 Relationship between Technical Affinity and the Appearance of Technostress

In order to measure the degree of technical affinity, the mean-value for each participant was formed. The general mean-value M=3 represents a neutral technical affinity. Individuals with a value below tend to have a lower affinity, whereas individuals with a score above tend to have a higher affinity. Table 3 shows the results of technical affinity.

Table 3. Results of Task Performance

Measure	Overall Time (min)	Overall Moves	Item	Time (min)	Moves
Test Group	03:29	47.75	Technical affinity	03:19	45.8
			Non-technical affinity	03:47	51
Control Group	03:10	47	Technical affinity	03:10	47
			Non-technical affinity	-	-

The test group's technical affine individuals performed with an average time of 03:19 min. Moreover, it took them 45.8 moves on average to complete the task. On the opposite, the test group's non-technical affine participants needed 03:47 min and used 51 moves on average to finish the online memory. The comparison of the results presents that the test group participants with a higher technical affinity performed better than the non-technical affine ones. The delta is 00:28 min and 5.2 moves. All participants of the control group tend to be more technical affine. No one showed a value below average. It demonstrates that the control group finished the task 00:09 min faster than the technical affine test group. Consequently, the higher the degree of technical affinity, the lower the level of perceived technostress. Based on these findings, H2: Technical affinity is negatively related to technostress is supported.

2.3.3 Relationship between Technostress and Task Performance

Table 3 also compares the overall task performance of the test group and the control group. The test group members fulfilled the task at 03:29 min, and it took them 47.75 moves on average. Without technostress's influence, the control group finished the task in 03:10 min and used 47 moves on average. The delta is 00:19 min and 0.75 moves. Comparing these measurements, it is evident that technostress has an impact on task performance. Therefore, H3: Technostress is negatively related to task performance is supported.

3. DISCUSSION

This experiment proposes seven hypotheses to understand the relationship between different personality traits on the appearance of technostress. Also, the influence of technical affinity on the appearance of technostress has been observed. Additionally, the impact of technostress on task performance was measured. The hypotheses H1a-e aim to answer the first research question. H2 strives to explain the second one, and H3 is related to research question three. According to the research model, only three hypotheses are supported, three hypotheses are partially supported, and one hypothesis is not. It leads to the answer to the research questions.

RQ1: "Which impact do personality traits have on the appearance of technostress?"

Past literature has revealed the impact of technostress creators and personality traits on outcomes such as job burnout and job engagement (Srivastava, et al. 2015). This study aimed to detect the relation between personality traits and technostress. The analysis of the hypotheses H1a-e determined that higher extraversion has a negative relation towards the appearance of technostress and plays a significant role. Neuroticism, openness, and conscientiousness show a tendency, but the hypotheses are only partially confirmed. Individuals with a higher score of neuroticism tend to experience technostress at a higher level. Open as well as conscientious individuals tend to perceive technostress at a lower level. The influence of agreeableness is not verified.

RQ2: "Which impact does technical affinity have on the appearance of technostress?"

Based on previous literature reviews, the impact of technical affinity was not examined within an experiment, yet. According to hypothesis H2, the research paper indicates the negative relation between technical affinity and technostress appearance. Surprisingly, the degree of technical affinity has a decisive influence. Therefore, the higher the degree of technical affinity, the lower the perceived technostress.

RQ3: "Which impact does technostress have on the task performance?"

Tams et al. investigated that individual technostress is negatively related to task performance (Tams, et al. 2018). This research paper came to a corresponding conclusion. Based on the findings of hypothesis H3, the test group performed worse than the control group in terms of task performance. In general, technostress reduces task performance.

Both previous studies and this study have shown that personality traits are partially related to technostress's appearance. These findings indicate that individual personality traits should be taken into account in the perception of technostress. Additionally, this research included the variable technical affinity as well. The result was that the higher the degree of technical affinity, the lower the technostress's perception.

4. CONCLUSION

This research paper contains certain limitations, so the results should be interpreted with caution. First and foremost, the small number of participants is the most significant limitation. Consequential only a few values can be assigned to many different variables and therefore, the hypotheses may only have limited validity. Future studies should implement a more significant sample to gather more comprehensive data to ensure a higher validity. Second, the position of the notifications was always on the right bottom of the screen. This may result in a habituation effect. For further research, the notifications could be projected on a random position on the screen to minimize such effects.

REFERENCES

Benzari, A. et al, 2020. The Rise of Technostress: A Literature Review from 1984 until 2018. *Proceedings of the 28th European Conference on Information Systems*. An Online AIS Conference.

Bhattacherjee, A. 2012. *Social Science Research: principles, methods, and practices*, *Book 3.*Global Text Project.

Brod, C. 1984. *Technostress: The Human Cost of the Computer Revolution*. Basic Books, New York City, USA.

Burton-Jones, A. and Straub, D. W., 2006. Reconceptualizing system usage: An approach and empirical test *Information Systems Research*. Vol 17, No 3, pp. 228-246.

Cassar, A. et al, 2009. Cheating in markets: A laboratory experiment. *Journal of Economic Behavior and Organization*. Vol 72, Issue 1, pp. 240-259.

Chandra, S. et al, 2015. Do technostress creators influence employee innovation?. *Pacific Asia Conference on Information Systems, PACIS 2015 - Proceedings*.

Costa, P. T. and McCrae, R. R., 1992. Revised NEO personality inventory (NEO-PI-R) and NEO five-factor inventory (NEO-FFI), *The SAGE Handbook of Personality Theory and Assessment.* Vol. 2, pp. 179-198.

Devaraj, U. S. et al, 2008. How does personality matter? Relating the five-factor model to technology acceptance and use. *Information Systems Research*. Vol. 19, No. 1, pp. 93-105

Graziano, W. G. and Eisenberg, N. H., 1997. Agreeableness: a dimension of personality. *Handbook of personality psychology*. pp. 795-824.

Karrer, K. et al, 2009. Technikaffinität erfassen – der Fragebogen TA-EG. *Der Mensch im Mittelpunkt technischer Systeme*. VDI Verlag GmbH, Düsseldorf, Germany, pp. 196-201.

Sarabadani, J. et al, 2018. 10 Years of Research on Technostress Creators and Inhibitors: Synthesis and Critique. *Twenty-fourth Americas Conference on Information Systems.* New Orleans, USA, pp. 1–10.

Schmitz, N. *et al,* 2001. Psychometric properties of the German version of the NEO-FFI in psychosomatic outpatients. *Personality and Individual Differences*. 31(5), pp.713-722.

Srivastava, S. C. et al, 2015. Technostress creators and job outcomes: Theorising the moderating influence of personality traits. *Information Systems Journal*, 25(4), pp. 355–401.

Tams, S. et al, 2018. Concentration, competence, confidence, and capture: An experimental study of age, interruption- based technostress, and task performance. *Journal of the Association for Information Systems*, 19(9), pp. 857–908.

Washburn, D. A. et al, 2007. A Species Difference in Visuospatial Working Memory: Does Language Link "What" with "Where"?. *International Journal of Comparative Psychology*. 20, pp. 55-64.

APPENDIX

Appendix 1. Results of NEOFFI of Test Group

Participants number	Standard Value Neuroticism	Standard Value Extraversion	Standard Value Openness	Standard Value Agreeableness	Standard Value Conscientiousness
1	41	59	38	43	52
2	55	44	51	34	34
5	62	45	49	58	38
7	58	64	53	61	54
9	38	51	54	45	47
10	49	50	33	58	55
11	34	64	64	69	80
12	32	58	47	38	57

FORCED ELEARNING USAGE: EXTENDING THEORY OF PLANNED BEHAVIOUR WITH PERCEIVED COST DURING COVID19 PANDEMIC

Samiaji Sarosa
Accounting Department, Atma Jaya Yogyakarta University
Jl. Babarsari 43 Yogyakarta 55281, Indonesia

ABSTRACT

Indonesian schools and universities were forced to suddenly changed from conventional classroom to full online classroom in late March 2020 to combat the spread of COVID19. The change has not been easy for many, yet it was the situation faced by people all over the world. One of the common early complain of fully online learning is the cost to acquire equipment and internet access. We use the Theory of Planned Behaviour extended with Perceived Cost to explore university student's behaviour in facing forced online learning. The result is similar to previous studies, but we found that Perceived Cost although influenced by Perceived Behavioural Control did not influence Intention.

KEYWORDS

Theory of Planned Behaviour, COVID19 Pandemic, Online Learning, Forced, Perceived Cost

1. INTRODUCTION

The use of technology in universities' classrooms are inevitable. The use of various hardware tools such as smartphone, tablet, and conventional computers are becoming common (Al-Emran et al., 2016; Brennan & Johnson, 2000; Cheon et al., 2012; Gikas & Grant, 2013; Popovici & Mironov, 2015). The usage of such gadgets has been used for accessing eLearning services such as Learning Management Systems, online classrooms, video meetings, file sharing, content sharing, and ultimately knowledge sharing (Cheon et al., 2012; Drennan et al., 2005; Popovici & Mironov, 2015). The combination of technology-based learning hardware and applications has created monikers such as blended learning, online classrooms, flipped classrooms, and providing support tools for distance learning (Chung-Yu et al., 2020; Elisabeth Counselman & Redcay, 2019; Kabassi et al., 2016; Nilsson et al., 2012; Talley & Scherer, 2013; Tomas et al., 2019).

Atma Jaya Yogyakarta University (UAJY) in Indonesia has decided to implement mandatory blended learning for all the courses and programs starting in the second semester of the 2019-2020 academic year[1]. All lecturers were required to have a minimum of one session and a maximum of four sessions out of fourteen lecture sessions per semester to have a non-face-to-face lecture. Initially, the non-face-to-face lecturer session could be synchronous (using video meeting application of choice) or asynchronous using the university's official learning management systems (LMS) that are based on modified Moodle. This was planned as a first step to adopt various modes of teaching and learning which ultimately would enable UAJY to provide a variety and customized learning experience for students.

In the first week of March 2020, the first case of Covid19 was announced by the Indonesian Government. It was immediately followed by the spread of the disease to all over 34 provinces in Indonesia by early April 2020. At the end of March 2020 following Government direction, UAJY switched all classes to online mode and made work and study from home mandatory. In the beginning, various tools were used at the lecturers' discretion in the absence of the university's direction. Various tools such as the official LMS, Zoom, Skype, instant messaging apps (WhatsApp, Line, Telegram, etc.) were used. The official LMS belong to the

[1] Indonesian academic year started in the middle of year, around mid-July for schools and between August-September for higher education institutions.

university were having difficulties coping with a sudden spike of workloads. Typical usage of the LMS was about 200-300 user's concurrent logon, however, during the first few weeks of forced online learning activities, the LMS could be used by more than 1000 concurrent users logon.

By the start of the first semester 2020-2021 academic year UAJY has been more prepared. It officially decided to use the enhanced LMS for asynchronous activities such as sharing lecture materials, assignment submission, exams, etc. For synchronous activities such as video meetings, real-time chat, and group work UAJY used Microsoft Teams (MS Teams). The MS Teams as part of the campus agreement license with Microsoft and has been available since 2018. A series of training to utilise both tools have been given to lectures and new students who were admitted in 2020 by mid-2020.

Using technology for teaching and learning along with changing the mode from conventional classroom to blended or flipped comes with various issues (Bouilheres et al., 2020; Khodabandelou et al., 2014; Nilsson et al., 2012). Suddenly and completely changed from conventional to online has exacerbated the problems. Many of the students were returning to their hometown that spread across all over Indonesia. The immediate problem was the availability, reliability, and quality of data communication infrastructure. Many students complaining that they often did not have sufficient internet connection to conduct real-time video meeting sessions. The next problem was the cost. For example, a typical one-hour video meeting session could consume up to 500 megabytes of data. A student could have up to 8 classes a week. If all the classes required them to have one-hour video meeting sessions, they could look at 4 gigabytes of data per week just for video meetings. A typical mobile internet package that accommodates such a need would cost a student about US$ 8 per month and a cable internet package would cost around US$ 20 per month. For comparison, the average minimum wage in Indonesia in 2020 is between US$ 127 to a bit above US$ 225 per month. Availability of reliable electricity also has been mentioned by a few students and lecturers. However, this was not deemed as a problem since both LMS and MS Teams client apps could be installed and used on mobile devices (smartphone, tablet, and laptop).

This study is trying to investigate the students' attitude toward using LSM and MS Teams for substituting conventional classrooms. We used Theory of Planned Behaviour or TPB as the main tool for investigation (Ajzen, 1991; Cheon et al., 2012; Fishbein & Ajzen, 1975; Pavlou & Fygenson, 2006; Redda, 2019; Schifter & Ajzen, 1985). We believe TPB could be used to explain the students' attitudes. We extend TPB by using perceived cost since it was one common complaint of using online learning technology (Wei et al., 2009).

2. THEORY OF PLANNED BEHAVIOUR

Theory of Planned Behaviour (TPB) was originally developed by Icek Ajzen to improve the predictive ability of Theory of Reasoned Action or TRA (Ajzen, 1991; Fishbein & Ajzen, 1975; Hrubes et al., 2001; HSU & CHIU, 2004). In TPB, an individual's intention and behaviour are influenced by attitude toward behaviour, subjective norms, and perceived behavioural control (Ajzen, 1988, 1991; Ajzen & Fishbein, 1980; Hrubes et al., 2001; Schifter & Ajzen, 1985). The core components of TPB are (Ajzen, 1988, 1991, 2005; Ajzen & Fishbein, 1980; Schifter & Ajzen, 1985; Sniehotta et al., 2014):

- Attitude Toward Behaviour is a degree of value seen by an individual in conducting a behaviour. The value could be positive or negative.
- Subjective Norm is a perception of an individual toward the pressure of the person's social environment in engaging a behaviour.
- Perceived Behavioural Control is a perception of individuals of their ability to perform certain behaviour.
- Intention is defined as an individual's readiness to conduct a certain behaviour. Intention is also an immediate antecedent of behaviour.
- Behaviour is defined as an observable manifestation of intention and influenced by Perceived Behavioural Control.
- Actual Behavioural Control is defined as everything needed by an individual to conduct a certain behaviour.

TPB has been used extensively in many academic publications in various disciplines such as health, technology adoption, environmental behaviour, etc. It is argued that TPB is better than TRA to explain behaviour of individuals without or with limited freedom of choice (Leone et al., 1999; Prapavessis et al., 2015), which is why it is chosen for this study.

As mentioned in the introduction, the cost is one of the common immediate complaints by students and lecturers alike when switching to online from conventional classrooms. The cost was seen by students as an additional financial burden since they already have paid their tuition fees for the semesters. Students who were recalled by their parent to their respective hometown (out of Yogyakarta as UAJY campus located and, in many cases, out of Java Island[2]) have already paid for their local accommodation near UAJY campuses. Internet connection costs were not a problem during the pre Covid19 academic years. Students could use an Internet connection on campus and use UAJY's computing facilities. When the campuses are closed due to Covid19 some students that were depending on UAJY computing facilities are forced to find alternative computing equipment. This too has put an additional burden financially on students. We defined cost in this study as the cost to acquire equipment (if not previously available or owned) and the cost of subscribing to Internet service for accessing online learning (LMS and MS Teams).

Cost or perceived cost factors have been included in many studies utilising TPB. A study in mobile commerce in Malaysia found that perceived cost has a negative impact toward intention (Wei et al., 2009). Perceived cost is also having a negative impact toward intention to use viral mobile marketing in the USA among young consumers (Yang & Zhou, 2011). We used Perceived Cost as antecedents of Perceived Behavioural Control (Ajzen, 1988, 1991, 2005; Hrubes et al., 2001). Our research model can be seen in figure 1 below.

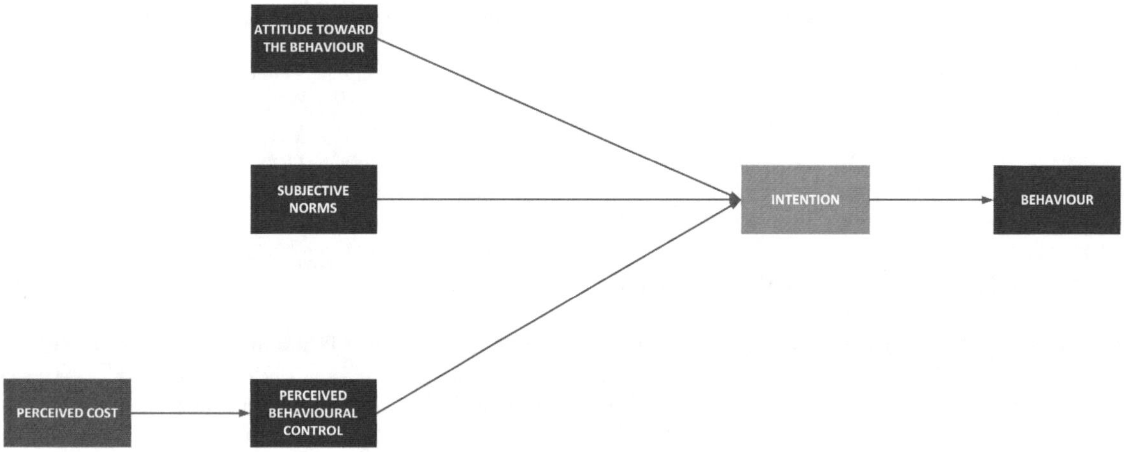

Figure 1. Theory of Planned behaviour with Perceived Cost As antecedent toward Perceived Behavioural Control

Based on the proposed research model, a series of hypotheses were developed. The hypotheses are as follows:

- H1 Attitude Towards Behaviour would positively influence Intention
- H2 Subjective Norms would positively influence Intention
- H3 Perceived Behavioural Control would positively influence Intention
- H4 Intention would positively influence Behaviour
- H5 Perceived Cost would negatively influence Perceived Behavioural Control

[2] UAJY is in southern coast in the middle of Java Island. Java is the main island and the centre of government, business, and education in Indonesia.

3. RESEARCH METHOD

The survey was developed based on the TPB model (Ajzen, 1988, 1991, 2005; Hrubes et al., 2001; Pavlou & Fygenson, 2006; Rehman et al., 2019; Xie et al., 2017). Perceived Cost was added and modeled antecedent of Perceived Behavioural Control (Ajzen, 1991, 2005; Wei et al., 2009; Yang & Zhou, 2011). The survey used Likert Scale with a range of 1 to 7, where 1 represents strongly disagree and 7 represents strongly agree. The survey was created and distributed electronically using Google Forms. The survey was conducted in the second half of the first semester 2020-2021 academic year in the last week of October to mid-November 2020. We sent a survey invitation using email to listed official students' emails[3]. We received 555 responses out of 10827 registered students or a 5.1% response rate. The respondents' profiles could be seen below in Table 1.

Table 1. Respondents' Profile

		Number	Percentage
Gender	*Male*	266	48%
	Female	289	52%
Level	*Undergraduate*	482	87%
	Master	73	13%
Program Disciplines	*STEM*	238	43%
	Social & Humanity	317	57%
Age range	*15-20*	354	64%
	21-25	167	30%
	>25	34	6%

For data analysis, we used Structural Equation Modelling or SEM using Partial Least Square or PLS and using SmartPLS version 3 software (Hair et al., 2017; Hair et al., 2019; Joseph F. Hair et al., 2017; Jr. et al., 2014; Ringle, 2015; Sarstedt et al., 2017).

4. DATA ANALYSIS

For SEM, the analysis using SmartPLS version 3 started by evaluating the model (Hair et al., 2019; Joseph F. Hair et al., 2017; Sarstedt et al., 2017). The evaluation was done by running PLS Algorithm. The first step is to evaluate indicator reliability which is available as Outer Loadings values. All outer loadings values for the indicators should not be below 0.70. The first run of PLS Algorithm's result shown there is few indicators that have a value below 0.70. Once the indicators were removed the second PLS Algorithm was conducted and the result can be seen in Table 2. Below

[3] The official email is provided based on Microsoft Outlook email service. The students are forced to use the email to access MS Teams and various online services.

Table 2. Outer Loadings

	ATT	Behav	Cost	Intent	PBC	SUB
ATT1	0.871					
ATT3	0.914					
ATT4	0.852					
BE2		0.743				
BE3		0.883				
BE4		0.904				
BE5		0.884				
BE6		0.714				
BE7		0.808				
BE8		0.868				
BIA1			0.937			
BIA2			0.953			
BIA3			0.891			
INT1				0.901		
INT2				0.781		
INT3				0.936		
INT4				0.901		
PBC1					0.776	
PBC2					0.773	
PBC5					0.831	
PBC6					0.770	
PBC7					0.806	
SN1						0.909
SN2						0.897

The next step is to evaluate internal consistency reliability and convergent validity. The complete result is provided in Construct Validity and Reliability as seen in Table 3 below. The rho_A values are above 0.7, all AVE values are above 0.5, and all Cronbach's Alpha values are above 0.6 (Hair et al., 2019; Joseph F. Hair et al., 2017; Ringle, 2015).

Table 3. Construct Validity and Reliability

	Cronbach's Alpha	rho_A	Composite Reliability	AVE
ATT	0.853	0.853	0.911	0.773
Behav	0.924	0.929	0.940	0.692
Cost	0.918	0.936	0.948	0.860
Intent	0.903	0.917	0.933	0.777
PBC	0.851	0.853	0.893	0.626
SUB	0.773	0.775	0.898	0.815

Hypotheses testing is conducted by running Bootstrap in SmartPLS version 3.0 (Hair et al., 2019; Joseph F. Hair et al., 2017; Ringle, 2015). The result can be seen in Table 4 below. A hypothesis would be supported if the original sample value is in the same direction as the hypothesis, T Statistics value greater than 1.64 (two-tailed test) and P Values less than 0.05 (Hair et al., 2019; Joseph F. Hair et al., 2017; Ringle, 2015).

Table 4. Path Coefficient

	Original Sample (O)	Sample Mean (M)	Standard Deviation (STDEV)	T Statistics (|O/STDEV|)	P Values
ATT -> Intent	0.219	0.217	0.059	3.714	**0.000**
Cost -> PBC	-0.187	-0.188	0.045	4.192	**0.000**
Intent -> Behav	0.682	0.684	0.027	25.378	**0.000**
PBC -> Intent	0.305	0.308	0.059	5.129	**0.000**
SUB -> Intent	0.313	0.312	0.063	4.966	**0.000**

- H1 Attitude Towards Behaviour would positively influence Intention is supported with Original Sample value 0.219, T Statistic value 3.714, and P value 0.000.
- H2 Subjective Norms would positively influence Intention is supported with Original Sample value 0.313, T Statistic value 4.966, and P value 0.000.

- H3 Perceived Behavioural Control would positively influence Intention is supported with Original Sample value 0.305, T Statistic value 5.129, and P value 0.000.
- H4 Intention would positively influence Behaviour is supported with Original Sample value 0.682, T Statistic value 25.378, and P value 0.000.
- H5 Perceived Cost would negatively influence Perceived Behavioural Control is supported with Original Sample value -0.187, T Statistic value 4.192, and P value 0.000.

The R-squared values are 0.465 for Behaviour, 0,523 for Intention, and 0.035 for Perceived Behavioural Control as seen in table 5

Table 5. R Squared

	R Square	R Square Adjusted
Behav	0.465	0.464
Intent	0.523	0.520
PBC	0.035	0.033

5. CONCLUSION AND FURTHER WORKS

The result of data analysis confirms that the Behaviour of using eLearning applications (in this case LMS and MS Teams) is influenced by Intention (Ajzen, 1988, 1991, 2005; Schifter & Ajzen, 1985). Intention was influenced by Attitude Toward Behaviours, Subjective Norms, and Perceived Behavioural Control (Ajzen, 1988, 1991, 2005; Schifter & Ajzen, 1985). Perceived Cost is negatively influencing Perceived Behavioural Control confirmed finding in previous studies (Wei et al., 2009; Yang & Zhou, 2011). This might be explained by the fact that students are forced to use online modes of teaching and learning due to the Covid19 Pandemic. They have no choice. The Indonesian government and UAJY itself has been trying to alleviate the problem. UAJY has provided financial assistantship for students that could not afford the cost of accessing online learning. The government have provided subsidies and forced state-owned telecommunication company to chip in by providing free or cheaper Internet subscription packages. The effort might be able to explain why Perceived Cost is not influencing Intention nor moderating the influence of Intention toward Behaviour. The R-squared values from this study are showing that Behaviour can be explained by 46.5% of the factors in this study, Intention could be explained by 52.3% of the factors in this study, and Perceived Cost influence toward Perceived Behavioural Control is account for 3.5%.

This study has been conducted with participants from only one university. We argue that it could portray the picture of Indonesia because UAJY students come from and currently reside all over Indonesia. We would continue the study by including students from other universities. We are also considering high school students' participation in our study to provide a wider understanding of students' experience in facing forced online learning environment.

REFERENCES

Ajzen, I. (1988). *Attitudes, Personality, and Behavior*. Open University Press.

Ajzen, I. (1991). The Theory of Planned Behavior. *Organizational Behavior and Human Decision Processes*, *50*(2), 179-211.

Ajzen, I. (2005). *Attitudes, personality, and behavior* (2nd ed.). Open University Press / McGraw-Hill.

Ajzen, I., & Fishbein, M. (1980). *Understanding attitudes and predicting social behavior*. Prentice Hall.

Al-Emran, M., Elsherif, H. M., & Shaalan, K. (2016). Investigating attitudes towards the use of mobile learning in higher education. *Computers in Human Behavior*, *56*, 93-102.

Bouilheres, F., Le Le Thi Viet, H., McDonald, S., Nkhoma, C., & Jandug-Montera, L. (2020). Defining student learning experience through blended learning. *Education and Information Technologies*, *25*(4), 3049-3069. https://doi.org/10.1007/s10639-020-10100-y

Brennan, L. L., & Johnson, V. E. (2000). Learning Technology While Teaching Technology Management: A Trial of Distance Learning in Higher Education. In M. Khosrowpour (Ed.), *Organizational Achievement and Failure in Information Technology Management* (pp. 39-60). IDEA Group Publishing.

Cheon, J., Lee, S., Crooks, S. M., & Song, J. (2012). An investigation of mobile learning readiness in higher education based on the theory of planned behavior. *Computers & Education*, *59*(3), 1054–1064.

Chung-Yu, L., Chung-Kai, H., & Chao-Jung, K. (2020). The impact of perceived enjoyment on team effectiveness and individual learning in a blended learning business course: The mediating effect of knowledge sharing. *Australasian Journal of Educational Technology*, *36*(1), 126-141. https://search.proquest.com/docview/2452445455?accountid=44396

https://ajet.org.au/index.php/AJET/article/view/4446/1609

Drennan, J., Kennedy, J., & Pisarski, A. (2005). Factors Affecting Student Attitudes Toward Flexible Online Learning in Management Education. *The Journal of Educational Research*, *98*(6), 331-338. https://doi.org/10.3200/JOER.98.6.331-338

Elisabeth Counselman, C., & Redcay, A. (2019). Understanding the Role of the Brick-and-Mortar Classroom in Course Design and Implementation of the "Flipped" Classroom: An Exploratory Case Study. *Journal of Teaching and Learning with Technology*, *8*(1), 42-59. https://doi.org/http://dx.doi.org/10.14434/jotlt.v8i1.26806

Fishbein, M., & Ajzen, I. (1975). *Belief, Attitude, Intention, and Behavior: An Introduction to Theory and Research*. Addison-Wesley.

Gikas, J., & Grant, M. M. (2013). Mobile computing devices in higher education: Student perspectives on learning with cellphones, smartphones & social media. *Internet and Higher Education*, *19*, 18-26.

Hair, J. F., Hult, G. T. M., Ringle, C. M., & Sarstedt, M. (2017). *A Primer on Partial Least Squares Structural Equation Modeling (PLS-SEM)* (2nd ed.). Sage.

Hair, J. F., Risher, J. J., Sarstedt, M., & Ringle, C. M. (2019). When to use and how to report the results of PLS-SEM. *European Business Review*, *31*(1), 2-24. https://doi.org/10.1108/EBR-11-2018-0203

Hrubes, D., Ajzen, I., & Daigle, J. (2001). Predicting Hunting Intentions and Behavior: An Application of The Theory of Planned Behavior. *Leisure Sciences*, *23*(3), 165-178.

HSU, M.-H., & CHIU, C.-M. (2004). Predicting electronic service continuance with a decomposed theory of planned behaviour. *Behaviour & Information Technology*, *23*(5), 359–373. https://doi.org/10.1080/01449290410001669969

Joseph F. Hair, J., Hult, G. T. M., Ringle, C. M., & Sarstedt, M. (2017). *A Primer on Partial Least Squares Structural Equation Modeling (PLS-SEM)* (2nd ed.). Sage.

Jr., J. F. H., Sarstedt, M., Hopkins, L., & Kuppelwieser, V. G. (2014). Partial least squares structural equation modeling (PLS-SEM): An emerging tool in business research. *European Business Review*, *26*(2), 106-121. https://doi.org/10.1108/EBR-10-2013-0128

Kabassi, K., Dragonas, I., Ntouzevits, A., Pomonis, T., Papastathopoulos, G., & Vozaitis, Y. (2016). Evaluating a learning management system for blended learning in Greek higher education. *SpringerPlus*, *5*(1), 1-12. https://doi.org/10.1186/s40064-016-1705-8

Khodabandelou, R., Habibah Ab, J., Wan Zah Wan, A., & Shaffe bin Mohd, D. (2014). Moderation Effect of Gender on Relationship between Community of Inquiry and Perceived Learning in Blended Learning Environments. *Contemporary Educational Technology*, *5*(3), 257-271. https://search.proquest.com/docview/2135157463?accountid=44396

Leone, L., Perugini, M., & Ercolani, A. P. (1999). A comparison of three models of attitude–behavior relationships in the studying behavior domain [https://doi.org/10.1002/(SICI)1099-0992(199903/05)29:2/3<161::AID-EJSP919>3.0.CO;2-G]. *European Journal of Social Psychology*, *29*(2-3), 161-189. https://doi.org/https://doi.org/10.1002/(SICI)1099-0992(199903/05)29:2/3<161::AID-EJSP919>3.0.CO;2-G

Nilsson, M., Östergren, J., Fors, U., Rickenlund, A., Jorfeldt, L., Caidahl, K., & Bolinder, G. (2012). Does individual learning styles influence the choice to use a web-based ECG learning programme in a blended learning setting? *BMC Medical Education*, *12*, 5. https://doi.org/10.1186/1472-6920-12-5

Pavlou, P. A., & Fygenson, M. (2006). Understanding and predicting Electronic Commerce adoption: an extension of the Theory of Planned Behavior. *MIS Quarterly*, *30*(1), 115-143. https://doi.org/10.2307/25148720

Popovici, A., & Mironov, C. (2015). Students' perception on using eLearning technologies. *Procedia - Social and Behavioral Sciences*, *180*(2015), 1514 – 1519. https://doi.org/10.1016/j.sbspro.2015.02.300

Prapavessis, H., Gaston, A., & DeJesus, S. (2015). The Theory of Planned Behavior as a model for understandingsedentary behavior. *Psychology of Sport and Exercise*, *19*. https://doi.org/10.1016/j.psychsport.2015.02.001

Redda, E. H. (2019). Attitudes towards Online Shopping: Application of the Theory of Planned Behaviour. *ACTA UNIVERSITATIS DANUBIUS*, *15*(2), 148-159. http://journals.univ-danubius.ro/index.php/oeconomica/article/view/5290

Rehman, S. U., Bhatti, A., Mohamed, R., & Ayoup, H. (2019). The moderating role of trust and commitment between consumer purchase intention and online shopping behavior in the context of Pakistan. *Journal of Global Entrepreneurship Research*, *9*(43). https://doi.org/10.1186/s40497-019-0166-2

Ringle, C. M., Wende, Sven, and Becker, Jan-Michael (2015). *SmartPLS Release: 3*. In SmartPLS GmbH. www.smartpls.com

Sarstedt, M., RIngle, C. M., & Hair, J. F. (2017). Partial Least Squares Structural Equation Modeling. In C. Homburg, M. KLarmann, & A. Vomberg (Eds.), *Handbook of Market Research*. Springer.

Schifter, D. E., & Ajzen, I. (1985). Intention, perceived control, and weight loss: An application of the theory of planned behavior. *Journal of Personality and Social Psychology*, *49*(3), 843–851. https://doi.org/10.1037/0022-3514.49.3.843

Sniehotta, F. F., Presseau, J., & Araújo-Soares, V. (2014). Time to retire the theory of planned behaviour. *Health Psychology Review*, *8*(1), 1-7. https://doi.org/10.1080/17437199.2013.869710

Talley, C. P., & Scherer, S. (2013). The Enhanced Flipped Classroom: Increasing Academic Performance with Student-recorded Lectures and Practice Testing in a "Flipped" STEM Course. *The Journal of Negro Education*, *82*(3), 339-347,357. https://search.proquest.com/docview/1462798738?accountid=44396

Tomas, L., Neus, E., Doyle, T., & Skamp, K. (2019). Are first year students ready for a flipped classroom? A case for a flipped learning continuum: Revista de Universidad y Sociedad del Conocimiento. *International Journal of Educational Technology in Higher Education*, *16*(1), 1-22. https://doi.org/http://dx.doi.org/10.1186/s41239-019-0135-4

Wei, T. T., Marthandan, G., Chong, A. Y.-L., Ooi, K.-B., & Arumugam, S. (2009). What drives Malaysian m-commerce adoption? An empirical analysis. *Industrial Management & Data Systems*, *109*(3), 370-388. https://doi.org/10.1108/02635570910939399

Xie, Q., Song, W., Peng, X., & Shabbir, M. (2017). Predictors for e-government adoption: integrating TAM, TPB, trust and perceived risk. *The Electronic Library*, *35*(1), 2-20. https://doi.org/10.1108/EL-08-2015-0141

Yang, H. C., & Zhou, L. (2011). Extending TPB and TAM to mobile viral marketing: An exploratory study on American young consumers' mobile viral marketing attitude, intent and behavior. *Journal of Targeting, Measurement and Analysis for Marketing*, *19*, 85-98. https://doi.org/10.1057/jt.2011.11

ASSESSING CUSTOMERS' CONTINUANCE INTENTION FOR M-PAYMENT USE FROM THE CROSS-NATIONALITY PERSPECTIVE: AN EMPIRICAL STUDY

Qian Huang, Mahbubur Rahim and Misita Anwar
Monash University
900 Dandenong Rd, Caulfield East VIC, Australia

ABSTRACT

Although mobile payment applications (m-payment) has been explosively used worldwide, the studies about the effect of national culture (differing among various nationalities) on m-payment are scarce. This study thus focuses on understanding the key factors that affect customers' continuance intention for m-payment usage from a cross-nationality perspective. A research model is proposed to investigate whether factors affecting m-payment continuance intention differs among two different nationalities (i.e. India, China). The findings reveal that the effects of integrated value (i.e. functional value and value for money) differ between Indian and Chinese students. The m-payment continuance intention is largely explained by social value and integrated value. The research results offer insights to m-payment providers in terms of the culture-based m-payment application strategy related to designing content and interface, so as to properly guide the momentum.

KEYWORDS

M-Payment, Continuance Intention, The Theory of Consumption Value, Cross-Nationality

1. INTRODUCTION

M-payment refers to the payment method for goods and services using mobile devices through wireless and other communication technologies(Al-Saedi et al., 2020). Some examples of m-payment apps are: Apple Pay, and mobile banking application. It is now considered as a more competitive payment method in the global society because: a) the high prevalent of mobile devices use provides more opportunities for mobile users to use m-payment, b) m-payment provides customers with increased convenience because they are not required to go to banks and c) customers find it easier to ubiquitously manage their money whenever and wherever they want (Al-Saedi et al., 2020). Despite such benefits, uptake of m-payment varies widely across countries. While m-payment has attracted popularity in some countries, its adoption rate is relatively lower in other countries (Johnson et al., 2018). For example, 68.67% of the total transactions on TaoBao (the largest online shopping website in China) was completed through m-payment during the "double eleven" festival (Cao et al., 2018). Whereas, the usage rate of m-payment in the USA is only about 12%. Similar trend of low usage rate is also observed in UK and France (Slade et al., 2015). In Australia, m-payment method had not been widely accepted in the past, but recent Australian reports showed the usage of this method is on the rise (Gao and Waechter, 2017).

In response to the wide variation in the acceptance of m-payment across various countries, several scholars have conducted research to explain the uptake of m-payment by individuals. Most studies are concerned with adoption intention of customers, whereas studies on the post-usage intention of m-payment is scarce. Decisions on continuance intention qualitatively differ from those of m-payment adoption since users have had immediate prior experience with m-payment at the post-adoption phase (Chen and Li, 2017). In addition, most of the studies on m-payment have been conducted from one single country. For example, Cao et al. (2018) studied the continuance intention of m-payment from trust perspective and find that trust has a significant influence on post-adoption intention in China. Johnson et al. (2018) report on the influence of perceived complexity and security, relative advantage, visibility on the usage intention of m-payment in USA. Factors that influences continuance intention for m-payment may vary across cultures (Chen et al., 2019). This calls for further research on comparing factors that effect on continuance intention for m-payment use in terms of different cultures. Furthermore, most studies largely rely on the perspective of customers (e.g. perceived ease of use, perceived security) to explain their m-payment adoption behavior. The financial, social desirability, quality, emotional, and context-specific values related to customers were not addressed. Much research in IS domain shows that perceived customer value is regarded as the important factor in customers' decision processes in pay-per-use service behavior (Turel et al., 2007). As a result, seeking the underlying values that drives customers to consume technology is essential.

Against this backdrop, we thus seek to evaluate continuance intention to m-payment applications (apps) by addressing the following research questions: a) how do various key factors affect continuation intention for m-payment apps? b) does the continuation intention for m-payment differ based on nationality (reflecting cultural backgrounds)? Using a qualitative method, our study seeks to identify and empirically assess a set of factors that influence the continuation intention for using m-payment from a contrastive perspective on the moderating influence of Indian and Chinese customers' experience on m-payment continuance intention. Based on our research findings, m-payment apps providers would learn how a set of integrated factors jointly influence continuation intention for this service use. Awareness of these factors would help providers customize their m-payment apps according to culture and their behavior, which would increase customer satisfaction, and hence promote the continuation intention of m-payment apps use.

2. LITERATURE REVIEW

2.1 Continuance Behaviors for M-Payment

Continuance intention of m-payment is defined as degree to which an individual currently using a m-payment has developed conscious plans to continue using it in the future (Setterstrom et al., 2013). Understanding m-payment continuance intention is important because of two reasons: 1) most of factors that influence continuance intention do not exist in initial intention. Given customers have had immediate prior experience with IT, which exerts an influence on their continuance intention decision. 2) m-payment continuance intention of consumers is crucial to the m-payment company's survival since previous papers have shown that the eventual success of a new IS depends heavily on continued use rather than initial adoption (Chen and Li, 2017). Publications on m-payment in top level of IS journals are scarce. A couple of examples are the papers of Mallat (2007) and Kazan et al. (2018). Mallat (2007) investigated factors that influence m-payment adoption using a qualitative study, which has been widely cited (e.g., google scholar citations: 1063) by other scholars. Kazan et al. (2018) used m-payment platforms in UK as examples to discuss disentangling digital platform competition. We find satisfaction as the most prominent factor for the context of customers' post-adoption of m-payment. While utilizing different theories, existing studies treat satisfaction as either a mediating factor or a driver directly influencing post-adoption intention. For example, Cao et al. (2018) apply satisfaction element from the extended theory of reasoned action to investigate the relationship between trust and continuance intention of m-payment. They report that satisfaction mediate between the trust and post-adoption of m-payment. Since satisfaction has been proved as a significant factor for m-payment continuance intention by many existing papers in terms of different contexts, it is excluded in our study to allow us to focus on other factors.

Few of extant literatures have considered factors that influence continuance intention in terms of different countries. For example, the study of Lu et al. (2017) investigate the difference of continuance intention toward m-payment between Chinese and American and found culture has a significant influence on m-payment continuance decision process both at the macro (country) and micro (individual) level. The study of Chang and Hsu (2019) suggest factors that influences continuance intention for m-payment may be different in terms of different cultures. For example, Korean customers are more sensitive to privacy and service quality whereas Chinese users are more attracted by some functions (e.g. red envelop) provided by m-payment. It is necessary for m-payment providers to study consumer mindset differences in terms of different cultures, and to propose a suitable product designs and marketing strategies in order to ignite adoption rates of m-payment (Hung and

Hsieh, 2010). According to extant literature, the penetration rate of m-payment in China is increasing significantly whereas the penetration in India is rising slowly (Chaurasia et al., 2019, Cao et al., 2018). As a result, it is necessary to understand mindset differences of customers between China and India.

The most used theory in customers' continuance intention of m-payments from the literature is UTAUT proposed by Venkatesh et al. (2003). For example, Lu et al. (2017) focused on perceived effort expectancy, performance expectancy, social influence, grouping variables (age, gender, experience) in UTAUT as the key determinants to investigate continuance intention in China and the USA. The study found the perceived effort expectancy and social influence were as mediating to impact on continuance intention of customers across two countries by influencing performance expectancy. The performance expectancy is a significant impact on customers' post-adoption intention whereas the grouping variables have weak influences on customers' behaviors. Slade et al. (2015) applied UTAUT to analyze customers' continuance intention of using m-payment in the UK. Their study reveals that performance expectancy and social influence has a significant influence on the continuance intention of using m-payment in the UK. However, UTAUT is developed to investigate the initial adoption decision rather than to explain disconfirmation of customer's beliefs or satisfaction changes. As a result, it is not strong enough to discover continuance decision scenario (Almazroa and Gulliver, 2018).

2.2 The Consumption Value Theory

The Consumption Value Theory (CVT) was originally developed by Sheth et al. (1991) understand the customers' choices of whether to buy or nor buy in the marketing field (Biswas and Roy, 2015). Then, Sweeney and Soutar (2001) modified the original model to evaluate buyers' perception of the value of consumer durable goods. Following its successful implementation, Turel et al. (2007) have employed the modified model in the mobile commerce field. We however use the modified version of model since it has been adapted into technology adoption context by removing or adding some new variables (Spink et al., 2011). According to Sweeney and Soutar (2001), CTV is a model that integrates components of various customers value models based on the assumption that customer choice is a function for multiple consumption values. Value is a subjective concept that contains some intrinsic needs such as knowledge concern, emotional aspects, as well as some implicit factors (e.g. experiential need or prestige associated with the component purchase) (Biswas and Roy, 2015). Four dimensions are included in the model, which encompass perceived value of a person towards her/his intention to engage in a behavior. Functional value dimension is fundamental value resulting from the fulfillment of products for functional, beneficial purposes required by customers. Emotional value dimension is the value relevant to emotion of customers affected by products or services. Regarding value for money, one of the dimension measures perception of consumers about the product performance with respect to price. Social value dimension is relevant to perceived utility derived from social groups that the consumer is in relation with. All four dimensions exert an effect on outcomes of behaviors (Turel et al., 2007). Existing studies in IS suggest the effect of dimensions vary in terms of different culture contexts. For example, Hung and Hsieh (2010) found Taiwanese customers regard the functional value highly than Japanese customers whereas Japanese customers put more focus on emotional value than Taiwanese customers in mobile commerce usage context.

3. MODEL DEVELOPMENT

Although CVT has not been used in m-payment, it has been served as an influential underpinning theory to explain mobile behavior of the customers (Aulia et al., 2016). For example, the study of Turel et al. (2007) suggested all of consumption values (i.e. functional value, social value, emotional value and value for money) affect users' acceptance of mobile-based SMS. Zolkepli et al. (2020) also deployed CVT to investigate consumption values on the behavior for mobile applications (mobile apps). They found that the rating of mobile apps is highly dependent on the four dimensions and consumers are likely to pay for mobile apps if they have reasonable rating. Therefore, CVT has been found to provide valid explanations for individual's behavior in relation to using different m-commerce applications. This is especially true in the pay-per-use context where value tradeoffs (i.e., price, social, emotional and quality) are essential drivers in the intention decision (Turel et al., 2007). M-payment app(s) is used in such a context. For example, before using a m-payment app, users should make the tradeoff between the cost of data to run the m-payment app(s) and expected benefits from the m-payment app(s). As a result, CVT is considered as the theoretical base for our conceptual model (Figure 1).

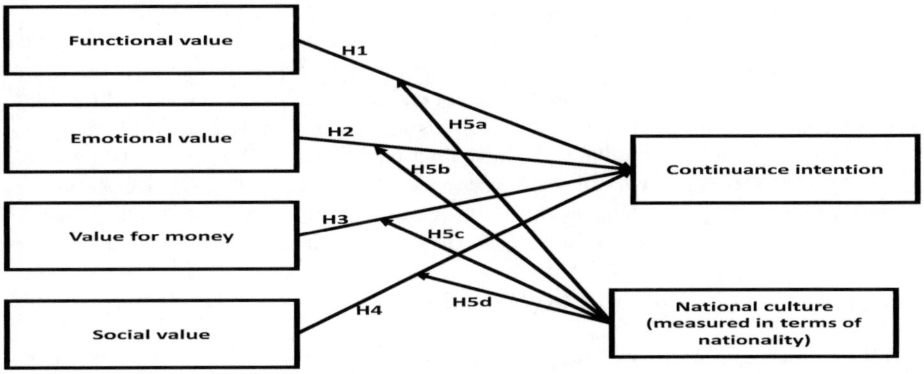

Figure 1. Conceptual research model

As indicated in the previous paragraph, the customers' continuance intention for m-payment need to be empirically evaluated in terms of the key constructs included in CVM. We have therefore derived eight hypotheses (shown in our research model - Figure 1) which are briefly described below.

Functional value: It refers to the perceived utility obtained from the efficient, consistent and effective performance of the services or products (Sheth et al., 1991). There are studies regarding that the functional value influences mobile services (Turel et al., 2007), use of mobile application (Zolkepli et al., 2020, Spink et al., 2011), information systems (Tzeng, 2011). Considering the studies performed, for m-payment context, we believe that the perception of customers about functional quality value would positively affect their continuance intention to use m-payment. Hence, the following hypothesis is proposed:

H1: Functional value will positively influence customers' continuance intention to use m-payment.

Emotional value: It is defined as the level of enjoyment, pleasure or anxiety a customer receives through using products or services (Sheth et al., 1991). It is related to the ability of products or services to mobilize the emotions. Emotional value is considered as an effective factor in building a loyal customer (Turel et al., 2007, Tzeng, 2011, Zolkepli et al., 2020, Spink et al., 2011). The more positive emotion derived from a product or service, the more likely that customers will continue to use the system (Goh et al., 2014). In the context of m-payment, we believe that emotional value would positively affect their continuance intention to use m-payment. Hence, the following hypothesis is proposed:

H2: Emotional value will positively influence customers' continuance intention to use m-payment.

Value for money: (Turel et al., 2007) defined value for money as the tradeoff between the quality of products or services (take) versus the cost of products or services (give). This should have a strong influence on the overall perceived value of m-payment, because it represents the main "take" component in the overall assessment. That is, the fee (e.g. fee for Internet connection) is charged and, in return, m-payment users receive emotional, social and function value (Spink et al., 2011, Turel et al., 2007). In the context of m-payment, we believe that value for money would positively affect their continuance intention to use m-payment. Hence, the following hypothesis is proposed:

H3: Value for money will positively influence customers' continuance intention to use m-payment.

Social value: It is defined as the value consumers gain from using products or services would increase their social status and approval (Turel et al., 2007). Social value in user decision making about IS continuance intention has been confirmed by several studies, such as mobile services (Turel et al., 2007), use of mobile application (Zolkepli et al., 2020, Spink et al., 2011), information systems (Tzeng, 2011). Adopting m-payment has growingly become a business trend as the mobile era evolves. Some consumers express uncertainty about the consequences of using m-payment; hence they may consult opinions or experiences from other consumers through social networks (Liébana-Cabanillas et al., 2013). The social environment of those who use m-payment significantly influence the usage attitudes of consumers. In order to develop favorable social impressions and approvals, consumers may prefer to be in line with others' behaviors through using m-payment (Gong et al., 2020, Liébana-Cabanillas et al., 2014). As a result, we believe that social value would positively affect their continuance intention to use m-payment. Hence, the following hypothesis is proposed:

H4: Social value will positively influence customers' continuance intention to use m-payment.

National culture: There have been multiple definitions of culture exist, but the most popular one is developed by Hofstede (1980). According to Hofstede (1980), culture is defined as the collective programming of the mind which differs the members of one group from another. Extant literature reveals the relationship between CVT variables to determine the moderating effect of national culture. Through an evaluation of Korea and Japan, Lee et al. (2002) reported values of the mobile Internet users significantly differ between two countries. For example, Korean users regard the emotional value highly than other values whereas functional value is considered as the most important value for Japanese users. Similar study also conducted by Hung and Hsieh (2010) and they found the culture has mediating influence on CVT from Japan and Taiwan context. According to exiting literatures, we can argue that some differences exist in the national role that moderates four dimensions influence on continuance intention. Hence, the following hypotheses are proposed:

H5a: The influence of functional value on continuance intention differs between Chinese and Indian consumers.

H5b: The influence of emotional value on continuance intention differs between Chinese and Indian consumers.

H5c: The influence of value for money on continuance intention differs between Chinese and Indian consumers.

H5d: The influence of social value on continuance intention differs between Chinese and Indian consumers.

4. METHODOLOGY

Continuance intention in this study is considered as a post-adoption intention of an individual for protracted use of a mobile payment application. This can be measured at any time once an individual user's initial adoption of that application has already taken place. Our study employs a quantitative research method. An online questionnaire was used as an instrument of data collection. Closed-ended questions, with a five-point Likert scale ranging from 1 (strongly disagree) to 5 (strongly agree), were included in the questionnaire. The questions involved in the questionnaire were totally from the extant literature (i.e. Gao et al. (2015), Yang et al. (2016)). A total of 150 online survey were randomly distributed among international students at an Australian university. 76 survey were given to Chinese students whereas others were given to Indian students. However, 125 completed responses were received, this yields a response rate 83.3%, which is considered quite satisfactory (Baruch and Holtom, 2008). Thirteen responses indicate that they are not m-payment app(s) users and remaining 112 are m-payment app(s) users. We note that a slight majority of the m- payment app(s) users are female (54.5%), a large percentage (71.4%) of the participants are aged between 24-29 years. Different from other studies, this study is unique as respondents are not living in their country of origin (China and India).

5. DATA ANALYSIS

Survey findings were analyzed using factor and reliability analysis and regression analysis. An exploratory iterative factor analysis was applied to the survey data collected from m-payment app(s) users (n=112) for the purpose of determining the discriminant validity of the research variables (Murtagh and Heck, 2012). Factor analysis was used to provide a description of variability among observed, correlated variables based on a potentially lower number of unobserved variables called factors (Sheppard, 1996). The reliability of each independent construct was also measured using Cronbach Alpha.

5.1 Reliability and Validity

The exploratory factor was performed on five items (e.g. functional value, trust, social value) representing four underlying independent constructs. According to the results, two factors (i.e. emotional value and social value) are empirically supported whereas two items (i.e. functional value, value for money) representing a single factor (i.e. Integrated value). It was noted that all the Cronbach Alpha values of these constructs are above 0.7, which is satisfactory (Murtagh and Heck, 2012). Drawing on the results of factor analysis and reliability analysis, most of factors in the research model were retained.

5.2 Survey Results

The regression analysis was applied to empirically evaluate relationships involved in the research model (Figure 1). The results indicate that integrated value has a large (31.9%) and significant ($p>.05$) influence on continuance intention for participants, whereas social value has a considerable variance effect on continuance intention (22.7%) and statistically significant ($p>.05$) effect on continuance intention. However, the analysis results find limited explanatory power of emotional value on the variation in continuance intention, and it is insignificant ($p= .01$). Three possible reasons potentially explain this result. Firstly, the sample size was not very large (e.g. not over 500). Secondly, there may be factors other than emotional value that may also affect continuance intention, which were not included in the model. This is because our study is concerned with CVT to investigate continuation to use m-payment, rather than other factors that are excluded from CVT. Thirdly, our study did not include participants from other cultural backgrounds. There is a possibility that this study could have provided dissimilar findings if it had also surveyed students from other cultural backgrounds (like Arab, English). Drawing on the survey results discussed above, the revised research model from general perspective has been further refined and are shown in Figure 2a.

In order to test whether national culture has a moderating impact, another two rounds of regression analysis based on nationality were performed. First round involved participation of participants from China (61) and second regression analysis involved participation of the remaining 51 participants from India. The results suggest that: a) For participants from India, only emotional value has statistically significant influence ($p <.05$) on continuance intention. For them, integrated value and social value have no effect on continuance intention ($p>.05$). b) For participants from China, however the effects of integrated value and emotional value have a significant impact on continuance intention ($p= .00$). But similar to Indian participants, social value has no impact on continuance intention ($p>.05$). Drawing on the survey results discussed above, the revised research model in terms of Chinese and Indian context have been further refined and are shown in Figure 2b ad Figure 2c.

The final research model is shown in Figure 2d. In this final model, the impact of emotional value on continuance intention is not considered as significant and hence it is shown as dotted line. However, further studies involving larger sample size will be done in the next stage to investigate this relationship.

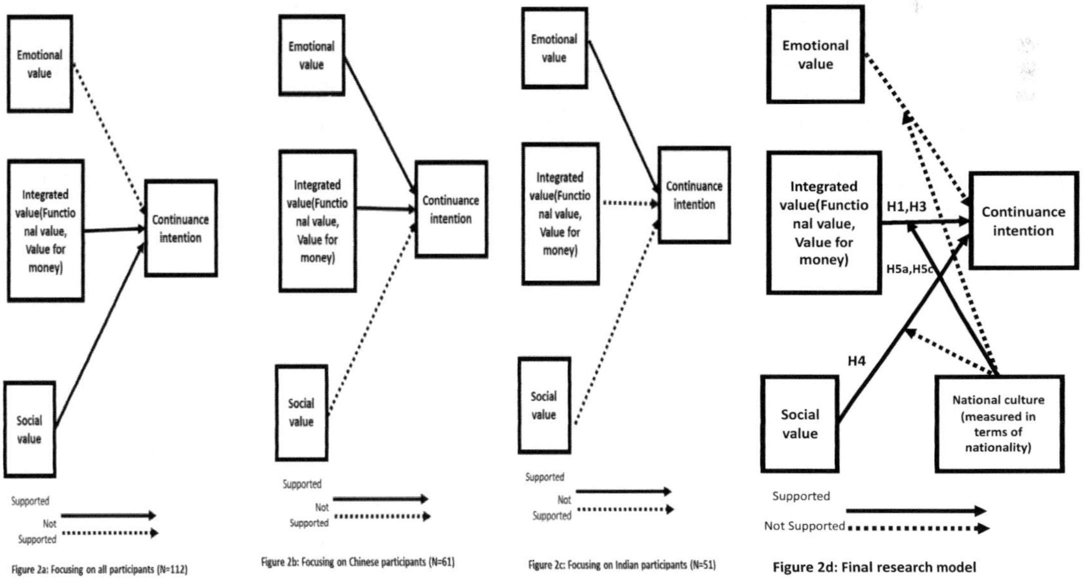

Figures 2a to 2d. The Research Models based on data analysis

6. DISCUSSION

Drawing on the analysis results, we provide insights into two main findings. First, out of eight proposed hypotheses (H1 to H4, H5a to H5d), five (H1, H3, H4 and H5a, H5c) were empirically supported by our survey findings. The implication is that CVT, in its current format, is partially able to explain customers' continuance intention. We found that one particular value perception (i.e., emotional value) with respect to m-payment continuance intention was not significant. In contrast, social value does play an important role in continuance intention for m-payment. These findings are different compared to those of Turel et al. (2007) but are consistent with Goh et al. (2014). This is due to the fact that Turel et al. (2007) have not examined how each value dimension relates to students' intentions and they do not focus on Chinese or Indian context. Despite this difficulty of direct comparisons, we find that consistent with their studies functional value (which has combined with value for money in the revised model) and social value appear to be more significant in explaining the relevance of CVT. This is also consistent with Zolkepli et al. (2020) who found functional value as well as social value have a positive influence on mobile app's usage.

Second, we can conclude that value structures, as derived from CVT, are somewhat different between Chinese and Indian participants. Results indicate that integrated value has an influence on continuance intention for m-payment for Chinese but no influence for Indian. This implies that Chinese customers are more likely to integrated value (i.e. perceive functional value and value for money) than Indian customers, the result makes sense that Chinese customers are willing to continue using m-payment if they are satisfied with the performance (e.g. effective, efficiency) of m-payment or they would consider it is worthy to deploy m-payment after the trade-off estimation between the price made by some risks (e.g. privacy risk) and continuing with deploying m-payment. This result is consistent with Lu et al. (2017) and Hung and Hsieh (2010) who suggest the value of mobile application customers between two cultures may be different. Furthermore, the emotional value has a significant impact on continuance intention for Chinese and Indian customers. The implication is that Chinese and Indian customers alike would continue using m-payment if they receive high level of enjoyment, pleasure through using this service.

7. CONCLUSION

Retaining users and facilitating their continuing use are crucial for m-payment service providers. Drawing on the theoretical justification, this research identified factors affecting continuance intention of m-payment use from cross-nationality perspective. A conceptual research model was developed based on CVT. A survey (with 112 set of responses) was then conducted and was statistically analyzed for model evaluation. We were able to obtain some findings that are useful to further refine the model. Results confirm that continuation intention is largely explained by integrated value (i.e. functional value and value for money) and social value. In contrast, emotional value has no significant impact on continuance intention to use m-payment app(s). In addition, cultural background (as represented by nationality) has a strong moderating effect on integrated value and continuance intention, but does not have significant influence on emotional and social value's effect on continuance intention. Due to the page limitation, the differences between these two cultures are not discussed in details. This study has several contributions. From a theoretical perspective, this study deploys CVT to address the continuance intention for the m-payment context using cross-nationality perspective. This is the first attempt not only to distinguish m-payment continuance intention across-culture, but also to explain these differences from cross-cultural perspectives with the CVT. For practical contribution, given the value structures are different between cultures, m-payment providers are required to consider some factors for specific country, such as integrated value is more important for Chinese customers. While this study considers only the background context of users, we acknowledge that there bound to be interactions with the m-payment context itself and this may have bearing on identified factors. This particular aspect is thus recommended for future studies.

REFERENCES

Al-Saedi, K., Al-Emran, M., Ramayah, T. & Abusham, E. 2020. Developing a general extended UTAUT model for M-payment adoption. *Technology in Society,* 62, 101293.

Biswas, A. & Roy, M. 2015. Leveraging factors for sustained green consumption behavior based on consumption value perceptions: testing the structural model. *Journal of Cleaner Production,* 95, 332-340.

Cao, X., Yu, L., Liu, Z., Gong, M. & Adeel, L. 2018. Understanding mobile payment users' continuance intention: a trust transfer perspective. *Internet Research.*

Chaurasia, S. S., Verma, S. & Singh, V. 2019. Exploring the intention to use M-payment in India. *Transforming Government: People, Process and Policy.*

Chen, S.-X., Wang, J.-Q. & Wang, T.-L. 2019. Cloud-based ERP system selection based on extended probabilistic linguistic MULTIMOORA method and Choquet integral operator. *Computational and Applied Mathematics,* 38, 88.

Chen, X. & Li, S. 2017. Understanding continuance intention of mobile payment services: an empirical study. *Journal of Computer Information Systems,* 57, 287-298.

Gao, L., Waechter, K. A. & Bai, X. 2015. Understanding consumers' continuance intention towards mobile purchase: A theoretical framework and empirical study–A case of China. *Computers in Human Behavior,* 53, 249-262.

Goh, T. T., Suki, N. M. & Fam, K. 2014. Exploring a consumption value model for Islamic mobile banking adoption. *Journal of Islamic Marketing.*

Gong, X., Zhang, K. Z., Chen, C., Cheung, C. M. & Lee, M. K. 2020. Transition from web to mobile payment services: The triple effects of status quo inertia. *International Journal of Information Management,* 50, 310-324.

Hofstede, G. 1980. Motivation, leadership, and organization: do American theories apply abroad? *Organizational dynamics,* 9, 42-63.

Hung, C.-L. & Hsieh, C.-Y. 2010. Searching the fit pattern between cultural dimensions and consumption values of mobile commerce in Taiwan. *Asia Pacific Management Review,* 15, 147-165.

Johnson, V. L., Kiser, A., Washington, R. & Torres, R. 2018. Limitations to the rapid adoption of M-payment services: Understanding the impact of privacy risk on M-Payment services. *Computers in Human Behavior,* 79, 111-122.

Kazan, E., Tan, C.-W., Lim, E. T., Sørensen, C. & Damsgaard, J. 2018. Disentangling digital platform competition: The case of UK mobile payment platforms. *Journal of Management Information Systems,* 35, 180-219.

Lee, Y., Kim, J., Lee, I. & Kim, H. 2002. A cross-cultural study on the value structure of mobile internet usage: Comparison between Korea and Japan. *J. Electron. Commerce Res.,* 3, 227-239.

Liébana-Cabanillas, F., Muñoz-Leiva, F. & Sánchez-Fernández, J. 2013. The impact of risk on the technological acceptance of mobile payment services. *Global Business Perspectives,* 1, 309-328.

Liébana-Cabanillas, F., Sánchez-Fernández, J. & Muñoz-Leiva, F. 2014. The moderating effect of experience in the adoption of mobile payment tools in Virtual Social Networks: The m-Payment Acceptance Model in Virtual Social Networks (MPAM-VSN). *International Journal of Information Management,* 34, 151-166.

Lu, J., Yu, C.-S., Liu, C. & Wei, J. 2017. Comparison of mobile shopping continuance intention between China and USA from an espoused cultural perspective. *Computers in Human Behavior,* 75, 130-146.

Mallat, N. 2007. Exploring consumer adoption of mobile payments–A qualitative study. *The Journal of Strategic Information Systems,* 16, 413-432.

Murtagh, F. & Heck, A. 2012. *Multivariate data analysis*, Springer Science & Business Media.

Setterstrom, A. J., Pearson, J. M. & Orwig, R. A. 2013. Web-enabled wireless technology: an exploratory study of adoption and continued use intentions. *Behaviour & Information Technology,* 32, 1139-1154.

Sheth, J. N., Newman, B. I. & Gross, B. L. 1991. *Consumption values and market choices: Theory and applications*, South-Western Pub. Cinicinnati, OH.

Slade, E., Williams, M., Dwivedi, Y. & Piercy, N. 2015. Exploring consumer adoption of proximity mobile payments. *Journal of Strategic Marketing,* 23, 209-223.

Spink, P., Rahim, M. M. & Singh, U. B. 2011. User intentions of downloading games on mobile phones: an empirical evaluation using consumption value model.

Sweeney, J. C. & Soutar, G. N. 2001. Consumer perceived value: The development of a multiple item scale. *Journal of retailing,* 77, 203-220.

Turel, O., Serenko, A. & Bontis, N. 2007. User acceptance of wireless short messaging services: Deconstructing perceived value. *Information & Management,* 44, 63-73.

Tzeng, J.-Y. 2011. Perceived values and prospective users' acceptance of prospective technology: The case of a career eportfolio system. *Computers & Education,* 56, 157-165.

Yang, X., Li, Y. & Liao, Q. 2016. Exploring continued use of mobile shopping channel in China: the effects of active coping and its antecedents. *Electronic Commerce Research,* 16, 245-267.

Zolkepli, I. A., Mukhiar, S. N. S. & Tan, C. 2020. Mobile consumer behaviour on apps usage: The effects of perceived values, rating, and cost. *Journal of Marketing Communications*, 1-23.

THE IMPACT OF SOCIAL MEDIA USE AND CONTENT ON THE YOUNGER GENERATION'S MENTAL HEALTH IN INDONESIA

Selina Maurizka, Putu Wuri Handayani and Widia Resti Fitriani
Faculty of Computer Science, University of Indonesia
Depok, Indonesia

ABSTRACT

This study aims to analyse the impact of social media use and content on the mental health of young people in Indonesia. This research uses a quantitative approach using an online questionnaire. There were 1,402 respondents who participated in this study. The collected data was analysed using a multiple linear regression method with a mediation relationship. The tool used to process the data was IBM SPSS version 25. This research shows that social media use, social media content, emotion regulation, perceived stress, and poor sleep affects depressive symptoms. The results of this study can help regulators and health service providers to provide better facilities for handling mental health cases, especially those due to the use and content of social media. The results of this study are expected to help social media developers develop features that provide a safe online environment for social media users.

KEYWORDS

Mental Health, Social Media, Social Media Use, Social Media Content, Young Generation, Indonesia

1. INTRODUCTION

Social media is now very knitted into the daily lives of most people. According to Clement (2020b), social media users will continue to increase, and the number is projected to be almost 3.43 billion in 2023. Indonesia ranks fourth highest in the world for Internet users (Clement, 2020a). Based on the results of a survey conducted by the Indonesian Internet Service Providers Association (APJII), the number of Internet users in Indonesia has reached 64.8% of the total population of Indonesia (APJII, 2018). APJII (2018) also found that the social media frequently visited by Indonesian residents were Facebook at 50.7%, Instagram at 17.8%, and YouTube at 15.1%. According to Kemp (2019), active social media users in Indonesia in 2019 numbered 150 million people, up 15% to 20% from 2018.

Mental health is a serious issue in Indonesia; the prevalence of severe mental disorders in Indonesia's population is 1.7% (Hartini et al., 2018). In addition, based on data from the Ministry of Health of the Republic of Indonesia, it is estimated that in 2018, 6.1% of the population aged 15 years and older had experienced depression. Social media users in children and adolescents number approximately 30 million people in Indonesia, according to the Ministry of Communication and Information, and the level of Internet addiction among teenagers in Jakarta has reached 31.4%, far surpassing the world's levels of 4.5–19.1 % and levels in young adults of around 0.7–18.3% (Napitupulu, 2019). According to the National Information and Communication Technology Board, during the COVID-19 pandemic, the use of the Instagram application rose 40% because many people used social media to communicate during quarantine. Based on these problems, an understanding of the impact of the use of social media and content on social media is needed, especially since Indonesia is currently experiencing a significant increase in the number of young people.

Although there is a correlation between the use of social media and mental health, the relationship between them is still considered unclear (de Calheiros Velozo & Stauder, 2018; Rasmussen et al., 2020). Moreover, the use of social media might be associated with negative mental health, such as suicide, loneliness, and lack of empathy (Berryman et al., 2018). In addition, Shensa et al. (2020) found that social media use is associated with depressive symptoms. Stress is also one of the factors associated with the use of social media (Rasmussen et al., 2020). Emotion and stress regulation is ultimately related to producing a higher likelihood of some mental disorders (Aldao et al., 2010). The use of social media is also often associated with the quality of one's sleep (Woods & Scott, 2016). Levenson et al. (2016) also found that the use of social media is associated with disruption of one's sleep time, including difficulties getting to sleep and poor quality of sleep. Further, Thompson and Lougheed (2012) found that social media users, especially young people, spend as much as 54% of their time accessing social media.

To date, there is not much research that addresses the effects of social media content on mental health. Coyne et al. (2020) found no influence of time spent on using social media on mental health. In addition, de Calheiros Velozo, and Stauder (2018) found that there was no relationship between viewing a person's content and emotional symptoms. In addition, there has been no research related to the relationship between social media content, poor sleep, perceived stress, and emotion regulation on the mental health of young people in Indonesia. Thus, this study aims to better understand the impact of social media use and social media content that can affect the mental health of the younger generations. This research is expected to benefit social media users, social media developers, and health workers by informing them about the impact of social media on mental health.

2. METHODS

2.1 Conceptual Model & Research Hypothesis

Social media use is an important element in the development of adolescents and young people because they can interact with others and present in creating their online identity (Bartsch et al., 2015). In general, social media use is associated with higher levels of anxiety and depression (Banjanin et al., 2015; Pantic et al., 2012; Woods & Scott, 2016). Research shows that there is a relationship between the time spent using social media and feelings of depression and anxiety in adolescents (Banjanin et al., 2015; Barry et al., 2017; Pantic et al., 2012; Woods & Scott, 2016). Further, Sujarwoto et al. (2019) found an influence between the use of social media and mental health in developing countries, such as in Indonesia.

Hormes et al. (2014) found that high social media use causes difficulties in emotion regulation. Emotion regulation is awareness, clarity, acceptance, access, ability to control, and ability to response through emotional responses (Gratz et al., 2004). Emotional regulation is considered important because excessive use of social media can cause depression, especially for people in developing countries, such as in Indonesia (Sujarwoto et al., 2019). In addition, Zahniser and Conley (2018) have shown that difficulties with emotion regulation are associated with indicators of stress or perceived stress in emerging adults.

Akin and İskender (2011) found an association between addictive Internet use with depression, anxiety, and stress. Young people in early adulthood experience extreme anxiety when their access to text messages is restricted and report feelings of stress and guilt when they do not immediately respond to messages (Thomée et al., 2010). Rasmussen et al. (2020) found that feelings of stress are related to problems with mental health. Having a good ability to self-regulate signifies the ability to remain calm in stressful situations or to withstand feelings of anger and frustration (de Calheiros Velozo & Stauder, 2018).

An et al. (2014) found a relationship between social media use and sleep disturbance. Social media is generally associated with poor sleep outcomes, specifically shorter sleep duration, delayed sleep time, and poor sleep quality (Levenson et al., 2016). Poor sleep quality is known to contribute to feelings of anxiety, depression, and low self-esteem in adolescents (Alfano et al., 2009). Research conducted by Nursalam et al. (2019) of Indonesian teenagers proved that the duration of use of social media affects the quality of sleep, which can cause insomnia. Problems with sleep quality can contribute to psychological problems such as depression (Eipstein, 2008).

H1. *Social media use (SMU) influences depressive symptoms (DS)*

H2. *Social media use (SMU) influences emotion regulation (ER) which will influence depressive symptoms (DS)*

H3. *Social media use (SMU) influences perceived stress (PS) which will influence depressive symptoms (DS)*

H4. *Social media use (SMU) influences emotion regulation (ER) which will influence perceived stress (PS), and in the end will influence depressive symptoms (DS)*

H5. *Social media use (SMU) influences poor sleep (PSL) which will influence depressive symptoms (DS)*

H6. *Social media use (SMU) influences poor sleep (PSL), which will influence perceived stress (PS), and in the end will influence also depressive symptoms (DS)*

Content is basically anything that touches or interacts with a targeted prospect, including online properties and everything on social media (Handley, 2014). Research by Viner et al. (2019) found that activities, such as watching dangerous content, could have direct harmful effects on mental health. One way that this can cause a negative impact on mental health relates to a person's inability to prove a trait or activity that is considered cool and the effort required to remain part of an online group (Mcdool et al., 2016). Exposure to various forms of media can be an effective means of manipulating a person's emotional mood (Zillmann, 2000), but an individual is not necessarily aware of how they use the media to regulate the state of their mood (Holger & Werner, 2008).

According to research by Rideout and Fox (2018), seeing too much negative news can make a person feel stressed and anxious. Thomée et al. (2010) found that stress can come from a never-ending flood of information that comes in the form of messages, emails, updates, etc. According to Rasmussen et al. (2020), stress plays a direct role in mental health problems. Awareness about stress events uploaded by others may also negatively affect someone's mental health, because through social media, users will be more aware of the struggles of the people in their network (Hampton et al., 2019).

Moreover, sleep disturbance due to notifications from social media content is one of the possible causes of the relationship between social media and poor sleep quality (Woods & Scott, 2016). Social media content on Instagram, Facebook, or Twitter can limit a person's sleep hours because they are compelled to check the content on an ongoing basis (Linetti, 2019). According to Harususilo (2018), some teenagers in Indonesia try so hard to maintain their existence on social media that it makes them lose sleep at night while they choose the best content to upload on Instagram; this can adversely affect teenagers. Harususilo (2018) shows that adolescents need 9.5 hours of sleep each night but only get 7.5 hours; the impact of this lack of sleep can make children tired, irritable, stressed, and prone to sickness.

H7. *Social media content (SMC) influences depressive symptoms (DS)*

H8. *Social media content (SMC) influences emotion regulation (ER) which will influence depressive symptoms (DS)*

H9. *Social media content (SMC) influences perceived stress (PS) which will influence depressive symptoms (DS)*

H10. *Social media content (SMC) influences poor sleep (PSL) which will influence depressive symptoms (DS)*

H11. *Social media content (SMC) influences emotion regulation (ER) which will influence perceived stress (PS), and in the end will influence depressive symptoms (DS)*

H12. *Social media content (SMC) influences poor sleep (PSL) which will perceived stress (PS), and in the end will influence depressive symptoms (DS)*

2.2 Research Instruments

This study divides the questionnaire into two parts, namely the demographic information and the statements related to the research, which involved 34 questions. The demographic section consists of respondents' gender, age, occupation, education, domicile of residence, use of social media, use of social media features, types of social media information that are frequently searched for, types of information that create stress, and sources of information that create stress. All sections except questions for depressive symptoms and one statement on poor sleep use a Likert scale of 1 to 5, starting from one that shows strongly disagree to five that shows strongly agree. The depressive symptoms section of respondents answered using a Likert scale from 1 to 3 and one question on the poor sleep section used a Likert scale from 1 to 4. A Likert scale of 3 has the correct, sometimes, and incorrect options. Likert scale of 4 adjusted to the context of the question where each scale will contain a time range.

2.3 Data Collection & Analysis

The questionnaire took approximately 10 minutes to complete and all respondents' answers were given anonymously. All respondents gave informed consent to fill out the questionnaires, which was followed by the questionnaire link being distributed through social media platforms such as Twitter, Facebook, Instagram, or dan LINE. Social media were chosen because they have the highest number of users in Indonesia. According to Müller (2019b), in 2018, social media users in Indonesia numbered 81 million people. Because of this high number, we set the target respondents for this study as young people who have used social media. The data processing method used was mediation relationship with multiple linear regression. The tools used to help process the data were IBM SPSS version 25 and, for processing data, an add-on in SPSS consisting of PROCESS macros created by Andrew F. Hayes.

3. RESULTS

The research questionnaire was distributed over three weeks online starting from February 20, 2020 to March 13, 2020 (23 days). We successfully obtained 1,402 complete questionnaires after we deleted invalid data. This research has fulfilled the requirements of the assumption test, namely multicollinearity test, homoscedasticity test and linearity test, independence test, and normality test (Hayes, 2018; Lund, 2018). Hypotheses 1 and 7 used a linear regression test without mediation. The hypothesis with one mediating variable has three direct effect relationships. Furthermore, the hypothesis with two mediating variables has six direct effect relationships. Indirect effect serves to describe the path effect from the independent variable to the dependent variable through mediating variables (Hayes, 2018). The results of the indirect effect can illustrate whether the effect of the independent variable on the dependent variable is transmitted through the mechanism represented by the causal chain of events (Hayes, 2018). Hypothesis testing is done in two directions (two-tailed). There are 12 accepted hypotheses that have p-values below 0.05 and t values greater than 1.96, and also for hypothesis with indirect effects can be accepted if the Effect value is between BootLLCI and BootULCI, which can be seen at Table 1.

Table 1. Indirect Effects

Relationship	Effect	BootLLCI	BootULCI
SMU -> ER -> DS	0,2736	0,2041	0,3558
SMU -> PS -> DS	0,0693	0,0153	0,1027
SMU -> ER -> PS -> DS	0,0622	0,042	0,0858
SMU -> PSL -> DS	0,0164	0,0049	0,032
SMU -> PSL -> PS -> DS	0,0238	0,0081	0,0409
SMC -> ER -> DS	-0,1883	-0,2284	-0,149
SMC -> PS -> DS	-0,054	-0,074	-0,0354
SMC -> PSL -> DS	-0,0091	-0,0174	-0,0029
SMC -> ER -> PS -> DS	-0,0427	-0,057	-0,0298
SMC -> PSL -> PS -> DS	-0,013	-0,0219	-0,0052

4. DISCUSSION

This study found that social media use has an influence on depressive symptoms (H1). This supports research by Banjanin et al. (2015), Barry et al. (2017), Pantic et al. (2012), and Woods and Scott (2016), which states that the time of use of social media has an influence on feelings of depression and anxiety. The use of social media on an ongoing basis is often blamed for causing problems with mental health, especially in young people and adolescents (Charles, 2019). In developing countries, increased use of social media, such as Facebook and Twitter, not only offers benefits, allowing individuals to connect with others, but can also have harmful effects on their mental health (Sujarwoto et al., 2019). The use of social media in Indonesia can negatively affect how users see the world, due to the high prevalence of negative news that is spread through social media (Müller, 2020).

Social media use also influences emotion regulation and affects depressive symptoms (H2). These results support previous research that emotion regulation plays a mediating role between the use of social media and mental health (Rasmussen et al., 2020). A high level of social media use is an example of engagement with an addictive activity, which suggests a lack of ability to regulate oneself (Lu et al., 2016). Further, Hormes et al.'s (2014) state that social media use causes difficulties for some people to regulate their emotions. Spending a lot of time on social media reduces self-control because users may start copying new behaviours from friends on social media (Linetti, 2019). According to Ministry of Communication and Information, with the increasing development of social media for use by young people in Indonesia, parents need to be stricter about the use of social media for their children. A duration of Internet and social media usage of more than 20 hours per week (Napitupulu, 2019) indicates that there is poor regulation of behaviour in relation to social media; if this pattern continues, it can have a negative impact on the person's mental health.

Furthermore, social media use has an influence on perceived stress and affects depressive symptoms (H3). These results support research by Akin and İskender (2011), which states that addictive use of the Internet is associated with depression, anxiety, and stress. Another cause of stress is the consciousness of the need to stop using social media, but which they have failed at, causing a person to feel more stress (Linetti, 2019). According to the 2018 Basic Health Research study conducted by the Ministry of Health, the number of Indonesian citizens who experience depression that leads to suicide is 6.1%, which is equivalent to 11 million people; this figure is for citizens over the age of 15 years.

In addition, social media influences emotion regulation and perceived stress, which affects depressive symptoms (H4). This supports previous research conducted by Rasmussen et al. (2020), which states that the ability of someone who uses social media to regulate their emotions affects the stress they face, which ultimately affects their mental health. Our analysis found that when comparing emotional and stress regulation pathways, emotional regulation pathways had a more significant influence than stress pathways. De Calheiros Velozo and Stauder (2018) state that a person's emotional regulation influences feelings of stress; for example, someone who has a good ability to self-regulate tends to have the ability to remain calm in stressful situations.

Social media use has an influence on poor sleep, which affects depressive symptoms (H5). These results support Woods and Scott (2016) research that found a significant relationship between the use of social media at night and poor sleep quality, which can cause feelings of anxiety and depression. This relates to studies by the University of Pittsburgh showing that the more time spent by young people on social media, the more likely they are to experience problems with sleep and show symptoms of depression (Levenson et al., 2016). According to Harvard Medical School (2019), one of the psychological effects of sleep deprivation is depression. In Indonesia, use of social media that exceeds 5 hours is associated with insomnia, which can cause mental health problems (Nursalam et al., 2019).

The fact that social media use has an influence on poor sleep and perceived stress affects depressive symptoms (H6). According to Levenson et al. (2016), people may have difficulty sleeping as a result of spending more time using social media; however, people with pre-existing sleep conditions can also use social media as a fun way to spend time when awake or to divert themselves from their difficulty of getting to sleep. According to Harvard Medical School (2019), problems with sleep are related to anxiety, depression, bipolar disorder, and attention deficit hyperactivity disorder (ADHD).

Furthermore, social media content has an influence on depressive symptoms (H7). Existing content on social media, such as harmful content (i.e. pornography, etc.), can affect one's mental health (Viner et al., 2019). According to Müller (2019a), false news that spreads online has a negative impact on Indonesians. Based on a survey conducted by Statista in 2019 in Indonesia, 58.3% of respondents said they read the latest news on social media (Müller, 2019a). Content that spreads on social media can also have a negative impact on the mental health of users (Hogenboom, 2018). Sujarwoto et al. (2019) found that news that spreads on social media contains mostly negative content, such as crime, corruption, and so on; news like that can make readers feel depressed.

Social media content influences emotion regulation and affects depressive symptoms (H8). This supports previous research that shows that people who are more selective of media content, using it to meet different needs, have a higher level of emotional regulation, which influences their ability to choose the content that is right for them (Schramm & Cohen, 2017). Content viewed by social media users can be an effective way to manipulate their emotional mood (Zillmann, 2000). Sukmayadi and Effendi (2018) found that many respondents of social media users felt frustrated and exhausted from the content and tone of the political environment in their social media timeline.

Furthermore, social media content has an influence on perceived stress and affects depressive symptoms (H9). This supports research conducted by Rideout and Fox (2018), which states that seeing too much negative content can make a person feel stressed and anxious. Thomée et al. (2010) says that stress arises when people view photo uploads, when they feel the need to follow uploads continuously via Twitter, or when they view activities that make them feel left behind by their friends. This result also supports research by Hampton et al. (2019) that shows someone's mental health can be affected by events uploaded by others in their network.

Next, social media content has an influence on poor sleep and affects depressive symptoms (H10). This supports previous research by Woods and Scott (2016) that social media, including notifications or content, is the cause of poor sleep quality. The results of this analysis test support the statement of Linetti (2019) that social media content on Instagram, Facebook, or Twitter can reduce people's sleep time, making their sleep quality worse. According to research by Nursalam et al. (2019), social media can make adolescents in Indonesia experience insomnia, while according to Alvaro et al. (2014), insomnia can have an impact on a person's psychology, causing issues such as depression, anxiety, withdrawal symptoms from addiction, and aggression.

The next result is that social media content has an influence on emotion regulation and perceived stress, which affects depressive symptoms (H11). Research from the UCLA Brain Mapping Center found that the number of 'likes' in a photo creates higher activity in the brain, so teenagers are more likely to give 'likes' to a photo regardless of the content, as they only care about the number of 'likes' (Sherman et al., 2016). The ability to regulate emotions can impact the existence of stressful feelings, as shown by the results of research by Zahniser and Conley (2018). Someone who can regulate emotions can regulate their affective circumstances, thereby reducing negative feelings and maintaining a positive mood (Zillmann, 2000). However, with the rapidly growing use of social media among young people, parental support and digital media integration are still lagging; therefore, efforts are needed to raise awareness for all groups.

Finally, social media content has an influence on poor sleep and perceived stress, which affects depressive symptoms (H12). The results of this analysis support research by Woods and Scott (2016) showing that a person can have poor sleep quality due to social media content or notifications that appear, which will lead to poor sleep that can trigger stress, which then has physiological and psychological consequences (Walker & Stickgold, 2006). High levels of adolescent addiction in Indonesia on social media among adolescents (Napitupulu, 2019) will have an impact on sleep duration and poor sleep quality. High levels of social media usage can cause anxiety, depression, and suicide for young people (McBride, 2011).

5. CONCLUSION

The results of the data analysis found that social media use can affect depressive symptoms through several channels, namely through emotion regulation, poor sleep, perceived stress, emotion regulation and perceived stress, and poor sleep and perceived stress. Further, social media content can affect depressive symptoms through emotion regulation, poor sleep, perceived stress, emotion regulation and perceived stress, as well as poor sleep and perceived stress. There needs to be a higher level of awareness and real action in developing social media applications to reduce the number of mental health patients. Social media users should also be more careful in using social media because excessive use can cause mental health problems. Future studies are expected to develop more specific social media content contexts.

REFERENCES

Akin A. et al, 2011. Internet addiction and depression, anxiety and stress. *International Online Journal of Educational Sciences, 3*(1), pp 138–148.

Aldao A. et al, 2010. Emotion-regulation strategies across psychopathology: A meta-analytic review. *Clinical Psychology Review, 30*(2), pp 217–237.

Alfano C. et al, 2009. Sleep problems and their relation to cognitive factors, anxiety, and depressive symptoms in children and adolescents. *Depression and Anxiety, 26*(6), pp 503–512.

Alvaro P. et al, 2014. The independent relationships between insomnia, depression, subtypes of anxiety, and chronotype during adolescence. *Sleep Medicine, 15*(8), pp 934–941.

An J. et al, 2014. Associations between problematic Internet use and adolescents' physical and psychological symptoms: Possible role of sleep quality. *Journal of Addiction Medicine, 8*(4), pp 282–287.

Asosiasi Penyelenggara Jasa Internet Indonesia [APJII], 2018. Penetrasi dan Perilaku Profil Pengguna Internet Indonesia. Jakarta: Asosiasi Penyelenggara Jasa Internet Indonesia.

Banjanin N. et al, 2015. Relationship between Internet use and depression: Focus on physiological mood oscillations, social networking and online addictive behavior. *Computers in Human Behavior, 43*, pp 308–312.

Barry C. et al, 2017. Adolescent social media use and mental health from adolescent and parent perspectives. *Journal of Adolescence, 61*, pp 1–11.

Bartsch M. et al, 2015. Technology and Self-Presentation. In *The Wiley Handbook of Psychology, Technology, and Society*, pp 339-357.

Berryman C. et al, 2018. Social media use and mental health among young adults. *Psychiatric Quarterly, 89*, pp 307–314.

Charles S., 2019. Social media linked to rise in mental health disorders. Retrieved from https://www.nbcnews.com/health/mental-health/social-media-linked-rise-mental-health-disorders-teens-survey-finds-n982526

Clement J., 2020a. Number of Internet users in selected countries 2019. Retrieved from https://www.statista.com/statistics/262966/number-of-internet-users-in-selected-countries/

Clement J., 2020b. Number of social media users worldwide 2010-2021. Retrieved from https://www.statista.com/statistics/278414/number-of-worldwide-social-network-users/

Coyne S. et al, 2020. Does time spent using social media impact mental health?: An eight year longitudinal study. *Computers in Human Behavior, 104*, 106160.

de Calheiros Velozo J. & Stauder J. E. A., 2018. Exploring social media use as a composite construct to understand its relation to mental health: A pilot study on adolescents. *Children and Youth Services Review, 91*, 398–402.

Eipstein L. J., 2008. Sleep and mood. Retrieved from http://healthysleep.med.harvard.edu/need-sleep/whats-in-it-for-you/mood

Gratz K. L. & Roemer L., 2004. Multidimensional Assessment of Emotion Regulation and Dysregulation: Development, Factor Structure, and Initial Validation of the Difficulties in Emotion Regulation Scale. *Journal of Psychopathology and Behavioral Assessment*, 26(1), pp 41-54.

Hair J. F. et al, 2019. *Multivariate data analysis.* Andover, Hampshire, United Kingdom: Cengage.

Hampton K. et al, 2019. Psychological stress and social media use. Retrieved from https://www.pewresearch.org/internet/2015/01/15/psychological-stress-and-social-media-use-2/

Handley A., 2014. Everybody writes: your go-to guide to creating ridiculously good content. New Jersey: John Wiley & Sons, Inc

Hartini N. et al, 2018. Stigma toward people with mental health problems in Indonesia. *Psychology Research and Behavior Management, 11*, pp 535–541.

Harususilo Y. E., 2018. Siswa Aktif Media Sosial Rentan Insomnia. Retrieved from https://edukasi.kompas.com/read/2018/09/19/19372001/siswa-aktif-media-sosial-rentan-insomnia-dan-cemas?page=all

Harvard Medical School, 2019. Sleep and Mental Health. Retrieved from https://www.health.harvard.edu/newsletter_article/sleep-and-mental-health

Hayes A. F., 2018. *Introduction to mediation, moderation, and conditional process analysis, second edition: A regression-based approach.* The Guilford Press.

Hogenboom M., 2018. The vital time you should not be on social media. Retrieved from http://www.bbc.com/future/story/20180110-the-vital-time-you-really-shouldnt-be-on-social-media.

Holger S. & Werner W., 2008. A case for an integrative view on affect regulation through media usage. *Communications, 33*(1), pp 27–46.

Hormes J. et al, 2014. Craving Facebook? Behavioral addiction to online social networking and its association with emotion regulation deficits. *Addiction, 109*(12), 2079–2088.

Kemp S., 2019. Digital 2019: Indonesia - DataReportal – Global digital insights. Retrieved from https://datareportal.com/reports/digital-2019-indonesia

Levenson, J. et al, 2016. The association between social media use and sleep disturbance among young adults. *Preventive Medicine, 85*, pp 36–41.

Linetti L., 2019. Why social media is boosting your stress. Retrieved from https://www.thejakartapost.com/life/2019/01/09/why-social-media-is-boosting-your-stress.html

Lu J. et al, 2016. Consuming, sharing, and creating content: How young students use new social media in and outside school. *Computers in Human Behavior, 64*, pp 55–64.

Lund A., 2018. *Multiple linear regression in SPSS statistics*. Retrieved from https://statistics.laerd.com/spss-tutorials/multiple-regression-using-spss-statistics.php

McBride, D. L., 2011. Risks and benefits of social media for children and adolescents. *Journal of Pediatric Nursing, 26*(5), pp 498–499.

Mcdool E. et al (2016). Social media use and children's wellbeing: IZA discussion paper No. 10412. Retrieved from https://www.sheffield.ac.uk/polopoly_fs/1.669622!/file/paper_2016011.pdf

Ministry of Health of the Republic of Indonesia, 2018. Riset Kesehatan Dasar oleh Badan Penelitian dan Pengembangan Kesehatan Kementerian RI tahun 2018. Retrieved from http://www.depkes.go.id/resources/download/infoterkini/materi_rakorpop_20 18/Hasil%20Riskesdas%202018.pdf

Müller J., 2019a. Indonesia: Most popular social media content 2019. Retrieved from https://www.statista.com/statistics/1050401/indonesia-most-popular-social-media-content-2019/

Müller J., 2019b. Number of social network users in Indonesia 2023. Retrieved from https://www.statista.com/statistics/247938/number-of-social-network-users-in-indonesia/

Müller J., 2020. Indonesia: Social media penetration 2019. Retrieved from https://www.statista.com/statistics/284437/indonesia-social-network-penetration/

Napitupulu E. L., 2019. Tingkat Kecanduan Remaja Indonesia pada Internet Sangat Tinggi. Retrieved from https://kompas.id/baca/humaniora/dikbud/2019/11/19/tingkat-kecanduan-remaja-indonesia-pada-internet-sangat-tinggi/

Nursalam N. et al, 2019. Association between insomnia and social network site use in Indonesian adolescents. *Nursing Forum, 54*(2), pp 149–156.

Pantic I. et al, 2012. Association between online social networking and depression in high school students: Behavioral physiology viewpoint. *Psychiatria Danubina, 24*(1), pp 90–93.

Rasmussen E. E. et al, 2020. The serially mediated relationship between emerging adults' social media use and mental well-being. *Computers in Human Behavior, 102*, pp 206–213.

Rideout V. & Fox S., 2018. *Digital health practices, social media use, and mental well-being among teens and young adults in the U.S.* San Francisco, CA: Hopelab and Well Being Trust. Available at: https://www.hopelab.org/reports/pdf/a-national-sur vey-by-hopelab-and-well-being-trust-2018.pdf.

Schramm H. & Cohen E. L., 2017. Emotion Regulation and Coping via Media Use. The International Encyclopaedia of Media Effects, pp 1-9.

Shensa A. et al, 2020. Emotional support from social media and face-to-face relationships: Associations with depression risk among young adults. *Journal of Affective Disorders, 260*, pp 38–44.

Sherman L. E. et al, 2016. The power of the like in adolescence: Effects of peer influence on neural and behavioral responses to social media. *Psychological Science, 27*(7), pp 1027–1035.

Sujarwoto S. et al, 2019. A tool to help or harm? Online social media use and adult mental health in Indonesia. *International Journal of Mental Health and Addiction, 17*, pp 1076–1093.

Sukmayadi V. & Effendi R., 2018. Social media emotion in politics: An Indonesian case study of political environment on Facebook. *IOP Conference Series: Earth and Environmental Science, 145*, 012009.

Thomée S. et al, 2010. Perceived connections between information and communication technology use and mental symptoms among young adults – A qualitative study. *BMC Public Health, 10*, pp 66.

Thompson S. H. & Lougheed E., 2012. Frazzled by Facebook? An exploratory study of gender differences in social network communication among undergraduate men and women. *College Student Journal, 46*(1), pp 88–98.

Viner R. M. et al (2019). Roles of cyberbullying, sleep, and physical activity in mediating the effects of social media use on mental health and wellbeing among young people in England: a secondary analysis of longitudinal data. *The Lancet Child and Adolescent Health, 3*(10), pp 685–696.

Walker M. P. & Stickgold R., 2006. Sleep, memory, and plasticity. *Annual Review of Psychology, 57*, pp 139–166.

Woods H. C. & Scott H., 2016. #Sleepyteens: Social media use in adolescence is associated with poor sleep quality, anxiety, depression and low self-esteem. *Journal of Adolescence, 51*, pp 41–49.

Zahniser E. & Conley C. S., 2018. Interactions of emotion regulation and perceived stress in predicting emerging adults' subsequent internalizing symptoms. *Motivation and Emotion, 42*, pp 763–773.

Zillmann D., 2000. Mood management in the context of selective exposure theory. *Annals of the International Communication Association, 23*(1), pp 103–123.

PROCESS MINING IMPLEMENTATION BENEFITS FOR ORGANIZATIONS USING ERP SYSTEMS

Effah A. Kadasah
King Saud University, Riyadh, Saudi Arabia

ABSTRACT

One of the most valuable assets of an organization is its organizational data. Enterprise recourse planning (ERP) is one of the information systems that can be a source for data and implemented processes for the most of the organizations. Business process management and data driven approach are combined in process mining to address the increasing needs of organizations. The core idea of process mining is to utilize ERP or any other information systems implicit data by using algorithms to create new process model, analyze a process model or enhance an existing process model. In this review paper, I will discuss how organizations benefit more from ERP in improving their business process by using process mining technique in business process management cycle. The paper contains examples of related work that use process mining in different business process that have been implemented in ERP.

KEYWORDS

ERP, Process Mining, Business Process Management

1. INTRODUCTION

Process mining is as one of leading innovations at business process management (BPM) field in 2012. IEEE has determined a Task Force who dedicated about process mining which has been lead by Wil van der Aalst, from Eindhoven University of Technology, The Netherlands (Van Der Alast et al., 2011). This task force published a Process Mining Manifesto where the process mining has been introduced as a research field which contains the main concepts description, principles guidance and related challenges (Van Der Alast et al., 2011).

Business process mining is a young research topic that related to both machine learning and data mining on area and process modelling and analysis on the area (Van Der Alast et al., 2011). ERP is a strategic tool which synchronizes, integrates, and streamlines data and processes of the organization into one single system to gain a competitive edge in the uncertain business environment (Madanhire & Mbohwa, 2016). The implementation projects of ERP systems are frequently considered as failure due to several reasons include: inherent complexity, resource intensity, required financial investment, required time, management challenges and risks and number of employees involved (Fleig, 2018). Chistian fleig and Dominik Augesnstein found out that the activities of doing the business process transformation and re-engineering are necessary in the actual ERP implementation or during the improvement of business process within the system (Fleig, 2018).

Ana Pajić and Dragana Bečejski mentioned that the organizations utilize Enterprise Resource Planning (ERP) systems to integrate the data and processes of organization into single database where those systems are handling a huge amount of data related to the actual execution of business processes and the goal is to discover from transaction log a model of how the business processes are actually completed (Pajić, & Bečejski, 2016). The main idea of business process mining is to extract the execution of business processes preserved in event logs which are available in information system like ERP in order to directly build the models of business processes, compare existing business process models with the new automatically constructed models to identify deviations and bottlenecks and to enhance the business processes (R'bigui & Cho, 2017).

This paper is organized as follows. Section 2 is presenting a brief description of an ERP system with related modules and details about BPM lifecycle phases. Section 3 contains the description of process mining and its related concepts, it's also shows how the process mining techniques can be implemented in each phase of BPM cycle. In section 4, the related works are discussed by presenting three examples that use process mining in different business processes that have been implemented in ERP. Also, in the same section which is section 4 I list the benefits the organizations gain from implementing process mining using their ERP. Concluding remarks are given in section 6.

2. ERP & BPM

According to American Production and Inventory Control Society, ERP is defined as a *"method for the effective planning and controlling of all resources needed to take, make, ship and account for customer orders in a manufacturing, distribution or service organization"* (Madanhire & Mbohwa, 2016). Ignato Madanhire and Charles Mbohwa list the basic modules which are consist in ERP as followed: *production planning module*, *purchasing module*, *ERP inventory control module*, *sales module*, *marketing module*, *ERP financial module* and *human resources module* (Madanhire & Mbohwa, 2016).

Izzeideen Alomari et al., researchers from University of Kebangsaan in Malysia, states that the ERP is playing an important role in supporting procedures of business by carrying necessary business process information and create changes on the activities of the business (Alomari et al., 2019). They mentioned that ERP is linked to business process highly by which the business process is a collection of interconnected activities that provide output of greater value than the inputs through one or more transference (Alomari et al., 2019).

There are various of definitions about process. Edyta Brzychczy mentioned that according to Grajewski, the process is defined as *"a chain of sequential activities that transform measurable inputs (materials, information, people, devices, methods) into a measurable output (products, services, information)"* (Brzychczy. 2017).

She considered that the major stage for process management in any organization is their identification which leads to process architecture development and presents a set of particular processes along with the sopecified relations between them (Brzychczy. 2017). Edyta Brzychczy and presents the BPM cycle (Figure 1) on her paper (Brzychczy. 2017). The BPM cycle includes the following phases: process modeling, process analysis, implementation, and process monitoring and controlling.

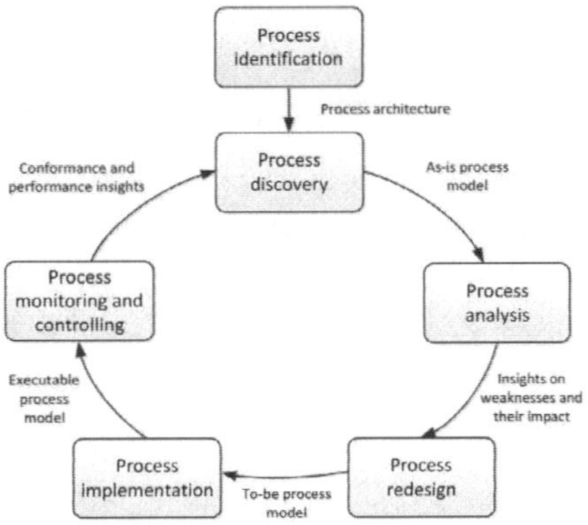

Figure 1. BPM Cycle (Brzychczy. 2017) [Source: http://bpmcenter.org/]

Process modelling (discovery) which involve the development of a process model which is an "as-is" that maps process realization in the organization (Szelągowski, 2018). *Process analysis,* this stage contains the identification and discovery of the problems related to the emerging process that have been identified and all documents related to it and procedures for the efficiency of the process. The result of this activity is that the organization obtains a set of problems associated with this process and is arranged according to their impact on the organization's results (Szelągowski, 2018). *Process redesign* which used for identifying the process changes that will support solving the problems that stand out and help the organization to accomplish the desired effects. The result of this phase is a process model of "to-be" process (Szelągowski, 2018). *Process implementation,* this phase involves the implementation of the resulted process from the process redesign phase (Szelągowski, 2018). *Process monitoring and control* contains the activity of data analysis during the implementation of the process in order to identify if the changes have produced the expected impacts and if the assumed objectives were achieved or not (Szelągowski, 2018).

3. PROCESS MINING

Process mining is a technique used in process management which can help the users to produce business processes in an objective manner by analyzing business data which can be extracted from event logs and visualize the actual process flows automatically (Park & Kang, 2016). The most suitable definition of process mining is the one that has been given in the Process Mining Manifesto: "*The idea of process mining is to discover, monitor and improve real processes (i.e., not assumed processes) by extracting knowledge from event logs readily available in today's (information) systems. Process mining includes (automated) process discovery (i.e., extracting process models from an event log), conformance checking (i.e., monitoring deviations by comparing model and log), social network/organizational mining, automated construction of simulation models, model extension, model repair, case prediction, and history-based recommendations.*" (Van Der Alast et al., 2011). (Figure 2) displayes process mining prerequisites (Van Der Alast et al., 2011).

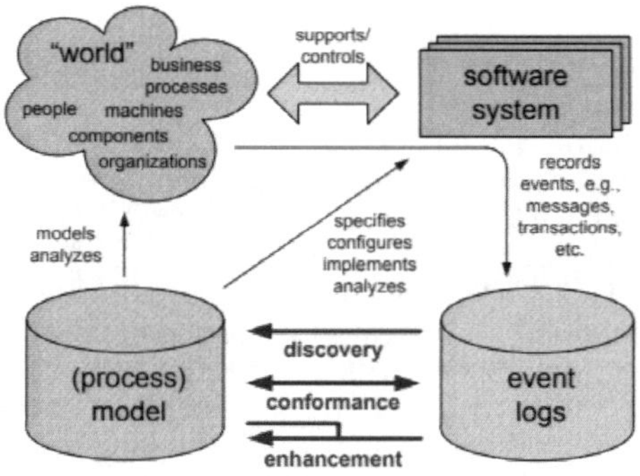

Figure 2. Process Mining Context (Van Der Alast et al., 2011)

3.1 Process Mining Concepts

Event can be defined as an activity corresponding to the starting point of the process mining, the sequential relation between events is required in process mining techniques where each activity is a unique process instance, i.e. it belongs to a specific event (Van Der Alast, 2012). Regarding what event log are actuating storing Dusanka Dakic et al., states that an event log are storing cases and activities information and also event performers information (like persons or devices), event timestamps or other recorded data of any of an event element (Dakic et al., 2018).

Dusanka Dakic et al., describe 3 process mining types: discovery, conformance and enhancement. *Discovery:* this technique is using to produce new process model based on data generated from event log, without depending on any prior information about the new process (Dakic et al., 2018). *Conformance:* this technique used to compare between an existing process model and data generated from event log of the same process which can be used to review the results of this process if it's exactly the same as recorded in event log (Dakic et al., 2018). *Enhancement:* this technique can be used to improve an existing process model depending on the actual process information which has been recorded in event log and the purpose is to change or a prior model (Dakic et al., 2018).

Van der Aalst et al., defined three different perspective that may covered by process mining which are process, organizational and case perspective. *Process perspective* which focuses on the control flow and the activities ordering. The aim of this perspective is to find the best description of all possible paths by using a Petri net or Event-driven Process Chain (EPC) (Van Der Alast, 2007). *Organizational perspective* which focuses on the originator field, the involvement of performers and relationship between them. The aim is to frame the organization by perform people classifications in terms of their roles and organization's units or to present relations between each one of the performers (Van Der Alast, 2007).*Case perspective* which focuses on properties of cases. Cases can be distinguished in the process by their path the process or they can be distinguished by the one who is working on a case. Moreover, cases can also be differentiated by the values of the identical data elements (Van Der Alast, 2007).

There are many of process mining software tools which are available for use. Aruna Devi et al., discussed on details about the software tools used for process mining which are ProM tool that developed at Eindhoven University of Technology, Disco which is a complete process mining software that offered by Fluxicon, Celonis Discovery which is a process mining tool provided by Celonis, Fujitsu Process Analytics, Rapid Mine, Process Gold Enterprise Platform and more (Devi, 2006). Dusanka Dakic et al., mentioned that there are 3 main types of process mining algorithms which are Deterministic algorithms (example of this is Alpha algorithm), Heuristic algorithms and Genetic algorithms (Dakic et al., 2018).

3.2 Using of Process Mining Techniques in BPM Cycle

Edyta Brzychczy presents the possibilities of using process mining techniques in the BPM cycle where she mentioned that the analysis can be performed using any of the process mining tools like ProM, Celinos or another tool (Brzychczy. 2017). Process modeling (discovery): there are several of algorithms that have been developed which can used to the construct process models based on event logs, examples of those algorithms are: Inductive Miner, Alpha Miner, Heuristic Miner (Brzychczy. 2017). Process analysis: in terms of process analysis, there are several useful techniques that can be used to visualize the event log like: dotted chart, Case flow visualization, Work hand-over graph (Brzychczy. 2017). Process implementation: contains the using of notation to draw and write executable process models like using the BPMN notation (Brzychczy. 2017). It contains the details of events types, activities, executing units and sources of data which can be applied in the organization after the phase of redesign (Brzychczy. 2017). Process monitoring and controlling: it is important in this phase to notice the differences between the realization of the process and the specified process model and the reference to process variation appears in this phase to enable the organization to take a corrective action (Brzychczy. 2017).

4. RELATED WORKS

This section shows a summary of several papers found that present an actual case studies related to implement process mining on organizations using ERP systems on some of their modules like financial module and purchasing module. These papers present on details how the data from ERP extracted and processed using process mining techniques and support the decision makers on developing a new business process, do enhancement in an existing process, or support on decision making for individualize or standardize the business process for organizations. First, I will discuss about two case studies from two different resources which present an actual implementation of process mining technique in two different business processes, first one for "purchase to pay" process and second one for "financial" process. In the second sub heading, I will list the benefits that the organizations gain from implementing process mining using their ERP data in improving the business process followed by the organization.

4.1 Examples of Implementing Process Mining on ERP

Christian Fleig, Dominik Augenstein and Alexander Maedche from Karlsruhe Institute of Technology in Germany studied an actual case study for a manufacturing corporation to demonstrate how process mining can be used for process decision making in an SAP S/4 HANA implementation project (Fleig, 2018). The corporation implements process mining for the analysis of the purchase to pay "Purchasing" process and the order to cash "Sales" processes to specify whether the new "to be" process should be standardized or to be individualized (Fleig, 2018). They described how the process mining can be used for business processes comparison and their variants against the different standards by following three steps which are: first, decide which standard is a nominee for implementation; second, contains the implementation of required deviations from the standard; third, contains the estimation of the impacts on an organization (Fleig, 2018). They found out that the use of process mining allows all variants to be considered in the decision to determine whether to individualize or standardize the process (Fleig, 2018). They mentioned that the managers from the corporation stated that process mining project helped them in utilizing BPM as an essence capability of their organization and to increase the "process oriented thinking" of themselves and their employees (Fleig, 2018).

Michael Werner from Auckland University of Technology in New Zealand discussed about how process mining can be used as an incoming technique for data analysis to support auditors in the context of financial and accounting structure (Werner, 2017). In his research, he investigates how process mining can be used to improve process audits that are an important part of financial audits where It focuses on source data from ERP systems and investigates how this data can be used in a novel way to produce less complex process models that provide precise information on the control flow from an accounting perspective (Werner, 2017).

Mahendrawathi ER, Shania Zayin and Firman Pamungkas promotes on their paper the use of process mining and root cause analysis from BPM field to make post implementation review of ERP implementation at the level of business process (Mahendrawathi et al., 2017). The case study company is a chemical company that is changing their old ERP system with SAP ERP. They presented how the event log for the process of procurement is generated from the activities data stored in SAP database (Mahendrawathi et al., 2017). They used the Disco tool to process the event log to conduct more analysis where they applied the fuzzy miner to discover the process model from event log (Mahendrawathi et al., 2017). They present that process mining helped them find out the bottleneck appears which related to technical issues, data migration issues and cultural issues like high dependency of hard copy approval (Mahendrawathi et al., 2017). Those results that they found helped them figure out the issues that they need to resolve so the company can realize the operational efficiency benefit and eventually long-term benefit of ERP implementation (Mahendrawathi et al., 2017).

4.2 Benefits of Process Mining for Organizations

Aruna Devi et al., list the benefits of process mining in four points. First, they considered that the objectivity is the main benefit of process mining because it helps the organizations to produce better process models for good productivity (Devi, 2006). Second, they mentioned that the time is major constraint in performing tasks, where the process mining techniques provide faster results if there is an accurate data used (Devi, 2006). Third, they notice that for any organization specially for the manufacturing industries, process mining offers the potential to find exceptions and allows to do conformance checking, so that it can avoid any deviation in production (Devi, 2006). The last benefit introduced by them is that the process mining has the ability to produce different opinions on the same data set (Devi, 2006).

5. RESULT

As a result of this review paper, the following (Figure 3) shows the relationship between the three main topics that I've been discussed about on this paper which are business process management (BPM), enterprise resource planning (ERP) and process mining.

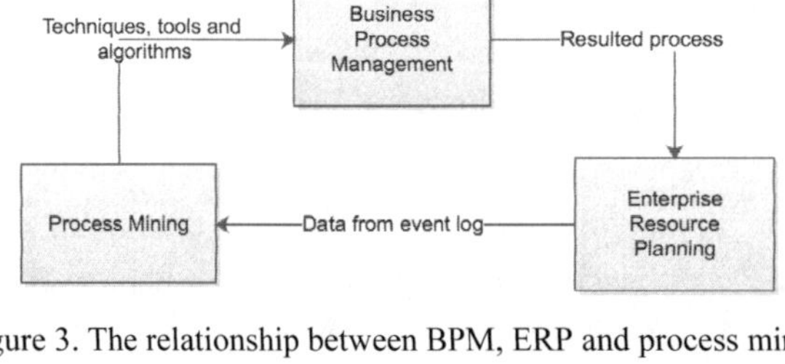

Figure 3. The relationship between BPM, ERP and process mining

The BPM produce a resulted process to be implemented in ERP as a new process or an enhancement in an actual process. Where from the ERP system we can extract the needed data from event logs that stored in the system as a history of people, data, time, and activities accomplished related to a specific process. The data that has been extracted from ERP are used in process mining by implementing their tools, algorithms and techniques to find the issues and gaps related to those data and processes by following the steps and phases of BPM lifecycle including: process discovery, process analysis, process redesign, process implementation and process monitoring and controlling. That step helps the high management or decision makers to make a decision on implementing a new process or an applying an enhancement in an actual process so this resulted business process can be again implemented in ERP system.

6. CONCLUSION

The goal of this paper is to gather information about how the organizations can benefit from ERP system data which can be extracted from event log and implement process mining techniques using extracted data from ERP in the phases of BPM cycle to came up with new process, or an enhancement for an existing process, or support on decision making for individualize or standardize the business process for an organization. The paper presented the relationship between the three main topics which are business process management, enterprise resource planning and process mining.

The three main theory backgrounds have been described in 3 separated sections. The business process management's role is to give context and setting for overall business process development and how the process mining techniques can be used through the BPM life cycle. Therefore, ERP systems act as a vital source of data, and where the improved process can be implemented. Finally, process mining context, is responsible of providing the analytical work to make the findings from ERP data to improve business processes.

REFERENCES

Alomari, I. A., Amir, A. M., Aziz, K. A., & Auzair, S. M. (2019). Enterprise resource planning system business process attributes: A research note. *IJAR*, *5*(3), 111-115.

Brzychczy, E. (2017). Use of Process Mining Techniques in an Enterprise. *Inzynieria Mineralna-Journal of the Polish Mineral Engineering SocietY*, (2), 237-244.

Dakic, D., Stefanovic, D., Cosic, I., Lolic, T., & Medojevic, M. (2018). Business Process Mining Application: A Literature Review. *Annals of DAAAM & Proceedings*, *29*.

Devi, A. T. (2006). An informative and comparative study of process mining tools. *Int. J. Sci. Eng. Res*, *8*(5), 8-10.

Fleig, C., Augenstein, D., & Maedche, A. (2018). Process Mining for Business Process Standardization in ERP Implementation Projects-An SAP S/4 HANA Case Study from Manufacturing. In *BPM (Dissertation/Demos/Industry)* (pp. 149-155).

Madanhire, I., & Mbohwa, C. (2016). Enterprise resource planning (ERP) in improving operational efficiency: Case study. *Procedia CIRP*, *40*, 225-229.

Mahendrawathi, E. R., Zayin, S. O., & Pamungkas, F. J. (2017). ERP post implementation review with process mining: A case of procurement process. *Procedia Computer Science*, *124*, 216-223.

Pajić, A., & Bečejski-Vujaklija, D. (2016). Metamodel of the artifact-centric approach to event log extraction from ERP systems. *International Journal of Decision Support System Technology (IJDSST)*, *8*(2), 18-28.

Park, S., & Kang, Y. S. (2016). A study of process mining-based business process innovation. *Procedia Computer Science*, *91*, 734-743.

R'bigui, H., & Cho, C. (2017). The state-of-the-art of business process mining challenges. *International Journal of Business Process Integration and Management*, *8*(4), 285-303.

Szelągowski, M. (2018). Evolution of the BPM Lifecycle. In *Federated Conference on Computer Science and Information Systems* (pp. 205-211).

Van Der Aalst, W. M., Reijers, H. A., Weijters, A. J., van Dongen, B. F., De Medeiros, A. A., Song, M., & Verbeek, H. M. W. (2007). Business process mining: An industrial application. *Information Systems*, *32*(5), 713-732.

Van Der Aalst, W., Adriansyah, A., De Medeiros, A. K. A., Arcieri, F., Baier, T., Blickle, T., ... & Wynn, M. (2011, August). Process mining manifesto. In *International Conference on Business Process Management* (pp. 169-194). Springer, Berlin, Heidelberg.

Van Der Aalst, W. (2012). Process mining: Overview and opportunities. *ACM Transactions on Management Information Systems (TMIS)*, *3*(2), 1-17.

Werner, M. (2017). Financial process mining-Accounting data structure dependent control flow inference. *International Journal of Accounting Information Systems*, *25*, 57-80.

A FRAMEWORK FOR IT PROJECT COMPLEXITY MANAGEMENT

Stefan Morcov[1], Liliane Pintelon[1]* and Rob J. Kusters[2]*
[1]Katholieke Universiteit Leuven, Belgium
[2]Open Universiteit Nederland, Netherlands
** Prof. Dr.*

ABSTRACT

Complexity is ubiquitous in modern IT engineering and project management. It is traditionally associated with risk and failure. But complexity also works: it delivers functionality, creativity, innovation. This paper proposes a conceptual framework to support IT Project Complexity Management in a structured, systematic way, consisting of the following processes: plan, identify, analyze, plan response strategies, monitor and control. The processes interact with each other and with other project management processes; they overlap, are incremental and iterative. They are described in terms of inputs and outputs, with a detailed inventory of available tools and techniques proposed for each process and step.

KEYWORDS

Project Management, Complexity, Complex Projects, Positive Complexity, Appropriate Complexity

1. INTRODUCTION

Contemporary IT projects are more and more challenging, larger, more complicated and complex. Project complexity is thus a topic of major interest in contemporary IT engineering.

Project complexity "makes it difficult to understand, foresee and manage a project's behavior, even when given reasonably complete information about the project system". It can be **structural** (i.e. consisting of many varied interrelated parts), or **dynamic** (i.e. referring to ambiguity, uncertainty, propagation, emergence, and chaos). Complexity strongly correlates with high cost, significant risk of failure, poor project management performance, and increased risk. Lack of understanding and recognition of system complexity is a critical cause of poor performance of large-scale IS/IT projects (Patanakul, 2014) (Montequín, et al., 2018) (Bjorvatn & Wald, 2018) (Głodziński, 2019) (Morcov, et al., 2020a).

While complexity is traditionally regarded as ***negative***, the benefits of technology to society and the economy are also significant. Complexity can have positive effects ("***positive complexity***"), or it can be ***appropriate*** (requisite). Positive and appropriate complexity are catalysts for opportunities (Maurer, 2017) (Morcov, et al., 2020b). A set of generic and specialized tools, guidelines, best practices, thumb rules are proposed by literature for managing project complexity (GAPPS, 2007) (PMI, 2013) (PMI, 2014) (Davies, et al., 2017) (Australian Government, Department of Defence, 2012) (Riis & Pedersen, 2003) (Remington & Pollack, 2007). Project managers currently apply these tools opportunistically - no structured approach being available (Botchkarev & Finnigan, 2015).

This paper proposes a framework to support IT Project Complexity Management in a structured, systematic way. It is a conceptual framework, in which to anchor specific tools and techniques; a high-level process design that helps add structure to the management of complex IT projects, and systematize concepts and practical approach. Project Complexity Management thus becomes a knowledge area that includes specific processes to understand, plan strategy and responses, monitor and control project complexity.

2. METHODS

The paper uses a qualitative approach based on design science, combined with a review of scientific literature related to IT project complexity management and management frameworks. Design science is a valid research methodology to develop solutions for practical engineering problems (Peffers, et al., 2007). Qualitative research helps develop initial understanding in a less explored area (Levitt, et al., 2018) (Gummesson, 2000).

The design of the management framework was based on a set of recognized management frameworks, including: project management, risk (PMI, 2017), vulnerability (Marle & Vidal, 2016); problem-solving; system engineering complexity management (Maurer, 2017), OODA loop (observe, orient, decide, act) (Boyd, 2018), Systems development life cycle (SDLC); Waterfall software development methodology, Object-Oriented Analysis and Design (Satzinger, et al., 2007), Scrum Agile (Schwaber & Sutherland, 2020), ADDIE and SAM models for instructional design (Allen & Sites, 2012), PDCA/OPDCA management method (observe, plan, do, check, act) - the Deming Cycle (Liker & Franz, 2011).

The inventory of tools and techniques was built based on a systematic literature review on project complexity. Systematic reviews are relevant methods for defining a framework of existing research, including gaps in existing research, in order to position and suggest future research (Kitchenham, 2004). The literature review used the search phrase: '(complex OR complexity) AND ("project management")', applied to the title and abstract on a large database of blind refereed research papers, extended by snowballing and additional areas such as Systems and IT Engineering (Morcov, et al., 2020a).

3. PROCESSES, WITH INPUTS, OUTPUTS, TOOLS AND TECHNIQUES

We define "Project Complexity Management" as the project management Knowledge Area that includes processes to understand, plan strategy and responses, and manage project complexity.

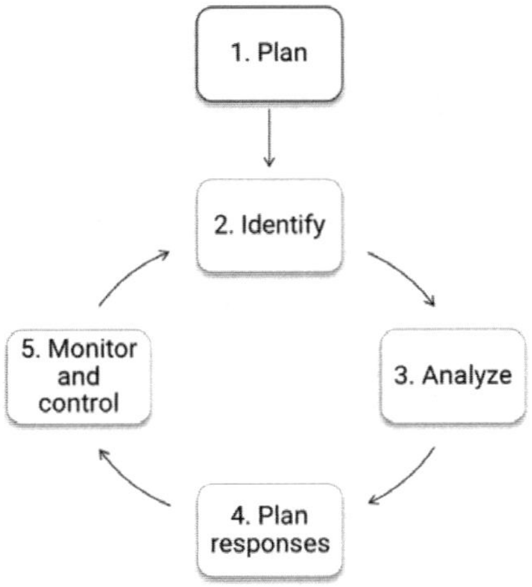

Figure 1. IT Project Complexity Management processes

The proposed IT Project Complexity Management framework consists of 5 processes (**Erro! A origem da referência não foi encontrada.**). The processes and steps interact with each other and with other management processes, are incremental and iterative.

1. **Plan IT project complexity management:** red-flagging complex projects, and deciding management strategies and tools.
2. **Identify IT project complexity**: listing the project complexity elements, i.e. detection and description of the problem.
3. **Analyze IT project complexity**: understanding the problem.
4. **Plan IT project complexity response strategy**: developing options and actions to enhance and use positive complexity, and to reduce or avoid negative complexity. It involves modeling and design of potential solutions.

5. **Monitor and Control IT project complexity**: the process of implementing response strategies, monitoring, controlling, and evaluating the overall effectiveness. It is a continuous activity.

The traditional methodologies for problem management require a 2-step process for **problem understanding**: a) identification and b) analysis (PMI, 2017) (Marle & Vidal, 2016). Complexity theory assumes strong structural variety and interdependence of the system's elements, as well as ambiguity and dynamic phenomena, therefore the identification and analysis of complexity cannot be performed in independent consecutive steps; they are intertwined.

Planning and understanding activities are done at the beginning of a project, but all activities are ubiquitous throughout all project phases. Throughout the project, the project manager should continue to understand project complexity better, by identifying additional complexity elements, and by analyzing and re-analyzing project complexity; replan and re-evaluate the process results. We propose therefore an iterative approach, where results of each step constitute valuable input to both subsequent, as well as previous steps.

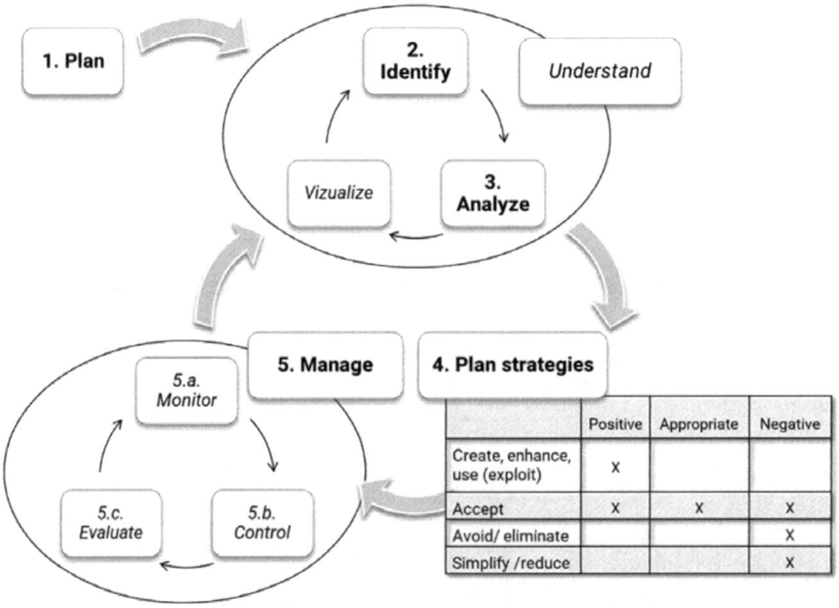

Figure 2. IT Project Complexity Management Framework - overview

Planning is performed at the beginning of the project, typically at the project approval gates: during the feasibility study, and/or project planning. The planning process includes: a) **measuring/assessing the complexity level**; red-flag the project if complex, with measurement tools such as the Crawford-Ishikura Factor Table for Evaluating Roles CIFTER, Vidal's Analytic Hierarchy Process, Hass' Project Complexity Model Formula (Morcov, et al., 2020a); and b) **deciding if complexity should be managed specifically**, and how, by choosing from the list of available tools at the disposal of the project manager. The decision of the tools and methods should be based on a cost-benefit analysis.

There are 2 specific moments when complexity assessment is particularly important: the initial go/no-go decision to start a project, and during the project planning phase.

Identification and analysis focus on objective, structural complexity, because structural complexity is less abstract, thus more discussable, analyzable, measurable, and manageable.

Qualitative analysis categorizes complexity based on effects, as positive, appropriate, or negative, e.g. using the Complexity Effect Scale - CES tool (Morcov, et al., 2020b). This analysis should be done primarily against the initial project objectives. Of course, the project objectives will be adapted, if new opportunities are uncovered during this analysis (PMI, 2017). **Quantitative analysis** can help prioritize and thus select the most useful subset of complexity items and tools to be applied. It includes quantifying the elements of complexity in numeric values, such as financial impact; similarly to the quantitative analysis of risks. It supports the application of numeric tools such as cost-benefit and Pareto. **Visualizing** IT project complexity is a general tool for analysis, especially suitable for engineering projects. System views help visualize both structural complexity and dynamic complexity.

The analysis relies on decomposition, which can be too granular, thus inefficient, or too superficial, thus not useful. A rule-of-thumb for deciding if an analysis is sufficiently detailed can be: *Detail until you know what is to be done*.

The potential **strategies for complexity management** (Figure 3) are designed based on the consideration that complexity is not always negative; that some elements of complexity are necessary and even produce positive effects. Traditionally, both research and practice focus on the negative effects of complexity, on the relationship between complexity, risk, and failure. Still, the complexity of IT projects and products is sometimes *appropriate*; and even *positive*. Complexity is needed to ensure system viability; it enhances creativity and innovation; offers functionality (Beer, 1972) (McKelvey & Boisot, 2009) (Floricel, et al., 2016) (Maurer, 2017). **Appropriate (requisite) complexity** is needed for the project to reach its objectives; its contribution to project success balances the negative effects. **Positive complexity** adds value to a project; its contribution to project success outweighs the associated negative consequences. Since it creates opportunity, it should be exploited rather than eliminated. Appropriate (requisite) and positive complexity are similar to the opportunities of risk management, and to antifragility (McKelvey & Boisot, 2009) (PMI, 2017) (Taleb, 2012).

	Response strategy	Complexity Effect		
		Positive	Appropriate	Negative
a.	Create, enhance	x		
b.	Use (exploit)	x		
c.	Accept / ignore	x	x	x
d.	Simplify / reduce			x
e.	Avoid / eliminate			x

Figure 3. The Mitigation Strategies Matrix – MSM (Morcov, et al., 2020b)

Complexity-related phenomena in one sub-system could lead to opposite effects in another sub-system, because of propagation phenomena (Marle & Vidal, 2016). Also, complex IT projects are emergent and dynamic, which requires a different paradigm than in a deterministic environment, since the project plan is known to be subject to change as it unfolds; not all activities can be foreseen; not all methods and objectives are known (Daniel & Daniel, 2018). Therefore, similarly as argued above regarding understanding and analyzing complexity, the plan should be detailed until it is clear what has to be done; but the level of detail required for a project plan is different for the different phases in a project lifecycle. The wave-crest planning model can support such an approach, where the activities of the near future are much more detailed than the activities planned for the distant future. This paradigm is a common practice in software engineering, which has long faced issues of complexity including uncertainty in methods and objectives, and has systematically experimented with and adopted flexible models, e.g. iterative, incremental, and agile development.

The process of **monitoring, controlling, implementing response strategies**, and evaluating the overall effectiveness is a continuous activity performed throughout the project's life, as part of a Monitoring and Controlling Process Group. The proposed inventory of tools focuses on objective, structural complexity, because structural complexity is less abstract, thus more discussable, measurable, and manageable. Dynamic complexity aspects are related to *"unknown unknowns"*; difficult to identify or plan. They behave like Black Swans and follow "Butterfly Effect" patterns (Lorenz, 1963) (Taleb, et al., 2009). Still, dynamic complexity aspects must be monitored, recognized, and identified as they occur, and the project should be prepared to deal with them. The main tool, in this case, is monitoring for change, especially in stakeholders, objectives, and the environment.

Table 1 and Figure 4 offer an overview of the proposed IT project complexity management framework, with inputs, outputs, tools and techniques, per phase.

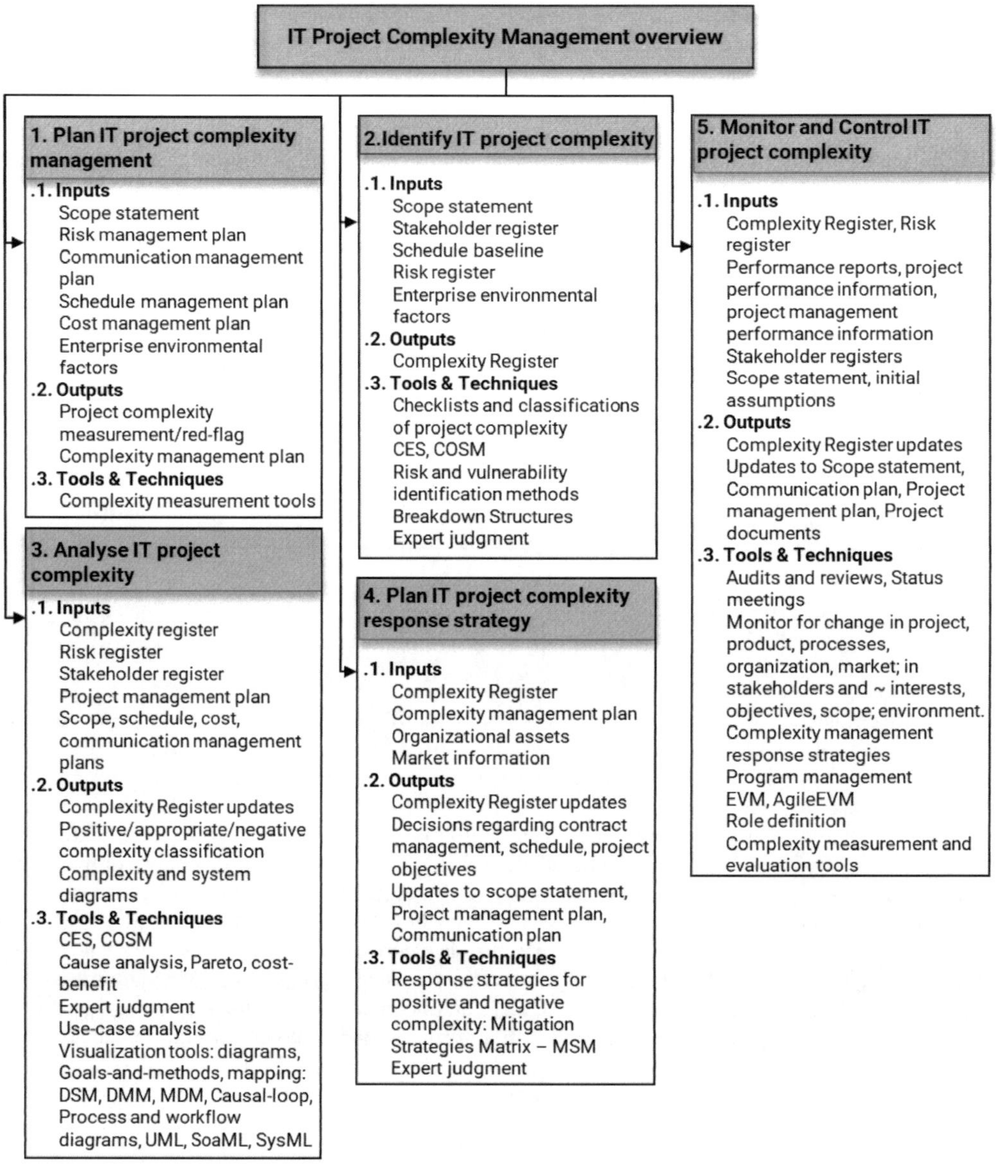

Figure 4. IT Project Complexity Management processes, inputs, outputs, tools and techniques

Table 1. IT Project Complexity Management framework, with inputs, outputs, tools and techniques, per phase

Inputs	Outputs	Tools and techniques
1. Plan IT project complexity management		
Scope statement Risk management plan Communication, schedule, cost management plans Enterprise environmental factors	Red-flag project as complex (complexity measurement) Complexity management plan	Complexity measurement and evaluation tools (Morcov, et al., 2020a): CIFTER scale, Hass, Vidal AHP scale, Morcov scale Simple, complicated, complex, really complex projects (Hertogh & Westerveld, 2010) (Bakhshi, et al., 2016).

2. Identify IT project complexity		
Scope statement, scope baseline Stakeholder register, communications management plan Schedule management plan, schedule baseline Risk management plan, risk register Project documents Market analysis Enterprise environmental factors	Complexity Register	Checklists and classifications of project complexity (Morcov, et al., 2020a) such as: • Technical vs. organizational complexity (Baccarini, 1996) • Related to ambiguity, uncertainty, propagation, or chaos; related to size, variety, interdependence, or context (Marle & Vidal, 2016) • Market, organization, process, product (Maurer, 2017) • Task-related complexity (business, external, organizational complexity) vs. system-related complexity (technological complexity) • TOE model - technological, organizational, environmental complexity (Bosch-Rekveldt, et al., 2011) Checklists of complexity indicators, dimensions, measures Complexity Effect Scale tool – CES, Complexity Source/Effect Segmentation Matrix tool – COSM (Morcov, et al., 2020b) Risk and vulnerability identification methods, SWOT analysis, WWWWHW, analysis of PEST, STEEP, STEEPLE, PERSI factors, Balanced Scorecard (Marle & Vidal, 2016) Systems engineering analysis (Maurer, 2017) X-BS: WBS Work Breakdown Structure, Risk BS, Resource BS, Product BS, Organization BS (Levine, 1993) Reference-class forecasting Audits, documentation reviews, assumptions analysis, Market analysis tools, External audits, Expert judgment
Inputs	**Outputs**	**Tools and techniques**
3. Analyse IT project complexity		
Complexity register Risk register Stakeholder register Project management plan Scope, schedule, cost, communication management plans	Complexity Register updates Positive/appropriate/ negative complexity classification Complexity and system diagrams	Quantitative & qualitative analysis of complexity effects and sources: CES, COSM Complexity measurement and evaluation tools – as checklists Root-cause analysis, fault-tree; cause-and-effect diagrams, Ishikawa, problem-tree, Toyota 5-Why's, Pareto, use-case analysis Cost-benefit analysis Project Systemic Vulnerability Analysis Market analysis tools, Delphi, focus groups, affinity diagrams, brainstorming Checklists, Expert judgment **Complexity visualization tools:** Diagramming techniques, system views help visualize both structural complexity and dynamic complexity Goals-and-methods matrix (Turner & Cochrane, 1993) Complexity mapping diagram (Remington & Pollack, 2007), dependency modelling, DSM, DMM (Maurer, 2017), MDM (Marle & Vidal, 2016) Causal-loop diagrams – Systems Thinking Use-case analysis, Graphs, mind-maps, UML, SoaML, SysML
4. Plan IT project complexity response strategy		
Complexity Register Complexity management plan Organizational assets Market information	Decisions and updates to Complexity Register, scope & objectives, schedule, PM & communication plans	Response strategies for positive and negative complexity: Mitigation Strategies Matrix – MSM (Morcov, et al., 2020b) • Create, enhance, use (exploit): positive complexity • Accept: positive, appropriate, or negative complexity • Avoid/ eliminate, simplify /reduce: negative complexity Expert judgment

5. Monitor and control IT project complexity		
5.a. Monitor		
Complexity Register Risk register Performance reports Change register & requests, configuration Stakeholder registers Scope statement & initial assumptions	Complexity Register updates	Audits and reviews Status meetings Monitor for change (Whyte, et al., 2016): • in project, product, processes, organization, market. • in stakeholders and stakeholders' interests, project objectives, and scope; environment. COSM Recheck assumptions
5.b. Control		
Complexity Register	Updates to Complexity Register, Scope statement (change requests), communication plan, PM plan	Implement complexity management response strategies Implement the project as a program (Remington & Pollack, 2007) Earned Value Management EVM (PMI, 2017) AgileEVM (Sulaiman & Smits, 2007) Integrating uncertainty into EVM (Pajares & López-Paredes, 2011). Role definition (Remington & Pollack, 2007)
5.c. Evaluate		
Complexity Register Performance reports	Complexity management plan updates	Audits and reviews Complexity measurement and evaluation tools

4. CONCLUSION

This paper proposes a conceptual framework for IT Project Complexity Management, in which individual specific processes and tools can be anchored and applied in a structured way.

The processes and steps interact with each other and with other project management processes; they overlap, are incremental and iterative. An inventory of tools and methods is proposed for each process and step in the framework. The inventory of potential tools and methods is not and cannot be exhaustive nor definitive; as all inventories of tools, it is a starting point: additional potential tools are continuously proposed; some tools are duplicated or are similar; there are different tools with the same name or similar tools with different names.

Complexity management contributes to the success of IT projects, reduces project risk, helps better project understanding, allows for better prioritization and planning of resources. The proposed framework aims to support practitioners to recognize, understand, analyze, and manage complexity more effectively, thus reducing associated risks and increasing project success rates. As with any tool or method, each organization and project manager should decide when and to what degree to apply a specific framework or set of tools to a particular portfolio or project.

REFERENCES

Allen, M. & Sites, R., 2012. Leaving ADDIE for SAM: An agile model for developing the best learning experiences. *American Society for Training & Development.*

Australian Government, Department of Defence, 2012. *Defence capability plan - public version.* [Online] Available at: http://www.defence.gov.au/publications/docs/CapabilityPlan2012.pdf [Accessed 19 May 2019].

Baccarini, D., 1996. The concept of project complexity, a review. *International Journal of Project Management,* 14(4), pp. 201-204.

Bakhshi, J., Ireland, V. & Gorod, A., 2016. Clarifying the project complexity construct: Past, present and future. *International Journal of Project Management,* Volume 34, p. 1199–1213.

Beer, S., 1972. *Brain of the Firm.* London: The Penguin Press.

Bjorvatn, T. & Wald, A., 2018. Project complexity and team-level absorptive capacity as drivers of project management performance. *International Journal of Project Management,* Volume 36, p. 876–888.

Bosch-Rekveldt, M. et al., 2011. Grasping project complexity in large engineering projects: the TOE (Technical, Organizational and Environmental) framework. *International Journal of Project Management,* Volume 29, p. 728–739.

Botchkarev, A. & Finnigan, P., 2015. Complexity in the Context of Information Systems Project Management. *Organisational Project Management,* 2(1), pp. 15-34.

Boyd, J., 2018. *A Discourse on Winning and Losing.* Maxwell AFB, Alabama: Air University Press.
Daniel, P. A. & Daniel, C., 2018. Complexity, uncertainty and mental models: From a paradigm of regulation to a paradigm of emergence in project management. *International Journal of Project Management,* Volume 36, p. 184–197.
Davies, A., Dodgson, M., Gann, D. & Macaulay, S., 2017. Five Rules for Managing Large, Complex Projects. *MIT Sloan Management Review,* 59(1), pp. 73-78.
Floricel, S., Michel, J. L. & Piperca, S., 2016. Complexity, uncertainty-reduction strategies, and project performance. *International Journal of Project Management,* Oct, 34(7), pp. 1360-1383.
GAPPS, 2007. *A Framework for Performance Based Competency Standards for Global Level 1 and 2 Project Managers.* Sydney: Global Alliance for Project Performance Standards.
Głodziński, E., 2019. Performance measurement of complex project: framework. *International Journal of Information Systems and Project Management,* 7(2), pp. 21-34.
Gummesson, E., 2000. *Qualitative Methods in Management Research.* London: Sage.
Hertogh, M. & Westerveld, E., 2010. *Ph.D. thesis: Playing with Complexity - Management and organisation of large infrastructure projects.* s.l.:s.n.
Kitchenham, B., 2004. *Procedures for Performing Systematic Reviews,* Keele, Staffs: Keele University.
Levine, H. A., 1993. Doing the weebis and the obis: new dances for project managers?. *PM Network,* 7(4), p. 35–38.
Levitt, H. et al., 2018. Journal Article Reporting Standards for Qualitative Primary, Qualitative Meta-Analytic, and Mixed Methods Research in Psychology: The APA Publications and Communications Board Task Force Report. *American Psychologist,* 73(1), pp. 26-46.
Liker, J. & Franz, J., 2011. *The Toyota Way to Continuous Improvement: Linking Strategy and Operational Excellence to Achieve Superior Performance.* s.l.:McGraw-Hill Education.
Lorenz, E. N., 1963. Deterministic Nonperiodic Flow. *Journal of the Atmospheric Sciences,* March, 20(2), p. 130–141.
Marle, F. & Vidal, L.-A., 2016. *Managing Complex, High Risk Projects - A Guide to Basic and Advanced Project Management.* London: Springer-Verlag.
Maurer, M., 2017. *Complexity Management in Engineering Design – a Primer.* Berlin, Heidelberg: Springer Berlin Heidelberg.
McKelvey, B. & Boisot, M., 2009. Redefining strategic foresight: 'Fast' and 'far' sight via complexity science. *L.A. Costanzo and R.B. MacKay (eds) Handbook of Research on Strategy and Foresight. Cheltenham, UK: Elgar,* p. 15–47.
Montequín, V. R., Joaquín, V. B., Sonia María, C. F. & Francisco, O. F., 2018. Exploring project complexity through project failure factors: Analysis of cluster patterns using self-organizing maps. *Complexity,* p. 17.
Morcov, S., Pintelon, L. & Kusters, R. J., 2020a. Definitions, characteristics and measures of IT Project Complexity - a Systematic Literature Review. *International Journal of Information Systems and Project Management,* 8(2), pp. 5-21.
Morcov, S., Pintelon, L. & Kusters, R. J., 2020b. IT Project Complexity Management Based on Sources and Effects: Positive, Appropriate and Negative. *Proceedings of the Romanian Academy - Series A,* 21(4), pp. 329-336.
Pajares, J. & López-Paredes, A., 2011. An extension of the EVM analysis for project monitoring: The cost control index and the schedule control index. *International Journal of Project Management,* 29(5), p. 615–621.
Patanakul, P., 2014. Managing large-scale IS/IT projects in the public sector: Problems and causes leading to poor performance. *Journal of High Technology Management Research,* p. 21–35.
Peffers, K., Tuunanen, T., Rothenberger, M. & Chatterjee, S., 2007. A design science research methodology for information systems research. *Journal of Management Information Systems,* pp. 45-77.
PMI, 2013. *Pulse of the Profession In-Depth Report: Navigating Complexity,* s.l.: s.n.
PMI, 2014. *Navigating Complexity: A Practice Guide.* Newtown Square, PA: Project Management Institute.
PMI, 2017. *A Guide to the Project Management Body of Knowledge (PMBOK Guide), Sixth Edition.* Pennsylvania: Project Management Institute.
Remington, K. & Pollack, J., 2007. *Tools for complex projects.* London: Gower Publishing Ltd.
Riis, J. O. & Pedersen, F. L., 2003. Managing organizational development projects by paradoxes. *Production Planning & Control,* 14(4), p. 349–360.
Satzinger, J. W., Jackson, R. B. & Burd, S., 2007. *Systems Analysis & Design In A Changing World.* Boston: Thomson Course Technology.
Schwaber, K. & Sutherland, J., 2020. *The 2020 Scrum Guide.* [Online] Available at: https://www.scrumguides.org/scrum-guide.html [Accessed 27 Dec 2020].
Sulaiman, T. & Smits, H., 2007. Measuring Integrated Progress on Agile Software Development Projects. *Methods & Tools,* 15(3), pp. 2-9.
Taleb, N. N., 2012. *Antifragile: things that gain from disorder.* New York: Random House.
Taleb, N. N., Goldstein, D. G. & Spitznagel, M. W., 2009. The Six Mistakes Executives Make in Risk Management. *Harvard Business Review.*
Turner, J. & Cochrane, R., 1993. Goals-and-methods matrix: coping with projects with ill defned goals and/or methods of achieving them. *International Journal of Project Management,* 11(2), pp. 93-102.
Whyte, J., Stasis, A. & Lindkvist, C., 2016. Managing change in the delivery of complex projects: Configuration management, asset information and 'big data'. *International Journal of Project Management,* 34(2), p. 339–351.

PATTERNS OF ADOPTION OF AGILE TOOLS

Roger Maull[1], Wendy Maull[2] and Alan Brown[1]
[1]*University of Exeter Business School, UK*
[2]*Maull Solutions Ltd, UK*

ABSTRACT

This short paper conducts a factor analysis of the adoption of Agile tools using data from the 14th state of agile survey. Our results suggest that organizations adopt combinations of tools that do not align to any Agile methodology and may reflect organizational role and historical development. Future research should focus on tool adoption not methodology.

KEYWORDS

Agile Methodology, Agile Techniques, Scrum, XP, Kanban

1. INTRODUCTION

Agile is now the preferred methodology for accelerated and risk-reduced software development with organizations of all sizes committed to Agile approaches to help themselves to compete, improve and transform. The key characteristics of agile methods were summarized and promoted through an "agile manifesto" (Fowler and Highsmith, 2001) created by a group of prominent software delivery experts They highlighted a set of values considered fundamental to these agile ways of working that encouraged a focus on: individuals and interactions over processes and tools; working software over comprehensive documentation; customer collaboration over contract negotiations and responding to change over following a plan.

This set of priorities led to an emphasis change in software delivery; a move away from heavyweight process-based methods towards more flexible experiment-based methods such as Scrum (Schwaber and Beedle 2002), Extreme Programming (XP) (Beck and Fowler 2001), Kanban (Anderson 2010) amongst many others.

The most comprehensive study into the adoption of agile approaches, now in its 14th year, is the State of Agile Report (digital.ai 2020). Accessing and downloading the full set of reports reveals some interesting observations. Over these 14 years the biggest change has been the increasing importance of agile to aligning the business and IT with a consistent increase in the number of teams adopting agile to the point where in the latest survey approximately 33% of respondents respond that *half of their teams have adopted agile* and around 20% saying *all their teams have.* The reasons why agile was chosen has remained consistent across the 14 years with the top reason being to accelerate time to market/software delivery followed by enhancing the ability to manage changing priorities, improving alignment between IT and the business and increasing team productivity.

However, the data on how organizations are approaching agile adoption offers a far more mixed picture. Over the 14 years Scrum has gradually increase from 40% of respondents to 58%, Kanban from a 0 to 7% in the same period, whilst noticeably Extreme Programming (XP) has moved from 23% to a barely negligible 1% in year 14. Over the 14 years there has also been an emergence of hybrid approaches such as ScrumBan from 0 to 10% at the same time as a rapid reduction in Scrum/XP from 23% 8%. At the level of the 'methodology' the picture appears clear: scrum is the dominant approach. However, this contrasts with questions posed around agile techniques and practices where for example the use of Kanban boards has moved from zero to 76% by year 14, with large numbers continuing to use XP methods such as Mapping tools (54%) re-factoring (26%) et cetera. Clearly, there is some significant blurring of the methodological distinctions and organizations are adopting a 'what works for us' approach.

In this short paper, we aim to use data from the state of agile report data to further investigate approaches to agile development through considering the differences between methodology and tools and techniques to begin to develop taxonomy of approaches to agile adoption. It is unclear from research what these combinations are and therefore our research question is: *what are the combinations of tools that organizations are adopting?*

2. LITERATURE

Agile methodologies contrast with the more traditional 'waterfall' approaches by accentuating aspects such as flexibility in scope and an ongoing continuous approach to design with an emphasis on engaging with the customer, allowing and even encouraging ambiguity and freezing the system design as late as possible (Serrador and Pinto 2015). In their article 'embracing agile' Rigby, Sutherland and Takeuchi (2016) claim that agile methods are a radical alternative to the traditional hierarchical project management techniques and have developed new sets of practices and principles that have revolutionized the technology industry and 'greatly increased' software development success rates over the last 25-30 years. Gandomani et al. (2013) identified four categories of challenges faced by organizations when migrating to agile: organization and management; people; process; and tools related challenges. Our focus in this short paper is on the tools related challenges.

Many of the published studies on approaches to agile focus on the overall methodology typically by comparing XP, Scrum and Kanban. Matharu et al (2015) has usefully described the distinguishing features of each. He typifies Scrum as having a focus on: cross functional teams; daily meetings; products and sprint backlogs and the identification of three primary roles, the product owner, development team and scrum master. The distinguishing features of XP are: the formulation of requirements using story cards; the simplest possible design: a continuous interaction with the customer: test driven development: re-factoring existing solutions and pair programming. Finally, Kanban is a method which emphasizes the delivery of software just in time for implementation. Its distinguishing characteristics are: the use of kanban boards; maximizing productivity by reducing idle time: the continuous delivery of software increments: the minimization of waste and the limitation of work in progress.

Hummel (2014) has summarized the literature on agile systems development from 482 papers reporting that despite the widespread popularity of Scrum in industry, most research was based on based on XP and particularly the practices of pair programming, unit testing and refactoring practices of which most studies of the last two were mainly conceptual.

In practice, differentiating between methodologies is difficult with organizations adopting a 'what works' and 'mix and match' approach. The literature is full of examples. For example, Azizyan et al (2011) note that summing the percentages of the Agile methods used in their survey results in 114%. implying that some organizations followed more than one Agile method. In specific case examples, Petersen and Wohlin (2009) reported that Ericsson used a hybrid agile methodology consisting of Scrum and XP as well as other general development practices and Murphy et al (2013) found no clear trends in practice adoption at Microsoft, concluding that tool availability may be a greater driver of practice adoption than methodology. Finally, Sjoberg, Johnson and Solberg (2012) report their case company stating that *being rigorous with agility just because it is written in theoretical books showing toy examples is of no business value.*

This paper focuses on the approach to agile, specifically tool use and the combination of tools that are used. It is our contention that grouping of tools may not be in alignment with any particular methodology but much more of a mix and match approach that adapts to the company need.

3. METHOD

To consider our research question we partnered with digital.ai. For the past 14 years, digital.ai has conducted an annual survey, The State of Agile which is widely quoted across the industry. The 2019 questionnaire asked 29 questions across seven broad areas: why agile; time and ability with agile; distributed teams and outsourcing; scaling agile; agile tools used, DevOps and the value and success of agile. We were provided with the raw data from the section on agile tools from the 14th survey to conduct our analysis.

The survey had 1121 completed questionnaires with the following characteristics. 41% of respondents were from companies between 1-1000 employees, 19% between 1000 and 5000, 15% between 5000 and 20,000 25% over 20,000. 41 % of the respondents were from North America, 31% from Europe, 13% from Asia and 15% from the rest of the world. In terms of their role, 37% were scrum masters or internal coaches, 14% project or programme managers, 13% development leadership, 7% development team member and 7% external consultants, 6% product managers and 18% other. Their main industry types were technology at 26%, financial services at 17% and professional services at 7%.

4. RESULTS

The general results from the survey (digital.ai 2020) show that the overwhelming methodology being used was Scrum at 59% of respondents and 77% in hybrid form with XP and Kanban. Most notably XP was now down at 1% suggesting that it is now more frequently being blended with other approaches.

Our analysis is at the level of agile tool. Here we saw much greater diversity. We downloaded the raw data from the 2019 survey into SPSS and we used factor analysis on the 22 variables containing responses to Q23 of the questionnaire: Which agile planning & delivery tools do you currently use or plan to use in the next 12 months? The responses were coded as 1: currently use, 2: plan to use, 3: do not use or plan to use, so a higher score represented a lower use of the technique. This was considered in interpreting the results.

1202 cases had enough responses to be included in the analysis (81 more than the fully completed questionnaires). The KMO measure of sampling Adequacy was .913 and Bartlett's Test of Sphericity yielded Approx Chi-square of 6427, df 231, sig .000. Five components had eigenvalues >1, explaining 51% of variance in these variables. These were then rotated using Varimax rotation to yield the table below. Coefficients below 0.4 have been suppressed for clarity.

Table 1. Factor Analysis

	Component				
	1	2	3	4	5
Automated Build Tool	0.828				
Continuous Integration Tool	0.777				
Unit Test Tool	0.714				
Release/Deployment Automation Tool	0.703				
Bug Tracker	0.648				
Wiki	0.553				
Automated Acceptance Test Tool	0.502				
Requirements Management Tool					
Story Mapping Tool		0.689			
Timecards		0.589			
Customer Idea Management Tool		0.574			
Refactoring Tool	0.455	0.532			
Spreadsheet			0.73		
Traditional Project Management Tool			0.683		
Static Analysis			0.462		
Taskboard					
Project & Portfolio Management (PPM) Tool				0.623	
Agile Project Management Tool				0.617	
Kanban Board				0.57	0.474
Index Cards					0.616
Product Roadmapping					0.573
Wireframes	0.41				0.458

5. ANALYSIS

Our analysis of the factors categorized the findings as follows.

Factor 1 Dev Ops

Fundamental to agile delivery scenarios, this set of tools are typical of those teams responsible for delivering a stream of quality features into production. The focus on Devops emphasizes a strong testing capability aligned with Continuous Integration and Continuous Delivery (CD/CI) practices.

Factor 2 Agile Planning

The use of combination of early-stage analysis tools is typical of those involved in agile planning activities. Here, close attention is paid to describing customer needs and to converting them into meaningful stories as the basis for further elaboration.

Factor 3 Traditional Quality Assurance and Project Management

Every large-scale organization has a heritage of common management tools and occupies substantial time creating spreadsheets for tracking progress. Much as agile purists rail against it, traditional project management persists and is ubiquitous. Their use is a daily reality for numerous individuals with management and quality assurance responsibilities.

Factor 4 Agile Project Management

As agile techniques become more widely adopted in an organization, the use of agile project management tools becomes common. These are essential to increase visibility and support agile rituals such as standup meetings, sprint reviews, and retrospectives.

Factor 5 Product Management and Design

The design, management, and delivery of products is central to agile approaches. The product manager holds a key role aligning customer needs, business priorities, and engineering capabilities. Support for product managers includes defining key product features and increasing the visibility of work in progress.

In their study Azizyan et al (2011) found that there were 32 different agile project management tools mentioned in their survey results which they grouped under five different types: agile project management tools for example scrum works; basic tools such as sticky notes: spreadsheets: traditional project management tools for example Microsoft project and finally custom built tools. This grouping seems somewhat simplistic and our groupings of 22 tools/techniques indicate a more complex set of combinations which do not appear to align to any methodological pure approach. This has important implications for those researching agile adoption, clearly pointing out that organizations are mixing tools and not adopting any pure methodological approach despite a large number identifying with a particular methodology (59% stated Scrum in this survey).

6. CONCLUSIONS

This research has provided strong evidence that organizations are adopting a mix and match approach to agile adoption and not following a 'pure' methodological approach. Our five factors show some intriguing combinations. For example, there is clear evidence of traditional approaches to project management continuing to exist under an agile banner. Furthermore, there is some indication that the remaining four are influenced by the different roles that respondents hold in an organization. This suggests that instead of a focus on the organization and its methodology, the focus may need to be on the individual role and the way in which participants view implications of agile techniques for each function. A second implication is that we may also be seeing the importance of the impact of organizational heritage and the influence that has on practices that are adopted in the organization. Although agile evangelists might argue for a focus on product not project, projects are the heritage and maintain a strong influence on techniques that are adopted.

There are some significant limitations in this research. Despite a relatively large sample we have no way of knowing if this is representative of the population of agile users and we have not tested our results against another population. We recognize that our factor analysis explains 51% variance and although each of the factors explains more than a single variable, they will require further analysis than are indicated in these preliminary results. Future work will be to investigate the data further. We have plans to look to cluster cases by using our five factors and the demographic data to identify clusters of cases, and therefore develop a more rigorous taxonomy of agile approaches.

REFERENCES

Anderson, D.J., 2010. Kanban: successful evolutionary change for your technology business. Blue Hole Press.

Azizyan, G., Magarian, M.K. and Kajko-Matsson, M., 2011, August. Survey of agile tool usage and needs. In *2011 agile conference* (pp. 29-38). IEEE.

Beck, K. and Fowler, M., 2001. *Planning extreme programming* (Vol. 200). Reading: Addison-Wesley.

Fowler, M. and Highsmith, J., 2001. The agile manifesto. *Software Development*, *9*(8), pp.28-35.

Gandomani, T.J., Zulzalil, H., Ghani, A.A.A., Sultan, A.B.M. and Nafchi, M.Z., 2013. Obstacles in moving to agile software development methods; at a glance. *Journal of Computer Science*, *9*(5), p.620.

Hummel, M., 2014, January. State-of-the-art: A systematic literature review on agile information systems development. In *2014 47th Hawaii International Conference on System Sciences* (pp. 4712-4721). IEEE.

Matharu, G.S., Mishra, A., Singh, H. and Upadhyay, P., 2015. Empirical study of agile software development methodologies: A comparative analysis. *ACM SIGSOFT Software Engineering Notes*, *40*(1), pp.1-6.

Murphy, B., Bird, C., Zimmermann, T., Williams, L., Nagappan, N. and Begel, A., 2013, October. Have agile techniques been the silver bullet for software development at microsoft?. In *2013 ACM/IEEE international symposium on empirical software engineering and measurement* (pp. 75-84). IEEE.

Petersen, K and C. Wohlin, "A comparison of issues and advantages in agile and incremental development between state of the art and an industrial case," Journal of Systems and Software, vol. 82, no. 9, pp. 1479-1490, Sept. 2009

Rigby, D.K., Sutherland, J. and Takeuchi, H., 2016. Embracing agile. *Harvard Business Review*, *94*(5), pp.40-50.

Schwaber, K. and Beedle, M., 2002. *Agile software development with Scrum* (Vol. 1). Upper Saddle River: Prentice Hall.

Serrador, P. and Pinto, J.K., 2015. Does Agile work?—A quantitative analysis of agile project success. *International Journal of Project Management*, *33*(5), pp.1040-1051.

Sjøberg, D.I., Johnsen, A. and Solberg, J., 2012. Quantifying the effect of using kanban versus scrum: A case study. IEEE software, 29(5), pp.47-53.

Stateofagile.com, accessed 31st December 2020.

THE HYBRID MAS APPROACH FOR INFORMATION SYSTEM DEVELOPMENT IN "CYBER TRAINER"

Agnese Salutari[1,2], Laura Tarantino[1], Mauro Evangelista[2] and Giulio Nazzicone[2]
[1]*Università degli Studi dell'Aquila – DISIM, Italy*
[2]*Reiss Romoli s.r.l., Italy*

ABSTRACT

Information storage, elaboration, and representation is a key point in developing and maintaining performing Information Systems and is becoming more and more challenging over time. In this paper we present the Multi-Agent Systems (MAS) based techniques being used for the refactoring and the expansion of the e-learning application "Cyber Trainer", in particular for specific ad-hoc modules focused on properly filtering and analyzing data. The MAS architecture is based on a set of different "agents", i.e., always running programs that can communicate with each other and work together in order to achieve their tasks. In this project, we used a novel hybrid approach blending MAS programming with Object and Event Programming techniques, taking the best from each one, to manage asynchronous events, communication between different modules, and data flows that need to be treated as big data. The Cyber Trainer "Reporting MAS" design has been focused on scalability, modularity, resistance to change and security. This last point, generally important for every real-world application, in our case is particularly crucial, since Cyber Trainer is distributed over many servers (Reporting MAS Server module agents themself can run on several machines as well).

KEYWORDS

Design and Development Methodologies and Frameworks, Multi-Agent Systems, Hybrid Approaches, E-learning, Agile Methodologies

1. INTRODUCTION

The very first step in a project design is choosing the proper technologies and frameworks to build it, hoping to make it as effective, maintainable and easy to develop as possible, generally facing some tradeoff involving costs, resources, performances and innovation. Usually, for academic projects developers prefer open source and free tools, maybe sacrificing security and performance, and strive for the research of innovative solutions. On the other hand, industrial projects tend to optimize development time and invest on paid tools in order to satisfy performance and security constraints, which means, sometimes, sacrificing the research of new solutions. Information Systems Development (ISD) is not an exception in this sense (Delone et al. 2016, Hassan and Mathiassen 2018, Sanchez et al. 2017) and, in particular, more and more often design choices of this kind have to be faced in ISD projects involving big data (Liang and Liu 2018, Sun 2018). Nowadays big data issues are pervasive in so many fields that they can be considered quite standard, requiring developers to design their applications by taking into account the relative best practices.

In this direction, Multi-Agent Systems (MASs) promise to offer efficient development approaches (Batkovskiy et al. 2019, Giannakis and Louis 2016) based on the integration of cooperating autonomous intelligent agents, with the advantages of the distribution of computational effort and the increase of overall robustness (Costantini 2016). Anyhow, though MAS programming has been largely used for simulations in academic contexts (e.g., Costantini 2017a, Costantini 2017b, Costantini 2020), only recently it is starting to appear in real world applications, and it is certainly a novelty in Information Systems Development. We have to observe that, if, on the one hand, MASs are very useful for managing asynchronous events and big data flows and increase modularity thanks to their very nature, on the other hand they have the disadvantage to be very often closed systems, e.g., programmed in logic programming languages like Prolog, Datalog or their derivatives. As a consequence, it may be burdensome integrating and managing MASs in real systems, especially after production.

The study presented in this paper goes in the direction of *conceiving novel MAS-based solutions trying to overcome such integrability problems*, by proposing *a novel hybrid approach blending MAS programming with Object and Event Oriented programming* and creating a module that can in this way easily interact with other (possibly already existing) ones. In particular, we present the first results achieved within the framework of Cyber Trainer, an ongoing project aimed at developing a Cyber Security e-learning platform, currently under refactoring and expansion at Reiss Romoli s.r.l. As to the choice of analytics and business intelligence platforms (Arnott 2017, Scholtz 2018, Trieu 2017), we initially considered the acquisition of Microsoft Power BI, Tableau and/or other commercial platforms, which, besides purchasing costs, has the disadvantage of requiring the installation of additional software (e.g., Power BI requires Microsoft OS on the hosting server). We hence opted for a development approach based on an ad-hoc novel solution to be internally developed with the following objectives: (1) the solution has to be fast to develop, (2) it should not require other software to be installed, (3) it has to be easily integrated in existing systems, and (4) it has to be fully customizable, modular, scalable and easily expansible during time.

The explored solution satisfying these requirements is a hybrid MAS programmed in Python 3.7, which properly interacts with pre-existing Cyber Trainer front-end and back-end modules via a message broker, exchanging data in Json format, collecting report information when some event occurs, and analyzing it in order to infer new information, making it available to the front-end, that has to draw corresponding diagrams and tables.

The remaining of this paper is structured as follows: Section 2 briefly sketches the Cyber Trainer system and introduces the Reporting MAS, Section 3 discusses the integration issues and underlines the advantages offered by the proposed hybrid approach, and finally in Section 4 conclusions are drawn.

2. THE CYBER TRAINER "REPORTING MAS"

Cyber Trainer is a Reiss Romoli s.r.l. project aimed at developing a Cyber Security e-learning platform where users attend Courses, carry out Laboratory activities, and participate in Team Challenges. Team Challenges are hacking competitions in which users are divided into two teams, attackers and defenders. In these challenges, users' machines and network ones are virtual machines hosted on servers, like for Laboratories, that can be performed in teams and are challenging too, but are not intended to be competitions: they are sections a user can access for training purposes.

Within this platform, the Reporting module is in charge of creating reports about platform users in order to evaluate their academic progresses, taking into account Courses they complete and Laboratories, Tests and Team Challenges they achieve. The module has to be developed and integrated with the pre-existing system, within a scenario of a system growing over time. Furthermore, the design has to be focused on scalability, modularity, resistance to change and security. This last point is particularly crucial since Cyber Trainer is distributed over many servers (and the Reporting MAS Server module agents have to run on several machines as well). Based on a MAS architecture, the Reporting module is organized as in Figure 1, showing the different agents, other system components, and their interaction.

To illustrate the MAS behavior, let us consider the example scenario in which a Cyber Challenge is finished, with an event triggering the system:

- A Cyber Challenge is finished, so the input Filter Agent has to update the Database about the Cyber Challenge itself and about the involved Users and their associated curricula.
- Then, one of these users asks for the percentage of completion of its general carrier, including Cyber Challenges too.
- So, the Reporting MAS module receives the request, it elaborates the needed Database data and sends its results in Json format to the front-end for graphical visualization or writes them on a file of the selected format.

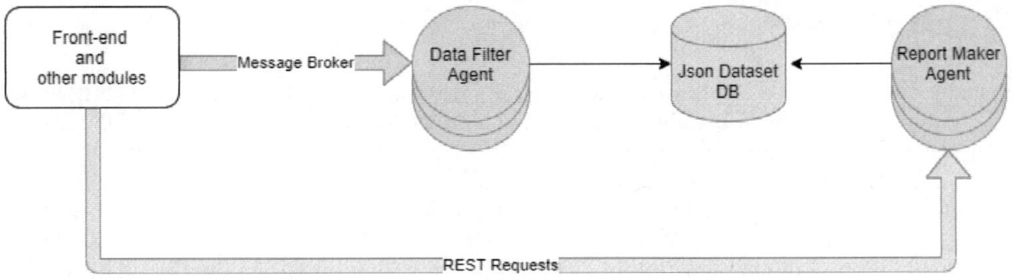

Figure 1. Reporting MAS module components

More in detail, *Data Filter Agents* are always listening on a message broker, waiting for events to occur. They have been developed in Python 3.7 using Faust (https://faust.readthedocs.io/en/latest/), a stream processing library. Faust applications can use different brokers, like Redis (https://redis.io/) or Kafka (https://kafka.apache.org/), that provide data encryption thanks to SSL and a queue for storing messages as a further data loss prevention technique which enables message retransmission thanks to a customizable retention policy. Each event can be categorized in order to be published on the proper dedicated broker topic, accordingly to the event type. Furthermore, each agent (or a group of agents) is listening to a specific topic that it is in charge of. Data Filter Agents have to filter incoming Json events information to store only needed data on the Database, eliminating all data that would be useless for reporting purposes. In our case, the broker is continuously crossed by a large amount of data flows that need to be treated as big data.

Data is stored in Json format on a *Database*. For our project, we used Couchbase (https://www.couchbase.com/), a NoSQL very efficient Database that can be configured to store multiple copies of the dataset in order to prevent data loss. Actually, agents can store data on many different databases, hosted on several servers, according to their configuration parameters. Json data can be seen as trees and their aggregations as graphs, so we focused on the proper way to represent them on the Database with the goal to easily aggregate and efficiently browse them after retrieving. *Report Maker Agents* are actually Python 3.7 apps responding to REST requests, developed using Falcon (https://falconframework.org/) and deployed on an uWSGI server. When needed, they analyze data from the database and extract new information thanks to crossings, relationships, combinations and comparisons among them. Output format is still Json or files of different format, like CSV.

3. INTEGRATION WITH OTHER MODULES

As previously observed, Reporting MAS has been added to the pre-existing Cyber Trainer system. In such a context, developers have to plug their work in a defined environment, and therefore they have constraints on the technologies to use. In our case, we decided to develop a MAS connected with a message broker in order to avoid conflicts with other software. Usually, MASs have their own message broker that is not compatible with most of the real applications and that does not address security concerns: agents communicate with each other sending clear messages over the communication channel. Obviously, this would be very harmful.

Another weak point of traditional MAS programming is the creation of files for Knowledge Base storage and agents reading and writing them to get or modify their information. On the contrary, in a hybrid context like ours, the MAS is perfectly integrated with other modules, including the Database, and no file is used for agent belief management: Datasets can be placed over Databases and can be shared outside the MAS too.

Another advantage is given by the fact that the Json format is compatible with almost every modern programming language and is particularly in line with Python 3 (e.g., it perfectly matches with its Dictionary type). Furthermore, Faust provides useful message handlers: retrieved messages can be casted in an Object-Oriented fashion, preventing any sort of data injection and allowing the definition of a proper semantic, by creating a Class for each message typology. Inside this Class, developers can enforce attributes type too. Messages that are not coherent are simply discarded, without triggering any error or malfunction.

4. CONCLUSION

In this paper we introduced a ISD technique based on Multi-Agent Systems and overcoming issues typically related to the integration with possibly pre-existing modules. In particular, we discussed the main features of the Reporting MAS module of the Cyber Trainer system, based on a novel hybrid approach offering scalability, modularity, resistance to change and security. The module is currently in pre-alpha release and needs to be extensively tested before the actual deployment on the production server. Future extensions will be focused on the analysis on users' preferences, in order to add user profiling capability (Bilal et al., 2019, Kichou 2020), and on the introduction of a recommender system in Cyber Trainer. Furthermore, Machine Learning techniques will be added, together with ad-hoc agents, in order to make the system able to make predictions and classifications over data.

REFERENCES

Arnott, D. et al, 2017. Patterns of Business intelligence Systems Use in Organizations. *Decision Support Systems*, Vol. 97, pp. 58-68.

Batkovskiy, A.M. et al., 2019. Sustainable Project Management for Multi-agent Development of Enterprise Information Systems. *Entrepreneurship and Sustainability*, Vol. 7, pp. 278-90.

Bilal, M., et al., 2019. Social Profiling: A Review, Taxonomy, and Challenges. *Cyberpsychology, Behavior, and Social Networking*, Vol. 22, No. 7, pp. 433-450.

Costantini, S. et al., 2016. Context and Action: A Unitary Vision Within A Logic-based Multi-agent Environment. In: Caporarello L.et al. (eds) *Digitally Supported Innovation*. Lecture Notes in Information Systems and Organisation, Vol 18. Springer, Cham, pp. 97-111.

Costantini, S. et al., 2017. Dali: A Multi Agent System Framework for the Web, Cognitive Robotic and Complex Event Processing. *Proceedings of Ictcs/Cilc 2017*, Naples, Italy, pp. 286-300.

Costantini, S. et al., 2017. Dali For Cognitive Robotics: Principles and Prototype Implementation. *Proceedings of International Symposium on Practical Aspects of Declarative Languages*. Springer, Cham, pp. 152-162.

Costantini, S. et al., 2020. Proposal of an Empathic Multi-agent Robot Design Based on Theory of Mind. *Proceedings of cAESAR 2020 - Workshop on Adapted intEraction with SociAl Robots,* Cagliari, Italy.

Delone, W.H. et al., 2016. Information Systems Success Measurement. *Foundations and Trends® in Information Systems*, Vol. 2, No. 1, pp. 1-116.

Giannakis, M. and Louis, M., 2016. A Multi-agent Based System with Big Data Processing for Enhanced Supply Chain Agility. *Journal of Enterprise information Management*, Vol. 29, No. 5, pp. 706-727.

Hassan, N.R. and Mathiassen, L., 2018. Distilling a Body of Knowledge for Information Systems Development. *Information Systems Journal*, Vol. 28, No. 1, pp. 175-226.

Kichou, S. et al., 2020. Tag's Depth-based Expert Profiling Using A Topic Modeling Technique. *International Journal on Semantic Web and Information Systems (Ijswis)*, Vol. 16, No. 4, pp. 81-99.

Liang, T.P. and Liu, Y., 2018. Research Landscape of Business intelligence and Big Data Analytics: a Bibliometrics Study. *Expert Systems with Applications*, Vol. 111, pp. 2-10.

Sanchez, O.P. et al., 2017. Cost and Time Project Management Success Factors for Information Systems Development Projects. *International Journal of Project Management*, Vol. 35, No. 8, pp. 1608-1626.

Scholtz, B. et al., 2018. A Business Intelligence Framework for Sustainability Information Management in Higher Education. *International Journal of Sustainability in Higher Education*, Vol. 19, No. 2, pp. 266-290.

Sun, Z. et al., 2018. Big Data Analytics Services for Enhancing Business Intelligence. *Journal of Computer information Systems*, Vol. 58, No. 2, pp. 162-169.

Trieu, V., 2017. Getting Value from Business Intelligence Systems: a Review and Research Agenda. *Decision Support Systems*, Vol. 93, pp. 111-124.

THE INSIDER THREAT MINIMIZATION AND MITIGATION FRAMEWORK

Ghassan (Gus) Jabbour[1] and Jason J. Jabbour[2]
[1]*Principled Innovation Institute, Fredericksburg, VA, USA*
[2]*University of Virginia, Charlottesville, VA, USA*

ABSTRACT

Countering the insider threat is a difficult and daunting task. Organizations concerned with the problem usually train their employees on security-related matters, rules of behavior policies, and the consequences of committing criminal activities. More technically-oriented solutions include enhanced credentialing and access control, and the use of monitoring tools that provide insight into the health and status of systems. This paper addresses the deficiency of widely-used monitoring tools and strategies. It proposes a solution that equips a system with innate self-defense mechanisms that relieve the system from having to rely on human intervention. The paper introduces the Insider Threat Minimization and Mitigation Framework. The framework equips systems with self-defense mechanisms such that a system can instantaneously respond to potential threats and defend itself against users who have unfettered access to it. The framework employs the autonomous demotion of power users' access privileges based on analysis and evaluation of the user's risk level. The paper presents the details of the proposed framework and simulates its effectiveness within a data center environment of mission-critical systems.

KEYWORDS

Insider Threat, Autonomous Computing, Self-Protection

1. INTRODUCTION

The Insider Threat continues to be a major risk to the security and financial stability of businesses. The most prevalent types of insider attacks are those associated with the theft of intellectual property, sabotage, fraud, and espionage. Countering such threats is a significant challenge. Today, there are a plethora of security software that offer system monitoring, incident management, and threat investigation capabilities. Usually, these are services provided by cloud service providers or vendors managing a data center. These tools constantly connect to and check system resources then generate alerts, notifications, and reports. The main use of such tools is to provide insight into the health and current state of a system. They do so by tracking specific system metrics in real time and generate alerts when certain readings exceed or fall below preassigned thresholds. This paper introduces the Insider Threat Minimization and Mitigation (ITMAM) Framework that goes beyond the usual monitoring of systems to enabling such systems with self-protection mechanisms. What distinguishes the ITMAM framework is that it inherently equips the system with defense capabilities allowing it to protect itself from potential insider attacks. Based on autonomous computing concepts, the ITMAM framework enables the system to intelligently deploy various levels of defenses in response to various potential threats without having to rely on human intervention. The use of autonomous computing capabilities provides a superior advantage over approaches that require human intervention. Conventional software monitoring tools are heavily deployed and used at data centers across the world. Companies rely on such tools to monitor the health of their systems, and to enforce and comply with recommended or federally mandated security requirements. Such requirements are either suggested by standards organizations such as NIST or the CERT Division at the Software Engineering Institute at Carnegie Mellon University, or they are federally mandated by laws such as the Federal Information Security Management Act (FISMA) of 2002. There is no doubt that such tools have been effective at detecting suspicious activities and malicious acts. They are also effective at alerting system owners of potential system failures. However, such tools do not address the crux of the issue that lies at the heart of the insider threat problem. As long as power users have unfettered access to the system they manage, they can inflict tremendous damage to it before they are caught. System, database, or network administrators have, by design, unfettered access to their systems. Therefore, they have the power to alter or damage the system instantaneously. Thus, as long as the defense mechanism lies outside the system that is being protected, there is no guarantee that the system will be protected. Autonomous computing equips the system itself with self-* capabilities (such as self-protecting, self-optimizing, self-managing, etc.) that move the control and command capability into the core components of the system itself. By doing so, the system can protect itself from actions that it deems potentially malicious or intended to damage it. Clearly, that comes with a certain level of restriction and limitation imposed on power users. However, those restrictions are specific to only certain system functions that are usually intrusive in nature. The idea is to create a balance between the act of self-defense and allowing administrators to perform their duties. We expect that if autonomic computing is properly designed and applied, such a balance can be struck. Monitoring tools are unable to prevent malicious actions by a power user who has unfettered access to the system. This deficiency is addressed by the ITMAM framework as it empowers a system to depend on itself rather than wait on delayed, or too late, human intervention. This paper presents the ITMAM framework and describes its various components. Also, it demonstrates its benefits by exercising its capability in a simulated data center environment.

2. LITERATURE REVIEW

The number of attacks committed by insiders, and the consequential damage, has been significantly rising in the past few years. In June of 2018, a former employee of Tesla allegedly "hacked the company's confidential and trade secret information and transferred that information to third parties" (Schwartz, 2018). In November of the same year, the hotel chain Marriott was hit by an insider attack where the records of 500 million customers had been compromised by an unauthorized party (BBC News, 2018). However, the insider attack committed against SunTrust Bank in 2018 was the costliest. The company, consequently, disclosed that one of its employees worked with outside criminals to gain access to, and compromise, the accounts of around 1.5 million clients (Weise, 2018). Moreover, the number of insider threat incidents and their related cost keeps rising year after year. According to Verizon's 2019 Data Breach Investigations Report, 34% of breaches that took place in 2018 were caused by insiders (Verizon, 2019). Notably, what elevates the insider threat problem to a much higher risk level is that a significant percentage of insider attacks are committed by power users. According to the 2019 Insider Threat Report produced by Cybersecurity Insiders, privileged IT users pose the biggest insider security risk to organizations (62% of total attacks) (Schulze, 2019). As such, companies cannot trust them with unfettered access to their systems. A system must be able to defend itself against power users. Any defense mechanism that leaves power users with unfettered access to the system is ineffective and weak. This validates the need for a framework that delegates the system protection task to the system itself. In order for that to work, the self-protection capability must be totally integrated into, and inseparable from the system that is being protected. Also, that capability must not be accessible by system administrators. There are many system monitoring tools on the market today that are being advertised as system protection and defense tools. However, almost all of these tools focus on monitoring the systems to allow administrators to manage their IT infrastructure efficiently, improve its uptime, respond to threshold alerts, and reduce cost. Many of these systems rely on analyzing system-generated data, identify vulnerabilities, identify potential threats, and report the findings to the data center leadership for their review and action (Ikany & Jazri, 2019), (Mavroeidis et al., 2018), (Ali et al.,2008). Others tackle the threat detection task by viewing it through different layers of the system namely the application layer, support layer, network layer, and perceptual layer (Kim et al., 2020). Some use situation-awareness technologies to detect an insider threat (Buford et al., 2008). Yet, other approaches focus on behavioral differences and social context variables using multidimensional classification systems that consider the severity (S), intentionality (I), type of employee norm violation (EV), and ethicality (E) of the incident (Schoenherr & Thomson, 2020). Lastly, some researchers have focused on developing a hierarchy-mapping-based insider threat model that described the kernel of threat detection, using sense and prediction to detect insider threats (Zhang et al., 2009). While such approaches have their merits, they are not effective in neutralizing or preventing an attack by an insider who has unfettered access to the system. Current monitoring tools leave it up to the system administrator to take action as discussed in Ali et al (2008), Paci et al. (2013), and Beena, Humayoon Kabir (2019). Such systems become obsolete and ineffective if the power user/administrator is the attacker. This is because a power user can perform an attack instantly thus rendering the alert and notification approach totally obsolete. This is supported by a study presented in Claycomb et al.

(2013), where the authors concluded that "the acts of IT sabotage often happened very close, if not in conjunction with, the moment of cyber damage to the organization". The same study also revealed that "90% of the cases studied will have an observable event indicating potential malicious activity prior to the moment of actual damage". This also validates the ITMAM framework, which allows the system to defend itself from within. This is supported in Chen & Lambright (2016), which argues that a self-protecting system "will perform reliably, trustworthily and resiliently even if it is compromised by cyberattacks". However, the ITMAM framework advances this notion by showing that a self-protecting system will not only perform resiliently but is also capable of completely preventing the occurrence of an insider attack even when attempted by the administrator of the said system.

3. THE ITMAM FRAMEWORK

The critical distinction between the ITMAM approach and that of other monitoring and threat detection tools is that the ITMAM capability lives inside of, and inseparable from, the system that is being protected. It simply delegates the task of protecting the system to the system itself. It does not require human intervention to invoke its defense capabilities to reject the action of a power user if deemed malicious. Also, the ITMAM self-defense capability is not accessible by the administrator. Technical details of how a defense mechanism is completely embedded into, and inseparable, from the system that is being protected are explained in Jabbour & Menasce (2009a) and Jabbour & Menasce (2009b). This paper argues that for any monitoring, threat detection, and mitigation methodology to be successful, it must be totally embedded and inseparable from, the system that is being protected. Moreover, the paper presents a detailed illustration of how the ITMAM framework works in equipping a system with self-protection capabilities. Expecting external monitoring and threat mitigation tools to fully protect the system is a weak and vulnerable protection mechanism. The reason is that such monitoring tools can be easily interrupted by the administrator. Alternatively, defense solutions based on the ITMAM framework are totally embedded into the system being protected and are inseparable from it. Once the solution is embedded into the system itself, the system will then be able to detect threats and protect itself without reliance on humans. It does so by predicting and rejecting unacceptable actions before they are even submitted. As discussed earlier, the ITMAM framework is designed for a data center environment where mission-critical systems reside. Such systems could potentially be the target of malicious attacks by insiders who wish to cause serious financial, social, or even national security damage. The ITMAM solution works by constantly collecting and analyzing user-related data to produce actionable information that give the system itself the power to autonomously detect and mitigate a potential threat before it happens. Insider attacks are usually committed by company employees who have elevated access privileges to mission-critical systems. However, elevated access privileges are intentionally given to employees to properly perform their duties. So, the consequences of such employees becoming malicious and committing criminal activities are significant and very costly. This paper argues that equipping the system with the ability to protect itself is much more effective. The ITMAM framework has two main components/modules that contribute to detecting, minimizing, or totally mitigating a potential insider attack. These are:

1) Collection, Aggregation and Synthesis of Employee-Related Actionable Information (CASAI): the CASAI component of the framework is tasked with collecting data from multiple sources to form a comprehensive and meaningful record of the risk level or threat status of an employee. The data sources are the company's various information systems as well as publicly available systems. Data is collected to enhance the understating of a potential threat level associated with an employee. The CASAI component only collects and stores data associated with positive hits or suspicious data that could lead to threat aversion. Once formed, an employee-related CASAI dataset is sent to the ADEMPT component for the investigation and mitigation of a potential threat.

2) Autonomic Detection, Evaluation, and Mitigation of Potential Threats (ADEMPT): the ADEMPT component equips the system with self-protection capabilities to counter any malicious action by power users. Equipped with built-in intelligent predictive analysis capability, strict business rules, and detailed security settings, the system invokes its self-protecting mechanism when needed to protect itself. Embedded self-protection mechanisms allow the system to detect a potential threat, evaluate possible countermeasures, assess unintended consequences, and take the appropriate steps to minimize or totally mitigate a threat. It performs assessments and predictions based on real-time access to employee and data center data.

Data is collected in real time from the various sources and assimilated to form the basis for predictive analysis of a user's risk level. The data sources are Data Center Point of Entry, Employee Performance

Appraisal Systems, Employee Grievance Management Systems, Employee's Corporate Email Traffic, Employee's Text Message using Corporate or Government Furnished Equipment (GFE), Internal Web Traffic, Public Social Media Sites, Financial Systems or Records, Law Enforcement Public Records, Network Traffic and Packets, System Event Log Files, Biometric Data Systems, and Data Center Physical Environment Sources including motion detectors, microphones, smart thermometers, and hygrometers. Existing tools also use such data; however, they use it in a reactive manner. They make the data available to managers or administrators to react to it. Instead, the proposed framework delegates that authority to the system itself. The rest of the paper presents the ITMAM Architecture and demonstrates its effectiveness in detecting and mitigating an insider attack.

4. THE ITMAM ARCHITECTURE

The ITMAM architecture is designed to empower a system with self-protection capability. Therefore, the system must be able to capture data from multiple sources and learn its environment and the actions of its power users. Based on that data, and in conjunction with predefined system security settings, the system is able to decide whether to accept or reject an action submitted by a power user. As discussed earlier, the components of the framework must be integrated into the system that is being protected. For example, in a Database Management System (DBMS), the components of the framework are codified into database objects at the system level, and are not available to the database administrator, but will control the actions of the database administrator to protect the system as explained in Jabbour & Menasce (2009a) and Jabbour & Menasce (2009b). A full depiction of the ITMAM architecture is shown in Figure 1.

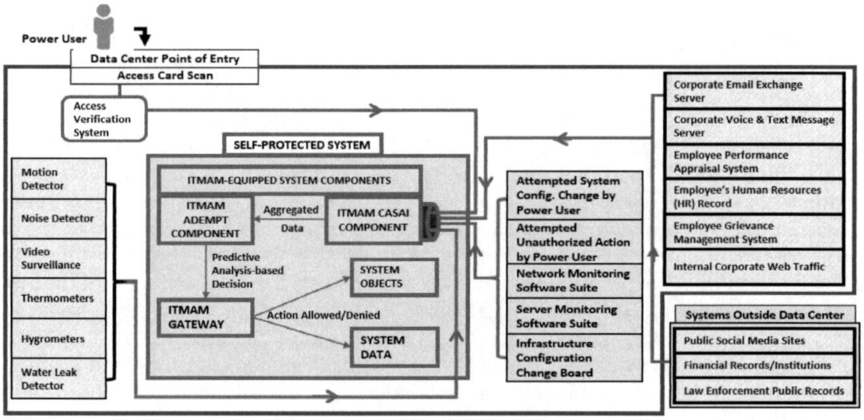

Figure 1. Architecture of the ITMAM framework

The architecture shows an ITMAM-equipped system residing inside a data center. The ITMAM components of the protected system gather data from internal systems as well as systems outside the data center for analysis. The protected system then performs predictive analysis to determine if an action is a threat. In response, the system acts instantaneously to neutralize or totally block an attack before it takes place. Systems on the left of the diagram are used to capture information on the state of the physical environment of the data center. That information is then combined with data from the other systems to form a complete understanding of what may be taking place inside the room. Systems on the right of the diagram are divided into two types. Some belong to the company and are hosted within the data center. Others are publicly available systems that are hosted somewhere outside the data center. It is important to note that the self-protected system could potentially be all of the systems within the data center. Figure 2 presents the Data Flow Diagram (DFD) of the ITMAM framework. Data collected from sensor devices, such as smart thermostats and noise and motion detectors, are fed into the CASAI module on an ongoing basis. However, data from the other systems (such as an employee's HR record) are requested in real-time as soon as the employee's identification information is captured at the data center's point of entry. At the same time, data from social media sites and other public websites are searched using bots.

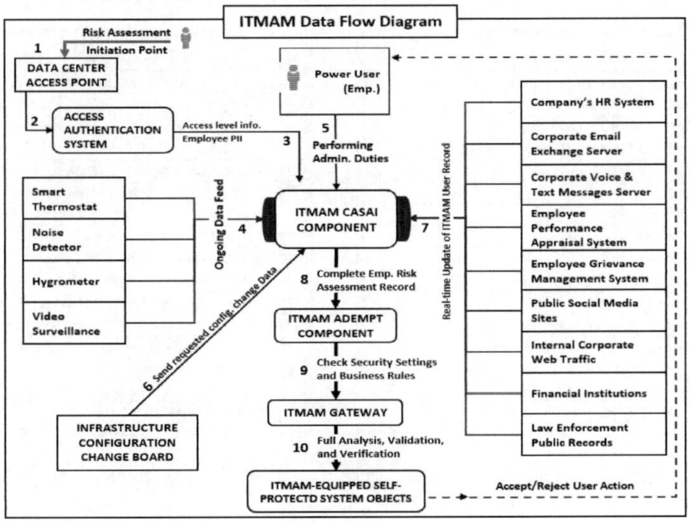

Figure 2. The ITMAM Data Flow Diagram

The data flow process is initiated when a power user accesses the data center at the point of entry as shown in step 1 of the DFD. At that point, an initial shell record of the user's data is created in the CASAI database. The employee's Personally Identifiable Information (PII) as well as data center access card authentication information are captured at the point of entry and sent to CASAI as shown in step 3. As soon as the user logs into the protected system (network, server, etc.) as depicted in step 5, the CASAI module requests and receives complimentary data from the other systems as shown in steps 6 and 7. The totality of the data received so far form the basis of the risk assessment in response to a power user submitting an action to the system (step 5). In this context, an action is any intrusive transaction that a user submits to the system such as a system configuration change, deleting system objects, injecting code, or installing or uninstalling unapproved software. The CASAI module collects the data, aggregates it with user actions, and sends it to the ADEMPT component for predictive analysis and decision making (step 8). Using the ITMAM GATEWAY, the ADEMPT component checks the predefined security settings and business rules stored within the system. It then uses that information to inform its analysis and decision-making process (steps 9 and 10). Depending on the result of the analysis of the complete user record, the self-protected system returns a decision to the user either accepting or rejecting the action.

5. FRAMEWORK SIMULATION AND VALIATION

To test the validity of the ITMAM framework, we simulate a data center environment where user-related data is collected, analyzed, and used to produce outcomes. The ITMAM interface allows the system owner to setup predefined security settings at the initial implementation and instantiation of the solution. Changes can later be made while the solution is already in operation, however, that change process follows a very strict and controlled path, where any change has to be approved by 3 or more members of the leadership team as discussed in Jabbour & Menasce (2009). For the purpose of this simulation, we chose 30 system security settings that, in normal setups, can be manipulated by a power user/system administrator at will.

Table 1. User actions and their corresponding threat level

	ACTION	Action Severity		ACTION	Action Severity
1	Install Malware on Network	H	16	Disable or Unistall Antivirus Software on Web Servers	H
2	Change password expiration period from 30 days to 45 days	L	17	Modify Domain Name System (add malicious domains)	H
3	Change password expiration period from 45 days to 30 days	L	18	Allow use of Portable Devices (USB Sticks, SD Cards, etc.)	H
4	Ignore Outdated or Unpatched Software when Prompted	M	19	Stop Data Backup Process	M
5	Disable Network Monitoring tools	H	20	Stop Transferring Backup Data to Secure Offsite Location	M
6	Disable Application Monitoring tools	H	21	Disable/Remove Network Encryption	H
7	Disable Database Monitoring tools	H	22	Use Credentials of a Different Power User	H
8	Upgrade Application Software	M	23	Disable Multi-factor Authentication	M
9	Update Security Certificates	M	24	Disable Password Expiration	M
10	Make Unauthorized/Unapproved Change of Firewall Config.	H	25	Install Approved Remote Desktop Software	L
11	Make Authorized/Approved Change of Firewall Config.	L	26	Install Unapproved Remote Desktop Software	M
12	Install Authorized & Approved Software on the Network	L	27	Enable Automatic Run/Open of Safe Files in Web Browsers	M
13	Install Authorized/Approved Software on Virtual Machines	L	28	Set Failed Login Attempt to Unlimited	M
14	Add Unauthorized/Unapproved Devices/Nodes to Network	H	29	Stop Database Audit Process	M
15	Disable or Uninstall Network Antivirus Software	H	30	Change/Elevate User Account Privileges	M
	Key: H = High M = Medium L = Low				

Most of the settings we selected are considered critical to the credibility, integrity, and availability of an information or network system. We also assigned a threat level to each parameter depending on the damage that the change of the security setting may cause if allowed. Those are presented in Table 1. The main threat levels we used for the simulation are Low, Medium, High, and Severe.

Table 2. Data elements of a user record

	USER RECORD DATA ELEMENTS	Description	Weighted Threat Level (Pts.)
1	USER_HR_FLAG	Background Check Red Flag, Unreported Job History, Employment-related Convictions, Discrepancy of experience vs. actual experience	30
2	USER_SENORITY_EXP	Unexperienced: ≤ 1Yr Mid Level Exp.: 1-5Yrs Senior Level: ≥ 5Yrs	1 Yr = 5 1 - 5 Yrs. = 15 > 5 Yrs. = 20
3	MISUSE_CORP_EMAIL	Comparison of email words to Predefined Ontology Repository	25
4	MISUSE_CORP_TXT	Comparison of text messages to Predefined Ontology Repository	25
5	MISUSE_CORP_VOICEMAIL	Comparison of recoded voice messages to Predefined Ontology	25
6	EMP_LAST_PREF_RATING	The employee's annual perforamnce rating	UNACCEPTABLE = 30 FAIR = 10 GOOD = 0 EXCELLENT = 0
7	EMP_GRIEF_CASE_6MO	Whether employee filed a grievance case in the past 6 months	20
8	MISUSE_CORP_WEB	Comparing visited sites against a repository of unfavorable sites to visit	25
9	EMP_FACEBOOK_POSTINGS	Whether employee posted derogatory words/phrases against company	15
10	EMP_TWITTER_POSTINGS	Whether employee posted derogatory words/phrases against company	15
11	SOCIAL_MEDIA_THREAT	Whether employee posted threat against specific employee(s)	YES/NO FLAG
12	CORP_ICCB_ACTION_APPROVE	If system change approved by Infrastructure Configuration Change	YES = 0 NO = 30
13	EMP_PUBLAW_VIOL_RECORD	Whether a criminal action has been recorded against the person	20
14	EMP_FINANCE_HARDSHIP	Bad credit or other negative financial information	10
15	RANDOM_SYS_FAILURE	Malfunctioning of the system due to failure not related to an attack	YES = 0 NO = 5
16	ROOM_TEMP	Data Center room temperature should not go above 82°F	≥ 82°F = 10
17	ROOM_NOISE_LVL	Normal range 40 - 70 dB but above 85 may be concerning	≥ 85dB = 10
18	DETECTED_WATER_LEAK	Whether the data center is experiencing water leak or flood	YES = 5 NO = 0

However, when combined with other data values collected from the various systems, a threat level can be demoted, elevated, or kept the same. For example, if elevated, a High threat level becomes Severe, in which case the self-protected system would totally lock the user out and promptly reject any submitted transaction. If changed, a threat level of Medium becomes either High, Low, Severe, or left unchanged. Next, we present in Table 2 the data elements that the CASAI module requests and receives from the various data sources that it interfaces with as shown in the data flow diagram. We assign a weighted value to each data element according to its relevance and the degree of impact it has on the decision of accepting or rejecting a user's action. Each data element is assigned a weighted score ranging from 1 to 100. The higher the score, the higher the risk. Depending on whether the overall weighted risk reaches or exceeds the allowable threshold of the ITMAM model, the threat level is elevated, demoted, or left unchanged. In response, the self-protected system invokes the appropriate outcome to deal with each specific threat. Table 2 shows 18 data elements that partially make up the user record that the ADEMPT module analyzes and investigates to determine the proper outcome. The table also includes the points associated with each data element. To cover the various security aspects of a data center, we have divided the threat assessment criteria into four categories. Those are shown in Table 2 as follows: Potential Insider Attack & Malicious Activity represented by data elements 1 – 14, Random System Failure or System Malfunction represented by number 15, and Physical Data Center Security represented by 16 – 18.

6. SIMULATION RESULTS AND FINDINGS

The simulation of the ITMAM framework utilizes a dataset of 150 records. The dataset is synthesized using realistic data center experiences of the relative occurrences of actions by system administrators. Also, the dataset is enriched with the initial system security settings and the outcomes associated with each action if allowed to be executed. Realistic and appropriate weights were assigned to each threat scenario. The simulation algorithm was designed and built to simulate the potential behavior of a power user from the moment he/she enters the data center. The algorithm generates one data record each time a user enters the data center. It then analyzes the complete user record to determine the risk level associated with the user. As a result, the simulation shows the outcome that the self-protected system undertakes to protect itself. The simulation algorithm also records the events, then uses that data to predict the next action of a power user. In this section of the paper, we present four instances from the simulated data and show how the system reacted to each one. In two cases, the self-protected system rejected the action and protected itself from the consequences. In the other two cases, the self-protected system allowed the action based on the overall analysis of the situation. Below are the four different scenarios:

```
Capture Employee ID: 8528
Employee profile found: [Name: Alisha Holland, HR Flag: False, Years Exp: 2, Perf. Rating: 4]
Capture threat information: Misuse Corp Email, Misuse Corp Text, Misuse Corp Voicemail,
Misuse Corp Web, Grief Case: 0,0,0,0,1
Misuse Facebook, Misuse Twitter, Direct Social Media Threat: 0,0,1
ICCB Action Approved, Law Violation, Financial Hardship, System Failure: 0,0,1,0
Room Temp, Room Noise, Detected Water Leak, Action id: 72,47,0,14
Action: Add Unauthorized/Unapproved Devices/Nodes to Network
Assessing threat severity...
[Weighted Threat: 80] [Default Severity: H] [Change Made: Increased by 1 Level] - [New Severity: S]
Outcome 1: USER REQUEST REJECTED
Outcome 2: USER ACCOUNT LOCKED ON ALL SYSTEMS. ENTRY TO DATA CENTER DISABLED
Outcome 3: Attn. Power User: Your account has been locked. Consult supervisor for next steps
Outcome 4: Alert sent to sec. team mobile device 3 times in 5 min and repeated in 5 min
Outcome 5: Urgent email sent to sup. & sec. team: Emp. Alisha Holland barred from
accessing all DC systems & physical access to DC revoked. Refer to ITMAM for incident details.
Outcome 6: Incident details have been stored in ITMAM for analytics & data mining purposes
```

Figure 3. Threat level elevated from High to Severe

Figure 3 shows a case where the threat level was elevated from High to Severe based on the insider's threat level. The action attempted by the power user was to add unauthorized devices/nodes to the network. A variable of the system algorithm, which stores data about a threat made by the user against a specific employee of the company was flagged. In this scenario, the initial threat level of the action was High. Based on the combined threat factors, the level was immediately elevated to Severe. Figure 4 presents a case where a Medium threat level has been elevated to High based on the context of all the data collected about the user.

```
Capture Employee ID: 2213
Employee profile found: [Name: Russell Morrison, HR Flag: True, Years Exp: 4, Perf. Rating: 1]
Capture threat information: Misuse Corp Email, Misuse Corp Text, Misuse Corp Voicemail,
Misuse Corp Web, Grief Case: 0,0,0,0,0
Misuse Facebook, Misuse Twitter, Direct Social Media Threat: 0,1,0,
ICCB Action Approved, Law Violation, Financial Hardship, System Failure: 0,0,0,0
Room Temp, Room Noise, Detected Water Leak, Action id: 70,61,0,19
Action: Stop Data Backup Process
Assessing threat severity...
[Weighted Threat: 125] [Default Severity: M] [Change Made: Increased by 1 Level] - [New Severity: H]
Outcome 1: USER REQUEST REJECTED
Outcome 2: USER ACCOUNT LOCKED ONLY USED SYSTEM UNTIL ALLOWED BY LEADERSHIP
Outcome 3: Attention Power User: Your account has been locked on this system. Action not allowed by
self-protected system without prior authorization.
Outcome 4: Alert sent to sup. & sec. team mobile device 3 times in 5 min
Outcome 5: Urgent email sent to sup. & sec. team: User account for employee Russell Morrison has been
locked on this system. Account can be unlocked if 3 ITMAM-assigned security members approve the unlocking
Outcome 6: Incident details have been stored in ITMAM for analytics & data mining purposes
```

Figure 4. Threat level elevated from Medium to High

Specifically, the user had an HR flag in his record and an unacceptable performance rating. In spite of being an experienced user, he intentionally attempted to disable system data backup, an action that was unapproved by the configuration change board. Data collected from external systems also revealed flags related to the misuse of Twitter by posting derogatory statements about the company. The aggregation and analysis of all the factors contributed to the elevation of the threat level. However, the algorithm did not elevate the threat to

Severe because the action initially had a Medium threat level if committed independently of other factors. Figure 5 depicts a situation where a Medium threat level was demoted to Low. The action was to ignore patching outdated software. The user had no HR flag in his record, and he had an excellent performance rating. However, company-related systems indicated that the user had submitted a grievance case against one of his peers. Since the action itself was approved by the configuration change board, and the initial threat level was not significantly exacerbated by other factors, demoting it to a lower threat level was justified.

```
Capture Employee ID: 9807
Employee profile found: [Name: Bradley Diaz, HR Flag: False, Years Exp: 4, Perf. Rating: 4]
Capture threat information: Misuse Corp Email, Misuse Corp Text, Misuse Corp Voicemail,
Misuse Corp Web, Grief Case: 0,0,0,0,1
Misuse Facebook, Misuse Twitter, Direct Social Media Threat: 1,0,0
ICCB Action Approved, Law Violation, Financial Hardship, System Failure: 1,0,0,0
Room Temp, Room Noise, Detected Water Leak, Action id: 71,57,0,4
Action: Ignore Outdated or Unpatched Software when Prompted
Assessing threat severity...
[Weighted Threat: 55] [Default Severity: M] [Change Made: Decreased by 1 Level] - [New Severity: L]
Outcome 1: USER REQUEST ALLOWED
Outcome 2: NO ACCOUNT LOCKING REQUIRED
Outcome 3: No alert displayed on screen. Action allowed to proceed
Outcome 4: No smart phone notification
Outcome 5: No email documentation required.
Outcome 6: Details on the user's action have been stored in ITMAM for analytics & data mining purposes
```

Figure 5. Threat level demoted from Medium to Low

Finally, Figure 6 illustrates how a threat level of Low was left unchanged. This inexperienced user had no HR flag in his record and had an excellent performance rating. Also, the action was approved by the change board, and a minor system failure was recorded. Although there was a misuse of corporate technology, the offense was not significant enough to warrant an elevation of the overall threat level.

```
Capture Employee ID: 7261
Employee profile found: [Name: Dennis Franklin, HR Flag: False, Years Exp: 0, Perf. Rating: 4]
Capture threat information: Misuse Corp Email, Misuse Corp Text, Misuse Corp Voicemail,
Misuse Corp Web, Grief Case: 1,0,0,1,0
Misuse Facebook, Misuse Twitter, Direct Social Media Threat: 0,0,0
ICCB Action Approved, Law Violation, Financial Hardship, System Failure: 1,0,0,1
Room Temp, Room Noise, Detected Water Leak, Action id: 59,56,0,11
Action: Make Authorized/Approved Change of Firewall Config.
Assessing threat severity...
[Weighted Threat: 30] [Default Severity: L] [Change Made: No Change] - [New Severity: L]
Outcome 1: USER REQUEST ALLOWED
Outcome 2: NO ACCOUNT LOCKING REQUIRED
Outcome 3: No alert displayed on screen. Action allowed to proceed
Outcome 4: No smart phone notification
Outcome 5: No email documentation required.
Outcome 6: Details on the user's action have been stored in ITMAM for analytics & data mining purposes
```

Figure 6. Threat level of Low kept unchanged

In addition to self-protection, the ITMAM framework incorporates business intelligence capabilities that deliver actionable information for making informed decisions. An analysis of the complete dataset showed a few relevant findings that a self-protected system will use to avert future actions as they progress. One finding reflected the correlation between the user's level of experience and the threat level. Assuming that the organization has a mostly experienced workforce, a Gaussian distribution was used to assign users a level of experience. The distribution was given a mean of 4 years and a standard deviation of 2. Scanning the full dataset revealed that only around 11% of the High or Severe threat level cases were attributed to inexperienced employees. This implies that the algorithm associated most of the insider attacks with more experienced users. Another finding linked the number of times a threat was elevated to a higher risk level with the decision rendered by the configuration change board regarding the action. In 35% of the recorded instances, the threat was elevated to a higher level at the time when the action was rejected by the configuration change board. This finding implied that power users, in our simulation, intentionally attempted to make a change to the system when they were explicitly told not to do it.

7. CONCLUSION

The paper introduced an autonomic framework designed to equip information systems with self-defense capabilities, to protect against a malicious action by an insider such as a system administrator. It simulated how an ITMAM-equipped system can protect itself against malicious actions by insiders. The paper also argued that such an approach is significantly more effective than other approaches that place the protection mechanism outside the system that is being protected. Simulation of a dataset of 150 records demonstrated how the system is able to protect itself against unauthorized actions. Future research related to this work will focus on building a more granular level of interdependencies between the weighted factors assigned to each action. Also, attention will be devoted to advancing the predictive analysis algorithm to establish a continuously growing intelligence base. This will allow the self-protected system to recognize early signs and extrapolate its self-defense attributes to avert an attack well before its occurrence.

REFERENCES

Ali, G., Shaikh, N. A., Shaikh, Z. A. (2008) Towards an automated multiagent system to monitor user activities against insider threat. *2008 International Symposium on Biometrics and Security Technologies, Islamabad*, 1–5.

BBC News. (2018) *Marriott hack hits 500 million Starwood guests* https://www.bbc.com/news/technology-46401890

Beena, A. L., Humayoon Kabir, S. (2019) Information Security Insider Threats in Organizations and Mitigation Techniques. *2019 International Conference on Recent Advances in Energy-Efficient Computing and Communication (ICRAECC)*

Buford, J. F., Lewis, L., Jakobson, G. (2008) Insider threat detection using situation-aware MAS. *2008 11th International Conference on Information Fusion*

Chen, Q., Lambright, J. (2016) Towards Realizing a Self-Protecting Healthcare Information System. *2016 IEEE 40th Annual Computer Software and Applications Conference (COMPSAC)*

Claycomb, W. R., Huth, C. L., Phillips, B., Flynn, L., McIntire, D. (n.d.). (2013) Identifying Indicators of Insider Threats: Insider IT Sabotage. *2013 47th International Carnahan Conference on Security Technology (ICCST)*

Ikany, J., Jazri, H. (2019) A Symptomatic Framework to Predict the Risk of Insider Threats. *International Conference on Advances in Big Data, Computing and Data Communication Systems (ICABCD)*

Jabbour, G., Menasce, D. (2009) Stopping the Insider Threat: The case for implementing integrated autonomic defense mechanisms in computing systems. *International Conference on Information Security and Privacy (ISP-09)*

Jabbour, G., Menasce, D. (2009) The Insider Threat Security Architecture: A framework for an integrated, inseparable, & uninterrupted self-protection mechanism. *2009 International Conference on Computational Science & Engineering*

Kim, A., Oh, J., Ryu, J., Lee, K. (2020) A Review of Insider Threat Detection Approaches with IoT Perspective. *IEEE Access*, *8*, 78847–78867

Mavroeidis, V., Vishi, K., Jøsang, A. (2018) A Framework for Data-Driven Physical Security and Insider Threat Detection. *2018 IEEE/ACM International Conference on Advances in Social Networks Analysis and Mining (ASONAM)*

Paci, F., Fernandez-Gago, C., Moyano, F. (2013) Detecting Insider Threats: A Trust-Aware Framework. *2013 International Conference on Availability, Reliability and Security*

Schoenherr, J. R., Thomson, R. (2020) Insider Threat Detection: A Solution in Search of a Problem. *2020 International Conference on Cyber Security and Protection of Digital Services (Cyber Security)*

Schulze, H. (2019) *2019 INSIDER THREAT REPORT*. Cybersecurity Insiders

Schwartz, M. J. (2018) *Tesla Accuses Insider of Stealing Gigabytes of Data—Former Employee Accused of Hacking Software as Tesla Warns of "Sabotage."* https://www.bankinfosecurity.com/tesla-lawsuit-alleges-insider-stole-gigabytes-data-a-11118, June 21, 2018

Verizon. (2019) *2019 Data Breach Investigations Report*. https://enterprise.verizon.com/resources/reports/2019-data-breach-investigations-report.pdf

Weise, E. (2018) *SunTrust said employee worked with outside criminal when info on 1.5M clients was breached*. USA TODAY. https://www.usatoday.com/story/tech/2018/04/20/many-1-5-million-accounts-may-have-been-compromised-suntrust-banks/535687002/

Zhang, H., Ma, J., Wang, Y., Pei, Q. (2009) An Active Defense Model and Framework of Insider Threats Detection and Sense. *2009 Fifth International Conference on Information Assurance and Security*

TRANSLATING GRAFCET SPECIFICATIONS INTO C/UNIX PROGRAM

Nacéra Benaouda and Abdelhafid Benaouda
SETIF-1 University, Algeria

ABSTRACT

This paper presents a method of simulating the operation of the control part of an automated system, modeled by a Grafcet. Our approach is to translate the Grafcet into C language, in a Unix environment. The resulting program simulates the operation of the automation in question. The first step is to establish the Grafcet / C generation schemes. A Grafcet put in internal form will be translated in C by a generating program, on the basis of the schemes previously found. This will allow the validation of the functional specifications of a sequential automation as, for educational purposes, the learning of the Grafcet formalism. Once the program has been configured, tested and validated, the object code can be implemented on a microcontroller of the actual control system.

KEYWORDS

Grafcet, Process, C/Unix

1. INTRODUCTION

Equipment manufacturers and automation engineers responsible for automated industrial installations must be able to understand the programs that drive their systems, in order to be able to carry out their corrective, adaptive or evolutionary maintenance missions (Benaouda. N, 2017). They want to do it without having to (re) program, especially since these programs often under treated, could use a variety of languages and libraries, depending as much on their provider's past as on the problem to be solved. At the programming languages Babel Tower, automation experts oppose the desire for specification formalisms, allowing them to dominate the situation, while expressing for each functionality all that they consider necessary, and nothing more.

In this work, we focus on sequential automated systems, where the control part is modeled by the Grafcet tool (Blanchard..M, 1994), (Reeb.B, Chèze, 2011). In an automated system, the control part is nothing else than the image of the operative part which concretely represents the automated machine. Before implementing the automation on actual installations, the simulation and validation of its operation is necessary. Simulating the operation of Grafcet amounts to translating it into appropriate languages which generate programs with the same semantics. These programs have shown their usefulness at several levels, namely, the validation of the design before the implementation of the automation on actual installations, in industrial maintenance tasks, with an educational aim for learning the Grafcet formalism, and also, once the program is configured, tested and validated, the object code can be implemented on the microcontroller of the control system itself. In our work, we have chosen a translation of Grafcet in C language in a Unix environment. The C language extended by the Unix library has all tools allowing to translate Grafcet, moreover, the required configuration for the realization is very simple: a personal computer with a linux distribution. To illustrate our work we begin by presenting some related works, showing their advantages and disadvantages. We then present our target language, C under Unix, emphasizing the tools for creating processes, communication between processes and timings. The following section contains a description of our simulation system. We continue with section 5 in which we present our approach in detail, by proposing an original approach that allowed us to develop the translation schemes of Grafcet in C. We end with a conclusion that encompasses the advantages and peculiarities of our work as well as a relevant perspective.

2. RELATED WORK

A big number of research work have been achieved to formalise the Grafcet. This research date back further, like (Remaki. Z and al., 1994), or in recent years such as (Gonzalez. E and al., 2016), (Julius.R and al., 2017), (Julius. R and al., 2019) and (Miguel-Escrig.O et al, 2020).

(Remaki.Z and al., 1994) have designed the translation schemes of the grafcet in Occam2 language which is executable on transputers. The authors have exploited the possibilities of expressions of parralel tasks offered in Occam2 to express the parallel tasks represented in the grafcet. The resulting program could be run on a parallel machine and simulated the actual operation of an automated system. With this work, we could from a grafcet in graphical or textual form obtain the equivalent Occam2 program that simulates the operation of the automation. By being a parallel language, Occam2 possesses the different tools that can translate a grafcet; but the resulting program can only be exploited if a parallel machine existed. Since parallel machines are only available in certain research laboratories or in specific industrial settings, such a program may have limited use.

(Gonzalez.E and al., 2016) have defined a semi-coarse ontology that they wrote in the web language of ontology. To test it, they integrated it into an already existing educational tool to teach Grafcet intended for use in programmable logic controllers. This ontology is OWL (Web Ontology Language) DL() based, a specific decidable fragment of first-order logic which is applied to OWL markup language. The objective of this method is to give a complement to other propositions previously defined by other authors, and in the same time to promote this type of techniques in the formalisation of the grafcet. Advantages of ontologies are numerous, they make the sharing of knowledge and the collaboration easier, they guarantee greater reliability, more over they assure to handle automatically any input change without having to recompile the processing code. The validation of the approach defined in this work was realized according to two criteria, accuracy and completeness.

(Julius.R and al, 2017) have defined an approach that automatically generates PLC (Programmable Logic Controller) code corresponding to a GRAFCET specification, with ST (Structured Text) as the target command programming language. The initial hierarchical structure of Grafcet is preserved by the resulting control program, and this without requiring standardization, as in the case of previous approaches. To avoid ambiguity in the interpretation of Grafcet dependency elements, the notion of hierarchical elements was used to extend the interpretation algorithm for Grafcet on sequential systems. The validation of the approach was carried out by making a comparison of the structure, the content and the behavior of the code generated automatically according to the adopted approach, with the code which had been implemented by human programmers of automatons and which are based strictly on the Grafcet specification.

The work presented in (Julius.R and al, 2019) can be considered as an extension of that presented in (Julius.R et al. 2017). It is always the automated generation of PLC code, from a Grafcet specification, and always having ST as target language, while preserving the initial hierarchical structure of Grafcet. But this time around, the approach is based on a model. The system produced includes a Grafcet editor and a rule-based ST code generator. Compared to (Julius. R and al. 2017), (Julius.R and al, 2019) includes temporal dependencies, and has been implemented using a model-based approach in the Eclipse environment via EMF and Acceleo. The authors presented a sample application to demonstrate the usability and accuracy of their approach.

Within (Miguel-Escrig. O et al, 2020) a new vision was adopted. From a Grafcet, the authors proposed the systematic implementation of the control software in IEC 61499. This constitutes a key advantage over previous Grafcet implementations, because it allows engineers to implement models of Grafcet, which are distributed over several devices, and at the same it keeps the initial centralized design. IEC 61499 has all the translation tools for most of the Grafcet elements. This work makes it possible to systematically translate grafcet and introduces several translation models. The disadvantage in IEC 61 499 lies in the fact that it is not possible to model the structuring mechanisms such as fences or forcing steps, moreover, the macros-steps that can be implemented are limited to simple sequences. The authors presented an example of application in which they show the main lines of their approach, illustrating the systematic implementation of Grafcet in IEC 61499.

3. WHY A TRANSLATION TO THE C LANGUAGE?

The Grafcet is a logical automatism description formalism, allowing to express competing processes. If a language has to translate it, it must be preferably parallel (Remaki.Z and al, 1994) and / or real time. In the choice of such a language, a factor such as the duration of the task's installation (or the task's switching time) is decisive. C/Unix (Stevens. W. R, Rago, 2004) was chosen, it presents advantages: portability, universality, control by a majority of computer scientists. Its disadvantage lies in the fact that Unix is not quite real time, because its too slow temporal primitives were defined according to the only problems of timeshare. The C language is located between the high-level languages, which it owns the data and control structures, and the HLMOL (High-Level Machine-Oriented Language) languages: it allows to define fields to bit close and Expanded by Unix libraries, C can provide on uniprocessor machines, the illusion of simultaneous execution of tasks, as shown by functions: FORK, WAIT, SLEEP, KILL(Stevens.W.R, Rago, 2004). The main means of communication between unix processes: pipes (Stevens.W.R, Rago, 2004). Several synchronization means are available under unix. In our study we have retained the WAIT function which constitutes the most basic mean of synchronization, and which makes it possible to synchronize a father process on the termination of its sons. Time management (Stevens.W.R, Rago, 2004) is carried out with the sleep() function : The call to the sleep(n) function suspends the calling process for a duration of n seconds. Since the second time unit is not realistic for many real-time scenarios, we use the macro tempo (), allowing us to do timers in microseconds.

```
#define tempo(n){
        clock_t reveil = clock()+n;
        while(clock()<reveil) sleep(0);
}/*n in microseconds */
```

Sleep(1) is then equivalent to tempo(1000000) . These timers are used in processes running in parallel and can limit the waiting time of certain events.

4. SIMULATION SYSTEM DESCRIPTION

The simulation system mainly consists of two subsystems:

- Grafcet entry : this first subsystem offers two possibilities :
    - Graphical input: based on a graphical editor, allows any Grafcet to be entered graphically, and outputs an image data structure of the entered Grafcet.
    - Text entry: in practice, rarely used, except for maintenance purposes; it allows to enter the Grafcet as a text, so requires a text analyzer that outputs, for the same Grafcet, the same data structure as the graphical editor receiving the corresponding Grafcet.
- Translation of the Grafcet: this second subsystem exploits the data structure resulting from the entry, and translates the Grafcet entered in the chosen target language, here C; two steps are possible:
    - Interpreter / simulator: A program that, according to the data structure, step by step executes the appropriate C sequences.
    - Generator: program that creates a complete C code image of all the Grafcet; the execution of this code constitutes the simulation of the automatism specified by the Grafcet (as long as this code is not configured according to real I / O).

In both cases, the translation requires, first of all, to find the generation schemes from Grafcet to C.

5. OUR APPROACH

5.1 Definition

To find the translation schemes of the Grafcet in C language, consists of finding for each basic element of the Grafcet, a scheme of program (macro, procedure, ...) in C which has the same semantics. The elements of the Grafcet are: the simple transition, divergences (AND, OR), convergences (AND, OR), the stage and the macro stage.

5.2 Preliminary Study

Let's consider the following scenario:

- rotating bar at a position x, y of the screen (successive display in x, y of characters -, /, |, \, -, /, ...),
- in case of no overflows, pressing the ↓, ←, →, ↑ keys causes the bar to move down, left, right and up, respectively,
- If the limits are exceeded, pressing the preceding characters will sound an audible signal and the bar will remain rotating in the same place.
- Pressing the character 'q' stops the scenario,
- Pressing any other character is ineffective.

Figure 1 shows the Grafcet describing the previous scenario.

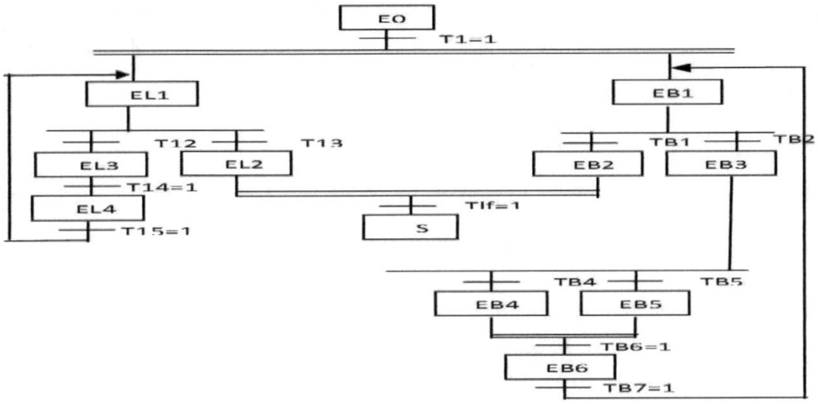

Figure 1. Grafcet associated with the rotating bar

nb. Let EB and TB be the stages and transitions of the rotating bar branch, and EL and TL are the stages and transitions of the reading characters branch.

(1) Stages
E0: initial stage, beginning of the program.
EB1 : rotating bar.
EB2 : end of the rotating bar process.
EB3 : Test of the character read in the pipe.
EB4: audible alarm.
EB5: moving the bar.
EB6: rest (sleep).
EL1: read and test the read character.
EL2: sending a KILL and exit.
EL3: write ↓, ←, →, ↑ in the pipe.
EL4: rest (sleep).
S: end of the scenario.

(2) Transitions
T1: pressing any key to start both processes.
TB1: reception of a KILL signal.
TB2: read ↓, ←, →, ↑ in the pipe.
TB4: overcoming limits.
TB5: no overflows.
TB6: = 1; TB7 = 1
TL2: read ↓, ←, → or ↑ from the keyboard.
TL3: reading of the 'q' character of the keyboard.
TL4 = 1; TL5 = 1; TLF = 1.

5.3 Principle of the Image Program

Once the program is launched, two processes are created and launched simultaneously. Note proc1 and proc2 these two processes. Proc1 is associated with the rotating bar, or standalone process. Proc2 is associated with the movement of the bar, or process under external influence. It is clear that at one point, the two processes proc1 and proc2 must act simultaneously on the coordinates (x, y) of the bar. A first solution is to create a critical section within each process to achieve mutual exclusion of both accesses (Raynal.M, 2013). The second would be to allow effective access to a single process, such as proc1, which will rotate and move the bar, proc2 reads the characters ↓, ←, →, ↑ considered as the move commands of the bar, and send them through a pipe to proc1 which will use them to move the bar in the desired direction, the end of the scenario will take place when proc2 reads the character 'q' key. We present in the table 1, the general processing algorithms of proc1 and proc2.

Since the program is modeled on the Grafcet, we make it a basis to deduce the basic translation schemes from the Grafcet into C. These schemes have been extended to the case of industrial processes where the system entries can be numerous and simultaneous and especially in real time; therefore push buttons and sensors have been integrated.

Table 1. The Parallel running of Proc1 and Proc2

Proc1	Proc2
At each position of the bar: • display the bar • look in p[0] if a character is placed in the pipe. • If yes the character is stored in cc1 and tested. • If exceeding the limits, warning sound, otherwise move in the desired direction. • rotation of the bar.	• Reads a cc character from the keyboard and test it • If cc ='q' then sends a SIGKILL to proc1 then EXIT. • If cc ='#' ,' ', '!' or "" then places cc in the inlet p[1] of the pipe; • If cc is other, ignore cc.

5.4 Grafcet-C Translation Schemes

5.4.1 Simple Transition

The simple transition is an external event, which can arise at any time from a sensor, a push button, etc ... To simulate it three cases arise:

(1) Keyboard

cc=getch()

(2) Order Box

Let boitcom the port address of the command box, reading 8 to 16 digital inputs. By assimilating all the bits to zero at the absence of an entry, we will have the scheme: *while(!(*boitcom)) sleep(0);*

These diagrams will be taken up and developed when a configuration language will cover the essential cases concerning the real-time management of arbitrary devices, which will be part of a realistic simulation; meanwhile, the input from the control box can be simulated by programming the keys of the keyboard, we associate in this case a sequence of bits: command [0] ... command [7], with command [i] = 1 hence the receptivity i is true; and command [i] = 0 for i = 1, ... , 7 means that no receptivity is true.

(3) always occurrent

t=1; which means that the sum of the internal and external receptivity conditions is 1; in this case, we will generate a comment: */* t=1 */* presumed zero cost, and facilitating research for development.

5.4.2 Divergences

Case of a transition followed by several stages

(1) AND Divergence

```
while (!t) sleep(0);
Rep=forkn(tab_fonc,nproc,tab_pid);
Rep1=wait(&status);
while((rep1 !=-1) wait(&status);
```

Where,

Tab_fonc is an Array of pointers to functions performed in the context of each process, Nproc is the number of the created processes, Tab_pid is pid chart of the created processes and Tab_fonc[i] is the pointer to the function executed by the process with the pid tab_pid[i]. the forkn () function based on the fork() function, it is used to create multiple processes (Stevens.W.R, Rago, 2004).

(2) OR Divergence

- **Exclusive OR**

```
while(!t1&&!t2&&!t3... &&!tn)sleep(0);
switch(transition){
  case t1 : p1();
  case t2 : p2();
  . . .
  case tn : pn();
}
```

with *pi ()* the procedure executed for the transition *ti*. There is no priming of new paths.

- **Inclusive OR**

```
while(!t1&& !t2&&... && !tn) sleep(0);
if(t1) p1();
if(t2) p2();
 ...
if(tn) pn();
/* the creative process enters the
zombie state */
rep1=wait(&status);
while (rep1 !=-1) wait(&status);
```

With pi(): the process creation procedure i. There is a boot of new paths.

We are here in the classical case of an input form, likely to have two images: A general image but expensive (competition diagram), or An effective image applicable under certain conditions: here, the alternative scheme, applicable if and only if the transitions are disjoined two by two.

In a generator, the evaluation of this question is the subject of a decision procedure, which in case of difficulties may substitute, the absolute criterion above, one or more sufficient conditions easier to evaluate. (For example here, if two transitions occur as products of elementary conditions, they are disjoint if the same condition is present in the two transitions in opposite forms, such that: T1 = x y z and t2 = x y z.

In the case of expectations with time-out, there is divergence with 2 issues, one of which carries the receptivity "event" and the other a receptivity "time limit"; since this can only be performed in excess, it is normal to consider the two as disjoint (in case of conjunction the event is considered to have happened after the prescribed duration). The quality of the decision procedure thus directly governs the quality of the code which may be inaccurate, correct but heavy, correct and effective, and even optimal for a perfect decision procedure. On the other hand, the generation with the divergences must be in agreement with the generation with the convergences.

5.4.3 Convergences

- **AND Convergence**

Two cases arise: a) pi have, as origin, the same divergence: the synchronization is done by WAIT. b) pi do not have the same origin: in this case, synchronization is mandatory. We describe below its principle.
Suppose for each father process, synchro a global variable.

i. Initially: synchro = number of incoming branches ;
ii. Once finished, each process simulating an incoming branch, must access synchro and decrement it.
iii. When synchro becomes null implies the end of all branches. It is clear that the access to synchro may be simultaneous; access to synchro must therefore be a critical section within each process; you must use either semaphores or locks (Raynal.M, 2013).

The Method Used

Choose a process, which we will call coordinator; take the one that simulates the most left incoming branch. When finished, the coordinator has to perform Algorithm 1.
Once it has finished, each of the other processes associated with other branches shall perform Algorithm 2:

Algorithm 1

```
/* scheme associated with coordinator*/
/*only The coordinator accesses synchro*/
int rep ;  char cc ;
...
/* as soon as it finishes, it
decrements synchro */
synchro-- ;
while(1){
   cc = ' ';
   dup(tube1[1]);
   close(tube1[1]);
   read(tube1[0],cc,1);
   if (cc=='f') synchro--;
   ...
   cc=' ';
   dup(tuben[1]);
   close(tuben[1]);
   read(tuben[0],cc,1);
   if (cc=='f') synchro--;
}/* finwhile */
/* synchro=0, le process p0 kills
 all the other processes and makes
  an exit */
    rep=kill(pid1, SIGKILL);
    rep=kill(pid2, SIGKILL);
    ...
    rep=kill(pidn, SIGKILL);
    exit();
```

Algorithm 2

```
/* scheme associated with other branches*/
/* let's suppose the process number i,
     other than the coordinator, sends the
     character 'f' in the pipe */

     dup(tubei[0]);
     close(tubei[0]);
     write(tubei[1],'f',1);
    /* infinite loop as wait */
     for( ; ;) sleep(0);
```

- **OR Convergence**

  i. Exclusive OR: In practice, this case comes down to the simple transition.
  ii. Inclusive OR: This case is discussed in the same way as AND convergence.

5.4.4 The Stage

The stage executes, within a process, and can be simulated by a message display specifying it, possibly a time-dependent timer associated with it, encapsulated in stage() procedure.

Void stage(num_stage, duration)
printf("stage %d",num_stage);
tempo(duration) ;

5.4.5 The Macro Stage

The macro-stage is translated using a procedure that is an image similar to the main program, because it is, in fact, a sub-Grafcet; obviously militates for a recursive generation.

6. THE NECESSARY CONFIGURATION FOR SUCH A SYSTEM

The necessary configuration may be: a) Unix or Linux system or any multitasking. b) A graphic screen for entering the Grafcet. c) As input device a keyboard and, if possible, a box of commands. d) As effectors: LEDs, bulbs, effectors.

Simulation process: The screen is divided into two windows: FEN1, for the drawing of the currently active Grafcet (command part). FEN2, specific to the messages illustrating the actions performed by the operative part. Initially, the Grafcet is animated from the initial situation; the arrival of the transitions of the keyboard or of the control box causes the evolution of the Grafcet, ie activation of the new, stage or stages (following the transition), and deactivation of the stage or stages, preceding. The active stages will be highlighted in FEN1, their associated messages in FEN2. The use of the order box is because it allows you to make several entries at once, a case that can be tested for OR divergences, transitions whose branches run in parallel. This will be a realistic simulation.

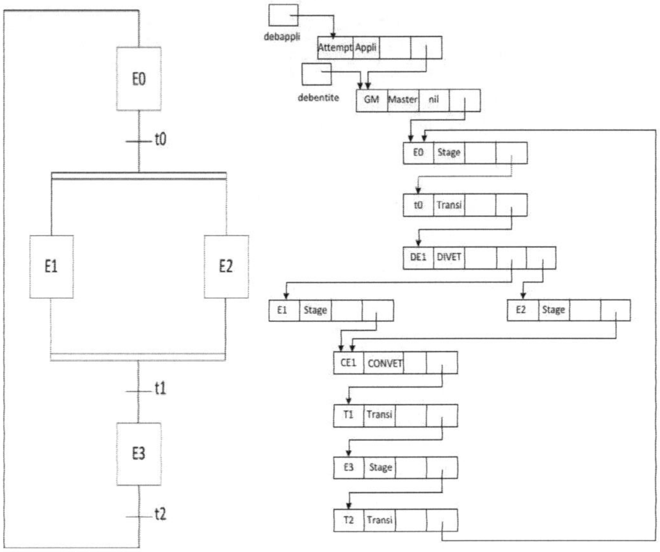


```
#include grafcet.h
Void p1();
Void p2();
Main() {
While (1) {
stage("E0", duration_E0);
Ctransimple;
Tab_fonc[0]=*p1;
tab_fonc[1]=*p2;
divet(2,tab_fonc,tab_pid);
stage("E3",duration_E3);      /*t=1*/
Reinitialize(); /* possibility of reinitializing the
automation or not by reading the variable reinit */
If (reinit==0) break;
}
}
void p1(){
stage("E1",duration_E1);
}
void p2(){
stage("E2",duration_E2);
}
```

a) The Grafcet   b) The internal form   c) The genarated C code scheme

Figure 2. From the Grafcet to the C program

7. CONCLUSION

The method followed, allows to translate many Grafcets, by composition of the most elementary elements. In practical terms, we have established a Grafcet.h library of translation schemes. This library has been tested on examples and is independent of the supposed internal form, it takes into account the automatisms described by a unique Grafcet; and can be extended to explicit macros and procedures relating to forcing processing, used in the case of a hierarchy of Grafcets. Starting from a graphic editor or specialized analyzers, our schematics will constitute a basis for the automatic production of C programs whose execution will behave according to the Grafcet treated. As a result, once the program has been configured, tested and validated, the object code can be implemented on a microcontroller of the actual control system, in particular by explaining everything that pertains to the execution configuration.

Our program can be widely used, because of the simple configuration, hardware and software, it requires: for instance, for educational purposes, for someone (high school student) who wants to learn the Grafcet formalism; or by an automation engineer in his research laboratory who wishes to validate the specifications of his automatism. All that is needed is a computer staff and a linux environment.

From a technical point of view, the adopted internal form can be used for automatic archiving of Grafcets. The archiving of Grafcets is a crucial task for automation engineers who still want to keep track of their initial designs of their automation systems in order to modify specifications when carrying out maintenance operations; or the extension of the functions of the automation to improve the efficiency of their installations. Our perspective in this work, is the translation of the Grafcet in Promela / SPIN. This time, our goal will be mostly formal verification of automation before its implementation on real installations.

ACKNOWLEDGMENT

Our tribute goes to Mr Louis Frécon, who was a professor at INSA / Lyon, and who died on November 11, 2018; for his competitions during the realization of this work.

REFERENCES

Benaouda.N., (2017). *Modélisation et Gestion des Activités de Maintenance dans les systèmes de Production*, doctoral thesis in computer science, SETIF-1 University, Setif, Algeria.

Blanchard. M, (1994). *Comprendre, maîtriser et appliquer le grafcet*, Cepadues, Toulouse. David, R. and Alla.H., (2010). *Discrete, continuous and hybrid Petri nets*. Springer-Verlag, Berlin.

Gonzalez.E, Marichal.R & Hamilton.A, (2016). Ontology-based approach to Basic Grafcet formalization, *Journal of the Chinese Institute of Engineers*, Taylor &Francis, Vol. 39, No. 8. pp. 946-953.

Julius.R, and al (2017). Transformation of GRAFCET to PLC code including hierarchical structures, *Control Engineering Practice,* Elsevier, Vol. 64, pp. 173-194.

Julius.R. and al. (2019). A model-driven approach for transforming GRAFCET specification into PLC code including hierarchical structures, *in IFAC- PapersOnLine*, Vol.52, No.13, pp. 1767–1772.

Miguel-Escrig.O and al (2020). Distributed implementation of Grafcets through IEC 61499. *Proceedings of 2020 25th IEEE International Conference on Emerging Technologies and Factory Automation (ETFA),* Vienna, Austria, 2020, pp. 402-409.

Raynal.M, (2013) *Concurrent Programming - Algorithms, Principles, and Foundations*, springer.

Reeb.B., Chèze.C., (2011). *Développement des grafcets. Des machines simples aux cellules flexibles, du cahier des charges à la programmation*, 2nd edition, ELLIPSES MARKETING.

Remaki.Z, and al (1994). Schémas de traduction grafcet Occam2, *3rd Maghreb Congress on Artificial Intelligence and Software Engineering*, Rabat.

Stevens.W.R, Rago.S.A., (2004). *Advanced Programming in the Unix Environment*, 3rd edition. The Addison-Wesley Professional Computing Series.

DIGITALIZATION OF ADMINISTRATIVE PROCESS IN THE GERMAN HEALTHCARE SYSTEM WITH THE FOCUS ON DENTAL PRACTICES

Karolin Bosch, Linda Mosenthin and Christian Schieder
Technical University of Applied Sciences Amberg-Weiden
Hetzenrichter Weg 15, 92637 Weiden, Germany

ABSTRACT

The digitization of processes in healthcare offers the opportunity to reduce costs and at the same time increase the quality of treatment. A large number of studies show how digitization can optimize and automate processes in healthcare. However, no study has yet addressed the specific requirements of processes digitalization in dental practices. This paper examines the status quo and opportunities of process digitization for dental practices in the German healthcare system.
A structured literature review was used to identify 25 previous relevant papers. Their categorization and analysis revealed existing research gaps, which were explored in detail based on semi-structured in-depth interviews with four dentists. The analysis shows that most organizations are at an early stage of digital transformation, but are actively working to improve the digitization of their processes.
Our findings provide a detailed description of the current challenges and starting points for process digitization and optimization in dentistry. They serve as a basis for further development and help to improve the quality and efficiency of processes in healthcare.

KEYWORDS

German Healthcare System, Dental Practice, Administrative Processes, Business Process Management, Business Process Automation, Process Digitalization

1. INTRODUCTION

Healthcare systems are facing a variety of challenges. The aging society and the increase in chronic diseases, even at a young age, pose major challenges for medical care. It must be provided in the best possible way under limited financial and human resources. Modern technology can help here. In addition to devices in diagnostics and treatment, technology can support the optimization of processes (Marsilio & Prenestini, 2020). To deal with this contradiction of efficiency and quality, process orientation has become increasingly important in recent years. Every healthcare organization should work in a process-oriented manner and align itself accordingly. On this basis, the targeted use of IT can enable the best possible design of processes from a cost and efficiency perspective. Therefore, dental practices are also challenged to become more process-oriented and digital. In order to get an overview of the current state of research on the subject, we conducted a structured literature review at the beginning of our work. This showed that some studies have already looked at the control and automation of processes in the health care sector. However, there are no studies on process management and process digitization in the dental field in the German healthcare system (de Koning et al., 2006; De Ramón Fernández et al., 2019; Mens et al., 2015; Müller & Rogge-Solti, 2011; Rolón et al., 2015). This study aims to close this gap and therefore examines the status quo of process digitization in dental practices. Semi-structured interviews were used to analyze the current perception and situation of different dental practices in the German healthcare system.

The remainder of this paper is organized as follows: Section 2 describes the methodology of the study, Section 3 briefly summarizes the related structured literature review and Section 4 provides insight into the theoretical background of the German healthcare system. The results are presented and discussed in Section 5 before we conclude the paper in Section 6 by highlighting the limitations of our research and providing an outlook for future work.

2. METHODICAL APPROACH

This section explains the methodological procedure in detail: For a focused research, we conducted a structured literature review at the beginning. Since no relevant work on process management and digitization in the German healthcare system was found, expert interviews with dental practices followed. These interviews were semi-structured and based on an interview guideline that was adapted to the respective expert group. The interview questions resulted from the research gaps identified in the literature review. Each interview was scheduled for one hour and was conducted online via video or telephone. The aim was to clearly define the administrative processes in dental practices and their interfaces, as well as the opportunities for optimization and automation through digitization. In order to obtain all the necessary information, the interview guideline was structured accordingly. The first step was to understand the role and task of the interviewee and his organization. Furthermore, all administrative processes in the organization as well as the interfaces between the dentists and all interfaces involved were to be recorded. In addition to the administrative processes, the aim was also to clarify the individual requirements of the participants. To this end, personal requirements for work and process optimization, the current status of digitization, the possibilities and opportunities of digitization, and personal attitudes toward digitization were asked (Barriball & While, 1994; Flick et al., 2004; McIntosh & Morse, 2015). When selecting the participants, care was taken to ensure that the individuals already had experience with the topic of digitization in the dental field or had already dealt with it. In the search for participating in dental practices, over 200 practices were contacted, most of which practice in the state of Bavaria. A total of four interviews (three female; one male interviewee) were conducted in the dental field. Three of the interviewees are practicing dentists, two of whom have a managerial position in a practice and are self-employed. The fourth person was a dental administrative assistant who gave us insights into her daily work.

3. STRUCTURED LITERATURE REVIEW FOR ANALYZING THE RESEARCH STATUS

As a basis for the research work, a structured literature review was conducted on the topic of process management in healthcare. The focus of the structured literature review was to provide a neutral overview of the topic by integrating different research findings and identifying the relevant research gaps to be addressed subsequently. In order to collect all relevant literature, the procedure followed the guidelines of a systematic literature review according to (Vom Brocke et al., 2009). To achieve the most comprehensive result possible, eleven of the most important databases for information systems served as the basis for the research. The following search string was defined: (Business Process* OR Workflow Management OR Process Management) AND (Healthcare).

Subsequently, all eleven databases were searched with the search string and additionally filtered by abstract, keywords, and title. Due to the high sum of papers found and the desired accuracy, the focus was placed on all results with the search string in the title. For further analysis, only papers published between 2015 and May 2020 and written in English were considered. In addition, only articles from peer-reviewed scientific journals and conferences were used to ensure high scientific standards. All results that did not meet the inclusion criteria were filtered out.

After this step, a subtotal of 363 results remained. These articles were manually evaluated by title, keywords, and abstract. The evaluation aimed to find articles suitable for the research topic. With this selection, we conducted a forward and backward search and determined the final corpus of articles (25 results).

The next step was to classify the results following Webster and Watson (Webster & Watson, 2002). The 25 papers on process management in healthcare were categorized according to the most frequently cited approaches to process management, such as business process management (BPM) in general, business process modeling (BPMod), business process improvement (BPI), and business process re-engineering (BPR). Additionally, they were clustered according to their application level. That is, whether the respective method was applied in a specific process, a department, or an entire organization, or even along with several organizations and their interfaces.

Table 1. Classification of previous research paper

Citation	*Methodology*	*Process orientation*						
		Process management				*Application level*		
		BPM	*BP Mod*	*BPI*	*BPR*	*System/ sector*	*Organi-zation*	*Unit*
(Ahmed et al., 2019)	literature review			x		x		
(Andreasson et al., 2016)	grounded theory	x	x				x	x
(Baldassarre & Ricciardi, 2016)	case study	x					x	x
(Buttigieg et al., 2016)	literature review	x				x		
(Cherni et al., 2019)	framework				x	x		
(de Koning et al., 2006)	case study	x					x	
(De Mast et al., 2011)	framework			x			x	
(De Ramón Fernández et al., 201	literature review	x					x	
(El Hadj Amor & Ghannouchi, 2	case study	x					x	
(Fältholm & Jansson, 2008)	case study	x					x	
(Goreva et al., n.d.)	survey	x				x		
(Hellström et al., 2010)	case study	x					x	
(Ilahi et al., 2014)	framework	x						x
(Khodambashi, 2013)	literature review				x		x	
(Lenz & Reichert, 2007)	none	x					x	
(Liu et al., 2017)	framework		x				x	
(Martinho et al., 2015)	case study	x	x					x
(Mens et al., 2015)	case study	x					x	
(Müller & Rogge-Solti, 2011)	proposal		x				x	
(Plsek, 1997)	theoretical			x			x	
(Reichert, 2011)	none	x					x	
(Rolón et al., 2015)	case study		x				x	
(Ruiz et al., 2012)	theoretical		x				x	
(Stephenson & Bandara, 2007)	action research		x				x	x
(Vest & Gamm, 2009)	literature review	x				x		

The following summarizes the findings from the structured literature review. The research devoted most application and attention to process management in hospitals. Processes within or between other types of healthcare organizations were not examined in the papers. The rationale for this is that process management is easier to implement in a specific unit than in a collaborative and complex system with different units (Andreasson et al., 2016; Hellström et al., 2010). In addition, process analysis and improvement focused on medical treatment rather than administrative processes. Measuring internal and external metrics or more real-world experimentation with new processes could lead to more comprehensive and detailed insights into the impact of process management in healthcare systems (Cherni et al., 2019; De Ramón Fernández et al., 2019; El Hadj Amor & Ghannouchi, 2017). Similarly, rigid planning of processes in healthcare is not productive because treatment must be different for each patient and standards are constantly evolving. The targeted use of novel technology could be the solution for flexibility and sustainability in the management of processes. Therefore, the definition of processes must be done first before implementing the appropriate IT (De Ramón Fernández et al., 2019; Lenz & Reichert, 2007; Reichert, 2011). Consequently, the digitization of processes in healthcare offers multiple potentials to optimize defined processes. There are research gaps in the application of process management and process digitization in various healthcare facilities outside the hospital. This paper, therefore, focuses on the current status and opportunities for the digitization of administrative processes in dental practices and their interfaces in the German healthcare system.

4. THEORETICAL STRUCTURE OF THE GERMAN HEALTHCARE SYSTEM IN RELATION TO DENTISTS.

In Germany, the healthcare system is part of the social insurance system. It is a federal system with a division of tasks and competencies at the national and state levels. All the different actors, institutions, and levels shape the complexity of the healthcare system in Germany. The state sets the framework conditions through laws and monitors compliance with them. Medical care is ensured by the self-administration of the most important players (associations for health insurances, hospitals, physicians and dentists). At the federal level, the Federal Joint Committee (G-BA) regulates all framework conditions for medical care within the framework of the laws and state supervision. At the state level, the government and associations are responsible for the regional organization of medical care (*Aufgaben Und Organisation Der GKV | BMG*, 2018; *Gesundheitswesen in Deutschland*, n.d.; Maier & Juschkat, 2020).

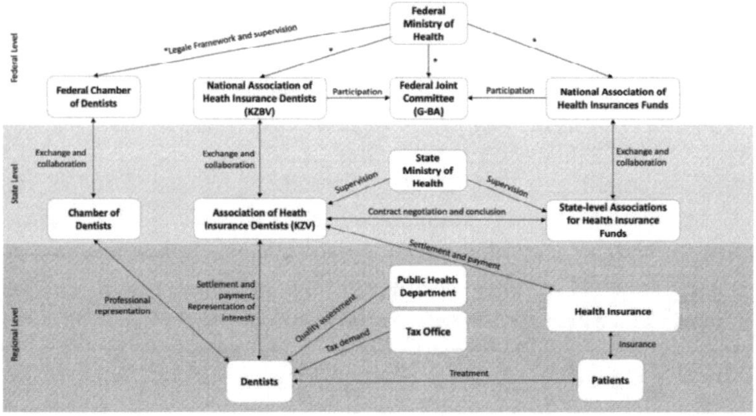

Figure 1. Sociogram of the organizations in the German healthcare in relation to dentists

Dentists are responsible for the prevention, treatment, and follow-up of teeth, jaws, and gums (*Was Macht Ein Angestellter Zahnarzt?*, 2018). The Kassenzahnärztliche Bundesvereinigung (KZBV) represents the interests of all dentists participating in contractual dental care in the treatment of patients with statutory health insurance (*KZBV - Kassenzahnärztliche Bundesvereinigung - Startseite*, n.d.). Besides, the Dental Association is the professional association of dentists (*Startseite: Bundeszahnärztekammer - Arbeitsgemeinschaft Der Deutschen Zahnärztekammern e.V. (BZÄK)*, n.d.). Both organizations are represented at the federal and state level. Figure 1 illustrates the sociogram of the various organizations in the German healthcare system in relation to dentists.

The basis for the digitization of the German healthcare system is the telematics infrastructure (TI). As a digital platform, it connects all organizations in the statutory health insurance system. Within the framework of the TI, patient information can be exchanged securely across the various sectors. The patient has control over his or her data and determines which applications are activated and who receives which data. Connection to the TI is mandatory for all healthcare providers, including dentists. For patients, on the other hand, participation is voluntary (*E-Health – Digitalisierung Im Gesundheitswesen*, 2020; *Telematikinfrastruktur*, n.d.).

5. RESULTS OF THE DEPTH-INTERVIEWS

This section explains and discusses the results of the conducted interviews. On average, the group of interviewees had 19.5 years of professional experience. This testifies a deep and large knowledge background. Concerning digitization, it is evident that the respondents find digitization helpful in their everyday lives, on a Likert scale of 1 to 10. They use digital technology in their everyday life outside the practices and enjoy learning about and trying out new products. In contrast to their everyday lives, however, the reality of the interview participants in the practices looks different. Here, the assessment of the degree of digitization is only just above half (on a Likert scale, 7.25 out of 10). Digitalization is already there, but its possibilities are far from exhausted.

Looking at the interfaces of dental practices with the German healthcare system, these are perceived as good by the respondents (on a Likert scale 7.75 out of 10). According to the information provided, the most important interfaces include the various health insurance companies, external laboratories and the KZV. Tax consultants, the tax office and the health office were listed among the general interfaces.

The current status of process digitization depends on various factors. These factors are the expertise of the staff, process orientation as a management task, the existing IT infrastructure, and the interfaces to other organizations in healthcare or in general. These factors in turn influence each other. The factors and their dependencies are shown in a graphic.

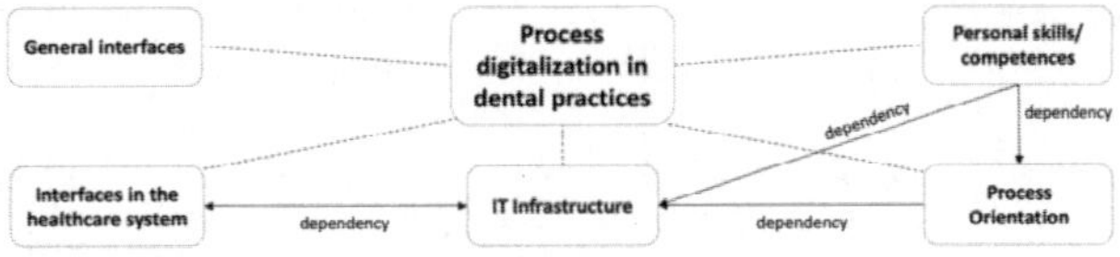

Figure 2. Influence factors of prozess digitalization

The status quo and possible optimization potentials of the influencing factors are presented individually below.

Personal competences

Among the interviewed persons and the staff in the practices, few competencies in process orientation, process management, and digitization are existent. Because of this gap, targeted digitization is a major challenge. The individual practices have to master the digital transformation with the given workforce and without prior knowledge. Therefore, this transformation is a major hurdle and challenge for the individual organization. Also, setting up, optimizing, and digitizing processes is more difficult when there is little knowledge in process management.

Possible starting points are the further training of staff in process management and the targeted digitization of a practice. Partnership-based collaboration and exchange between individual practices on digitization could build up and disseminate the necessary knowledge. Collaborative networks for the digitalization of practices could provide additional knowledge, guidance, and exchange of experience. Another possibility is for long-established associations or state government policies to install experts to serve as advisors.

Future work could analyze the various possibilities and develop a possible concept for professional competence enhancement. As already mentioned, existing expertise affects how process management is conducted. Consequently, personnel competence can be regarded as the basis for process management.

Process management

Despite the low application of process management, five different processes can be defined as areas in the administrative work of dental practices. Scheduling appointments with patients is one of them, as are materials planning, accounting, quality management and personnel management.

Appointments are made by telephone. Digitization and automation of appointment scheduling is not considered possible, as too many parameters have to be taken into account in the targeted scheduling of appointments by trained employees. Material planning is currently done in a hybrid format. As inventory becomes more depleted, order cards are collected manually and orders are placed digitally by the responsible personnel. Accounting is done manually through the tax office. The two processes could thus be fully digitized and automated. Personnel management is partially digitized, depending on the software used. The health department's specifications and guidelines for quality management are made available digitally.

One solution and topic area for future work may be the use of artificial intelligence in making appointments or intelligent help in managing material inventories.

IT infrastructure

There are already initial software solutions that facilitate the daily work in a dental practice and patient education. DAMPSOFT and synMedico should be mentioned here. DAMPSOFT offers a specialized software solution for the billing system required in dental practices and for the entire practice management. This is a modular software system in which the functions can be put together individually. synMedico focuses on patient education and accurate information about the costs incurred for the customer. Both software solutions would be of great advantage for the daily work of any dental practice, but the introduction of such software is fraught with challenges. Apart from the high costs that a dental practice has to incur for the introduction, there is a lack of trained personnel who can both a lack of trained personnel who can manage both the target-oriented implementation and the handling of the new. Also, end-to-end software support often requires practices to restructure. For dental practices, confidence in data security also plays an important role. From their point of view, there is a great risk of data misuse concerning the practice data itself, but also for the patients' data. During the conversion from analog to digital, both in patient education and in areas of material ordering, all files must be kept twice.

A purely digital workflow management with a ticket system and digital inbox would be a welcome solution to simplify the various administrative and medical processes. This would give everyone involved in the process an overview of patient history and the current status of treatment at any time. In addition, everyone can quickly and easily get an overview of the upcoming administrative tasks.

Interfaces in the healthcare system

As mentioned above, dental practices have the most interfaces in the health care system with the state's KZV, health insurance companies, and dental laboratories. Most interfaces to the health insurances exist via the KZV as an intermediary.

Practices send their invoices digitally via the KZV to the respective health insurer. The insurance pays the costs after a verification. The money is paid to the KZV, which forwards the money to the practice. As a result, this process is already fully digital. The exception is if the health insurance has queries during the billing verification. The clarification of the queries is done manually by mail.

Billing reports from each practice are sent collectively in PDF format via the KZV to one health insurance fund per federal state. Based on the PDF reports, the insurance company carries out the performance audits. In the future, performance audits could be completely digitalized.

The approval of dental prostheses by the health insurance fund is currently still done manually. Here, the treatment plans are sent by post either by the patient or the practice to the relevant health insurance company. Some health insurers digitize their incoming mail and process the plans internally digitally, but the original treatment plans still have to be approved and returned. Larger health insurers are working on digitizing the approval process by exchanging treatment plans digitally between practices and the health insurer in the future.

Consequently, dental practices, KZV, and health insurance companies have many interfaces that can be digitized. Here, a joint approach is necessary for a holistic transformation, as the various systems of the organizations must be compatible to achieve frictionless and secure digitization and automation. The focus here is primarily on the protection of personal health data as well as joint goal orientation. Through the TI, the legislature has provided a platform for the digital exchange of health data between the individual service providers. Simultaneously, health insurers and practices are striving to digitize process flows.

Here, a uniform approach is the best possible solution and, at the same time, the greatest challenge. The analysis of possible solutions for the joint transformation of the entire system can be the content of future research work.

General interfaces

In addition to the interfaces in the healthcare system, there are a large number of general interfaces that have a low level of digitization.

These include the interface to courts, tax offices, and tax consultants. The challenge here is to find the right approach between analog and digital and to be able to guarantee data completeness. In this case, many invoices, treatments data, and other data take months to retrieve and review. Finding a digital solution and sending the required files to the tax advisor is almost impossible. For this reason, a possible digital solution for the entire billing and court processes would be a huge. This includes all general areas and interfaces that are necessary to operate a business in Germany.

From the generated results of the interviews with dental practices, it is clear that these interfaces can in principle be easily digitized. However, the German judicial and tax systems are established systems that are similar in complexity to the healthcare system. Therefore, the digital transformation of these areas and interfaces is a holistic challenge that will take a long time. The basis here is that each dental practice is supported in this process and has clear contact persons.

In summary, it can be said that there are various starting points for increased and targeted digitization of administrative processes in dental practices. The possibilities presented for the respective factors stand for themselves as starting points. When analyzing and pursuing these, the dependencies on the other factors must be taken into account.

Dental practices hope to build a better relationship with their patients through digitization. This would lead to more transparency, targeted support of medical treatment and education, and thus to shorter treatment times and costs.

6. LIMITATIONS AND CONCLUSIONS

This work focused on the German healthcare system and dentistry there. Therefore, no conclusions can be drawn for other countries or medical fields. The lack of a view from the perspective of patients, health insurers, the Association of Statutory Health Insurance Dentists, and the federal government represents an opportunity for further research.

In addition, a more detailed listing of all administrative processes in the practices would be useful to gain an even better insight into the daily work of medical staff in the dental field. For this, a larger number of participants would be important, as well as the exact elaboration of the individual roles and requirements. Our work can be a basis for further research in the field of digitalization and automation of processes in dentistry. The study of the processes and the problems of dental practices have given the first insight into this area and shows many approaches to optimize the processes. The development of a maturity model for process digitization in the healthcare system and specifically for dentists is required as a theoretical framework. Based on this theoretical background, further steps and scientific work could be derived.

To shape the future of a digital, targeted, and modern healthcare system, the points mentioned in the paper should be elaborated, deepened, and implemented. Digitalization is a topic that affects everyone and also has an impact on all areas of life. For this reason, dentistry must not be left out and digital and innovative solutions should be developed for this area in the future.

REFERENCES

Ahmed, E. S., Ahmad, M. N., & Othman, S. H. (2019). Business process improvement methods in healthcare: a comparative study. *International Journal of Health Care Quality Assurance*, *32*(5), 887–908. https://doi.org/10.1108/IJHCQA-07-2017-0116

Andreasson, J., Eriksson, A., & Dellve, L. (2016). Health care managers' views on and approaches to implementing models for improving care processes. *Journal of Nursing Management*, *24*(2), 219–227. https://doi.org/10.1111/jonm.12303

Aufgaben und Organisation der GKV | BMG. (2018). https://www.bundesgesundheitsministerium.de/themen/krankenversicherung/grundprinzipien/aufgaben-und-organisation-der-gkv.html

Baldassarre, F., & Ricciardi, F. (2016). Business process management to manage clinical risk: a case study in the healthcare sector. *Conference" Excellence in ..., September*, 37–50. http://www.toulonveronaconf.eu/papers/index.php/tvc/article/view/400

Barriball, L., & While, A. (1994). Collecting data using a semi-structured interview: a discussion paper. In *Journal of Advanced Nursing* (Vol. 19).

Buttigieg, S., Dey, P. K., & Gauci, D. (2016). Business process management in health care: current challenges and future prospects. *Innovation and Entrepreneurship in Health*, *January*, 1. https://doi.org/10.2147/ieh.s68183

Cherni, J., Martinho, R., & Ghannouchi, S. A. (2019). Towards Improving Business Processes based on preconfigured KPI target values, Process Mining and Redesign Patterns. *Procedia Computer Science*, *164*, 279–284. https://doi.org/10.1016/j.procs.2019.12.184

de Koning, H., Verver, J. P. S., van den Heuvel, J., Bisgaard, S., & Does, R. J. M. M. (2006). Lean six sigma in healthcare. *Journal for Healthcare Quality : Official Publication of the National Association for Healthcare Quality*, *28*(2), 4–11. https://doi.org/10.1111/j.1945-1474.2006.tb00596.x

De Mast, J., Kemper, B., Does, R. J. M. M., Mandjes, M., & Van Der Bijl, Y. (2011). Process improvement in healthcare: Overall resource efficiency. *Quality and Reliability Engineering International*, *27*(8), 1095–1106. https://doi.org/10.1002/qre.1198

De Ramón Fernández, A., Ruiz Fernández, D., & Sabuco García, Y. (2019). Business Process Management for optimizing clinical processes: A systematic literature review. *Health Informatics Journal*. https://doi.org/10.1177/1460458219877092

E-Health – Digitalisierung im Gesundheitswesen. (2020). https://www.bundesgesundheitsministerium.de/e-health-initiative.html

El Hadj Amor, E. A., & Ghannouchi, S. A. (2017). Towards KPI-Based Health Care Process Improvement. *Procedia Computer Science*, *121*, 767–774. https://doi.org/10.1016/j.procs.2017.11.099

Fältholm, Y., & Jansson, A. (2008). The implementation of process orientation at a Swedish hospital. *The International Journal of Health Planning and Management*, *23*(3), 219–233. https://doi.org/10.1002/hpm.884

Flick, U., von Kardorff, E., & Steinke, I. (2004). *Wolff in Flick et a . July*, 178–183. https://www.researchgate.net/profile/Stephan_Wolff2/publication/305496229_Wolff_in_Flick_et_a/links/5792046008aec89db77fca3c/Wolff-in-Flick-et-a.pdf#page=268

Gesundheitswesen in Deutschland. (n.d.). Retrieved August 10, 2020, from https://vbw-zukunftsrat.de/Gesundheit-und-Medizin/Analyse?box=56&box_56=Gesundheitswesen-in-Deutschland

Goreva, N., Mishra, S., Draus, P., & Caputo, D. (n.d.). *Impacts of Organizational Structure and Business Processes on Effective Security Governance in Healthcare Organizations*. 1–12. http://proxy1.ncu.edu/login?url=http://search.ebscohost.com/login.aspx?direct=true&db=bth&AN=116211858&site=eds-live

Hellström, A., Lifvergren, S., & Quist, J. (2010). Process management in healthcare: Investigating why it's easier said than done. *Journal of Manufacturing Technology Management*, *21*(4), 499–511. https://doi.org/10.1108/17410381011046607

Ilahi, L., Ghannouchi, S. A., & Martinho, R. (2014). Healthcare information systems promotion: From an improved management of telemedicine processes to home healthcare processes. *ACM International Conference Proceeding Series*, *June 2016*, 333–338. https://doi.org/10.1145/2669711.2669920

Khodambashi, S. (2013). Business Process Re-engineering Application in Healthcare in a Relation to Health Information Systems. *Procedia Technology*, *9*(2212), 949–957. https://doi.org/10.1016/j.protcy.2013.12.106

KZBV - Kassenzahnärztliche Bundesvereinigung - Startseite. (n.d.). Retrieved August 8, 2020, from https://www.kzbv.de/

Lenz, R., & Reichert, M. (2007). IT support for healthcare processes - premises, challenges, perspectives. *Data and Knowledge Engineering*, *61*(1), 39–58. https://doi.org/10.1016/j.datak.2006.04.007

Liu, C., Xiong, H., Papadimitriou, S., Ge, Y., & Xiao, K. (2017). A Proactive Workflow Model for Healthcare Operation and Management. *IEEE Transactions on Knowledge and Data Engineering*, *29*(3), 586–598. https://doi.org/10.1109/TKDE.2016.2631537

Maier, C., & Juschkat, T. (2020). Digitization in the German Health Care System - An Analysis of the Status Quo Using the Example of the Dental Sector. *European Journal of Business and Management Research*, *5*(3). https://doi.org/10.24018/ejbmr.2020.5.3.331

Marsilio, M., & Prenestini, A. (2020). Making it happen: Challenges and transformations in health care processes, people management, and decision-making. *Health Services Management Research*, *33*(2), 53–54. https://doi.org/10.1177/0951484820906314

Martinho, R., Rijo, R., & Nunes, A. (2015). Complexity Analysis of a Business Process Automation: Case Study on a Healthcare Organization. *Procedia Computer Science*, *64*, 1226–1231. https://doi.org/10.1016/j.procs.2015.08.510

McIntosh, M. J., & Morse, J. M. (2015). Situating and constructing diversity in semi-structured interviews. *Global Qualitative Nursing Research*, *2*. https://doi.org/10.1177/2333393615597674

Mens, J., Ahlers, B., van Hattem, B., & Ravesteyn, P. (2015). Value-Based Healthcare Through a Standardised Process Management Model. *ECMLG 2015 Proceedings*, 8.

Müller, R., & Rogge-Solti, A. (2011). BPMN for Healthcare Processes. In *undefined*. http://spz.charite.de

Plsek, P. E. (1997). Systematic design of healthcare processes. *Quality and Safety in Health Care*, *6*(1), 40–48. https://doi.org/10.1136/qshc.6.1.40

Reichert, M. (2011). What BPM technology can do for healthcare process support. *Lecture Notes in Computer Science (Including Subseries Lecture Notes in Artificial Intelligence and Lecture Notes in Bioinformatics)*, *6747 LNAI*, 2–13. https://doi.org/10.1007/978-3-642-22218-4_2

Rolón, E., Chavira, G., Orozco, J., & Soto, J. P. (2015). Towards a Framework for Evaluating Usability of Business Process Models with BPMN in Health Sector. *Procedia Manufacturing*, *3*(February 2016), 5603–5610. https://doi.org/10.1016/j.promfg.2015.07.748

Ruiz, F., Garcia, F., Calahorra, L., Llorente, C., Gonçalves, L., Daniel, C., & Blobel, B. (2012). Business process modeling in healthcare. *Studies in Health Technology and Informatics*, *179*(May 2014), 75–87. https://doi.org/10.3233/978-1-61499-086-4-75

Startseite: Bundeszahnärztekammer - Arbeitsgemeinschaft der Deutschen Zahnärztekammern e.V. (BZÄK). (n.d.). Retrieved August 8, 2020, from https://www.bzaek.de/

Stephenson, C., & Bandara, W. (2007). Enhancing best practice in public health: Using process patterns for business process management. *Proceedings of the 15th European Conference on Information Systems, ECIS 2007*, *2007*, 2123–2134.

Telematikinfrastruktur. (n.d.). Retrieved August 10, 2020, from https://www.gematik.de/telematikinfrastruktur/

Vest, J. R., & Gamm, L. D. (2009). A critical review of the research literature on Six Sigma, Lean and StuderGroup's Hardwiring Excellence in the United States: The need to demonstrate and communicate the effectiveness of transformation strategies in healthcare. *Implementation Science*, *4*(1), 1–9. https://doi.org/10.1186/1748-5908-4-35

Vom Brocke, J., Simons, A., Niehaves, B., Riemer, K., Plattfaut, R., & Cleven, A. (2009). Reconstructing the giant: On the importance of rigour in documenting the literature search process. *17th European Conference on Information Systems, ECIS 2009*.

Was macht ein angestellter Zahnarzt? (2018). https://www.deutscher-zahnarzt-service.de/blog/was-macht-ein-angestellter-zahnarzt

Webster, J., & Watson, R. T. (2002). Analyzing the past to prepare for the future : Writing a literature review Reproduced with permission of the copyright owner . Further reproduction prohibited without permission . *MIS Quarterly*, *26*(2), xiii–xxiii. https://doi.org/10.2307/4132319

OPEN SPATIAL DATA FOR DECISION MAKING – REQUIREMENTS AND QUALITATIVE CONSIDERATIONS

Hardy Pundt
Harz University of Applied Sciences
Friedrichstr. 57-59, 38855 Wernigerode, Germany

ABSTRACT

Open data play an increasing role in various societal fields, administration, economy, science and others. This concerns also open, spatial data which can be used in space-related decision-making. Open spatial data will be introduced as an important source of information. However, open spatial data must meet specific qualitative requirements. Pros and Cons will be identified and recommendations will be given which characteristics should be considered when using such data. The experiences described are based on the results of a transdisciplinary project that was aimed at deciding on prioritized climate change adaptation measures.

KEYWORDS

Spatial Decision Support Systems, Open Data, Geographical Information Systems, Web Mapping, Geodata

1. INTRODUCTION

"Data is a key resource in the modern world" (Kitchin 2014). Open data, however, has raised interest during the last decade in various sectors, administrations, as well as enterprises. Especially in society, open data play an important role because they can be accessed and used by citizens in a manner that is only possible through the wide spread of Web- and mobile applications. Open data has various advantages that makes them an adequate resource to support computer-aided data analysis and decision-making. Open spatial data, as a specific type of open data, can be used widely in different sectors, such as science, governmental administration, business, and by citizens in view of the saying that more than 80 % of decisions made in economy and administration rely, at least to a certain extent, on spatial information.

Benefits of using open data concern, among others, (no) costs and large reuse potential, availability and accessibility, whereas risks are seen concerning privacy and fraud, inaccuracy and legality. But there are more constraints and considerations that have to be taken into account when evaluating the benefits of open, spatial data. Furthermore, the usage of such data should be seen from different perspectives, because the requirements in business, government, science or concerning the usage by citizens are diverse.

This paper will introduce briefly what open, spatial data means in terms of different data types, e. g. qualitative vs. quantitative data, structured, semi-structured and unstructured data, captured, exhaust, transient and derived data, and others, as Kitchin (2014) proposes such categories. The paper will summarize some benefits, as well as risks of applying open data. It will describe an example that explains difficulties and opportunities of developing a Web-based, online mapping system that includes, among others, open spatial data. The example is thought to demonstrate that openness can lead to more effective decision making, if specific quality constraints are considered. This will lead to conclusions that affect the ongoing discussion on proper usage of open data to support spatial analysis and decision making.

2. OPEN, SPATIAL DATA

Open data are seen commonly as data that are published on the Internet in a way that anyone can freely use, re-use and redistribute this data (Open Knowledge Foundation 2021). Open government data is data that is owned by a public sector body (Kucera & Chlapek, 2014), whereas open data in business means often each kind of data that is abundant and free which makes it a potential source of great opportunities for all businesses, regardless of their location, size or sector (NibusinessInfo 2021). Open, spatial data include "volunteered geographic information (VGI)" a term that was introduced by Goodchild (2007).

Van Loenen et al. (2018) have emphasized that, "in a rather naïve way, it was thought that open data could be used directly by everyone, by all citizens and businesses" but they conclude that this is not the case. This citation confirms experiences that were gathered during a project ("BebeR") that was based on a living lab approach thus including actors from administration, organizations, education and citizens (Pundt and Heilmann 2020). It will be described later in more detail. The steps to establish such a "common data platform" to serve all "concerned parties" raised some challenges that were not expected at the beginning of the project. At the end, however, it was discovered that specific problems that occurred were due to lacking "openness" of data. Discussions of the problems led to the result that open data require the proper consideration of qualitative, security and other constraints, otherwise the acceptance of potential data users is low. Reliability of open data, however, becomes a central quality constraint at that point. Reliability concerns different components, such as the data collection procedures, quality management, data security and others.

In general, open, spatial data can be provided in two ways, by default and by request. Figure 1 is presenting the approaches. Whereas in the first case data are collected and provided without considering who possibly will use the data, the second case describes a situation in which a user asks for the provision of specific data for particular purposes. In such a case, data will only be provided if a formally correct request has been sent.

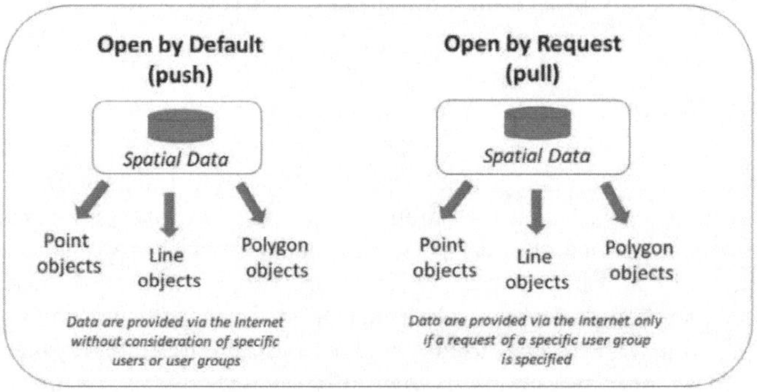

Figure 1. Open data by default and by request (Hörster and Kärle (2019), modified). Adopted concerning a focus on open, spatial data, thus representing point-, line- or polygon objects

Klessmann et al (2012) summarized some pros and cons of open data. Table 1 presents an extended version, including aspects suggested by the Open Knowledge Foundation (OKF 2021), Jackson et al. (2013) and own experiences related to the BebeR-project.

Table 1. Pros and cons of open spatial data: experiences from Klessmann et al (2012), Jackson et al. (2013) and the BebeR-project

Pros	Cons
Klessmann et al. 2012:	*Klessmann et al.2012:*
Re-use and access	Assessment of quality is difficult
Achieving greater audience	Metadata often lacking
Enhances overall information basis	Context-knowledge often not available, which raises the danger of data misuse
Jackson et al.2013:	
Open spatial data and VGI means to bring the general public into the realm of map production functions traditionally reserved for official agencies	*Jackson et al.2013:* Spatial errors between different open datasets Differences in completeness

Open data and VGI can extend helpfully official, administrative datasets *BebeR (Pundt 2018; Pundt and Heilmann 2020):* Supporting integration of different datasets (data sharing and redistribution) Enabling integration of spatial layers that would possibly be disregarded Supporting multi-perspective view on problems and problem solutions Improving of decision making, possibly accomplish information benefits due to adding open data Possibly more current data compared with official datasets Easing data acquisition due to voluntary citizens that act as data collectors or "sensors"	Volunteered data is usually provided with little to no information on mapping standards, quality control procedures, and metadata in general *BebeR (Pundt 2018; Pundt and Heilmann 2020):* Reliability of data in terms of quality parameters and security is difficult, if not impossible, to evaluate (e. g. completeness, spatial accuracy, currentness of data) Insufficient spatial accuracy Improper spatial reference systems or scales Unsureness concerning professional data collection procedures

3. INTEGRATION OF OPEN DATA IN AN ONLINE MAPPING SYSTEM

3.1 Project Background

From 2017 – 2020, the "BebeR-project" has been carried out. The project was aimed at developing and assessing the vulnerability of mountainous areas concerning soil erosion taking into account the challenges provoked by climate change. The investigation area for the development of vulnerability assessment methods was the administrative district of Mansfeld-Südharz, situated in the south of the German federal state of Saxony-Anhalt. Within the framework of carrying out computer simulations it appeared that heavy rainfall events in the concerned region might increase in future. Heavy rainfall, however, can lead to cumulative soil erosion which can, in turn, cause damages in terms of soil loss, as well as damages to infrastructures such as roads, bridges, or houses. These possible future events require decision making to mitigate the threats. This cannot be done without considering the different interests in the region: water management, nature protection, agriculture and forestry, regional planning, settling, urbanization and economy. Due to this situation, various partners were collaborating in the BebeR-project to discuss related problems and alternative solutions, taking into account possibly occurring and varying climate change scenarios (Pundt 2018).

3.2 Integration of Different Kinds of Spatial Data in an Online Mapping System

Spatial decision making in multi-actor projects must necessarily be based on comprehensive and adequate data. Within the BebeR-project, establishing such a comprehensive spatial database was an important step to enable the participating stakeholders, including scientists, different administrational and further partners, to use the data from not only one, but all concerned sectors. The intention is, that looking across sectoral borders may lead to more comprehensive and qualitatively better decisions instead of wearing sectoral blinkers. The database was conceptualized and implemented during a foregoing project, and further developed during the BebeR-initiative (Pundt and Heilmann 2020; Pundt 2018). It resulted finally in an interactive, online mapping system including a great variety of spatial datasets (layers) from different sectors. To implement the system, standardized Geographical Information Services were used. The aim was to enable users to overlay different spatial data layers aiming at the analysis of data from different perspectives and thus broadening the information basis for decision making. In such a way, the concept of the online mapping system follows the "Open by Default"-approach, as described in figure 1. The integration of spatial data from different sources was appreciated very much by the project partners because before starting the project most actors had only access to their "own" data, which implied a relatively "closed view" ("blinkers") on the problems that occur due to climate change. Using the data from the online mapping system, it was possible, for example, to integrate data in such a way that areas vulnerable to soil erosion were identified under consideration of water-, soil-, geological-, agricultural-, vegetation-related, infrastructural-, and other information. The growth of the database increased the opportunities for participants to look on the different data layers in a kind of a "holistic" information platform. The system enabled users to integrate datasets aimed at more sophisticated analyses. This led to new maps, which, in turn, could be provided for other users via the same system. In such a way, the online mapping system was soon accepted as an ideal basis for discussion of problem solutions, and alternative approaches, considering not only a "sector-wise", but varying perspectives and scenarios. The maps became decision support tools on the one hand, and information means for the actors, as well as the public.

However, in some cases, it was not easy to convince administrational officers to provide their datasets as "open" layers in the mapping system due to legal and security reasons. Apart from such official datasets, openly accessible spatial data was integrated, e. g. topographical data from the world-wide OpenStreetMap project, "a map of the world, created by people like you and free to use under an open license" (OSM 2021), and data from citizen-based mapping initiatives to collect information on invasive species (KORINA 2021; see Figure 2).

Figure 2. Official, administrative data (dark area objects: *flooding areas*), as well as open, spatial data (point objects: *invasive species* and underlying topography: *OpenStreetMap*) in one map. Both kinds of data are integrated and used by different stakeholders to support decision making in spatial planning

3.3 Special Considerations Concerning Decision Making

During workshops, the maps and different alternatives of measures to reduce soil erosion in view of climate chnge were discussed intensively within the framework of the BebeR-project. Selected measures to reduce soil erosion in vulnerable areas were prioritized and those considered as being the "most important and feasible" measures were selected to be realized within the next few months or years in the pilot region. The following list mentions some of the discussed options:

- Minimization of soil erosion through change of agricultural practices
- Storage of great water amounts occurring during heavy rainfall events
- Reduction of flow velocity in rivers to reduce erosion potential
- Analyzing habitats of invasive plants based on various spatial datasets; developing concepts to mitigate invasive species in certain areas, followed by afforestation or reafforestation aimed at reducing soil erosion

The online mapping system served as a comprehensive and reliable data basis to analyze data and compose maps that were used as basis for discussion, and (visual) decision support. Different stakeholders were applying the system for a variety of purposes, but foremost as a means to understand the different perspectives and opportunities, thus coming finally to *common* results.

4. CONCLUSIONS

Based on an "Open by Default" – approach, the BebeR-online mapping system provides both, open spatial data, as well as official administrative data and data from other providers. Open spatial data result from well-known initiatives as OpenStreetMap (OSM), the "fastest growing community mapping project of all times" (Digital Geography 2021), as well as data provided from citizen-science (or VGI-) initiatives (KORINA 2021). When implementing the system, the main difficulties occurred not technically. Due to the usage of standardized Geographic Information Services, the technical problems were predominantly solved. However, the discussions with stakeholders to convince them to provide the data in an open, commonly accessible web-based system were quite time consuming in some cases. Even the arguments that good decisions on spatial problems require the availability of at least all data that concern the problem to be solved, was sometimes not enough to persuade representatives. Therefore, the online mapping system, originally planned as "completely open", was secured in a way that users only could access data when registering as a legal user, by Email address and Password. Jackson et al (2013) hint on differences between web-based spatial datasets concerning accuracy and completeness, and that the "vagueness can be degradation in the utility of VGI for decision making; however, these effects have not been studied" (Jackson et al 2013). This deficit does probably not only affect positional accuracy and completeness, but more, e. g. semantic accuracy, granularity of attributes describing spatial objects, and reliability, as well as data security aspects. This needs further research in future.

Finally, the users of the BebeR-system were well-disposed to the application because it contains both, official, administrative data, and open spatial data. But it must be added with emphasis, that open data are only accepted as information basis, if specific qualitative requirements are fulfilled. Clearly, the stakeholders participating in BebeR uttered that they would prefer to renounce on the usage of open data, if such quality parameters are not ensured. Especially concerning administrative decision-making, open spatial data can hardly be included in analyses and resulting maps, and therefore in decision-making, if they do not serve the corresponding legal, and qualitative requirements.

REFERENCES

Digital Geography, 2021, *How to use OpenStreetMap*, guides for beginners and advanced users. https://digital-geography.com/use-openstreetmap-guides-beginners-advanced-users-learnosm-org/ (accessed 09-01-2021)

Goodchild, M., 2007. Citizens as Sensors: The World of Volunteered Geography. *GeoJournal 69(4)*, pp 211-221.

Horster, E., Kärle, E., 2019. *Braucht der Tourismus Open Data*? Open Data Germany. https://open-data-germany.org/braucht-der-tourismus-open-data/ (accessed 19-01-2021)

Jackson, S.P., Mullen, W., Agouris, P., Crooks, A., Croitoru, A., Stefanidis, A., 2013. Assessing Completeness and Spatial Error of Features in Volunteered Geographic Information. *ISPRS Int. Journal of Geo-Information 2*, pp. 507-530.

Kitchin, R., 2014. *The Data Revolution*. Big Data, Open Data, Data Infrastructures and their Consequences. SAGE Publications, London.

Klessmann, J., Denker, P., Schieferdecker, I., Eschulz, S.E., 2012. Open Government Data Deutschland.

KORINA, 2021. *Koordinationsstelle Invasive Neophyten in Schutzgebieten Sachsen-Anhalts*. https://www.korina.info/ (accessed 05-01-2021)

Kucera, J., Chlapek, D., 2014. Benefits and Risks of Open Government Data. *Journal of Systems Integration 2014/1*, pp. 30-41.

NibusinessInfo, 2021. *Open data opportunities for business*. https://www.nibusinessinfo.co.uk/content/open-data-opportunities-business (accessed 01-11-2020)

OKF, 2021. Open Knowledge Foundation - The Open Data Handbook. Available from: https://opendatahandbook.org/guide/en/ (accessed 15-01-2021)

OSM (2021): OpenStreetMap. https://www.openstreetmap.org/ (accessed 20-01-2021)

Pundt, H., Heilmann, A., 2020. Building Collaborative Partnerships: An Example of a 3rd Mission Activity in the Field of Local Climate Change Adaptation. In: Leal, W.F., Alves, F., Azeiteiro, U., Manolas, E.: *Universities as Living Labs for Sustainable Development. Supporting the Implementation of the Sustainable Development Goals: Vol. II.*, Springer Nature Switzerland, Cham, pp 621-636.

Pundt, H., 2018. Collaboration of Science, Practice and Citizens in the Field of Climate Change Adaptation, supported by Interactive GI-Tools. *21st Int. Conference on Geographic Information Sciences Lund/Sweden. Proceedings*, https://agile-online.org/programme-2018/accepted-papers-and-posters-2018.

Van Loenen, B., Vancauwenberghe, G., Croempvoets, J., 2018. *Open Data Exposed*. Information Technology and Law Series, Vol. 30. T.M.C. Asser Press, Springer.

USE OF ARTIFICIAL INTELLIGENCE TECHNOLOGIES IN E-COMMERCE AND BUSINESS PROCESSES

Anna Nikolajeva
Rezekne Academy of Technologies
Atbrīvošanas aleja 115, Rezekne, LV- 4601, Latvia

ABSTRACT

The research is endeavoured to explore artificial intelligence technology adoption in electronic commerce and business processes. The research dedicated to the author's doctoral theses it is in its opening stage. The author's doctoral thesis meant to be about digital marketing personalization using artificial intelligence technologies. The doctoral thesis will aim to collect and analyze specific e-commerce company marketing and sales data and create a machine learning algorithm that will increase key performance indicators by personalized marketing. Machine learning technologies algorithm will initiate in inner website upsells, cross-sells, down-sells, popups and banner display settings. Artificial intelligence technologies today are in all areas. Important to understand what is happening in different industries and markets currently to prove that personalization is the key to a successful marketing strategy almost in all areas and especially in e-commerce to justify the author's doctoral theses topicality.

KEYWORDS

Machine Learning, Artificial Intelligence, Electronic Commerce, Digital Marketing, Business Processes

1. INTRODUCTION

A business process defines a set of interrelated or interacting actions - methods, steps, and activities. All business processes must be related to the organization's goals and built to add value and include human resources and technologies managed by human resources (Röglinger et al. 2012). Artificial intelligence technologies can optimize many business processes by decreasing human resource necessity and the human factor.

Electronic commerce (e-commerce) is the selling of goods and services via computer networks. Internet commerce considered to be the most popular industry in e-commerce. The benefits of Internet e-commerce lie in the global advantage and accessibility of the Internet, where entrepreneurs acquire this commerce on an unlimited geographical scale (Khurana, 2019).

Digital marketing is a form of marketing that focuses on marketing activities in the digital environment, meaning several key activity platforms - email marketing, web browser marketing, social network marketing, smartphone marketing (Yannopoulos, 2011). Digital marketing is an advertising channel in e-commerce. If e-commerce business uses an effective marketing strategy, a consumer will have a relevant product or service. Until the goods arrive, they take the long way to their customer, and in these processes, artificial intelligence technology is an essential part.

Artificial intelligence is a wide-ranging branch of computer science concerned with building smart machines capable of performing tasks that typically require human intelligence. Artificial intelligence is an interdisciplinary science with multiple approaches. Advancements in machine learning and deep learning currently are creating a paradigm shift in virtually every sector of the tech industry (Schank, 1991). An important subsector of artificial intelligence is machine learning - learning from experience, not from direct programming. Machine learning algorithms subordinate to new data, applications learn, grow, change and evolve themselves (Wang et al. 2019).

Tasks of the research:

1. To study the current situation in the influence of artificial intelligence technologies in different industries.
2. To draw conclusions substantiating the topicality of the topic of the doctoral thesis.

Research object: explore artificial intelligence technology adoption in electronic commerce and business processes.

The subject of the research: topicality of the doctoral thesis. Research methods:

1. Synthesis method used to re-analyse and compare published studies to produce a personal interpretation of the current market situation using AI technologies in different industries.
2. Analysis method used to analyse and compare published studies to prove topicality of the doctoral theses in the current market situation in e-commerce using AI technologies in digital marketing tools.

The theoretical base consists of theoretical literature of foreign authors, materials published in Internet resources, scientific articles of foreign authors, statistical data, personal experience of the author.

The empirical basis of the research: World.

Study period: September 2019 – October 2020.

2. BODY OF PAPER

As a result of the research, industries that use artificial intelligence technologies were analyzed. For example, Global Positioning System navigation. If current location and speed are known, that data is used to create a map of the current traffic. Machine learning in such cases helps to estimate all possible scenarios (Wang et al. 2018). Online transport networks: When booking a trip, the app calculates the cost of the trip. Jeff Schneider, head of Uber's Advanced Technologies Group, revealed in an interview that they are using machine learning technology to determine price rises over time, forecasting demand (Martin, 2019). New commercial aeroplanes use a combination of Flight Management System, Global Positioning System, motion sensors and computer systems to track its location in flight. So the pilot spends only seven minutes flying the plane manually, and most of those minutes are spent during landing. Corporations such as Mercedes, Tesla, Google, BMW are developing their autonomous vehicles. Alphabet's Waymo, GM's Cruise, Argo AI, Intel's Mobileye, and Tesla have all pushed forward in the autonomous-mobility business (DeBord, 2019). The product route begins when the supplies are purchased and the design formed. Production and optimization of production processes meeting the need to meet different inside countries standards, international standards, and consumer standards. Finding the right target audience for the product and presenting it in a way that makes sense of its benefits: developing a marketing strategy. Logistics chain management delivers the product to the consumer as quickly as possible. Things mentioned have to be achieved at the same time company has limited resources and must profit, along motivating its employees, providing job security and paying taxes. Depending on the industry, these processes can be much more intense with higher risk factors, that why artificial intelligence is a resource, which is a real opportunity for all industries.

Social networks such as Facebook, Instagram, and Twitter analyze hundreds of variables and predict the order in which a user should display posts in the personal news feed. Learning from user reaction - read by clicking on an article, leaving a comment. Also pressing the reaction buttons - like, hide, spam. Algorithm attributes match points to ads that help not only users but also marketers to outline the precise ads for their products (Kalyanam, 2017).

Artificial intelligence use can help in surgical operations - heart, colorectal and thoracic. Artificial intelligence with robots in surgery provides greater accuracy, lower risk of infection, less blood loss, shorter hospital stays and faster recovery time. Another innovation for patients and professionals is automated digital medical records. Electronic health records use a machine-learning algorithm to help document, organize, and save records in a digital form. It helps reduce the time it takes to find information, and digitalized health records make it easier for patients to access their data (Future Healthcare Jurnal, 2019).

Educational sector developed - parents can see how their children are doing at school anytime using online systems. iTalk2Learn is an online learning system designed for primary school students. A joint project developed in Europe requires that machine learning used to compile personal lesson plans for students. In 2016 Duolingo announced iPhone-compatible chatbots for learning to speak fluently in French, Italian, and Spanish. Following conventional bots, users proceed with the application using hints in their native language (Guilherme, 2019).

In the employment sector, artificial intelligence used to automate the initial recruitment process and select suitable candidates from an existing database such as ZipRecruiter. Artificial intelligence automated tools scan candidate profiles to find industry-specific keywords helping find the right candidates while filtering unsuitable ones. Within seconds, the algorithm can review hundreds of candidates profiles and offer the most fitting candidates (Dowling, 2019).

In logistics, artificial intelligence technologies used with new intensity. Artificial intelligence technology is used in warehouse automation to predict demand for particular products. Based on this data, it is possible to modify the demand for goods required by a specific time, for example, more fans in summer. Forecasting this demand and planning logistics means lower logistics costs. Ocado is a supermarket chain that has developed an automated warehouse. The system is based on a robot and can handle 65,000 orders a week. The robot's main task is moving, sorting and lifting goods in the warehouse. Ocado automation reduces the need for a large staff and lead times (Kleinman, 2018).

Personalizing site content using artificial intelligence technology can automatically generate content such as archive updates, sports reports, news. Such services provide tools such as Quill. Quill can identify the hidden potential of data and allow people to understand the exact meaning of the text. Advanced machine learning technology learns from scratch using algorithms that generated initially. Robot software learns from its data and interactions with people who start to contact them. In this way, it learns to communicate and create its own text (Shum et al. 2018). Chatbot based on artificial intelligence technology includes the ability to discuss using specific objects. For example, if someone asks, "Can you eat the house?", Mitsuku looks for "house" properties. Finds "as containing" set to "bricks" and answers "no" because the house is inedible.

Artificial intelligence is the technology used to learn about people and the basic things that interest people, what makes people what they are today. It goes far beyond age or gender generalizations, with machine learning technology it is possible to understand if a person is a cartoon, dog or cat fan, but granted that all of these people have the same hair colour (Davenport et al. 2020). In the e-commerce space, artificial intelligence use to find out what customers prefer and how they want to see the information to purchase. Personalization and recommendations are the most popular trends in the global e-commerce space. Large amounts of data can thoroughly present the online activities of hundreds of millions of users using. It is possible to create data-based product recommendations tailored to a specific user or group of users by automatically segmenting them. By analyzing the data collected on websites, you can determine which subpages the users were using. Based on a variety of information: past user activity, preferences, decisions, social media data, location, whether - results will be aggregated and reflected. Referral systems are a contribution to the Internet store's ability to activate and retain customers. 56% of customers are more likely to return to a site that offers product recommendations. 75% of citizens expect a personalized shopping experience from e-commerce websites (Segmentify, 2019).

On average, every Internet user spends more than six hours a day on the Internet per year. That means that more than one hundred days per year spent on the Internet (Hughes, 2019). In 2020, advertising spending projected to grow by 6% to $ 656 billion, driven partially by the USA presidential election and the Summer Olympics (Handley, 2019). The author presumed that advertising, consciously or unintentionally, shape purchasing choices. Today's consumers may not like advertising, but they still need to agree and trust that advertising is a requirement in the reality of 2020. Advertising is one of those necessities, that affect consumer's experiences every day sometimes without realizing it. Current marketing trends are for more trustworthy customer experience. The e-commerce revolution began with the improvement of digital technology and automation, while the renaissance started today with the appearance of machine learning technologies.

3. CONCLUSION

Based on the analysis of the research, the author's personal experience and work on a doctoral thesis, the author came to conclusions:

1. Personalization is about better customer experience because the aim of the entrepreneur is profit.
2. Digital Marketing is already in a new era based on artificial intelligence technologies.
3. Artificial intelligence technologies can automatically generate content by teaching the algorithm to compose texts.

4. Social networks have long been analyzing all possible information that provides users with access to relevant news, goods, services.
5. Artificial intelligence algorithms and their applications can quickly analyze large, diverse data sets, improving demand forecasting accuracy.
6. The use of robotic software reduces the incidence of human error in medicine.
7. In the employment sector, artificial intelligence is used to automate recruitment processes.
8. In logistics, artificial intelligence technology is used to automate warehouses and anticipate possible increases or decreases in demand for goods.
9. Author presumed that inner website advertisement personalization can increase conversions and lower bounce rate.
10. The theme of the doctoral thesis is relevant and purposeful.

REFERENCES

Andreasen, A., R. 2018. *Social Marketing. Theoretical and Practical Perspectives*. Psychology Press, USA.

Davenport, T. et al. 2019. The potential for artificial intelligence in healthcare. *Future Healthcare Journal*. Vol. 6, No. 2, pp 2-3.

Davenport, T. et al. 2020. How artificial intelligence will change the future of marketing. *J. of the Acad. Mark. Sci.* Vol 48, pp. 24 - 42. https://doi.org/10.1007/s11747-019-00696-0

DeBord, M. 2019. *Here are the executives running the biggest and most important self-driving-car companies* https://www.businessinsider.com/self-driving-car-company-executives-who-is-running-them-2019-7 viewed 19.09.2019.

Dowling, S. 2019. *Recruitment Startups Realize, With The Help Of AI, Less Is More*. https://news.crunchbase.com/news/recruitment-startups-realize-with-the-help-of-ai-less-is-more/ viewed 25.10.2019.

Enberg, J. 2019. *Digital Ad Spending* https://www.emarketer.com/content/global-digital-ad-spending-2019 viewed 25.12.2019.

Guilherme, A. 2019. AI and education: the importance of teacher and student relations. *AI & Society*. Vol. 34. No. 2, pp. 47–54.

Handley, L. 2019. *Global ad spend has slowed but 2020 looks set to be a bumper year* https://www.cnbc.com/2019/10/24/global-ad-spend-has-slowed-but-2020-looks-set-to-be-a-bumper-year.html viewed 22.12.2019.

Hughes, T. J. 2002. Marketing principles in the application of e-commerce. *Qualitative Market Research: An International Journal*. Vol. 5, No. 4, pp 252 - 260.

Kalyanam, J. 2017. *Machine Learning and Applications on Social Media Data. UC San Diego.* https://escholarship.org/uc/item/6545w71z viewed 12.12.2019.

Khurana, A. 2019. *E-Commerce Basics. Types, Trends, and How Transactions Work* https://www.thebalancesmb.com/let-s-ask-the-basic-question-what-is-ecommerce-1141599 viewed 11.01.2020.

Kleinman, Z. (2018). The Ocado robot swarms that pack your shopping https://www.bbc.com/news/technology- 43968495 viewed 19.09.2019.

Martin, E. 2019. *AI Has Entered Our Daily Lives More Than You Know* https://www.opennebraska.io/ai-has-entered- our-lives-more-than-you-know/ viewed 29.10.2019.

Röglinger, M. et al. 2012. Maturity models in business process management. *Business Process Management Journal. Emerald Publishing Limited*. Vol. 18, No. 2, pp. 328-346.

Schank, R., C. 1991. Where's the AI. *AI Magazine*. Vol. 12, No. 4, pp. 5-38.

Segmentify. 2019. *3 Ecommerce Personalisation Stats You Need to Know* https://www.segmentify.com/blog/23-ecommerce-personalisation-stats-you-need-to-know-in-2019/ 25.12.2019. viewed 19.09.2019.

Shum, H-Y. et al. 2018. From Eliza to XiaoIce: Challenges and Opportunities With Social Chatbots. *Frontiers of Information Technology & Electronic Engineering,* Vol. 19, No.1, pp 10-26.

Siau K. et al. 2018. Building Trust in Artificial Intelligence, Machine Learning, and Robotics. *Cutter Business Technology Journal,* Vol. 31, No. 2, pp 47-53.

Wang, W. et al. 2019. Artificial Intelligence, Machine Learning, Automation, Robotics, Future of Work, and Future of Humanity – A Review and Research Agenda. *Journal of Database Management*. Vol. 30, No. 1, pp 2-6.

Yannopoulos, P. 2011. Impact of the Internet on Marketing Strategy Formulation. *International Journal of Business and Social Science*. Vol. 2, No. 18, pp 1-7.

A CALL FOR MORE SOCIOMATERIALITY AND ITS USAGE IN RESEARCH ON DIGITAL TRANSFORMATION

Sven Packmohr
Malmö University, Dept. of Data Science and Media Technology (DVMT)
Nordenskiöldsgatan 1, 211 19 Malmö, Sweden

ABSTRACT

Sociotechnical and sociomaterial perspectives are tools for research on Information System. As Digital Transformation is a research area related to IS, this paper takes these two perspectives into account for a literature review. The explicit use of both perspectives is rather limited. Still, sociotechnical is the broader perspective. A call for more sociomateriality in research on Digital Transformation is the aim of this reflection paper.

KEYWORDS

Sociotechnical, Sociomaterial, Digital Transformation

1. INTRODUCTION

Although digital transformation (DT) is a rather young field, recent reviews found 73,244 publications in the realm of management literature dating 20 years back (Hausberg *et al.*, 2019). Other reviews claim a superior amount of case studies as research methods (Reis *et al.*, 2018). The latter shows the maturity of the field, which seems to be in the phase of exploration. DT can be seen as a further development of the use of information systems. For research on information systems and organization, Orlikowski and Scott (2008) propose sociomateriality to develop the field in research further.

This paper reflects upon sociomateriality as a perspective for research in the field of DT. Therefore, the research questions are: How is sociomateriality used in research on DT? How can sociomateriality be framed better to help researchers in applying this perspective in research on DT?

To conclude, short introductions on the terms sociomateriality and digital transformation are given. A literature search is conducted to present how common combinations of these two and related terms are. The results from the search are the base for the later discussion and conclusion.

2. SOCIOMATERIALITY

Leonardi (2012) defines and relates different concepts in the realm of sociomateriality. Sociotechnical system (STS) is the older term coined by Trist and Bamforth. They argue for an interrelation of technological and social systems. The STS approach became common in IS and organizational studies (Cecez-Kecmanovic *et al.*, 2014). As the older and broader term, STS is the general recognition of a non-simultaneous interconnection between social and technical elements on an abstract level. Whereas sociomateriality is the specific "enactment of a particular set of activities that meld materiality with institutions, norms, discourses, and all other phenomena we typically define as 'social' ". A prerequisite for this is materiality. Materiality is defined as the composition of a technological system (artifact). Such a system contains features, which are somewhat stable over time and significant to users. Sociomateriality is the imbrication of the social agency and the material agency, which influences the social subsystem and is influenced by it (Leonardi, 2012).

3. DIGITAL TRANSFORMATION

Reis et al. (2018) review and analyze different definitions of Digital Transformation (DT). According to the smallest common meaning, DT uses "new digital technologies that enable major business improvements and influences all aspects of customers' lives." This definition shows three elements: (1) technology, (2) organization, (3) customer.

DT is a relatively new field. Although first publications date back to 1968, it is first around 2015 that it became a topic of interest in academic research.

Digital Transformation includes technology such as Information Systems (IS). Nolan and Wetherbe (1980) define IS as an "integrated, man/machine system for providing information to support the operation, management, and decision-making functions in an organization." O'Brien and Marakas (2011) add data input, processing, and output of information products.

4. USAGE OF BOTH PERSPECTIVES IN THE ACADEMIC LITERATURE

The author conducted different searches via the Scopus database by the beginning of 2020. The aim is to get an impression of how the usage of a sociomaterial perspective evolves in literature. The searches focus on the article's title, abstract, and keywords. The first search on DT and sociomateriality found only one article by Barata and Da Cunha (2018). The sociotechnical counterpart generated 43 results. Sometimes, the terms sociomateriality and sociotechnical are spelled with a hyphen. Although some authors call for spelling without a hyphen, both versions were included in the search. Otherwise, no time, language, or other limits were set.

A broader search and included both American and English spelling of digitali(z/s)ation leading to 8 new results and a total of 9 resources. The sociotechnical counterpart generated 115 results.

As the term digital transformation is rather new, the author conducted searches on organi(z/s)ation and IS. Primarily, search number 8 would need some refinement. Areas like health-care and farming show up, in which sociotechnical imaging / sociotechnical imaginaries are addressed. These terms address a system thinking, too. They do not necessarily include information systems.

Therefore, searches number 9 and 10 were conducted. These searches show the overlap between searches on organization and IS. The search results show the dominance of the sociotechnical view.

Table 1. Scopus search results

#	Search string	Results
1	"digital transformation" AND (sociomateriality OR socio-materiality)	1
2	"digital transformation" AND (sociotechnical OR sociotechnical)	43
3	("digital transformation" OR digitalization OR digitalisation) AND (sociomateriality OR socio-materiality)	9
4	("digital transformation" OR digitalization OR digitalisation) AND (sociotechnical OR sociotechnical)	115
5	"information systems" AND (sociomateriality OR socio-materiality)	157
6	"information systems" AND (sociotechnical OR sociotechnical)	1703
7	(organization OR organisation) AND (sociomateriality OR socio-materiality)	150
8	(organization OR organisation) AND (sociotechnical OR sociotechnical)	2644
9	(organization OR organization) AND ("information systems") AND (sociomateriality OR socio-materiality)	57
10	(organization OR organization) AND ("information systems") AND (sociotechnical OR sociotechnical)	571

The following section will summarize the resources found in the third search to overview the kinds of research and the applied procedures.

Klischewski (2019) addresses the issue that information systems become more and more autonomous. The author uses a sociomaterial perspective to research the interconnection between human action and technology performance in the area of digitalized governmental systems. Drawing on models from

Mintzberg, challenges are identified. A way to solve the marginalization of humans is a more aligned composition of the system, reflecting the human and the machine agency.

Knights and Latham (2019) research the distribution of computers for social interactions given to disabled people by using a case study design. The selection procedure is administrated by an allocation assessment form. The authors analyze how the form, the allocation procedure, the distributors, and the solicitors influence each other.

Barat and Da Cunha (2018) examine the transformation of traditional industries towards Industry 4.0 as it claims a new perspective on the social and the material. The authors use an action research approach to explore how product life-cycles evolve through the social and the material. The results are aggregated into roadmaps.

Morland and Pettersen (2018) aim to understand how clinical work is changed by technology and the usage of medical personal. In a case study, the authors analyze the use of a speech recognition system through the lenses of an actor-network theory approach. Results show the importance of powerful actors and their influence on system development and usage.

Samdanis and Lee (2017) use a case study of a leading architect to investigate the interplay between technology and architects. This interplay influences how space is designed and experienced. Results show the importance of uniqueness as well as the development of a personal digital system for design.

Furthermore, power relations play an essential role in developing digital materiality. Bader and Kaiser (2017) look more in-depth into paradoxes provoked by an interplay between technology and individuals, such as greater autonomy and greater control. The authors examine different degrees of the autonomy-control paradox, which are (1) independence of autonomy and control, a (2) hybrid degree on an individual level, or (3) dominance of one aspect. The hybrid paradox on the individual level is influenced by social norms. This research informs managers who seek to influence specific rationalities in paradoxes.

Panourgias, Nandhakumar, and Scarbrough (2014) research how the interplay between creativity and digital technology shapes the development of computer games. The researchers use data from three leading development studios to show how new development technologies and development practices influence creativity and are influenced by creativity. In this work, creativity is understood as a process triggered by a creative starting event.

Hedman, Srinivasan, and Lindgren (2013) survey literature in leading IS journals to analyze how researchers work with data on digital traces. For this, they developed a classification for data. Their results show that digital data-traces are underused. They suggest being more aware of these data sources as they are the result of a sociomaterial process.

For their panel, Barret et al. (2012) connect service innovation and digitization to focus the panelist perspective onto the multiple contexts of a service exchange between customers and suppliers. It leads to a paradigm shift if the social-material and tangible-tacit dynamics of exchange are considered for concepts and models of service-design.

5. DISCUSSION

Table 1 shows that a sociotechnical perspective is more common in research than sociomateriality. This might seem logical for the literature search in the fields of information systems and organizations. These fields are more mature and had more time to develop a sociotechnical perspective as it is the older term. When looking at DT, which is a younger research area, the same pattern applies. Potentially, the number of results between both terms could be distributed equally. Both terms were known in epistemology when research on DT got on track. Still, the focus is on research addressing a sociotechnical perspective. Although DT is not that mature as the field of organization or information systems, researchers might feel more used to the sociotechnical view. Critics claim that sociomateriality has some drawbacks, such as a lack of understandability of certain information systems (Mutch, 2013). It might help to induce sociomateriality into a broader picture. (Creswell, 2013) proposes a dependency on the researchers' perspective and experience with philosophical assumptions and interpretative frameworks. This leads to research strategies and approaches, which, in return, lead to methods of data collection and analysis. In the end, all these levels influence the practices of interpretation and evaluation. If sociomateriality and STS could be placed in this model in a coherent way, it might help researchers in getting more familiar with these terms. The resources in section 4 show that some studies follow a case study or an action research approach. Such as Panourgias, Nandhakumar, and Scarbrough (2014), who ask the following research question concerning sociomateriality: "How does a focus on the 'sociomaterial entanglements' of human and material agencies enhance our understanding of this interaction between the creative agency and the design of digital technologies?" A research question is influenced by the researching subject as well as her/his philosophical assumptions and interpretative frameworks. (Creswell, 2013) lists nine frameworks. Out of these nine, four are focusing on the empowerment of marginalized groups, leaving five frameworks that might be applicable for DT research, which are post-positivism, constructivism, transformative/postmodern, and pragmatism. Looking upon ontology, epistemology, axiology, and methodology, it seems sociomateriality fits best with constructivism. Thus, interactions with technologies need to be included in this framework. Although, some authors question the fit of a constructivist framework (Orlikowski and Scott, 2008). Sociomateriality could become part of the researching subjects' beliefs (Creswell, 2013) that individuals and technology are part of an interdependency. Beliefs and experiences take a longer time to change. This might also be an argument for less sociomateriality in research in general.

Another aspect is bound to different types of research. Descriptive research clarifies the characteristics of a phenomenon. In comparison, normative research explains how a certain status evolves (Meirovich, 2015). A description of a specific phenomenon can be done on a very aggregated level. E.g., without looking at certain technologies in detail. With normative research, a black-box perspective, e.g., on technology, will less likely generate reliable results. For normative frameworks within DT, the digital aspects need to be materialized within research projects. Here, researchers can draw insights from a design point of view. Some of the reviewed resources take a design view into account. These design insights found entry to IS research already (Chandra, Seidel, and Gregor, 2015). Therefore, a call to adopt a sociomaterial perspective in research on DT is needed.

6. CONCLUSION AND OUTLOOK

Results show that sociomateriality lacks behind. Researchers use this perspective less than the sociotechnical perspective. Sociomateriality could give valuable insights. DT, as a new field, gives the chance to experiment with more sociomateriality-focused approaches. In DT, three views come together, making it more complex. This complexity opens up for an even more entangling approach.

This reflective paper gives first insights on sociomateriality in the field of DT. A more comprehensive model on how to specifically use sociomateriality needs to be developed. A start is to work backward from existing publications and evaluate in greater detail how sociomateriality fits into models of a research process and how normative perspectives can evolve (Creswell, 2013). Furthermore, this preliminary and descriptive literature review could be developed into a broader systematic review, including more induction and interpretation of the results to compare, oppose or complement arguments (Petticrew and Roberts, 2006).

REFERENCES

Bader, V. and Kaiser, S. (2017) 'Autonomy and Control? How Heterogeneous Sociomaterial Assemblages Explain Paradoxical Rationalities in the Digital Workplace', *Management Review*, 28(3), pp. 338–358.

Barata, J. and Da Cunha, P. R. (2018) 'Understanding sociomaterial transformations in industry 4.0: An action research study', in *Proceedings of the Thirty-Ninth International Conference on Information Systems* (ICIS), San Francisco.

Barrett, M. et al. (2012) 'Being innovative about service innovation: Service, design and digitalization', in *Proceedings of the Thirty-Third International Conference on Information Systems* (ICIS), Orlando.

Cecez-Kecmanovic, D. et al. (2014) 'The Sociomaterialty of Information Systems: Current Status, Future Directions', *MIS Quarterly*, 38(3), pp. 809–830.

Chandra, L. et al. (2015) 'Prescriptive Knowledge in IS Research: Conceptualizing Design Principles in Terms of Materiality, Action, and Boundary Conditions', in *Proceedings of the 48th Hawaii International Conference on System Sciences* (HICSS), pp. 4039–4048.

Creswell, J. W. (2013) *Qualitative inquiry and research design: choosing among five approaches.* 3rd ed. Los Angeles: SAGE Publications.

Hausberg, J. P. et al. (2019) 'Research streams on digital transformation from a holistic business perspective: a systematic literature review and citation network analysis', *Journal of Business Economics*, 89(8–9), pp. 931–963.

Hedman, J. et al. (2013) 'Digital traces of information systems: Sociomateriality made researchable', in *Proceedings of the Thirty-Fourth International Conference on Information Systems* (ICIS), Milan.

Klischewski, R. (2019) 'Will the Government Machine Turn into a Monster?', in *20th Annual International Conference on Digital Government Research*, Dubai, United Arab Emirates: ACM Press, pp. 306–313.

Knights, D. and Latham, Y. (2019) 'Disabled People and Digitalization: Disruptive documents in distributing digital devices', *Organization Studies*, 41(6), pp. 855-872.

Leonardi, P. M. (2012) 'Materiality, Sociomateriality, and Socio-Technical Systems: What Do These Terms Mean? How are They Related? Do We Need Them?', in Leonardi, P. M. et al. (Eds.), *Materiality and Organizing: Social Interaction in a Technological World*. Oxford: Oxford University Press, pp. 25-48.

Meirovich, G. (2015) 'Normative and Descriptive Aspects of Management Education: Differentiation and Integration', *Journal of Educational Issues*, 1(1), pp. 97–113.

Morland, C. and Pettersen, I. J. (2018) 'Translating technological change – implementing technology into a hospital', *International Journal of Productivity and Performance Management*, 67(6), pp. 1000–1015.

Mutch, A. (2013) 'Sociomateriality — Taking the wrong turning?', *Information and Organization*, 23(1), pp. 28–40.

Nolan, R. L. and Wetherbe, J. C. (1980) 'Toward a Comprehensive Framework for MIS Research', *MIS Quarterly*, 4(2), pp. 1-19.

O'Brien, J. A. and Marakas, G. M. (2011) *Management information systems*. New York: McGraw-Hill.

Orlikowski, W. J. and Scott, S. V. (2008) 'Sociomateriality: Challenging the Separation of Technology, Work and Organization', *The Academy of Management Annals*, 2(1), pp. 433–474.

Panourgias, N. S. et al. (2014) 'Entanglements of creative agency and digital technology: A sociomaterial study of computer game development', *Technological Forecasting and Social Change*, 83, pp. 111–126.

Petticrew, M. and Roberts, H. (2006) *Systematic Reviews in the Social Sciences: A Practical Guide*. Oxford: Blackwell Pub.

Reis, J. et al. (2018) 'Digital Transformation: A Literature Review and Guidelines for Future Research', in Rocha, Á. et al. (eds) *Trends and Advances in Information Systems and Technologies*. Cham: Springer International Publishing, pp. 411–421.

Samdanis, M. and Lee, S. H. (2017) 'White space and digital remediation of design practice in architecture: A case study of Frank O. Gehry', *Information and Organization*, 27(2), pp. 73–86.

PANDEMIC LEARNING ONTOLOGY: METHODOLOGICAL ASPECTS TO ASSESS SKILLS IN A PUBLIC HEALTH EMERGENCY

Marcos Lévano[1], Billy Peralta[2] and Gabriel Venegas[1]
[1]*Computer Engineering Department, Catholic University of Temuco, Ave. Manuel Montt 56, Mailbox 15-D, Temuco, Chile*
[2]*Departamento de Ciencias de la Ingeniería, Universidad Andres Bello, Antonio Varas 880, piso 6, Providencia, Región Metropolitana, Chile*

ABSTRACT

The purpose of this work is to show the experience of methodological aspects which were used to assess competencies with regard to conceiving, designing, implementing and operating (CDIO), in a curriculum for competencies in the face of state of emergency in public health due to coronavirus. The situation and advances are displayed as a case study, in training civil engineering professionals in computer science at the Catholic University of Temuco (CUT) in Chile.
The questions intented to be resolved are: Is it possible to improve the capacities of students from the Araucanía region (Chile) in a social-economic-cultural system, through teaching and learning based on education which allows them to discover, expand and exploit the improvement of the training of professional human capital with competencies in an emergency situation in public health due to coronavirus?. The process of validation of competencies responds to conceive, design, implement and operate (CDIO) being adapted. The way in which the transition in the levels of competencies that the progressing student advances occurs is achieved in different teaching and learning activities through online training. The implementation of competency validation is produced in different contexts in the phases: conceive, design, implement and operate, which have had to be faced by teachers, instructors, assistants for the achievement of students.

KEYWORDS

Coronavirus, Pandemic, Educational Evaluation, Competency Training, CDIO, Ontology

1. INTRODUCTION

On March 18, 2020, a state of constitutional catastrophe exception was decreed in Chile, due to public calamity in the territory of Chile.

Due to the COVID-19 coronavirus pandemic, a virus which has produced a global alarm (Chen et al., 2020; Geldsetzer, 2020). Educational institutions throughout the country were closed and all: boys, girls and young students, as well as the general population (except those who performed essential services), were ordered to remain confined to their homes, until the end of the state of alarm, given this seems to be the most effective non-clinical measure to stop the advance of the pandemic (Choe, & Choi, 2020; Kim et al., 2020; Prem et al., 2020).

Teachers had to innovate in the short term with the means at their disposal, a structure which has allowed a good part of the students of all educational stages to continue learning. Since the beginning of the pandemic, 1,200 university students have already dropped out in the case of the Catholic University of Temuco, of which 85% suspended their studies.

Several trends have boost changes in teaching ways around the world. Some of these trends are globalization, advancements in technology and the new organizational structures of companies and job organization (Lévano & Herrera, 2012). A variety of international initiatives have ended up becoming models, methodologies, and educational practices that have been incorporated to higher education. A common denominator in many of these educational proposals is the orientation towards education based on competences or skills. Competences are those behaviors, abilities, and visible aptitudes that people contribute in a specific field of activities to function effectively and successfully.

The alumni from computer engineering of our university poses a good background in basic sciences, engineering sciences, management of specific contents (Lévano & Herrera, 2012). The new setting (Lévano, 2017) of the program was developed by making questions to employers, ex-students, other universities, international organizations specialized in the area of computer engineering science (mainly from the Association for Computing Machinery), consultations on studies about teaching engineering (CDIO model) (Crawley et al., 2007), and studies about higher education in Chile and some future changes (OCDE -Organization for Economic Co-operation and Development, and World Bank) (OCDE, 2009), (CNIC, 2010).

This study addresses the process in which how to evidence cognitive and metacognitive processes is demonstrated (Lévano & Fernández, 2015) in order to achieve the competences. The process of evidencing competences meets with the model CDIO being adapted to the program. The progression of it in the validation of competences is reached through a number of activities of teaching, and learning and the implementation of this process is achieved in several moments during the program in the four stages of CDIO (Crawley et al., 2007).

The present work introduces, firstly, the educational model of Catholic University of Temuco by competencies, then an ontology of validation of competences in times of pandemic for the adapted CDIO, afterwards the progress of results, then the conclusions and future work. Finally, the references.

2. UCT EDUCATIONAL MODEL

In our university, we define competence as: "to know how to behave, using our own means and outside resources in order to solve real problems in an effectively and ethically responsible manner" (Lévano & Herrera, 2012). We also distinguish two kinds of competences or skills, generic competences, which are shared among all the programs and the specific competences which are directly related to the areas of study of each program.

The educational model in our university is based on five axes. Therefore, the Engineering Computer program is set in the same way (Lévano & Herrera, 2012; Lévano & Fernández, 2015).

1) Model of education based on competences: we are committed to managing the quality of learning, so we have implemented four specific competences that are vital for the education and development of the students and ten generic competences stipulated by the university.

2) Significant learning focused on students.

3) Ongoing education: we hope that our students keep studding after they graduate, in post graduate levels that develop and increase the complexity of the development of the human resources among the students.

4) Information technologies in the process of learning and teaching: based on what is stipulated in the curriculum, we have intensively incorporated ICT as an important part of the evaluation and teaching processes in all the subjects of the program.

5) Humanistic and Christian education: our globalized society demands ethical professionals with robust knowledge about their specific area of study, ability to face problems from different perspectives, and a high capacity for handle a variety of competences or skills.

These abilities are developed throughout the five years of study by the validation of the generic competences.

2.1 Engineering Computer Science Program

The curriculum program operates based on four specific competences according to the stipulations of the university (Lévano, 2017; Herrera et al., 2018).

Software development: The students are able to give solutions by the development of software for specific problems, by using a software engineering approach integrating technical, ethical, social, legal and economic aspects.

ICT management: The students are able to manage hardware and software technology systems in an organized way, in order to automate management systems and production processes.

Modeling and application of computer science procedures: The students create and apply solutions related to informatics to solve real problems, applying computer science methods, taking care of abstract, logical, and scientific aspects of science. To do so, they use algorithmic methods in the automation process of engineering information.

Application of engineering science: The students implement mathematical and engineering models, as well as models from basic sciences by using logical and reasoning skills, in order to engage themselves in problems of analysis and design of technological systems based on software, linked to engineering special areas.

3. ONTOLOGY FOR VALIDATION OF COMPETENCIES

The competences validation process was developed based on the following strategies and developed by the work methodology which consists of 5 situations: Situation 1: Online classes; Situation 2: Forums; Situation 3: Follow-up controls; Situation 4: Group tasks; Situation 5: Group project.

Strategies

Work meetings: these meetings are performed by an executive board of teachers in the area of computing and other disciplines. The function of these meetings is to evaluate and discuss some situations like: how to distinguish learning difficulties among students, how to generate communication between teachers, choosing advanced students to assist partners having difficulties, developing projects to support the student community, discussing about mechanisms to validate skills and competences and to develop evaluation guidelines.

The topics can be gathered as followed: Problems of specific students (check behavior in each group); Methods to validate generic competences; Performance of each group; Discussion of topics in a vertical way.

There is a coordinator who keeps records of these issues and who moderates and prioritizes topics addressed and the actions to be derived from these meetings. The development strategy was adapted in meetings via Google meet / Zoom / Collaborate.

Integration of competences workshops: Evaluation processes have been carried out every year to evaluate the integration of the development of competences in a horizontal way. They are practical workshops to generate challenges, creativity, and innovation among students in several ways, for example, on a personal or attitudinal level, and how to use their knowledge. The development strategy was Google Meet for presentations and GIT and GITKRAKEN for version control of software product design processes.

Feedback: feedback is done at every moment, in all the subjects. It is accomplished through a learning resource center and also, it is done by all teachers. Feedback takes place in mixed hours, in which the teachers work individually or in groups with the students, as stipulated by the educational model. The objective is to solve analytic, application, or knowledge problems. The development strategy was carried out via webinars and Telegram/WhatsApp.

Peer tutoring: it is developed in each subject that allows intervention of other students. The objective is that older or advanced students help their partners. To do so, focused peer tutorials and tasks with the learning resource center are promoted. The development strategy was carried out via webinars.

Advisory services for teachers: every year, this strategy allows teachers to improve their pedagogical practices. They participate in workshops, training and guided classes. They are supported by the teaching innovation center of the university. The development strategy was carried out via webinars, and academic council meetings of professors via Google Meet. Messaging via LMS Blackboard.

Record book: we keep track of all the generated and validated knowledge that students achieve in the different topics of the educational process. It allows validating competences, making self-assessments and making interventions in weak areas in medium term. The development strategy was carried out using Google DRIVE, Dropbox as digital repositories.

Control and tracking of professional training: in this stage of the educational process, we check, orient, guide and evaluate the validation of the competences in the work place. The evaluations are made taking into account our own formative discipline and the rules of each place of work in which the professional training is done. The strategy, in situations according to the type of practice, has been to establish work in online mode.

Learning guidelines: it is based on the triple instrument according to the methodology, the assessment and learning outcomes or objectives of the subjects. To develop the guidelines, we worked on activities based on the development of the knowledge of knowing, being, and making. The strategy aims to generate and design e-learning material and VLO (virtual learning objects).

3.1 Alignment of CDIO with the Curriculum

The alignment of the process of CDIO (Crawley et al., 2007; Lévano, 2020) with the curriculum has been implemented based on the development of the graduated profile. A Computer Engineer graduated from UCT has a set of competences and a robust basis in engineering sciences that allows him to work in the areas related to software development and ICT. To enhance characteristics that are highly demanded by the working market, and to promote the identity seal of the university, we have boosted the competences of team work, creativity, and innovation.

3.1.1 Scheme of Competences Development

The process of developing competences in environments occurs in the classrooms, laboratories, visits, professional job practice, workshops, seminars, and final papers, all as described in the educational model proposed by the university. The process of experiencing the developing of competences goes along with the contexts of active, reflexive, conceptual and application experimentation, see figure 1.

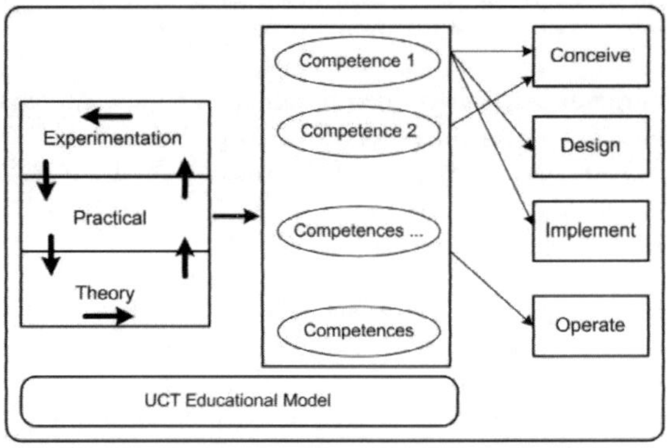

Figure 1. Scheme of competences development in the educational guideline

In table 1, the relationship between specific competences and CDIO model is shown. Generic and specific competences go along together during the process of validation, and each subject can incorporate two or more generic or specific competences.

Table 1. CDIO Model and Specific Competences

Specific Competences	Conceive	Design	Implement	Operate	Generic competences in the curriculum	Levels		
ICT management	X	X	X	X	Ethical Action; Respect and appreciation of diversity; Collaborative work; Creativity and innovation; Autonomous Learning.	1	2	3
Modeling and application of computer science		X	X			1	2	3
Software development	X	X	X	X		1	2	3
Application of engineering science		X	X	X		1	2	3

3.1.2 CDIO in the Development of Specific and Generic Competences

During the first year "to operate" is worked, while "to implement and to operate" are worked during the second and third year. During the fourth year "to design, to implement and to operate" are worked. Finally, during the fifth year "to conceive, to design, to implement and to operate" are worked altogether. During first year we begin with the vertical implementation and during second year we implement the horizontal integration of competences. This process is sequential and it is also combined along the subjects and the years. For example in figure 2, basic science knowledge is developed in activities inside the subject, because that course is focused on fundamental knowledge. That knowledge is manifested in a horizontal way of competences. In the figures 3 and 4 below we can observe what happens during the rest of the years.

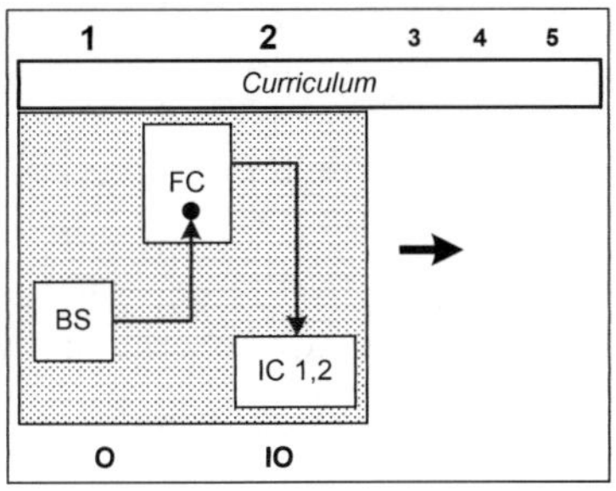

Figure 2. To operate (O); to implement and to operate (IO)

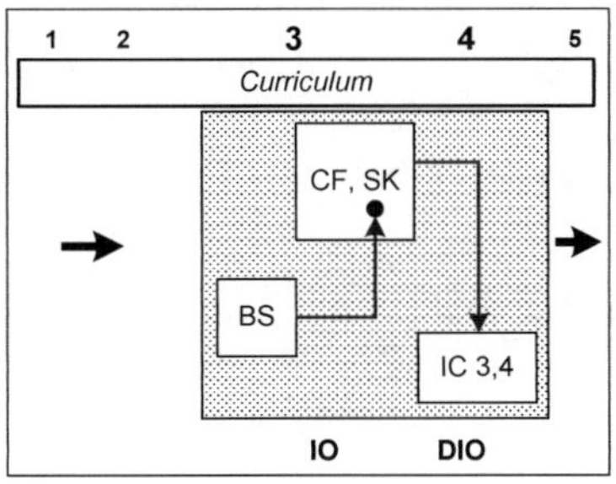

Figure 3. To implement and to operate (IO); Design, Implement and Operate (DIO)

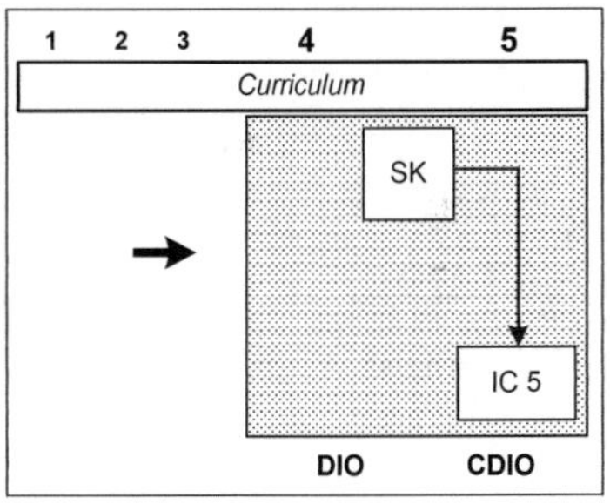

Figure 4. Design, Implement and Operate (DIO); Conceive, Design, Implement and Operate (CDIO)

Notes: (FC) fundamental knowledge; (BS) basic sciences; (IC) integration competences; (SK) specialty knowledge.

4. RESULTS AND DISCUSSIONS

The progress of the results achieved were implemented in the semester II-2020 in the Civil Engineering in Computer Science degree at Catholic University of Temuco (CUT). To show the progress made, it was applied in four subjects.

Data Description,

Table 2. Description of the data under study

Subject	Total Students	General competencies	Level of competence	Year on the curriculum
Introduction to databases	10	Autonomous Learning	1	1
Integration Workshop II	34	Creativity and innovation Collaborative work Oral and written communication	2	2
Computer Theory	32	Appreciation and respect for diversity	1	4
Business Intelligence	24	Ethical Performance	2	4
Total	100	6 competencies		

Incidence of causal variables, which worried the students. In the figure 6, we can see that contagion and uncertainty are over 60% of concern in the face of the pandemic, (see figure 5).

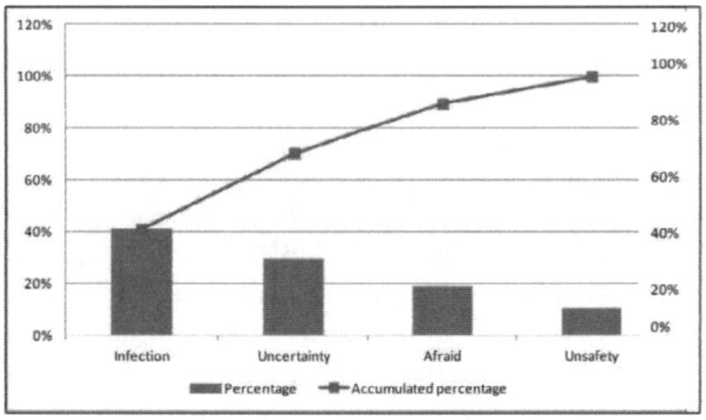

Figure 5. Pareto diagram regarding causal variables

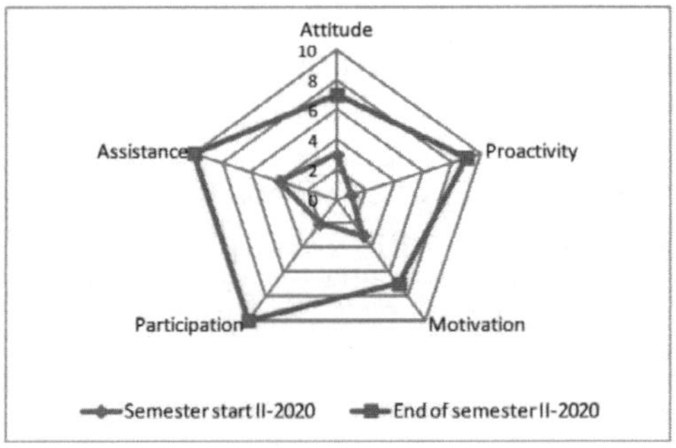

Figure 6. Radial diagram of teacher perception belief

In figure 6, we can observe the perception of professors regarding the teaching and learning process of students, referring to achievement learning (see figures 7, 7(a), 7(b), 7(c) y 7(d)). See also focus groups in the table 3.

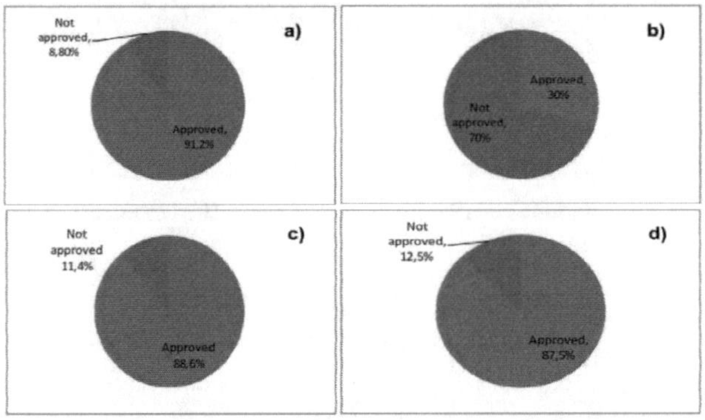

Figure 7. a) Approval in progress of Integration Workshop II, $\mu = 5.6, \sigma = 1.8$; b) Approval in progress of Introduction to Databases, $\mu = 2.7, \sigma = 4.7$; c) Approval in progress Computer Theory, $\mu = 5.1, \sigma = 1.6$; d) Approval in progress Business Intelligence, $\mu = 5.6, \sigma = 3.4$

Table 3. Focused discussion

Focus group	Design	Questions	Analysis
1	10 students; Age 18 to 20; Duration 15 minutes; Number of courses: 2 Courses: Introduction to Database Systems and Integration Workshop II.	How did you perform during the Pandemic learning process?	In this sample, deficiency is reported due to a large number of people who failed. Implication due to motivation and attendance.
		Whose pressure do you feel to study?	It is observed that from their parents and / or guardians they feel pressure due to the cost of the degree.
		Have you felt assisted by the professor in the learning and teaching processes?	They are aware they had the necessary and frequent support from their professors. Implication of affect due to attitude and participation.
		Were the remote support hours sufficient?	They assume the channels existed, but they still feel a difference because of the digital divide.
2	20 students; Age 2 to 25; Duration 20 minutes; Number of courses: 2 Courses: Business Intelligence and Computer Theory.	Was the methodology applied adequate to develop your skills?	It is believed the instances of: online classes; forums; follow-up controls; group tasks; and group project, give a balance and adequate aspects for their learning experience.
		Was the academic demand from professors excessive or low?	They complain saying some professors exceeded the product and the estimated timing.
		Do you think you have acquired knowledge in "knowing" and "doing"?	They are aware they reached their goal. In some cases, they still feel they need the physical classroom, since they think they missed completing some tasks *in situ* and having their professors physically present for support.
		Have the technological platforms used been consistent with the teaching and learning process?	They are aware the study media and artifacts, through the LMS Moodle platform and Blackboard, allowed a substantial and situational support instance.
		Was the leadership style they performed more transactional, transformational, or liberal?	They believe in group work; they have grown in the way they face situations. Other students still require record of attendance.

5. CONCLUSIONS

It is interesting to note the students adapted to the situations of the evaluation methodology and styles. They mention the resources provided by professors should be of support to their PLE and PLN (Castañeda et al., 2016; Dabbagh, Fake, & Zhang, 2019). They suggest short video files of 10-15 minutes. So they also consume more files with content. On the other hand, they themselves map out a constructivist vision which feeds their PLE and then this is shared in their PLN.

Professors and instructors have had to move from a belief and habit in the traditional way to build their materials for teaching and learning. This has led them to develop divergent creativity, to exploit the use and application of ICT tools. Given that currently formators face pressure and adaptation in a VICA world (Bauman, 2007).

The social action theory of E. Goffman (Goffman, 2010) indicates human behavior depends on its settings and on personal relationships. This has helped the apprentice to strengthen ties of ties between people and their acquaintances, since the subject does not exist in isolation.

Through this work ontology, a mechanism is intended to validate general competencies in the curriculum for a major in computer engineering in times of emergency due to coronavirus, where the CDIO process is performed. This does not limit the trainer to innovate new strategies which help in the teaching and learning process of students.

REFERENCES

Bauman, Zygmunt, Miedo líquido. *La sociedad contemporánea y sus temores*, Paidos, Barcelona, 2007.

Castañeda, L., Cosgrave, M., Marín, V., & Cronin, C. (2016). Personal Learning Environments: PLE Conference 2015 *Special Issue Guest Editorial*. Digital Education Review, 29. Retrieved from http://greav.ub.edu/der

Chen, Y., Jin, Y. L., Zhu, L. J., Fang, Z. M., Wu, N., Du, M. X., ... & Yao, Y. S. (2020). The network investigation on knowledge, attitude and practice about COVID-19 of the residents in Anhui Province. *Zhonghua yu Fang yi xue za zhi Chinese Journal of Preventive Medicine*, *54*(4), 367-373. http://doi.org/dtqg

Choe, Y. J., & Choi, E. H. (2020). Are We Ready for Coronavirus Disease 2019 Arriving at Schools? *Journal of Korean Medical Science*, *35*(11). http://doi.org/ggq848

Crawley, E., Malmqvist, J., Östlund, S., Brodeur, D. (2007). *Rethinking engineering education: The CDIO approach*. Vol. 14, 286 p.

CNIC. (2010). Agenda de Innovación y Competitividad 2010-2020. CNIC: Consejo Nacional de Innovación para la Competitividad, 2010, Chile.

Dabbagh, N., Fake, H., & Zhang, Z. (2019). Student Perspectives of Technology Use for Learning in Higher Education. RIED. *Revista Iberoamericana de Educación a Distancia*, 22(1), pp. 127-152. doi: http://dx.doi.org/10.5944/ried.22.1.22102

Geldsetzer, P. (2020). Use of Rapid Online Surveys to Assess People's Perceptions During Infectious Disease Outbreaks: A Cross-sectional Survey on COVID-19. *Journal of medical Internet research*, *22*(4), e18790. http://doi.org/ggq7t8

Goffman, E. (2010). Comportamento em lugares públicos: notas sobre a organização social dos ajuntamentos. Vozes.

Jieming Ma, Chili Li, Hai-Ning Liang, "Enhancing Students' Blended Learning Experience through Embedding Metaliteracy", *Education Research International*, vol. 2019, Article ID 6791058, 8 pages, 2019. https://doi.org/10.1155/2019/6791058

Kim, S., Kim, Y. J., Peck, K. R., & Jung, E. (2020). School Opening Delay Effect on Transmission Dynamics of Coronavirus Disease 2019 in Korea: Based on Mathematical Modeling and Simulation Study. *Journal of Korean medical science*, *35*(13). http://doi.org/dtqx

Kristina Edström (2020) The role of CDIO in engineering education research: Combining usefulness and scholarliness, *European Journal of Engineering Education*, 45:1, 113-127, DOI:10.1080/03043797.2017.1401596

Levano, M. (2017). Methodology for Knowledge Management and Self-Directed, Science Program Engineering Computing. In Issa, T., Kommers, P., Issa, T., Isaías, P., & Issa, T. B. (Eds.), *Smart Technology Applications in Business Environments* (pp. 63-81). IGI Global. http://doi:10.4018/978-1-5225-2492-2.ch004

Levano M., Fernández C. (2015) A Model for a Physical and Virtual Environment for Extreme Feedback in the Development of the Metacognition Supported by TICS: The Computer Engineer Career as Case of Study. In: Park J., Stojmenovic I., Jeong H., Yi G. (eds) Computer Science and its Applications. *Lecture Notes in Electrical Engineering*, vol 330. Springer, Berlin, Heidelberg. https://doi.org/10.1007/978-3-662-45402-2_187

M. A. Lévano, "Effects of Cycle Evaluation on Peer Learning: Competency Assessment, Case Study, Catholic University of Temuco, Chile," *2020 11th International Conference on Information, Intelligence, Systems and Applications (IISA*, Piraeus, 2020, pp. 1-6, doi: 10.1109/IISA50023.2020.9284369.

M. A. Lévano and O. A. Herrera, "Validation Strategies of Competences in a Computer Science Curriculum," *2012 31st International Conference of the Chilean Computer Science Society*, Valparaiso, 2012, pp. 9-11, doi: 10.1109/SCCC.2012.8.

O. A. Herrera, M. Lévano and J. Rojas-Mora, "Evaluating achievement of competences through integration workshops: an approach with strategies supported by ICT," *2018 37th International Conference of the Chilean Computer Science Society (SCCC)*, Santiago, Chile, 2018, pp. 1-7, doi: 10.1109/SCCC.2018.8705267.

OECD/The World Bank (2009), La Educación Superior en Chile, Revisión de Políticas Nacionales de Educación, Ministry of Education, Chile, Santiago de Chile, https://doi.org/10.1787/9789264054189-es.

Prem, K., Liu, Y., Russell, T. W., Kucharski, A. J., Eggo, R. M., Davies, N., ... & Abbott, S. (2020). The effect of control strategies to reduce social mixing on outcomes of the COVID-19 epidemic in Wuhan, China: a modelling study. *The Lancet Public Health*. https://www.thelancet.com/action/showPdf?pii=S2468-2667%2820%2930073-6

REPROGRAMMING CORRECTIONAL EDUCATION: A CONCEPTUAL FRAMEWORK FOR THE IMPLEMENTATION OF ADAPTIVE LEARNING TECHNOLOGIES IN PRISONS

Shahram Amiri[1], Joseph Woodside[1] and Humberto J. Soares[2]
[1]*School of Business Adminstration, Stetson University Deland, FL 32723, USA*
[2]*Division of Business and Finance, Brandeis University Walham, MA 02453, USA*

ABSTRACT

Considering the probability of reinstatement of the Pell Grant Program, the debate to advance educational programs in prisons has flourished. Extensive evidence shows that the availability of learning opportunities in correctional facilities drastically diminishes the prisoner's probabilities of recidivism and, augments the likelihood of positive social re-integration. However, the effectiveness of these educational programs depends greatly on the methods of instruction offered. Therefore, the real issue lies on the selection of the appropriate method of instruction. The aim of this paper is to indicate the value of adaptive learning technologies (ALTs) to enhance a prisoner**'s** learning abilities, by designing a theoretical framework for the implementation of ALTs in prisons. This framework draws its basis from theories of machine learning, adaptive learning, and information technology. The **intention of this paper is to be** used as a preliminary, conceptual framework, which can then be adapted as empirical studies are developed.

KEYWORDS

Adaptive Learning, Correctional Education, Recidivism, Prison, Information Technology

1. INTRODUCTION

1.1 Recidivism and the Purpose of Education in Prison

Recidivism is defined as the return to criminal behavior after release, measured by a *rate of recidivism* (Esperian, 2010) Multiple factors are attributable to the re-offense of prisoners, such as (but not limited) to: (1) socio-economic status, (2) effectives of post-release supervision, (3) length of incarceration, (4) severity and seriousness of offense committed, and (5) education achieved of each individual. Extensive evidence shows that the availability of learning opportunities in correctional facilities, drastically diminishes the prisoner's probabilities of recidivism and, augments the likelihood of positive social re-integration. (Davis et al, 2013; Owens, 2009; Makorios, Travis, 2010; Lahm, 2009; Harlow, Jenkins, Steurer, 2010; Wilson et al., 2010) However, the effectiveness of these educational programs depends greatly on the methods of instruction offered in correctional facilities. From children, students of higher education, to prisoners, effective methods of instruction are the basis of quality learning. To this end, adaptive learning technologies (ALTs) can provide the appropriate method of instruction for all different types of learners, which is clearly needed within any correctional facility. Natriello (2013) defines ALTs as a system that performs under the "current learner performance and adapt accordingly to support and maximize learning." These technologies are programmed to deliver personalized educational experiences for each learner. This will be the operating definition of ALTs throughout this paper. These ALTs provide the ability and flexibility for instructors to cater to the specific need of the student, without compromising the level of quality of the program; while also considering the intricate variables such as the academic background, social and the socioeconomic conditions that affect the learning process of students. (Natriello, 2013)

1.2 Current State of US Prisons

Understanding the current state of the educational profile of American prisoners is critical, especially before questioning and/or improving the current system. To that matter, Davis et al. (2017) performed an examination of the educational profile of prisoners in the U.S. According to their demographic study, 64% of adult prisoners have a high school credential, and 30% are reported to have less than a high school degree. Only 6% were reported to have an associate degree or higher. In addition, the study reported five proficiency levels for numeracy and literacy (in ordinal values of Level 1 through 4/5). The demographic analysis found that 52% scored below Level 2 on numeracy and that 29% of prisoners scored below Level 2 in literacy. Understanding the educational needs of prisoners allows software engineers, correctional officers, teachers, and policy makers to understand the parameters that should be involved in creating/implementing/funding these educational services. The understanding of these educational profiles is especially important when experimenting with the use of adaptive technologies, where the software must be adequate to the capabilities and current knowledge of correctional students.

1.3 The Present Study

The view that prison is usually perceived as a long-term storage locker by policy and decision makers, clearly demonstrates the necessity to develop studies that focus on the reformation of correctional education. (Esperian, 2010) Prisoners should spend their sentence learning to become law-abiding citizens. Prisons should not focus on maintaining individuals in solitary, adrift, developing anger towards society. Considering that correctional education deems a revamp, the purpose of this research papers is to provide a technological approach to prisoner's education. The framework offered has the intention to be used as a foundation for future research and empirical studies on the effect of ALTs on prisoner's recidivism and positive social reintegration. Even though the model to be presented in this paper draws its foundation from clearly successful programs in higher education, we believe that its implementation will still pose as a challenge for correctional facilities. These challenges, logically, are related to the intellectual capabilities, technological literacy, and personal stances of prisoners towards education. Regardless, this paper has the potential, given its solid foundations based on early and current prison education research, to influence correctional facilities, local, state, and national government of the benefits of a technological approach to education, specifically using ALTs.

2. LITERATURE REVIEW

2.1 Relationship between Education and Recidivism

Early history of correctional rationale suggested that retribution and punishment were the quintessential attributes of appropriate correctional practices. Fortunately, this rationale quickly changed after the 13th century, were penitentiaries were seen as places where offenders could reflect on their mistakes and prepare to live life as law-abiding citizens. (Esperian, 2010) The critical shift occurred in the late 18th century, as correctional facilities embodied the Middle Ages' desire to reform prisoners. (Esperian, 2010; Clear and Cole, 1994) After the 19th century, America borrowed this concept of reformation of the offender, leading to the rationale that education can improve the conditions of prisoners after release. Currently, multiple authors have concluded that education is an essential component for any effective rehabilitation process for offenders. Davis et al. (2013) from the RAND Corporation, avowed that prisoners that undertake educational services on their correctional facilities, are less likely to relapse and return to prison. According to the analysis, prisoner that participate in these educational programs have a 43% lower probability of recidivating than prisoners that did not. The educational goals of these programs can be divided into two main streams: academic and vocational training. Both programs have the common goal to prepare the inmate for their success in the free world. Academic training, as the words suggests, allows prisoners to take courses/classes/activities that will facilitate their entry/preparation into a General Educational Development (GED) program, high school equivalency, or a college level educational program. On the other hand, vocational training is composed of courses/classes/activities that prepare prisoners to take on labor/technical activities when leaving prison. These can undertake a variety of forms, but most commonly are: "Autobody, auto mechanics, building maintenance, electronics, office services, plumbing, and others." (Hill, 2008)

Education holds true universal benefits for prisoners. Linton, Lockwood, Nally, & Steurer, (2010) cleverly state that "education of prisoners not only provides job skills, knowledge and a positive behavioral disposition toward work, but also supports security and safety within the prison and outside in the community and improves the economy by improving chances for prisoners to fill jobs." Regaining self-confidence and self-sufficiency, are one of the most valuable social skills that can be gained from education in the correctional facility. More specifically, the report found that prisoners that have been previously exposed to educational experiences (High school education, General Education Development, college, etc.) have a lower probability of recidivating than others. In addition, prisoners that participated in vocational, or professional development programs increased their post-release employment probabilities by 28% in comparison to others. Strictly related to this study, the meta-analysis concluded that computer-assisted instruction improves academic performance slightly, in comparison to other methods of instruction.

2.2 History and Current State of the Pell Grant Program

An important initiative for prisoner's education started with the Pell Grant program. Established by Congress on 1972, the Federal Pell Grant Program aimed to provide low-income students (which included those in prison) funds to pay for postsecondary education. The program initiated its success early on, by 1982 there were 350 postsecondary programs in prison, enrolling 27,000 incarcerated students. By the early 1990s, prison programs surpassed 700 within 1,300 correctional facilities. (Robinson, English, 2017). However, the loss of Pell Grants for prisoners in 1994, due to Congress passing the Violent Crime Control and Law Enforcement Act (VCCLEA) revoking funding, was a somber moment for prisoner education. A provision of the VCCLEA, however, allowed for funding for postsecondary education, thanks to the Higher Education Act of 1965. Several changes have taken place to the Pell Grant Program. Currently, a bipartisan bill called The Restoring Education and Learning (REAL) has been introduced to the senate. If approved, it would be effective for the 2019-2020 academic year. This bill signifies a political desire to continue the Pell initiative, which started on 2016 with the Second Change Pell pilot Program.

2.2.1 Challenges of Education in Prison

Although the benefits of education are clear, providing effective educational environments to offenders is rightfully viewed as challenge. Prisoners' educational profiles usually include learning disabilities, behavioral disorders, and mental illness. (DelliCarpini, 2008; Shermer, 2011) Challenges are twofold: Firstly, correctional facilities are not the most inducing learning settings; the social dynamics behind bars altogether with the intricate background variables within every inmate, greatly affect their learning capabilities. In most cases, these facilities do not provide the habitat to foster positive learning environments. In addition, the diversity of educational needs and personal backgrounds of the prisoners, and often the numerosity of these individuals, disallows the possibility of providing a universal educative system that considers the needs/abilities/pace of each student. Technologies are proven to facilitate the learning process, regardless of the barriers mentioned above.

As McCulley et al. (2014) states, a blended classroom (one that combines the use of technology and a physical instructor) is proven to generate higher engagement and success rates within students, especially prisoners. Wade, Bohac, and Platt (2013) explain the numerous technological methods that can be applied to facilitate the learning experiences for individuals in correctional facilities. As the authors imply, correctional settings require systematic changes from their traditional teaching model, in order to mold to the modern, diverse student population. In this case, the use of technology allows professionals to address these changes more effectively. Software and hardware such as e-learning, videoconferencing, virtual observations, virtual reality and portable hardware such as tables and laptops, allows a more effective immediate feedback on instructional delivery. Online instruction, specially, has appealed greatly to correctional planners due their inherent flexibility.

Secondly, the current policymaker's opinion on correctional education greatly damper its objective. Particularly, these negative views are centralized on two different themes: Cost (the use of the taxpayer's dollar) and effectiveness (due to public perception on the appropriate methods of penitentiary service). In terms of cost, policy maker's reproach the use of taxpayer's dollars for education, signified by a clear intention of not approving Pell Grant funding. Davis et. al (2013) among their other findings, state that providing education to prisoners is a financially sound solution. The study compared the direct costs of correctional education programs versus the direct costs of incarceration, with a hypothetical pool of 100 prisoners using a three-year reincarceration rate. The results were very significant. Three-year reincarceration costs for the prisoners that did not receive correctional education were between $2.94 million and $3.25 million. Contrastingly, reincarceration costs for those that undertook educational programs ranged between $2.07 million and $2.28 million, significantly less. The study's estimated a cost for education per inmate to range between $1,400 and $1,744 or, $140,000 to $174,400 for the hypothetical pool of 100 prisoners (Davis, et al., 2013). Sellers (2016) reemphasizes the argument above and provides findings supporting the financial benefits of implementing educational technologies in prison. Sellers (2016) states that "the cost of instruction decreases significantly with the use of online learning," while being more economical than both onsite and offsite face-to-face classes. Therefore, we can state that education with a technological approach is desirable for facilities, given that these solutions are financially sound and feasible (Sellers, 2016). Sellers (2016) reemphasizes the argument above and provides supplemental findings to support the financial benefits of implementing educational technologies in prison.

Sellers (2016) states that "the cost of instruction decreases significantly with the use of online learning," while being more economical than both onsite and offsite face-to-face classes. Therefore, we can state that education with a technological approach is desirable for facilities, given that these solutions are financially sound and feasible. Cost is the overriding factor in any attempt to foster fiscal stability. Yet, almost ironically, spending for education is exactly what must be promoted. (Esperian, 2010) Public opinion fails to realize that individuals that have been incarcerated face significant barriers to success, including lack of resources, lack of education, and an engraved criminal history. (Shermer, 2011) If these barriers fail to be addressed, ex-prisoners face a greater probability of recidivating. Low literacy rates and lack of abilities to be employed highly diminish the prisoners' success. (Makorios, Steiner, Travis, 2010) Therefore, and despite its inherent challenges, education proves to be the soundest solution to lower recidivism rates. The solution lies on increasing the availability of education and vocational training in prison.

2.3 Use of Technology in the Delivery of Education in Prison

2.3.1 Curriculum

Hopkins and Farley (2015) explain that the core curriculum of correctional educative programs should be based on the disciplines of humanities. They argue that this focus is effective, not only these programs can be "completed in relative isolation, without field work, complex technologies or compulsory practicum components", but because it offers students the opportunity for nonmaterial activities, such as self-understanding, self-expression, and self-growth. This, logically, allows students to reflect and reconsider their mistakes, and contextualize their actions on the basis of "morality, culture, personal history and social positioning." (Hopkins and Farley, 2015) However, we disagree slightly. We suggest that the core curriculum should, aside from focusing on humanitarian disciplines, focus on the integral sciences such as mathematics, or "contextual" subjects like history, which help develop the practical skills valuable in the workplace. A higher probability of post-release employment is, undoubtedly, the panacea for high levels of recidivism. Regardless of the curriculum chosen, researchers, correctional institutions officials, and policy makers need to be aware that the ability of students to learn is strictly related with social, cultural, political, and economic aspects of prisoners. (Selwyn, 2000; Alexander, 2006; Maltby & Mackie, 2009) Although the thoughts of these authors were intended for students outside correctional facilities, their recommendations are easily applicable for prisoner students.

2.3.2 Categories for Methods of Instruction

Blended Classrooms

A blended classroom uses both technology and the physical learning guidance of a teacher. In this type of setting, a professor easily facilitates and incentivizes student engagement of the curriculum, attributable to the mixture of technology and physical teaching being offered. A blended classroom should achieve the following goals: (1) enhance pedagogy, (2) increase access and flexibility, (3) improve cost-effectiveness and resource use. (Graham, Allen, and Ure, 2005; Porter, Graham, Spring, Welch, 2014) A study conducted by the

University of Central Florida (UCF) determined that students that took courses with a blended learning component, surpassed the comparable success of students only exposed to face-to-face or fully online courses. (Dziuban et al., 2004) Successful implementation of the blended classroom setting must be a combined effort of all agents involved in the education of prisoners. Fortunately, this type of instruction method is gaining momentum in the US as a preferred method of instruction in prisons. (McCulley, 2014; Varlas, 2011)

Individualized training

Although blended classrooms are proven to be more effective than its traditional counterpart, individualized, adaptable, and digitalized instruction methods specifically can improve the re-integration of prisoners to society. Efforts to correlate individualized training with successful understanding of educative material, have long been the role of academic studies in correctional education. One of the earliest contemporary efforts to achieve this is described by Muse (1998), where he explained the positive relationship with individualized teaching of incarcerated youth and their success within the educative program. In his study, Muse (1998) concluded that "individualized instruction represents the preferred method of instruction for at-risk, troubled, and underachieving youth" prisoners. However, Muse (1998) acknowledged that "individualized instruction is not a prescription." Rather, it is a special process that must equate with the intricate variables present in the minds and lifestyles of each inmate. As discussed earlier, the effects of the social dynamics in prison altogether with the background of the prisoners, must be considered for the creation of a singular method of instruction, accommodated to each correctional facility and its prisoners.

2.4 Usage of Information Technology

Information technology is a crucial component to improve, and effectively utilize, individualized training. However, according to the U.S. Department of Education (2015), the availability of technology in correctional education is inadequate and insufficient. On this study, based on a pool of 42 correctional facilities, the most common instruction method was on-site classes. Davis et al. (2014), cited by the Department of Education, states that only 2% of academic programs offers an interactive internet-based method of instruction. In addition, only 2% has one-way interned-based (defined as non-interactive, instructor-only online teaching system) method of instruction. As mentioned, one of the primary concerns of implementing educative technologies in prisons are security issues, especially abuse and security breaches, according to the U.S. Department of Education (2015). To complement this, these methods of instructions are rather static (and do not provide the flexibility of the learning environment) having 93% of the hardware being desktop computers. On the contrary, only 24% of the correctional facilities studied in the report use tablets as their technology of preference.

In terms of the type of network used, 62% use a Local Area Network (LAN) to provide all their connectivity needs. On the other side, only 26% employ a state-wide or Wide Area Network (WAN) to provide their connectivity needs. In terms of access to the internet, 73% have restrictions except for the instructors, which are providing the material live. A staggering 62% does not let students access the internet (or even a censored version of it), while only 14% allow prisoners to have a restricted live access. This overview of the technologies used in correctional facilities allows us (the researchers) to see two common things: (1) Extreme restricted access to internet connectivity (which some can be justified), and (2) there's no existent evidence that supports the idea of machine learning, and adaptive technologies. The internet is the gate to access much of the material and software tools that aid the educational process. In terms of abuse, which is of great concern in correctional facilities, the access to the vastness of content (either instructional or unsuitable) has been prohibited or is highly inaccessible, for understandable reasons. Allowing a free and unsupervised use of the Internet to uneducated, and principle-lacking prisoners can lead to disastrous outcomes.

Despite the fact that technologies are proven to facilitate the learning environment, there exists little to no effort to include such in correctional facilities. McCulley et al. (2014) states that a blended classroom (One that combines the use of technology and a physical instructor) is proven to generate higher engagement and success rates within students, especially prisoners (McCulley et al., 2014). Wade, Bohac, and Platt (2013) explain the numerous technological methods that can be applied to facilitate the learning experiences for individuals in correctional facilities. As the authors imply, correctional settings require systematic changes from their traditional teaching model, in order to mold to the modern, diverse student population. In this case, technology allow professionals to address these changes more effectively. Software and hardware such as e-learning, videoconferencing, virtual observations, virtual reality and portable hardware such as tables and laptops, allows a more effective immediate feedback on instructional delivery. Online instruction, specially, has appealed greatly to correctional planners due their inherent flexibility (Wade, Bohac, and Platt, 2013).

2.5 Usage of Machine Learning and Adaptive Learning Systems

Although technology and individualized training can have significant positive effects on prisoners; adaptive learning technologies specifically are intrinsically more effective. These technologies are proven to hold benefits for the individual, the instructor, and the institution (McLaren, 2013). These technological systems achieve this by utilizing computer programs that adapt to the student's ability and intellectual level. Furthermore, such 'adaption' is attained because computer systems "refine the selection of items on the basis of a student's response and provides a mechanism, for identifying the particular abilities and potential problem areas within the domain of assessment" (Shapiro and Gebhardt, 2012).

McLaren (2013) provides a comprehensive assessment of the purpose of an adaptive learning system. Such system must base itself from the present knowledge of the student, and feed that knowledge, "with new material and/or problems to solve that are just at the edge, or just beyond the edge, of the student's demonstrated knowledge and understanding." The software, by design, scaffolds the learning process of the student. The author argues why adaptive learning is so valuable to the educational environment. Given the intricate and different variables present in a traditional classroom, altogether with the natural burden of instructors in terms of time, proposed method of instruction, learning style, class size and, their unsustainable desire to teach to the velocities of each student (which in reality, those desires are farfetched); adaptive learning technologies are emerging to complement instructors by providing catered content, which is directly based on the student's knowledge, motivation, and learning style (McLaren, 2013).

Adaptive educational methods have been tested in correctional facilities before; however, not with the intensity or software complexity desired. McCulley et al. (2014) provided statistical evidence that an adaptive educational software possesses benefits to the learning experience of prisoners and educators alike. On their study, the authors developed a "Text-to-Speech" software that improved the reading skills for prisoners that were generally accustomed to the use of electronics in their lives. This proved to be successful tool for prisoners (McCulley et al., 2014). Leading in into the discussion component of this research paper, it is noticeable from the literature that technology, and more specific, adaptive learning technologies, are very efficient methods to enhance an inmate's educative experience; however, these technologies lack presence in the correctional educational environments. Therefore, the following portion of this research paper will be to discuss the role of educative adaptive learning technologies (successful in other areas of education) into the correctional facility. In addition, the availability of private companies developing technologies to further education in correctional facilities will be discussed.

3. CONCLUSION

3.1 Theoretical Implementation of Machine Learning on Education

The most appropriate method of artificial intelligence for educational purposes, must be based on a supervised model of learning. A supervised model is defined as a task executed in machine learning were the understanding of a function maps an input to an output based on example input-output pairs, and labelled training data. (Russel and Norvig, 2010) After a sufficient number of examples and iterations of data are provided, the network of data is able to predict, with accuracy, any prolongations or potential outputs of such data. The relevancy of supervised models of learning is that they can produce statistical guesses on a given input data pattern. Therefore, these models allow us to classify patterns into a set of pre-defined classes. (Tuomi, 2018) These models are able to improve the user's experience based on historical patterns, or iterations of previously inputted data, exactly what is required for learners. The process by which a supervised model of learning works, can be described as follows: The learner, in this case the machine, is required to approximate the behavior of a certain function. Then, the system should map a vector into several groups, by observing at multiple input-output examples of the desired function.

3.2 ALTs & Policy

Although it is widely recognized within the correctional literature that an amplified use of education and technology, increases the chances of positive social re-integration; the literature does not offer a "guideline" or a universal criterion that can help implement these blended classrooms (mainly consisted of instructors and some form of adaptive learning technology) in correctional facilities throughout the country. Therefore, the purpose of this section of the paper is to offer that sought-after theoretical guideline.

Acknowledging that educational programs in correctional facilities are beneficial, is the first step towards developing educational programs, and even further, policy. The second step is to understand what characteristics these programs should have. Lopez (2015) describes that the effectiveness of a correctional education program is a function of the following variables: the program objectives, the curriculum, the faculty roster, the prisoner students, the facilities and equipment, other services and, financial support. Although the paper reflects the Filipino context, it can certainly be transcribed to the American context. A first step towards such guideline is to include a universal procedural design of such adaptive software. As discussed in the body of this paper, McKee & Clements (2000) provide a comprehensive system design to tackle the issue. Any educative adaptive method should follow that guideline, in order to be effective and efficient. Correctional facilities can decide whether to use a general placement test, or the prisoner's Test of Adult Basic Education (TABE) which provides classification recommendations for placement in academic and/or vocational/training programs.

In terms of the content of such educative systems, one should take into consideration which design provides the best cost and results-effective combination. The research suggests that such systems should be design with the intent to prepare the prisoner for vocational or job training, with the supplemental value to teach them to be proficient with IT systems and computers. In addition, these systems must consider the effects of the social dynamics in prison altogether with the background of the prisoners, which must be accommodated and customized to each correctional facility.

Regarding governmental involvement, we can trace ideas and mirror the success of the Australian project "Making the Connection" developed by the University of Queensland. Such partnerships with universities help reduce costs while providing valuable educative and vocational training for prisoners. In addition, the role of government should be to provide economic incentives to those entrepreneurs to develop target-specific technologies that can be used by prisoners to enhance their learning experience. In other words, companies such as Virtual Rehab (mentioned in this research paper) should be economically incentivized to manufacture and design these technological aids. The role of such technologies should be to allow a flexible and, modifiable educational environment that best address the needs, and limitations of both the prisoners and the correctional facility.

3.3 Potential of ATLs on Data Collection and Analysis

Natriello (2013) emphasizes the role of adaptive learning technologies on data collection and analysis. Since these technologies are able to record and collect data from the individual student's performance, the systems are able to create immense datasets and data entries to databases for educational research. Evidently, there are infinite benefits to gain from the implementation of adaptive learning technologies, especially regarding the data interpretation and future design stages of educative programs. As Natriello (2013) suggests, the implementation of these technologies give rise to three pathways for educational research: 1) It allows researchers and instructors examine problems and issues previously unexamined in other data sets, 2) It allows the formulation of new research questions, previously concealed on data sets hankering for empirical examination, and lastly 3) these technologies permit the formulation of new research questions given the examination of larger, newer datasets.

The use of adaptive learning technologies can pose immense benefits to the instructive process of correctional facilities. It encompasses benefits for the prisoner, the instructor and, the institution. In terms of the students, prisoners are provided with individualized learning systems that are proven to be more effective, and more engaging than traditional teaching methods. In addition, the technology is able to cater and nurture several areas of development behind bars, including: 1) Post-release employment opportunities, 2) academic development and/or continuousness, 3) positive social re-integration, and lastly data analysis can be reviewed on the prisoner's learning feedback process.

In terms of the value-added for the instructor, adaptive learning technologies provide the versatility and individualized attention that most prisoners require, but not many teachers are able to provide. Given the fact that adaptive learning technologies build on the learner's current knowledge, and advance based on the learner's pace and ability to grasp information; these technologies allow instructors to do their work more efficiently while focusing on the important tasks of their job: designing educative programs that affects prisoners positively. These technologies also provide great benefits to the institution given their cost-effectiveness. An investment in such equipment are proven to provide sound financial solutions to the most effective methods of maintaining lower recidivism rates, read education. In addition, by making the investment to make the institution's best tool to keep recidivism rates low, institutions now can spend less on faculty, staff and prison maintenance if educative programs keep plausible recidivating criminals away from prison. Also, these technologies allow the possibility to gather innumerate amounts of data that can be used to provide immediate feedback to the effectiveness of these programs. Therefore, allowing the feedback cycles to be significantly shorter, and make systematic changes faster.

REFERENCES

Alexander, P. M. (2006). Virtual teamwork in very large undergraduate classes. *Computers and Education, 47*(2), 127-147.

Allred, S. L., Harrison, L. D., & O'Connell, D. J. (2013). Self-Efficacy. *The Prison Journal, 93*(2), 211-233. doi:10.1177/0032885512472964

Alper, M., & Durose, M. (2018). Update on Prisoner Recidivism: A 9-Year Follow-up Period (2005-2014). In *Bureau of Justice statistics*. Washington, D.C.: The Bureau.

Clear, T. R., & Cole, G. F. (1994). *American Corrections*. Belmont, CA: Wadsworth Pub.

Champion, N., Edgar, K. (2013) "Through the Gateway: How Computers Can Transform Rehabilitation." London: Prison Reform Trust and Education Trust.

Davis, L. M. (2013). *Evaluating the effectiveness of correctional education: A meta-analysis of programs that provide education to incarcerated adults*. Santa Monica, CA: RAND Corporation.

Davis, L. M., Tolbert, A. M., & Mizel, M. (2017). Correctional Education Projects. Retrieved 2020, from https://www.rand.org/well-being/justice-policy/portfolios/correctional-education/projects.html

DelliCarpini, M. (2008, August 31). Creating Communities of Professional Practice in the Correctional Education Classroom. Retrieved 2020, from https://eric.ed.gov/?id=EJ814389

DelliCarpini, M. (2010, November 30). Building a Better Life: Implementing a Career and Technical Education Program for Incarcerated Youth. Retrieved 2020, from https://eric.ed.gov/?id=EJ971297

Durose, M., Cooper, A., & Snyder, H. (2014). Recidivism of Prisoners Released in 30 States in 2005: Patterns from 2005 to 2010. Retrieved 2020, from http://www.bjs.gov/content/pub/pdf/rprts05p0510.pdf

Durose, M., Snyder, H., & Cooper, A. (2015). Multistate Criminal History Patterns of Prisoners Released in 30 States. Retrieved 2020, from https://www.bjs.gov/content/pub/pdf/mschpprts05.pdf

Dziuban, C., Hartman, J., Moskal, P., Sorg, S., & Truman, B. (2004). Three ALN modalities: An institutional perspective. *Elements of quality online education: Into the mainstream*, *5*, 127-148.

Esperian, J. H. (2010, November 30). The Effect of Prison Education Programs on Recidivism. Retrieved 2020, from https://eric.ed.gov/?id=EJ971299

Graham, C., Allen, S., & Ure, D. (2005, January 01). Benefits and Challenges of Blended Learning Environments. Retrieved 2020, from https://www.igi-global.com/chapter/benefits-challenges-blended-learning-environments/14246

Harlow, C., Jenkins, H., & Steurer, S. (2010, February 28). GED Holders in Prison Read Better than Those in the Household Population: Why?. Retrieved 2020, from https://eric.ed.gov/?id=EJ971289

Hill, E. (2008). From Cellblocks to Classrooms: Reforming Inmate Education to Improve Public Safety. Retrieved 2020, from https://lao.ca.gov/2008/crim/inmate_education/inmate_education_021208.aspx

Hopkins, S., & Farley, H. (2015, January 01). E-learning incarcerated: Prison education and digital inclusion. Retrieved 2020, from https://eprints.usq.edu.au/28730/

James, L. (2012, January 01). Evaluation of an Adaptive Learning Technology as a Predictor of Student Performance in Undergraduate Biology: Semantic Scholar. Retrieved 2020, from https://www.semanticscholar.org/paper/Evaluation-of-an-Adaptive-Learning-Technology-as-a-James/387a82a87bb12a9583e31ec96c9ac88c07fd79f3

Lahm, K. F. (2009). Educational Participation and Inmate Misconduct. *Journal of Offender Rehabilitation, 48*(1), 37-52. Retrieved 2020, from https://www.tandfonline.com/doi/abs/10.1080/10509670802572235?journalCode=wjor20&

Lewis, J. (2006). Correctional Education: Why it is Only 'Promising7' - JSTOR. Retrieved 2020, from https://www.jstor.org/stable/23282803

Linton, J., Lockwood, S., Nally, J., & Streurer, S. (2010). The top-nine reasons to increase correctional education ... Retrieved 2020, from https://www.thefreelibrary.com/The+top-nine+reasons+to+increase+correctional+education+programs.-a0236026979

Lopez, E. (2015). Management of the Correctional Education Program for Students Behind Bars. Retrieved 2020, from http://www.ajmse.leena-luna.co.jp/ajmsevol4n1.php

Maltby, A., & Mackie, S. (2009). Virtual learning environments – help or hindrance for the 'disengaged' student? *ALT-J, Research in Learning Technology, 17(1),* 49-62. Retrieved 2020, from https://files.eric.ed.gov/fulltext/EJ831099.pdf

Makarios, M. & Steiner, B. (2010). Examining the Predictors of Recidivism Among Men and Women Released from Prison in Ohio - Matthew Makarios, Benjamin Steiner, Lawrence F. Travis, 2010. Retrieved 2020, from https://journals.sagepub.com/doi/abs/10.1177/0093854810382876

Makorios, M., & Travis, L. F. (2010). From the Classroom to the Community. Retrieved 2020, from https://www.urban.org/sites/default/files/publication/30671/411963-From-the-Classroom-to-the-Community.PDF

McCulley, Y., Gillespie, C., & Murr, A. (2014, April 30). Assessing the Effectiveness of Text-to-Speech Software in Incarcerated Adult Literacy Education. Retrieved 2020, from https://eric.ed.gov/?id=EJ1185239

McLaren, B. (2013). Adaptive Online Learning: The Present and Future of Education. Retrieved 2020, from https://issuu.com/wiley_publishing/docs/whitepaper_v7

Muse, F. (1998). A Look at the Benefits of Individualized Instruction in a Juvenile Training School Setting: How Continuous Progress Accelerates Student Performance. *Journal of Correctional Education, 49(2),* 73-80. Retrieved 2020, from https://www.jstor.org/stable/pdf/23292236.pdf

Natriello, G. (2013). Adaptive Educational Technologies: Tools for Learning, and for Learning About Learning. Retrieved 2020, from https://files.eric.ed.gov/fulltext/ED574477.pdf

Owens, C. D. (2009, November 30). Social Symbols, Stigma, and the Labor Market Experiences of Former Prisoners. Retrieved 2020, from https://eric.ed.gov/?id=EJ871288

Porter, W. W., Graham, C. R., Spring, K. A., & Welch, K. R. (2014, March 12). Blended learning in higher education: Institutional adoption and implementation. Retrieved 2020, from https://www.sciencedirect.com/science/article/pii/S0360131514000451

Russell, S., & Norvig, P. (2010). Artificial Intelligence: A Modern Approach. Retrieved 2020, from http://aima.cs.berkeley.edu/

Schwarzer, R., & Jerusalem, M. (1995). The General Self-Efficacy Scale (GSF) - PCNA. Retrieved 2020, from https://pcna.net/wp-content/uploads/2018/12/16e_the_general_self_efficacy_scale.pdf

Selwyn, N. (2000, April 05). Researching computers and education - glimpses of the wider picture. Retrieved 2020, from https://www.sciencedirect.com/science/article/abs/pii/S0360131500000063

Shapiro, E., & Gebhardt, S. (2012). Comparing Computer-Adaptive and Curriculum-Based Measurement Methods of Assessment. Retrieved 2020, from https://www.tandfonline.com/doi/abs/10.1080/02796015.2012.12087510

Tsend-Ayush, G. (2019, October 04). The Impact of Information and Communication Technologies on Prison Institutions. Retrieved 2020, from https://williamlockitt.co.uk/download/the-impact-of-information-and-communication-technologies-on-prison-institutions/

Tuomi, I. (2018). (PDF) The Impact of Artificial Intelligence on Learning, Teaching, and Education: Policies for the Future. Retrieved 2020, from https://www.researchgate.net/publication/329544152_The_Impact_of_Artificial_Intelligence_on_Learning_Teaching_and_Education_Policies_for_the_Future

U.S. Department of Education (2015). "Educational Technology in Corrections." Office of Career, Technical, and Adult Education. Washington, DC

Varlas, L. (2011). Getting to graduation: Can blended learning curtail the dropout crisis. Retrieved 2020, from http://www.ascd.org/publications/newsletters/education-update/aug11/vol53/num08/Getting-to-Graduation.aspx

Wade, W., Bohac, P., & Platt, J. S. (2013). Technology-Based Induction: Professional Development ... Retrieved 2020, from https://www.jstor.org/stable/26508105

Wilson, K., Gonzalez, P., Romero, T., Henry, K., & Cerbana, C. (2010, May 31). The Effectiveness of Parent Education for Incarcerated Parents: An Evaluation of Parenting from Prison. Retrieved 2020, from https://eric.ed.gov/?id=EJ971291